International Conference on Interfaces and Human Computer Interaction 2016, International Conference on Game and Entertainment Technologies 2016 and International Conference on Computer Graphics, Visualization, Computer Vision and Image Processing 2016

Held at the Multi-Conference on Computer Science and Information Systems (MCCSIS 2016)

Madeira, Portugal
1 – 4 July 2016

AA005322

Editors:

Katherine Blashki
Yingcai Xiao
Piet Kommers
Pedro Isaias
Luis Rodrigues

ISBN: 978-1-5108-6527-3

Printed from e-media with permission by:

Curran Associates, Inc.
57 Morehouse Lane
Red Hook, NY 12571

Some format issues inherent in the e-media version may also appear in this print version.

Copyright© (2016) by International Association for Development of the Information Society (IADIS)
All rights reserved.

Printed by Curran Associates, Inc. (2018)

For permission requests, please contact International Association for Development of the Information Society (IADIS) at the address below.

International Association for Development of the Information Society (IADIS)
Rua Sao Sebastiao Da Pedreira
No. 100, 30, 1050-209
Lisbon, Portugal

Phone: 351 21 3151373
Fax: 351 21 3151244

secretariat@iadis.org

Additional copies of this publication are available from:

Curran Associates, Inc.
57 Morehouse Lane
Red Hook, NY 12571 USA
Phone: 845-758-0400
Fax: 845-758-2633
Email: curran@proceedings.com
Web: www.proceedings.com

INTERNATIONAL CONFERENCES ON

INTERFACES AND HUMAN COMPUTER INTERACTION 2016

GAME AND ENTERTAINMENT TECHNOLOGIES 2016

and

COMPUTER GRAPHICS, VISUALIZATION, COMPUTER VISION AND IMAGE PROCESSING 2016

part of the

MULTI CONFERENCE ON COMPUTER SCIENCE AND

INFORMATION SYSTEMS 2016

PROCEEDINGS OF THE INTERNATIONAL CONFERENCES ON

INTERFACES AND HUMAN COMPUTER INTERACTION 2016

GAME AND ENTERTAINMENT TECHNOLOGIES 2016

and

COMPUTER GRAPHICS, VISUALIZATION, COMPUTER VISION AND IMAGE PROCESSING 2016

Madeira, Portugal
JULY 1 - 4, 2016

Organised by
IADIS
International Association for Development of the Information Society

Sponsored by

TURISMO DE PORTUGAL madeira islands

Official Carrier

TAP PORTUGAL
with arms wide open
A STAR ALLIANCE MEMBER

Copyright 2016

IADIS Press

All rights reserved

This work is subject to copyright. All rights are reserved, whether the whole or part of the material is concerned, specifically the rights of translation, reprinting, re-use of illustrations, recitation, broadcasting, reproduction on microfilms or in any other way, and storage in data banks. Permission for use must always be obtained from IADIS Press. Please contact secretariat@iadis.org

Volume Editor:
Katherine Blashki
Yingcai Xiao

Computer Science and Information Systems Series Editors:
Piet Kommers and Pedro Isaías

Associate Editor: Luís Rodrigues

TABLE OF CONTENTS

FULL PAPERS

INTERFACES AND HUMAN COMPUTER INTERACTION

SHORT PAPERS

INTERFACES AND HUMAN COMPUTER INTERACTION

GAME AND ENTERTAINMENT TECHNOLOGIES

COMPUTER GRAPHICS, VISUALIZATION, COMPUTER VISION AND IMAGE PROCESSING

REFLECTION PAPERS

INTERFACES AND HUMAN COMPUTER INTERACTION

POSTERS

INTERFACES AND HUMAN COMPUTER INTERACTION

GAME AND ENTERTAINMENT TECHNOLOGIES

COMPUTER GRAPHICS, VISUALIZATION, COMPUTER VISION AND IMAGE PROCESSING

DOCTORAL

GAME AND ENTERTAINMENT TECHNOLOGIES

FOREWORD

These proceedings contain the papers of the International Conferences on Interfaces and Human Computer Interaction 2016, Game and Entertainment Technologies 2016 and Computer Graphics, Visualization, Computer Vision and Image Processing 2016 which were organised by the International Association for Development of the Information Society, from 2 - 4 July, 2016. These conferences are part of the Multi Conference on Computer Science and Information Systems 2016, 1 - 4 July, which had a total of 606 submissions.

The Interfaces and Human Computer Interaction (IHCI) 2016 conference aims to address the main issues of concern within Interface Culture and Design with a particular emphasis on the affective aspects of design, development and implementation of interfaces and the generational implications for design of human and technology interaction. This conference aims to explore and discuss innovative studies of technology and its application in interfaces and welcomes research in progress, case studies, practical demonstrations and workshops in addition to the traditional submission categories.

This conference seeks to cover both technological as well as non-technological issues related to these developments.

Submissions were accepted under the following topics:
- Affective User-Centred Analysis, Design and Evaluation
- The Value of Affective Interfaces / Systems / Application / Interaction
- Generational Differences and Technology Design
- Measurement of Success of Emotional Technology / Interfaces
- Supporting User Populations from Specific Generations
- Supporting User Populations with Physical Disabilities
- Supporting User Populations with Intellectual Disabilities
- Creativity Support Systems
- Emotional Design Issues / Methods / Experiences for Novel Interfaces including Tangible, Mobile and Ubiquitous Computing, Mixed Reality Interfaces and Multi-Modal Interfaces
- Usability
- User Studies and Fieldwork
- Methodological Implications of Emotional User Studies
- Participatory design and Cooperative Design Techniques
- Ethical Issues in Emotional Design
- HCI and Design Education
- Eliciting User Requirements

The Game and Entertainment Technologies (GET) 2016 conference aims to bring together research and practice from creative, social and business practitioners and researchers in this challenging field. The focus of this conference is on design, development and evaluation of games, entertainment technologies and the nature of play.

Known to have been enjoyed since at least 30 BC, games and entertainment are a universal part of human experience and present in all cultures. Games and entertainment activities contribute to the social, emotional, psychological and physical well-being of human society. As game and entertainment technologies become increasingly more pervasive we are continually challenged in our work, learning and personal life by increased access to virtual spaces and communities that offer opportunities for everyday needs and aesthetic experiences. The 'Creative Industries' require design and development structures, techniques and methodologies that enrich, enhance and encourage new interaction modes, metaphors and in-depth co-creation.

Topics of interest include, but are not limited to the following areas:

- Development Methodologies
- Design Issues
- Controversial Issues – we welcome debate and dissension, for example; games as art, entertainment as purely for monetary returns etc
- Special Effects
- Animation
- Mobile and Ubiquitous Games and Entertainment
- Serious Games –Applications, Critiques
- Philosophical Issues
- Prototypes
- Social and Cultural Uses of/for Play
- Tools and Technologies
- Skills, Strategy, Rules and Chance
- Genre
- Immersiveness and Engagement
- Research methodologies in Creative Practice
- Usability and Playability
- User/Player Centered Design
- Psychological, Social, and Cultural Differences in Perception and Participation
- Communities, Networks, Social Interaction and Social Capital
- Cross-Cultural and Intercultural Approaches
- Assessment of Exploratory Learning Approaches
- Emerging Practices

The Computer Graphics, Visualization, Computer Vision and Image Processing (CGVCVIP) 2016 conference intends to address the research issues in the closely related areas of Computer Graphics, Visualization, Computer Vision and Image Processing. The conference encourages the interdisciplinary research and applications of these areas.

Submissions were accepted under the following 5 main topics:

- Computer Graphics
- Visualization
- Computer Vision
- Image Processing
- Other Related Topics

These events received 192 submissions from more than 30 countries. Each submission has been anonymously reviewed by an average of five independent reviewers, to ensure that accepted submissions were of a high standard. Consequently, only 29 full papers were approved which means an acceptance rate of 15%. A few more submissions were accepted as short papers, reflection paper, posters and doctoral paper. An extended version of the best papers will be published in the IADIS International Journal on Computer Science and Information Systems (ISSN: 1646-3692) and/or in the IADIS International Journal on WWW/Internet (ISSN: 1645-7641) and also in other selected journals, including journals from Inderscience.

Besides the presentation of full papers, short papers, reflection paper, posters and a doctoral consortium, the conferences also included two keynote presentations from internationally distinguished researchers. We would therefore like to express our gratitude to Professor Jan Gulliksen (KTH Royal Institute of Technology, Sweden) and Professor Alfred Inselberg (Senior Fellow San Diego, Supercomputing Center & Computer Science and Applied Mathematics Departments, Tel Aviv University, Israel) for accepting our invitation as keynote speakers.

This volume has taken shape as a result of the contributions from a number of individuals. We are grateful to all authors who have submitted their papers to enrich these conferences proceedings. We wish to thank all members of the organizing committee, delegates, invitees and guests whose contribution and involvement are crucial for the success of the conference.

Last but not the least, we hope that everybody has a good time in Madeira, and we invite all participants for the next edition of these conferences.

Katherine Blashki, Noroff University College, Norway
Interfaces and Human Computer Interaction 2016 Program Chair
Game and Entertainment Technologies 2016 Program Chair

Yingcai Xiao, The University of Akron, USA
Computer Graphics, Visualization, Computer Vision and Image Processing 2016 Program Chair

Piet Kommers, University of Twente, The Netherlands
Pedro Isaías, Universidade Aberta (Portuguese Open University), Portugal
MCCSIS 2016 General Conference Co-Chairs

Madeira, Portugal
July 2016

PROGRAM COMMITTEE

INTERFACES AND HUMAN COMPUTER INTERACTION

GAME AND ENTERTAINMENT TECHNOLOGIES

PROGRAM CHAIR

Katherine Blashki, Noroff University College, Norway

COMPUTER GRAPHICS, VISUALIZATION, COMPUTER VISION AND IMAGE PROCESSING

PROGRAM CHAIR

Yingcai Xiao, The University of Akron, USA

MCCSIS GENERAL CONFERENCE CO-CHAIRS

Piet Kommers, University of Twente, The Netherlands
Pedro Isaías, Universidade Aberta (Portuguese Open University), Portugal

INTERFACES AND HUMAN COMPUTER INTERACTION

COMMITTEE MEMBERS

Aidan Rowe, University of Alberta, Canada
Alexander Gelbukh, Instituto Politécnico Nacional, Mexico
Alexander Kröner, Technische Hochschule Nürnberg Georg Simon Ohm, Germany
Ana Cristina Bicharra Garcia, Universidade Federal Flumninese, Brazil
Antonio Maria Rinaldi, University Napoli Federico II, Italy
Arcadio Reyes, Universidad de Malaga, Spain
Arianna D. Ulizia, IRPPS-CNR, Italy
Aris Alissandrakis, Linnaeus University, Sweden
Arttu Perttula, Tampere University of Technology, Finland
Bruno Santana da Silva, Federal University of Rio Grande do Norte, Brazil
Caterina Senette, Istituto di Informatica e Telematica, CNR (Pisa), Italy
Celia Martinie, Universite Paul Sabatier, France
Connie Veugen, Vrije Universiteit Amsterdam, The Netherlands
Daniela Trevisan, Universidade Federal Fluminense, Brazil
Eduardo Tanaka, Universidade Estadual de Campinas, Brazil
Elaine Hayashi, University of Campinas, Brazil
Evan Golub, University of Maryland, USA
Florian Reinfrank, TU Graz, Austria
Francisco Jurado, Universidad Autónoma de Madrid, Spain
Francisco Madera Ramirez, Universidad Autonoma de Yucatan, Mexico

Hanan Salam, University of Pierre And Marie Curie-Paris 6, France
Hanna Wirman, The Hong Kong Polytechnic University, Hong Kong
Heiko Hornung, University of Campinas, Brazil
Isabela Gasparini, Universidade do Estado de Santa Catarina (UDESC), Brazil
Jesuk Ko, Gwangju University, South Korea
Joe Dumas, User Experience Consultant, USA
José Antonio Macías Iglesias, Universidad Autónoma de Madrid, Spain
José Luis Tapia Fabela, Universidad Autónoma del Estado de México, Mexico
Junia Anacleto, Federal University of Sao Carlos, Brazil
Kathia Oliveira, Université de Valenciennes et du Hainaut-Cambrésis, France
Keith Nesbitt, University of Newcastle, Australia
Khaled Khankan, Taibah University, Saudi Arabia
Larbi Esmahi, Athabasca University, Canada
Leonelo Almeida, University of Technology, Paraná, Brazil
Lucia Vilela Leite Filgueiras, Escola Politécnica da Universidade de São Paulo, Brazil
Luciana Romani, Embrapa Agricultural Informatics, Brazil
Maki K. Habib, The American University in Cairo, Egypt
Manuel Ortega Cantero, University Castilla – La Mancha, Spain
Marcelo Romero Huertas, Universidad Autonoma del Estado de Mexico, Mexico
Marco Antonio Ramos Corchado, Universidad Autonoma del Estado de Mexico, Mexico
Marina Buzzi, Istituto di Informatica e Telematica, CNR, Italy
Marja Kankaanranta, University of Jyvaskyla, Finland
Matjaz Gams, Jozef Stefan Institute, Slovenia
Maxim Bakaev, Novosibirsk State Technical University, Russia
Michael Hobbs, Deakin University, Australia
Michael Hohl, Anhalt University of Applied Sciences, Germany
Monica Bordegoni, Politecnico di Milano, Italy
Nadine Vigouroux, IRIT, CNRS, Paul Sabtier University, France
Nayat Sanchez-Pi, Universidade do Estado do Rio de Janeiro, Brazil
Niklas Ravaja, University of Helsinki, Finland
Nitendra Rajput, IBM Research, India
Nuno Otero, Linnaeus University, Sweden
Otniel Portillo Rodriguez, Universidad Autonóma del Estado de México, Mexico
Panagiotis Germanakos, Department of Computer Science, University of Cyprus, Cyprus
Pauliina Tuomi, Tampere University of Technology, Finland
Philip Breedon, Nottingham Trent University, UK
Philippe Gorce, South Toulon University, France
Pilar Lacasa, University of Alcala, Spain
Radoslaw Niewiadomski, University of Genoa, Italy
Roberto Pereira, University of Campinas (UNICAMP), Brazil
Rodrigo Bonacin, DSSD – CTI Renato Archer, Brazil
Rommert Casimir, Tilburg University, The Netherlands
Sandro José Rigo, Unisinos, Brazil
Silvio Cazella, Ufcspa , Brazil
Toni Granollers, University of Lleida, Spain
Vagner Figueredo de Santana, IBM Research, Brazil
Xiaokun Zhang, Athabasca University, Canada

GAME AND ENTERTAINMENT TECHNOLOGIES

COMMITTEE MEMBERS

Abdennour El Rhalibi, Liverpool John Moores University, UK
Alf Inge Wang, Norwegian University of Science and Technology, Norway
Ali Arya, Carleton University, Canada
Anastasios Karakostas, Aristotle University of Thessaloniki, Greece
Anthony Whitehead, Carleton University, Canada
Areti Damala, University of Strathclyde, UK
Armelle Prigent, Universite de La Rochelle/L3I, France
Arttu Perttula, Tampere University of Technology, Finland
Carla Hoekendijk, Independant consultant/developer, The Netherlands
Castulus Kolo, Macromedia University of Applied Sciences, Germany
Christos Bouras, University of Patras and Computer Technology Institute, Greece
Connie Veugen, Vrije Universiteit Amsterdam, The Netherlands
Daniel Cermak-sassenrath, IT University of Copenhagen, Denmark
Ellen Brox, Norut – Northen Research Institute, Norway
Emanuele Carlini, ISTI, CNR, Italy
Eric Gressier, Cnam – Cedric, France
Erik Van Der Spek, Eindhoven University of Technology, The Netherlands
Eva Hudlicka, Psychometrix Associates, USA
Gabriele D`Angelo, University of Bologna, Italy
Hanna Wirman, Hong Kong Polytechnic University, Hong Kong
Harry Agius, Brunel University London, UK
Ian Marshall, Coventry University, UK
Isabelle Astic, Cnam, France
James Bowman, University of Advancing Technology, USA
Jesper Juul, Royal Danish Academy of Fine Arts, School of Design, Denmark
Jouni Smed, University of Turku, Finland
Kai Kimppa, Turku School of Economics, Finland
Laura Ricci, University of Pisa, Italy
Louis-martin Guay, University of Montreal, Canada
Magnus Johansson, Stockholm University, Sweden
Marcia Medeiros, UFC – FANOR(Devry), Brazil
Marcos Rodrigues, Sheffield Hallam University, UK
Melinda Jacobs, Subatomic, The Netherlands
Michael Katchabaw, University of Western Ontario, Canada
Michel Simatic, Telecom Sudparis, France
Mikael Collan, Lappeenranta University of Technology, Finland
Monica Gavrielidou, University of Thessaly, Greece
Niklas Ravaja, University of Helsinki, Finland
Pauliina Tuomi, Tampere University of Technology, Finland
Pilar Lacasa, University of Alcala, Spain
Richard Bartle, University of Essex, UK
Roberto Beauclair Seixas, National Institute of Pure and Applied Mathematics, Brazil
Rommert Casimir, Tilburg University, Netherlands
Ruck Thawonmas, Ritsumeikan University, Japan
Spyros Vosinakis, University of the Aegean, Greece
Stefano Ferretti, University of Bologna, Italy

Thrasyvoulos Tsiatsos, Aristotle Univerisity of Thessaloniki, Greece
Torill Mortensen, University of Copenhagen, Denmark
Vagelis Kapoulas, Computer Technology Institute & Press "Diophantus", Greece
Windson Viana , UFC, Brazil
Yoshihiro Okada, Kyushu University, Japan

COMPUTER GRAPHICS, VISUALIZATION, COMPUTER VISION AND IMAGE PROCESSING

COMMITTEE MEMBERS

Adrian Jarabo, University of Zaragoza, Spain
Aiert Amundarain, Ceit, Spain
Alessandro Rizzi, Università degli Studi di Milano, Italy
Arcadio Reyes Lecuona, Universidad de Málaga, Spain
Belen Masia, Universidad de Zaragoza, Spain
Brian dAuriol, Kyung Hee University, South Korea
Bruce Campbell, Rhode Island School of Design, USA
C. C. Lu, Kent State University, USA
Carina Gonzalez, University of La Laguna, Spain
Carla Binucci, Università degli Studi di Perugia, Italy
Carlo Nati, Working Group for the development of tecnoscientific knowledge, Italy
Chang Ha Lee, Chung-Ang University, South Korea
Charalampos Georgiadis, The Aristotle University, Greece
Chien-hsing Chou, Tamkang University, Taiwan
Christos Gatzidis, Bournemouth University, UK
Creto Vidal, Federal University of Ceará, Brazil
Daniel Thalmann, Nanyang Technological University, Singapore
Dariusz Frejlichowski, West Pomeranian University of Technology, Poland
David Wortley, Immersive Technology Strategies, UK
De-Yuan Huang, National Central University, Taiwan
Dmitriy Vatolin, Moscow State University, Russia
Fatima Nunes, University of São Paulo, Brazil
Francisco Gonzalez Garcia, Next Limit Technologies, Spain
Gaetano Impoco, Co.R.Fi.La.C., Italy
Galina Pasko, Uformia, Norway
Gilles Gesquiere, Liris, France
Giovanni Farinella, University of Catania, Italy
Giovanni Puglisi, University of Cagliari, Italy
Giuseppe Patanè, CNR-IMATI, Italy
Hans-Jörg Schulz, University of Rostock, Germany
Helmuth Trefftz, Eafit University, Colombia
Igor Sevastianov, Nvidia Corp, USA
Ingemar Ragnemalm, Linköping University, Sweden
Isaac Rudomin, Barcelona Supercomputing Center, Barcelona
Jairo Sanchez, Vicomtech-IK4, Spain
Jian Chang, Bournemouth University, UK

Jon Goenetxea, Vicomtech-ik4, Spain
Jose Ignacio Echevarria, Universidad de Zaragoza, Spain
José Pascual Molina Massó, Universidad de Castilla-la Mancha, Spain
Jose Remo Ferreira Brega, Sao Paulo State University, Brazil
Josip Almasi, VRSpace, Croatia
Juan Manuel Gonzalez Calleros, Meritorious Autonomous University of Puebla, Mexico
Jyoti Singhai, Maulana Azad National Institute of Technology Bhopal, India
Kadi Bouatouch, Irisa, University of Rennes 1, France
Karolj Skala, Rudjer Boskovic Institute, Croatia
Krzysztof Okarma, West Pomeranian University of Technology, Poland
Krzysztof Walczak, Poznan University of Economics, Poland
Kurt Debattista, The University of Warwick, UK
Leandro Fernandes, Federal Fluminense University, Brazil
Lihua You, Bournemouth University, UK
Linda Giannini, Teacher, eTwinning Ambassador , Italy
Luca Grilli, Universita degli Studi di Perugia, Italy
Luciano Soares, Insper Instituto de Ensino e Pesquisa, Brazil
Luis Unzueta, Vicomtech-IK4, Spain
Marc Daniel, Ecole Superieure D'Ingenieurs de Luminy, France
Marcelo Guimaraes, UNIFESP / FACCAMP, Brazil
Marla Schweppe, Rochester Institute of Technology, USA
Marta Fairen, Universitat Politècnica de Catalunya, Spain
Mauricio Hess-Flores, University of California, Davis, USA
Mubbasir Kapadia, Rutgers University, USA
Mu-Chun Su, National Central University, Taiwan
Nadia Ambrosetti, Universita Degli Studi Di Milano, Italy
Nicoletta Adamo-Villani, Purdue University, USA
Paolo Pingi, CNR – ISTI, Italy
Pascual González López, University of Castilla-La Mancha, Spain
Patrick Gioia, Orange Labs, France
Pawel Forczmanski, West Pomeranian University of Technology, Poland
Peter Dannenmann, RheinMain University of Applied Sciences, Germany
Pierre-frederic Villard, University of Lorraine, France
Piotr Lech, West Pomeranian University of Technlogy, Poland
Quan Wen, University of Electronic Science and Technology of China, China
Rene Rosenbaum, University of Rostock, Germany
Richard Kulpa, M2s University of Rennes 2, France
Robert Laramee, Swansea University, UK
Roman Durikovic, Comenius University in Bratislava, Slovakia
Sandra Morales, Polytechnic University of Valencia, Spain
Shaun Bangay, Deakin University, Australia
Simon Richir, Arts et Metiers ParisTech, France
Stratos Stylianidis, Aristotle University of Thessaloniki,, Greece
Theresa-marie Rhyne, Computer Graphics Consultant, USA
Valery Adzhiev, Bournemouth University, UK
Victor Debelov, Institute of Computational Mathematics and Mathematical Geophisycs, Russia
Xenophon Zabulis, FORTH, Greece

Xiaogang Jin, Zhejiang University, China
Xiaosong Yang, Bournemouth University, UK
Xuejun Hao, Columbia University, USA
Zhong-hui Duan, University of Akron, USA
Zongyi Liu, Microsoft, USA
Zoran Ivanovski, Faculty of Electrical Engineering and Information Technologies, Macedonia

KEYNOTE LECTURE

HUMAN COMPUTER INTERACTION AND SOCIETAL IMPACT – CAN HCI INFLUENCE PUBLIC POLICY MAKING AND IT POLITICS?

Professor Jan Gulliksen, KTH Royal Institute of Technology, Sweden

ABSTRACT

Research and research funding organizations are becoming more and more aware of the need to conduct research that proves some form of utility to the society and has some form of practical impact. There are several different ways of making research that has practical relevance and that can contribute to changing and improving society. This talk aims at discussing ways to plan, conduct research with the aim of improving the society and also show how we should make use of our research knowledge and positions to influence politics and public policy making.

Full Papers

WHEN DESIGNERS ARE NON-DESIGNERS: OPEN ENDEDNESS VS. STRUCTURE OF DESIGN TOOLS

Alma Leora Culén[1], Andrea Gasparini[1], Pavla Minaříková[2], Roman Novotný[2],
Sumit Pandey[1] and Ladislava Zbiejczuk Suchá[2]
[1]Department of Informatics, University of Oslo, P. Boks 1080, 0316 Blindern, Oslo, Norway
[2]Department of Information and Library Studies, Masaryk University, Arna Nováka 1/1, Brno, Czech Republic

ABSTRACT

In this paper, we explore types of toolsets that are suitable for design thinking processes, when design teams consist of non-designers. We have conducted a series of workshops to experiment with open-ended, semi-structured and structured tools, using design thinking for libraries as a research case. Our results clearly indicate that semi-structured tools fare best regarding variety of outputs, breadth of ideas and engagement of participants.

KEYWORDS

Design thinking, team creativity, tools for design thinking.

1. INTRODUCTION

Design thinking (DT) provides a tremendous opportunity for designers and non-designers alike to create new and sustained creative and innovation-oriented practices. Design thinking has been advocated across many areas of business, e.g., (Brown, 2009; Lockwood, 2009; Martin, 2009) and has emerged as a desirable orientation towards innovation within many organizations. DT has been outlined as a co-design method in teams, often multidisciplinary and including users and other stakeholders. It has been framed as a process, both in the academic literature (Bjögvinsson et al., 2012; Cross, 2011, 1982; Schön, 1983) and in the commercial design practice (IDEO, 2014). While framing of the process as a design practice may differ among authors, it can be described as a sequence of actions related to problem definition (understanding of the problem space, users and their needs), ideation, prototyping, and evaluation. These practices that are based on DT processes are supported through use of diverse methods, tools and techniques, frequently including design ethnography, different forms of mapping (affinity, mind, concept), brainstorming, visual representations of ideas (sketching, storyboarding), prototyping and evaluation techniques (ranging from rapid idea evaluation, to prototype testing).

The design thinking approach to innovation has been in focus within several different academic fields, design (Buchanan, 1992; Cross, 2011), service design (Polaine et al., 2013; Stickdorn and Schneider, 2012), management (Johansson-Sköldberg et al., 2013; Lockwood, 2009) and interaction design and HCI (Culén and Følstad, 2015; Finken et al., 2014) among others. However, findings from these diverse fields, especially when it comes to multidisciplinary teams, their creativity and tools that should support it, are still not fully explored. In particular, little research is drawn from fields such as psychology or creativity studies that address team compositions and tools that support design-thinking practices in organizations. The importance of team composition and tools that the team works with grows when teams include non-professional designers or are even exclusively composed of non-designers.

In this paper, then, we focus on how to make tools that are suitable for DT processes when design teams consist of non-professional designers, supported by at least one researcher experienced in DT, and with at least one member with background in either design or art. As all authors are researchers engaged with design thinking and design thinking practices in the context of libraries, DT tool set design for libraries was chosen as a case for this paper. The paper describes reflections and lessons learned from three workshops that were conducted with four matched teams of participants. The teams included library employees, students in library and information sciences, graduate students in interaction and HCI design, researchers experienced in DT, designers or artists (not necessarily familiar with innovation through DT processes). At least one library employee on each team was familiar with DT, and at least one participant was a novice to DT. What is important to mention is that, in addition to findings from the literature on DT and team work, e.g., (Toh and Miller, 2015) that support similar choices, this team composition corresponds to how we commonly compose teams in our own innovation through DT library work.

Multiple toolkits, e.g., ("Design Kit"; "frog Collective Action Toolkit | frogdesign.com"; "Use our methods") have been designed to support DT processes in organizational settings, where more frequently than not, novices to design thinking are part of the design team. Some of the toolkits were made specifically for supporting design thinking within libraries ("EN | Libdesign"; IDEO, 2014). While these toolkits on design thinking may be useful on occasions of starting a new project(s), they are not enough to create sustainable innovation and prototyping practices in the library (Pandey, 2015). In his paper, Pandey suggests that these toolkits are too abstract and too far removed from actual organizational work practices to be adoptable for sustained organizational innovation and to become a source of change in non-design practice (ibid.). Therefore, he argues that DT tools and methods need to be kept semi-structured by design, allowing for collaborative co-shaping, appropriation and improvisation during use by participants involved. Extending this line of argumentation, our concern was the level of open-endedness vs. structured guidance that the tools that we designed afforded during the DT process. However, as we consider tools to be inseparable from the group of people using them, we also were concerned with how concepts of openness to experience and conscientiousness, correlated to abilities of divergent and convergent thinking within the field of personality psychology, trying to use this research to make team compositions that support different styles of thinking. At the same time, the teams were to have approximately the same sets of skills and abilities. Their work, then, could be used to discuss how tools mediate interactions within teams and how are expected outcomes related to the use of more structured vs. more open tools when working with multidisciplinary teams.

Our paper contributes to better understanding of design thinking tools, when multidisciplinary teams composed of non-designers use them. In particular, open-endedness opposed to fully structured tools was explored. We also make a contribution by actively using the research from psychology and creativity studies. We believe that both fields have much to contribute in helping shape creative practices when working on design with non-designers. Findings indicate that semi-structured tools work best with respect to generating outputs, breadth of ideas and engagement of participants.

The paper is structured as follows: the next section provides a short background for this paper. Section 3 presents our case, including methods, participants and tools. Section 4 presents findings and discussion. Conclusion ends the paper.

2. BACKGROUND

Amabile (Amabile, 1983) conceptualized a framework for creativity, consisting of domain-relevant skills, creativity-relevant skills, and task motivation, which represent a set of necessary and sufficient components of creativity. These cognitive abilities, personality characteristics, and social factors were seen as contributors to creative process. In line with Amiabile's framework, recent research in psychology shows that there is increasing evidence suggesting that individual differences in creativity reflect particular combinations of thinking styles, affective dispositions, and motivational preferences, e.g., (Soroa et al., 2015). Some researches also addressed issues of creativity within design teams, e.g., Toh and Miller (Toh and Miller, 2015) who used personality traits and risks attitudes on creative concept selection to study creativity of engineering teams. Since (Costa and McCrae, 1992) introduced the five factor model (openness to experience, conscientiousness, extraversion, agreeableness, and neuroticism) of basic personality traits, the model has been subject of discussion, refinement, attempts to quantify, correlate and measure diverse related characteristics. Some of this research has direct relevance for design thinking processes. For example, divergent and convergent thinking, both crucial to successful outcomes of design thinking, have been strongly correlated to openness to experience and conscientiousness, respectively (Kaufman et al., 2013; Kaufman, 2013; Mussel et al., 2011). Kaufman refines the concept of openness to experience, and looks at how its four facets (explicit cognitive ability, intellectual engagement, affective engagement, and aesthetic engagement) affect creative achievements.

Furthermore, recent discourses on creativity include not only balancing of spontaneous (divergent, open) and controlled (structured) processing of creative cognition (Mok, 2014), but also how creativity expresses itself in everyday life. In her paper (Tanggaard, 2013), Tanggard goes beyond considering convergent and divergent thinking, anchoring creativity in social practice and suggesting that 1) creativity is an everyday phenomenon resulting in continual processes of "making the world" 2) there is a close relationship between human beings and material tools in the creativity process and 3) there is a close relationship between continuity and renewal, meaning that materials, tools, things, institutions, normative practices and "ways of doing" already in the world are taken as starting points for new creations. The second point that Tanggard makes was of a particular interest for this paper, as we wanted to deepen our understanding of how to work best with tools for DT and also how to design them for other non-designers to use as tools for sustained innovation practices, in line with Tanggard's points 1) and 3). Similar findings have also been made by Pandey (Pandey, 2015), where the author states: *"for catalyzing sustained reflexive and collaborative transformation of work practices, design thinking practices need to be transformed into proto-practices, i.e., design methods novel to an organization need to be integrated with familiar elements from the context and the practice of the organizational communities involved"*. Pandey has explicitly studied prototyping practices in the library settings, and appropriated the sustainable practice design framework from (Kuijer et al., 2008) with the DT approach to frame new practices that can take root at the library. Involving bodily performances, creating crisis of routines and generating a variety of performances are highlighted by both Pandey and Kuijer et al. as means of configuring new practices and hence are also considered in this paper as tools that help creative processes. We describe the use of these factors in detail in the context of our case study in the following section.

3. DT IN LIBRARIES: INTERPLAY BETWEEN TOOLS AND PEOPLE

This section describes our case, which focuses on the use of design thinking in libraries, and presents our method to explore the relation between tools, group composition and both creative and new knowledge production related to the process. Recently, design thinking has become one of the important ways that libraries try to use to innovate their services and improve user experiences. Libraries are also in the process of re-evaluating their role in community lives, affected strongly by the recent advances of technology (Culén and Gasparini, 2015, 2014; IDEO, 2014). Therefore, libraries are, a very good case for methodological and work-practice related studies examining the implementation of design thinking as a way of fostering changes and establishing innovative practices that are not disruptive, but rather sustainable over time.

3.1 Method

In this research, we have used a workshop format to explore expected outcomes of DT processes when tools used for DT varied in the degree of open-endedness. Three workshops were carried out, the first one using the structured and semi-structured tool set, the second used completely open-ended tools, and the third workshop repeated a session with semi-structured tools, but used a different research facilitator and new participants. All workshops gave 15 minutes long introduction to DT, for participants who were not familiar with it; followed by 45 minutes of DT process work based on a given task.

The first workshop was run in two sessions. Two teams (5-6 participants per team, including facilitators) participated in each session, see Figure 1. The first session was facilitated by the research team one (RT1), while the second session was run by the research team 2 (RT2). The team with 5 participants had one facilitator, and the larger team two. Both research teams have long experience with DT, but are not trained as professional designers, exception being one of the researchers on RT2 who also has design background.

Figure 1. The participants of the first workshop. Method cards on the right, one card per team, were used to formulate a design brief: use the card, as a departure point of DT process, to create an online presentation of the method on the card

During the first 45 minutes session, both design teams were led by RT1 and both used *structured* tools inspired by (IDEO, 2014), see Figure 2. The method cards shown in Figure 1, right, were designed by some of the authors (Zbiejczuk Suchá et al., 2015). The cards were used as part of the design brief. The design teams were to use DT to find out how to best represent one of the method cards on some digital platform. After a break, the second 45 minutes session, facilitated by RT2, was carried out. This time, both teams used a *semi-structured* approach that incorporated diverse bodily performances, creating crises of routines and generating variety of performances. Subsequently, RT1 and RT2 facilitators joined for a reflection on actions and discussion of outcomes. RT2 facilitated the second workshop couple of weeks later. The workshop had a total of 6 participants, whose skills and background matched participants of the first workshop. The format of the workshop and the design brief were the same as for the first workshop (15 minutes long introduction in DT for novice team members, followed by a 45 minutes long design process). This time an *open* approach was used. Reflection and discussion of achieved results concluded the workshop. RT1 facilitated the third workshop, with total of five participants. This workshop took place at the same time as the second one, but they were not co-located. Everything was done in the same way as before, but the *semi-structured* approach was repeated in order to see how well it worked under different facilitation.

3.2 Participants

20 individuals in total, divided into four design teams, participated in the above-described workshops, and as specified in the Table 1. Two teams participated in two design sessions each, while the third and the fourth team had a single design session. Teams were matched by their background as follows: 1 participant on each team had art or design background (although some, at present, were pursuing different education), at least 1 was a library employee with prior experience from at least three DT workshops, at least 1 team member was a novice to DT and was either a library employee or a student, and finally, at least one (and at most 2) members were research facilitators. These background combinations were intentional, ensuring that each team would have a person skilled in divergent thinking, and a person skilled in convergent thinking. Since research facilitators were familiar with those who had previous experience with DT in libraries, their engagement level, motivation and cognitive skills observed during other workshops were also taken into account. Teams were to be as equal as possible regarding skills and personality traits, so that the differences in outcomes could be co-related with qualities of tools and, as little as possible, differences among teams.

3.3 Tools and Sessions

As mentioned, the main differentiator between sessions 1-3 was openness of tools and support they provided in creative processes. Session 4 was carried out to verify results from the first workshop.

What we call tools in this paper, are objects, such as method cards, verbal and written instructions to follow, canvases providing a way to organize input or ideas, visual tools, such as sketches, post-its and other things that influence productivity and creativity during the design process.

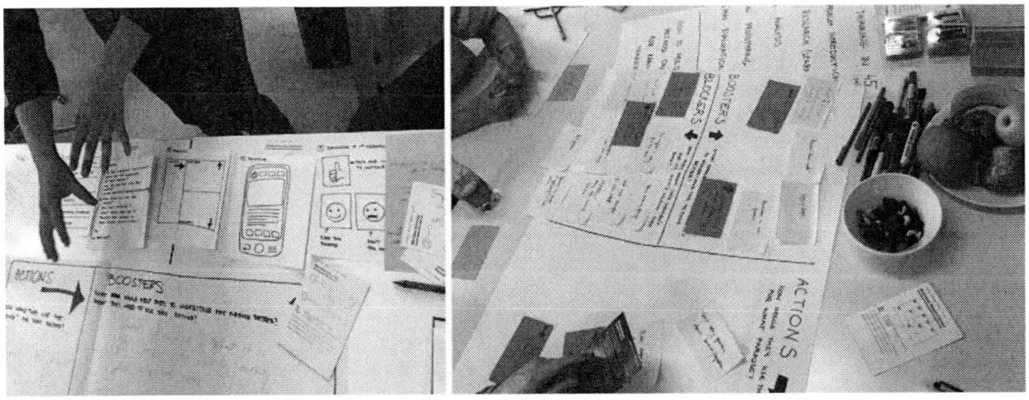

Figure 2. Guided work during the Session 1, with the tools inspired by IDEO: a set of method cards by LibDesign, an interview guide, boosters, blockers and actions map, a quick evaluation of generated ideas guide

A set of tools used in conjunction with different sessions is provided in Table 1.

Table 1. Summary of workshop sessions, approach and tools used

	Facilitators	Approach	Participant teams	Tools
1st session Workshop 1	Research team RT1	Structured approach	T1 (5): 3 researchers, 1 novice student, 1 librarian. T2 (6): 3 researchers, 1 librarian, 2 novices	Focused sheet with research questions, post-its, markers, pre-designed canvas, cards
2nd session Workshop 1	RT2	Semi-structured approach	T1 and T2, same as above	Post-its, whiteboard, index cards, markers, cards
3rd session Workshop 2	RT2	Open approach	T3 (6) 3 researchers, 2 librarians, a novice student	Markers, paper, whiteboard, cards
4th session Workshop 3	RT1	Semi-structured approach	T4 (5) 2 researchers, 1 librarian, master students (novice and some experience)	Post-its, whiteboard, index cards, markers, cards

Method cards (Zbiejczuk Suchá et al., 2015) were given to each team in all sessions. The card set is to be digitized and the activity in all sessions focused on how to represent the method cards digitally. Each team got one card to work with. Participants were to use quick ethnography and interview someone outside the workshop on how they understand the method card. Are images clear? Are they self-explanatory? Is the text clear, do they understand the essence of the method? Workshop participants had 10 minutes to complete this task. As the workshop took place at the university, potential interviewees were sitting in their offices, just outside the workshop location. The team members could interview people in any constellation they found desirable, either individually, in pairs or the whole team, if that was preferred. After the interviews were done, the teams were to work on a canvas inspired by the Value Proposition Canvas (Osterwalder et al., 2014) with booster, blocker and action fields. This type of coding and categorizing could be labeled as a "structural coding" or "protocol coding" according to Saldaña (Saldaña, 2013). It is based on the categorization of data according to the pre-established system represented here by the canvas. This type of coding is appropriate for some disciplines with previously developed coding systems, something that was field-tested, but the pros and cons of its use in design thinking are still unexplored. After the use of Canvas, the teams shifted to prototyping.

Figure 3. Session 2 had much less structure. Each participant was to think of some ideas individually, then all were to cluster them, standing, moving, discussing – using the space also vertically

While the second session closely followed the structure of the first session, the tools and methods used were changed to a semi-structured format. Using the ethnographic data from session 1, the participants were taken through a series of rapid design exercises that used constructive materials like post-its, index cards, whiteboards and markers rather than pre-defined templates. The form and structure of the outcomes from these exercises was largely generative while the nature of content expected was briefly introduced at the beginning of each exercise as opposed to highly directed and regulated actions. In other words, participants were provided with materials for each exercise and *'what'* outcomes they were expected to generate with these materials but not directed on *'how'* they should generate these outcomes. This was in line with the notion of generative materials and semi-regulated actions used in conjunction with specially configured spaces (Pandey, 2015). Some functional constraints were also suggested as appropriate for each exercise. This helped in eliciting a variety of improvised performances from the workshop participants due to a crisis of routine that was triggered by an absence of a formal structured process directing each exercise. The first exercise started with identifying all possible insights and putting them on post-its, which were finally put up on a vertical surface, to stimulate bodily engagement, see Figure 3 and Figure 4, and a fuller range of movement from the participant's side. Participants were asked to put only one insight on each post-it so they could be moved around and clustered, following the principles of open coding, into emergent categories corresponding to themes brought up by the informants. Using these themes as points of departure, each participant was asked to work individually using index cards and generate 6 or more possible solutions to the design brief under consideration. Most participants kept standing up while ideating so as to be able to move through the identified themes and notes from the previous exercise. The ideas generated during this exercise were also clustered collaboratively after discussions, highlighting possible explorations and directions that could be incorporated into the final concept. Finally, relevant ideas and themes explored and clustered were combined together into possible feature proposals for a digital platform, as in session 1.

Figure 4. Standing, sitting varying positions around work, and the room. Freely drawing, ideating

4. DISCUSSION

In our work to prepare for the workshops, we have thought of the necessary and sufficient components of creativity given by (Amabile, 1983). Domain relevant skills were represented well by including librarians and researchers and students in information and library sciences. Creativity-relevant skills were taken care of by including people with art and design background, as well as interaction design researchers and practitioners. The task motivation, we hope, was provided by interest in innovation in the library at the first place, meeting between different disciplines and, perhaps, somewhat by a really good pizza. These task motivations were in part intrinsic (for some participant) and extrinsic only for others.

The outcomes of the first three sessions were really interesting, in terms of numbers and variety of ideas, broadness of ideas and engagement of participants. Although discussions during Session 1 were interesting, people have remained fixed to their seats and to instructions and canvas provided. The session gave some outputs and some paper prototypes were made, but it was clear that the output was constrained by the Canvas tool used. Session 2 provided most diverse ideas, the most interesting prototypes and has engaged people both mentally and physically.

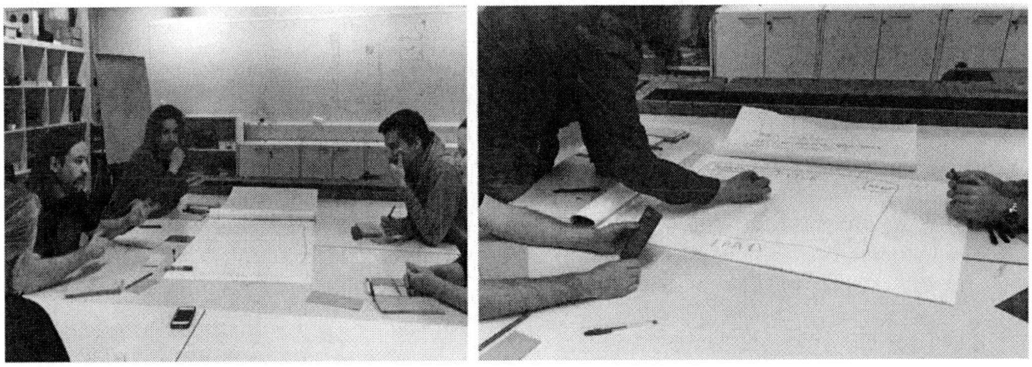

Figure 5. Session 3 did not use pre-made tools or instructions. Total lack of structure actually hindered creativity

Session 3 provided no particular instructions for participants on how to proceed after the quick ethnography session (instructed in the same way as in the workshop 1, lasting 10 minutes). The facilitator did not lead the ideation, but rather participated in line with others. The mini ethnography session was done in two groups. One group had two novices who had problems understanding the method card themselves. "How are we going to interview people, when we do not know what this is about ourselves?" one of them asked. In the end, the results of their interview corresponded to how they felt – their interviewee did not understand the sketches on the card, and in 10 minutes did not manage to make sense of it. The second group though, had interview findings that were about that we saw earlier. This example shows that one group did not have a proper motivation for mini ethnography. During ideation activities, many short stretches of silence broke discussions that were barely trickling. In spite of facilitators' encouragements to freely use the space, write on the blackboard, use flip charts, only after direct prompts, one librarian with DT workshop experiences stood up and tried to use flipchart to put down the ideas. 45 minutes did not suffice to finish making a paper prototype. When the workshop ended, a short (3 minutes) paper prototyping session was introduced. A structure for prototyping (a drawing of an iPad), was provided, and the participants were asked to quickly sketch and interface for the method card they worked with. Suddenly, participants had many ideas and in less then 3 minutes, one reasonable paper prototype was made. This last exercise showed that the problem was not with the team, but with the openness of the process when all participants were non-designers. Al least, a small guidance through the process was required. Figure 5 shows well the contrast between this session and the previous ones.

In Session 2, a researcher with design background led one of the design teams. This team performed better than the other one in terms of the range of ideas considered, and the ability to converge to solution that was subsequently prototyped. Both teams, though, outperformed results from Session 1 in terms of variety, breadth of ideas. In order to make sure that results similar to those of the first workshop, if conducted with a matched team but with another facilitator team, were obtainable, workshop 3 was organized, see Figure 6.

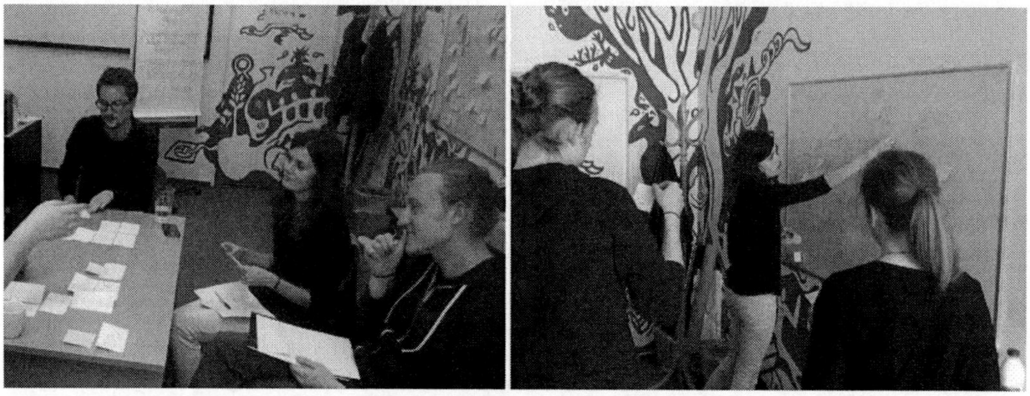

Figure 6. Session 4. Semi-structured workhop. Veryfying the 2nd session

Also in this workshop, engagement was excellent, and the ideation broad. These findings indicate that indeed semi-structured approach works well, confirming Pandey and Tanggard assumptions (Pandey, 2015; Tanggaard, 2013). Thus, as predicted by (Toh and Miller, 2015) no structure does not work for non-designers, while a strict structure bounds them to only what is asked of them.

5. CONCLUSION

Whenever working with design thinking, one should consider the composition of design teams, as well as tools that are to be used in the process. Cross-disciplinary research may be challenging, but it also hides a lot of potential for design processes, as people often have different thinking stiles and different affinities towards analysis or synthesis. In this paper, we focused on how tools, in terms of their open-endedness, influence the design process, when the attempt is made to keep design teams as similar as possible. Three workshops with matched teams were conducted. Both convergent and divergent thinking were represented in each team, as well as novel influences by including novices to DT. Semi-structured tools have given the best output.

ACKNOWLEDGEMENT

This work was conducted as part of the project LibDesign, Design Thinking as a service quality improvement tool in specialized libraries, under EEA and Norway Grants CZ 07 Scholarship Program & Bilateral Scholarship Program number NF-CZ07-ICP-4-4932015.

REFERENCES

Amabile, T.M., 1983. The Social Psychology of Creativity: A Componential Conceptualization.

Bjögvinsson, E., Ehn, P., Hillgren, P.-A., 2012. Design Things and Design Thinking: Contemporary Participatory Design Challenges. Des. Issues 28, 101–116.

Brown, T., 2009. Change by design: how design thinking can transform organizations and inspire innovation. HarperCollins Publishers, New York, NY.

Buchanan, R., 1992. Wicked Problems in Design Thinking. Des. Issues 8, 5–21.

Costa, P.T., McCrae, R.R., 1992. Four ways five factors are basic. Personal. Individ. Differ. 13, 653–665.

Cross, N., 2011. Design Thinking: Understanding How Designers Think and Work. Bloomsbury Academic, Oxford ; New York.

Cross, N., 1982. Designerly ways of knowing. Des. Stud. 3, 221–227.

Culén, A.L., Følstad, A., 2015. Innovation in HCI - What Can We Learn from Design Thinking. Interact. Des. Archit. J. 27, 109–114.

Culén, A.L., Gasparini, A., 2015. HCI and Design Thinking: Effects on Innovation in the Academic Library, in: Proceedings of the International Conferences on Interfaces and Human Computer Interaction. Presented at the IHCI 2015, IADIS Press, pp. 3–10.

Culén, A.L., Gasparini, A., 2014. Find a Book! Unpacking Customer Journeys at Academic Library, in: The Seventh International Conference on Advances in Computer-Human Interactions. Presented at the ACHI 2014, ThinkMind, pp. 89–95.

Design Kit [WWW Document], 2016, URL http://www.designkit.org/ (accessed 5.6.16).

EN | Libdesign, 2016, URL http://libdesign.cz/en/(accessed 5.6.16).

Finken, S., Culen, A.L., Gasparini, A.A., 2014. Nurturing Creativity: Assemblages in HCI Design Practices, in: Proceedings of DRS 2014. Presented at the Design: Big Debates, Design Research Society, Umeå, pp. 1204–1217.

frog Collective Action Toolkit | frogdesign.com, 2016, URL http://www.frogdesign.com/work/frog-collective-action-toolkit.html (accessed 5.6.16).

IDEO, 2014. Design Thinking for Libraries. URL http://designthinkingforlibraries.com/ (accessed 5.6.16).

Johansson-Sköldberg, U., Woodilla, J., Çetinkaya, M., 2013. Design Thinking: Past, Present and Possible Futures. Creat. Innov. Manag. 22, 121–146.

Kaufman, J.C., Pumaccahua, T.T., Holt, R.E., 2013. Personality and creativity in realistic, investigative, artistic, social, and enterprising college majors. Personal. Individ. Differ. 54, 913–917.

Kaufman, S.B., 2013. Opening up Openness to Experience: A Four-Factor Model and Relations to Creative Achievement in the Arts and Sciences. J. Creat. Behav. 47, 233–255.

Kuijer, L., Jong, A. de, Eijk, D. van, 2008. Practices As a Unit of Design: An Exploration of Theoretical Guidelines in a Study on Bathing. ACM Trans Comput-Hum Interact 20, 21:1–21:22.

Lockwood, T., 2009. Design thinking: integrating innovation, customer experience and brand value. Allworth Press, New York, NY.

Martin, R.L., 2009. Design of business: Why design thinking is the next competitive advantage. Harvard Business Press.

Mok, L.W., 2014. The interplay between spontaneous and controlled processing in creative cognition. Front. Hum. Neurosci. 8, 663.

Mussel, P., Winter, C., Gelléri, P., Schuler, H., 2011. Explicating the Openness to Experience Construct and its Subdimensions and Facets in a Work Setting. Int. J. Sel. Assess. 19, 145–156.

Osterwalder, A., Pigneur, Y., Bernarda, G., Smith, A., Papadakos, T., 2014. Value Proposition Design: How to Create Products and Services Customers Want, 1 edition. ed. Wiley, Hoboken.

Pandey, S., 2015. Proto Design Practice: translating design thinking practices to organizational settings. Interact. Des. Archit. J. 129–158.

Polaine, A., Løvlie, L., Reason, B., 2013. Service design: from insight to implementation. Rosenfeld Media.

Saldaña, J., 2013. The coding manual for qualitative researchers /, 2nd ed. ed. SAGE Publications, Los Angeles [i.e. Thousand Oaks, Calif] :

Schön, D.A., 1983. The reflective practitioner: How professionals think in action. Basic books.

Soroa, G., Balluerka, N., Hommel, B., Aritzeta, A., 2015. Assessing interactions between cognition, emotion, and motivation in creativity: The construction and validation of EDICOS. Think. Ski. Creat. 17, 45–58.

Stickdorn, M., Schneider, J., 2012. This is Service Design Thinking: Basics, Tools, Cases, 1 edition. ed. Wiley.

Tanggaard, L., 2013. The sociomateriality of creativity in everyday life. Cult. Psychol. 19, 20–32.

Toh, C.A., Miller, S.R., 2015. Creativity in design teams: the influence of personality traits and risk attitudes on creative concept selection. Res. Eng. Des. 27, 73–89.

Use our methods [WWW Document], 2016, d.school. URL http://dschool.stanford.edu/use-our-methods/ (accessed 5.6.16).

Zbiejczuk Suchá, L., Novotný, R., Minaříková, P., Šimková, G., Chodounská, A., Horák, M., 2015. Libdesign: 35 methods for better services, QQML Conference 2015, Paris, France.

INVOLVING SENIORS IN THE DESIGN OF HOME-BASED WELFARE TECHNOLOGIES: A REVIEW OF EXISTING RESEARCH

Rune B. Rosseland
Department of Informatics, University of Oslo, Boks 1072 Blindern, 0316 Oslo, Norway

ABSTRACT

This paper introduces a set of guidelines for involving seniors in participatory design (PD) of home-based welfare technologies. The guidelines are produced through a literature review of existing research and focus on the practical experiences of involving seniors in participatory design activities. The guidelines suggest that the design process should be tailored to the needs and abilities of the participants in a way that supports the development of trusted relationships, and facilitates learning and understanding among researchers and participants. The guidelines are useful for researchers and designers intending to involve seniors in the design of home-based welfare technologies, and give recommendations regarding the recruitment, motivation, and engagement of seniors in participatory design activities.

KEYWORDS

Participatory Design, welfare technology, seniors, elderly, configuring participation

1. INTRODUCTION

Approximately half of the adult population of Norway is over 50 years, and by 2050, "the number of people over the age of 67 will have doubled" (The Norwegian Design Council, 2010). There is a growing interest in ICT-based solutions that can assist seniors in maintaining normal lives in their own homes, and avoid or reduce dependence on health care services (Vines et al., 2012). The term home-based welfare technology is used to signify any ICT-based technology that can help give seniors living at home a better quality of life (Teknologirådet, 2009). Existing efforts to produce home-based welfare technologies for seniors often have a technology-centered focus that neglects to consider the everyday, situated use of such technologies (Huldtgren et al., 2013). As a result, many technological solutions are difficult to incorporate into the daily lives and routines of the intended users. This can lead to incorrect use, or even a refusal to use such technologies (Ballegaard et al., 2008).

To ensure that the proposed solutions will be accepted and used by senior citizens, participatory design (PD) emphasizes the importance of involving users in all stages of the design of new technologies, from early ideation to final evaluation (Dickinson et al., 2003; Eisma et al., 2003; Uzor et al., 2012). However, involving seniors in the design of innovative home-based welfare solutions is not straightforward. As Grönvall and Kyng (2012) points out, little research has focused on PD studies within home-based healthcare. Research on home-based settings is fundamentally different from organizational and workplace settings, which has been the domain of PD over the last 40 years (Grönvall and Kyng, 2012; Iversen et al., 2004; Lindsay et al., 2012a, 2012b). People arrange their homes and conduct their lives in a variety of ways, and this diversity must be acknowledged in PD-projects focusing on home-based welfare technologies (Grönvall and Kyng, 2012).

Furthermore, many current seniors have very limited experience with modern digital technologies and have difficulties envisioning how it can be used to improve their daily lives (Eisma et al., 2004; anonymous, 2014). Some reject the idea that they need any technological aid (Aarhus et al., 2010). Thus, seniors' lack of knowledge, experience, and interest in new technologies complicates their involvement in the design and development of welfare technologies.

There is a lack of research on, and guidelines for, involving seniors in PD-activities focusing on home-based welfare technologies. There are some examples of very good work that specifically addresses this issue (e.g. Aarhus et al., 2010; Brandt et al., 2010; Chen and Wang, 2012; Dickinson et al., 2003, 2003; Eisma et al., 2004; Grönvall and Kyng, 2012; Huldtgren et al., 2013; Lindsay et al., 2012a, 2012b), as well as other work that touch upon the subject in related research (Culén and Velden, 2013; Davidson and Jensen, 2013; De Schutter and Vanden Abeele, 2008; Massimi et al., 2007; Massimi and Baecker, 2006; Uzor et al., 2012; Vines et al., 2012; Xie et al., 2012).

Given the unique challenges researchers experience when conducting PD with seniors, it is important to evaluate what has been done so far and see how we can improve our methodological approach. This paper attempts to sum up current knowledge on the subject and produces a set of guidelines for how to involve seniors in PD. (See also Grinter (1997) for a similar approach to workplace studies, or Ertner et al. (2010) on empowerment in the PD discourse.)

2. APPROACH

Google Scholar, ACM Digital Library, and PDC proceedings were searched for papers containing the keyword *participatory design*, and at least one of the following: *elderly, senior, older, aging, or gerontechnology*. The search results were scanned for abstracts relating to the subject of involving seniors in participatory design of home-based welfare technologies. The initial search yielded 35 papers. After careful reading, 10 papers were excluded due to lack of descriptions of recruitment and involvement of senior participants. The identified papers can be categorized into one of two general categories. The first category (n=10) includes papers that focus on a specific design context and employ participatory design methods in order to produce either: prototypes of products, or design guidelines for the specific design context. Many of these papers give short descriptions or recommendations regarding the involvement of senior participants, but do not go into much detail on these topics. The second category (n=15) includes papers that focus specifically on issues regarding the involvement of seniors in participatory design processes. These papers identify a range of different challenges and benefits of involving senior participants and examine these in much greater detail than those in the first category.

Several papers emphasize the importance of involving all relevant stakeholders when doing care-related PD (Aarhus et al., 2010; Eisma et al., 2003; Huldtgren et al., 2013). While acknowledging the importance of involving other stakeholders, due to space limitations, this paper focuses exclusively on the involvement of seniors in PD activities.

3. FINDINGS

This section describes the findings of the literature review. It is divided into 12 themes that have emerged through the analysis. The themes and resulting guidelines are grouped into the following three categories: *selecting and recruiting participants*, *motivating participants*, and *engaging participants*.

3.1 Selecting and Recruiting Participants

The selection and recruitment of participants are crucial to any participatory design process, and particularly so when it comes to old or frail participants (Eisma et al., 2004).

3.1.1 Avenues of Recruitment

Finding potential participants is not an easy task, and should be carefully considered as it has important implications for the subsequent design process (Brandt et al., 2010; Eisma et al., 2004; Lindsay et al., 2012a). There are a number of different avenues of approaching potential participants: Word-of-mouth (Davidson and Jensen, 2013); distributing flyers and posters (Uzor et al., 2012); mail shots, telephone calls, and personal visits to different organizations, clubs, residential homes, day centers (Eisma et al., 2004); charities, support groups, health professionals (Lindsay et al., 2012a); and established research panels (Vines et al., 2012).

The chosen method of approach may influence potential participants' ability to perceive and understand what they are being asked to take part in. For example, letters are difficult to read for people with visual impairments, and telephone calls can be challenging for those who are hard of hearing (Lindsay et al., 2012a). Several papers report good experiences from asking professionals, as well as different organizations and groups that work with seniors to help identify suitable participants (Eisma et al., 2004; Grönvall and Kyng, 2012; Lindsay et al., 2012a).

3.1.2 Clarify Assumptions, Expectations, Purpose, and Goals

During the recruitment process, it is necessary to explain and clarify what participation will entail, both to potential participants and to people who provide access to potential participants. It is, therefore, important that the researchers can give a clear account of the purpose and goals of the process, the structure and timing of activities, and level of engagement they expect from the participants. It is crucial to be as honest as possible and not promise more than can be delivered, as unmet expectations can quickly lead to waning interest and withdrawal from the project (Aarhus et al., 2010; Huldtgren et al., 2013).

Furthermore, the framing of the project and the words used to describe its purpose and goals play an important role in how people respond when being recruited. Ballegaard et al. (2008) and Brandt et al. (2010) underline the potential stigmatizing effects of being recruited to a study focused on age-related diseases and disabilities, or simply based on stereotypical understandings of what it means to be old.

3.1.3 "Seniority"

Brandt et al. (2010) and Huldtgren et al. (2013) emphasize that there are no typical users of welfare technology for seniors. 'Senior citizens' is not a specific and easily identifiable group of people, but an incredibly diverse and heterogeneous group with a wide range of needs and abilities. Therefore, simply recruiting people based on their biological age may not ensure that the participants are suited for the subject of the research (Vines et al., 2012).

Rather than focusing on biological age, Brandt et al. (2010, p. 402) argues for using the term situated elderliness: "With situated elderliness we refer to practices that for some reason or another has become more challenging or perhaps even impossible to carry out by himself or herself." Situated elderliness thus allows us to focus on the everyday practices that our participants engage in and address the specific challenges they experience.

3.1.4 Group Composition and Ability to Participate

Several papers report difficulties coordinating suitable times for the participants to meet, and to get commitments for continued involvement (Aarhus et al., 2010; Vines et al., 2012). Grönvall and Kyng (2012) found that the health conditions of their elderly participants varied from day to day, making it difficult to schedule PD sessions. One participant terminated her involvement because the PD activities were too exhausting. Ballegaard et al. (2008) suggest taking the daily lives of participants as a starting point and making sure that the development process fits well with all participants' daily activities.

Moreover, it is important to consider group composition. Clashes of personalities and interests may occur, with adverse effects on the scheduled activities and their outcomes (Lindsay et al., 2012b). Lindsay et al. (2012a, p. 528) found that working with pre-existing groups was very beneficial in this regard: "The environment in these groups lent confidence to the participants and they were able to support each other when articulating their thoughts". By recruiting existing support groups, and only those groups that unanimously agreed to participate, they were able to ensure that the participants were comfortable with each other and that they were able to work together. However, working with pre-existing groups introduces potential issues with representability and conflicting group interests that need to be considered (Grönvall and Kyng, 2012).

Sustar et al. (2013) found that the most productive workshop groups were composed of a mix of designers and older participants. By comparing the number of topics covered and turns taken (during discussion) by differently composed groups of participants, they found that "more topics and a higher number of turns were developed by mixed groups than by older people or designers working on their own" (ibid, p. 653).

When it comes to the ideal number of participants in groups, the prevalent notion seems to be to keep groups small in order to enable all participants to contribute. Sustar et al. (2013) had 1-2 participants working together with 1-2 designers per groups of 3, Uzor et al. (2012) used 3 – 4 participants and 2 facilitators per group. Lindsay et al. (2012b) recommends 4 – 5 participants per group, but also recommends over-recruiting in the case of last minute cancellations.

3.2 Motivating Participants

Multiple papers underline the importance of motivating seniors to take part in PD activities and processes (Eisma et al., 2004; Grönvall et al., 2010; Grönvall and Kyng, 2012). Hence, it is useful to be aware of some motivational factors that can inspire seniors to engage in PD. Furthermore, it is important to deliver on the promises that are made in the recruitment process in order maintain participants' interest and engagement (Eisma et al., 2004). If participants' expectations are not met, they are likely to lose interest and might withdraw from the project (Grönvall et al., 2010; Huldtgren et al., 2013). This also underlines the need to be clear about expectations, purpose, and goals of the project during the recruitment process.

3.2.1 Social Contact

Many participants enjoy the social aspect of taking part in co-design activities. New acquaintances are made, and new friendships are forged. Several authors recommend either making the activities themselves into pleasurable social events (Davidson and Jensen, 2013; Vines et al., 2012) or providing designated time for socializing (Eisma et al., 2004). It is also recommended that researchers, in addition to facilitating social interaction among the participants, try to build good relationships with the participants. This helps participants feel more comfortable and helps build a level of trust that is crucial to their successful participation (Grönvall et al., 2010; Lindsay et al., 2012a). Eisma et al. (2004) found that the good relationships they were able to establish with some of the participants made it possible to involve them at a higher level: One participant volunteered to administer a questionnaire to her contacts, while another agreed to speak on behalf of the users at an industry seminar. Blythe et al. (2010, p. 169) also underline the importance of connecting with the participants: "If we have succeeded at all in enhancing our participants' experience of ageing through technological interventions, it is not by observing users, identifying needs, goals and activities, then specifying the requirements of design solutions. It is by spending time, living with them a little, and by letting our relationship grow to a point where we could respond empathically with something. The form of response was less of a solution to a problem and more like a gift."

However, building intimate and trusted relationships with the participants can also become problematic. Grönvall et al. (2010) found that their close connection to their participants made it difficult to collect data and conclude the study.

Finally, it is important to be aware of potential pitfalls regarding participants' need for social interaction. Some see their engagement in the design process as an opportunity to socialize, which may make it difficult to maintain focus (Eisma et al., 2004; Grönvall and Kyng, 2012).

3.2.2 Learning

Several authors point to learning as an important motivation for seniors to participate in PD activities (e.g. Eisma et al., 2004; Grönvall et al., 2010). Participants see their involvement as an opportunity to learn about new technologies and the possibilities they represent. "In our experience the enjoyment that people get from learning about new products and technologies is an important motivation to participate, and to participate again. This is especially true of the hands-on activities" (Dickinson et al., 2003, p. 5).

While learning about new technology can be a strong motivator in itself, it also enables older participants to understand and connect with younger, more tech-savvy generations (Massimi and Baecker, 2006). Thus, learning about technology becomes an identity-forming activity. By better understanding popular new technologies they are able to connect with and relate to their children or grandchildren on a different level than before.

However, as underlined by Dickinson et al. (2003, p. 2) "many older people do not feel comfortable 'learning while doing' in unsupported environments" and require assistance and guidance in order to learn. This may present opportunities for researchers to motivate continued participation by arranging activities in a way that allows participants to learn about technology under the guidance of researchers. It can also be an opportunity to develop personal relationships and trust between participants and researchers.

3.2.3 Appreciation of Contribution

People take pride in their contributions, and it is important to show participants that their input is valued and respected. Participants are likely to be de-motivated if they experience that their input is not acted upon or incorporated into mock-ups and prototypes (Huldtgren et al., 2013). Conversely, participants feel valued and develop a sense of ownership of the designs when they experience that their input is taken seriously (Taylor et al., 2012).

It is important to help participants appreciate that their opinions matter: "The lack of confidence felt by many older people about technology meant that it was important to provide an atmosphere within focus-groups encouraging participants to value their own opinions, express themselves honestly, and enjoy their experience" (Eisma et al., 2004, p. 135).

3.2.4 Regular Contact and Information about Progress

It is important to nurture and maintain participants' interest and motivation throughout the entire process. "Disillusionment and waning interest [can] occur if there [is] a delay between the initial contact and any particular project activity" (Eisma et al., 2004, p. 134). They distributed a quarterly newsletter to all participants, which resulted in a number of requests for technological assistance. By visiting participants and helping them with their problems, the researchers were able to develop participants' interest and loyalty to the project. These visits also provided good opportunities for the researchers to gain insights into participants' issues and concerns (Eisma et al., 2004).

It is important to establish channels of communication and to keep them open throughout the entire process (Huldtgren et al., 2013). Lindsay et al. (2012a) established consistent points of contact for each group of participants. The consistent point of contact would facilitate the group meetings and was the closest member of the design team to the participants. Thus, all participants had one member of the design team as their main contact, leading to the development of trusted relationships: "Because of insights into the participants lives gained from active debates with them, the consistent point of contact found that they became an advocate for the participants at design team meetings that were conducted without them, where their opinions might otherwise have been marginalized" (Lindsay et al., 2012a, p. 528).

3.3 Engaging Participants

This section looks at themes related to how participants are engaged in the PD process. There are many methods and approaches available for PD researchers, but there is not enough existing research to give a coherent analysis of how well the different approaches are suited for working with older participants. Therefore, rather than focusing on specific methods, this section looks at different ways of communicating and interacting with older participants in order to maximize the benefits of their involvement.

3.3.1 Practicalities

In choosing a location for the activities, it is important to consider accessibility and travel options for the participants, taking care to accommodate any mobility problems or other special needs the participants may have (Uzor et al., 2012). Rooms should be well lit, quiet, and free from distractions, and restrooms should be easily accessible (Lindsay et al., 2012b). Providing refreshments may be necessary, depending on the duration of the activities, and also serves an important purpose in creating a social and enjoyable atmosphere for the participants (Davidson and Jensen, 2013; Vines et al., 2012). Finally, PD activities can be tiresome and it is important to adjust the duration and timing to suit the participants (Blythe et al., 2010; Eisma et al., 2004). Even when sessions are going well, it is important to respect the pre-set schedule in order to avoid putting pressure on participants to spend more time than was originally agreed (Lindsay et al., 2012b).

3.3.2 Adapt Methods to Participants and Context

Typical PD methods include ethnographic observations and field studies, questionnaires, interviews, focus groups, future workshops, and design of and experimenting with physical and computer-based prototypes (Ballegaard et al., 2008; Davidson and Jensen, 2013; Dickinson et al., 2003; Verdezoto and Wolff Olsen, 2012). Several authors underline the need to modify and adapt these methods when working with older participants in order to maximize the benefits of the activities (Blythe et al., 2010; Vines et al., 2012; Xie et al., 2012). "When questionnaires were personally administered by researchers, spontaneous excursions into users' own experiences and demonstrations of various personal devices were relatively common and provided many useful insights" (Eisma et al., 2004, p. 135).

Blythe et al. (2010) found ethnographic interviews difficult because some of the older participants were suspicious of the interviewer, and grew tired and sometimes distressed by the questions they were asked. It was, therefore, necessary to adapt the methods to suit the participants.

3.3.3 Use of Language and Things to Talk With

The use of language and hands-on activities with artifacts or prototypes are recurring themes in many papers. It is imperative that researchers and participants are able to understand each other and communicate effectively, and the use of technical jargon and intangible concepts and metaphors can often have an alienating effect on older participants: "'Computer-speak' is not simply confusing, but can act as a significant barrier both to technology use and to communication about technology" (Eisma et al., 2004, p. 138).

Having tangible artifacts to manipulate, test, explore, and critique is very helpful in overcoming language problems and promoting creativity. It also helps participants understand the possibilities of the technologies much better than any verbal explanation can (Eisma et al., 2004). For example, when Vines et al. (2012) allowed participants to use and explore prototypes of digital cheques, the seniors were able to articulate the usefulness of the technology far more succinctly than the researchers had been able to do. Lindsay et al. (2012a, p. 522) describes how the development of individually tailored prototypes during the later iterative stages of the project allowed for "an in-depth exploration of individual's thoughts and experiences with the prototypes".

The artifacts become things to think and talk with. It reduces the strain of having to mentally envision intangible concepts and future uses and lets participants focus on concrete properties and possible uses of the artifacts. Hands-on sessions with physical artifacts also make it possible for the researcher to observe differences between what people say they do and what they actually do (Eisma et al., 2004).

However, as Blythe et al., (2010, p. 163) noted when discussing the use of artifacts as so-called *tickets to talk*, it can be equally important to have tickets to be silent: "Often during interviews and even during 'ticketed' talk there is an obligation to keep the conversation going which could be overly demanding for these residents. Tickets to be silent were as important as tickets to talk in this setting."

Furthermore, some people are not comfortable with expressing their opinions during group sessions and must be called on to contribute to the discussion. Davidson and Jensen (2013, p. 8) found it necessary to call on some participants in order to get them to talk: "As with any group setting, some people talk more than others, however we found that the 'non-talker' had valuable insights."

Another way of facilitating discussion and communication is through co-questioning (Lindsay et al., 2012a). By allowing the participants to ask each other questions based on a thematic guide, researchers are able to pull into the background and listen and observe the development of the discussion. There is a good chance that this will uncover misunderstandings that need to be addressed, as well as generate novel insights and new questions that can form the basis for future discussions.

Lindsay et al. (2012a, p. 528) also point to some dangers regarding analysis and interpretation of workshop transcripts: "The analysis could, inadvertently, disempower the participants and undermine our relationship with them if we took action on our analysis too early in the process". Accordingly, it is important to discuss interpretations and analyses with participants to ensure that their input is not misrepresented.

3.3.4 Realistic Context

The context of the different PD activities can play an important role in the outcome of the activities. Several papers recommend conducting interviews and observations in the homes of the participants, or in a realistic setting, particularly during information gathering activities and during evaluation and testing of different mock-ups and prototypes (Aarhus et al., 2010; Ballegaard et al., 2008; De Schutter and Vanden Abeele, 2008; Eisma et al., 2004). This allows researchers to gather qualitative data and gain insights into the everyday lives of the participants that would not otherwise have been possible (Dickinson et al., 2003). "In-home interviews [...] produced many stories about how the equipment in the home was obtained, how people learned to use it, who supported them, and the reporting of a variety of both good and bad experiences" (Eisma et al., 2004, p. 136).

Contextual inquiries are also useful for uncovering underlying motives and capture the true meaning of participants' statements. For example, De Schutter and Vanden Abeele (2008) learned that one participant's love of Tai Chi, and another's passion for news were both rooted in a desire to connect and spend time with friends and family.

Finally, it is imperative to respect the rituals of hospitality when visiting the homes of participants. The home is the occupants' refuge from the outside world and is closely tied to their identity and sense of self. Inviting strangers into the home can be intimidating and draining, and it is important that researchers do not overstay their welcome (Grönvall et al., 2010). "Apparently insignificant actions like refusing a cup of tea can make a tremendous difference to the comfort of your host" (Dickinson et al., 2003, p. 4).

4. GUIDELINES

The twelve themes identified in the literature review have been condensed into twelve guidelines on how to involve seniors in PD with a focus on home-based welfare technologies.

4.1 Recruiting Participants

- Carefully consider how potential participants are identified and recruited, and how their inclusion may affect the outcome of the process. Try to enlist the help of professionals and other people who have a network of, and regular contact with, potential participants.
- Be as clear and concise as possible when describing the purpose and goals of the project, and make sure that participants understand what participation will entail for them. Take care not to offend or stigmatize potential participants by explicit or implicit assumptions.
- Seniors are not a homogenous group. Biological age may not be a suitable criterion for recruiting participants. Participants and potential future users should be selected by focusing on situated challenges and everyday contexts. Try to understand the problem space through the lived experiences of participants.
- Consider potential participants' physical and mental ability to take part in the planned PD activities. Make efforts to adjust the timing of activities to suit the participants other daily activities. Keep groups small in order to allow all participants to be heard, and to foster open and productive discussions. Recruiting pre-existing groups can help ensure open and productive group sessions, and prevent breakdowns.

4.2 Motivating Participants

- Facilitate informal social interaction during meetings. Provide refreshments. Try to establish trusted relationships with and among participants, but beware of potential pitfalls.
- Arrange the design activities in a way that allows participants to learn and develop themselves. Provide guidance and assistance, and an environment that is conducive to exploration and learning. Use the opportunity to develop good relationships with participants.
- Allow all participants to express themselves, and be to be heard, without fear of ridicule or embarrassment. Show that their input is valued.
- Make sure participants are informed about project progress and future plans. Establish consistent points of contact for participants in order to reduce complexity and stress for the participants. Keep lines of communication open throughout the entire process.

4.3 Engaging Participants

- Carefully consider transportation, accessibility, light and noise levels, access to restrooms, etc. when choosing a location. Adjust duration and timing to suit participants.
- Participants' wellbeing is more important than strict methodological protocol. Combine and adapt methods to suit context and participants.
- Use clear and understandable language. Avoid the use of technical jargon, metaphors, and intangible concepts. Use artifacts extensively as things to talk about, explore, and critique. If possible, consider

developing individually tailored prototypes to gain more detailed insights. Verify transcripts and interpretations with participants to avoid misunderstanding and misrepresentation.

- Try to conduct interviews, observations, and hands-on explorations and evaluations in the homes of participants, or in other realistic contexts. This is likely to produce richer and more detailed insights into the lives of the participants than more neutral lab settings. Be sensitive when entering the homes of participants and respect the rituals of hospitality. Do not overstay your welcome.

5. CONCLUSION

Given the increasing interest in technologies that can help prevent or delay the onset of age-related health challenges and relieve the strain on public healthcare resources, it is critical to understand how welfare technologies can become meaningful and helpful parts of seniors' everyday practices. Participatory design promotes the involvement of potential and future users in the entire design process to ensure that the end result will meet the users' situated needs and demands. This paper gives an overview of current knowledge and provides some important points to consider for anyone intending to involve seniors in PD of home-based welfare technologies. The guidelines are generally applicable to participants of all ages but are particularly important to take into account when involving seniors in PD. The guidelines are not intended as a step-by-step guide for conducting PD with seniors but as points of departure for researchers and designers intending to involve seniors in PD. Some of the points will be more relevant than others, depending on the intentions and resources of the project. It is, therefore, necessary to carefully reflect on how the guidelines apply to specific projects. Furthermore, the guidelines suggest that the design process should be tailored to the needs and abilities of the participants in a way that supports the development of trusted relationships, and facilitates learning and understanding among researchers and participants. Hence, it is vital that the project organization is flexible enough to accommodate participants' needs and abilities, and to adapt to unforeseen challenges and obstacles. Accordingly, project planning and management, as well as proactive facilitation of activities, are critical to the successful involvement of seniors.

REFERENCES

Aarhus, R., Grönvall, E., Kyng, M., 2010. Challenges in participation. *Proceedings of the 4th International Conference on Pervasive Computing Technologies for Healthcare* (PervasiveHealth). pp. 1–4.

Ballegaard, S.A., Hansen, T.R., Kyng, M., 2008. Healthcare in everyday life: designing healthcare services for daily life. *Proceedings of the SIGCHI Conference on Human Factors in Computing Systems*. pp. 1807–1816.

Blythe, M. et al., 2010. Age and experience: ludic engagement in a residential care setting. ACM Press, pp. 161–170. doi:10.1145/1858171.1858200

Brandt, E. et al., 2010. Communities of everyday practice and situated elderliness as an approach to co-design for senior interaction. *Proceedings of the 22nd Conference of the Computer-Human Interaction Special Interest Group of Australia on Computer-Human Interaction*. pp. 400–403.

Chen, P.-C., Wang, X., 2012. Design for well-being in China: lessons learned from exploratory workshops. ACM Press, pp. 81–84. doi:10.1145/2348144.2348170

Culén, A.L., Velden, M. van der, 2013. The Digital Life of Vulnerable Users: Designing with Children, Patients, and Elderly, in: Aanestad, M., Bratteteig, T. (Eds.), *Nordic Contributions in IS Research, Lecture Notes in Business Information Processing*. Springer Berlin Heidelberg, pp. 53–71.

Davidson, J.L., Jensen, C., 2013. Participatory Design with Older Adults: An Analysis of Creativity in the Design of Mobile Healthcare Applications. *Proceedings of the 9th ACM Conference on Creativity & Cognition, C&C '13*. ACM, New York, NY, USA, pp. 114–123. doi:10.1145/2466627.2466652

De Schutter, B., Vanden Abeele, V., 2008. Meaningful play in elderly life. *Proceedings of ICA.*

Dickinson, A. et al., 2003. Domesticating technology. In-home requirements gathering with frail older people. *Proc. of 10th International Conference on Human-Computer Interaction HCI*. pp. 827–831.

Eisma, R. et al., 2003. Mutual inspiration in the development of new technology for older people. *Proceedings of Include*. pp. 252–259.

Eisma, R. et al., 2004. Early user involvement in the development of information technology-related products for older people. *Univers. Access Inf. Soc. 3*, 131–140. doi:10.1007/s10209-004-0092-z

Ertner, M., Kragelund, A.M., Malmborg, L., 2010. Five enunciations of empowerment in participatory design. *Proceedings of the 11th Biennial Participatory Design Conference*. pp. 191–194.

Grinter, R.E., 1997. From Workplace to Development: What Have We Learned So Far and Where Do We Go? *Proceedings of the International ACM SIGGROUP Conference on Supporting Group Work: The Integration Challenge,* GROUP '97. ACM, New York, NY, USA, pp. 231–240. doi:10.1145/266838.266917

Grönvall, E. et al., 2010. The intrinsic fragility of elderly care networks: five challenges in participatory design practices. *Ther. Strateg. Chall. User Involv*. Des. 20–23.

Grönvall, E., Kyng, M., 2012. On participatory design of home-based healthcare. *Cogn. Technol. Work* 1–13.

Huldtgren, A. et al., 2013. Towards Community-Based Co-creation. In Holzinger, A., Ziefle, M., Hitz, M., Debevc, M. (Eds.), *Human Factors in Computing and Informatics*. Springer, Berlin, Heidelberg, pp. 585–592.

Iversen, O.S., Kanstrup, A.M., Petersen, M.G., 2004. A Visit to the "New Utopia": Revitalizing Democracy, Emancipation and Quality in Co-operative Design. *Proceedings of the Third Nordic Conference on Human-Computer Interaction*, NordiCHI '04. ACM, New York, NY, USA, pp. 171–179. doi:10.1145/1028014.1028040

Lindsay, S. et al., 2012a. Empathy, participatory design and people with dementia. ACM Press, pp. 521–530. doi:10.1145/2207676.2207749

Lindsay, S. et al., 2012b. Engaging older people using participatory design. *Proceedings of the 2012 ACM Annual Conference on Human Factors in Computing Systems*. pp. 1199–1208.

Massimi, M., Baecker, R., 2006. Participatory design process with older users. *Proc. UbiCoomp 2006 Workshop on Future Media*.

Massimi, M., Baecker, R.M., Wu, M., 2007. Using participatory activities with seniors to critique, build, and evaluate mobile phones. *Proceedings of the 9th International ACM SIGACCESS Conference on Computers and Accessibility*. pp. 155–162.

Sustar, H., Jones, S., Dearden, A., 2013. Older People as Equal Partners in Creative Design. In Holzinger, A. et al. (Eds.), *Human Factors in Computing and Informatics, Lecture Notes in Computer Science*. Springer, Berlin, Heidelberg, pp. 649–656.

Taylor, A. et al., 2012. TeleWEAR: Engaging Users and Suppliers of Telecare in Product Design. *CHI '12 Extended Abstracts on Human Factors in Computing Systems, CHI EA '12*. ACM, New York, NY, USA, pp. 2637–2642. doi:10.1145/2212776.2223849

Teknologirådet, 2009. Rapport-Fremtidens-alderdom-og-ny-teknologi.pdf [WWW Document]. URL http://teknologiradet.no/wp-content/uploads/sites/16/2013/08/Rapport-Fremtidens-alderdom-og-ny-teknologi.pdf (accessed 2.27.14).

The Norwegian Design Council, 2010. *Innovating with people: The business of inclusive design*. The Norwegian Design Council, Oslo, Norway.

Uzor, S., Baillie, L., Skelton, D., 2012. Senior Designers: Empowering Seniors to Design Enjoyable Falls Rehabilitation Tools. *Proceedings of the SIGCHI Conference on Human Factors in Computing Systems, CHI '12*. ACM, New York, NY, USA, pp. 1179–1188. doi:10.1145/2207676.2208568

Verdezoto, N.X., Wolff Olsen, J., 2012. Personalized Medication Management: Towards a Design of Individualized Support for Elderly Citizens at Home. *Proceedings of the 2nd ACM SIGHIT International Health Informatics Symposium, IHI '12*. ACM, New York, NY, USA, pp. 813–818. doi:10.1145/2110363.2110463

Vines, J. et al., 2012. Cheque Mates: Participatory Design of Digital Payments with Eighty Somethings. *Proceedings of the SIGCHI Conference on Human Factors in Computing Systems, CHI '12*. ACM, New York, NY, USA, pp. 1189–1198. doi:10.1145/2207676.2208569

Xie, B. et al., 2012. Co-designing an e-Health Tutorial for Older Adults. *Proceedings of the 2012 iConference, iConference '12*. ACM, New York, NY, USA, pp. 240–247. doi:10.1145/2132176.2132207

MODELS AS BRIDGES FROM DESIGN THINKING TO ENGINEERING

Hilda Tellioğlu
Vienna University of Technology, Multidisciplinary Design Group
Favoritenstrasse 9-11/187, A-1040 Vienna, Austria

ABSTRACT

In this paper we address the critical link between design thinking (DT) and software engineering by investigating the role of models as artifacts crossing the boundaries from designers to other disciplines like engineering. We introduce our approach (*mDT, multidisciplinary Design Thinking*) by describing its methods. We show how the results of a DT process can be handed over to others. We focus on the characteristics of the artifacts DT induce. We suggest using *design models* (i.e., use, systems and interaction models) to create a smooth transition from design to engineering and other disciplines. We illustrate our *mDT* by giving some examples from a previous DT project before concluding the paper.

KEYWORDS

Design Thinking, Models, User-Centered Design, Innovation.

1. INTRODUCTION

More and more "radical innovations" are needed "in our connectivity infrastructure" (Weiser and Brown, 1996). This is because of the imbedding, invisibility and the ease-of-use requirements to technologies that we use in our everyday life. Several theories like sociotechnical systems (Cherns, 1976), actor network (Callon, 1987), activity (Engeström et al., 1999; Nardi, 1995) or other methodology centered ones like participatory (Bodker et al., 2004), user-centered (Cooper et al., 2007) or contextual design (Beyer and Holtzblatt, 1998) try to bring user, use and context issues into the design and development of systems. They inform software engineering about user needs, user capabilities and use context restrictions and affordances. Creativity and innovation were subject to art and economy related disciplines. The increase of technology use everywhere in the last years made it essential to invest more into innovation and creativity in product and service management. At this point, design thinking (DT) became an interesting approach as a new way of thinking. Facilitating innovation and idea generation was originally motivated by economic factors. It was studied to create new forms of managing business. It enables improvements in innovation management, but it is still unclear to many managers which DT approach is most useful and effective for their business (Tschimmel, 2012).

It is for sure that creative supporting environments are needed to design and develop interactive computer systems of future. Such environments enable foster, promote, improve, and increase creative experiences, processes, products, or services. To create and maintain such environments is still a challenge for most companies, especially if there are several teams working on different parts in a design and production workflow. In most cases, innovatively created new ideas need to be handed over to engineering teams. Interaction between designers and engineers must be smooth and continuous by avoiding misunderstandings and disagreements that would have impact on the quality of the product-in-development or on the production process as a whole. Besides cultural differences the language, the artifacts and the representations of work differ in design and engineering teams. Conflicts that occur because of these differences can create big problems during the entire process, which might be the reason for a failure at the end. This is exactly the challenge we are dealing with in our research.

In this paper we address this critical link between design thinking (DT) and software engineering in product and service development. We introduce our approach (*mDT, multidisciplinary Design Thinking*) by describing the methods as well as their relation to each other in a time line. The focus of *mDT* is providing means to improve the communication among stakeholders involved in a design project by creating and maintaining common understanding among all. It applies well-known and -established artifacts like models for the mediation and exchange, which is scientifically and empirically well-informed by our investigations so far. Furthermore, *mDT* systemizes models based on their purpose and content to express the areas of communication like use aspects, system properties and functions as well as interaction mechanisms. This is the main difference of *mDT* to other DT approaches known so far that mainly focus on economic factors.

After the introduction of the *mDT* we show how the results of DT process can be handed over to engineering teams. We focus on the characteristics of the artifacts DT induce. We suggest ways to create a smooth transition from design to engineering, especially by creating three different types of models: use, systems and interaction models. We illustrate our *mDT* by giving some examples from a previous DT project before concluding the paper.

2. RELATED WORK

User participation has been explored and further developed in computer science for a very long time (Bodker et al., 2004). By means of principles user participation in a project can be defined and kept throughout a process as well as the nature and content of outcomes. Besides being a mutual learning process, active genuine user participation increases the potential of visions produced by a project and then of the systems to be used according to their intentions.

The principle of firsthand experience can be realized especially during the in-depth analysis phase of a project. It builds on the proposition that to understand any phenomenon one needs to experience it firsthand. This can be done by qualitative methods, like observation, shadowing, in situ interviews, and thinking-aloud experiments, followed by systematic analysis and presentation of the gathered information. Models are very powerful tools for the representation of work, for the presentation of ideas and for the articulation of activities (Tellioğlu, 2013; Schmidt et al., 2009). Finally, anchoring vision involves informing target group about the project's goals, visions, and plans, and again getting their feedback.

Besides ethnographic qualitative methods (like participatory observations, in-depth open interviews, data analysis) several innovative methods have been established in participatory IT design, partly stemming from other disciplines: cultural probes (to understand the cultural context of users), provocative requisites (to achieve provocation, ambiguity, inspiration in context) (Dahley et al., 1998), design games (as a playful way to gain design ideas) (Brandt, 2006; Pedersen and Buur, 2000), narrative posters (to tell the whole story on one sheet) (Sandelowski, 1991), design workshops (to be creative and explore ideas in a team), technology probes (to get a hint about real life interaction). These methods can be applied to facilitate participatory explorative design by involving users, also from other disciplines. They at the same time guarantee that solutions developed fit to users' skills, environments and requirements.

DT was introduced as a cognitive process of designers two decades ago (Cross et al., 1992; Eastman et al., 2001). The goal was to understand design creativity and to improve design-thinking abilities. Today, DT is defined as "a complex thinking process of conceiving new realities, expressing the introduction of design culture and its methods into fields such as business innovation" (Tschimmel, 2012, p.2). The most popular DT models are: the 3 I Model (Inspiration, Ideation, Implementation) by IDEO (2001) (Brown and Wyatt, 2010, 33ff); the HCD Model (Hearing, Creating and Delivering) again by IDEO; the model of Understand, Observe, Point of View, Ideate, Prototype and Test by Hasso-Plattner Institute (Thoring and Müller, 2011); the 4 D or Double Diamond design process model (Discover, Define, Develop, Deliver) by British Design Council (2005); the Service Design Thinking Model (Exploration, Creation, Reflection, Implementation) by Stickdorn and Schneider (2010).

Seen from actor network theory point of view (Callon, 1987), intermediaries created by applying DT impact the setting in which they evolve so they influence the design process as such. Being part of the network, intermediaries are related to activities or actors. Activity theory (Engeström et al., 1999) "focuses on practice, which obviates the need to distinguish 'applied' from 'pure' science – understanding everyday practice in the real world is the very objective of scientific practice. … The object of activity theory is to understand the unity of consciousness and activity." (Nardi, 1995). Besides involving users in design processes we believe that DT is a very helpful approach to design sociotechnical systems. "Design thinking is a human-centered approach to innovation that draws from the designer's toolkit to integrate the needs of people, the possibilities of technology, and the requirements for business success." (Tim Brown, IDEO).

The exploration of the role and potential of DT within organizations has changed the original objective of this research (Brown, 2009; Martin, 2009). So, "DT is not only a cognitive process or a mindset, but has become an effective toolkit for any innovation process, connecting the creative design approach to traditional business thinking, based on planning and rational problem solving" (Tschimmel, 2012, p.2). This shifted DT from design disciplines more and more to the fields of management and marketing. In this paper, we want to investigate DT again in the context of design of systems, products or services, especially in the field of systems design and development. If we take DT as an approach seriously and apply (all) its methods thoroughly throughout the whole design process, we can easily follow the goal of understanding of the everyday practice and its actors. This would lead us furthermore to design of systems that consider the context of use, user experiences, and the needed technology support. Our objective in designing systems is being innovative and improving user experience. We think this can be done only by understanding the actors, their actions, their use context, and of course by including them as experts into the design process.

3. *mDT* – YET ANOTHER DESIGN THINKING APPROACH

We have created and established our own version of design thinking as an approach to enable design among designers, students, and companies for a decade now. We call it *multidisciplinary Design Thinking* (*mDT*). It uses several methods (for details see Table 1). The design process we have established so far is iterative and user-centered by supporting creativity and innovation. *mDT* not only shows how to design for users it also involves them in the entire design process. We understand *mDT* as a summary of several design methods accompanying a design process from the idea creation, through shaping and detailing design parameters, to the exact configuration and description of the properties of a system that has to be finally engineered. The methods shown in Table 1 are in a chronological order, whereas some of the design-evaluate-redesign methods are applied repeatedly in several iterations of the process. Steps listed for each method are supposed to serve as a guideline for designers.

Table 1. Design thinking methods applied in *mDT* (*media.tuwien.ac.at/designthinking*)

Method	Steps
The Very First Idea Description: Brainstorming the very first associations and impressions in team Goal: Gather all associations and possible ideas based on images and impressions Type: Idea generation Example of use: Very early stages of idea generation or orientation	1. After a discussion in the project team, create associations to the subject 2. Brainstorm (brainwrite and brainsketch) different ideas, also by using images or impressions from media 3. Map all results in a shared representation of ideas and associations 4. Start thinking further on ideas following up the collected associations and impressions 5. Document all relevant data for further reference
Literature Review Description: Effective evaluation of selected digital, analog, scientific, or non-scientific documents on a research topic Goal: Assure that the idea is relevant and unique Type: Data inquiry and knowledge generation method Example of use: Early stages of idea generation or orientation	1. Prepare: setup a due date, create a precise focused question to base the review on, create select criteria, consider synonyms and translations as well, define the scope of the literature to review, identify the sources of literature 2. Search on identified sources by using the select criteria 3. Select the most relevant documents from the result list, repeat 2 and 3 as long as necessary 4. Procure the selected documents 5. Document the most relevant data from the literature reviewed
Expert Interviews Description: Gathering data from experts Goal: Consider experts' knowledge to the very first idea and research alternatives Type: Qualitative method Example of use: Ethnographic field work	1. Prepare interview guideline by formulating questions based on hypothesis 2. Locate and contact experts of interest 3. Carry out semi-structured or in-depth open interviews and, if possible, record the interview, make notes 4. Transcribe the interview, analyze it in relation to questions and hypothesis, write down the analysis results
Observations with Video Analysis Description: Creating views of real scenarios Goal: Observe and understand the context, use, or other aspects of design; analyze interaction, requirements, evaluation, usability; document or illustrate Type: Data inquiry and recording method Example of use: Workplace studies	1. Find the place and/or people for the observation 2. Setup the video equipment 3. Carry out the observation and recording, if needed, repeat it several times or change the location and time of recording 4. Analyze the material qualitative and quantitative, select relevant parts, and create a short video to visualize the most relevant observations
Cultural Probes Description: Understanding the cultural context of future users Goal: Create qualitative approach to understand the user, inspire the design functionally and aesthetically, evoke creative reaction of (potential) users, support the creation of design material Type: Experimental research method Example of use: Early stages of user-centered design processes	1. Define data to inquire via the probe 2. Design probe elements, consider corporate identity, visuals, sounds, tangible elements, and texts 3. Create a cultural probe package for distribution 4. Distribute the probe to users 5. Analyze the data gathered in probes: qualitative, ask for clarification if needed, compare, extract particular occurrences including emotions, ideas, and inspirations 6. Document the analysis and comparison without interpretation
Provocative Requisites Description: Provocation, ambiguity, inspiration in context Goal: Represent a design idea creative and playful, question and discuss the design ideas by letting them experienced in context, create inspiration for design Type: Experimental research method Example of use: Dealing with ambiguity and dubiety of the idea	1. Define a situation, a scenario, or a context for the requisite 2. Design the requisite, populate it with data, play it or set it up 3. Observe the requisite in action 4. Document the scenario, the observation, the interaction with the requisite 5. Analyze and explain in relation to the design idea

Design Games Description: Playful way to gain design ideas Goal: Generate design ideas, concretize a design idea in form a party game, play different options of interaction, experiment with use and functionality of design elements Type: Design creation method Example of use: Create playful elements of a design idea	1. Define the goal of a design game 2. Document the process of creation of the design game, also the dismissed ideas 3. Describe the game with all elements (props, content, rules, etc.) 4. Play several times with the design game 5. Document the games played, describe how it was perceived by the players 6. Adapt the game if necessary 7. Analyze the game, its components, the interaction, etc. 8. Document the analysis and extract issues for the design idea
Scenarios Description: Scenarios of use context with personas and actions Goal: Identify problems and search for solutions in certain settings, provoke ideas Type: Experimental research method Example of use: Product design, interaction design	1. Define the goal, context, prerequisites, actors, interactions, and processes of a scenario 2. Start with a rough scenario 3. Observe and play the scenario, analyze, and refine it 4. Create a positive scenario: Adapt the scenario as long as it does not contain any negative aspect any more 5. Create a negative scenario: Adapt the scenario as long as it does not contain any positive aspect any more 6. Analyze the results and their impact onto the design idea 7. Document all actions and results
Narrative Posters Description: Telling the whole story on one sheet Goal: Tell a general or specific story about the design, its use, and context, visualize the design process and its elements to reflect on in form of a poster Type: Experimental narrative method Example of use: Visualize design elements and process for reflection	1. Sort and organize the design material created so far in the design process 2. Construct a story based on the material gathered 3. Visualize the story in form of a poster
Design Workshops Description: Being creative and exploring design ideas in team, or exploring options for systems design Goal: Communicate different views to the design idea in a group, generate new ideas in a team, discuss different perspectives to the design-on-table in a group, explore different options for systems design based on a decided idea at a later stage of a design process Type: Design in team Example of use: Create common understanding of a (rather complex) design idea in a team, e.g., in product design	1. Define the goal of the workshop 2. Select the participants of the workshop and define their role 3. Set up a place, date, and process for the workshop 4. Prepare the necessary material like models, plans, creative material, etc. as well as devices for audio/video recording and photos 5. Carry out the workshop: introduction of participants and process, brainstorming related to the defined goal, working on different ideas, discussion and refinement of ideas come up during the workshop 6. Identify and document results of the workshop
Sketches Description: From the idea to the first low fidelity design artifacts Goal: Sketching the design ideas, for an overview but also for details Type: Design generation and evaluation method Example of use: User-centered design projects, prototyping	1. Create sketches of interaction, with different details 2. Compare and update sketches, explain their use 3. Evaluate critical sketches with users 4. Document the evaluation results
Wireframes Description: From sketches to more linked organized design artifacts Goal: Design structures, control elements, contents as a blue print Type: Design generation and evaluation method Example of use: User-centered design projects	1. Create wireframes to cover all parts of the system 2. Link all parts of the system with the wireframes, including the navigation 3. Evaluate the wireframes with users 4. Document the evaluation results 5. Update the wireframes based on the evaluation results
(Video-)Mockups Description: From wireframes to the first prototypical systems Goal: Create look and feel of the design with visual and audio elements Type: Design generation and evaluation method Example of use: User-centered design projects	1. Create mockups to visualize the look and feel for the interaction with the system 2. Use video and audio elements if needed 3. Evaluate the (video) mockups with users 4. Document the evaluation results 5. Update the mockups based on the evaluation results
Technology Probes Description: Getting a hint about real life interaction Goal: Examine and experiment a challenging technology implementation as a possible solution to the design idea Type: Experimental technology application in field Example of use: User-centered design projects	1. Select a relevant technology for the system-in-development 2. Select an interaction aspect of the system-in-development 3. Set up the technology infrastructure and implement the selected interaction 4. Evaluate the technology probe with users 5. Document the evaluation results by stressing out the pros and cons of the technology selected for evaluation
Prototypes Description: The first impression of the last design step Goal: Create 2D, 3D or executable prototypes to illustrate the idea as an interactive artifact Type: Executable design generation and evaluation method Example of use: Product design	1. Gather all positively evaluated design ideas 2. Define the most important functions of the system-in-development 3. Implement a prototype by focusing on the selected functions and applying look and feel from the positively evaluated mockup 4. Evaluate the prototype and update it 5. Describe the final prototype
Product and Design of Corporate Identity Description: Designing the whole story Goal: Define and present the product as a result of the whole design process Type: Product and context definition Example of use: Product design	1. Define all interactions, functions and interrelated systems, including hard facts like costs and target users 2. Finalize the visual and technical design all product components 3. Describe the use and administration of the product with a guide/handbook 4. Design a corporate identity for the product, apply it for its presentation 5. Create a product folder with all data relevant for target stakeholders

To summarize, *mDT* can be presented as a road map from a very initial idea to a product that is ready for engineering and deployment. Figure 1 shows an overview of *mDT* in a chronological order.

The results that are sent to engineering teams are in form of, as we call them, *design models*. There are three types of design models:

- *Use models* – These are personas, scenarios, use cases, flow models, storyboards, narrative posters, mainly presented as models and descriptions by using a standard modeling language like UML (Unified Modeling Language). The aim of these models is to detail and describe the design to make it understandable for others who are not involved in the design process.
- *Systems models* – These are interface and interaction visualizations, technology probes as well as (hi-fidelity) executable 2D or 3D prototypes showing how the original idea looks like in action in the envisioned context.
- *Interaction models* – These are product descriptions and presentations with final corporate identity elements, demonstrating the use and features of the product, pricing, and measures for dissemination. They show the idea of the final product or service, by referring to its technology features, interfaces, architectural elements or its real time use.

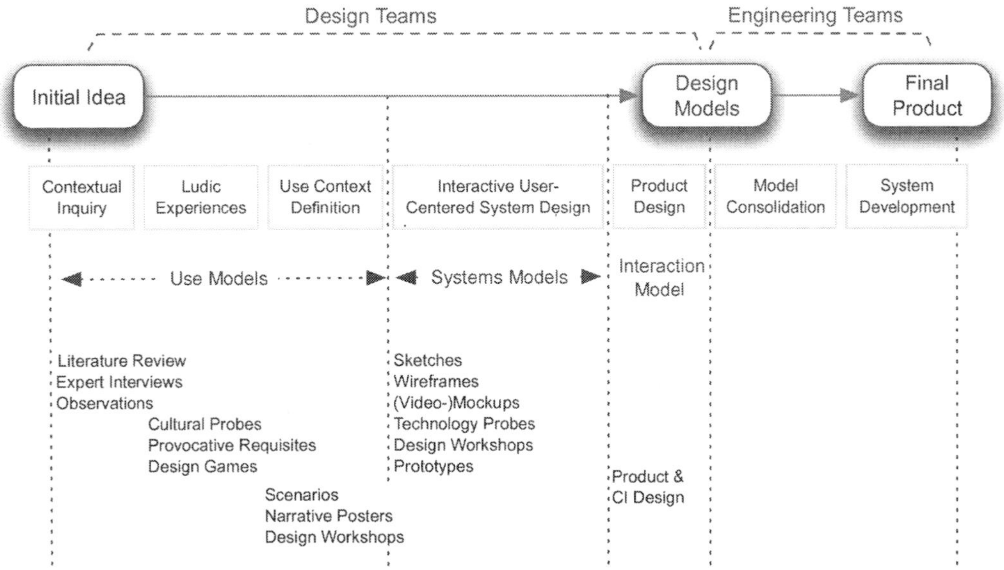

Figure 1. Overview of *mDT*

In this section we presented our *mDT* as a set of methods to guide and facilitate innovation and creativity in design teams, to document the intermediaries developed and to create artifacts to bridge boundaries to other communities of practice, like engineering teams. In the next section we will discuss some relevant aspects for a successful implementation of the design thinking approach in software projects.

4. DISCUSSION

Designing for use requires user involvement in design processes. By being aware of that users are not designers but experts in using the artifacts designers create, user contribute to the design in two ways: First of all, they communicate their requirements to the systems-in-design and their use context including the restrictions and conditions that might have impact on several properties of the system. Second, they evaluate the intermediaries created during a design process and give their feedback to the features, interactions and interfaces of the system. Timing of user involvement and ways of gathering the user experience during a design process must be planned properly. Methods applied must be selected and compiled carefully to make the best use of the gathered context data.

Software engineering deals with several problems of requirement gathering and analysis, design and development issues. But, its primary focus does not lie on the idea creation at the first place and continuous adaption during the design process based on user feedback and use context considerations. While software engineering deals with engineering methods and technologies, DT tackles the challenges before the prospect software is engineered.

Since two decades we have been studying several design and engineering teams, their obstacles, communication problems not only within their project teams but also with externals, and all the effort that was in vain because it was based on false assumptions, lack of communication and misinterpretations. In this paper, we introduced and showed our design methods (used in *mDT*) to describe how design thinking might look like and be integrated in software projects. *Design models* help translate the design ideas into the language of engineers by avoiding information gaps and misunderstandings.

mDT integrates user involvement into its methods and through this into the whole design process. *mDT* is based on important principles of sociotechnical approaches. Considering the sociotechnical design principles defined by Cherns (1976), we found out that *mDT* is in line with the principles of sociotechnical systems, especially with the ones that are related to processes: compatibility, minimal critical specification, design and human values, and incompletion. By considering these principles in design and development of systems we believe that we move the engineering process further into the direction of a process that produces more innovative and usable systems for the anticipated target group.

- *Compatibility* – Design thinking facilitates a process, which is compatible with its objectives (Tellioğlu et al., 2012). For instance, if the design objective is a playful system, the process needs to be playful by facilitating playful working and playful intermediaries. If the objective is the highest degree of usability, the process must be opened for users and their evaluation of single design artifacts.
- *Minimal critical specification* – This principle says that no more should be specified than is absolutely essential. This means the design process must be kept open and flexible as long as possible. Options should be not closed, each design decision should be challenged, and alternatives should always be offered. Design thinking supports this principle completely.
- *Design and human values* – Design must put human values to the center. Design thinking offers a complete model to design, which makes designing sociotechnical systems possible. The goal is to improve the quality of users' life.
- *Incompletion* – Finally, design is a reiterative process. As soon as design (intermediaries) is implemented, its consequences indicate the need for redesign. "The multifunctional, multilevel, multidisciplinary team required for design is needed for its evaluation and review." (Cherns, 1976, p.791). This is exactly how design thinking sees the design process.

mDT fulfills the above listed principles, and furthermore it communicates its results by using design models. To illustrate how diverse the artifacts, as instantiations of these design models, look like depending on the idea that the design process was based on, we present some examples from one student project carried out two years ago. It is about enabling free speech and democracy and the ways to create a public space in which citizens can stress their thoughts to a given common subject. A group of five students[1] applied *mDT* throughout two semesters in their media informatics study. The goal was to create and evaluate a new idea to support practicing democracy in the society. After the first semester the team ended up with the design idea that supports the expression of one's (political) opinion in a public space. After the second semester, a product – the so-called *Meinungsbilder*, meaning *images of opinion* as well as *opinion former* – was created.

(a) (b) (c)

Figure 2. *Use models*: Contextual inquiry with a publicly placed cultural probe (a), ludic experience with a design game to express one's political opinion (b), narrative poster illustrating the use context and the functionality to be achieved if one wants to communicate a publicly relevant opinion with others (c)

Figure 2 shows some example artifacts or intermediaries that we see as *use models* to hand over from design to engineering. They are results of contextual inquiry, e.g., a publicly placed cultural probe (a), and results of the ludic experience phase, e.g., a design game to express one's political opinion (b). A narrative poster illustrates the use context and the functionality to be achieved if one wants to communicate a publicly relevant opinion with others (c). Figure 3 shows some of the *systems models* created during the project: Iterative user-centered system design with sketches, wireframes and models of the product (in this example a mushroom-shaped kiosk to stress one's own opinion to a common subject) showing different details explicitly. The first ideas were withdrawn during the course of the design process, based on the evaluation and feedback given by users. Figure 4 shows the final *interaction models* of the project: (a) the model of the

[1] Michael Dichtl, Markus Hametner, Janis Meißner, Rafael Mitterlehner, Gözde Taskaya

product with concrete measures for production (in this case the mushroom-shaped kiosk), (b) the computer model to visualize the entire shape of the mushroom, (c) interfaces implemented in four compartments of the mushroom showing the interaction possibilities for users, and finally (d) the logo and corporate identity of the product.

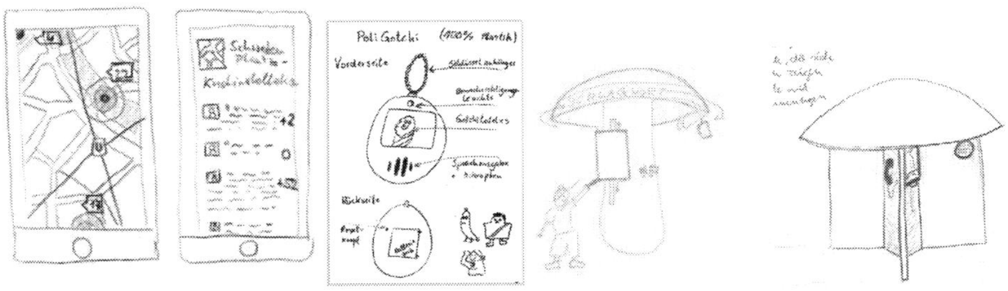

Figure 3. *Systems models*: Iterative user-centered system design with sketches, wireframes and models of the product (in this example a mushroom-shaped kiosk to stress one's own opinion to a common subject) showing different details

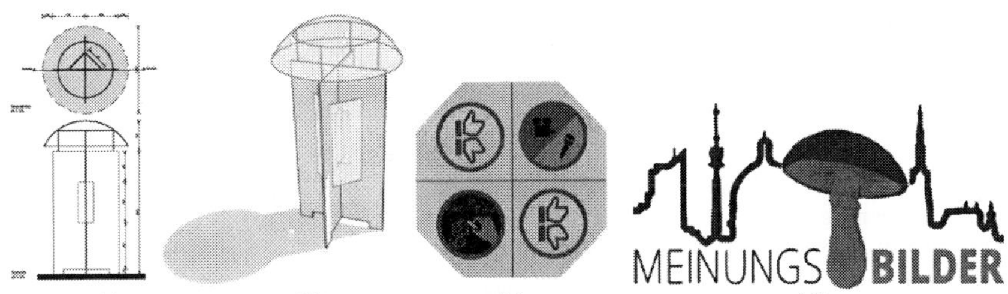

(a) (b) (c) (d)

Figure 4. *Interaction models*: Model of the product with concrete measures for production (in this case the mushroom-shaped kiosk) (a), computer model to visualize the entire shape of the mushroom (b), interfaces implemented in four compartments of the mushroom showing the interaction possibilities for users (c), the logo and corporate identity of the product (*Meinungsbilder*) (d)

This example tries to represent the introduced design models that *mDT* delivers to help understand, use and further develop in engineering teams.

5. CONCLUSION

We succeeded in several industrial as well as educational projects by considering design thinking as a holistic approach to design sociotechnical innovative systems. We contributed to DT research by proposing *design models* as an interface and communication channel to cross the boundaries to other disciplines like engineering, management or marketing. Nevertheless, our development of DT methods and processes are ongoing. Next, we plan to describe best practice examples to provide more insights to design teams. We are aware of the difficulty to evaluate this approach in a real context. We are currently developing measures for the evaluation of *mDT* in design projects what we plan to present in our future work.

Our goal is not addressing managers to offer an easy access of several DT tools and methods by providing a guideline how to do this. Our objective is rather to contribute to the integration of DT driven design process with the following engineering and final production and deployment process by explicitly determining the interfaces facilitated mainly by model-based artifacts, like we put them into the categories use models, systems models, and interaction models. We think the only way to achieve the goal of an innovative design and development process is a holistic integrated approach to design and engineering what, we think, can be implemented by means of models and DT process we introduced in this paper.

REFERENCES

Beyer, H. and K. Holtzblatt (1998). *Contextual Design: Defining Customer-Centered Systems.* Morgan Kaufmann, San Francisco.

Brandt, E., 2006. Designing Exploratory Design Games: A Framework for Participation in Participatory Design? *Proceedings of the Ninth Conference on Participatory Design: Expanding Boundaries in Design,* PDC'06, Vol. 1.

Bodker, K. et al., 2004. *Participatory IT Design. Designing for Business and Workplace Realities.* The MIT Press, Cambridge.

Brown, T., 2009. *Change by Design. How Design Thinking transforms Organizations and inspires Innovation.* Harper Collins Publishers, New York.

Brown, T. and Wyatt, J., 2010. Design Thinking for Social Innovation. *Stanford Social Innovation Review,* pp.31-35.

Callon, M., 1987. Society in the Making: The Study of Technology as a Tool for Sociological Analysis. *In The Social Construction of Technological Systems: New Directions in the Sociology and History of Technology,* Bijker, W. et al. (eds.) London: MIT Press, London, pp. 83–103.

Cherns, A., 1976. The principles of sociotechnical design. *In Human Relations.* Vol. 29, No. 8, pp.783-792.

Cooper, A. et al., 2007. *About Face 3: The Essentials of Interaction Design.* 3rd Edition, Wiley.

Cross, N. et al. (Eds.), 1992. Research in Design Thinking. Delft: Delft University Press.

Dahley, A. et al., 1998. Water Lamp and Pinwheels: Ambient Projection of Digital Information into Architectural Space. *CHI'98,* April 18-23.

Eastman, C. et al. (Eds.), 2001. *Design Knowing and Learning: Cognition in Design Education.* Elsevier Science Ltd., Oxford.

Engeström, Y. et al., 1999. *Perspectives on Activity Theory.* Cambridge University Press.

Martin, R., 2009. *The Design of Business. Why Design Thinking is the next Competitive Advantage.* Harvard Business Press, Boston, Massachusetts.

Nardi, B., 1995. *Context and Consciousness: Activity Theory and Human-Computer Interaction.* MIT Press.

Pedersen, J. and Buur, J., 2000. Games and Movies - Towards Innovative Co-Design with Users, *CoDesigning.*

Sandelowski, M., 1991. Telling Stories: Narrative Approaches in Qualitative Research. *In Journal of Nursing Scholarship,* Vol. 23, Nr. 3.

Schmidt, K. et al., 2009. Asking for the moon. Or model-based coordination in distributed design. *Proceedings of the 11th European Conference on Computer Supported Cooperative Work (ECSCW'09),* September 7-11, 2009, Vienna, Austria, pp.383-402.

Stickdorn, M. and Schneider, J. (Eds.), 2010. *This is Service Design Thinking. Basic – Tools – Cases.* BIS Publisher, Amsterdam.

Tellioğlu, H., 2012. About Representational Artifacts and Their Role in Engineering. *Chapter in the IGI book on Phenomenology, Organizational Politics and IT Design: The Social Study of Information Systems.* Viscusi, G. et al. (eds.), IGI Global, pp.111-130.

Tellioğlu, H. et al., 2012. Multimodality in Design of Tangible Systems. *In Journal ICOM Special Issue on AAL,* i-com, 11/3, November, pp.19-23.

Thoring, K. and Müller, R. M., 2011. Understanding the Creative Mechanisms of Design Thinking: An Evolutionary Approach. *Proceedings of the DESIRE'11 Conference Creativity and Innovation in Design.* ACM, Eindhoven, pp.137-144.

Tschimmel, K., 2012. Design Thinking as an effective Toolkit for Innovation. *Proceedings of the CCIII ISPIM Conference: Action for Innovation: Innovating from Experience.* Barcelona, pp.1-20.

Weiser, M. and Brown, J. S., 1996. Designing Calm Technology. *In PowerGrid Journal,* Vol. 1.01, July.

A HAPTIC DISPLAY FOR THE SIMULATION OF SOFT TISSUE PALPATION IN CHAI3D

Jan Hergenhan and Heinz Wörn
Institute for Anthropomatics and Robotics (IAR) – Intelligent Process Control and Robotics (IAR)
Karlsruhe Institute of Technology (KIT), Engler-Bunte-Ring 8, 76131 Karlsruhe, Germany

ABSTRACT

This paper presents a novel haptic input device for haptic feedback in soft tissue palpation. Our Haptic Display features seven pins mounted on compression springs that can be pre-loaded with servo motors. Each pin has a stroke of 10mm and a maximum counterforce of 1.1N. An additional force of 0.7N per pin can be applied by servo motors. This technique allows for simultaneous stimulation of kinesthetic as well as tactile perception. The control software of the haptic display has been implemented in the open-source haptics library CHAI3D. We extended the framework with an adapted Mesh Tool that realistically represents the hardware. Our simulation environment features a deformable mass-spring based virtual soft tissue with multiple adjustable parameters. We evaluated this software in a user study with 15 participants in order to demonstrate the usability of the haptic display. With 90% of successful hits, we are confident that sensible haptic feedback can be generated with the presented device.

KEYWORDS

Haptic display, haptic feedback, CHAI3D, deformable body, mass-spring-model

1. INTRODUCTION

Palpation is an important diagnostic tool in medicine. It serves to determine structure and consistency of tissue. In that manner, hard inclusions in soft tissue such as lymph nodes or tumors can be detected. In open surgery, tissue can be palpated easily. However, in minimally invasive surgery (and other teleoperation scenarios), palpation plays a minor role. Due to the laparoscopic instruments and friction in the trocar, forces at most can be sensed (Greenwald et al. 2012). In robot-assisted minimally invasive surgery (e.g. with the daVinci Surgical System), force feedback is impossible without further ado.

Figure 1. The haptic display with seven spring mounted pins for palpation training in CHAI3D environment

There are various approaches to re-establish haptic feedback in robot-assisted minimally invasive surgery (Westebring-van der Putten et al. 2008), (Okamura 2009). Generally, a system with at least two components is required: a sensor and device on the outside to stimulate the surgeons' haptic perception. Haptic or tactile sensors basically measure forces as a function of indentation in a certain area. In (Beccani et al. 2013), a single point sensor has been developed that the surgeon manually pushes into the tissue repeatedly in the relevant area. The more common approach is a sensor array which is mounted on the tip of a tool specially for sensing (Gwilliam et al. 2010), (Talasaz & Patel 2012), (Xie et al. 2013). The advantage of single point sensors is that they can be used on non-planar surfaces whereas sensor arrays are prone to the curvature of the surface. On the other hand, it takes way more time to scan a certain area with a single point sensor.

Haptic input devices for force (= kinesthetic) feedback are already commercially available (Force Dimension omega/sigma, Geomagic Phantom). Basically, they are joysticks for six or seven degrees of freedom (translation and rotation plus gripper). Each degree of freedom is powered with a motor that can exert a certain force against the users' input to generate the feedback.

In contrast, devices for tactile feedback are still in prototype state. Many approaches feature multiple mechanically actuated pins in an array of $\approx 1\text{cm}^2$. The high density of moving stimulators requires either small actuators (piezoelectrics (Kim et al. 2009), dielectric elastomers (Koo et al. 2008)) or decoupling of the actuators and the pin array (motor driven bowden cables (Sarakoglou et al. 2012), (Roke et al. 2013), pneumatic or hydraulic actuation (Santos-Carreras et al. 2010), (Goethals et al. 2008)).

The more challenging task is to combine the two parts of haptic feedback. One possibility is to install a tactile display onto a haptic input device. This requires small overall dimensions of the tactile display of $\approx$30mm$\times$30mm$\times$30mm without limiting its capabilities. Moreover, the hardware for the tactile feedback has to cope with the forces that the user exerts on both devices to manipulate the haptic input device (up to 20N).

Another approach are devices that are specialized for palpation feedback. A very recent approach for remote palpation was presented in (Pacchierotti et al. 2015). In this work, a finger-mountable device with a small actuated platform was presented. The platform rests below the users' finger and can be pulled up with three servo motors via attached strings to present 3-DoF force feedback. The device serves to present data recorded with a BioTac tactile sensor. The goal is to deform the users' fingertip similarly to the sensor during palpation. However, this device only allows global deformation of the fingertip.

For simulation of soft tissue palpation, (Genecov et al. 2014) presented a very promising approach. Their device is made up of a silicone bubble with a diameter of 4cm filled with coffee grounds. When a vacuum is created inside the bubble, the coffee grounds will jam and hence become a hard inclusion. The size of the jammed lump can be controlled with the magnitude of the vacuum. The lower half of the bubble is enclosed in a pressure chamber. With the applied pressure, the stiffness of the silicone bubble can be controlled. In this way, the Haptic Jamming device can present very realistic sensations. On the downside, the inclusion will always be at the same place which makes it unnecessary to search for the inclusion.

The main contribution of our work was to develop and construct a novel device that is specialized on soft tissue palpation (see Figure 1). The haptic display can be used very intuitively as palpation with the haptic display is performed just as palpation on a human organ. The forces on the finger are controlled precisely to create realistic kinesthetic and tactile feedback. The virtual environment with a virtual soft tissue was implemented in CHAI3D. The virtual soft tissue with encapsulated tumors is made up of a mass-spring-based body that is realistically deformable. The avatar in the virtual environment has been adapted to the special layout of the haptic display. The graphics and haptic rendering are each executed at adequate rates to reduce latency. To evaluate the haptic display and the software, a user study was performed with very promising results.

2. HARDWARE

Prior to the development and construction of the haptic display, we analyzed how palpation works and which dimensions of indentations and forces were to be expected. Our medical partners provided us with a so called haptic phantom which is used for training purposes. It is made up of a soft silicone with included small wooden balls and roughly imitates tumorous liver tissue. We performed force-indentation measurements on the haptic phantom and found that indentations of up to 1cm were necessary to "see" the inclusion in the data and measured force differences of up to 1N.

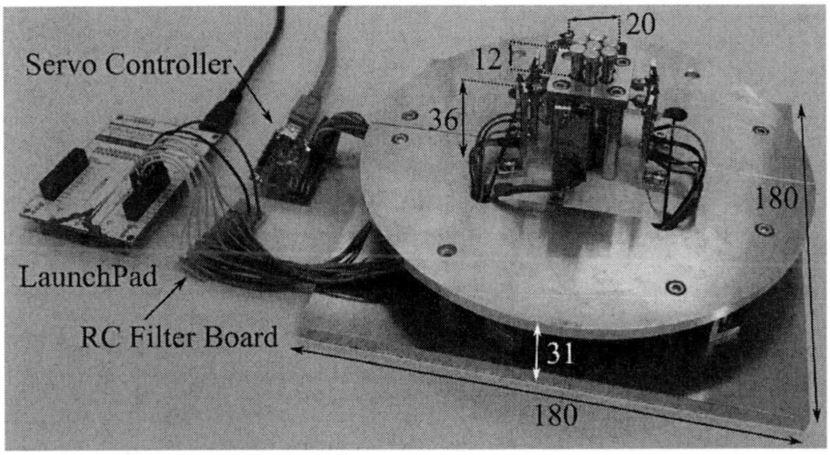

Figure 2. Full setup of the haptic display. The servo motors rest below the circular hand rest, the controller boards are shown on the left side. All dimensions in mm

Our haptic display consists of seven pins in hexagonal layout with a total diameter of 2cm (see Figure 2). The layout and size were chosen to fit the nearly circular shape of the human finger pad. Each pin rests on a compression spring and can be pushed down for 10mm with linearly increasing force (kinesthetic feedback). Additionally, the basis of each spring can be pushed upwards with a servo motor leading to locally increased forces. Each servo motor is controlled separately, so the counterforce of each pin can be adjusted individually. This causes local deformations of the skin (tactile feedback) enabling the user to locate inclusions and to determine their properties (also see Figure 3).

The inner workings of the haptic display are depicted on the final single-pin prototype for better clarity (see Figure 4). The main components of the assembly are a digital servo motor, a linear potentiometer, a compression spring, a sleeve and the pin itself. Plastic sliding bearings ensure that the pins and the sleeves move smoothly. All parts were manufactured from aluminum except for the sleeves. In order to reduce the friction of the bolt inside the sleeve, steel was used here.

The servo motor (Gaupner/SJ GmbH DES 476 BB) generates a holding force of 18N/s, and has a rotational speed of 0.11s for 40°. It is controlled with a Pololu Mini Maestro 12-Channel USB Servo Controller. The servo motor moves the sleeve with a horn with a length of 37mm. The servo motors are controlled with a frequency of 250Hz. This is sufficient for the stimulation of the mechanoreceptors involved in palpation: Merkel cells for static pressure, Meissner corpuscles for slow movement (frequencies of up to 50Hz) and Ruffini endings for shear forces. The Paccinian corpuscles which are most sensitive to vibrations around 300Hz (from friction between a sliding finger and the surface) are not involved.

The spring is prevented from buckling out by a long bolt that is guided inside the sleeve. The bolt also protects the spring from becoming compressed too heavily. The spring has a maximum force of 1.77N and a maximum travel of 18.22mm, resulting in a spring rate of 0.97N/cm. The spring is pre-strained with a force of 0.17N to overcome remaining friction forces when the pin has to be pushed back to starting position. Without the servos taking action, a counterforce of 1.1N per pin (7.7N in total) can be realized. This leaves a reserve of 0.7N for each servo for the tactile stimulation. According to our measurement data, the total maximum counterforce of 12.4N at 10mm is sufficient for sensible feedback.

To generate appropriate counterforces with the motors, the pins' positions have to be measured at any time. We use linear potentiometers with a priority on low operation forces (ALPS RDC1022A05). These forces add to the unavoidable friction forces inside the bearings and the sleeves. The friction increases the force on the pin when it is pushed downwards by the user and decreases the force when the pin is pushed upwards by the springs. This hysteresis effect diminishes the user's sensation and has to be minimized. The chosen potentiometers' operation force was specified with <0.25N, the measured forces (0.03N) were even less. The potentiometer has a travel of 22mm and a linearity of ±0.5%.

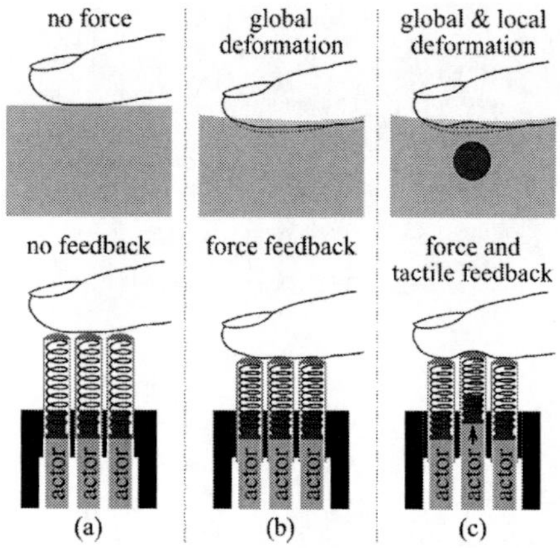

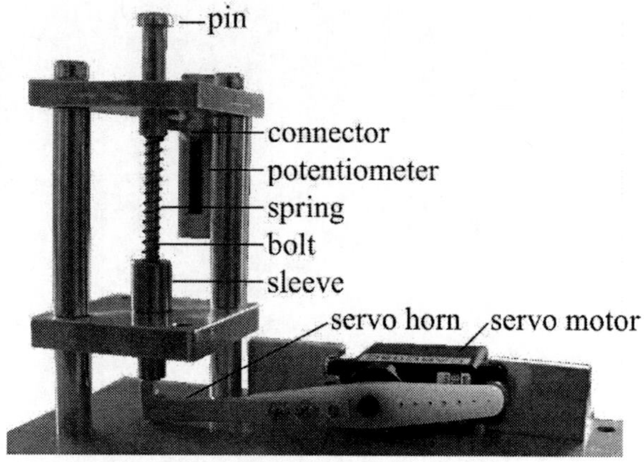

Figure 3. (left). The upper half shows the palpation process of soft tissue with and without a hard inclusion. The lower half shows the concept of the haptic display simlating this process.

Figure 4. (right). Composition of components for each pin demonstrated on the final single-pin-prototype

To read out the potentiometers' positions, a TI MSP430F5529 LaunchPad evaluation board is used. It features a 12bit ADC with 16 input channels. The potentiometers are supplied with 3.3V from the LaunchPad which is also used as reference voltage for the ADC. To reduce noise in the signal, an RC filter was integrated into the circuit. The micro controller reads the voltages and converts them. Using the TI MSP430 USB API, a special driver for the LaunchPad was created. When connected, the board is identified as a communications device which results in a virtual COM port on the USB host. It allows to reliably send and receive the converted voltage data with a rate of 1000Hz.

The arrangement of potentiometers around the pins appears rather bulky but was unavoidable: Each potentiometer needs a rigid connection to its corresponding pin and has to be placed close and parallel to the pin. The potentiometers to the outer pins are arranged circularly. For the central pin, we had to find a place for the potentiometer which allows the connection rod to move inside the gap between two outer pins. Similar difficulties occurred on the bottom side with the servo horns and the corresponding sleeves. Again, the components were arranged circularly. The consequence was a rather large overall size of the haptic display of 18cm×18cm.

3. SOFTWARE

The haptic display was integrated into CHAI3D, (chai3d.org) version 3.0.0, an open-source multi-platform C++-library (Conti et al. 2003). CHAI3D allows to implement both haptic and graphics rendering of objects in order to create real-time simulations. It has a modular architecture which allows to add functionality. It supports different commercial haptic input devices and offers a variety of classes and algorithms that can be used or extended such as collision detection, file support, timers and extensions.

Due to its special design, the haptic display had to be implemented as a new haptic device. During the initialization phase, a connection to both controller boards (LaunchPad for potentiometers, Mini Maestro for servo motors) is established. The converted voltage data of the pins sent by the LaunchPad are extracted and converted to a pin travel. In order to reduce the remaining noise in the signal, we apply a binomial filter with width N=4. The seven pin positions are used to calculate the shape of the tool or avatar (see section 3.2). To control the global position of the tool, the mouse is used: To move the tool in a plane parallel to the surface, the user clicks and drags anywhere in the scene. The user can toggle between tool and camera control by clicking the respective buttons in the GUI to control the camera's angle and zoom.

In every cycle, the position and shape of the tool are processed in graphics and force rendering. This results in the deformation of the virtual soft tissue, the visual output and in target forces for each pin. The target force is decreased by the force the user already exerts on the pin resulting in the force the motor has to bring up. A PID controller has been implemented to avoid oscillations when the user pushes his finger down quickly. The resulting force is converted to a motor position and sent to the servo controller which moves the servo motors accordingly. The interaction of the individual components is shown in Figure 5.

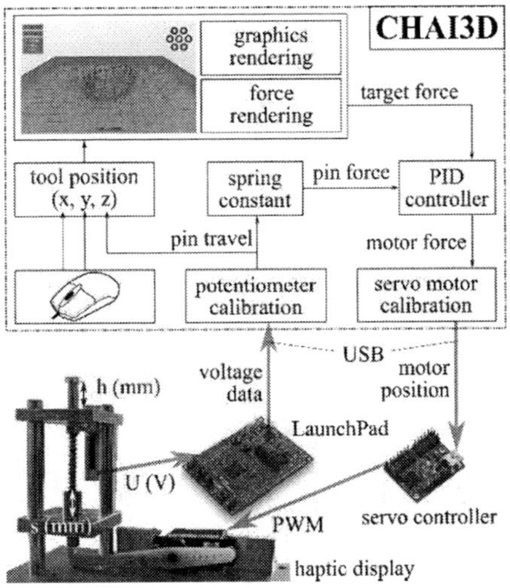

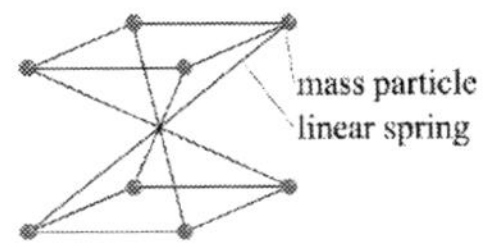

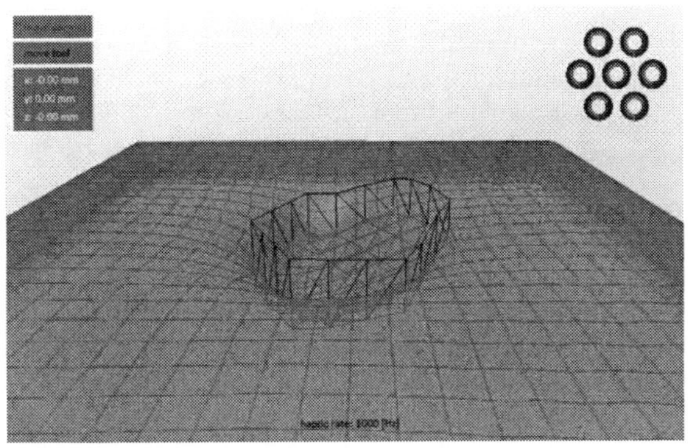

Figure 5. (left). Interaction of hardware, electronics and software
Figure 6. (top right). One element of the lattice structure of the virtual soft tissue
Figure 7. (bottom right). Mesh Tool interacting with the deformable virtual soft tissue

3.1 Virtual Soft Tissue

The palpation simulation program uses the GEL module of CHAI3D. This module provides several possibilities to create deformable objects rather than rigid objects made of plain meshes. Both models are mass-spring-based with different physical complexity. The physically more realistic model is the Skeleton Model. It features skeleton nodes with mass, radius and damping factors for translational and rotational movement. The model allows to fix the positions of nodes individually. Gravity can be used as additional external force. The skeleton nodes are linked with massless skeleton links. These are described with an initial length and constants for elongation, flexion and torsion. The skeleton links are rigidly linked to the skeleton nodes.

The simpler model, the so called Mass Particle Model, is made up of mass particles with reduced physical properties and linear springs. The mass particles are described with a mass and a damping factor for translational movement only. Rotational movement is not considered as the particles are point-shaped and have no spatial dimension. The mass particles are linked with linear springs which only have a constant for elongation. They are linked to the mass particles but can rotate freely around them. The main advantage of this model is the largely reduced effort for dynamics calculation, as only forces between particles have to be considered. On the downside, the physical behavior is not always realistic.

Our main concern with the software was to reach the necessary calculation rate of 1000Hz which is considered the minimum for haptic feedback and is also necessary for proper deformation simulation. Furthermore, we wanted to have a large number of nodes in our model to generate smooth deformations. For that reason, we chose to use the Mass Particle Model and cope with its inconveniences. In our current setup, the virtual soft tissue is made up of 24×24×5 mass particles and has a size of 7cm×7cm.

We "moved" the damping property from the particles to the springs, as we need to create local inconsistencies to be able to simulate the tumor. Secondly, we needed to find means to circumvent the missing inner stability of bodies made up of the mass particle model. The missing stability comes from the lack of rotational forces between mass particles and linear springs. As a first step, we figured out a suitable structure to link the mass particles (see Figure 6). We use a cubical arrangement of the particles and link the particles in the planes parallel to the surface. The horizontal links between layers have been replaced by diagonal links.

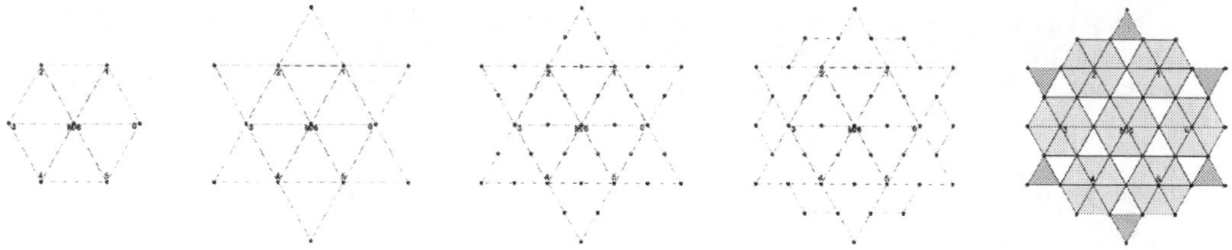

a b c d e

Figure 8. Composition of the mesh tool. The blue faces in the figure on the right side represent the seven pins

Additionally, we implemented a holding structure around the actual virtual soft tissue which does not interact with the tool. It only serves to hold the tissue in position and support the inner forces by pulling the mass particles at the surfaces back into their initial position. The support structure is made up of fixed mass particles and is linked to mass particles at the surface with linear springs. The properties of these springs differ, as they have a larger damping factor. On the plus side, this concept also allows to adjust the viscosity (or relaxation times after deformation) of the tissue over a large range.

The tumors are simulated by increasing the elongation constant of certain springs inside the tissue. The shape (rectangle or sphere), location and size of the tumors are defined via text files. Multiple tumors with different properties can be placed in the tissue at the same time. For more realistic behavior of the virtual soft tissue, the springs in the top surface also have increased elongation constants to create a tough skin. To adjust the parameters of the different spring types, we use a genetic algorithm. The algorithm optimizes a score that is calculated from global tissue behavior under a predefined indentation pattern. In this way, we can realize different tissue properties (soft, hard, elastic, viscous…) or tumor properties with different parameter sets.

3.2 Mesh Tool

Out of the box, CHAI3D has only one tool that serves as avatar for the input device in the virtual environment. This so called haptic point has the shape of a sphere with definable radius. It is moved with the input device and collides with the meshes in the scene. The forces between the haptic point and the object are calculated and sent to the input device (if actively controllable degrees of freedom are featured). The haptic points can be multiplied if more than one input device is connected or if the input device has a gripper. However, our haptic device with its unique shape called for a completely new type of avatar.

Our new tool that allows to model the shape of the finger while pushing the pins and thus interacts with the virtual soft tissue more realistically (see Figure 7). Our Mesh Tool is made up of a triangular mesh with the shape of a hexagon. The general layout as a projection to the xy-plane is shown in Figure 8e. As a first step, a hexagon with six triangles is generated (a). The corners and the middle represent the middles of the seven pins. The area of the hexagon has to be enlarged in order to cover the whole touching area. Therefore, the triangles are folded to the outside which yields a star shaped figure (b). The z-values of these additional points are calculated from the mean value of the adjacent points and its absolute difference from the middle. Hence, the corners of the star always point upwards (away from the virtual soft tissue) in order to imitate the shape of the fingertip on the pins. Afterwards, the Loop subdivision algorithm (Loop 1987) is applied once to the mesh which results in a smoother mesh and more vertices and triangles (c). In a last step, the vertices between the star tips are interpolated (d) and the outermost triangles are neglected (e). At each side, six triangles in vertical direction are added to receive a three-dimensional shape. The positions of the vertices are recalculated in every cycle according to the pins positions and the global position of the tool. Following the rearrangement, the bounding box of the mesh is updated.

To calculate the interaction between the Mesh Tool and the virtual soft tissue, the Finger Proxy Algorithm (Ruspini et al. 1997) that comes with CHAI3D is used in a modified form. This algorithm is a penalty based method to circumvent the problem that haptic input devices cannot render infinite forces that are necessary when a haptic point collides with a stiff object. While the goal position can go inside the object, its proxy always stays on top of the surface. The algorithm moves the proxy along the surface in order to minimize the distance to the goal. The final vector from goal to proxy defines the magnitude and the direction of the force rendered on the input device.

For our Mesh Tool we inverted the algorithm. This means, we use it to calculate the proxy of the mass particles that are in contact with our Mesh Tool and hence the force between tool and each particle. In an iteration loop, all mass particles that can come in contact with the tool (the ones on the top surface) are checked for collision with the mesh of the tool. This is done with a simple collision check of the mesh and a line segment going straight down from the mass particle's position. To apply the Finger Proxy Algorithm, an initial proxy outside the mesh is necessary. The placement depends on the direction from which the particle entered the tool. The algorithm then successively improves the proxy's position on the tool's mesh. Finally, the proxy is in contact with up to three triangles. The index of these triangles is used to assign the force between mass particle and its proxy to one of the seven pins. Over one iteration, the forces for each pin are summed up and result in the target force. The forces on the individual mass particles are used as external forces for the dynamics calculation which leads eventually to the deformation of the virtual soft tissue over time. Although the algorithm seems cumbersome, it executes quickly enough for an overall rate of 1000Hz on a laptop computer.

The adaptable shape of the avatar and the deformation of the virtual soft tissue enable the user to immediately see the impact of his or her actions. The realistic reactions of the virtual environment measure up to the user's expectations and allow to get accustomed quickly. Although the user can move the hand freely in a regular palpation process, the mouse control does not diminish the experience. It is only used to reposition the initial point where the user starts pushing down the finger, but it does not interfere with the process itself. The visual output also allows the user to judge the deformation of the tissue by sight. This creates a certain redundancy to the haptic output and helps the user to intuitively use the haptic display.

4. EVALUATION

An evaluation of the haptic display and the simulation environment has been carried out with an older version of the software. The main difference was the use of a static model with no visible or physical deformation. The tool made up of seven haptic points could penetrate the virtual soft tissue while the forces were calculated by the overlap of the spheres making up the soft tissue. The evaluation served to determine, if the participants were capable of using the haptic display properly and if they could feel the differences in the forces on the pins.

15 people with technical or medical background between 27 and 34 years participated in the evaluation. It was divided into several parts but the common task was to find a hidden tumor in the virtual soft tissue by palpation. In the first part, the tumors had different properties (stiffness, size, depth in the tissue) but were rather large (about the diameter of the tool). The participants had little problems to find tumors close to the surface or with a high stiffness. In the other cases however, they had problems to distinguish if the tumors were rather soft or were deeper in the tissue. The hit rates was also slightly lower.

In the second part, a rod shaped tumor with increasing depth had to be found. The participants were only told that the point closest to the surface lies rather central. The correct answers were close to the average but it took the participants quite some time to find the tumor and determine the direction.

The last part of the evaluation was to find a single-node tumor (diameter of less than 1cm). Astonishingly, only one person did not find the tumor. However, some participants searched for the tumor for more than four minutes which is not realistic for a real palpation.

Overall, the results of the evaluation are very positive. With hit rates of 90% over all tasks, we can conclude, that the users are very capable of using the haptic display and the simulation software. None of them had problems with the bimanual control or complained about counterintuitive handling. Another pleasant result was that the medically experienced participants stated that the feedback and "feeling" of the haptic display was very realistic.

5. CONCLUSION

In this paper, we have presented a novel haptic input device specially tailored for the haptic feedback of soft tissue palpation. We achieved to construct a device that can reproducibly render intended forces by minimizing friction between the components and thus hysteresis. With an RC filter and a binomial filter we could suppress the noise of the pin position measurement and the implemented PID controller avoids possible oscillations of the motors. Additionally, we extended our virtual environment based on CHAI3D with a special tool that represents the hardware more realistically. The Mesh Tool interacts with the virtual soft tissue made up of a simple deformable mass-spring-model at a rate of 1000Hz. With these improvements, we seek to further improve the quality of the haptic feedback while our previous evaluation shows that we are on the right track.

ACKNOWLEDGEMENT

The authors would like to thank Andreas Jelinek for his countless hours in the workshop to manufacture the individual parts of the haptic display and its prototypes.

REFERENCES

Beccani, M. et al., 2013. Wireless Tissue Palpation: Proof of Concept for a Single Degree of Freedom. *In IEEE International Conference on Robotics and Automation*. pp. 703–709.

Conti, F. et al., 2003. The CHAI libraries. In *Proceedings of Eurohaptics 2003.* pp. 496–500

Genecov, A.M., Stanley, A. A. & Okamura, A.M., 2014. Perception of a Haptic Jamming display: Just noticeable differences in stiffness and geometry. *In 2014 IEEE Haptics Symposium (HAPTICS).* Ieee, pp. 333–338.

Goethals, P. et al., 2008. Powerful Compact Tactile Display with Microhydraulic Actuators. *In EuroHaptics 2008.* pp. 447–457.

Greenwald, D., Cao, C.G.L. & Bushnell, E.W., 2012. Haptic Detection of Artificial Tumors by Hand and with a Tool in a MIS Environment. *IEEE Transactions on Haptics*, 5(2), pp.131–138.

Gwilliam, J.C. et al., 2010. Human vs. robotic tactile sensing: Detecting lumps in soft tissue. *2010 IEEE Haptics Symposium (HAPTICS)*, pp.21–28.

Kim, S.-C. et al., 2009. Small and lightweight tactile display(SaLT) and its application. *In World Haptics 2009.* Ieee, pp. 69–74.

Koo, I.M. et al., 2008. Development of Soft-Actuator-Based Wearable Tactile Display. *IEEE Transactions on Robotics,* 24(3), pp.549–558.

Loop, C.T., 1987. Smooth Subdivision Surfaces Based on Triangles. M.S. Mathematics thesis, *University of Utah.*

Okamura, A., 2009. Haptic feedback in robot-assisted minimally invasive surgery. *Current opinion in urology*, 19(1), pp.102–107.

Pacchierotti, C., Prattichizzo, D. & Kuchenbecker, K.J., 2015. Cutaneous Feedback of Fingertip Deformation and Vibration for Palpation in Robotic Surgery. *IEEE transactions on bio-medical engineering*, PP(99), pp.1–10.

Roke, C. et al., 2013. The effects of laterotactile information on lump localization through a teletaction system. *In 2013 World Haptics Conference (WHC).* Ieee, pp. 365–370.

Ruspini, D.C., Kolarov, K. & Khatib, O., 1997. The haptic display of complex graphical environments. *In ACM SIGGRAPH.* pp. 345–352.

Santos-Carreras, L. et al., 2010. Design and psychophysical evaluation of a tactile pulse display for teleoperated artery palpation. *In IEEE/RSJ International Conference on Intelligent Robots and Systems*. Ieee, pp. 5060–5066.

Sarakoglou, I. et al., 2012. A High Performance Tactile Feedback Display and Its Integration in Teleoperation. *IEEE Transactions on Haptics*, 5(3), pp.252–263.

Talasaz, A. & Patel, R., 2012. Integration of Force Reflection with Tactile Sensing for Minimally Invasive Robotics-Assisted Tumor Localization. *IEEE Transactions on Haptics*, 6(2), pp.217–228.

Westebring-van der Putten, E.P. et al., 2008. Haptics in minimally invasive surgery - a review. *Minimally invasive therapy & allied technologies: MITAT: official journal of the Society for Minimally Invasive Therapy*, 17(1), pp.3–16.

Xie, H. et al., 2013. Fiber Optics Tactile Array Probe for Tissue Palpation during Minimally Invasive Surgery. *In IEEE/RSJ International Conference on Intelligent Robots and Systems*. pp. 2539–2544.

A DYNAMIC INTERFACE ADAPTATION APPROACH FOR ACCESSIBLE IMMERSIVE ENVIRONMENTS

Ioannis Paliokas[1], Sofia Segkouli[1], Dimitrios Tzovaras[1] and Charalampos Karagiannidis[2]
[1]*Information Technologies Institute-ITI Centre for Research and Technology Hellas-CERTH*
6th km Charilaou-Thermi Rd P.O. Box 60361, GR 57001 Thermi, Thessaloniki, Greece
[2]*Department of Special Education, University of Thessaly, Argonafton & Filellinon, Volos, Greece*

ABSTRACT

Current trends in context-aware computing have altered the static nature of interfaces and equipped them with the ability to adapt to the physical or social context. This paper investigates new paradigms towards cognitive context-awareness which relies on adaptation and personalization factors of more explicit interfaces oriented by individuals' cognitive processes. The main objective is to propose a smooth transition from existing interface design practices to advanced adaptation techniques concerning interfaces' design, based on cognitive abilities' inclination. To prove this, a group of young users, elderly and MCI positives, were asked to perform series of common tasks in a Metaverse interface design. A prediction model was developed to categorize users based on the way they interact with the interface. The outcomes of the interaction pattern analysis serve as the criterion based on which the proposed novel interaction-aware interface can adapt users' abilities to maximize accessibility and comfort.

KEYWORDS

Context-aware Computing, Interaction Patterns, MCI, Adaptive Interface Design, Metaverse

1. INTRODUCTION

Users' ability to drive interfaces effectively seem to be affected by aging [Heijkers et al., 2013] and disability factors [Ferreira et al., 2012]. Modern interface features as the orientation switching of the screen, map rotation and adapting zoom depending on user's location are quite common. Adaptive User Interfaces (AUI) are defined to adjust to the user's goals and abilities according to the continuous user and current state monitoring [Lavie & Meyer, 2010] and context is usually specified by physical or social criteria which are utilized as sensors resulting in the appropriate interface adaptation. The present paper extends the idea of the context-aware AUI design considering individuals' cognitive state affected in MCI and Mild Dementia, the transitional state between the cognitive changes of normal aging and very early dementia, recognized as a risk factor for Alzheimer disease [Grundman, 2004]. The emphasis is put on the use of interaction patterns driven by human factors as context acquisition criteria. User's behavior patterns matched with the appropriate accessible interface design can lead to an adaptive functionality for inclusion, especially for social networks and games, for high motivation and effective user's engagement [Kamieth et al., 2010].

2. PREVIOUS WORK AND PROJECT POSITIONING

One of the major challenges in Human–Computer Interaction (HCI) is to deal effectively with individual differences, preferences, experience [Lavie & Meyer, 2010] and cognitive flexibility that may associated with a variety of different user behaviors [Gonzalez, 2013]. Traditional AUI approaches classify users according to their profile and perceived behaviour [Feng, 2015]. However, cognitive capability considerations made UI design further challenging [Kim & Yoon, 2005], especially for immersive interfaces used in game-like applications in which both the UI and the game content should be adapted to people with cognitive decline.

Previous work on AUI monopolizes adaptation to physical and social contexts through the design of pervasive games [Guo et al., 2012] while demographics can play an important role in user clustering [Yee et al., 2012]. Interface adaptation is getting more challenging when user profiles are not defined in advance. Known approaches to this problem include the concept of Non-Obvious Profiles (NOPs) [Mushtaq et al., 2004] used in web applications on the basis of clustering by behavior [Hoebel & Zicari, 2007] and the *READ* technique proposed by Cerny et al. [2013] which has provided different UI presentation examples for children, elderly, adult and experienced users but with focus on GUI usability issues, not accessibility. Nebeling and Norrie [2011] have proposed a crowdsourcing model in which end users could participate in adaptation process. Moreover, the Context-Sensitive User Interface (CSUI) proposed by Vanderdonckt et al. [2005] was driven by a model-based approach to manage various reconfigurations of the UI.

This study goes one step beyond current solutions by proposing the adaptation of both the interface and the Metaverse content based on a user classification engine able to drive a run-time interface adaptation mechanism robust to reasonable turbulence on human factors. According to Jameson [2007], there are interfaces which support the user by undertaking parts of the tasks to be performed while others target the information acquisition processes. The proposed AUI strategy focus to Metaverse content and UI structure adaptation oriented by critical parameters like users' reaction time and the degree of performed activity as markers of cognitive processes to support the information acquisition and 3D navigation processes. Also the present effort aims to enrich research experience with proactive inclusion rules for more effective and accessible immersive interfaces. Next sections describe how the proposed methodology meets those requirements, present experimental results and propose an evidence-based interface adaptation structure to be applied in other similar ICT fields.

3. MATERIALS AND METHODS

Despite the variety of interface designs still the remaining question is: which interface is proper for use according to specific user cognitive conditions? The intelligence of the proposed method refers to the ability of the system to categorize new-coming users based on their interaction pattern according to data made available by past users. A prove-of-concept intelligent interface was developed, trained by real users and tested against users of varying cognitive ability. This test was set to collect initial data regarding interaction patterns of different user groups (fig.1), retrieve information and develop the novel interface design.

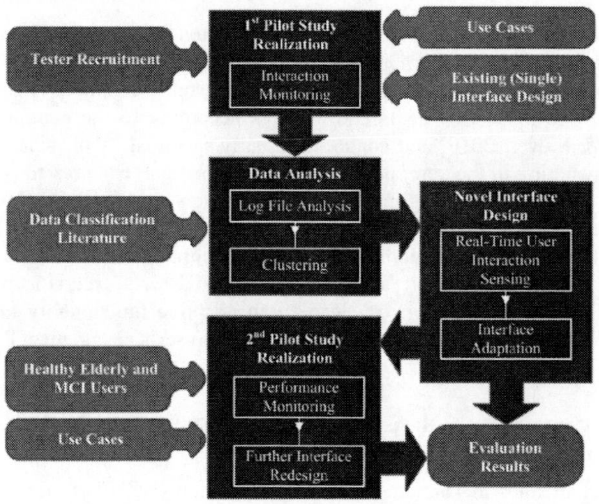

Figure 1. Overall approach and major steps

3.1 Used Tools and the Testbed Application

As a testbed application, the 'Second Life' (SL) environment, developed by Linden Lab, was chosen mainly as one of the most typical Metaverse environments and its potentiality to be customized for the study purposes. The default SL interface design was used as the most suitable for young and middle aged populations. Another two designs of the SL interface were created in order to comply with the needs of healthy elderly people and people with cognitive decline caused by Mild Cognitive Impairment (MCI). The accessible interface designs of the SL Metaverse application was developed using the OpensSim server platform and the open source code version of the official SecondLife Viewer application. Those interface designs were developed and evaluated in a previous related work [*Reference removed for review process*], thus considered in here as appropriate interfaces for their respected target audiences (fig. 2). An additional software tool was developed in order to capture the Operating System (OS) messages containing end-device interruptions (mouse clicks, keystrokes, cursor moves, etc), running in the background. This tool was used for user monitoring purposes in this experiment.

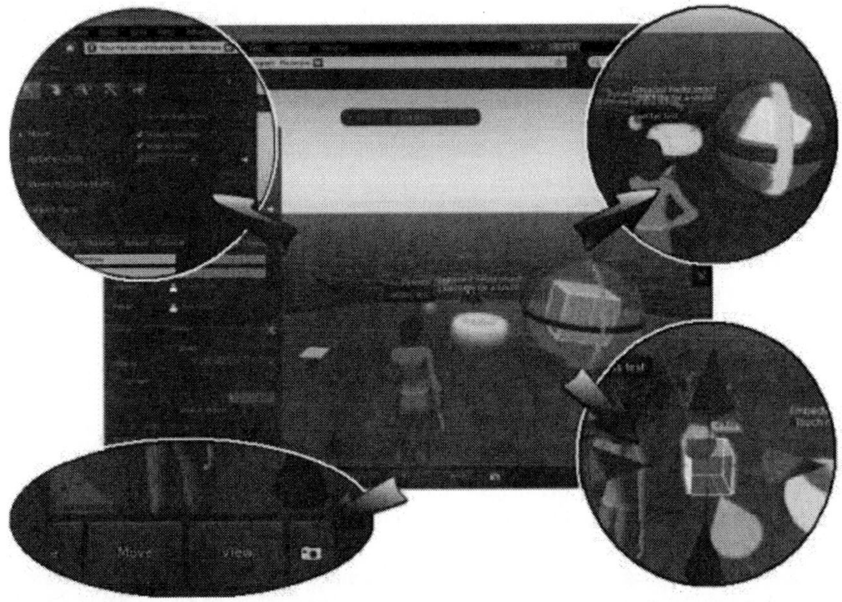

Figure 2. Multiple interface designs. Multiple interface designs (views) of the SL Metaverse environment: a. 40% font size increment (upper-left), size and contrast increment (upper-right) for elderly users, b. 300% button size increment (bottom-left), saturation and size changes in navigation indicators and 3D-object manipulation visual controls (bottom-right) for MCI users

3.2 Algorithmic and Methodological Approach

The route from interaction pattern sensing to user categorization and interface adaptation goes through a standard data classification process. Cluster analysis was used to separate the patterns of interaction into k (k>1) groups (clusters) by using p (p>0) variables. The number of clusters in this study is predefined and it is matched one-by-one to the 3 main user categories: a. young & middle aged users, b. healthy elderly and c. people with MCI. Possible variables used for classification were performance indicators of: a. time needed for tasks completion, b. the number of interaction events triggered during a task session (e.g. the total mouse down, mouse up, key-down and key-up events during the user authentication process). The duration of a task was measured in milliseconds and the starting point was the time of the related triggering event (e.g. a click on the 'change outfit' button, or the first move-avatar action in a 3D navigation task). The end point was indicated by the start point of the next task, so users should be kept busy.

Among various clustering techniques, a centroid-based clustering approach was considered as the most appropriate for this study. Evaluation and assessment of the clustering results followed in order to compare how well the selected clustering algorithm performs on the given tasks and also to evaluate how well the selected tasks challenge users to differentiate their behavior. This is of high importance, as apart from the strong internal similarity expected in young and middle aged groups other groups may not shape dense and well-separated clusters. Having also in mind that a k-means clustering approach will be applied, the clustering results will be evaluated by the silhouette coefficient [Rousseeuw, 1987; Kaufman & Rousseeuw, 1990] and no other internal criteria like the Davies-Bouldin [1979] or the Dunn index [Dunn, 1974].

3.3 Interaction Pattern Recognition and Classification of Users

User groups were defined on the basis of a simple rule: variability of records within a hosting cluster will be reduced and at the same time the variability between different clusters will be maximized. Although the proposed deterministic approach is highly probabilistic, it is expected that will work in real world examples even with high false positives. In other words, it is expected that perceived delays in user's responses attributed to reasons other than pure cognitive conditions will exert pressure towards categorizing users as people with MCI or healthy elderly. Users who have a better cognitive condition and computer driving ability than the system thinks of them will be able to perform unhindered in the accessible interface design.

Thus, given a set of interaction session observations (I1, I2,.., In) created by n users over an interface design during a given task, we need to partition the n observations into k sets where k < n. In this particular experiment, k = 3 which produce S = {Sy, Se, Scd} sets for the three user groups: young & middle aged, healthy elderly users and MCI respectively. Partitioning in those groups (clusters) had to be performed in such a way, that each interaction session observation will have the minimum distance to one of the mean clusters. The followed algorithm will be used to generate clusters by optimizing a criterion function. Now, consider the following equation which tries to minimize a function f(x):

$$argmax_S\, f(x) := \{x \mid \forall y: f(y) \leq f(x)\} \quad \{1\}$$

where f(x) is the mean distance to either of the two evaluation parameters which are the duration and the interaction volume. A k-means clustering algorithm was applied using equation (1), which finally becomes:

$$argmin_S \sum_{i=1}^{k} \sum_{x \in S_i} \|x - \mu_i\|^2 \quad \{2\}$$

Equation (2) was used in order to calculate mean values of performance indicators, where μi is the mean of observations in Si. Clusters were shaped around their central points (centroids) which represent subject groups. Manual insertion of initial central points was not eligible because this clustering process is planned to be fully automated in the near future. So, random initial centers were selected by the clustering algorithm and at every next pass (10 maximum iterations), cluster centers were updated. After clustering has been completed, each couple of values, namely the duration (in msec) and the interaction volume (in number of interaction events) were projected in a 2D plane using Euclidean distances to centroids. The system was trained on existing data derived from the first pilot study and later called to find the closest cluster for new-coming users of unknown profile. Indeed, for a new record R(t,e) created by a new user who performs a given task, the Euclidean distance to the j cluster centroid was calculated. The problem is that the Euclidean distance cannot be used for calculation of the closest cluster because records in clusters may have different deviations. To overcome this issue, Euclidean distances were divided by the standard deviation of each cluster values to give the normalized distances given by:

$$d_{Nj} = \sqrt{\left(\frac{x_j - x}{\sigma_{jx}}\right)^2 + \left(\frac{y_j - y}{\sigma_{jy}}\right)^2} \quad \{3\}$$

$$\text{with } \sigma_{jx} = \sqrt{\sum_{i=1}^{N_1} \frac{(x_1 - x_i)^2}{N_1}} \quad \{4\} \text{ and } \sigma_{jy} = \sqrt{\sum_{i=1}^{N_1} \frac{(y_1 - y_i)^2}{N_1}} \quad \{5\}$$

For each new-coming user, the min(dN1, dN2, dN3) was calculated to find the closest cluster. This model was trained on the 75% of the available data and tested on the rest of the 25%. Clustering quality here is expressed by the silhouette measure of cohesion and separation (SMCS). This was used as a simple numerical indication of how well the clustering solution fits the data and it is given by the simple formula:

$$SMCS = \sum_{i=0}^{Nj} \frac{(D_{cl} - D_i)}{max(D_{cl}, D_i)} \quad \{6\}$$

where Di is the element's distance to the centroid of the hosting cluster and Dcl is the distance to the nearest cluster centre other than the hosting cluster. The SMCS takes values in the range [-1, 1] and every value greater than 0.5 indicate a satisfactory solution quality. According to this, cluster validation in all tested tasks resulted to an accepted quality.

3.4 Pilot Study Participants, Experimental Conditions and Use Cases

The pilot tests were performed with a group of volunteer users (N=32), from young adulthood to elderly (26 to 78 years old). All users gave an MCI screening test as cognitive ability evidence. For this purpose, the short Boston Naming Test (30BNT) was chosen as a well-established instrument to screen for MCI conditions. Thus, the group of participants was divided into three subgroups:

Group A: Eleven (N=11) young to middle-aged adults, free of disabilities or disorders. Subjects of this group were very efficient computer users and needed no help, interface adaptation or assistive technologies to perform the 100% of the required tasks on expected times.

Group B: This group consisted of twelve (N=12) healthy elderly users who manage to perform all tasks but needed some more time in comparison to group A. The aging threshold was regulated in 60 years in order to separate the elderly users from young and middle aged.

Group C: Users of this group (N=5) were elderly with MCI who needed more time than both of the previous groups to perform the required tasks. Group C users produced noisy results (unnecessary interaction events like double or triple clicks) and they did not managed to complete all given tasks. The criterion for separating healthy elderly from those having MCI was set to 25/30 in the BNT scale.

Group D: Users of this group (N=2) were people already progressed to mild Dementia at the time of the experiment. Inclusion criteria were based not only to BNT test, but mainly to recent health records.

After a short introduction to the scopes of the experiment, participants had a demonstration of the default Metaverse viewer and enough free time to navigate around in order to ensure that all feel confident in using the interface. Finally, participants were asked to follow nine (9) common and relatively easy scenarios of Metaverse tasks as seen in Table 1.

Table 1. Common tasks used in the experiment as typical examples of Metaverse interaction

No.	Description of Metaverse tasks
T1	User authentication using username and password (login process)
T2	Change avatar's appearance based on a menu (choose outfit)
T3	Upload files from local disks to the share information space of the Metaverse
T4	Create new 3D objects based on primitives (e.g. a 3D cube of size 1x1x1 meter)
T5	Scale, rotate and move 3D objects (the cube created at the previous step)
T6	Navigate avatar in 3D space (walk to a target area)
T7	Trigger objects to respond back (multimedia objects)
T8	Locate other users and initiate text-based communication
T9	Share a folder with other users (send sharing privileges)

4. RESULTS

Ideally subjects would be grouped in their respected groups based on their performance on the scenarios presented in Table1. After the final cluster centers (centroids) were calculated by the k-Means algorithm described earlier, a set of ANOVA tests was performed to estimate the cohesion of the clusters. After ANOVA analysis of the results of the 1st scenario (user authentication), it became obvious that durations were stronger separators than the number of events.

As an example, a plot diagram from scenario 1 (user authentication) is cited in fig.3 to show how the clusters were shaped by a typical user authentication procedure. Well-shaped clusters were noticed on the bottom left part of the diagram representing the young and middle aged users who need less time to login. There was some diaspora on the x axis mainly because some users needed to correct the language settings on their keyboards and they had to delete and retype their username and password.

In overall, it was found a good cognitive decline condition prediction. For evaluation purposes, the sensitivity (Sn) and specificity (Sp) of the prediction model of the 1st scenario are graphically presented in fig. 4. It was found that the prediction mechanism underestimates the performance of people with cognitive decline because of some extreme performance scores, so forming the 4 groups (A, B, C & D) only by monitoring the user authentication process may not be possible at one stage. On the other hand, it was possible to apply both cognitive health and aging criteria at once by keeping groups A and B as independent clusters but merging C and D groups. This way, cognitive decline was predicted in a much better accuracy, having Sn≈.09 for healthy people and Sn≈.06 for cognitive declined.

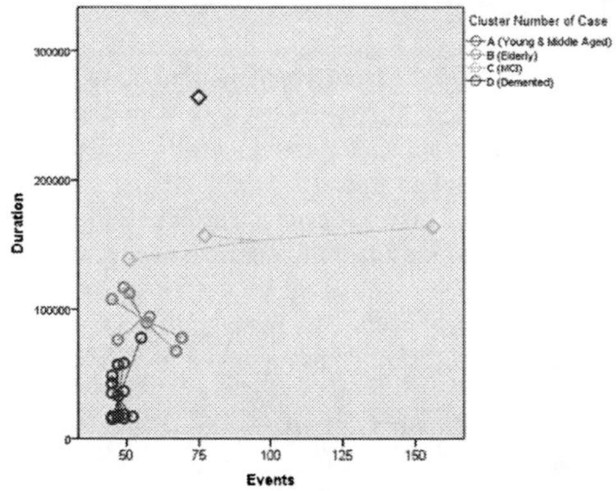

Figure 3. P-P plot of the scenario 1 results (clusters). Y-axis: task duration (msec), X-axis: number of interaction events

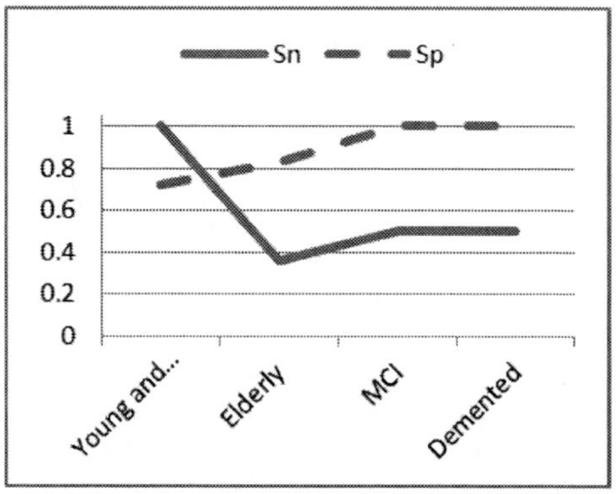

Figure 4. Sensitivity (Sn) - Specificity (Sp) plots for the prediction evaluation of the 1st scenario

In overall results (table 2), the interaction volume followed task durations with a much lower cluster forming power. The same pattern was repeated in all of the rest ANOVA results, except for S7 (dynamic objects).Table 2 also presents results of the quality assessment of the clusters. The SMCS was found over 0.5 in all clustering cases (all scenarios) and this indicates a good fit of the clustering solution to the data. In overall, young and middle aged users were categorized in a group of high intra-cluster similarity (low intra-cluster distances). On the other hand, users with MCI and Mild Dementia covered a wider area, sometimes spread to the X axis indicating over-interaction, but more frequently in Y axis indicating longer task sessions.

Table 2. Results of the 2nd study performed on the accessible interface

Scenario	Interaction Metrics	Final Cluster Centers A	B	C&D	ANOVA Results F	p	Cluster SMCS
S1	Duration (in msec)	28541	90811	153411	2636257	<.001	.70
	Interaction volume	47	55	95	8.715	<.05	
S2	Duration (in msec)	7552	38012	67531	248.628	<.001	.75
	Interaction volume	11	12	16	29.359	<.001	
S3	Duration (in msec)	30301	111447	163914	130.903	<.001	.80
	Interaction volume	19	26	25	2.426	>.05	
S4	Duration (in msec)	22563	49083	81094	44.196	<.001	.60
	Interaction volume	10	13	16	3.609	<.05	
S5	Duration (in msec)	20469	64170	126976	52.376	<.001	.60
	Interaction volume	13	15	27	8.358	<.05	
S6	Duration (in msec)	11156	30097	56029	95.399	<.001	.65
	Interaction volume	15	30	42	3.192	>.05	
S7	Duration (in msec)	3787	15828	24875	72.413	<.001	.80
	Interaction volume	4	5	16	121.443	<.001	
S8	Duration (in msec)	20292	49809	83135	80.737	<.001	.65
	Interaction volume	21	28	30	2.288	>.05	
S9	Duration (in msec)	31236	93821	189969	56.258	<.001	.60
	Interaction volume	29	36	47	1.335	>.05	

Pearson test for correlation between durations and number of interaction events was performed to evaluate variable independence and conclude on the necessity to keep both variables in the prediction model. It was found a strong positive correlation in 8 out of 9 scenarios, having the S5 (r=.805, p<.001) and S7 (r=.849, p<.001) the two strongest cases. On the other hand, the less strong correlation was found on S9

($r=.363$, $p<.05$). In 'closed tasks' (those performed in a very specific way without obvious alternatives of doing the same thing), the correlation between duration and interaction volume was high. In the contrast, when tasks were more 'open' or Operating System operations were included like in locating a file in local disk (S9), the degrees of freedom for each single user were getting higher. In such cases, the higher interaction events did not get followed by longer times.

Users' performances depend on the kind of the task, so performance analysis results of one task cannot be transferred to another and conclusions cannot be generalized arbitrarily. The most effective tasks were tasks which were well defined and there was a unique or an obvious way of doing them. In any case, a SMCS measure lower than 0.5 indicated that the task may not be eligible for being a user's screening task. Mixed correlation test results indicated that it was not always safe to omit the number of interaction actions and consolidate the prediction model exclusively on the task duration metric.

4.1 Machmaking

After the prediction engine was set, a matchmaking algorithm was developed to match users with the accessible interface designs. The interface adaptation mechanism was based on a simple rule: at given times, the most appropriate interface design becomes visible ('running'), while other sibling interface designs enter their 'runnable' mode. When certain conditions met, UI designs come to foreground and become visible to serve interaction-specific needs. As long as the system recognizes a certain type of interaction pattern the Interface Manager (IM) will project to users the winner interface design. Having interaction patterns predefined (in training), IM dynamically change the interface designs at run-time according to the equation:

$$I(i) = \begin{cases} I_0, & if\ c(t,e) = C_0 \\ I_1, & if\ c(t,e) = C_1 \\ I_n, & if\ c(t,e) = C_n \end{cases} \quad \{7\}$$

where $I(i)$ is the winner interface, I_0, I_1, I_n are n instances of the interface (or n interface designs), t is the task duration, e is the number of interaction events, c(t,e) is a function which finds the cluster centroid with the minimum distance to the R(t,e) record during the testing phase. Distances to cluster centroids are calculated based on the normalized Euclidean distances as described in equation {3}.

According to the proposed matchmaking schema, for those users currently working on interface I_n, some may need to be redirected to interface I_{n+1}, or to downgrade to interface I_{n-1}. For the last interface (I_{max}), the one designed for the most severe users, further adaptation to accessibility rules may not be possible because it is a 'roof' accessible interface view. While in such border conditions, if some users from this group perform much better than the average in-group user, then they will downgrade to interface I_{max-1} after some while (monitoring quota). These interface transactions would be normally expected especially for some time after entering the Metaverse in order to classify users with greater confidence. After a number of interface adaptation transactions per user (Itr=3 in here) the IM became inactivated to prevent users' inconvenience.

5. CONCLUSION

Cognition has been used in interface design to better sense users [Dong et al., 2009] while affect, a new emerging factor touched sporadically, is used to evaluate and judge. In this line, an AUI for accessibility adaption is proposed to make a nice match between user groups and the pool of available interface designs.

The prediction ability of the interaction-aware interface strongly depends on the design of the interface and the common tasks to be performed in there. Based on our experimental results, the task duration was found to be a strong separator both for cognitive health status and for age. Thus, in future experiments, user's clustering could be performed only with the duration variable without losing much of the clustering accuracy for casual infotainment environments, like the SL Metaverse used in this experiment, separation into major cognition health statuses and age groups was made possible. More advanced grouping may require stressing the users with more demanding tasks and longer screening times. Moreover a larger sample of the group with mild dementia may illuminate subjective experiences of cognitive oriented interfaces.

Delays generated not by causing factors (distraction, short brakes, etc.) may create frequent flips in back and forth interface designs until a stable user interface is created. In addition, a portion of wrong classification results (e.g. false MCI positives) do not cause any inconvenience to healthier and younger populations as they will be able to drive UIs designed for seniors or for cognition declined individuals. This feature brings the overall concept closer to what Lieberman et al. [2004] has proposed for 'soft fails' in intelligent user interfaces. Selecting separate competitive interface views in real time in the current approach is perceived as a rough change from the user's point of view. Therefore, future plans include the use of smooth adaptation techniques to maximize convenience and comfort for a variety of electronic device users.

REFERENCES

Cerny, T., Cemus, K., Donahoo, M.J. & Song, E., 2013. Aspect-driven, Data-reflective and Context-aware User Interfaces Design. *Applied Computing Review*, 13(4), pp. 53-65.

Davies, D.L. & Donald, W., 1979. A Cluster Separation Measure. *IEEE Transactions on Pattern Analysis and Machine Intelligence*, PAMI-1 (2), pp. 224–227.

Dong, A., Kleinsmann, M. & Valkenburg, R. 2009. Affect-in-Cognition through the Language of Appraisals. *Design Studies,* 30, pp. 138–153.

Dunn, J., 1974. Well separated clusters and optimal fuzzy partitions. Journal of Cybernetics, 4, pp. 95–104.

Feng, J., & Liu, Y., 2015. Intelligent Context-Aware and Adaptive Interface for Mobile LBS. *Computational Intelligence and Neuroscience,* Article ID 489793.

Ferreira, S.B.L., Nunes, R.R., Silva, D. & (da) Silveira D.S., 2012. Aligning Usability Requirements with the Accessibility Guidelines focusing on the Visually-Impaired. *Procedia Computer Science*, 14, pp. 263-273.

Gonzalez, C. A., Figueroa, I. J., Bellows, B. G., Rhodes, D. & Youmans, R. J., 2013. A new behavioral measure of cognitive flexibility. *Engineering Psychology and Cognitive Ergonomics*, pp. 297-306.

Grundman, M., Petersen, R.C., Ferris, S.H. et al, (2004). Mild cognitive impairment can be distinguished from Alzheimer disease and normal aging for clinical trials. Archives of neurology, 61(1), 59-66.

Guo, B., Fujimura, R., Zhang, D. & Imai, M. (2012). Design-in-Play: Improving the Variability of Indoor Pervasive Games. *Multimedia Tools and Applications*, 59(1), pp. 259-277.

Hoebel, N. & Zicari, R.V., 2007. On Clustering Visitors of a Web Site by Behavior and Interests. In Wegrzyn-Wolska K.M. & Szczepaniak P.S. (Ed.), *Adv. in Intel. Web, ASC 43*, pp. 181–188.

Heijkers, J., Rietsema, J., (de) Witte, L. et al., 2013. Supporting Autonomy in the Aging Population by using an Accessible Information System on Comfort Products and Assistive Technology. *Assistive Technology: From Research to Practice*, pp. 917-923.

Jameson, A., 2007. Adaptive Interfaces and Agents. In A. Sears & J.A. Jacko (Ed.), *The Human-Computer Interaction Handbook: Fundamentals, Evolving Technologies and Emerging Applications*, pp. 305–330.

Kamieth, F., Arca, A., Villalar, J. L. et al. 2010. *Exploring the Potential of Virtual Reality for the Elderly and People with Disabilities.* INTECH Open Access Publisher.

Kaufman, L. & Rousseeuw, P., 1990. *Finding Groups in Data: An Introduction to Cluster Analysis.* London: John Wiley & Sons.

Kim, H. & Yoon, W.C., 2005. Supporting the cognitive process of user interface design with reusable design cases. *Int. J. Human-Computer Studies,* 62(4), pp. 457-486.

Lavie, T. & Meyer, J. (2010). Benefits and costs of adaptive user interfaces. *Int. J. Human-Computer Studies*, 68(8), pp. 508-524.

Lieberman, H., Liu, H., Singh, P. & Barry, B., 2004. Beating Common Sense into Interactive Applications. *AI Magazine,* 25(4), pp. 63–76.

Mushtaq, N., Tolle, K., Werner, P. & Zicari, R., 2004. Building and Evaluating Non-Obvious User Profiles for Visitors of Web Sites, San Diego. *IEEE Workshop on Hot Topics in Web Systems and Technologies – HOTWEB*, pp. 9-15.

Nebeling, M. & Norrie, MC. (2011). Tools and Architectural Support for Crowdsourced Adaptation of Web Interfaces. In S. Auer, O. Diaz & G.A. Papadopoulos (Ed.), *ICWE 2011, LNCS 6757*, pp. 243-257.

Rousseeuw, PJ., 1987. Silhouettes: a Graphical Aid to the Interpretation and Validation of Cluster Analysis. *Computational and Applied Mathematics*, 20, pp. 53–65.

Vanderdonckt, J., Grolaux, D., Van Roy, P. et al., 2005. A Design Space for Context-Sensitive User Interfaces. *International Conference in Intelligent and Adaptive Systems and Software Engineering-IASSE 2005*, pp. 207-214.

Yee, N., Ducheneaut N., Shiao, H.T. & Nelson, L., 2012. Through the Azerothian Looking Glass: Mapping In-Game Preferences to Real World Demographics. *CHI 2012*, Austin, pp. 2811-2814.

International Conferences Interfaces and Human Computer Interaction 2016,
Game and Entertainment Technologies 2016 and
Computer Graphics, Visualization, Computer Vision and Image Processing 2016

'SIMON SAYS' "USE HUMANOID ROBOT TO TEACH CHILDREN" – A CASE STUDY OF EXPECTATIONS AND REALITY

Kaberi Naznin, Dr. Vivienne Farrell, Dr. Karola von Baggo and Dr. Clinton Woodward
Swinburne University of Technology, PO Box 218 Hawthorn, Victoria 3122, Australia

ABSTRACT

There are rising expectations from educational bodies, governments, and parents, for teachers to integrate emerging technology into their everyday teaching. Introducing new technology is not always an easy task for the school, the teacher or the students. The aim of this paper is to present our initial work in developing a system to integrate an emerging technology, the humanoid robot, into learning environments in a manner that encourages the learners to engage with and reflect on the learning activity. This paper describes our attempt to develop a classroom activity using the humanoid NAO robot to help students learn a second language. We found that although individual functions were theoretically supported by the software and hardware, we felt that the programming requirements and problems with the reliability of the technology meant this type of technology is likely to be beyond what could be reasonably expected from people without good technical or programming skills.

KEYWORDS

Teaching, Usability, and Human Robot Interaction

1. INTRODUCTION

Schools and other governing bodies are endeavouring to exploit the D-generation's (Campbell 2009) acceptance of technology and rapidly advancing technological capabilities to create engaging and effective learning environments. However, before introducing a new technology into a school, both technological and human resources need to be considered. Poor implementation could easily impact negatively on both teacher and student experience.

New technology seldom comes cheaply, nor does the infrastructure that surrounds its use, including software, upgrades, maintenance, set up, training of technicians and training of teachers who are already time poor (Billig, Sherry & Havelock 2005). Before we can promote the use of any technology to students we must consider how it will be used and whether it will be accepted by the teachers in a positive, encouraging and constructive manner. If teachers feel uncomfortable with the technology, then this could adversely on the effectiveness of technologically intensive learning activities. A final consideration is that any new classroom activities must align with required learning outcomes of the school and governing bodies.

This paper reports our attempt to prepare an emerging technology for a simple classroom activity for primary school aged children in order to assess the likelihood of a classroom teacher being able to do the same. Firstly, we review the factors that influence student learning in relation to emerging technology and how we came to investigate the NAO humanoid robot as an emerging technology. Secondly, we describe our attempt to program the robot for use in a simple lesson plan. Finally, we make some recommendations on what would be required to successfully use robots in the classroom.

2. DETERMINATION OF THE TECHNOLOGY

Our review of the literature is presented in Table 1, found three main factors in the effective uptake and use of technology in schools: School level, teacher level, and student level factors.

Table 1. Different level of factors (school level, teacher level and student level)

School Level Factors	*Teacher Level Factors*	*Student Level Factors*
Curriculum: Mandatory curriculum requirements do not leave many opportunities to undertake activities that do not meet learning outcomes. Therefore, it is necessary to ensure that any use of technology supports curriculum requirements. **Right tool for the job**: It is important to match suitable educational technology to learning outcomes. (Martin 2000) (Simon 2012, Mouza 2005, Turbill 2001). **Use technologies to aid learning**: How best to use technologies to aid learning and what types of learning we should facilitate with computers (Clarke and Zagarell 2012, Simon 2012, Campbell 2009, Cordes and Miller 2000, Mouza 2005, Fischer 2009). **Physical Environment**: Creating an environment that enables the use of the technology to be optimised. This may include aspects such as space, noise, visibility etc. **Maximising use of available resources**: School facilities are limited and ensuring that the funding and resources allocation are carefully planned and executed, which are essential for the viability of the school.	**The right teacher**: Teachers who support constructivist learning have been found to strongly align with the use of computers in the classroom. In contrast, the traditional teacher-centered approach seems to have a negative impact on the computer integrated classroom (Francis-Baldesari and Pope 2008). **Up to date information**: Teachers need to be aware of new and emerging technology tools that are available to them for teaching. Using technology in education, "it is a journey, not a destination" (Simon 2012, 29, Mumtaz 2000). **Effective training**: Suitable and effective teacher training on how to utilize the technology to augment their lessons (Clarke and Zagarell 2012) (Simon 2012) (Clements and Sarama 2002, Ntuli and Kyei-Blankson 2012) Danielowich and McCarthy 2013, Campbell 2009). **Ongoing Support**: This may include before, during and after the introduction and training of the technology. Further lesson plans and suitable software to enhance the learning tool may be required. Technical support must be available when 'things go wrong'. **Time Allowance**: Teachers need time allowances to reassessing teaching practices, learn about new technologies, train with new technologies and/or research new lessons.	**Social interaction**: Computers can act as facilitator of social interactions. In previous comparative studies it has been found that "Children spent nine times as much time talking to peers while on computers than while doing puzzles and compared to more traditional activities, such as puzzle assembly or block building, the computer elicits more social interaction and different types of interaction" (Clements and Sarama 2002, p.341). **Cognitive development**: Using technology can support a child's cognitive development in three ways: (a) it helps students to create environments where students can learn by doing; (b) it helps students visualize difficult-to-understand concepts and (c) it highlights traditional developmentally appropriate activities. Students need opportunities to learn by doing via interacting, exploring, and manipulating real world objects (Mouza 2005). **Duration of Exposure to Technology**: This is about the amount of time children should spend using technology. For example, previous studies have shown that "the use of technology in one teacher-directed activity should not exceed 20 minutes" (Simon 2012, p. 44, Clarke and Zagarell 2012). Each new technology will need to be assessed for the duration that it can hold a child's attention for any given activity. **Novelty**: When does an emerging technology start to lose its interest for the children or can it be reused in various ways so that the novelty does not wane?

We considered a range of emerging technologies in relation the three factors noted above (Table 1). After reviewing the manufactures specifications, we selected the NAO humanoid robot. Such humanoid robots can act and speak in ways that represent canonical behaviours of an autonomous, thinking, feeling, social, and moral human being. In this sense, they can be viewed as offering the same social affordances as a human and thus elicit or merit the same moral considerations (Magyar 2014). The potential richness of humanoid robot behaviours offers exciting opportunities to integrate them into key curriculum requirements such as teamwork, project management, problem solving, oral language (speaking and listening) and communication skills. In addition, humanoid robots are yet to become common in the day-to-day lives of students (unlike the iPad and other similar tablet technology). This allowed us to research a technology that was new to both teachers and students.

Literacy is a key component of the curriculums of many countries. Thus, we decided to build a simple lesson plan using the robot to help children to improve their language skills. Our idea was to engage the children in literacy tasks by asking them to teach the robot language skills through such games as 'Simon Says' and teaching it simple words, names and objects. Such activities should encourage students to consider engage deeply with the material in order to give proper instruction to the robot and to reflect on the verbal responses they received before offering a further response. The first step in developing our learning activity was to assess the ability of the NAO robot and develop a model and functional requirements of the system.

2.1 Employing the NAO robot

The NAO robot, designed by Aldebaran, is 58cm tall and includes two cameras, four microphones, two IR emitters and receivers, one inertial board, nine tactile sensors, eight pressure sensors, a voice synthesizer,

LED lights, and two speakers (Hughes 2013). The NAO robot is programmed through the software development kit Choreographe which is a drag and drop editable programming tool with a 3D simulator using C++ libraries or Python and .Net.

According to the manufacturer specification, the NAO appears to offer many opportunities to develop activities to support student learning in a positive way. In a typical class room situation, the teacher instructs the student. However, we envisaged an approach where the robot is the learner and the child act as a 'student teacher' who helps to instruct the robot in tasks they themselves are learning. The 'student teachers' learn from the experiences they have gained in the teaching interaction (Nilssen 2010) and to do this task will require the children to reflect on, and deeply understand the task they are trying to teach. To act a learner, the robot will need to utilise many of its advertised capabilities including visual object recognition, human face recognition, gesture recognition, natural language processing and physical decision-making. We envisaged that ability to do these human-like tasks would enable the robot to play language games, such as 'Simon Says'.

Features and Possible Interactions

To assist us to develop our lesson plan, we talked with 10 current primary school teachers who taught between the grades 2 and 6. We showed them a video of the NAO and asked them how they felt the robot could be used in their classroom. Following these discussions, four stages of interaction complexity were identified for the initial work. **Elements**: basic letters and pictures from flash cards; **Components**: words, names, and objects; **Compound** sentences, context and grammar; **Game play**: turn-based interaction using elements, components and compound stages (for example, the game 'Simon Says').

Some technical challenges remained to support all of the interaction models, which will be explained later in this paper. The four stages of descriptions and example interactions are presented in Table 2. The teachers were shown the four stage descriptors and asked if they could identify any foreseeable concerns with either the technology or their requirements to interact with the technology. None of them was identified and the teachers agreed that these would be useful activities meeting curriculum requirements and that the children would benefit from enabling multiple repetitions.

Table 2. The description of four stages and examples of interactions

Stage 1: *Letter and Number Recognition (elements)* This stage involved teaching the robot to recognise and name basic letters and numbers. Letters and numbers are provided on flash cards to make the task technically robust. N.B. the student while acting as the teacher is referred.	*Student teacher: "I want to teach you a letter."* *Robot: "Okay. Please show me the letter."* *Student teacher: Selects and holds up flash card for the robot to see.* *Robot: Moves head to track the flash card.* *Robot: When letter identified says, "What is the letter?"* *Student teacher: "It is the letter 'A'."* *Robot: "A"* *Student teacher: "Yes – that's it!"* *Robot: "I think I know it now. Want to test me?"* *Student teacher: "Well done!"*
Stage 2: *Words, Names and Objects (components)* Building on the outcomes of Stage 1, the aim of this stage was to learn words, names and other objects. Once the robot has been taught and has a working database, it can be questioned about what it knows. If movement and object manipulation is technically robust at this stage it could also be incorporated.	*Student teacher: "What colour is a strawberry?"* *Robot: "It is red."* *Student teacher: "That's right. Can you find something that is red?"* *Robot: "I'll have a look". It searches for a red object and turns body until it finds a red ball. It walks to ball, picks it up, and returns to the previous position.* *Student teacher: "Can I have it?"* *Robot: "Yes". Offers the object with an open hand.* *Student teacher: "Well done!"*
Stage 3: *Sentence Construction, Context and Grammar (compound)* Extending Stage 2, this stage could involve specific lessons and interaction about the structure of a sentence. For example the student teacher could teach and ask the robot to identify in a sentence. The dialog to support this (example omitted for brevity), while still structured, requires a strong internal model of the learning within the programming of the robot.	*Robot: Let do some grammar now. Give me a sentence problem* *Student teacher: Carefully listen the sentence: I have a red ball.* *Robot: what do you want me to do with the sentence?* *Student teacher: find noun and pronoun from that sentence.* *Robot: 'I' stands for a pronoun, ball is a noun. Learning Grammar is interesting for me. Was it correct?* *Student teacher: yes, you are very intelligent.*
Stage 4: *Game Play (game)* Our initial planning and development focused on support of the Simon Says game, where the robot is able to perform either the role of 'Simon' or a follower. This requires not only the ability to understand the dialog interaction with the human student teacher, but also the body position of the human. The robot also needs to be able to apply the rules of the game in a meaningful and robust manner.	*Student teacher: "I want to play Simon says."* *Robot: "Do you want me to be Simon or do you want to be Simon?"* *Student teacher: "I want to be Simon."* *Robot: "Okay, I'll follow what you say."* *Student teacher: "Simon says 'Raise your left hand'." (Robot lifts his left hand).* *Robot: "Did I perform the action correctly?"* *Student teacher: "Yes. Well done!" (Robot dances.)*

At the conclusion of this activity, we determined that the functional requirements needed to support our research activities were: **Recognize and remember letters, words, faces and objects**: For example the robot needs to be able to learn the alphabet from student teachers and remember the name of the student; **Initiate and lead a conversation with emotional expression**. For example, the robot should be able to sound like a human in a friendly tone and manner; **Follow and continue a basic dialog**. This would be required for simple game play (Simon Says); **Walking while avoiding objects and falls**; **Pick up, manipulate and place objects**; **Detect (locate), track and focus (head movement) on a person using audio and video signals**. This can be extended to identification of subject body position (pose) and tracking of change (movement); **Memory (database) of interaction session**. As the robot learns from the student teacher the data needs to be stored and access to enable sensible interaction; **Adaptive scripting of interaction session**. Essentially the interaction should be scripted to follow a standard form, as well as being robust and flexible to handle the natural variation of human interactions. This will be supported by researcher supervised monitoring and override control if needed; **Remote recording and operation**. Ideally, the human teacher would be able to interact with the robot without excessive interference by a supervisor. Finally, during interaction sessions, data learnt by the robot is stored in a database. Observations and decisions made by the robot will be recorded for analysis.

3. RESULTS OF THE DEVELOPMENT AND TRIAL PROCESS

There were many issues and challenges that occurred during the development and testing of the project as well as some pleasing outcomes which are described in this section.

From the description and basic tutorial of Choreographe (the robot programming environment) it was considered that the functional requirements we had set for the robot were achievable. The development team was a group of 4 final year undergrad robotics and computer science students. The students worked with the robot over a year covering two units of study. The students were required to present substantial documentation of project plans, requirements, testing plans, etc. The research team was the client for the project whose position was to ensure specifications were met and developed to a good level of usability.

The development team had no knowledge of the robot or its capabilities before starting the project. This included no knowledge of its set up or the software Choreographe used to run the robot. It was felt that this was essential to emulate the classroom teacher's first introduction to the technology and the software.

Programming skills required

The initial programming of the robot using Choroeographe was quite basic. It was found that programming movements such as waving, talking, dancing was simple and obvious and provided an excellent demonstration of the robot capabilities. The visibility of the system was clear as instant feedback was received by observing the movement of the limbs or use of verbal response as each runtime occurred. The icons used to represent the movement actions were obvious and the stringing together of a sequence of actions was easily created by drag and dropping the icons to the workspace and using connectors to link the actions. Overall it was easy to do the most basic of pre-programmed activities. The level of difficulty for a non-programmer occurred after this stage as we tried to implement the interactions required for our language activities. The descriptions in the table below (Table 3) rate the various levels of programming skills that were required to achieve actions or interactivity with NAO. This is to demonstrate what a teacher would be able to achieve for their classroom depending on their programming skills.

Things that went wrong.

Setup Connectivity was an issue as the robot required a connection from the laptop through Wi-Fi. The connection was often lost and the NAO required technical assistance in reconnecting. Eventually, after quite a bit of research, it was found that a separate router provided the stability required for a continuous reliable connection. This activity also required technical support in the form of router configuration.

Balance was an issue with any movement such as raising limbs and walking on surfaces such as carpet and some vinyl. This forced the developers to consider minimising movement and selecting floor coverings that could be rolled out for the demonstration. This would need to be considered in a classroom where the floor has carpets.

Table 3. The three levels of programming skills, which required achieve during interactivity with the NAO robot

Level 1:	**Level 2:**	**Level 3:**
Before commencing the development of the interactions it was necessary to learn how to program Choreographe to interact with NAO to undertake each of the individual activities. This included such activities as verbal response and prepared dialogue with prompts, decision making and iteration, teaching to recognise shapes, walking, picking up items, facial recognition and movement of limbs. These were easy enough to teach NAO in isolation from the easy to use tool kit of Choreographe. It was simply a case of dragging the appropriate action from the library and attaching the required dialogue and activity path.	Next level was to set conditions and loops requiring a knowledge of programming practices but not necessarily the coding skills. Conditions needed to be set for the robot to recognise the objects, person or to know how to respond to various input such as which limb to move. Repetition occurred when the robot searched for another item etc.. It was possible to set conditions for these activities without opening the source code and editing as there were selections to enable number of repetitions, conditions etc..	A level of difficulty was identified when the developers attempted to combine the activities into a flowing interaction that offered the affordance of a human interaction. This level of programming required the user to edit the source code or to write small routines that would enable out of the box activities or combinations of activities that were reliant on previous conditions. This level would require basic coding skills to quite extensive coding skills depending on the activity.

Speech during the Simon Says game the robot did not recognise the natural speech of the user due to the limitations of the built-in speech recognition in naoqi, which requires a list of words to be input to use as a comparison. We tried with words and the speech recognition box however Choreographe could not handle the list. To overcome this initially, we required the users to speak loudly and clearly and to ensure that they started talking after the beep as anything said before the beep was not "heard" by the robot. This still led to many misinterpretations. If the robot did not respond it generally meant that the voice level was too low and would require the user to repeat what was said. The next work around this was to employ the Google Chrome Web Speech Recognition API which is a built-in function in the Google Chrome browser. This did increase the word recognition but did not really enable free flowing natural speech.

Once the Simon Says game starts, the robot would ask if 'you want to be Simon' or if you want 'me' to be Simon. In this case, the robot was listening only for the words "me", "I" and "you", to increase versatility. So a response should include one of those words such as: "I want to be Simon", "make me Simon" or "you be a Simon". While these all make perfect sense to a child they were not suitable to initiate an action from the robot. Phrases such as "I would like to be Simon" instead of "I want to be Simon" were misunderstood. To make the robot understand a wider variety of phrases which would reduce the feeling of scripted conversation and allow the conversation to feel more natural, 'word spotting' was used which would find certain words in what was said and react accordingly to that. We also found:

- Using word spotting and the words - "I", "me" and "you" all provided the same response irrespective of where they appeared in the phrase used by the child. Using word spotting was effective and very robust. It misunderstood more often than a set phrase but the robot understood a far greater variety of phrases.
- Offering alternative words for the same action such as when the child does not want to continue they could say either, "no more", "stop", "enough" and "no" and any of these will end the game, anything else, will start another round.
- The learners will need to be supplied with lists of words and phrases that are understood by the robot. For our project the list included phrases such as raise your right hand, raise your left hand, look to your left, look to your right, crouch, both hands up, wave, turn around, point left, point right, moo like a cow, go to sleep, swing your arms, pat your head, click your fingers, dance, play air guitar, play air drums, and sing.
- If users paused too long within their sentence when talking to the robot, the robot would think that they had finished talking and would only interpret the first part of what was said. This was especially relevant in Simon Says where the user frequently paused after saying "Simon says" and before saying the instruction.

From interviews with other developers, it was found that issues regarding common speech with the NAO are common and often lead to presenters reverting to a "Wizard of Oz" type demonstration, where the voice response of the robot is being directly manipulated by a programmer in response to the child's conversation.

This can be seen in many public demonstrations of the humanoid robots where the interaction appears to flow in response to the casual conversation. More so in the case of children where they may not stay on the topic ever mind following a limited vocabulary conversation.

Performance issues with software

There were performances issues when first opening the Simon says files as there were many action boxes causing Choregraphe to not respond without any feedback for a few minutes. This may cause issues within the classroom context.

4. DISCUSSION

Learning takes on many forms and different methods may be accepted or rejected by individual students. Early adopters of technology are often open to experimentation that generally offers insight into the positives and negatives of the technology. Controlled research and experimentation before deployment of technology, or any new teaching method, helps to minimise the risks to the children, obtain richer data and enhance the positive experiences for both the teachers and the children. The main goal of this research was to gain an understanding of what is necessary to support a teacher who undertakes to include an emerging technology into their classroom activities. In particular, we have considered the humanoid robot, the expectations of this emerging technology and the realities required for its use as a classroom learning tool.

The humanoid robot is portrayed as an easy to use, almost infallible technology. Further to the media hype, the fact that the robot is humanoid and appears to have human characteristics generates the expectation that it is just like a real human or small child. This includes the ability to learn and reason through normal verbal and physical interfacing rather than a computer terminal. From this expectation, it seems reasonable that the inclusion of a tool such as a humanoid robot that will engage children's imaginations, undertake repetitive tasks and be totally non-judgemental of failure would be seen as an asset to the classroom.

From the discussions with others who have deployed or attempted to deploy the humanoid robot in the classroom and the outcomes of our attempts to build an easy to use, interactive lesson based on the robot's capacity we can draw the following conclusions in Table 4 regarding deployment in the classroom. These consider the average classroom teacher without a programming background.

Table 4. Our recommendations to the teachers, who wants to start using a NAO robot in classroom

<table>
<tr>
<td>Level 1:
The pre-programmed actions from Choreographe can be achieved through a basic level of training in Figure (a). Setup of wifi connection (although not reliable) and drag and drop pre-programmed actions.
Support required: Basic training, technical assistant prior for setup and during session for loss of connection and resetting. Ensure non-slip surface.
Expected Training: Approximately 4 hours to familiarize with connection and actions.</td>
<td>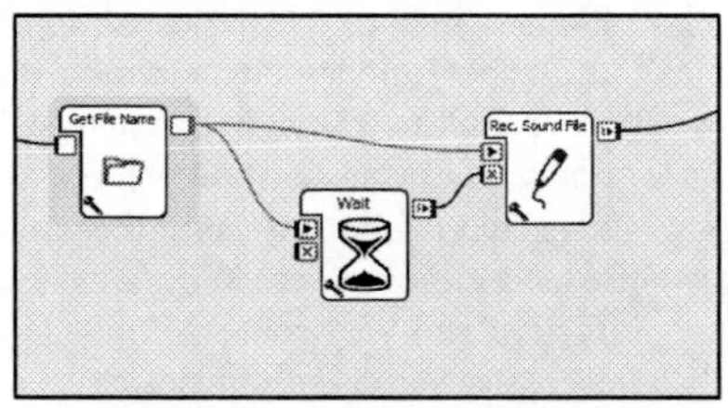

Figure (a). Words Reading Handwritten</td>
</tr>
<tr>
<td>Level 2:
Simple interactions can be achieved where basic pre-programmed actions are linked in Figure (b).
Support required: As per Basic but with further training to explain some basic programming practices such as conditions and loops. Further training may be required of the technical assistant or teacher to cover the exceptions which have not been covered in the preparation.
Expected preparation: Approximately 40 hours for the initial 1 hour lesson, approximately 2 hours per 1 hour after the 1st hour.</td>
<td>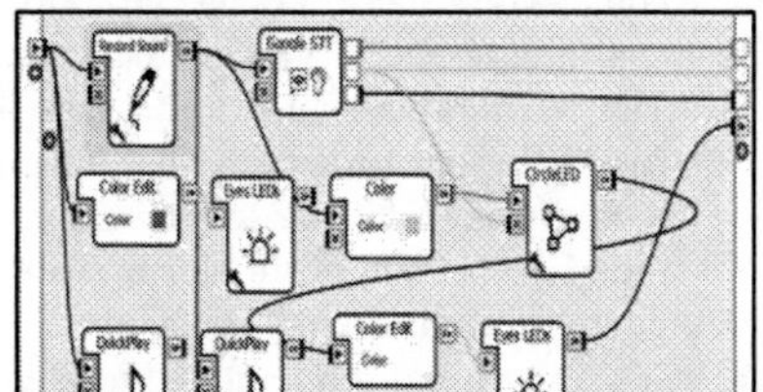

Figure (b). Words Verbal Speech to Text</td>
</tr>
</table>

<table>
<tr>
<td>Level 3:
Advanced Interactions enable fluid conversations and activities often associated with a “thinking” humanoid robot.
Support required: We did not get to this stage and found that many others have not either but have improvised along the way to give the impression of the human aspect of the robot. This level requires substantial programming in Figure (c) and testing in a variety of situations that can occur in the classroom.</td>
<td>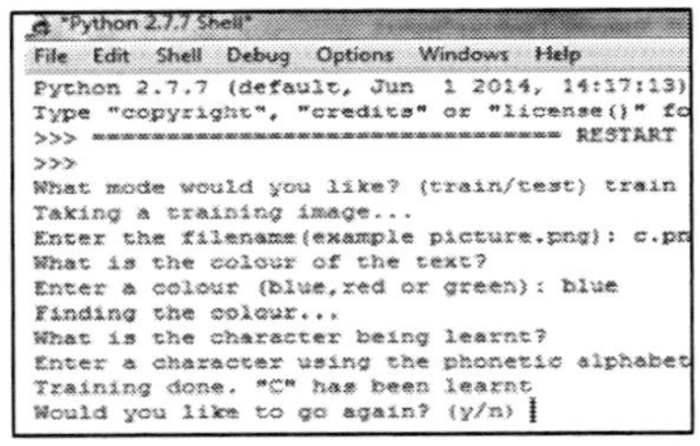

Figure (c). The python code for the NAO robot</td>
</tr>
</table>

As was identified by other researchers, it is very difficult to create responses that replicate what people expect from a humanoid form. The conclusion made by our group, and others who have trialed the robot, is that successful student-robot interactions will need to be supported by the team associated with the development; the technician within the school to ensure the connectivity; the teacher who works with the children and the robot will need to be tested in the physical space where it is to be used.

For our simple exercises, the time outlay was substantial but what was more of a concern is that in all but the first level of interaction, the software was not suitable for a non-programmer teacher to be able to competently perform without any assistance or intervention. This is not to say that better software cannot be written, or that a more stable and reliable connectivity be established, only that the customisation of programs to suit individual needs is not as simple as it appears in the demonstrations.

It is understandable that users expect humanoid robots to be a walk up and use technology. This expectation is not only from the developers and the media but generally because the affordance of human behaviors creates an expectation of intelligence and reasoning rather than just responding to developed instructions. So why does it look so easy in the media? In many cases, the dialogue is scripted and has had many hours of work behind the scenes to make it look as though it is a natural free flow interaction. Furthermore, the videos have been cut and pasted to appear fluid (as we have done in our own demonstration videos). None of this assists in setting a realistic view of the real ease of use of the robot for non-programmers or non-technical users and can create unrealistic expectations in schools and teachers.

5. CONCLUSIONS AND FURTHER WORK

The curriculum in primary school education offers many opportunities for the introduction of technology that can take on the job of repetitive activities, offer novel interfacing with students and provide a human-like face to a technical interaction.

Although, we were not able to easily develop the interactions required for language learning, in the domain of computer science, the current capabilities of the robot does offer the opportunity for students to learn logic, basic programming techniques, group work and many other skills as seen in the example of the second-graders at the Northwoods Elementary School of Technology and Innovation in Onslow County, North Carolina (Curtis 2012). This example was the seen by many of those who had trialed the NAO robot as the most impressive part of using the robot. The imagination and problem solving, trialing and refining the interaction and a renewed enthusiasm towards computer science are valuable skills, knowledge and attitudes that make the use of NAO and other robots worthwhile even in these still early stages. While the robotic engineers are ensuring the robustness of the robots and the programmers are developing software that is reliable, the use of robots in the classroom still offers excellent opportunities for students to experiment with the robots while learning new skills.

This is not to say that the excellent programs and trials that are currently occurring should not continue but that it should be recognized that there is a lot of support and knowledge to get the robots to do what we are expecting and the lack of ease of use may currently render the robots beyond what should be expected of the non-tech, non-programmer.

From the cases discussed it is evident that our teachers are undertaking their own path of discovery learning and require support and encouragement to do so. We are still at the early stages of discovering how technology can aid and encourage our children to learn in ways we are yet to understand.

Our main concern with the expectations created by emerging technologies is that they will be seen as an "easy add-on" to the teaching tool kit. Unfortunately, this has not been our experience. However, it is hoped that false expectations do not discourage teachers and schools from investing both time and money on equipping their schools and classrooms with the best educational tools they can afford and that teachers are well supported in their attempts to experiment with new emerging technologies.

Even if it is difficult to adapt the NAO to assist with the learning of literacy, there may still be many opportunities to use the NAO in the classroom for teaching computer science given that this is fast becoming a core in many curriculums. Our next study will consider if putting the child in control of the robot rather than the teacher will provide an engaging computer science experience for the child. This idea has resounded the most with our study and will drive us to further research into the use of robots in teaching and learning.

REFERENCES

Billig, S. H., Sherry, L., and Havelock, B. 2005. Challenge 98: Sustaining the Work of a Regional Technology Integration Initiative. British Journal of Educational Technology, 36(6), 987-1003.

Bransford, J.D., Brown, A. and Cocking, R. 2000. How People Learn: Mind, Brain, Experience and School, Expanded Edition. DC: National Academy Press, Washington.

Campbell, A. 2009. Learning with Technology for Pre-service Early Childhood Teachers. Australasian Journal of Early Childhood no. 34 (2), 11-18.

Creemers, P. M. 2008. The Dynamics of Educational Effectiveness: A Contribution to Policy, Practice and Theory in Contemporary Schools. Edited by Leo Nidas Kyriakide s, Contribution to Policy, Practice and Theory in Contemporary Schools, London.

Clarke, G., and Zagarell, J. 2012 Technology in the Classroom: Teachers and Technology: A Technological Divide, Childhood Education no. 88 (2):136-139.

Clements, D. H., and Sarama, J. 2002. The Role of Technology in Early Childhood Learning. (Early Childhood Corner). Teaching Children Mathematics no. 8 (6):340.

Clements, D. H., Bonnie, K. N., and Swaminathan, S. 1993. Young Children and Computers: Crossroads and Directions from Research. Young Children.

Danielowich, R. M., and McCarthy, M.J. 2013. Teacher Educators as Learners: How Supervisors Shape Their Pedagogies by Creating and Using Classroom Videos with Their Student Teachers. Action in Teacher Education no. 35 (3):147-164. doi: 10.1080/01626620.2013.806231.

Engel, L., Kington, A. and Mleczko, A. 2013. The Influence of Education on Community Cohesion: Adaptation of Policy to Practice. The Journal of Educational Research no. 106 (5):408-418. doi: 10.1080/00220671.2012.753862.

Francis-Baldesari, C. and Pope, C. 2008. Using a Social Constructivist Model of Teaching to Create a Learning Community. The Journal of Nursing Education 47(3): 143.

Gurney, J. 2014. http://www.telegraph.co.uk/education/educationnews/10923190/Welcome-to-Nao-your-robot-teacher.html.

Hughes, A. 2013. What Is A Humanoid Robot? (2013, May 3). Retrieved from Idaho National Laboratory. https://inlportal.inl.gov/portal/server.pt?open=512&objID=539

Martin, T. 2000. Organizing Pediatric Education to Meet the Needs of Infants, Children, Adolescents, and Young Adults in the 21st Century. (The Future of Pediatric Education, part 2). Pediatrics no. 105 (1):S160.

Mouza, C. 2005. Using Technology to Enhance Early Childhood Learning: The 100 Days of School Project. An International Journal on Theory and Practice 11(6): 513-528.

Mumtaz, S. 2000. Factors Affecting Teachers' Use of Information and Communications Technology: A Review of the Literature. Journal of Information Technology for Teacher Education no. 9 (3):319-342.

Ntuli, E., and Kyei-Blankson, L. 2012. Teacher Assessment of Young Children Learning with Technology in Early Childhood Education. International Journal of Information and Communication Technology Education no. 8 (4):1.

Nilssen, V. 2010. Encouraging the Habit of Seeing in Student Teaching, Teaching and Teacher Education 26, 591–598.

Sammons, P. 2009. The Dynamics of Educational Effectiveness: A Contribution to Policy, Practice and Theory in Contemporary Schools." School Effectiveness and School Improvement no. 20 (1):123-129.

Simon, F. 2012. Digital Decisions: Choosing the Right Technology Tools for Early Childhood. Edited by Karen N. Nemeth. Lewisville, NC: Lewisville, NC: Gryphon House.

Turbill, J. 2001. A Researcher Goes to School: Using Technology in the Kindergarten Literacy Curriculum. Journal of Early Childhood Literacy 1(3): 255-279.

AN INVESTIGATION OF VISUAL APPEAL AND TRUST IN WEBSITES

Marian McDonnell and Alex Lee
Institute of Art, Design and Technology, Kill Avenue, Dun Laoghaire, Co Dublin, Ireland

ABSTRACT

As businesses of all types increasingly rely on webpages as their first point of contact with customers, the importance of users' first impressions of websites continues to grow. The current study aimed to examine factors which influence users' early impressions of websites, and therefore the probability that they will engage in custom with a business. The study focused on the factors of Visual Appeal and Trustworthiness. Sixteen participants took part in the rating of website visual appeal. A further 71 participants took part in the rating of website trustworthiness under two conditions, short exposure and long exposure. There was a significant relationship between visual appeal and both trustworthiness ratings. Visual appeal accounted for 56% of the variation in trustworthiness rating in the long exposure condition. Trustworthiness in the short exposure condition accounted for a further 11% of variation in trustworthiness rating in the long condition. Based on these results, it was concluded that user evaluation of website trustworthiness has begun after just 200ms of viewing time, and is heavily influenced by the visual appeal of a website.

KEYWORDS

Visual Appeal, Trustworthiness, Website First Impressions, Precognitive Response, Website Genre

1. INTRODUCTION

When individuals browse the internet, they continuously assess each website they visit, deciding whether to further explore the site or move on to another website (Lindgaard et al., 2011). Impressions of the quality of a website begin to form before a user has had time to read information (Lazard & Mackert, 2014). Impressions of website quality play an important role in business performance (Lee & Kozar, 2006). One factor that has been shown to have a positive impact on users' first impressions of a website, and thus entice them to further explore the website, is visual appeal (Lindgaard, et al., 2006). Another factor which is of importance to users' attitudes towards business websites is trustworthiness (Mou et al., 2015). Trustworthiness can be defined as the extent to which a user is willing to depend on a website, when there is a perceived risk (Roghanizad & Neufeld, 2015). The level of risk can vary. Low risk online situations include investing the time to read a website, as there is the potential that the information attained will be factually incorrect. An example of a high risk activity is divulging sensitive personal information such as credit card details or bank account information. The following literature review will outline research in the areas of visual appeal and trustworthiness, with a focus on users' first impressions of websites.

1.1 Background

Visual appeal (VA) can be viewed as "an immediate pleasurable subjective experience that is directed toward an object and not mediated by intervening reasoning." (Moshagen et al., 2010, p. 690). The phrase 'visual appeal' is used interchangeably with beauty (Schenkman & Jönsson, 2000) and aesthetics (Thielsch et al.,2014) in scientific literature. The importance of VA in forming positive attitudes towards websites has been recognised for some time (Schenkman & Jönsson, 2000).

In order to form theoretical frameworks, and provide guidelines to website designers, VA has been divided into a number of categories, including Symmetry (Wang & Emurian, 2005), Visual Complexity, (Tuch et al., 2012; Reinecke et al., 2013; Deng & Poole, 2012), Colourfulness (Reinecke et al., 2013) and Prototypicality (Tuch et al., 2012). Identifying distinct subcategories of VA has enabled researchers to create theoretical frameworks which can be used to accurately predict users' ratings of a website's VA (Reinecke et al., 2013). However, for the purposes of some types of experimental research, it is not unusual for researchers to treat VA as a simple variable, without further subdivision (Cyr, 2008; Lindgaard et al., 2011; Tractinsky et al.,2000). Due to the nature of the current study, VA will be treated as a simple variable.

Once it had been established that VA was the primary factor in determining users' first impressions of websites, research began to focus on just how quickly this impression could be formed. Lindgaard et al. (2006) found that users make reliable judgements of VA after viewing a static image of a webpage for just 50ms. This short period of time indicates that impressions of VA are formed through precognitive processes similar to those identified during research on the mere exposure effect (Bornstein, 1992). The mere exposure effect induces neural activity which takes place early in the encoding and retrieval process, and leads to an affective interaction with a stimulus (Lindgaard et al., 2006). By observing participants' reactions to visual stimuli after exposure times of fractions of seconds, researchers have been able to investigate the initial, precognitive response to that stimulus.

Trustworthiness is important for business websites, as it has an effect on the likelihood that customers will use their products or services (Gefen, 2000). Trust also determines whether users will remain loyal to a website, which is important for customer retention (Flavián, Guinalíu & Gurrea, 2006).

Website owners rely on a number of different mechanisms to instil trust in their users (Bart et al., 2005; Wang & Emurian, 2005). Extensive research has been carried out in the area of trust and websites, with an emphasis placed on Trust in an E-commerce context (Jourdan & Ingram, 2011; Beatty et al., 2011; Karimov et al., 2011). Wang et al. (2014) proposed that Trust is a triple-dimensional construct, consisting of integrity, benevolence and ability. They found that integrity and benevolence are most important for consumers for the formation of trust in the hotel industry.

The dominant view held by researchers in the field of website trust is that users employ 'deliberative reasoning' during the trust formation process (Roghanizad & Neufeld., 2015). Deliberative reasoning involves making a complex decision after taking all relevant information into account. Roghanizad and Neufeld criticised this approach, arguing that researchers have biased results by providing participants with instructions which explicitly ask them to investigate pertinent elements of websites such as security certificates. This undermines the ecological validity of results. In real world situations, the majority of users do not take the time to read through website security certificates. Herley (2009) found that monitoring all security information on a website is not an economical use of users' time, as the amount of time required to read and evaluate all relevant information is greater than the amount of time lost to untrustworthy websites.

In low risk situations, where the accuracy of information is the important factor, users have been shown to scan and reject websites after just thirty seconds (Lindgaard et al., 2011), which is shorter than the time required to make a decision using deliberative reasoning. To address this gap in the literature, Roghanizad and Neufeld (2015) proposed a dual-process reasoning theory to better explain the way users form trust in an online setting. By introducing the concept of 'associative reasoning' to the trust formation process in an online setting, it is possible to account for occasions when users decide to trust websites without being able to provide a logical explanation. Roghanizad and Neufeld (2015) found that associative reasoning is used to decide how trustworthy a website is in situations involving risk and ambiguity.

Visual appeal has been shown to positively influence ratings across other variables such as trustworthiness and usability (Li & Yeh, 2010; Lindgaard et al., 2011; Tractinsky et al., 2000). In a cross cultural study, Cyr (2008) found VA to be a key factor contributing to website trust in Canada, Germany, and China.

In a review of the empirical literature on the formation of trust in websites, Karimov et al. (2011) identified a scarcity of research into the effect VA has on trust formation when users first view a website. They described first impressions of trust as 'initial trust', to distinguish them from impressions of trust formed after interacting with a website over a prolonged period. Although research on initial trust in websites is rare, research has been conducted on initial trust in other areas.

Willis and Todorov (2006) demonstrated that VA is a predictor of perceived trustworthiness when viewing images of human faces for a time of just 100ms. The short exposure times in this experiment indicates that trust begins to form at a precognitive level (Bornstein, 1992). Yu et al. (2014) demonstrated that first impressions of trustworthiness formed while viewing an image of a person's face are predictors of perceived trustworthiness after interacting with that person in a trust based game, regardless of whether the person behaved in a trustworthy manner. These experiments indicate that initial trust in a person is influenced by VA, formed precognitively, and affects trust after interacting with that person.

Another example of the effect of VA is Tractinsky et al.'s (2000) experiment, which demonstrated that VA is a predictor of first impressions of usability in ATM machine interfaces. These first impression of usability were shown to be predictors of perceived usability after prolonged use, regardless of the actual usability of the ATM machine interface, as measured by the System Usability Scale.

Lindgaard et al. (2011) carried out an experiment investigating the relationship between VA and trustworthiness of websites. During the experiment, participants were exposed to static images of website homepages for a time of 50ms, and asked to rate them on either VA or trustworthiness. There was a strong correlation between ratings of VA and trust, indicating that VA has an influence on initial trust, and that this interaction takes place precognitively. However, research of this kind is scarce in the area of initial trust in websites. Lindgaard et al. (2011) suggested the inclusion of website genre as a variable in future research. Flanagin and Metzger (2007) found significant differences in trust across different genres of website. However, their study involved high levels of interaction between the participants and the websites, and they used just two websites from each genre.

1.2 The Current Study

It has been shown that impressions of VA are partially formed by precognitive processes (Lindgaard et al., 2006), and first impressions of trust in websites are at least partially affected by VA (Lindgaard et al., 2011). However, there is a lack of research investigating whether precognitive impressions of trust in a website are predictors of impressions of trust that have been formed after a longer exposure. There is also a lack of research investigating whether website genre has an impact on perceived VA or perceived trustworthiness. The current study will address these gaps in the literature, by building upon the experimental model used by Lindgaard et al. in 2011, in attempting to answer the following three questions:

1. Is visual appeal a predictor of initial trust?
2. Do impressions of trustworthiness that are formed precognitively predict impressions of trustworthiness that are formed after a longer viewing time?
3. Does the website genre affect impressions of visual appeal or trustworthiness?

These questions will be answered by testing the following hypotheses:

H1: There will be a strong positive relationship between visual appeal and trust, demonstrating visual appeal to be a predictor of trustworthiness.

H2: Trust after a short exposure time (200ms) is a predictor of trust after a longer exposure time (7s).

H3: There will be a significant difference in visual appeal of websites across different genres of website.

H4: There will be a significant difference in trustworthiness of websites across different genres of website.

2. METHOD

2.1 Design

The first part of this study is a correlational, within subjects design, analysing the relationship between two independent variables and one dependent variable. The independent variables are Visual Appeal (VA) and trustworthiness rating after a short exposure (Trustworthiness Short [TS]). The dependent variable is trustworthiness rating after a long exposure (Trustworthiness Long [TL]).

The second part is a quasi-experimental, within subjects design which will analyse the effect of website genre (k=3, healthcare, educational, financial) on the variables of VA, TS and TL.

2.2 Participants

In order to attain an independent rating for visual appeal, 16 second year Creative Computing students were recruited as raters using purposive sampling. These students were selected as they have a theoretical understanding of the factors which contribute to visual appeal in a website.

A total of 71 participants (male = 36, female = 35) were recruited to provide trustworthiness ratings. Participants were selected using convenience sampling. All participants were undergraduate students, attending one of three different courses; Creative Computing (n = 37), Applied Psychology (n = 31), and Applied Entrepreneurship (n = 3). Ages ranged from 18-52, (M = 22), with 83% of participants falling into the 18-22 band. All participants and their data were treated in accordance with the ethical guidelines of the Psychological Society of Ireland.

2.3 Materials and Apparatus

A total of 30 websites were selected for inclusion in this study. All websites selected fell under the category of 'company pages' (Roth et al., 2010). All sites were targeted at an Irish audience, in order to rule out cultural differences as a confounding variable. In order to facilitate testing of the independent variable website genre, 10 websites were selected from the genres of healthcare, education and financial advice. To minimise the risk that participants were familiar with any of the images used, sites were checked for popularity using the online service provided by ranking.com, and excluded from use in the study if they achieved an Irish popularity rank higher than 10,000 or a global popularity rank higher than 1,000,000.

The prototyping software application Axure RP Pro7, version number 7.0.0.3174, was used to construct the experiment. This programme was selected as it provides a high degree of experimental control, allowing for the manipulation of image exposure time to the nearest millisecond.

A pilot study was carried out with 15 participants a week before data collected commenced. Minor issues such as typos in the instruction sheet and minor bugs in the experiment website were identified by participants, and later corrected.

2.4 Procedure

Data for visual appeal was collected separately from data for trustworthiness. For the collection of visual appeal ratings, participants were approached during class in a computer lab. They were provided with a participation pack, which included an information sheet, two consent forms, an instruction sheet, and a debrief sheet. Participants were given a unique identifier code in order to allow for their data to be anonymised. Participants opened the website at bit.do/visappeal, which was designed in order to facilitate this part of the data collection. Here, participants could view static images of the 30 websites selected for inclusion in the study. Participants viewed each image for as long as they wanted before providing a visual appeal rating ranging from 1 (extremely unappealing) to 7 (extremely appealing). After participants had rated all 30 websites, they were debriefed and thanked for their participation in the study.

Trustworthiness ratings were gathered in a similar manner to visual appeal ratings. Participants were approached during class and provided with an information pack similar to the one used in 2.4.1. Notable differences are the inclusion of a demographic data questionnaire and modified information, instruction, and debrief sheets. Ratings for trustworthiness were collected in two phases. After opening the website at bit.do/trustex, participants began phase 1 of the experiment. During this phase, a blank white screen was displayed for a time of one second, followed by an image of the website homepage for 200ms, and then a blank white screen for one second. Participants were then asked to provide a rating of trustworthiness from 1 (extremely untrustworthy) to 7 (extremely trustworthy). Participants were given 5 practice images at the start of the phase. Results were not recorded for the practice images. Once all 30 test images were rated in phase 1, phase 2 of the experiment began. During this phase, images were displayed for a time of seven seconds. Participants were again given 5 practice images before viewing and rating the 30 test images. Images were shown in different, random orders across phase 1 and phase 2, to control for the order effect.

3. RESULTS

3.1 Visual Appeal and TS as predictors of TL

The relationship between VA and TL can be seen in Figure 1, while the relationship between TS and TL can be seen in Figure 2. Overall mean scores were 3.54 (*SD* = .82, *n* = 30) for VA, 3.98 (*SD* = .55, *n* = 30) for TS, and 3.95 (*SD* = .65, *n* = 30) for TL.

In order to test the interrater reliability and internal validity of the variables VA, TS and TL, Intraclass Correlation Coefficients (ICC) were computed for each variable (Shrout, & Fleiss, 1979). There was a high ICC value for VA (ICC (2,16) = .865, 95% CI [.779, .928]), TS (ICC (2,16) = .938, 95% CI [.902, .966]), and TL (ICC (2,16) = .946, 95% CI [.912, .972]). Van Ness et al. (2008) consider an ICC value between .40 and .75 to be "good", therefore all ICC values were considered "good". This indicates that there was a very high level of agreement between raters for all three variables; VA, TS and TL.

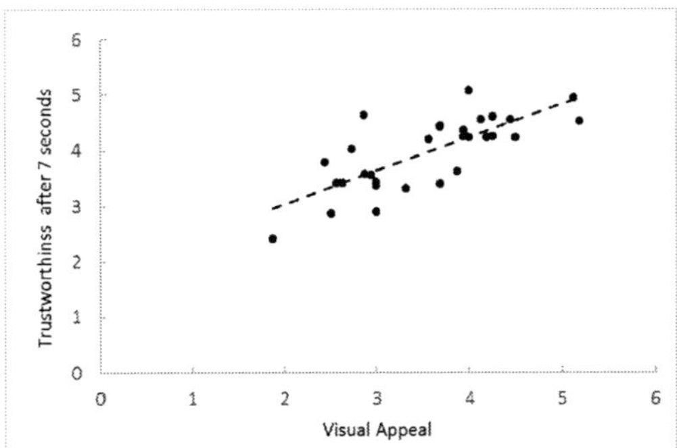

Figure 1. Scatterplot visualising the relationship between VA and TL. Pearson's r = .75

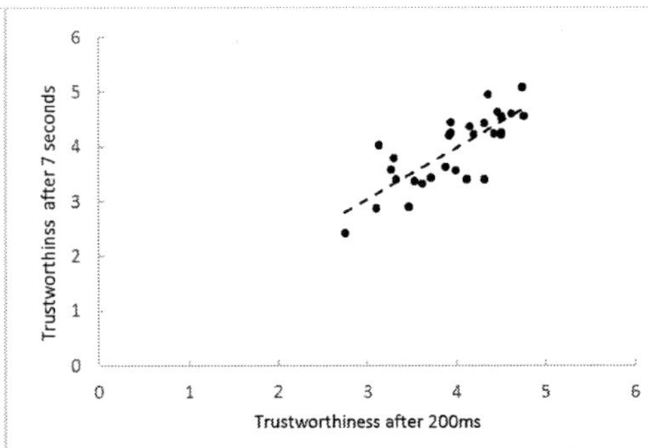

Figure 2. Scatterplot visualising the relationship between TS and TL. Pearson's r = .79

Hypothesis 1 looked to examine whether VA is a predictor of TL. Hypothesis 2 was directed at determining whether TS was also a predictor of TL. Both of these hypotheses were tested using a Hierarchical Multiple Regression (HMR) analysis. The data were tested to ensure that the assumptions of a HMR were met. An analysis of standard residuals was carried out, which showed that the data contained no outliers (Std. Residual Min = -2.101, Std. Residual Max = 2.131). The data met the assumptions of collinearity (VA, Tolerance = .39, VIF = 2.54; TS Tolerance = .39, VIF 2.54) (Marquaridt, 1970). The data met the assumption of independence of observation (Durbin-Watson value=1.48). Visual inspection of the histogram of standardised residuals indicated that the data contained approximately normally distributed errors. The scatterplot of standardised residuals indicated that the data met the assumptions of homoscedasticity and linearity.

The results of the HMR showed that VA explains a significant amount of the variance in TL (F (1, 28) = 36.28, $p < .000$, $R^2 = .56$). This result allows for the acceptance of H1. The combination of VA and TS was also found to have a significant effect on TL (F (2,27) = 27.61, $p < .000$, $R^2 = .67$). These results allow for the acceptance of H2. There is an increase in R^2 of 0.11, which means there was an increase of 11% in predictability of TL. Based on the results of The MRC, it can be stated that both VA and TS are strong predictors of TL. Therefore, hypotheses 1, and 2 were accepted.

3.2 The Effect of Website Genre on Ratings of VA, TS and TL

The independent variable, genre, consisted of three levels; healthcare, education and financial. There were ten websites in each genre. The means plot in figure 3 below shows the average score for the dependent variables VA, TS and TL in each genre. Hypothesis 3 proposed that website genre would have a significant effect on VA ratings, while hypothesis 4 proposed that trustworthiness ratings would be significantly affected by website genre. A series of one-way ANOVAs were conducted to investigate whether this is the case. The data were tested to ensure that the assumptions of a one-way ANOVA were met. There were no significant outliers. Levene's test for homogeneity of variance indicated that there were equal variances for TS and TL, although VA broke the assumption of homogeneity of variance. A lowered acceptable alpha value of .017 was adopted to control for the increased risk of a type 1 error from carrying out 3 ANOVAs in parallel. Three one-way within subjects ANOVAs were conducted to determine whether website genre (K=3) has an effect on VA, TS or TL, respectively. There were no significant differences in VA (F (2, 27) = 2.4, $p > .017$), TS (F (2, 27) = 3.16, $p > .017$, or TL (F (2, 27) = .82, $p > .017$). Based on these results of the three one-way ANOVAS, hypotheses 3 and 4 were rejected.

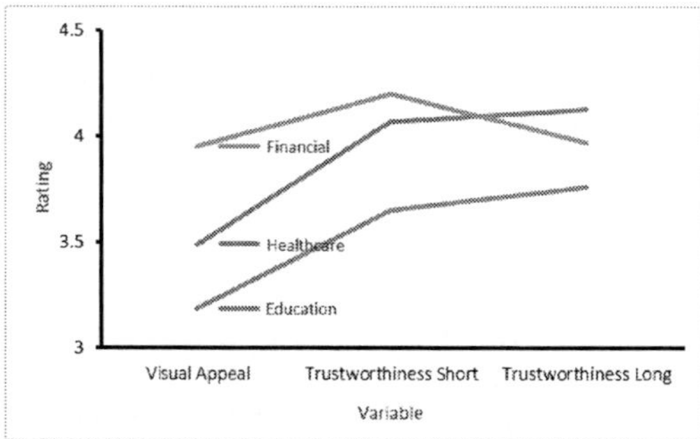

Figure 3. Mean Rating for VA, TS and TL Across Website Genre

4. DISCUSSION

The current study investigated the relationship between VA, TS, and TL. Genre was also included as a variable, to investigate whether ratings of VA, TS or TL change significantly across different genres of website. Results of a HMR indicate that both VA and TS play a significant role in predicting the value of TL. This is in line with expectations, which were based on previous research in the area (Lindgaard et al., 2011).

When ratings of VA, TS and TL were compared individually across genre of website using one-way ANOVAs, no significant differences were found. These findings will be discussed in greater depth below.

4.1 Interpretation of Results

Results of the HMR indicate that the VA of a website plays a significant role in predicting a user's rating of trustworthiness for that website. Websites with higher VA received higher ratings of TL.

When TS was combined with VA in the HMR, it had a significant positive effect on the predictability of TL. This, in turn, indicates that the impression of trustworthiness formed after viewing a website for just 200ms plays an important role in the formation of trust over a longer period of time. From this, it can be said that trust formation in websites involves precognitive processes, an area which has received very little attention from researchers in the area of initial trust in websites (Karimov et al., 2011).

There was no statistically significant difference for VA, TS or TL across different genres of website. Therefore, expectations that website genre would affect ratings of VA, TS and TL were not met. This implies that the results of the current study are applicable across numerous different genres of website. It is interesting to note that visual inspection of means plots comparing VA, TS and TL across website genre show a tendency for websites in the educational genre to have lower scores across all three variables. However, caution is advised when interpreting results for the effect of website genre, as there were numerous weaknesses in this part of the study. These are addressed below.

4.2 Strengths, Weaknesses and Future Research

There was a high level of interrater reliability, as measured by ICC. VA was shown to predict 56% of variation in TL, and the inclusion of TS increased this value by a further 11%. This, combined with the fact that all of the assumptions of a Hierarchical Multiple Regression Analysis were met, means that the results concerning the interaction between VA, TS and TL have a high degree of internal validity.

The current study took into account criticisms of previous experiments on trustworthiness in websites raised by Karimov et al. (2011). By providing participants with a simple definition of trustworthiness, instead of explicit instructions for ascertaining trustworthiness, the current study ensured a higher level of ecological validity. Due to the ambiguity of the instruction 'Provide the trustworthiness rating you feel is most appropriate', participants were forced to rely on their own schema, rather than a set of artificially constructed schema, when coming to a decision on trustworthiness.

When testing differences between different website genres, the sample size was small, with just 10 websites in each category. In addition, the website selection process was not highly developed, failing to take into account variables such as the absence or presence of faces, which has been shown to effect perceived trustworthiness (Cyr, Head, Larios, & Pan (2009)).

The convenience sampling method used to recruit participants lead to a highly homogenous sample, with the majority of raters falling into a narrow demographic of 18-22 year olds studying technology oriented courses in the Institute of Art, Design and Technology.This weakens the external validity of results, as the sample was not representative of the population of interest, which was all internet users.

The current study did not allow for participants to interact with websites, instead asking them to base their impressions on viewing a static image for just seven seconds. While this was necessary for the purposes of collecting a large amount of empirical data for use in inferential analyses, it has a negative impact on the ecological validity of results.

This study relied on participants' ratings of static images of websites. Future research in the area should take this into account, comparing initial trust ratings to trust ratings provided after participants complete a number of simple tasks on a live version of the website. Tractinsky et al.'s (2000) experiment on the effect of visual appeal on impressions of usability form a suitable template for future research in the area.

A more in depth empirical test for differences between website genres should be conducted, taking into account the weaknesses highlighted above. Research in this area is scarce, and the current study contradicts existing research (Flanagin & Metzger, 2007). More experimental research is required to clarify whether perceptions of trust or visual appeal vary significantly across genres.

4.3 Conclusion and Implications

Trustworthiness is an important factor in customer retention (Flavian et al., 2006), and intention to buy (Gefen, 2000), which are both significant contributors to the success of any businesses. This study has shown that visual appeal is a significant predictor of initial trust, meaning that the visual appeal of a company website can be considered highly important to the success of a business. This study has also shown that impressions of trustworthiness are formed by precognitive processes, a concept that has not previously received widespread attention (Karimov et al., 2011: Lindgaard et al., 2011). This information is of value to business owners when deciding whether to invest in improving the visual appeal of their company website. However, further research is required to investigate whether initial trust is a predictor of trust after prolonged use of a website.

REFERENCES

Bart, Y. et al, 2005. Are the drivers and role of online trust the same for all web sites and consumers? A large-scale exploratory empirical study. *Journal of marketing*, *69*(4), pp. 133-152.

Beatty, P. et al, 2011. Consumer trust in e-commerce web sites. *ACM Computing Surveys*, *43*(3), pp. 1-46.

Bornstein, R.F., 1992. Subliminal Mere Exposure Effects. In *Perception Without Awareness: Cognitive, Clinical, and Social Perspectives,* R.F. Bornstein and T.S. Pittman (Eds.), pp. 191-210 (New York: The Guilford Press).

Cyr, D., 2008. Modeling Web Site Design Across Cultures: Relationships to Trust, Satisfaction, and E-Loyalty. *Journal Of Management Information Systems*, *24*(4), pp. 47-72.

Cyr, D. et al, 2009. Exploring human images in website design: a multi-method approach. *MIS quarterly*, pp. 539-566.

Deng, L., and Poole, M. S., 2012. Aesthetic design of e-commerce web pages – Webpage Complexity, Order and preference. *Electronic Commerce Research And Applications*, *11,* pp. 420-440.

Flanagin, A. J., and Metzger, M. J., 2007. The role of site features, user attributes, and information verification behaviors on the perceived credibility of web-based information. *New Media & Society*, *9*(2), pp. 319-342.

Flavián, C. et al, 2006. The role played by perceived usability, satisfaction and consumer trust on website loyalty. *Information & Management*, *43*(1), pp. 1-14.

Gefen, D., 2000. E-commerce: the role of familiarity and trust. *Omega*, 28(6), pp. 725-737.

Herley, C., 2009*. So long, and no thanks for the externalities: the rational rejection of security advice by users. *Proceedings of the 2009 workshop on New security paradigms workshop* (pp. 133-144). ACM.

Jourdan, Z., and Ingram, W. R., 2011. *Trust in e-business: A cross-disciplinar y analysis of the literature.* Working Paper.

Karimov, F. et al, 2011. THE EFFECT OF WEBSITE DESIGN DIMENSIONS ON INITIAL TRUST: A SYNTHESIS OF THE EMPIRICAL LITERATURE. *Journal Of Electronic Commerce Research*, *12*(4), pp. 272-301.

Lazard, A., and Mackert, M., 2014. User evaluations of design complexity: The impact of visual perceptions for effective online health communication. *International journal of medical informatics*, *83*(10), pp. 726-735.

Lee, Y., and Kozar, K. A., 2006. Investigating the effect of website quality on e-business success: An analytic hierarchy process (AHP) approach. *Decision support systems*, *42*(3), pp. 1383-1401.

Li, Y. M., and Yeh, Y. S., 2010. Increasing trust in mobile commerce through design aesthetics. *Computers in Human Behavior*, *26*(4), pp. 673-684.

Lindgaard, G. et al, 2011. An exploration of relations between visual appeal, trustworthiness and perceived usability of homepages. *ACM Transactions on Computer-Human Interaction (TOCHI)*, *18*(1), p. 1.

Lindgaard, G. et al, 2006. Attention web designers: You have 50 milliseconds to make a good first impression! *Behaviour & information technology*, *25*(2), pp. 115-126.

Marquaridt, D. W., 1970. Generalized inverses, ridge regression, biased linear estimation, and nonlinear estimation. *Technometrics*, *12*(3), pp. 591-612.

Moshagen, M., and Thielsch, M. T., 2010. Facets of visual aesthetics. *International Journal of Human Computer Studies*, *68*(10), pp. 689-709.

Mou, J. et al, 2015. Trust and risk in consumer acceptance of e-services. *Electronic Commerce Research*, pp. 1-34.

Reinecke, K. et al, 2013. Predicting users' first impressions of website aesthetics with a quantification of perceived visual complexity and colorfulness. *Proceedings of the SIGCHI Conference on Human Factors in Computing Systems* (pp. 2049-2058). ACM.

Roghanizad, M. M., and Neufeld, D. J., 2015. Intuition, risk, and the formation of online trust. *Computers In Human Behavior*, *50,* pp. 489-498.

Roth, S. P. et al, 2010. Mental models for web objects: Where do users expect to find the most frequent objects in online shops, news portals, and company web pages?. *Interacting with computers*, *22*(2), pp. 140-152.

Schenkman, B. N., and Jönsson, F. U., 2000. Aesthetics and preferences of web pages. *Behaviour & Information Technology, 19*(5), pp. 367-377.

Shrout, P. E., and Fleiss, J. L., 1979. Intraclass correlations: uses in assessing rater reliability. *Psychological bulletin*, *86*(2), p. 420.

Thielsch, M. T. et al, 2014. User Evaluation of Websites: From First Impression to Recommendation. *Interacting with Computers*, *26*(1), pp. 89-102.

Tractinsky, N. et al, 2000. What is beautiful is usable. *Interacting with computers*, *13*(2), pp. 127-145.

Tuch, A. N. et al, 2012. The role of visual complexity and prototypicality regarding first impression of websites: Working towards understanding aesthetic judgments. *International Journal of Human-Computer Studies*, *70*(11), pp. 794-811.

Van Ness, P. H. et al, 2008. Testing Measurement Reliability in Older Populations Methods for Informed Discrimination in Instrument Selection and Application. *Journal of Aging and Health*, *20*(2), pp. 183-197.

Wang, L. et al, 2014. Scale development of perceived eTrust in the hotel industry: The perspective of Internet users. *International Journal of Hospitality Management*, *43*, pp. 35-46.

Wang, Y.D., and Emurian, H. H., 2005. Trust in E-Commerce: Consideration of Interface Design Factors. *Journal Of Electronic Commerce In Organizations*, *3*(4), pp. 42-60.

Willis, J., and Todorov, A., 2006. First impressions making up your mind after a 100-ms exposure to a face. *Psychological science*, *17*(7), pp. 592-598.

Yu, M., et al, 2014. Developing trust: First impressions and experience. *Journal of Economic Psychology*, *43*, pp. 16-29.

COMPUTATIONAL PRODUCTION OF COLOUR HARMONY USING A GENETIC ALGORITHM

Paul Lyons and Giovanni Moretti
CSIT, Massey University
Private Bag 11-222, Palmerston North, New Zealand

ABSTRACT

The Colour Harmoniser creates *abstract colour schemes* by applying conventional rules of colour harmony to features of an interface or web page; the user then converts these to *concrete colour schemes by* modifying the scheme's overall colour cast, overall saturation, and light-dark distribution. The results are both harmonious and usable.

We present a set of criteria underlying the Colour Harmoniser. We describe the tool and some experiments that suggest that the tool functions more effectively than anticipated, producing colour schemes with higher quality than those produced by random choice, by humans who self-classify as non-artists, and by humans who self-classify as artists.

KEYWORDS

Color, harmony, abstract, concrete, GUI, Genetic

1. INTRODUCTION

When designing computer interfaces or websites, it is very easy to choose colours that are difficult to use, or positively repellent. Thus, many designers stick to bland colours, and HCI guidelines generally recommend deploying no more than six or seven (Shneiderman, 1998).

Colour harmony rules can be expressed mathematically, so software to capture designers' personal taste without violating the rules of colour harmony is possible. We have implemented a prototype tool that assists in the chromatic design of computer interfaces and webpages. It incorporates pragmatic considerations such as text legibility, and allows designers some freedom to express personal colour preferences. Empirical evaluation of the resultant colour schemes showed that they significantly exceeded expectations.

Colour selection tools for most general-purpose applications fall into three main categories (Lyons & Moretti, 2004): *one-colour-at-a-time* (PowerPoint, Photoshop, *inter alia*), *prepared colour scheme* (PowerPoint), and *colour wheel/colour harmony/restricted colour set* (Adobe Kuler) tools. Users who use *one-colour-at-a-time* tools may spend hours selecting and rejecting colours. Prepared colour schemes reduce the decision-making; they make sense for images with a standardised format, but are clearly not adapted to a free design environment. Tools of type 3, the colour wheel/colour harmony/restricted colour set produce sets of colours that conform to the standard rules of colour harmony (Hu et al., 2014). The user positions a rotary control (straight line, Y-shape, etc.) over 2D colour wheel and can rotate it to specify two of the three dimensions of colour, usually hue and saturation. We are not aware of any such tools that consider the areas of image components, or text readability.

We have developed a type 3 tool for applying the rules of colour harmony to computer interfaces and web pages, following (Tractinsky, Katz, & Ikar, 2000)'s principle "What's Beautiful is Usable." The tool uses genetic optimisation to produces an *abstract colour scheme* and then converts the abstract scheme to a *concrete colour scheme* based on designers' personal preferences. It uses – and extends – Munsell's colour harmony theory. Here we describe the background to the tool, its functionality, and an evaluation of it.

Ideas about colour harmony have largely been based on pronouncements by respected commentators. Empirical discoveries such as simultaneous contrast (Chevreul, 1839) and investigations such as (R. G. Kuehni, 2001, 2014; Nemcsics, 2007, 2008a, 2008b, 2009, 2010, 2011) have not yet been incorporated into colour harmony theory.

The theory of colour harmony has had some important contributors. When Newton bent his colour wheel into a circle, he made the concept of complementary colours possible. Runge generalised Newton's wheel to a colour sphere (Birren, 1969) with a central black-grey-white spine threaded through a stack of colour discs, each with the same lightness as the grey at that level. In 1810, Goethe (von Goethe, 1991) described experiments with complementary colours, anticipating Ewald Hering's 1892 opponent colour theory (Hering, 1964). In realistic art, colours are dictated by "the model" (the painter's recollection of nature), but van Gogh, a more figurative artist, selected *colour combinations he liked rather than colour combinations seen in the model* (Sloane, 1991, p. xxii). The roughly contemporaneous discovery of simultaneous contrast (Chevreul, 1839) influenced other artists to use non-naturalistic simultaneous contrast to induce colours that were not present in reality.

In 1905, Albert Munsell (Birren, 1969) codified the idea that complementary colours harmonise, producing a hue-independent formula for achieving balance between a pair of complementary colours that can be rendered as $A_1V_1C_1 = A_2V_2C_2$, where A_n is the area of colour$_n$, V_n is its value, and C_n is its chroma (roughly, the saturation). At that time, applying this formula required an infeasible amount of calculation, but simplified versions of his ideas became canonical: geometric shapes within a three-dimensional colour solid could be used to define sets of harmonious colours, and such harmony would be invariant under hue rotation. Itten, for example, *(Itten, 1970)* described *complementary* and *split-complementary* schemes, and some special cases of a general principle: colour harmony exists in any set of colours at regular intervals around an oval in the colour solid (plus black and white).

Munsell's and Itten's rules are commonly visualised as rigid "wireframes" that rotate about the centre of a colour wheel (Figure 1). At any orientation of the wireframe, the small black circles attached to the wireframe define a harmonious set of colours.

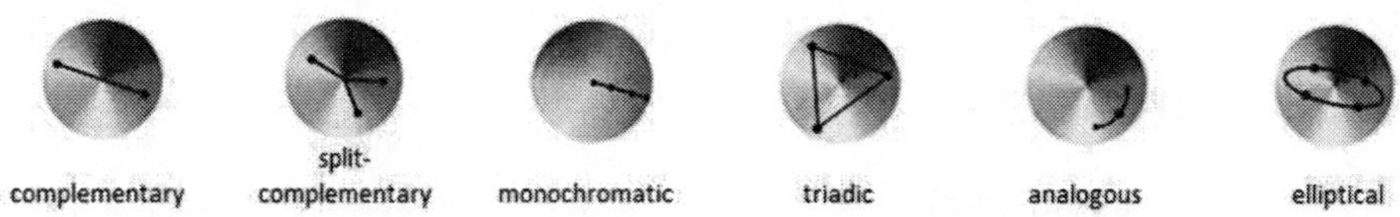

Figure 1. At any angle, the positions of the dots on the "wireframes" defines harmonious colour schemes

(Albers, 2006) takes a contrary view. He states that *no mechanical color system is flexible enough to precalculate the manifold changing factors... in a single prescribed recipe*, and advocates that *any color "goes" or "works" with any other color*. Certainly, colour combinations that induce feelings of disquiet, alarm, or excitement may "work" in some situations (a horror film, perhaps, or heavy metal concert). (Sloane, 1991) claims that societal norms change, rendering scientific theories about beauty untenable. Notwithstanding Albers and Sloane, we take the view that producing colour harmony (semi)automatically is feasible. We have developed a software tool that handles manipulates colour areas, saturations, hues and value, and geometric models of colour harmony, without preventing designers from expressing personal preferences.

2. SHORTCOMINGS OF CURRENT TOOLS

Some computer-based tools for achieving colour harmony incorporate separate controls dedicated to saturation and brightness, but most are based on a 1D colour model, which is summarized neatly, but inaccurately, in the help system for one of them: *While your color scheme can use any tints, shades, and tones, color theory pays attention only to the hue component* (QSK Software Group) (Lyons & Moretti, 2004). Rotating a rigid wireframe about the centre of the colour wheel should, in principle, "choose" a set of harmonious colours. However, colour wheels are inconsistent – so each tool must produce a unique result – and perceptually non-uniform – so the subjective colour differences between constant point-to-point distances will change as the points move within the space. Perceptually uniform colour space has a strange bulbous shape (see (R. Kuehni, 2010)) but only in such a space will rotating a wireframe produce a consistent set of harmonious colours. None of the tools surveyed conform to that requirement, and many only show two of the three dimensions of colour.

Next, the interface to these tools is typically based on a dialog box that requires the user to work out of the context of the image component that is being coloured, which makes it difficult to make subjective judgements of the holistic effect of the mutual interaction of several colours. Ideally, the systems that were surveyed would update the user's image in real time, but none link to the user image.

Finally, most of the approaches are restricted to a small number of colours; images with a large number of differently-coloured items are outside of their scope.

3. MUNSELL'S MODEL OF COLOUR HARMONY

Manual application of the Munsell-derived equation $A_1V_1C_1 = A_2V_2C_2$ to complex images is prohibitive, but today, such tedious problems are easily handled by computers. Consequently, our software incorporates Munsell's principles of colour harmony, extended to deal with the legibility of text, but we do not contend that his principles are always "right." For example, colour scheme appeal is age-specific (Nemcsics, 2009); children prefer vivid discordant schemes (Morriss, Dunlap, & Hammond, 1982); their appeal peaks at age 12–14, and is uncommon in adults (Palffy, 1976). Futher, the formula deals only with two colours; realistic images have many more colours than two.

3.1 Criteria for a Colour Harmonisation Tool

We have therefore assembled a set of criteria (Table 1) for the construction of a colour harmonisation tool.

Table 1. Desiderata for a colour harmonisation tool for interfaces and websites

Consideration	The tool should…
Hue-independent colour harmony rules can map onto rotary wireframes within a perceptually uniform colour space. They can only define hue, saturation, and value if the space is 3D.	**... perform colour harmony calculations based on a rotary wireframe model, within a 3D, perceptually uniform, colour space.**
Colour strength should be inversely related to area (Birren, 1969).	**... be able to measure the areas of interface components.**
Notwithstanding HCI guidelines, many-coloured interfaces can be usable.	**... be able to handle an arbitrary number of colours.**
Subtle colour preferences are unlikely to be perfectly modelled by a computer system.	**... capture æsthetic input from the designer.**
Various colour harmony principles exist (Caivano, 2004).	**... implement rules as plugin modules.**
The tool is initially targeted at software and website design, but others targets areas such as interior and product design are possible.	**... be able to incorporate specific rules (e.g., for legibility of text) for particular application areas.**
It is frequently desirable to colour-code a set of items that share a common property.	**... be able to treat multiple items as a single entity**
It is frequently desirable to colour code items to ensure that they are visually distinguishable (Brown, 1998).	**... allow a user to specify that the colours for a given pair of interface items should be sufficiently different to distinguish them.**
Design is holistic and iterative (Meskens, Luyten, & Coninx, 2009). Changes should occur in context, and without delay.	**... update the colours of the designer's actual image in real time, at design time.**
Interfaces whose colours change at runtime are distracting.	**... not update dynamic images at runtime or while downloading.**
Colour harmony is hue- and value-independent (Caivano, 2004).	**... allow the designer to personalise the wireframe's hue-angle and value-angle.**
A wireframe that fits within the space would not reach the extremes of the colour space, which would prevent a user from selecting full saturation colours.	**... allow the wireframe to be lengthened and shortened to fit within the limits of the colour solid at any given orientation.**

4. THE COLOUR HARMONISER

The tool that we have developed (G. Moretti, Lyons, & Marsland, 2013) presents a list of the visual components to the designer, who specifies

- any pairs of items that should be identically coloured,
- any pairs of items that should remain visually distinct,
- items that are textual,
- the type of colour harmony rule to apply (monochromatic, complementary, etc.)

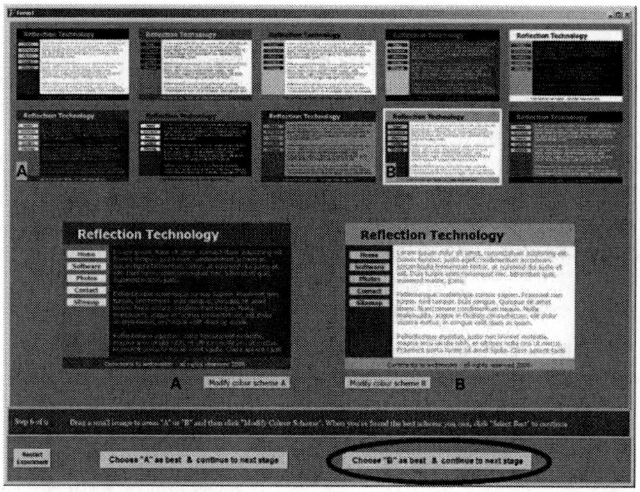

Figure 2. Evaluation screen showing several Colour Hamoniser outputs and the facility for evaluators to modify the schemes by inverting light and dark, and/or increasing or decreasing saturation

The Colour Harmoniser also determines the area of the components (text is treated as a small component, whatever its overall extent). The software then runs a genetic algorithm that optimises a set of 10 independently generated preliminary colour schemes. The optimisation ranks successive generations of colour schemes using an overall fitness score $F = w_1C + w_2W + w_3D + w_4R$, where C, W, D, and R are independent scores for colour balance (the Munsell formula, augmented with colours along the black-white axis), wireframe alignment, component distinguishability and readability respectively. To validate the fitness function , twelve subjects each ranked a sixteen sets of six colour schemes. Each set contained one scheme from each of six fitness bands. Spearman correlation coefficients show high correlation between human and the function (Figure **3**).

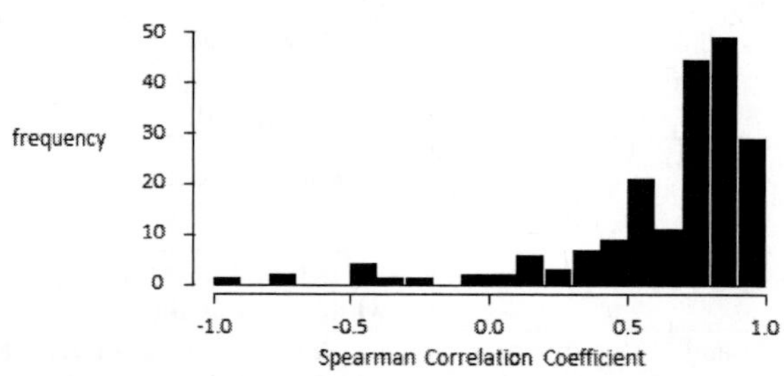

Figure 3. Correlation between fitness function and human rankings

The colour schemes produced at this stage, are *abstract colour schemes*. That is, the software has determined the position of a point on the wireframe corresponding to each interface component, so the colour relationships between components are fixed. However, the orientation of the wireframe has not been fixed in the colour space; the user is free to rotate it about the vertical axis of the space, repositioning the points within the colour space – which updates the hues of the colours in the user's image in real time – without changing their positions on the wireframe – thereby leaving the colour harmony intact. In addition, although value (light-dark) differences are very important for creating a mental model of a scene, in non-realistic scenes, it is not so important *which* items are dark and *which* are light (although text is generally more readable when represented as dark letters on a light background), so the user can also flip the molecule in the light-dark dimension.

Each colour combination produced by these user actions is a *concrete colour scheme* and the system thus allow the user to express personal preferences for the hues in the image, and to change its overall light-dark feeling.

Two sets of evaluation experiments were undertaken ((G. Moretti, Marsland, & Lyons, 2013), Massey University HEC approval #04-184) The first, dubbed Compare The Methods, measured the usability of the Colour Harmoniser method of colour selection in comparison with a standard approach;. It was a within-subjects design in which 39 female and 34 male subjects created one colour scheme using a standard approach and another using the Colour Harmoniser, and completed quality and usability questionnaires for both approaches. The subjects were not chosen for their design skills, and although using the Colour Harmoniser involves inputting some data about the interface, no knowledge of colour theory is required.

The second experiment, dubbed *Compare The Results,* measured the quality of the colour schemes. 127 participants with an approximately equal gender split, and ages from 5 to 65+ scored colour schemes created in five different ways in terms of four criteria. We feel that abstract images are an unrealistic test for a system like this, so the participants were presented with a realistic but simple web interface with seventeen colourable elements: body text, body background, header text, header background; footer text, footer background; five navigation panel buttons (text and background) and navigation panel background. The backgrounds and text for the buttons were treated as single areas, which reduces the number of colours required to seven. With 24-bit colour, the number of possible colourings is 2**24**7 ($\sim 4 * 10^{50}$). Within this enormous search space, good colour schemes are rare. A set of 14 million randomly generated schemes which were grouped into 6 fitness bands contained none in the two highest fitness bands.

The experimental environments were uncontrolled but typical of those used by home users and non-professional developers; lighting was indirect and was most commonly daylight or a daylight/artificial light combination.

The *Compare The Methods* trial took place in five stages:

- introduction to the experiment and the identity and organisational affiliation of the experimenter
- capture of subjects' demographic information
- creation of one colour scheme by conventional means and another using the Colour Harmoniser
- post-questionnaire, concerning usability of the tool and quality of the results
- post-questionnaire, concerning relative usability of the tools and comparison between quality of the two schemes the subjects had produced.

In summary, (see (G. S. Moretti, 2010) for full description) participants stated that the Colour Harmoniser:

- made it easier to find good looking schemes
- was more likely to yield professional looking colour schemes
- had colouring controls that were easy to understand, and
- produced results that were comparable in quality to colour schemes produced manually.

In the evaluation experiment (a between-groups design using the previously constructed colour schemes) each of the 127 evaluators (who did not include any who had participated in the first experiment) was presented with an individualised set of 15 schemes, 3 selected at random from each of the 5 following sets:

- randomly chosen colours (100 schemes)
- colours chosen by people who self-classified as non-artists (93 schemes)
- colours chosen by people who self- classified as artists (48 schemes)
- colours chose by the Colour Harmoniser, without "tweaking" (80 schemes)
- colours chosen by the Colour harmoniser and "tweaked" (62 schemes)

Tweaking is the process whereby users express their personal preferences by altering the hue angle of the wireframe and/or flips the wireframe end-for-end so that light colours become dark and vice versa.

The users ranked the quality of the colour schemes they were presented with, with respect to four criteria: visual appeal, professionalism, "artisticness" and web-suitability. The reason we included – and distinguished between – colour schemes created at random, by non-artists and by artists is that there was no pre-existing quality scale for colour schemes. As we expected, the quality scores increased in the order *random* < *non-artist* < *artist*, so we could use colour schemes of those three types as fixed points on a quality scale against which to assess the Colour Harmoniser colour schemes. We hoped that untweaked Colour Harmoniser colour schemes would be as good as, or nearly as good as, nonartists' schemes, and that tweaking might improve the Colour Harmoniser schemes so that they ranked higher than non-artists' schemes. In the evaluation, the raw Colour Harmoniser schemes were ranked at least as high as artists' schemes (higher, in fact, on three out of four criteria), and the tweaked schemes were ranked higher on all four criteria.

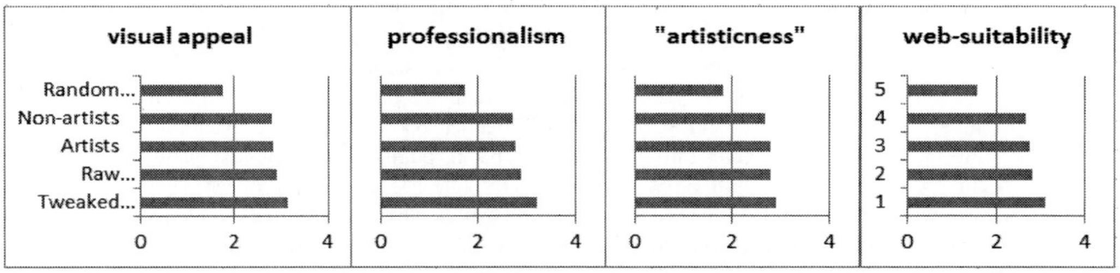

Figure 4. Quality evaluations for colour schemes produced by various methods including untweaked (raw) and tweaked Colour Harmoniser schemes

The results presented here are necessarily very brief. A more extensive treatment is given in (G. S. Moretti, 2010), which includes statistical data that establishes the statistical significance of the results.

5. CONCLUSIONS

This research has demonstrated that

- It is possible to design a computationally tractable model of colour harmony that can be used to evaluate interface colour schemes
- It is possible to create harmonious colour schemes in an abstract colour space
- It is possible to build a software tool for creating colour schemes that incorporates a model of colour harmony, augmented to include pragmatic considerations such as text readability
- Unskilled users of an algorithmic colour harmony tool can achieve successful designs
- The Colour Harmoniser method produces good colour schemes, and
- The Colour Harmoniser method of colour adjustment makes finding good colour schemes easier

REFERENCES

Albers, J. (2006). *Interaction of Color: Revised and Expanded Edition*: Yale University.

Birren, F. (1969). *MUNSELL: A Grammar of Color*: Van Nostrand-Reinhold.

Brown, C. M. (1998). *Human-Computer Interface Guidelines*: Intellect, Limited.

Caivano, J. L. (2004). *GAC Revista* (No. ano 7, no19): Grupo Argentino del Color.

Chevreul, M. E. (1839). *The Principles of Harmony and Contrast of Colours and their Applications to the Arts*.

Hering, E. (1964). Outlines of a Theory of the Light Sense (L. M. Hurvich & D. Jameson, Trans.) (pp. 49): Harvard.

Hu, G., Pan, Z., Zhang, M., Chen, D., Yang, W., & Chen, J. (2014). An Interactive method for Generating Harmonious Color Schemes. *Colour Research and Application, 39*(4), 18.

Itten, J. (1970). *The Art of Color*: Wiley.

Kuehni, R. (2010). Color Spaces. Retrieved 4 July, 2010, from http://www.scholarpedia.org/article/Color_spaces

Kuehni, R. G. (2001). Colour Space and its Divisions. *Color Research & Application, 26*(3), 14.

Kuehni, R. G. (2014). Unique Hues and Their Stimuli—State of the Art. *Color Research & Application, 39*(3), 9.

Lyons, P., & Moretti, G. (2004). *Nine Tools for Generating Harmonious Colour Schemes*. Paper presented at the Proc 6th Asia Pacific Conference on Computer Human Interaction (APCHI 2004).

Meskens, J., Luyten, K., & Coninx, K. (2009). *Shortening user interface design iterations through realtime visualisation of design actions on the target device*. Paper presented at the 2009 IEEE Symposium on Visual Languages and Human-Centric Computing (VL/HCC).

Moretti, G., Lyons, P., & Marsland, S. (2013). Computational production of colour harmony. Part 1: A prototype colour harmonization tool. *Color Research and Application*, 38(3), 15.

Moretti, G., Marsland, S., & Lyons, P. (2013). Computational production of colour harmony. Part 2: Experimental evaluation of a tool for gui colour scheme creation. *Color Research and Application*, 38(3), 11.

Moretti, G. S. (2010). A Calculation of Colours: Towards the Automatic Creation of Graphical User Interface Colour Schemes. Unpublished Ph.D., Massey University, Palmerston North.

Morriss, R. H., Dunlap, W. P., & Hammond, S. E. (1982). Influence of Chroma on Spatial Balance of Complementary Hues. *The American Journal of Psychology, 95*(2), 323-332.

Nemcsics, A. (2007). Experimental Determination of Laws of Color Harmony. Part 1: Harmony Content of Different Scales with Similar Hue. *Color Research and Application, 32*(6), 477-488.

Nemcsics, A. (2008a). Experimental determination of laws of color harmony. Part 2: Harmony content of different monochrome color pairs. *Color Research and Application, 33*(4), 8.

Nemcsics, A. (2008b). Experimental determination of laws of color harmony. Part 3: Harmony content of different hue pairs. *Color Research and Application, 34*(1), 33-44.

Nemcsics, A. (2009). Experimental Determination of Laws of Color Harmony. Part 4: Color Preference and the Color Harmony Content. *Color Research and Application, 34*(3).

Nemcsics, A. (2010). Experimental determination of laws of color harmony. Part 5: The harmony content of the various hue triads. *Color Research and Application*, 13.

Nemcsics, A. (2011). Experimental Determination of Laws of Color Harmony. Part 6: Numerical Index System of Color Harmony. *Color Research & Application*.

Palffy, Z. (1976). Age-specific characteristics in sensitivity to harmony of colours. *Magyar Pszichologiai Szemle, 33*(6), 562-570.

QSK Software Group. Color Wheel Pro. Retrieved 21 August, 2010, from http://www.color-wheel-pro.com/

Shneiderman, B. (1998). *Designing the User Interface: Strategies for Effective Human-Computer Interaction* (3 ed.): Addison Wesley Longman.

Sloane, P. (Ed.). (1991). *Primary Sources: Selected Writings on Color From Aristotle To Albers* (1 ed.): Design Press.

Tractinsky, N., Katz, A. S., & Ikar, D. (2000). What is Beautiful is Usable. *Interacting With Computers, 13*(2), 18.

von Goethe, J. (1991). Theory of Colours. In P. Sloane (Ed.), *Primary Sources: Selected Writings on Color From Aristotle To Albers* (pp. 21). New York: Design Press.

ASPECT ORIENTATION AS A NEW APPROACH FOR CONTEXT DEPENDENT HMI ADAPTATION

Sebastian Heinze, Jens Ziegler, Markus Graube and Leon Urbas
Chair of Process Control Systems Engineering
TU Dresden, Germany

ABSTRACT

This article presents a concept to improve the collaborative, task-centered work in all phases of the lifecycle of a production site. Key feature of this concept is a shared access to an integrated, semantically connected information space for all users. The interaction with the information space is facilitated by means of an adaptive HMI which reconfigures itself at runtime to fit the users' needs in their current context of use. The HMI is implemented with readily available concepts and technologies of concurrent responsive web design that make it possible to also accommodate the properties of different device classes and sizes.

KEYWORDS

HMI Adaptation; Responsive Design; Collaborative Work; Information Spaces; Semantic Web

1. INTRODUCTION

The significance of collaborative work and job processing in modern productions sites is continuously growing. The software used to fulfill these tasks today is using proprietary and highly specialized technologies as well as inconsistent or even incompatible, non-interoperable HMIs. Negatively affecting the usability of the system, also interactions with by persons working in the plant are restrained by using these HMIs. Combining data from separated and semantically incompatible information spaces creates a massive negative impact on the usability of the data access. Graube et al. (2015) proposed a solution to overcome these limitations and a contribution to the operating efficiency is the integrated information- and interaction space. This concept introduces the approach of aspect orientated HMI adaption to adapt the fundamentally consistent user interface to certain parameters beyond the properties of the particular device at hand (Ziegler et al., 2015). Depending on its role, task, place of work and device the user requires different views on the integrated information space and information concerning other people working in the same context. The information display is optimized for the current task, without changing the underlying structure or interaction concept.

An extensive adaptive system is enabling cross device usage as well as multi device usage, while current solution still need several applications to fulfill this task. Cross and multi device use cases favor collaborative and especially migrative workflows, whereas multiple non adaptive applications cannot fully support such a use case. A reduction of the cognitive workload of the user generated by the high usability can lead to less errors and in conclusion to a better product quality. A better user experience can rise the user's satisfaction, leading to a higher motivation. The flexibility of a highly adaptive system can favor the systems possibility for evolution in a highly manner.

Given the example use case of the process industry, complex problems in the production phase can be solved collaboratively and on the fly by experts without necessary preparation. All available devices can be used to display smaller parts or the big picture of the necessary information. This enables a much faster reaction time to possible endangerments. In contrast to the prevalent, hard coded user interfaces, the progress in the context of highly adaptive and device border crossing concepts is far developed in the field of web design and technologies (Gardner, 2011). Looking at the use case of a process control user interface, the conventional and static design in style of VDI 3699 (2014) can be drastically improved by the introduction of these ideas. Still, the adaptation of user interfaces in web design is determined on adapting to the device,

device properties like dpi or the preferences set by the user and saved locally, e.g. cookies. To adapt also to the task and the context of usage, the existent concepts have to be extended.

This article provides a concept for an integrated interaction space that utilizes modern web technologies for presentation and interaction and is based on a semantically integrated information space. Section 2 describes relevant technologies related to these technologies. The concept is presented in detail in section 3. Section 4 handles aspects of HMI adaptation. The article concludes with a case study in the process industry domain in section 5 and a view on the current status of the approach and future research challenges in section 6.

2. STATE OF THE ART

Adaptation is one of the key features of modern web design technologies and frameworks. The main goal is to enable end users to access to relevant content on as many devices as possible, thus the different natures and qualities of the devices have to be taken into account. Marcotte (2011) coined the term *responsive web design* for combining artistic elements and technical descriptions of existing technologies to react to different devices, like *liquid* and *adaptive design*. The concepts and ideas of responsive web design not only found their way into modern web design, but also in more holistic approaches (Voutilainen, Salonen and Mikkonen, 2015; Taivalsaari, Mikkonenand Systä, 2014). The approach of many existent web technologies is to fit a predefined user interface (web page) to the capabilities of the current device. This concept can so be reused to overcome the current problems and limitations of existing UI technologies when supporting cross-device concepts (Ziegler et al., 2015). In order to adapt the user interface to the current situation, the system has to know or infer which information is relevant. Towards that end the system an information model is necessary that represents "concepts, relationships, constraints, rules, and operations a chosen domain of discourse" (Lee, 1999). For non-trivial scenarios, usually several different information models are necessary. They are provided by an information system and form an information space as understood by Nemby (Newby, 1996). Multiple authors extend this rather general concept of an information space and take the distributed nature of the information concepts into account, e.g. Hilbert (2015). This makes it necessary to interlink the single concepts and describe both the links and the concepts themselves semantically. This provides the basis for an external system with linked information to derive the meaning of the referenced concepts. Exactly this feature will become more and more necessary in future decentralized automation systems (Obst et al., 2015).

Collaborative work in interdisciplinary teams requires a continuous exchange and alignment of knowledge of all members in order to create a common ground of situation awareness. The structure of tasks and situation, the content and its development, as well as the temporal course of processes need to be commonly understood by all team members. This is largely supported by explicit and implicit interpersonal communication and behavior. In spatially distant teams, these channels are unavailable and need to be replaced by means of technologically mediated communication, coordination and interaction. Web conference systems, project management platforms and collaborative office tools are prominent examples. These tools combine means for synchronous and asynchronous collaboration in an integrated environment that provide various visual (or multimodal) cues to represent the team members' situations and actions and the relations between them. There is good scientific evidence for the benefits of technologically mediated cooperation (Wilson, 1991).

Modern collaborative software tools primarily use self-managed databases. Although these services provide a multitude of import and export options, complex industrial tasks still cannot be done in integrated collaborative environments. Current integration approaches are usually based on remote desktop tools which, however, are hardly suitable for collaborative work because of the lack of the necessary mechanisms to create team situation awareness and coordination (Dourish and Bellotti, 1992).

3. THE INTEGRATED INFORMATION- AND INTERACTION SPACE

3.1 Information Space

The information space needed for an adaptive and flexible interaction has to meet several requirements in order to make the interaction space most usable at runtime and highly flexible at development time.

First of all, it has to provide access to information coming from different data sources as shown in Figure 1. Complex tasks in a plant may need the user interface to visualize highly aggregated indicators which base on information of multiple underlying systems. With respect to the trend of further outsourcing some service, as health monitoring, this data can also come from outside the own organization. Hence, the data has to be semantically described providing the comprehension about concepts and properties of information in order to allow computers to sophisticatedly operate on this information. In addition to the semantic description the information entities have to be interlinked. The links to other information entities have to carry semantics in order to distinct different kinds of relation to other information.

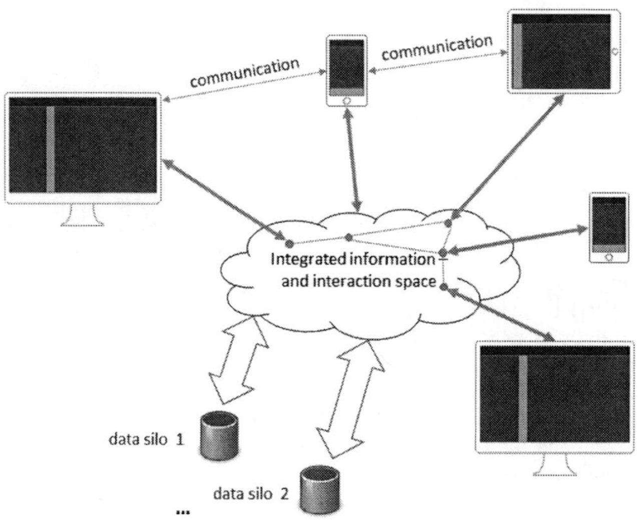

Figure 1. Integrating information spaces and interaction spaces

Further needed is a unified information access mechanism to different kinds of data, while the instances and the meta models are important to create highly flexible user interfaces. For collaboration, the users communication is inevitable. It can be realized be integrating it into the information space. This makes it possible to interlink past conversations about an occurred problem and its solution to the related device. Afterwards, depending on the actual situation this communication and the involved persons can be displayed when a user is facing a similar problem. Since the high dynamics, there is a need for a flexible and seamless way to integrate new data silos as well as giving transparent access to information spaces. To offer the needed level of consistency, revision control has to be supported by the information space.

Currently, the most readily available tools only partly meet the requirements described above. However, some technologies for creating such a distributed information space exist. Graube et al. (2012) introduced the concept of linked enterprise data that provides an excellent basis for mobile applications in plant maintenance (Graube et al., 2013) and plant operation (Pfeffer et al., 2015) that have requirements quite similar to the ones presented in this paper. It uses Linked Data as base technology which transfers the principles of the WWW to a web of data (Prud'hommeaux, and Seaborne, 2008). The concept includes building adapters for all relevant data sources which lift necessary data into a semantic information space. The flexibility to express all different information is achieved by using the Resource Description Framework (RDF) as base data format and light-weight ontologies based on RDFS and OWL. The data from the different sources is directly integrated on data level by introducing links which are a primary element in RDF.

The actual access to the data is realized using the SPARQL query language (Prud'hommeaux, and Seaborne, 2008), which allows complex queries as well as an interface for federated queries in the distributed information space. Established communication protocols like XMPP are used for inter-human communication, with a possible direct integration into the Linked Data space using additional modules. Furthermore, the messages can be enriched by links to specific resources in the information model. These can not only be RDF resources identified by URIs but also OPC UA nodes identified by their node id or browse path. A further OPC UA adapter allows to access OPC UA nodes via a REST interface which seamless integrated into the Linked Data environment.

Advanced security mechanisms and revision control mechanisms can be integrated into the SPARQL interface. These features exploit that graph theoretical concepts can be applied to RDF. Hence, it is also possible to use graph grammars for model transformation and model synchronization which is another key requirement to achieve a powerful information space.

3.2 Interaction Space

The availability of an integrated information space allows to create a highly flexible, dynamic, and adaptive shared interaction space that can be accessed by multiple persons with multiple roles using a variety of interaction devices. The availability of an integrated information space allows to create a highly flexible, dynamic, and adaptive shared interaction space that can be accessed by multiple persons with multiple roles using a variety of interaction devices in order to collaboratively cope with a complex task. A major challenge for provide suitable collaborative workspaces is the variety and diversity of entangled tasks. In the example of collaborative fault diagnosis, there may be workplaces for process control, alarm management, maintenance management, asset management, web conferencing and remote maintenance control. Users should be able to easily switch between workspaces, preserving their current informational context.

The area of interest of the users often extend well beyond their current workspace. In the given example, the task of the operators would obviously be to operate the faulty plant. However, the reorganization of the maintenance plan by the other team members might be of great interest for the operator, since it is crucial to know when they will be able to return to normal operation. Opening multiple workspaces in parallel, however, quickly results in information overload for the user. The use of an overview-detail pattern with graded density of information and interaction can be useful here. Figure 2 shows our proposed design. A single working area contains active workspace that provides all content and controls that are necessary to actively contribute to a collaborative task. One or more context (b) areas each contain an observed workspace providing reduced content and controls that can be used to modify the active workspace only. Finally, a single overview area (d) contains highly generic views on all available workspaces and show significant situational changes in an overview. This area can be used to quickly switch between workspaces. Other components in the design resemble and notification bar (a) and a navigation bar (c). The structural layout of these components highly depends on the user's context of use and can be adapted to each device.

In the above example, an operator might actively work in the process control workspace while observing the maintenance management workspace. When the user notices that the current plan needs some corrections, he or she activates the previously observed workspace. The Process Control Workspace turns into a context area. All team members are getting notified of this structural change in the group work.

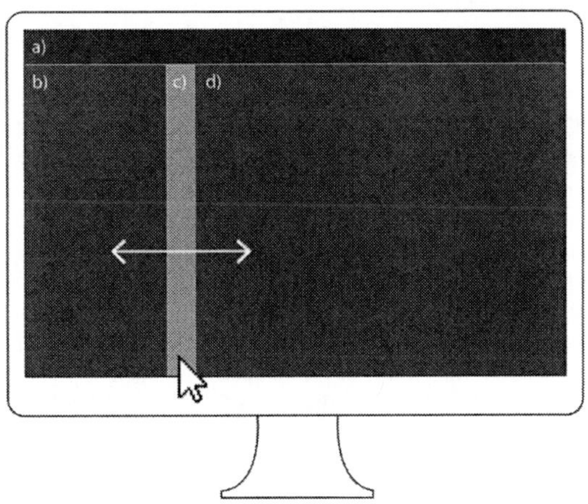

Figure 2. Screen layout on a desktop pc

Collaborative environments provide visual and other cues to highlight activities of other team members. This includes changes on the content the user is working on, but also changes on related content, or situational or structural changes that might be beneficial for the user's situation awareness. According to the current task, different aspects of the work of other team members can be important for the user's situation awareness in order to collaboratively cope with a complex task. A major challenge for collaborative working environments is the variety and diversity of entangled tasks. An integrated collaboration environment must provide suitable workspaces for each of these tasks. In the example of collaborative fault diagnosis, there may be workplaces for process control, alarm management, maintenance management, asset management, web conferencing and remote maintenance control. Users should be able to easily switch between workspaces, preserving their current informational context.

4. ASPECTS

4.1 Needs for HMI Adaptation

The user interface to a shared interaction space should be platform independent and migratory. Users should be able to seamlessly switch between different target devices to accomplish their tasks. Depending on the task and context at hand, target devices may be office PCs, mobile devices or even wearables. Data and services should be provided anywhere and anytime, and always in the best suited representation mode (Pernici and Krogstie, 2006). This also imposes an adaptation to the user role and the task at hand. Different views might be presented to different users according to their specific responsibilities and permissions in their occupied role. If explicit task or workflow models are available (e.g. as BPMN models), the views might be aligned with the modelled informational needs and message flows as well. A shared interaction space might further be responsive to the current environmental constraints such as noise, lighting, weather conditions or user behavior.

4.2 Aspects

Aspects represent the visual model of the information contained in the system. Their selection is vastly depended of the use case of the system. Aspects establish a basis for the interactions and enable algorithms to adapt the model to the needs of the current execution context, which includes additional parameters like the used device and its properties, environmental conditions and even preset preferences of the user. All aspects share this execution context, but while the configuration of each aspect will enable the view on different parts of the information space. For the influence of the aspects onto each other we coin the term aspect entangling.

Aspect orientation is a well-known paradigm in programming (Kiczales et al., 1997). Its objective is the addressing of cross-cutting concerns, a term describing the issues of software development, that can't be modularized, due to the lack of compatibility with conventional approaches like object orientation. Issues like safety and security are usually hard to comply, when the corresponding functionality is distributed in the whole system (Rashid et al., 2010). Aspect oriented programming centralizes certain functionality and combines it with rules for a suitable application.

The concepts presented in this paper expand the concept of cross-cutting concerns on information also to the user interface. This enables the comprehensive adaption to the aspects, e.g. a user's role. The main paradigm is to unravel information inside the information space and interaction in the interaction space as late as possible, namely at runtime. This enables the support of weakly structured or non-structured tasks with a high complexity.

The visual presentation of the aspects uses different parts of the UI with different adaptation possibilities. The overview area with its generic views on the data can be used to select the detail areas data and point of view. Its adaptation uses the dependency of the role of the user as well as the current task of the user. The adaptation is not limited to a change of the level of detail but explicitly includes changes in the arrangement or presence of user interface elements. The detail area of the user interface enables the interaction with the information space and is adapted on a basis of user role, the task of the user and additionally the current execution context to tailor the granularity to the given possibilities of the display.

4.3 Aspect Entangling

By sharing the execution context, aspects are able to combine the shown information and create a highly adapted access to information suitable for the current user needs. While not adding new data to the information space, the entanglement of aspects has its strength at filtering and faceting information, simplifying the information access. While sharing one execution context, the overview area filters data of the information space and puts it into display on the detail area by using the generic view to make a choice based on the current possibilities of the user. The displayed data at the detail area is facetted, taking into account the execution context. The flow of information can be reverted to also using the view in the detail are to facette data in the overview area, e.g. by highlighting.

5. CASE STUDY

5.1 Context of Use

Context of the case study is a plant of the process industry. Its environment has a broad spectrum of conditions. From the quietness of the enclosed control room with its operators into the field with maintenance technicians facing potential endangerments like high temperatures, erroneous gas and fluid leaks, accessing exposed platforms or difficult to access process elements.

Operators control the complete plant while centralizing more and more of the information accruing in the runtime of the process plant. The given toolset is mainly several specialized programs based on proven concepts like VDI 3699 (2014). The proceeding information centralizing rises high challenges for the existing system, missing the necessary flexibility to the new principle.

Maintenance technicians are highly demanded during their on-site work, consisting of plant maintains, repairs and overhauls of the process equipment. To fulfill these task, a wide spectrum of tools and equipment is necessary. Assuring the personal safety by wearing protective clothing in different expansion stages, from protective gloves and a helmet up to a completely sealed overall, the safety equipment can differ as well as the environment conditions at the site. In the course of their work, the maintenance technicians have to handle a big amount of data, from task lists to manuals of the process equipment to complex engineering and process data of the site. With their work, they assure the correct and error free plant operation.

The context of process industry enables the view on different aspects of the information. As the base for all tasks, a hierarchical view on the plant is useful. In the overview area, a tree view of the plant with its sub plants gives the possibility to navigate through the plant following the hierarchy. The detail area is best used as a hierarchy view resembling the piping and instrumentation diagram with an enriched information (Graube et al., 2015). This view can be scaled to many different sizes, showing different levels of information, from the piping and instrumentation view to details and load diagrams of and single plant equipment, which was enlarged on the screen.

Main control and monitoring tool in a conventional control room is the alarm & event list. To expand the hierarchical view, an asset view with the focus on single process elements could be used to show the overview of all available process assets grouped by their type. The detail screen shows a selected part of the plant with its details, connected information and persons, e.g. the responsible maintenance technician. The view can differ from a single, file card like display for a single equipment to an enriched list, if more assets were selected, e.g. by selecting a sub plant. For planning longer running tasks or even work days for workers, a task display can show tasks set for persons, as well as tasks set for assets, e.g. regularly done maintenances. Considering other data sources of the process industries, many views may be taken into account after an analysis of the information demand, some examples are views like Analysis of past event signals, a key performance indicator (KPI) view or a more process orientated view for the current running recipe or batch.

To forward the collaboration, the communication between persons can be carried out with a text based messaging service, shown in the detail area of the screen. The Overview shows the contacts available for communication.

5.2 Workflows

The plant's operator is located in the control room, working on a desktop pc environment. He works on at least one screen and a mouse and keyboard. Entry point of the operators system is a display, which shows the necessary overview for the daily tasks. It is composed out of the alarm details and the hierarchy overview, so the typical and well known use case for an alarm and event list is still in use. When an alarm enters the system, it is displayed inside the alarm list to be acknowledged by the operator. If a further investigation is needed, the alarm can be marked. In the current display configuration, the hierarchy overview would highlight through the aspect entangling the corresponding equipment in the hierarchy to enable a better classification of the abnormal state.

With the ongoing error investigation, the need for more detailed information rises and can be satisfied by the operator by using the detail asset view. Navigation to this view can be started directly in the alarm list with a link to the erroneous device. The system has adapted its granularity for the operator and shows load and timing diagrams as well as the current condition of the process equipment. By looking at the last executed maintenances, the operator can draw conclusions whether to directly contact the responsible technician or just set a note for the next scheduled maintenance. In the hierarchy overview, a whole sub plant can be selected and will be displayed in the assets detail in reduced information complexity, still containing the information to decide whether one asset is operating outside of its range. When a current state of the plant or an event can be discussed by persons with access to the control room, each member of the discussion can use their currently available device to contribute to the conversation. As it's typical for a control room to contain a big screen, the operator, who has previously worked at its desktop pc can bring the context of the error to the big screen. Other people, currently only carrying their smartphone, can use the pc to display their own sight, which helps them, to visualize the problem on a way, which suits them best.

As the operator decided to contact the responsible technician because of a defective pump, the overview area is switched to contacts. Sharing the context with the current asset details view, the responsible worker is filtered out of all connected persons and a conversation can be started. As the topic of the defective pump is set, all past conversations about this pump, and possibly its problems, are shown above the current conversation. Necessary steps can be discussed within the system and later be realized by the technician.

The usage of the information system of the maintenance technician differs in the usage of mobile devices to access the information needed as well as in a task based approach of work scheduling. So the key display is the overview of tasks, scheduled for the current day and the detail screen with descriptions of each task, as well as additional information like specifications, montage instructions or an overview of the last maintenances with the notes of the technician. After finishing each task, notes and and result rating can be saved to each task, which enables later evaluation of the work.

In case of unplanned events, the technician can be contacted from the operator or another supervising person. During the conversation via text or audio/video chat, new tasks can be defined and later be accessed in the tasks aspect.

6. SUMMARY

This paper presented a new concept to adapt human machine interfaces to the current needs of the user. The widely known adaptation on devices and device properties of web sites in mind, the adaptation was extended to also consider the current task and the context of the system use. To realise this adaptation, an integrated information and interaction space was created using semantic web technologies. The visuals were designed with the most flexibility in mind and help to cross the boundaries of current systems as well as enabling the possibility to use the most fitting device for each use case. The adaption is based on the selection of aspects of the user's tasks and contexts. The case study was settled in the process industry. Using two use cases, it showed the possible utilization of aspect entangling while also giving insights on the aspect selection process.

The concept of aspect oriented hmi adaption enables complex system to a much higher level of flexibility, while enabling new ways of accessing information which. Reducing the complexity of such a safety and security relevant user interface enables an error free and less cognitive exhausting usage. Future research will focus on the definition of algorithms for a generic approach to the aspect oriented adaptation as well as integrating the technical and methodical requirements of such algorithms in the visualization prototype.

ACKNOWLEDGEMENT

We are grateful to Stefan Bamberger and Georg Kluge for their support and the valuable discussions.

REFERENCES

Beck, K., Ralph, J., 1994, "Patterns Generates Architectures". *Proceedings of European Conference of Object-Oriented Programming.* Bologna, Italy, pp. 139-149.

Berners-Lee, T., 2006. *Design Issues - Linked Data.* Available from: http://www.w3.org/DesignIssues/LinkedData.html

Dourish, P., Bellotti, V. ,1992, Awareness and coordination in shared workspaces. *In Proceedings of the 1992 ACM conference on Computer-supported cooperative work. Toronto, Canada,* pp. 107-114.

Gardner, B. S., "Responsive Web Design: Enriching the User Experience", *Sigma.*, vol. 11, pp. 13-19, Oct. 2011

Graube, M. et al., 2012. "Linked Data as Integrating Technology for Industrial Data", *International Journal of Distributed Systems and Technologies (IJDST)*, vol. 3, no. 3, pp. 40–52.

Graube, M. et al., 2013 "Linked Data as Enabler for Mobile Applications for Complex Tasks in Industrial Settings," in Proceedings of IEEE 18th Conference on Emerging Technologies & Factory Automation (ETFA 2013).Cagliari, Italy, pp. 1–8.

Graube, M.et al., 2015, "Integrierter Informations- und Interaktionsraum. Modularisierung und Digitale Anlage von der Leitwarte bis ins Feld". *Tagungsband GMA-Kongress Automation 2015.* Baden Baden, Germany.

Hilbert, F., 2015. *Kontextabhängige Informationsräume - Unterstützung interdisziplinärer Bauinformationsprozesse durch eine kontextbewusste Informationslogik.* Technische Universität Dresden, Dresden.

Kiczales, G. et al., 1997, "Aspect-Oriented Programming". *Proceedings of the 11th European Conference on Object-Oriented Programming.* Jyväskylä, Finland, pp. 220 – 242.

Lee, Y. T., 1999, "Information modeling: From design to implementation". *Proceedings of the second world manufacturing congress*, pp. 315–321.

Marcotte, E., 2011. *Responsive Web Design.* A Book Apart.

Newby, G. B., "Metric Multidimensional Information Space," *Proceedings of The Fifth Text REtrieval Conference TREC.* Gaithersburg, USA.

Obst, M. et al., 2015, "Semantic description of process modules - Towards an open implementation for plug and produce in process plants". P*resented at the Conference on Emerging Technologies & Factory Automation ETFA*, Luxembourg, Luxembourg.

Pernici, B., Krogstie, J.,2006. *Mobile information systems.* Springer-Verlag, Berlin.

Pfeffer, J.et al., 2015, Towards collaborative plant control using a distributed information and interaction space. *Proc. IEEE Conf. Emerging Technologies & Factory Automation (ETFA).* Luxembourg, Luxembourg.

Prud'hommeaux, E., Seaborne, A., 2008. *SPARQL Query Language for RDF. W3C Recommendation.* Available at: http://www.w3.org/TR/rdf-sparql-query/

Rashid, A. et al., 2010, "Aspect-Oriented Software Development in Practice: Tales from AOSD-Europe". *Computer* 43(2), pp. 19 – 26.

Taivalsaari, A., et al., 2014., "Liquid Software Manifesto", *Proceedings of the 38th Annual International Computers, Software and Applications Conference.* Vasteras, Sweden, p. 338 - 343

VDI/VDE 3699 – Process control using display screens. Beuth Verlag, Berlin, 2014.

Voutilainen, J. P. et al., 2015, On the Design of a Responsive User Interface for a Multi-device Web Service. *Proceedings of the 2nd ACM International Conference on Mobile Software Engineering and Systems MOBILESoft.* Florence, Italy, p. 60-63.

Wilson, P. ,1991. *Computer supported cooperative work: An introduction.* Springer Science & Business Media.

Ziegler, J. et al., 2015, "Using Semantic and Responsive Web Design Technologies for Cross-Device Interactions in Industrial Applications". *Workshop on Interacting with Multi-Device Ecologies in the Wild.* ACM International Conference on Interactive Tabletops and Surfaces 2015.

ECO-A: CHILDREN'S ENGAGEMENT IN ENVIRONMENTAL AND CLIMATE ISSUES

Alma Leora Culén, Ingeborg Eilertsen, Lone Lægreid, Sumit Pandey, Magnus Søyland and Ingrid Smørgrav Viddal
Department of Informatics, University of Oslo, P. Boks 1080, 0316 Blindern, Oslo, Norway

ABSTRACT

The paper describes experiences with Eco-A, an interactive installation for children and youth. The installation was designed to engage children and youth in active conversation around environmental and climate issues. It was developed using research through design (RtD), i.e., the practice of using design thinking, design processes and artifacts as inquiry methodology. Eco-A was made to help us to explore design spaces for youth and children's engagement with environmental issues and climate change. The installation was used as part of a larger exhibit City Kids at Sentralen, a culture house in Oslo. The paper summarizes our findings from observing Eco-A in use by children and youth, reflections on how well our design decisions supported the desired engagement, and knowledge gained towards future design.

KEYWORDS

Design for engagement; research through design; youth and sustainability; interaction design

1. INTRODUCTION

Our planet is changing rapidly, mainly due to human activities that are having a global impact. The extent of changes is so profound that the term Anthropocene era (Waters et al., 2016), referring to an epoch of human-induced changes in Earth's geology and ecosystems, is being increasingly used. Concerns around environmental and climate changes, in particular, often bring to mind the question *"What kind of world are we leaving to our children?"* The motivation for our work arose from turning the question into *"What kind of world the children see for their future selves and how their actions today impact that future world?"* We started by looking in the direction of design activism (Fuad-Luke, 2013) among Norwegian children and youth who are concerned with these issues. More specifically, we were interested in exploring why and how some children and youth get engaged with organizations acting on these matters, such as Miljøagentene ("Eco-Agents," 2016) and how could this activism and engagement be spread more widely. As we work within the field of interaction design and Human-Computer Interaction (HCI), we were also interested in the role of technology, beyond social media and the Internet, in catalyzing and researching this motivation, the level of understanding of issues at hand by those aged 13 and under, and opportunities for direct engagement.

This paper describes our attempt to explore children and youth's relation to environmental problems using research through design approach. The artifact designed and studied in real-life use, is an installation that we named Eco-A, a name inspired by Miljøagentene (Eco-Agents in English). Eco-A was used during the exhibit City Kids, and is shown in Figure 1. City Kids was an exhibit organized by Oslo Children's Museum and had numerous hands-on activities for children, focused on learning through play, tinkering, mastering etc. Eco-A was places in a separate room, a bit outside of the area of main activities. It consisted of three components. The first component of the installation aimed to create a shared information space (Bannon and Bødker, 1997; Hornecker et al., 2007) related to diverse issues pertinent to climate changes and presented at a level understandable for children. The second one took a critical approach, probing and questioning children's existing and future habits that impact the environment. The third component of Eco-A, inspired by design activism, aspired to engage youth and children in voicing their opinions on climate change and other environmental issues.

The Research through Design (RtD) approach was chosen because, as argued by Zimmerman and Forlizzi (Zimmerman and Forlizzi, 2014, p. 168), it engages with both what is (the present) and what can be (the future), while also creating opportunities of an ongoing dialog between the two. Thus, we present our findings and reflections on the installation's real life use situation, and our interpretation of how this dialog went in this particular case.

Verbeek, arguing for a post-interactions view in design, centered on mediation and mediation theory rather than interaction between technology and humans, points out that "*what is being designed, then, is not a thing but a human-world relation in which practices and experiences take shape*" (Verbeek, 2015, p. 28). In this sense, Eco-A was designed to be a mediation platform. The interaction bit in itself (with different parts of the exhibit) was not particularly novel. However, what interested us were the reactions and actions that were consequences of experiences with Eco-A. Reflective considerations over the exhibit as an artifact could bring forth many limitations with respect to its design and interactions that it facilitates. The strength of the installation, and what we wish to emphasize through this paper, is in the potential of the design space that Eco-A opens. Observing children's engagement with the exhibit gave us insight into what matters for deepening the engagement of young visitors to exhibits such as City Kids.

Figure 1. The image shows the three members of the team preparing for the opening of the exhibit. The informative videos are shown on the right, the critical questioning through the quiz on the left, while the possibility to voice opinions by speaking or writing a bottle-mail, was in the back. A glass side of the room provided a good spot for observations

The paper is structured as follows: in the next section, we provide a short background on RtD. In Section 3, we describe the installation. Section 4 explains our research design, while the Section 5 presents discussion and interpretation of our findings. Conclusion closes the paper.

2. BACKGROUND

Over the last ten years, both interaction design and HCI have engaged in considerable research activity in order to find out how to tackle environmental and other sustainability related issues. These research activities have resulted in multiple approaches and an evolving framing of sustainable interaction design or sustainable HCI within these fields, e.g., (Blevis, 2007; Brynjarsdottir et al., 2012; DiSalvo et al., 2010; Dourish, 2010; Pierce et al., 2008). When it comes to sustainable HCI related to youth and children, research directions such as education for sustainability (Sterling and Huckle, 2014), gamification (Culén et al., 2015), awareness systems at home (Horn et al., 2015), family living styles (Håkansson and Sengers, 2013) and others have been explored. However, sustainable design for and with the youth and children that goes beyond learning and gamification is still largely under-researched.

RtD provides a way for human-computer interaction practitioners to reconcile research and design practices that are both needed when designing and making new technological artifacts. Many researchers and designers have actively advocated this approach that employs methods and processes from a design practice, e.g., (Fallman, 2007; Gaver, 2012; Stolterman et al., 2009; Zimmerman and Forlizzi, 2014). The reflective practice (Schön, 1983) is a fundamental part of RtD, and is a fundamental way of producing new knowledge about design (methods or processes), the artifact itself, and what gets mediated through the artifact.

Zimmerman and Forlizzi (Zimmerman and Forlizzi, 2014) describe the evolution of RtD, and frame three different design research practices that emerged as influential in RtD. These are the Lab, the Field and the Showroom. The Lab practice, native to Netherlands, combines design with experimental evaluation. The Field practice utilizes the user-centered and/or Scandinavian participatory design perspective, where the researchers try to identify design opportunities in order to improve the state of the world. Finally, the Showroom practice builds on the design of critical and speculative artifacts that challenge the current situation. In making Eco-A, we have used the Field practice, lightly touching and examining Showroom practice as well, in the second component of Eco-A.

In addition to the above mentioned literature, we also use work on ecologies of interactive spaces (Culén and Rosseland, 2014) and its components (physical space, technologies, people, activities and values), as well as Kaptelinin and Bannon's work on creating technology-enhanced activity spaces (Kaptelinin and Bannon, 2012). The physical space, for Eco-A exhibit, implied making only small changes to the room (due to the limited resources for the project) to visually better support the theme of the exhibit. A door decoration was made and the modern light fixtures were covered with green, organic looking fabric (see Figure 1). The other components, technologies, users, activities and values are addressed in the next two sections, woven into the description of Eco-A, or in the discussion.

3. ECO-A

This project was initiated as part of a larger Creative Europe project that explores diverse forms of participation in culture and civic life. The Norwegian subproject is concerned with children and youth's participation and engagement in urban culture; activism being a part of this engagement. The initial work on the project was done as part of the interaction design course that four co-authors were taking during the fall of 2015. The remaining two co-authors were teaching the course and supervised design efforts. Several alternative designs of Eco-A were created during that time period.

Starting from the Field practice, and as is customary in the Scandinavian tradition, getting to know the user is important. Since we wanted to design for engagement and activism, initial contact with Miljøagentene ("Eco-Agents," 2016) was established. They are a small organization dedicated to giving children and youth an opportunity to voice their opinions regarding important debates around the environment. More than that, they strive to increase understanding around sustainability and promote active engagement in caring for the environment, involving thousands of children and their teachers or parents in meaningful activities. One of their actions that took place during the fall of 2015, was to collect opinions of children all over Norway on climate change (these were later actually delivered to politicians at the climate panel in Paris ("Barnas Klimapanel møtte FNs klimapanel i Paris - Miljøagentene," 2015)). This activity coincided with the start of the interaction design course, and the initial idea that the project group had was to cooperate with Miljøagentene and provide a platform for supporting the climate panel initiative by Miljøagentene. However, the work soon took a different turn, because of the interest in a broader age group, and particularly in children not already involved in activities such as those that Miljøagentene support. Thus, a public space installation was seen as a good way to reach this broader audience.

The design phase started with preparatory research, including informal research on what children know about climate changes and other related environmental and sustainability issues that we are face today. Ethnographic work and observations of how Miljøagentene operate and what they actually do followed. An interview with one of their employees was conducted. Then a focus group (a group of 6 children) and a workshop (5 children) were conducted with members of Miljøagentene, where the focus was on understanding what it is that motivates them and how other children who are not already active in the organization could be motivated to join and help build a more sustainable future. Regular contact with this group of youth was established and some of them helped during the design process with valuable input on several occasions. Two of them also attended the City Kids exhibit. To reach those who are not already engaged, 17 children from the 7th grade (approximately aged 12) were also interviewed. Data gathered from these sources was combined and analysed. We found that the children knew more than we thought about climate change. However, the 7th graders did not seem to actively engage with what they knew. The knowledge did not seem to affect their actions in everyday life. Thus, the student design team wanted to make something that would present the facts in different, more experiential and fun ways inspiring personal and emotional engagement. The details of the design process itself are outside the scope of this paper. What is presented here is the work done after the course was over, and interaction design students were hired as creative professionals and researchers to continue the work on the project. Apart from interaction design, the team includes a practicing artist and a designer.

Figure 2. The photo shows images from three different video clips, providing information on climate and environmental issues. The small image shows tangible interaction form that was chosen to open and close videos

The skills available within the group played an important role in deciding on the form and shape of information given to the children. The common information space took the form of short, funny and informative videos that used both artistic and animation skills available within the group. Tangible interaction was chosen as a way of controlling the choice of a video. Placement of a ball into the glass container started a video. Containers were identical, and there was, intentionally, no information on the kind of video that will play. This choice was to promote curiosity and make the children try them all. Videos were shown on a large TV screen (see Figure 2).

Figure 3. The intention with questions was to challenge children to discuss and reflect on their own behaviors. Are they, and their families "green"? Questions could be answered with "yes", "no" or "I do not know"

The second part of the exhibit was designed as a series of small questions intended to trigger reflection. The questions were posed as in a quiz, a familiar format for children, but the purpose was not to test their knowledge or play. The questions were intended as an impetus to reflect over and discuss their own habits and those of their families. The questions were answered by pressing a large leaf-shaped button with "Ja" (yes), "Nei" (no) or "Vet ikke" (I do not know), causing a leaf in the same color to appear on the tree at the screen, giving immediate visual clue as to how green their choices were overall (see Figure 3, image on the left). Some questions led to a heated exchange with friends, (Figure 3, in the middle). Example questions are: "Would you mind getting second-hand stuff as a Christmas gift?", "Would you be willing to buy less stuff to in order to reduce climate changes?" or "Do you think that it is better to walk or cycle to school, rather than driving in a car?"

After watching the videos and spending time going through a sequence of speculative and critical questions, the children could sit down and write messages to policy makers, parents, or whoever they thought could be responsible for helping them to shape a better future for themselves. They could use ordinary paper and pencils, or they could talk into the bottle, recording their message (see Figure 4). Bottles were then deposited in a deposit bin (see Figure 4, on the right).

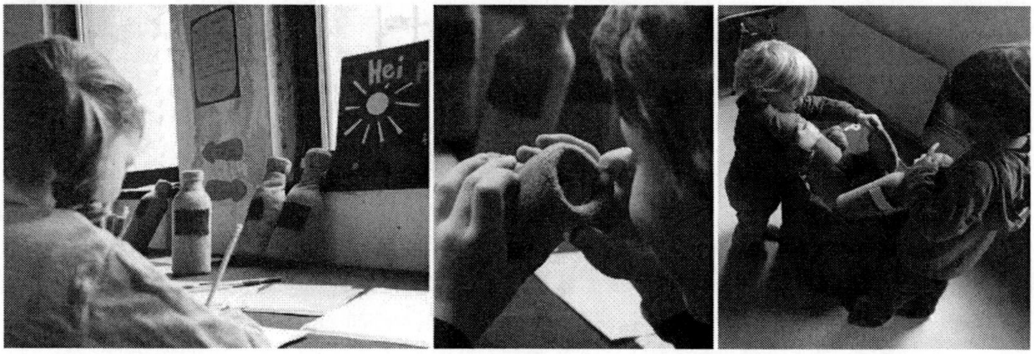

Figure 4. The "activist" part: write a bottle post, or say it into the bottle and deposit in the deposit bin!

During the design phase, the prototype of the installation was tested at the Norwegian Museum of Science and Technology in Oslo (see (Smørgrav Viddal et al., 2015), the final report is in Norwegian, but the Tumblr blog is in English). It was observed then that during working days, audiences consisted mainly of school classes. This was not an optimal situation for this installation. As our aim was to potentially catalyze new domestic practices related to the improvement of the environment, parents' engagement with the exhibit, alongside their children, was seen as a positive trait.

4. METHOD

We have chosen qualitative and interpretative methods to study the use of Eco-A. Activities in the Eco-A exhibit room were followed, using *formal and informal observation*, over a period of two days. The first day's informal observations (no documenting took place, either in the form of field notes, photos or videos), were serving as a basis of reflection, and guidance over choices of methods and tools for the next day. For example, we discussed some a-priori categories that could guide our observations. Those categories were *engagement, playful interactions, aesthetics, exploration, learning and activation*. Reflecting on these choices after the informal observations made on the first day, aesthetics and learning were dropped. This is because we understood that engaging visitors directly in the research through questionnaires, or short interviews would likely be taking away from their experience of the installation itself. The environment was rather hectic and somewhat noisy (videos playing, people talking and discussing), and their stay in the room was relatively short. We deliberately decided to stay away from interrupting the children's exploration and interaction with the installation. Flexibility in research design, based on reflection and adaptation to the actual use context was preferred instead. *Engagement, exploration, playful interactions and activations were judged to be a good framework* for evaluating how well the installation mediates our intentions.

In order not to influence visitors' behavior, fly-on-the-wall observations were chosen for data gathering, behind the glass door and through the glass panels (see Figure 1, the photo on the right). Some of the team members were available in the room to help visitors if needed (not more than one or two at the time), but they did not collect data from visitors. *Engagement* was measured by the length of time spent in the room over the period of 30 minutes. *Playful interactions* were measured by noting social behaviors; *exploration* by number of installation components used and the number of quiz questions or videos explored. Finally, *activation* was about children engaging in telling their own opinions, either using bottle-mail, or other people in the room. These were also taken over a 30 minutes period. This was done as a way of validating what we observed, and very simple descriptive statistics (average) were used. Given our study preferences, some of the gathered data, such as quiz logs that were collected automatically, were also left out for the purposes of this paper.

In addition, Mara (name changed, a 13-year-old girl), one of the Miljøagentene, joined the team. Towards the end of the day, Mara was interviewed using the open interview method.

Lastly, the children's bottle-mails (see Figure 5) were gathered and the texts were analyzed within three age group categories - aged up to 7, 8-10 and 11-13 years. If more than one child wrote a message together, the age of the oldest child determined the category.

5. FINDINGS AND DISCUSSION

As mentioned in the introduction, this installation was part of a larger City Kids exhibit and its activities. Firstly, observing the visitors' movement patterns and activities, we were happy to conclude that the decision to place the installation in a separate room and out of the main action site for City Kids was the appropriate one. Secondly, we could observe during the first day that the space that Eco-A created indeed seemed to foster *engagement*, *exploration*, *playful interactions* with others (both among children and intergenerational) and that it moved the children to express their opinions (*activation*). Thus, those were found to be appropriate as an evaluation framework for gaining insight in how well the installation fulfilled its design intentions.

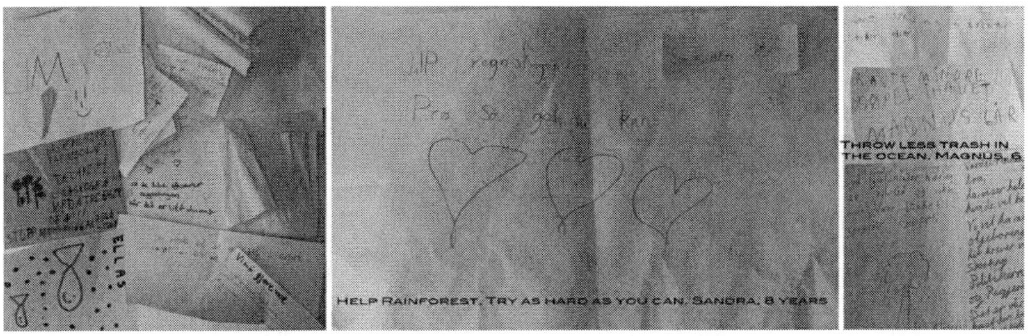

Figure 5. The photo shows a selection of collected messages. Couple of them translated from Norwegian by authors

There were no difficulties that we could observe in accessing and engaging with the activities. The children understood the actions needed – all of them pressed the buttons, or could understand that the video changes when the ball was transferred from one glass jar to another. However, in a case of the youngest children, reading questions from the screen was hard and some were interested in hearing them, while others chose to leave. In one case only, a child who looked old enough to be able to read requested assistance with reading questions. He then went through all the questions. The bottles caused much curiosity. They were just a prototype, with LED lights lighting up, and what the child said was actually recorded by us. Some of the older children managed to figure this out; see Figure 4, the central image. The lights inside two bottles stopped working and the software crashed once during the 2-day period. The prototype was indeed sturdy enough to last for a while, including glass jars (none was broken). So, the technology in itself was not a problem regarding affordances, entry and access points (Hornecker et al., 2007).

5.1 Length of Engagement

We start with observations on the number of visitors to the room and the length of stay. Within 30 minutes, 34 people came by, and 26 of them chose to come into the room. Others looked in and walked away. Most visitors were families. Two girls came alone during the observation period, but this was their third visit that day. The longest stay lasted 23 minutes (the second longest nearly 16 minutes), and the shortest one about 30 seconds. The average stay was approximately 9 minutes long. A stopwatch was used to record the time, but since multiple actions were taking place simultaneously, the time could not be registered very precisely. However, it is a close enough approximation for the purpose of providing an idea of how long the engagement lasted, typically, over both days.

5.2 Exploration and Playful Interactions

Those families or children that stayed longer typically used all three components of the installation and they watched all three videos (with two exceptions, the two girls who came in alone and who, during the observation time, used only one component and one family who stayed with the bottle-mail for the duration of their visit). Interestingly, most visitors, without any guidance, did this in the order intended - videos, questions and then bottle-messages, allowing enough time for a child to write, draw or tell what they think. The two girls, who came alone, used their time on questions, reflecting on their choices and discussing them together (Figure 3, the central image). Another young girl used about 10 minutes just to deposit bottles (with repeated messages) into the deposit bin. From this short observation period, we learned that those who did enter the room and engaged with the installation stayed long enough to explore and playfully interact with the exhibit. The ones who stayed for a short period were mostly parents with very young children. Again, taking times and noting activities were helpful in confirming what we observed during the two days otherwise.

5.3 Effect of Engagement and Age on Activation

Looking at the bottled messages best indicated the level of learning and ability to reflect on the issues we wanted the visitors to engage with. All messages were gathered after the second day and separated by the age of participants. The youngest group was aged up to 7. Many children in this age group still do not write well or gladly. So many messages with simple drawings were placed in this category, although they did not have anything written on them. One team member was tending to the children writing messages (explaining how to "record the message", or write their thoughts on the paper and then send it off to those who can help with climate issues). The children 5-7 in this group, who could write, were clearly influenced by the videos they saw and what they learned from them. For example, Ella (5) just drew fishes in the polluted ocean (Figure 5, left bottom corner). She made two drawings with similar motives. Peder (7) drew a large fish eating a huge piece of plastic. A smaller fish was drawn swimming close to the plastic. It smiled a huge smile. Perhaps Peder thought that a piece of plastic saved the life of the smaller fish.

Those aged 8-10 were both reflecting on own actions and could add an environmental tip or two of their own. *"I deposit my bottles and press the Red Cross button* (note: bottle return stations in most supermarkets in Norway have an option to play lottery for the value of the returned bottle. This is a form of donation to the Red Cross, a humanitarian agency) *and I do not throw trash in the nature". "A bit less oil drilling. Save the light (bulbs). Less driving. Walk and bike more. Be smart and recycle the trash"* (Alexandra (6 ½) and Vilhelmine, (8 ½)). This note also had a drawing of a tree.

Older children, aged 11-13, were more assertive and expressed more radical opinions. Two girls, Ella (10 ½) and Ella (11), wrote: *"We believe that one should stop cutting down the rainforest. Also, we can stop eating food with palm oil. We also believe that everyone should recycle. And stop throwing trash into the sea. Everyone can help by removing the trash from the beach."* Kristina (12 ½) and Sara (13) wrote: *"Ball-burning is good, then the whole of Norway shows what they want* (note: vardebrenning or ball burning has become a political symbol and lately serves as an expression of the Norwegian populations' desire to keep the Lofoten islands free from oil drilling). *We want less oil drilling; we demand that from our parliament. The politicians must hear. This is our future, do not throw it away and remember that time passes fast!"* (the message is on the far right, bottom, of Figure 5).

The most active, helpful and radical person that day was Mara (13), from Miljøagentene. She has been with Miljøagentene for nearly four years. She described her experience during the day at City Kids: *"There were many kids here, and I tried to help. However, many children were not interested in the video. They were more interested in the ball, and moving it from one of the glass containers to the other or in pushing buttons. However, after a while when they got an explanation, they followed more closely, learned a bit more, and began to draw and write, and deposit bottles. They were then very engaged. It was fun to go around and help. Many still have no idea what climate is and why is it important. It is nice for them then to see the video."* (a direct translation from Norwegian)

Mara would, thus, gladly see more people who, like her, provide explanations for younger children. When asked about what could be done with the prototype to make the children understand consequences of climate changes better, she answered: *"You should make more videos that present more facets of the problem. It is important to talk about this* (climate change) *more in the media and have it be more present in everyday life".*

The age of children emerged as a parameter that was important, especially about the ability to reflect on the environmental and climate issues. The installation was fun even for some of the youngest children with regards to playing, exploration and engagement. Smaller children took changing videos by placing the ball in different jars as a game, and the little boy in Figure 4, on the right, spent quite a bit of time putting the bottles in and then taking them out of the bin. In one case, an approximately two-year-old boy, who came in with his mother, used the ball used to select a video, but rather than watching the video as all others have done, he ran out of the room with the ball and had much fun being chased all over the building. Finally, saying or writing down an opinion and placing it into the bottle, the children found to be fun. Just as it often is, there were also exceptions. One such example is of a girl who sat down at the table and wrote: *"miljø suger"* (environment sucks). When asked why the environment sucks, the girl replied that her mom dragged her to the City Kids, when she did not wish to go at all. She thought that the whole exhibit was just something for small kids.

Analysis of bottled messages shows that children did remember what they saw in videos. According to their age and developmental capabilities, they could also reflect on their practices and those of their families, and yes, they would take action and speak up if offered a chance.

6. CONCLUSIONS AND FUTURE WORK

RtD was used to reflect on the Eco-A interactive installation and ways in which the installation mediated understanding of climate changes for children and youth. Our findings show that the installation in itself may have limitations, but it opens a previously underused design space for children and youth's activism related to climate and environmental issues. Additionally, we highlight that the installation had the components that were needed: the information in the form that is accessible and appropriate for the age group, engaging interactions and questions intended to catalyze reflection. We could observe that parents and their children engaged reflectively with the questions. Some children discussed questions with others (than parents) as well. Mara sometimes initiated discussions, in particular when she saw that children needed a nudge to think, highlighting the positive role of having young activists as a catalyst in such conditions.

The question that we reflect over and discuss in the paper is related to what the installation mediated, and finally activated, through engagement, exploration and interactions that we designed for. Given that each prototype is a concrete embodiment and instantiation of a range of ideas and that, in the process of *prototyping one idea*, we have eliminated many other possible alternatives. We could clearly see some limitations of the prototype. Even Mara could do that, e.g., how our choice of three videos and questions delineate and simplify the problem space and how more themes and issues need to be explained.

Future work in this area could explore speculative and critical design and its effects in activating this age group more explicitly.

ACKNOWLEDGEMENT

This project was, in part, financed by the EU Creative Europe project "The People's Smart Sculpture", under the grant number EC-EACEA 2014-2330. We are deeply grateful to one person in particular, who made this exhibit possible, Katie Coughlin, the leader of Oslo Children's Museum and the organizer of the City Kids exhibit. Katie has also initiated our contact with Miljøagentene. The organization Miljøagentene also deserves our deep gratitude for their input and contribution to the project. We are also grateful to the two young agents who visited the installation.

REFERENCES

Bannon, L., Bødker, S., 1997. Constructing Common Information Spaces, in: Proceedings of the Fifth European Conference on Computer Supported Cooperative Work. Springer Netherlands, pp. 81–96.

Barnas Klimapanel møtte FNs klimapanel i Paris - Miljøagentene [WWW Document], 2015 URL http://miljoagentene.no/nyheter/barnas-klimapanel-motte-fns-klimapanel-i-paris-article3509-6.html (accessed 15.6.16).

Blevis, E., 2007. Sustainable Interaction Design: Invention & Disposal, Renewal & Reuse, in: Proceedings of the SIGCHI Conference on Human Factors in Computing Systems, CHI '07. ACM, New York, NY, USA, pp. 503–512.

Brynjarsdottir, H., Håkansson, M., Pierce, J., Baumer, E., DiSalvo, C., Sengers, P., 2012. Sustainably Unpersuaded: How Persuasion Narrows Our Vision of Sustainability, in: Proceedings of the SIGCHI Conference on Human Factors in Computing Systems, CHI '12. ACM, New York, NY, USA, pp. 947–956.

Culén, A.L., Pandey, S., Srivastava, S., Coughlin, K., 2015. Can Games Motivate Urban Youth for Civic Engagement?, in: Zaphiris, P., Ioannou, A. (Eds.), Learning and Collaboration Technologies, Lecture Notes in Computer Science. Springer International Publishing, pp. 549–560.

Culén, A.L., Rosseland, R., 2014. Ecologies of spaces for enjoyable interactions. Int. J. Adv. Netw. Serv. 6 3 4 361–373.

DiSalvo, C., Sengers, P., Brynjarsdóttir, H., 2010. Mapping the Landscape of Sustainable HCI, in: Proceedings of the SIGCHI Conference on Human Factors in Computing Systems, CHI '10. ACM, New York, NY, USA, pp. 1975–1984.

Dourish, P., 2010. HCI and environmental sustainability: the politics of design and the design of politics, in: Proceedings of the 8th ACM Conference on Designing Interactive Systems. pp. 1–10.

Eco-Agents, 2016. . Wikipedia Free Encyclopedia, URL https://en.wikipedia.org/wiki/Eco-Agents (accessed 15.6.16).

Fallman, D., 2007. Why research-oriented design isn't design-oriented research: On the tensions between design and research in an implicit design discipline. Knowl. Technol. Policy 20, 193–200.

Fuad-Luke, A., 2013. Design Activism: Beautiful Strangeness for a Sustainable World. Routledge.

Gaver, W., 2012. What Should We Expect from Research Through Design?, in: Proceedings of the SIGCHI Conference on Human Factors in Computing Systems, CHI '12. ACM, New York, NY, USA, pp. 937–946.

Håkansson, M., Sengers, P., 2013. Beyond Being Green: Simple Living Families and ICT, in: Proceedings of the SIGCHI Conference on Human Factors in Computing Systems, CHI '13. ACM, New York, NY, USA, pp. 2725–2734.

Horn, M.S., Leong, Z.A., Greenberg, M.D., Stevens, R., 2015. Kids and thermostats: Understanding children's involvement with household energy systems. Int. J. Child-Comput. Interact. 3–4, 14–22.

Hornecker, E., Marshall, P., Rogers, Y., 2007. From Entry to Access: How Shareability Comes About, in: Proceedings of the 2007 Conference on Designing Pleasurable Products and Interfaces, DPPI '07. ACM, New York, NY, USA, pp. 328–342.

Kaptelinin, V., Bannon, L.J., 2012. Interaction Design Beyond the Product: Creating Technology-Enhanced Activity Spaces. Human–Computer Interact. 27, 277–309.

Pierce, J., Strengers, Y., Sengers, P., Bødker, S., 2008. Introduction to the Special Issue on Practice-oriented Approaches to Sustainable HCI. ACM Trans Comput-Hum Interact 20, 20:1–20:8.

Schön, D.A., 1983. The reflective practitioner: How professionals think in action. Basic books.

Smørgrav Viddal, I., Lærgreid, L., Søyland, M., Eilertsen, I., 2015. Eco-agents. URL http://www.uio.no/studier/emner/matnat/ifi/INF2260/h15/presentations/Eco-agents/index.html

Sterling, S., Huckle, J., 2014. Education for Sustainability. Routledge.

Stolterman, E., McAtee, J., Royer, D., Thandapani, S., 2009. Designerly Tools. Presented at the Undisciplined! Design Research Society Conference 2008, Sheffield Hallam University, Sheffield, UK.

Verbeek, P.-P., 2015. Beyond interaction: A Short Introduction to Mediation Theory 12, 26–31.

Waters, C.N., Zalasiewicz, J., Summerhayes, C., Barnosky, A.D., Poirier, C., Gałuszka, A., Cearreta, A., Edgeworth, M., Ellis, E.C., Ellis, M., Jeandel, C., Leinfelder, R., McNeill, J.R., Richter, D. deB, Steffen, W., Syvitski, J., Vidas, D., Wagreich, M., Williams, M., Zhisheng, A., Grinevald, J., Odada, E., Oreskes, N., Wolfe, A.P., 2016. The Anthropocene is functionally and stratigraphically distinct from the Holocene. Science 351, aad2622.

Zimmerman, J., Forlizzi, J., 2014. Research Through Design in HCI, in: Olson, J.S., Kellogg, W.A. (Eds.), Ways of Knowing in HCI. Springer New York, pp. 167–189.

DESIGNING FOR TECHNOLOGY ENABLED CONSTRUCTIVISM LEARNING: EXPLORING A MANGROVE FOREST BIOME

Kaberi Naznin, Dr. Vivienne Farrell and Dr. Karola von Baggo
Swinburne University of Technology, PO Box 218 Hawthorn, Victoria 3122, Australia

ABSTRACT

Museums are places that can provide children with a vast and exciting world of information. However, constructivist learning theory suggests that static information displays are not the best way to help the children learn about the worlds being presented and that good learning outcomes occur when the learner directly interacts with, and reflects on, the subject material. In this research, the authors explored using new technologies to enable a constructivist learning environment for subject matter that children would not otherwise be able to interact with physically. We worked with a museum to construct a prototype interactive display to help children learn about the mangrove forest. Our evaluation of the prototype found that users were satisfied with the natural touch screen, the persistence of vision, media, storytelling, collaborative learning, and interactive artifacts. Issues included target age group, the shape of multi-touch tabletop, and story type. The technology offered opportunities to provide constructivist learning and was engaging and intuitive.

KEYWORDS

Constructivist learning, Museums' Application, Interactive Storytelling, Tangible User Interface, and Interactive Tabletop

1. INTRODUCTION

Constructivist learning theory suggests that for learning to occur, the student must be actively involved in the process of acquiring knowledge together with reasoning. Constructivism is not prescriptive in how it is implemented, nor how the student attains, manipulates or organizes the knowledge and can be as simple as listening to a lecture. According to the constructivist approach, as long as the student is actively reorganizing the information in a way that enables the knowledge to 'make sense', learning will occur. Typically, constructivist learning involves the physical engagement of the student in an activity that connects the mind and the body to the knowledge.

Activity based learning (where the learners physically engage with learning activities) occurs in an environment where students are encouraged to be active learners rather than passive observers. Children can develop knowledge and understand about the world through personal, social and culturally mediated experiences (Piscitelli et al. 2003). Field excursions are a good example of a constructivist learning environment where students are engaged both mentally and physically, using the senses of touch, feel and smell to aid discovery and where they are able to experience and determine locations, facts and develop situational emotions in context. Unfortunately, activity based learning activities are not always an available option for teaching children due to practical constraints (i.e., traveling 1,000's of kilometers to a mangrove forest to learn about ecosystems). In the past text books and images have been employed to passively provide information about a study topic (such as ecosystems). However, emerging technologies, such as tangible user interfaces, offer new opportunities for children to interact in an environment that is tactile, relevant and interactive.

Museums provide an important learning landscape for children as, rather than just reading about an object in a book, children can see the objects of study in 'real life'. Many museums are recognizing the important role they can play in learning by changing their educational programs to a more dynamic, engaging and enjoyable experience through the use of technology. In this way they hope to raise awareness of ecological challenges, human rights, globalization, tourism, gender aspects and so on.

The purpose of this research is to consider how technology can be used to encourage constructivist learning. In particular we examined the challenge of educating children about mangrove forests. Mangrove forests are complex and sensitive environments which are economically "worth an estimated US$ 180 billion and yet 50% of the world's mangrove forests have been destroyed over the past century" due to the construction of shrimp ponds, industrial developments, biological unbalance, global warming and more (Datta, 2008; Alongi, 2002; Muhibbullah, Amin, and Chowdhury, 2005). The mangrove forest is an important biome and of vast importance to mankind and however it is inaccessible for many to experience first-hand. This paper discusses the design of a learning space to encourage children to interact with physical objects related to the mangrove biome and receive digital feedback to enable constructivist, and active learning through developing the mind-body connection during the learning process (Anderson, Piscitelli and Everett 2008).

This paper will initially assess a variety of different learning methods in regards to their ability to provide a constructivist learning environment and their suitability to technical solutions for interactivity. Design concepts for a tangible user interface on the topic of the mangrove biome were developed and reviewed by museum staff and subject matter experts. Finally, a low fidelity prototype of our design concept was tested with a small group of users to assess if the design encourages active learning (Jokela 2003).

2. CURRENT USE OF TECHNOLOGY TO ENCOURAGE LEARNING THROUGH CONSTRUCTIVISM

An initial review of current literature relating to several learning methods, their relevance to constructivism and their suitability to possible technical solutions was undertaken. Twenty-six papers of various current technologies and relevant learning methods were analyzed for their suitability to encourage learning through constructivism. The authors recognize this is not an exhaustive list of the current literature, rather a strategic sample of relevant rigorously tested material that is presented in the Appendix A (please click this link, https://www.dropbox.com/s/9ci0yoo2ry26xo3/Appendix_Designing%20for%20Technology%20Enabled%20Constructivism%20Learning.docx?dl=0).

Tangible user interface technology was identified as a candidate technology for its ability to represent and provide educational material for children in a fun filled physically interactive way. From the literature review (see Appendix A), we found that the majority papers dealt with tangible tabletop systems, the benefits of which are defined by Garber (2012) as: nearly 50 people can interact with a tangible tabletop system simultaneously; it can be used as a table, hung on a wall, or embedded in other objects such as furniture; "You get your hands and brain working together" (Garber 2012, p.17). According to Sifteo's Merrill, tabletop systems encourage constructivist and active learning due to the enhanced mind-body connection. They also enable one hand and two handed interactions (Garber 2012).

The literature regarding current technologies and their suitability to facilitate various learning methods was analyzed. Table 2 shows the main findings from the literature review (Table 1 in the Appendix A) and presents a clear line from the past literature findings to current design consideration. It shows a summary of the constructivism learning methods to be employed in this research and the identified technology that will be used in the interactive learning space for this research.

Table 2. The purposes of using technologies

Learning Method	Technologies
Provides a physical connection and between the real and a virtual world	Tangible User Interface, Augmented reality Interactive diorama
Encourages students to verbalise and contextualise their understanding of the required knowledge	Interactive Storytelling
Visualizing art	Interactive Art

Figure 1. Our proposed initial design: A diorama for visualizing mangrove forest

3. INITIAL DESIGN CONCEPT

Our initial design concept was based on a combination of interactive art, interactive storytelling, tangible user interface (RFID chip) technology, and an interactive diorama (Table 2). An interactive diorama was used for visualizing information using storytelling concept incorporating the tangible user interface and RFID technology.

The design concepts of the proposed interactive diorama are described in Figure 1. The design concept was of a digital screen displayed on the top of the diorama showing an animated video of a mangrove forest environment (Part: a). In the middle of the diorama (Part: b), 3D objects create a physical view of a mangrove forest that offer a tangible interface (i.e. if someone touches those objects they can listen to a story and view video related to the object on the digital screen).

In the design concept, objects in the diorama are fixed and smaller than actual size; there are symbols of various species of mangrove trees and animals living in the forest. The artificial soil and river chain are used to make a more natural atmosphere and at the end of river chain as it meets to the ocean. Children can manipulate the objects by the magical tool (a reader). The magic tool (Part: g) has the shape of a leaf of a mangrove tree. There is a small sign (Part: f) in front of every object that contains the scientific name, family and other information related to the object. Children need to touch the level with the magical tool object in order to listen and view the relevant animated video. At the bottom (Part: c), the roots of mangrove trees and some species of fishes are displayed using an image (mangrove forest under the water). There is a button to listen to a biological description and ecosystem for those species. Instruction is available (Part: d) as a text and audio; and in (Part: e), users can listen to an ending story about the mangrove forest as a text or audio.

When the user attaches the entrance card of the museum with the magic tool (reader), the system can scan and read the user data which can be used to record the users' learning outcome and their attitude and interest in the content by analyzing their visit in terms of whether they required assistance, the time duration spent with the system and more.

The data collected from users' interaction would include:

- how much the user has learned from the system
- the most interesting features to the users: visualization or objects.
- the number of children who interacted with the system out of total number of children attending exhibition (i.e., percentage of interested children).
- the users' learning outcome/efficiency level (i.e., how many problems are solved and time is taken by the user).
- feedback provided for users based on correct answers and how many attempts to solve the problems.

4. FEEDBACK FROM EXPERTS AND RE-DESIGN

To further refine the requirements of the mangrove forest design, expert feedback was sought through focus groups. To facilitate the focus group, professionals were invited from the museum staff at the Übersee-Museum, Bremen, Germany and the disciplines of ecology and, technology from the University of Bremen, to walk through issues and implications of the initial design concept. The focus groups revealed the following:

Content:

- The content was considered to be interesting and important for children to learn. Nevertheless, it was considered essential to provide freedom to choose any mangrove forest in the world.
- The addition of a storyboard for users who are interested in listening to a short game based story to involve them more with the system. The addition of an ecosystem into the story would enable learning of dependencies and interconnectivities between humans, trees, and animals.

Interaction:

- Children's involvement in the system was to be explorative and not replicate the classroom environment.
- More interaction was considered necessary in order to involve the children with the system.

- The collaboration was considered advantageous for children's learning process; therefore, a multi-user functionality to be included.

Technical perspective:

- Need to do more research on advanced technologies in museums and build a standard model that will be fit for mangrove forests in any region.

Museum Installation:

- Installation of interactive diorama would be useful for children to allow them natural interactions.
- Only using the magic tool will not be sufficient for interactive learning for children.
- Concept designer should mention the size of diorama with each part.

Re-design of the initial design concept

The initial concept was re-designed to incorporate expert recommendations. As recommended, the redesign incorporated an interactive tabletop to enhance the interactive diorama. The interactive tabletop is also a type of interactive diorama as is found from the diorama table (Takahashi and Sasada 2005). With the tabletop system, children can explore and undertake different interactions using the multi-touch functionality allowing 50 children to work collaboratively (Kim et al. 2007). The tangible tabletop, interactive storytelling, interactive art and user profile have been included in the re-design; these being the various fields of technology identified, that encourage learning through constructivism for children in a fun way in museums. We envisage that a one-handed gesture technique will be used to control the system and the interactions (Kim et al. 2007). In the final system, the user will use the move, zoom-in, zoom-out, left-rotation, right-rotation instructions to control of the interactive tabletop to visualize the mangrove forest as shown in Figure 2 (Kim et al. 2007). In the next section we well describe our second design concept.

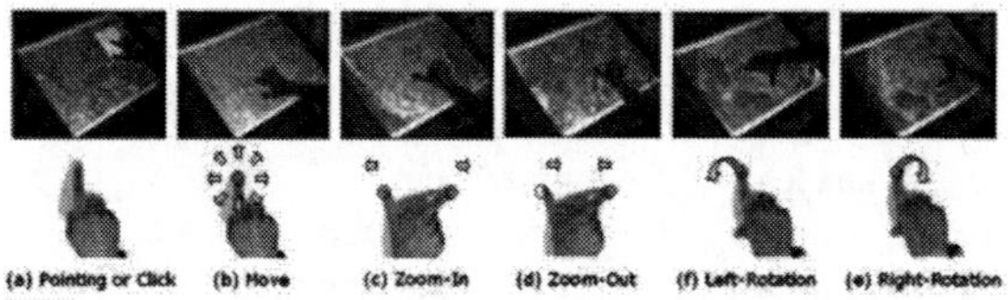

Figure 2. One handed instruction set (Kim et al. 2007, p.393)

4.1 Design Scenarios for Our Proposed Second Design Concept

In our second design concept, a ferocious royal Bengal tiger is shown on the screen of the interactive table with sound to attract children to the system. When children touch the screen, the background screen is changed and one animated leaf pops up with the name and character fields. The fingerprint of the user is captured to track individual activities with the system. Children are asked to enter their name and a password into the system and to choose a character to travel with into the forest (i.e., an avatar). They are then presented with a menu that looks like the road to a mangrove forest made from bamboo and wood, different species of mangrove trees line the road. There are four items that appear in the menu: Travel to World Mangrove; Story time; Tell Story and Pop quiz.

Travel to World Mangrove: Users can explore the mangrove forest by selecting their preferred region through the world map. The mangrove forests are represented by mangrove trees. After choosing the region, users will listen to information about the transportations available to reach the desired destination. Users can travel by: boat (journey by river); ladder (climbing trees); clock (changing daylight); hand (keeping hands on mud or sand, users will see the changes of behavior and shape on that surface); circle (viewing objects from different angles); underwater helmet to watch and understand the spectacular underwater life (Kaufman 2010). The user can explore the forest with their chosen character (3D avatar). It is possible for an avatar to move east, west, north and south using various interaction tools. Zoom in and out are also possible. For Information Visualization, X (all media: video, audio and text) and Y (different objects' names) axis are used; choosing X and Y axis, users can view the related information on the screen, see Figure 3 (this figure is from the paper mockup design of the evaluation).

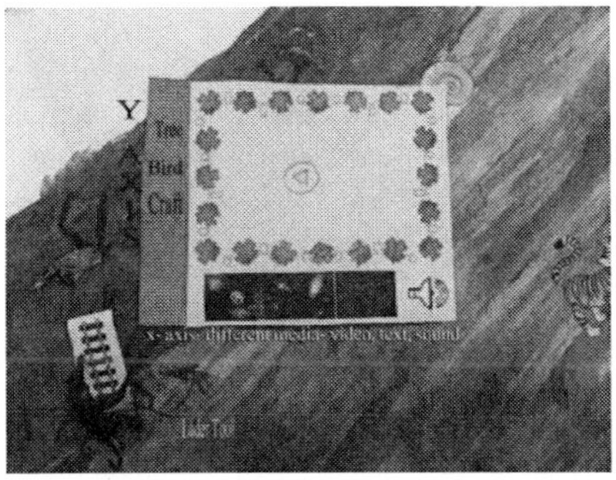

Figure 3. Travel to world mangrove: For information visualization, x-axis and y-axis and, interaction tool- ladder (from our mock-up)

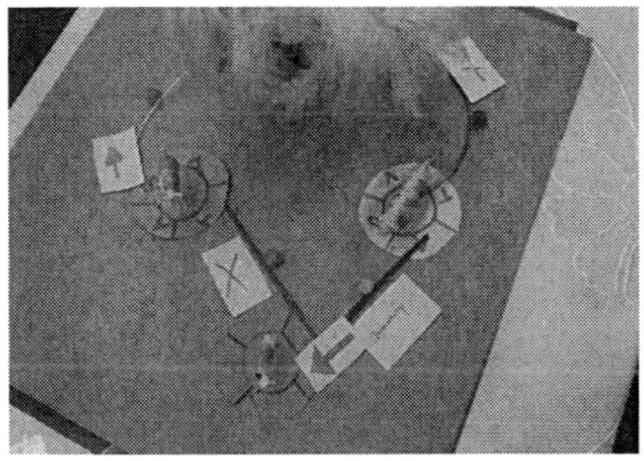

Figure 4. Physical POV on the screen of interactive tabletop during Story time (from our mock-up)

Story time: Users will listen to a story from speaking animals who introduce themselves, their eating habits, living places, behavior, favorite things and so on. The avatar will act as an instructor for the users at each level. The avatar will give instruction on creating the environment of a forest using 3D physical objects (POVs) on the screen see Figure 4 (Jordà 2010). After putting an object on the interactive table, a circle will appear around the object with four different media (video, audio, sound and text). Users can obtain information related to the object in their preferred media type. In the same way, information will be visible for more objects. Users can generate connecting lines between POVs by finger and stories will be played for similarities and conflicts between objects. In this case, users can listen to a story based on organism, population, community or ecosystem (Barange et al, 2010).

Tell story: Users can produce their own mangrove forest, tell stories, record their own voices and save their story. They also have the opportunity to listen to the stories of others.

Pop quiz: Users will find a Pop quiz and balloons. They can shoot these balloons to open images for each balloon; the avatar will then ask questions to test their learning. Questions will be based on animals and tree species, soil and water, organism, population, community, ecosystem and so on. The avatar will congratulate the user when they answer the question correctly.

4.2 Developing Final Prototype

To assist in evaluating our conceptual design, a mock-up prototype was developed. In this step, it was necessary to decide what aspects of the system should or should not be prototyped as the proposed system. We decided to prototype Travel to World Mangrove, Story Time, Tell Story and Pop Quiz.

User Activities

There are four different types of activities in the prototype. The first task for users exploring the mangrove forest is to select a specific region to visit. While traveling through the mangrove forest, participants will view objects and listen to stories on various objects (e.g., mangrove trees, animals and other living and non-living). Their main task is to attain information about mangrove forests, if they travel into the forest using various interaction tools and listen to the information carefully, they should be able to answer questions which are available in the Pop Quiz activity. If they answer the pop quiz correctly, they will receive a prize (real present). This was to help encourage the student's participation for a prolonged time while testing.

To assist in the process, a scenario was developed to assist in creating a single focus for all participants reducing the variable that may bias the data.

Scenario

Thirteen years old girl named Alexandra is in a science museum to visit an exhibition. She is very curious about different technologies and nature. Alexandra has visited various illustration, interactive diorama, and demonstrations. Alexandra also wants to explore herself with the technologies that are used in the museum, as she has already achieved some knowledge about science and technology in school. Now, she is in front of the amazing interactive tabletop, and a mysterious forest is projected on the wall. In this forest, she has found a ferocious tiger. She enjoys the tiger's roaring and the nature on the digital screen. This mysterious forest makes her inquisitive to know more about this interactive system and a nature of the mangrove forest.

She has found a large interactive table that includes a touch screen to explore the details. A welcome message with a green leaf appears for entering name and character. She writes her name and chooses a monkey as a 3D character. In this way, she has just logged into the system.

Wow, it seems like the entrance road of a mangrove forest, one road is made of bamboo and wood. She has found four options such as Travel to World Mangrove Forest, Story Time, Tell Story and Pop Quiz. She selects Pop quiz but an avatar appears and advises her to visit 'Travel to World Mangrove Forest' first. Now she selects Travel to World Mangrove Forest. She is very excited ends up completing Story Time, Tell Story and Pop Quiz.

Create Paper Prototype

Based on the scenario discussed above, a paper prototype was developed with interactions. Different materials were used to make it attractive for children such as colorful images, water colors for drawings, colored pencils, wood, different kinds of colorful papers, scissors, glue, children's toys (3D toys of various animals), and decorative items such as paper made flowers, circles shaped colorful cottons and clothes. Some interactions and features were not possible to construct due to the difficulty of implementation using paper prototype and the time constraint. This included the secondary display of this concept, under water interaction, a complex game based questions and so on.

4.3 Usability Test

To test the prototype, primary and secondary stakeholders were identified. Early secondary school age children were identified as the primary stakeholders, because of the nature of the topic requires a basic scientific knowledge and reasoning as well as a capacity to retain some scientific knowledge regarding mangroves such as genus, species, and scientific names. Further, it was preferred that students have some experience in the use of technology. Two secondary school students aged 12 and 16 years were chosen from the International school in Bremen, Germany to represent the primary stakeholder group; Two university students were included as secondary target users, who would potentially be involved in designing for technology in future careers, further one technical expert from University of Bremen actively working in this field was also included in the testing team. A facilitator interviewed the five participants for the duration of approximately half an hour each. The aim of this evaluation was to investigate the impact of the workflow of the interactive tabletop on the different users in order to complete their task. Interactions with the system were also observed and feedback about the story, game and so on. During the testing session 'think aloud techniques' were used while an observer took notes and the session was recorded by video. At the end of the sessions, participants were rewarded with prizes for the correct answers to the quizzes.

The following are the steps necessary to reach their destination and to complete the activities (Figure 5).

Travel to World Mangrove Forest: Different users selected different regions and explored the mangrove forest with various interactions. They found several interactive tools while traveling in the forest, hear stories about trees, animals, soil, water, and watch animals from every angle.

Story Time: Users kept physical objects on the screen and made the connection by finger to listen to the relevant stories representing a more abstract level. Stories based on organism, population, community and ecosystem.

Tell Story: Users generated and recorded their own story.

Pop Quiz: The participants needed to solve questions using a Pop quiz. If answered correctly, the student received a prize. This was the final step of this test.

Figure 5. The four steps: a) Travel to world mangrove, b) Story time, c) Tell story, and d) Pop quiz

After the test, the users were interviewed about their experience, workflow, content, interactions, and their opinions about identifying suitable target groups. The analysis results of test session are described in the next section.

4.4 Discussion

Three categories of users participated in the prototype test: two children (primary target users), two university students (secondary target users) and one design expert. Some important feedback from users was obtained from the interviews and text session and is summarized here.

Issues and Feedbacks from Users

The following observations and feedback was obtained from the user interviews:

Draw the path you took with the system.

Two school children were able to draw a picture of their progress through the system and to talk about deeper activities that were inside each. Students from the university explained the detailed workflow by telling a story that covered the whole working process of the system.

What were the special things with this learning space technology?

One child talked about natural touch and the need for a little bit bigger screen and different types of interactions to make the system special. She also mentioned about the four types of media (video, audio, text and sound) as she found that listening to the information was a special feature of the system.

What did you like most and what did you like the least?

Users identified various features. Their favorite things included the screen design, animals in the forest, speaking animals that introduce themselves and tell stories, interactive circle for moving animals (possibly to view animals from every angle), ladder (climbing trees), the four types of media, using of POVS, and collaborative learning. They liked the biological context of the mangrove forest: trees, animals, nature. The users also identified features they felt were not as useful such as the camera, which is available in the Tell Story activity; unexpected touch (it is a large screen and users were concerned they would touch something they did not want to). In the Story Time stage, children may put objects on the screen of the multi-touch table that has no digital information attached to it.

If you were a designer, how would you build your mangrove forest concept?

One student offered that she would do the same as the existing concept, but that the Pop Quiz questions would be more complicated.

Views on the Interactive storytelling

Children recommended to add an adventure story, such as game based stories where there is functionality hidden behind the animals; the ability to play with the animals; and create steps, where after every step the users have to do something for the story to be continued.

Preferred target group? Do you think that target group 12 to 16 is suitable for this system?

16 years old children may find the display boring; however, it may be suitable for 14 or 15 years olds.

Would you prefer a book or an interactive system to assist you in learning about mangroves? If an interactive system then why would you prefer it to a book?

Interactive systems were preferred by participants as it enables learning with fun. Children could view and listen to the sounds of animals, and explore things by themselves rather than being told by a teacher.

Others

Environment: This system could be used in a climate house that would be like a mangrove forest.

Table shape: Another shape, rather than a regular table, use one that would look more like a mangrove.

From the above discussion, users were more or less satisfied with many aspects of the mangrove forest prototype such as the various interaction possibilities (ladder, circle, hand and so on), natural touches with bigger screen, using POVS the four different media for obtaining information (video, audio, text and sound), storytelling concept, collaborative learning, interactive artifacts, biological context (mangrove forest: trees, animals, natures) and so on. However, there were some issues not as positive for users such as the: age range of target group (12 to 16 years); table shape (why a regular table); and story type. Based on users' feedback, the target users' age range may be reduced (12 to 15 years or 12 to 14 years); game based (hide and seek), adventure stories can be suitable for other interactions and step the user through the stages of the interface; a more realistic shape could be overlaid on the table to change the shape and make it more relevant to the mangrove and interesting for the children.

5. CONCLUSION

The main focus of this paper was to explore the use of interactive technologies to support learning for children through constructivism. Constructivist learning practice was matched with current technologies and tools that were adaptable to establishing an integrated work space where children could engage in developing the 'mind-body connection' for example touching physical objects, listening stories, and doing natural interactions to enhance the learning process. Our tangible interface prototype of a mangrove forest appeared to be well received by the small group of users we investigated. The children's excitement and concentration during the test sessions evidenced their eagerness to engage with the tangible learning space. Together with the positive feedback received from the children and the designers it appears that this use of technology could be used to enhance a child's museum experience and give them an experience that would be difficult to articulate or present in books.

The results of this study would be of interest to educators, educational media designers and for those who wish to present areas of interest using a virtual tangible interface that represents the physical environment.

The authors of this study are aware that further work will need to be undertaken to ensure that the eagerness of the students was not merely a novelty and anticipation of rewards from the quiz. Further, the authors recognize the limitations of the results given; that not all of the features were developed at this stage; that the results are reliant on a small population of the potential stakeholders and that the testing was with a prototype version of the learning space. However, despite these limitations, the positive feedback and the ease with which the children interacted with the prototype continue to motivate us to experiment with tools and technologies designed to encourage constructivist learning.

REFERENCES

Anderson, D., Piscitelli, B. and Everett, M. 2008. Competing Agendas: Young Children's Museum Field Trips. Curator: The Museum Journal, 51, 3, 253–273.

Alongi, D. 20002. Present State and Future of the World's Mangrove Forests. Environmental Conservation. 29, 3, 331–349.

Barange, M., Field, J., G. and Harris, R., P. 2010. Marine Ecosystems and Global Change. Oxford University Press.

Datta, R., K. 2008. Coastal Ecosystems: Hazards, Management, and Rehabilitation. Centre for Science & Technology of the Non-Aligned and Other Developing Countries (NAM & S&T Centre).

Garber, L. 2012. Tangible User Interfaces: Technology You Can Touch. Computer, 45, 6, 15 –18.

Ishii, H. 2008. The Tangible User Interface and Its Evolution. Communication ACM 51, 6, 32–36.

Jordà, S. 2010. The Reactable: Tangible and Tabletop Music Performance. In Proceedings of the 28th of the International Conference Extended Abstracts on Human Factors in Computing Systems, 2989–2994. CHI EA '10. New York, NY, USA: ACM.

Jokela, T.et al. 2003. The Standard of User-centered Design and the Standard Definition of Usability: Analyzing ISO 13407 against ISO 9241-11. Proceedings of the Latin American Conference on Human-computer interaction. ACM.

Kaufman, H. 2010. The Lightness of Your Touch. In ACM SIGGRAPH 2010 Art Gallery, 398–399. SIGGRAPH '10. New York, NY, USA: ACM.

Kim, J., Park, J., Kim, H., K., and Lee, C. 2007. HCI (Human Computer Interaction) Using Multi-touch Tabletop Display. In IEEE Pacific Rim Conference on Communications, Computers and Signal Processing, PacRim, 391 –394.

Muhibbullah, M., Amin, S., M., N., and Chowdhury, A., T. 2005. Some Physico-chemical Parameters of Soil and Water of Sundarban Mangrove Forest, Bangladesh. Journal of Biological Sciences, 5(3), 354–357.

Piscitelli, B., Everett, M., Weier, K., and QUT Museums Collaborative Enhancing Young Childrens Museum Experiences: a Manual for Museum Staff. Brisbane. QUT, (2003).

Takahashi, K., and Sasada, S. 2005. Diorama Table. In Proceedings of the 13th Annual ACM International Conference on Multimedia, 1077–1078. Multimedia'05. Hilton, Singapore: ACM.

REFLECTIONS ON COST-BENEFIT ANALYSES CONCERNING UNIVERSAL DESIGN OF ICT SOLUTIONS

Till Halbach and Kristin Skeide Fuglerud
Norwegian Computing Center, Oslo, Norway

ABSTRACT

The proper calculation of the return on investment into universally designed ICT products and services is of interest to the public and private sector alike. This work overviews the findings of related research and a number of available case studies, discusses outcomes, categorizes reported effects, and suggests future research topics and suitable research methodology. Conducting cost-benefit analyses appears to be a very complex area due to the vast number of influencing factors. The effects have to be differentiated for all stakeholders, such as users, service providers, society, etc., and they have to be related with uncertainty estimations and associated sensitivity calculations. All review articles and case studies show that the benefits of universally design solutions outweigh their initial investment.

KEYWORDS

Cost, benefit, ROI, bottom-line, universal design

1. INTRODUCTION

When asked why universal design of ICT solutions is an important and meaningful goal, advocates of accessibility technologies and universal design in the ICT domain often argue with international legislation, such as the UN Convention on the Rights of Persons with Disabilities (United Nations 2006), or national bills like the Americans with Disabilities Act in the U.S. (U.S. Congress 1990) or the Anti-Discrimination and Accessibility Act in Norway (Norwegian Ministry of Children and Equality and Social Inclusion 2014). In fact, in Norway fines could be given to violators of the Regulation regarding Universal Design of ICT Solutions (Ministry of Local Government and Modernisation 2014). Norwegian legislation specifies that new electronic solutions of both public and private service providers must be universally designed, with the goal to contribute to a higher motivation for new, inclusive solutions. The legislation is operationalized by referring to the most widely accepted standard in this area, namely the W3C WCAG 2.0 guideline which was adopted as an ISO/IEC International Standard (ISO/IEC 40500:2012) in October 2012. However, the law has not been enforced very strictly, and the mechanism of fines has so far not been used.

While social inclusion, equality of opportunities, and anti-discrimination are honorable goals in themselves, it is our impression that they are not viewed as weighty enough by the industry to be taken seriously. Moreover, research has shown that there is a negative attitude towards universal design (UD), for instance that it is seen as expensive (Eikhaug, Onny and Gheerawo 2010), and that it leads to boring and unaesthetic solutions (Dong et al. 2004). The latter work also explicitly mentions the lack of business cases to promote the advantages of UD.

To convince the public and particularly the private sector to develop universally designed solutions, cost-benefit analyses (CBAs) explicitly showing the benefits and expenses of UD are necessary, as well as business cases suggesting how to achieve a positive bottom line.

This work overviews some of the previous research regarding cost-benefit analyses of UD, discusses the research findings, and, based on that, provides suggestions for research methodology and further work. The remainder of the article is structured in a straight-forward manner: A number of related studies and case studies is surveyed and discussed, after which suggestions for further research on this topic are formulated. The conclusion is drawn in the end. The major contributions of this work are the overview of related research in this area and the suggestions for future research topics based on a thorough discussion of the findings.

2. COST-BENEFIT ANALYSES

One of the first impact analyses of the consequences of Norway's new legislation regarding universal design of ICT is a report considering the transformation of an existing website with content management system from a low degree of universal design to a high degree (Halvorsen & Andersen 2007). The report looks at a number of activities with impact for an overall cost increase, including an analysis of existing content, acquirement of (external) technical expertise, acquirement of new tools for content generation and management, modification of existing tools, and testing and quality assurance. Some of these tasks can be seen as one-time expenses, while operation and maintenance of the new solution are claimed to outweigh one-time investments in terms of much higher costs. It is also argued that obviously costs must be seen in relation to how many people work with the development of UD inside a company. Another aspect is in how far assistive technology (AT) can be applied to reach over the inaccessibility gap. The authors argue that the use of AT may save a lot of money as compared to an entire redesign of the solution, which is estimated to be very costly. The report further summarizes some earlier international cost estimates. The presented numbers are based on interviews, partly with IT engineers and advisors, partly with buyers, sellers, and manufacturers of web solutions, and partly with representatives for companies which help other companies to increase the inclusiveness of their web site, such as Deque (Brodkin 2007). The authors also shed some light on the socio-economic analysis of the benefits of accessibility, but concentrate on simply listing the benefits and rather refers to (Boardman et al. 2006) for the proper methodology with cost-benefit analyses.

Another work by the Agency for Public Management and eGovernment, here dubbed Difi, estimates the one-time expenses of requiring WCAG 2.0 for public organizations' web portals and the continuous yearly costs for multimedia production (Direktorat for forvaltning og ikt 2009). The calculations distinguish between costs related to existing solutions vs. new equipment/tools, costs which must be seen in relation with a one-time upgrade of content vs. the continuous preparation of multimedia, and costs associated with training. With other words, there are expenses for the provider of the content management systems (CMSs), and expenses for the content publisher. The report also differentiates between internal costs and expenses for buying external services. The calculation model recognizes, by means of a simple multiplication factor, that web sites from discerned organizations, such as companies, schools, small and big municipalities, etc. vary in size and complexity. The uncertainty in the estimates is quantified by means of Monte Carlo simulations, resulting in range of costs where the estimate will lie with a probability of for instance 90%. Regarding possible benefits, the report restricts itself to listing of a number of arguably non-measurable qualitative advantages, which are mostly related to benefits for the society.

In another analysis regarding the impact of implementing UD in web solutions (Standard Norge 2010), the estimation of expenses follows Difi's derivation of costs, while mentioning that the starting point for the improvements is important, too: Does the solution fulfill WCAG yet, or does it have to be built from scratch? The authors do not fail to consider costs related to buying new tools such as for publication, testing, and content management. However, the main value of this report is to extend the scope of CBAs to include private entities, to quantify the savings/benefits, and to consider the three guidelines WCAG 2 (all three levels), ATAG 1, and ISO 8241-20. The report also fills in some of the estimated parameters in Difi's models with actual measurements, by means of a process dubbed Unified Web Evaluation Methodology (UWEM), while properly discussing the uncertainty of the approach. Two cases are mentioned as examples for the quick and positive return on investment that follows increased accessibility, one from the public and one from the private sector.

Difi's first report is extended to include companies and private organizations in a follow/up report (Direktorat for forvaltning og ikt 2010b). The authors use roughly the same methods and models, and follow otherwise the considerations of the last report, replacing some estimated parameters with more accurate, measured values, where known. However, this work goes a bit more into detail and discusses matters like what is the definition of the main solution (a requirement in the Regulation), how much content is going to be produced in the future, and what are the costs of buying a new CMS vs. the costs for a major upgrade. It is also mentioned that the expenses for user testing need to be part of the equation. Taking all these aspects into account, they argue that a sensitivity analysis as mandated previously is not meaningful since many relevant parameters cannot be quantified, or may even be hidden. This report is a bit more detailed than the previous one by diversifying benefits for users, service providers, and society. But as done elsewhere before, the authors claim that quantifying the benefits of UD is not reliable enough in order to provide useful results.

An impact study regarding the consequences for self-service machines is given in another report (Vista Utredning AS 2010). This work employs a welfare economics analysis (Longva & Tverstøl 2014), utilizes the findings from a survey among people with visual impairment (MMI 2004), and applies these findings to visually impaired, dyslectics, and elderly. The authors calculate costs and benefits for the machine types ATM and ticket, while for queuing and goods there was not enough user behavior data to give a proper estimate. Where given, the benefits outweigh the costs. The calculation of costs is based on the comparison of a universally designed alternative and a version without particular UD measures, accounting for a natural progression towards more universally designed solutions. The estimation of benefits considers advantages for users with and without impairments, and for the machine-owning organization as well. However, both costs and benefits estimations are bound to many uncertainties and assumptions, and this is also honored in the included sensitivity calculation.

Yet another impact study considers the implementation of a guideline for the design of electronic forms in the public sector (Direktorat for forvaltning og ikt 2010a). Here, it is argued that a quantitative analysis would not lead to meaningful results, and therefore the work concentrates on the qualitative effects. However, the study lacks a real cost-benefit analysis, and important organizations like the Norwegian Labor and Welfare Administration have been omitted from the expert panel. Other shortcomings are that the study has neither referred to relevant work nor taken into account previous impact analyses.

Although being rather generic, the topic cost estimations of software projects is related, and fruitful conclusions can be drawn from considerations regarding the proper estimation of return on investment (ROI) in IT projects and be applied to development processes dealing with universally designed software solutions. One particular work discusses numerous approaches to computing reliable and sustainable cost estimates, such as the use of estimation models vs. expert assessment (Jørgensen 2008). There appear to be many aspects and degrees of freedom in the course of choosing a proper strategy to calculate an estimate, each with their own advantages and drawbacks, like for instance following an analytical approach and even using plain intuition.

In another publication, the same author lists a number of influencing factors, such as direct vs. indirect effects, quantifiable vs. non-quantifiable effects, short-term vs. long-term impact, high-risk vs. low-risk, and others (Jørgensen 2011). In particular the impact for internal processes is mentioned to increase the problem complexity of estimate computation considerably. The author also points at the necessary combination of skills, knowledge, and IT investments for getting the most out of IT projects. It is furthermore relevant to know that IT projects faced with a high degree of uncertainty and measurement problems, as often the case in UD projects, typically overestimate the ROI. According to the author there is no well established way for the calculation of the ROI, but it is advisable to combine several methods and compute a number of ROI values with associated confidence intervals. For good examples, it is referred to (Senter for statlig økonomistyring 2009).

The recognition of universal design in the requirement specification and its subsequent implementation on the ICT sector can also be seen as a simple IT investment. This is especially true for software-only projects but depends when it comes to self-service machines and other products which involve hardware. However, if this is a valid assumption, some results from previous research are related as well (Brynjolfsson & Hitt 1996), detailing that the gross marginal product for computer capital is 81%, and that the return on IT investment exceeds that of non-IT capital investment. While this basically means that the investment of IT capital is low as compared to the revenue generated by IT, the study must be interpreted with care. First, measuring a company's productivity has changed considerably since this study was conducted, with the arrival of the Web, Internet points of sale, online customer support, and so on. Second, the marked has changed a lot too, with the arrival of many services (as compared to previous products). Also, the study considers only companies and does not include the public sector. The consequences for society are neither of concern.

Another related research field to seek inspiration from is architecture and the design of physical environments, as this is also where UD originates from. One particular case study considers a building claimed to be universally designed (Danford 2003). Four populations of individuals are involved during the evaluation, three with various impairments, and one control group without impairments. The participants' activities are quantified in terms of their (subjective) perception and (objective) performance by means of different measures/metrics. The former is called Environmental Utility Measure (EUM), and the latter is dubbed Functional Performance Measure (FPM). The study compares the collected data regarding the building of concern to the metrics measured for "most other buildings".

Yet another work considers four artificial buildings with different degrees of universal design (Grimble et al. 2010). The work involves users with temporary and permanent conditions and impairments, and a control group without impairments. A number of subjective and objective metrics for all buildings are then compared with each other.

A rather extensive analysis of the economic effects of UD for buildings is given in (Medby et al. 2006). This work concentrates on a thorough discussion of the topic and establishing the proper methodology first. A number of important questions are formulated and answered, like what is a universally designed solution, which parameters to acknowledge in the calculations, and how to deal with risk, among others. The authors also argue that the given constraints, such as whether a reference point for measurements exists, may be dominant in the proper choice of methodology, be it cost-benefit, cost-efficiency, or cost-effect. Finally, the work gives two interesting case studies; one for the upgrading of an existing environment, and one for involving UD as a process in a project from scratch.

The costs related to excluding people from certain products and services is found to be important to justify measures to increase the accessibility of buildings, as an earlier study shows (National Council of Disability 2001). In the authors' opinion, existing civil-rights laws typically put too much emphasis on the direct costs of inclusive design while failing to highlight the economical consequences of inaccessible design in order to determine the efficiency of accessible-accommodations strategies.

3. CASE STUDIES

In addition to cost-benefit analyses, we have surveyed a number of case studies, 15 in total, and organized their outcomes into a few main categories. These case studies involve the following actors (TNO STB 1998),(OneVoice for Accessible ICT 2010): British Telecom, Telefónica, NCR (owned by AT&T, produces ATMs, software and web design for bank applications), Siemens, Philips Design, Landmark (small independent design company), Visual Position Ltd, HM Revenue & Customs, Legal & General, BBC, The British Museum, IBM's intranet, CNET's website, Tesco's online home grocery service, and Virgin's website.

There is a great variety of approaches to achieve universal design and accessibility. WCAG (2) is typically regarded as the de facto standard in this area. It is, however, often not documented to what extent the resulting product or solution does conform to these guidelines, and if other (and which) methods have been used to measure the degree of UD.

In addition to social, ethical and humanitarian benefits of UD, the case studies supply us with a number of business-related outcomes, here organized into six main categories to ease the overview:

1. **Improved products and services**
    - More accessible mainstream products: Improved product with accessibility features, such as better displays, synthetic voice option, more accessible keyboards, tactile mark on keyboard no 5, wheelchair access, insert coins without force (only gravity), large keyboard, allow plug in of ear phones, have voice-over (audio instructions when moving finger over screen) , street phones has features to increase volume for the hearing impaired (or in noisy environments), light on landline phones indicating ringing (for deaf people or in quiet environments) (BT, NCR, Telefónica)
    - Potential spin-offs
    - New access technologies: alternative versions of information material: Braille, large print, audio (BT), or picture telephone and a home assistant (Siemens)
    - Improved quality of service: the same quality of service for anyone who needs or prefers to customize their computing devices, use assistive technologies (ATs), or requires clear, easy to follow content (HMRC)
    - Increased speed of service: all customers can now self-serve through channels open 24 hours a day, seven days a week (HMRC), and improved quality of service

2. **Market and customer satisfaction**
    - Increased marketability: by increasing functionality for all users
    - Increase international marketability: More and more countries introduce UD and accessibility into their legislation, and thus, to be able to sell across international markets, it is necessary to consider these aspects.
    - Improved customer satisfaction: best scores in usability ratings (VP)
    - The website is future proofed for new technologies (VP)
    - Increased the customer growth rate with between 100 and 200 percent (Telefónica)
    - Reach new markets and attract more customers (Bias & Mayhew 2005)
    - Retain customers (Bias & Mayhew 2005)
    - Support for people with temporary difficulties: Including features that make products and services usable for persons with disabilities will also make them easy to use for people with temporary difficulties, such as a broken arm, lost glasses, walking with at pram or luggage etc.
    - Increase market share (Bias & Mayhew 2005)
    - Reduce user errors and time to complete tasks (Bias & Mayhew 2005)
    - Increase success rate and user satisfaction (Bias & Mayhew 2005)
    - Increase ease of use, ease of learning and trust (Bias & Mayhew 2005)
    - Increased number of visits, return visits, and length of visits (Bias & Mayhew 2005)
3. **Community relations and reputation**
    - Built a reputation of an exemplar public body: engaging and consulting all our customers as to the way we do things, and building trust that we are a responsible organisation (HMRC)
    - Increased the number of people that they reach through awareness campaigns and external presentations (BT)
    - Grown reputation: credibility from the social responsibility stance (VP)
    - Raised brand awarenes: a market leading website according to BBC radio and TV review, judged to be easier to access and use compared to other sites.
    - Great feedback from the web community (BBC)
    - Great recognition from winning the Jodi Award, judges stated: "a high profile international museum, setting new standards in what should be in place in our online sectoral provision" (BM)
    - Contributed to wider inclusion objectives by promoting cultural identity on the web and raising awareness of the ICT barriers to the experience of culture, to help overcome digital exclusion (BM)
    - Responded to an increasingly socially minded and demanding audience (BM)
4. **Internal processes and employees**
    - Maximized employee engagement and productivity
    - Improved supply chain management
    - Incorporated international and in-house accessibility standards, and regular user consultancy (HMRC)
    - Developed innovation and skills - making customisable web pages that are usable and accessible by all, with an expert accessibility team (BBC)
    - Improved service provision and delivery - with solutions captured as practice guidelines for other customisable developments (BBC)
    - Advance research - surveying UK disabled communities to gain a better understanding of assistive technologies (BBC)
    - Stimulation to design, develop, communicate and interpret the service of accessible online experiences (BM)
    - Pursue new customers - a clear practice for reaching new users, using expert partners and working to high international standards (VP)

5. **Financial effects**
   - Increased revenue: the take-up of some financial products via the website increased by 300% (L&G); a 90% increase in online life insurance sales (L&G); a £13 million increase in annual revenue from a £35,000 investment to develop an accessible website (Tesco); 68% uplift in revenue to £62 million after a redesign to incorporate accessibility standards. (Virgin); new channels to market/higher website traffic (VP)
   - Improved ROI: the Design for all approach also resulted in content that was more accessible and usable across a wide array of networks and devices (BBC); a 95% increase in online life quote requests (L&G); a 100% return on investment in five to six months. (L&G); by advertising quick wins from innovative, accessible websites to other stakeholders in the museum (BM)
   - Reduced costs: decrease support costs (Bias & Mayhew 2005); support costs were cut as there were zero complaints from people using handheld devices (L&G); web transactions cost approximately £0.27 each, compared with £3.22 for the phone and £6.56 for face to face (HMRC); an estimated saving of 66% a year on website maintenance as speed/effort required to manage content was reduced from an average of five days to half a day per job (L&G); lower website maintenance and server load costs, (VP); Reduce maintenance costs and save redesign costs (Bias & Mayhew 2005)□; a decrease in demand for alternative format materials e.g. printed materials in large print/embossed Braille as the website user is able to enlarge the font or use a screen reader (HMRC); by winning over key influencers, hence reaching whole communities at a relatively low expense (BM); a 40% reduction in bandwidth costs after introducing an accessible solution (IBM); reduce training and documentation costs (Bias & Mayhew 2005)
   - Increased cost efficiency: utilizing previous experience and guidelines ensured well targeted test and development costs (L&G); involving the accessibility team with prior experience of the broad range of users' needs throughout the development was crucial in keeping down cost of the number of user tests (L&G)
   - improved cash flow: easier for customers to pay the tax and duty they owe and receive the credits and payments due to them (HMRC)
6. **Legislation**
   - Avoid legal action/cost/damage by conforming to accessibility legislation

4. DISCUSSION

Industrial CBAs is a vast and well researched field, but the review of related literature in this work shows that only few attempts have been made when it comes to CBAs regarding UD of ICT solutions. We found it useful, though, to seek inspiration from other research areas, notably the return of IT investments, the costs of software projects, and universal design in housing and architecture.

Most of the overviewed papers deal with websites and webpages, but a few also consider self-service machines. Currently, there is no general methodology which the scientific community agrees upon. Some common conclusions can be drawn, though: It makes sense to classify costs into once-only investments and continuous efforts. The most important single-time cost contributors are acquisition of new software (and potentially hardware), use of external knowledge and services, as well as training of staff and developers. Operation, maintenance, and user involvement are the major contributors to the continuous costs, including the proper preparation of accessible content, and testing and quality assurance, as well as various user evaluations. To quantify the validity and reliability of such calculations, it is absolutely crucial to include proper uncertainty computations and to use control groups. Numerous works further agree upon that one of the first obstacles to be solved in such calculations is to address how to measure the degree of universal design. Suitable metrics have been proposed in the literature, but they have to be adapted specifically to UD and accessibility. Also, more work is needed when it comes to more detailed estimates of the benefits of UD on an individual, organizational, and societal basis.

There are critical voices that the aforementioned approach to quantify the benefits of UD for different entities (person/organization/society) would not lead to meaningful results due to the plethora of influencing factors, potentially hidden parameters, and the high degree of uncertainty in the computations. However, other researchers do think that it is indeed possible and meaningful to quantify the return on investment by using multiple methods and statistically combining their results and confidence intervals.

When a CBA attempt is made, the majority of reviewed studies estimates that the benefits of universally design solutions outweigh their initial investment without exception.

The main reasons for universally designed ICT solutions appear to be reaching broader audiences and complying with legislation. Many of the case companies consult experts in universal design (or do similar approaches), and/or they cooperate with user groups and interest organizations. Many of the case studies have been taken from major corporations with a long design tradition. They have large budgets, the means to involve multi-disciplinary teams, and opportunities for extensive testing and systematic utilization of user feedback. However, because the ICT design business is highly competitive, design processes and activities can also be spread out over networks of smaller companies (TNO STB 1998). While each company can only influence a very small proportion of the total development of products and services, the processes and practices of smaller companies are at least as important as that of the larger companies.

Management commitment towards UD is mentioned as important in several of the cases. Particularly, large companies have established organizational units or positions that have special competence and knowledge about UD. In most of the cases, special thought have been given to sharing that knowledge within the organization. Examples include having people from the UD unit participating in development projects. Interdisciplinary work is mentioned as important, and various forms of awareness activities are also mentioned.

User-centered design activities are frequently mentioned among the UD approaches used, such as focus groups, field observation, interviews with customers, and customer panels etc. The most common evaluation techniques are testing for compliance with relevant guidelines, expert evaluation, and usability testing.

Regarding the six categories of case study outcomes, the first category (products and services) covers both improved mainstream products and new or improved access technology (e.g., special purpose assistive technology). The second category (market and customers) is about the effects that UD may have on market shares, customer satisfaction, and customer efficiency. The third category is about reputations and relations with partners and community. The fourth category deals with effects on internal processes and employees, such as improved or more efficient development routines, and increased competence and engagement among the employees. The fifth category is about financial effects, such as increased revenue, improved ROI, and a decrease in support costs. The sixth and final category is to avoid legal action cost or damage by conforming to legislation.

5. CONCLUSION

This work has reviewed some related research regarding cost-benefit analyses of universal design in the ICT domain, and 15 related case studies were examined and categorized. There seems to be agreement on that it is far from trivial to study effects or to perform cost-benefit analyses of universal design. Real world cases are always affected by a number of uncertainties. To be able to arrive at meaningful results regarding the effects of universal design, it is necessary to get details on the company in question, its products and market, its organizational characteristics, the specific UD process and techniques that are applied, as well as surrounding and contextual factors that might influence the outcomes. Any findings should not only be viewed in terms of business parameters, but should also be seen in the light of accessibility and usability of the resulting ICT solution.

ACKNOWLEDGEMENT

The authors thank Ingvar Tjøstheim and Stein Erik Skotkjerra for their cooperation in the original project, and the Delta Centre at the Norwegian Directorate for Children, Youth and Family Affairs for original funding.

REFERENCES

Bias, R.G. & Mayhew, D.J., 2005. Cost-justifying usability: An update for the Internet age, Elsevier

Boardman, A.E. et al., 2006. Cost-Benefit Analysis: Concepts and Practice

Brodkin, J., 2007. Blind Americans demand Web access; Target fights back. *NetworkWorld*

Brynjolfsson, E. & Hitt, L., 1996. Paradox Lost? Firm-Level Evidence on the Return to Information System Spending. *Management Science*, 42(4), pp.541–558

Danford, G.S., 2003. Universal design people with vision, hearing, and mobility impairments evaluate a model building. Generations, 27(1), pp.91–94

Direktorat for forvaltning og ikt, 2009. Konsekvensvurdering av universell utforming på offentlige virksomheters nettsider 2009 – Standardiseringssekretariatet

Direktorat for forvaltning og ikt, 2010a. Konsekvensvurdering: ELMER som obligatorisk forvaltningsstandard for innbyggerskjemaer

Direktorat for forvaltning og ikt, 2010b. Krav til universell utforming av nettsider: Konsekvensvurdering av WCAG 2.0 AA

Dong, H., Keates, S. & Clarkson, P.J., 2004. Inclusive Design in Industry : Barriers , Drivers and the Business Case. , (C), pp.305–319

Eikhaug, Onny and Gheerawo, R., 2010. Innovating with People - The Business of Inclusive Design, The Norwegian Design Council

Grimble, M.D., Danford, G.S. & Schoell, D.M., 2010. The Effectiveness of Universal Design: Case Study Demonstrations

Halvorsen, R. & Andersen, C., 2007. Konsekvensanalyse av tilgjengelighetskrav til IKT i forslag til ny diskriminerings- og tilgjengelighetslov

Jørgensen, M., 2011. Lønner det seg å investere i IT-prosjekter? Hva vet vi om ROI prediksjoner?

Jørgensen, M., 2008. Prinsipper for Estimering av Utviklingskostnader i IT-prosjekter

Longva, P. & Tverstøl, A., 2014. Prinsipper og krav ved utarbeidelse av samfunnsøkonomiske analyser mv. , pp.1–8.

Medby, P. et al., 2006. Samfunnsøkonomiske effekter av universell utforming

Ministry of Local Government and Modernisation, 2014. Regulation regarding universal design of information and communication technology (ICT) solutions

MMI, 2004. Undersøkelsen blant synshemmede, *Telefonintervjuundersøkelse utført av MMI på oppdrag fra Norges Blindeforbund*

National Council of Disability, 2001. The Accessible Future, Washington, USA

Norwegian Ministry of Children and Equality and Social Inclusion, 2014. Act relating to a prohibition against discrimination on the basis of disability (*Anti-Discrimination and Accessibility Act*)

OneVoice for Accessible ICT, 2010. Accessible Information and Communication Technologies. Benefits to Business and Society

Senter for statlig økonomistyring, 2009. Samfunnsøkonomisk analyse og gevinstrealisering av IKT-prosjekter

Standard Norge, 2010. Universell utforming – samfunnsmessige konsekvenser ved innføring av pliktige standarder for web

TNO STB, 1998. Design for All and ICT business practice: Addressing the barriers. Examples of Best Practice, *Report produced by TNO STB on request of the European Commission, DG XIII C5.Telematics Applications Programme. Disabled and Elderly sector*

U.S. Congress, 1990. Americans with Disabilities Act

United Nations, 2006. Convention on the Rights of Persons with Disabilities

Vista Utredning AS, 2010. Samfunnsøkonomisk analyse av krav til universell utforming av selvbetjeningsløsninger

THE ROLE OF MATERIALS IN DESIGN OF FAMILIAR AND CONTEXTUAL ASSISTIVE TECHNOLOGIES

Suhas Govind Joshi and Heidi Bråthen
Department of Informatics, University of Oslo, Norway

ABSTRACT

This paper reports on an exploration of the role of materials in the design of assistive technologies for elderly people. The research aim was to investigate whether expectations and choices of materials could help raise the perceived familiarity and context-suitability of assistive technologies. Data was gathered through five different methods involving 42 participants residing or working in two local care homes in Oslo, and later thematically analyzed. The results provided several important examples of how material plays an important role in how the elderly participants experienced the design. Our findings suggest that material properties such as aesthetics qualities and texture strongly influence the perceived familiarity of the design and the technology's ability to properly blend into the home environment and not disrupt the home context.

KEYWORDS

Assistive technology, material, elderly people, tangible interaction

1. INTRODUCTION

Assistive technology has the potential to improve the daily lives of elderly people by extending and supporting their functional and cognitive capacities. Over the last four years, we have researched the design of tangible alternatives to current touch-screen based assistive technologies such as tablets and televisions. However, our prior research has also largely demonstrated that not all elderly people end up using designed assistive technologies. One reason for not partaking is because they deliberately abstain from using available technology due to stigmatizing and sometimes alienating designs or design practices (Joshi 2014). Another explanation is the reported tendency within the design of assistive technology to create designs that support physical and cognitive functioning without considering other dimensions of the aging experience, e.g., social, emotional, and environmental factors (Joshi 2015, Hirsch, Forlizzi et al. 2000). One such dimension is the material of designed assistive technologies.

In this paper, we present a material exploration in the context of assistive technologies for elderly people. Our findings expand on our current research on designing tangible assistive technologies with a particular focus on habits, familiarity, and context (Joshi 2016). An important point of departure for the research presented in this paper has been to explore the relationship between familiarity and context on one hand, and the users' perceptions, expectations, and choices of materials on the other. Data has been gathered from 42 participants (M = 80 years) residing or working at two care homes in Oslo through five methods of investigation: interviews, focus groups, material testing, and two types of usability tests of a prototype named GLiMT. GLiMT has previously been presented in (Joshi and Bråthen 2016). The results and thematic analysis are structured around the two topics of interest, i.e., familiarity and context, and we end the paper by discussing the significance and limitations of our findings. Our work contributes by exploring the role of materials in the design processes of assistive technology. Based on our findings, we argue that addressing material aspects during the design process allows assistive technology to be perceived as more familiar and simultaneously better adhere to the context in which it will reside.

2. RELATED WORK

Hirsch, Forlizzi et al. (2000) have studied design of eldercare technologies focusing on different dimensions of the aging experience. They emphasize that designers of eldercare technologies should consider the users' individual perception of the aging experience as encompassing more than the decline in physical and cognitive function. Rather, it constitutes a complex interweaving of social, emotional and environmental factors. Failure to consider the aging experience as a whole might prohibit adoption and use of assistive technologies, even when the user has a need for the assistance provided by the technological device.

In their investigation into what matters most to elderly users of assistive technology and the materiality of assistive technologies, Greenhalgh, Wherton et al. (2013) argue that the material features of technologies have an important impact on whether and how they will be used. They also point to the sociological aspects of materiality and how materiality can convey cultural meaning such as status and independence, or adversely, dependence and stigma. Hirsch, Forlizzi et al. (2000) found that elderly users' own perceptions of their abilities are often misconceived as below or above their actual capabilities; assistive technologies have a significant influence on the self-perception of elderly users. Users' aesthetic requirements should guide the form of a device and aesthetic considerations like materials, size and «look and feel» are equally important components in assistive technologies as product function (ibid). While good usability ensures that a product can be used, they claim that aesthetic factors determine whether a product will be used.

Materials might be especially useful when designing for usability. An interface that draws on elderly users existing habits and competences has been shown to lower thresholds of use (Joshi 2015). Krasner (2006) analyses the meaning of materiality to elderly people and states that the habits of elderly people tend to be anchored in the material in the home; the tangibility of the home and immediate surroundings offers the elderly comfort and support their habits, enabling them to mirror their identities and life stories. The familiarity and tangibility of their home and immediate surroundings support elderly people function by providing a "smooth path"; a habitual routine when moving around in the material environment of the home that sometimes enables elderly to function above their level of ability (ibid). However, with declining function, the range of movement tends to contract and the immediate physical environment tends to become more important. It is important that assistive technologies designed for use in the home of elderly are unobtrusive and designed to blend in with the context (Hirsch, Forlizzi et al. 2000). Research on assistive technologies for patients suffering from dementia has also shown that familiar representations in the immediate physical surroundings of these users' help make sense of sensory input (Fay, Fleming et al. 2010).

The topic of materials has become gradually more important within design fields over the last years, yet there is still a need for a better scientific apparatus to describe how materials matter in design processes (Fernaeus and Sundström 2012, Wiberg 2014). Döring, Sylvester et al. (2012) present material-centered design concepts for tangible interaction through theories from material iconography. Their work explores how material aspects influence the users, e.g., by discussing how materials can strongly influence body movement and manipulation and stimulate engagement. Furthermore, Vallgårda and Redström's (2007) understanding of materials in interaction design and Wiberg's (2014) suggested framework for a methodology of materials in HCI design offers some guidelines regarding a methodological application of materials in the design process.

3. RESEARCH METHODS

3.1 Empirical Context

Our study is part of a larger research project focusing on assistive technology in cooperation with Oslo Municipality. Two local care homes for residents with cognitive and physical impairments served as the primary locations for our empirical research. Visitors at a local daytime activity center for citizens above the age of 60 served as our control group during the usability tests. Many of these participants lived in their private homes and came to the care home in the daytime to participate in scheduled activities and sharing meals. The study included 42 participants; 25 in the experiment group and 17 in the control group. The participants were between the age of 67 and 92 years old (M = 80). The residents of the care homes had lived there for between nine months and three years. We also consulted three domain experts through interviews in the various phases of the research, aged 23 to 54 years old. We recruited our participants through the method of convenience sampling by visiting the care facilities and joining activities in the common rooms. We aimed at achieving a balanced and representative distribution of age and gender within the target population, but the gender balance was skewed towards women (61%).

3.2 Data Gathering

The data was gathered over a period of three months in the autumn of 2015. Using a mixed-method approach, we conducted semi-structured interviews with a combined total of 10 participants. This included six individual interviews and two sessions of group interviews. We also conducted an experimental blindfold testing with material samples and performed two usability tests, namely one formative test and one summative evaluation, on the GLiMT prototype. Table 1 gives a summary of involved methods and participant distribution from the experiment group and control group respectively.

Table 1. Overview of methods involved in the study showing participant distribution

#	Method	N *Experiment group*	N *Control group*	Collected data	Inquiry method
A	Interviews	6	-	Photographs, field notes, probes	Semi-structured interview
B	Focus group	5	5	Photographs	Semi-structured group interview
C	Material test	5	-	Field notes	Blindfolded material testing
D	Formative test	11	8	Photographs, field notes	Observation, think out loud, interview, task performance testing
E	Summative test	3	4	Video, photographs, field notes	Task performance testing

3.2.1 Interviews and Focus Group

The *semi-structured interviews* and *focus group* were conducted in the common rooms of the care homes and activity center. The interviews were held over the course of three weeks where we visited the care home on five separate occasions to take part in daily activities like dinner in the cafeteria, afternoon coffee, and reading group in the library of the care home. The aim of this research was to learn about the challenges with the use of current assistive technologies. We asked open-ended questions about what technological devices they used regularly, as well as related questions regarding social aspects, daily activities, routines, and communication with relatives. We also observed the daily life in the common rooms of the care home and discussed their current assistive technological devices. In addition to photographs and fields notes, other probes such as activity leaflets, food menus, facility brochures, etc. were also collected.

3.2.2 Material test with Blindfolds

The blindfold test of material samples was conducted in the same facilities and during the same period as the interviews. Vallgårda and Redström (2007) argue that materials in design are chosen to a large degree because of their properties and that these choices are made with respect to the focal points of interest to reflect the concerns at hand. We explored potentially suitable materials by gathering objects placed in ordinary homes. We utilized a bricolage approach (Louridas 1999) to explore combinations of our chosen digital "material", e.g., sensors, Arduino, and different traditional materials. To generate and communicate ideas regarding surface, size and shape we used wood, play dough, polymer clay, paint, stickers, yarn, fabric, canvas, and cut paper to make quick and expendable prototypes. Some of these material ideas are illustrated in Figure 1.

We conducted blindfold testing of samples of contrasting materials with five residents. The aim was to explore what the elderly users associated with different materials and what the perceived as desirable concerning the experience of manipulating a physical object with their hands; the focus was on the experience of the surface of the materials, the natural first contact with the material (Vallgårda and Redström 2007). As both the texture and color are related to the experience of materials, the participants were blindfolded to avoid that the visual appearance of the material sample affected the immediate experience of the material. The test was performed with one participant at the time. The material samples were covered with a cloth; the participant was blindfolded, and one researcher handed pieces of materials to the user's one at the time. The user was then asked about their immediate impression of the sample and asked to associate freely for a short while. Then they were asked what they thought of the material in their hands in regards to an assistive technology product that they would enjoy using. They got to see the material samples afterward and comment further if they wished to do so.

Recruiting participants for the blindfold tests was challenging due to potential participants being uncomfortable with the concept of using a blindfold. However, the goal of this experimental study was to explore whether the materials could influence perceived familiarity or context at all rather than drawing strong conclusion in any direction from these data. While its main function was to contribute to our overall results with empirical observations, this small experiment also resulted in interesting preliminary data regarding the method of blindfold testing materials themselves which is suitable for further investigation or future work. It also yielded some interesting findings concerning the perception of the material samples, although the sample size was too small to be conclusive.

Figure 1. Using a bricolage approach, we explored combinations of digital and traditional materials by generating quick and expendable prototypes from cardboard, wood, yarn, polymer clay and silicone

3.2.3 Usability Testing

We conducted formative usability tests and a summative evaluation of tangible prototype named GLiMT (see Figure 2). GLiMT is a prototype designed as a tangible alternative to services currently offered through touch-screen interfaces such as tablets. Designed as a small wooden cube, it receives online information through a wireless configuration, and the cube has four sides with corresponding symbols to represent the four categories of information; the information is identical to the information offered through an existing touchscreen-based tablet currently in use in one of the care facilities. Incoming messages are indicated as the corresponding side of the cube lights up. The four chosen categories of information included social messages, organizational information, and home care services (Joshi and Bråthen 2015). The message can be displayed on a bigger screen that the residents are comfortable with, like the TV, the tablet, and cell phone by placing the lighted side of the cube next to the screen. The small screen embedded on the top of the device displays the sender of the message. The base station contains inductive charger and a separate control unit for TV. GLiMT has been previously described in (Joshi and Bråthen 2016). We do not claim this prototype to be a definite piece of technology; instead, it serves as a demonstrative prototype in exploring the role of materials in the design of assistive technologies for elderly users.

Figure 2. The prototype GLiMT was used during both formative and summative usability testing

The aim of the usability test was twofold. The aim of the usability test was twofold. Firstly, we wanted to compare a representation of a current touchscreen-based interface, i.e., the tablet with our tangible alternative GLiMT. Secondly, we wished to further explore how the materials chosen for our tangible interface and its resulting appearance were perceived by the elderly users. To measure performance, we asked the participants who struggled to use the touchscreen-based interface to carry out two sets of daily tasks. Open-ended questions about the users' perception of the appearance of the GLiMT prototype complemented the set of tasks. They were also encouraged to think out loud while performing tasks to uncover expectations and opinions about the prototype.

4. RESULTS AND FINDINGS

4.1 Familiarity

When blindfolded during the material test, the participants experienced the material with their tactile sense exclusively. While the blindfold test did not reveal any materials as unanimously favored, the participants expressed enthusiasm towards different material properties. We registered a strong relationship between the material properties, e.g., the finishing of the object's surface, and the perceived familiarity. For instance, when asked to feel a brushed steel cup, a material usually associated with coldness, several participants described it as warm and comfortable. This was surprisingly similar to the feedback for other materials, i.e., wood, silicone and crochet fabric. At the same time, two samples of wood with different finishes, one varnished bowl and one rough block of wood rendered very different associations from the participants although being the same material. These two cases demonstrated to us how the finishing of the surface would influence the texture of the material to such a degree that the materials were no longer perceived as similar. During interviews, the participants explained that trying to identify the purpose or application of the material further affected their ability to identify the material; expectations of intended application could potentially yield confusions about the material itself. Similar objects were identified as ranging from a lid (woman, 81) to a ball (man, 79), and their perception of the material was very different due to this conflicting interpretation of purpose. Besides the surface, the form of the object also played into the experience of the material. One participant explained how the smoothness of materials was a key factor as it influenced resistance and ability to grip (man, 84) while another participant related their perception and preference to the physical shape of the material (man, 80). However, most results suggested that participants favored materials that were perceived as warm and smooth such as wood and silicone.

The GLiMT-prototype used in the usability tests further allowed us to explore material properties such as weight and size. Through testing various shapes and sizes, we ended up with a form that all participants were able to handle, i.e., lift and hold (Joshi and Bråthen 2016). However, certain participants with psychomotor challenges expressed concerns with the weight of the material: "I have arthrosis, so it is a bit heavy for me, but I can do it." (woman, 79). Another participant struggled with the size due to challenges with dexterity: "My fingers are a little stiff, but I can manage this." (man, 86). The participants' perception of the material properties was not a static and definitive relation; it evolved along with changes to bodily capacities.

4.2 Context

Interviews and usability tests revealed how the aesthetics properties of the material were of importance to the participants. This was the motivation for also facilitating blindfold testing where preferences towards aesthetics properties would not bias their tactile experience of the material. A material particularly favored by several participants was wood. One of the main comments during the usability testing of the GLiMT-prototype was that they enjoyed that the prototype was neat and simple, frugal, and Nordic in its design. The simple and Nordic design was explicitly associated with the wooden material: "It is very nice and neat. This is what you associate with the Norwegian; it is wood." (woman, 87). Interviews revealed that the aesthetics were a part of how they experienced the object in relation to its surroundings, a factor that for most participants heavily influenced the perception of the material. Most comments on appearance revolved around envisioning how the material properties of the exterior of the prototype would fit in their homes. For certain participants, the material would decide whether it needed to be stowed away during visits: "It is not ugly, either, it could very well be left out on the table." (woman, 89). The participants associated technology with certain materials and colors and materials that would remind less of assistive technology would be easier to have laying around. This was to them an advantage of the design that the younger participants did not perceive as equally necessary or important.

The difference in preferences between generations was further strengthened by the statements from the domain experts who were very much satisfied with the cold, shiny, and sharp look of existing technology: "It should be black and look more like the other technological devices I have so that it would fit in my home" (domain expert, 45). We also registered a difference in expectations between the younger and older participants within the user group (67-92 years). While the oldest participants preferred simple and traditional aesthetics, the preferences of the younger participants aligned more with the views of the domain expert: "It should be black or light so it could go with anything. Then it would be more appropriate in my home" (woman, 67).

Finally, the intrinsic value of using certain materials in assistive technologies played an important role to the participants. In contrast to most screen-based interfaces, GLiMT was described during the usability tests as "something real, not just a screen" and favored due to its material properties. Interacting with physical components in a physical environment yielded a different experienced compared to performing similar tasks on a screen-only device, and the material properties of the physical components stimulated particular emotions. In our case, the participants described the wooden material as fun and playful, thereby inviting to interaction. Participants explained that the physical and material properties triggered a curiosity and that the shape and material invited to play: "I feel like a child playing with blocks! It is fun!" (woman, 83).

4.3 Findings

The qualitative data from both the individual and the group interviews, as well as from the usability tests, were analyzed using the thematic analysis procedure described by Braun and Clarke (Braun and Clarke, 2006). Using open coding, the data sets were initially read carefully to identify and code for patterns in the data. The resulting 22 codes were reduced to two main themes by ordering and clustering them. We chose to focus our analysis on the theme of familiarity and context within the data to answer our initial questions about assistive technology and materiality. The categories and themes were selected based not on quantitative measures of prevalence, but of salience to our research question. We chose to subject all our different types of data to an analysis that had its point of departure from our research question and chose the theme based on what Braun and Clarke terms "keyness". A summary of the two thematic areas along with main findings is presented in Table 2.

Table 2. Overview of main findings

Thematic area	*Main findings*	*Source method*	*Key observations*
Familiarity	▪ Familiarity with materials is tied to experience and expectations	[C], [D], [E]	▪ Expectations of the purpose or application affected the tactile experience of the material
	▪ Material properties such as texture influence the perception of material type		▪ Different textures conveyed different meanings when using the same material
	▪ Perception of material changes along with the bodily changes		▪ Participants with psychomotor challenges expressed concern with long-term use due to bodily capacities
Context	▪ There were strong preferences and objections towards the aesthetics	[B], [C], [D], [E]	▪ Wood as a material was appreciated for its simple, frugal, and clean aesthetic properties.
	▪ Expectations regarding appearance seemed to be different between age groups		▪ Domain experts preferred ergonomic values while elderly participants focused on simplicity
	▪ The opinions of material were largely dependent on the intended use context		▪ Shaping an opinion on a material was difficult without understanding the context as the material had to "blend in" with the environment

5. DISCUSSION

5.1 Designing for Familiarity

Our goal was to explore how materials could support habits and capacities. Incorporating materials in the design of assistive technologies for elderly people has contributed something more than the mere pleasure of inviting aesthetics. Our application of materials in the design process also aligns with the notion of the texture as central to the communication of a material's properties to the user through its surface and appearance (Vallgårda and Redström 2007, Wiberg 2014).

We found a clear tendency between the tactile experience of the material and what the participants believed the intended purpose of use to be. Furthermore, it is the characteristics of materials as well as the material itself that anchor habits and bodily capacities, something that is particularly true in cases where the users are experiencing declining function (Krasner 2006). We also found that exploring materials helped to invoke not only a familiar association but also appropriate associations. Familiarity may help the user relate to the technology and perhaps even provide usability. However, usability alone does not guarantee that the technology will be used (Hirsch, Forlizzi et al. 2000) as the material features of technologies has an important impact on whether and how they will be used (Greenhalgh, Wherton et al. 2013). We saw how certain aesthetics properties of materials carried stigmatizing and undesired signals discouraging use, e.g., technologies built with material that reminded the participants of their own helplessness. This low use rate due to stigmatizing has been previously observed in our empirical context (Joshi 2014). A material explanation for low use rates is that certain designs look like they belong in a hospital and that their presence and use bring the users "one step closer to institutional care or death" (Greenhalgh, Wherton et al. 2013). Similarly, we registered how certain materials such as wood yielded encouraging designs, something Hirsch, Forlizzi et al. (2000) argue can add dimensions to the design that contributes to a positive self-image of mastery and a more positive perception of own abilities by empowering the user.

Furthermore, certain materials afford certain actions or behaviors through expectations of the material properties. This phenomenon is for instance mentioned by Döring, Sylvester et al. (2012) who observed in their studies that users interacting with soap bubbles as the material would act cautious and calm in response to the fragility of the material.

Besides discovering the appropriate material itself, the use of the material may highly influence the experienced familiarity. Physical objects naturally link visual appearance with other characteristics such as weight, material, texture, and sound (Djajadiningrat, Wensveen et al. 2004), and directly engaging with materials alters our relationship to and experience of materials (Wiberg 2014). Removing visual stimuli from material exploration allowed us to explore isolated characteristics of materials (e.g., the surface) by exploring the surface as the material's interface to its surroundings (Vallgårda and Redström 2007). The blindfold testing in our study revealed different associations for similar materials based on the texture of the material. Based on our findings, we argue that all material dimensions such as aesthetics and functionality need proper exploration in order to communicate appropriately with old habits and familiar gestures.

5.2 Designing for Context

Even though new technological designs cannot directly represent the past and the lived life of an elderly user, the design may support the elderly by building on a metaphor that reminds the user of familiar things and blends into a cherished tangible environment to avoid disruption. The aesthetics of the material were important to the participants and all participants who expressed a preference or objections on the aesthetic properties of the GLiMT-prototype evaluated it explicitly in the context of their homes. It became challenging to disentangle the material from the context, and it was hard to discern whether it was the material or the finished product in their homes that were being evaluated by the users, even during the blindfolded test. Their main concerns were linked to how well the design would blend in or not, and whether it could be "left in plain sight" without disrupting their home aesthetics. Krasner (2006) argues that the immediate tangible surroundings provide comfort and support their habits by "enabling them to mirror their lived lives and their identities". By their very nature, older adults' memories and stories can highlight their identity in terms of their home. Often, the home is where people age and ''what has happened in life is increasingly likely to have happened in this place'' (Rubinstein, Kilbride et al. 1992). Thus, the disruption of the aesthetic harmony in the homes of the users should be avoided when designing assistive technologies. This importance of the home to elders is also emphasized in the in the EAT guidelines for designing for Alzheimer patients (Fay, Fleming et al. 2010), and Greenhalgh, Wherton et al. (2013) describe how assistive technology left in homes can disrupt the equilibrium by making the room untidy or cluttered.

Another reason that the home becomes gradually more important to elderly people in need of assistive technology is that many elderly people find their surrounding space narrowing down. The accessible world often shrinks with declining functioning abilities, including their immediate surroundings, their homes, and often also parts of the home, e.g., the kitchen or the living room (Krasner 2006). Accordingly, the presence and influence of the assistive technology become stronger as the space shrinks.

6. CONCLUSION

The aim of this paper was to explore the role of material in the design of assistive technologies, and whether incorporating materials more actively in the design process can contribute to increased familiarity and context-suitability. The results from our five data gathering methods indicated strong correlations. The blindfolded material testing yielded varying opinions and preferences towards the expectations and preferences towards different materials, and interview sessions revealed that most participants desired to influence the choice of materials. Several material characteristics such as aesthetic properties as well as texture, size, weight, and color contributed to individual preferences. Our findings suggest that there is a strong relationship between choice of materials and the perceived familiarity; designing around appropriate materials can help users build on old habits and experiences. Furthermore, the participants expressed concern with the designed technology's ability to "blend in" with their existing home context. To not disrupt their home aesthetics, as well as their routines and organization, the selection of material stood out as a key dependency. While our work has focused on the exploration of materials' role in the design process, we aim to further investigate material composites (Vallgårda and Redström 2007) and material transformation (Robles and Wiberg 2010) in our future work.

REFERENCES

Braun, V. and Clarke V, 2006, "Using thematic analysis in psychology", *Qualitative research in psychology*, 3(2), p. 77-101.

Djajadiningrat, T., S. Wensveen, J. Frens and K. Overbeeke, 2004, "Tangible products: redressing the balance between appearance and action." *Personal and Ubiquitous Computing* 8(5): 294-309.

Döring, T., A. Sylvester and A. Schmidt, 2012, Exploring material-centered design concepts for tangible interaction. *CHI '12 Extended Abstracts on Human Factors in Computing Systems*. Austin, Texas, USA, ACM: 1523-1528.

Fay, R., R. Fleming and A. Robinson, 2010, Design for dementia: Sustainability and human wellbeing, *Australian and New Zealand Architectural Science Association* (ANZAScA).

Fernaeus, Y. and P. Sundström, 2012, The material move how materials matter in interaction design research. Proceedings of the Designing Interactive Systems Conference. Newcastle Upon Tyne, United Kingdom, ACM: 486-495.

Greenhalgh, T., J. Wherton, P. Sugarhood, S. Hinder, R. Procter, R. Stones, 2013, "What matters to older people with assisted living needs? A phenomenological analysis of the use and non-use of telehealth and telecare", in Social Science & Medicine, Vol.93, pp.86-94.

Hirsch, T., J. Forlizzi, E. Hyder, J. Goetz, C. Kurtz, J. Stroback, 2000, "The ELDer Project: Social, Emotional, and Environmental Factors in the Design of Eldercare Technologies", in *Universal Usability: Proceedings on the 2000 conference, (CUU '00)*, pp.72-79.

Joshi, S.G., 2014, "Emerging ethical considerations from the perspectives of the elderly", in *Ninth International Conference on Culture, Technology, and Communication 2014.* Culture Technology Communication, pp. 186 – 203.

Joshi, S.G., 2015, "Designing for Experienced Simplicity. Why Analytic and Imagined Simplicity Fail in Design of Assistive Technology", in *International Journal on Advances in Intelligent Systems,* vol. 8 (3-4), pp. 324- 338.

Joshi, S.G., 2016, "Re-establishing Interaction Through Design of Alternative Interfaces",in eTELEMED 2016, *The Eighth International Conference on eHealth*, Telemedicine and Social Medicine, pp. 220 – 229.

Joshi, S.G. and Bråthen, H., 2016, "Lowering the Threshold: Reconnecting Elderly Users with Assistive Technology through Tangible Interfaces", 2nd International Conference on Human Aspects of IT for the Aged Population, HCII2016

Krasner, J., 2006, "Accumulated Lives: Metaphor, Materiality, and the Homes of the Elderly" In *Literature and Medicine*, Vol.24(2), pp.209-30.

Louridas, P., 1999, "Design as Bricolage: Anthropology Meets Design Thinking"

Redström J., A.Vallgårda, 2007, "Computational Composites" in *Proc. CHI 2007, Design Theory*, San Jose, USA, 513-522.

Robles, E. and M. Wiberg, 2010, Texturing the "material turn" in interaction design. *Proceedings of the fourth international conference on Tangible, embedded and embodied interaction.* Cambridge, Massachusetts, USA, ACM: 137-144.

Rubinstein, R., J. Kilbride and S. Nagy, 1992,"Choice, independence, and aging", Elders living alone: frailty and the perception of choice. New York NY: Aldine de Gruyter.

Vallgårda, A. and J. Redström (2007). Computational composites. Proceedings of the SIGCHI conference on Human factors in computing systems, ACM.

Wiberg, M., 2014, "Methodology for materiality: interaction design research through a material lens", in *Personal and Ubiquitous Computing*, pp. 625-636, Springer-Verlag, London, UK.

MASTERBLIND - TESTING THE USABILITY OF AUDITORY FEEDBACK IN A COMPUTER GAME FOR BLIND PEOPLE

Ana Rita Teixeira[1, 2], Ana Carvalhal[1], Filipe Abrantes[1], Vladimiro Lourenço[1], Anabela Gomes [3, 4] and João Orvalho[1]
[1]*Master in Human Computer Interaction (HCI), Polytechnic of Coimbra,*
Rua Dom João III – Solum 3030-329 Coimbra, Portugal
[2]*Institute of Electronics and Informatics Engineering of Aveiro – University of Aveiro*
Campus Universitário de Santiago, 3810-193 Aveiro – Portugal
[3]*Engineering Institute of Polytechnic Institute of Coimbra*
Rua Pedro Nunes, Quinta da Nora, 3030-199 Coimbra, Portugal
[4]*Centre for Informatics and Systems – University of Coimbra*
Pólo II - Pinhal de Marrocos, 3030-290 Coimbra

ABSTRACT

The present study presents an adaptation of the Mastermind board game for blind users - Masterblind. Given the focus on visual information in the original game, the game mechanics were simplified and auditory feedback introduced. The research object was to understand what kind of sounds would work better to help blind people play the game. Three versions were presented to the subjects - pentatonic notes, animal sounds and vowels - to help users recall previous steps in the game. The main hypothesis predicted that blind users would consciously benefit from the auditory feedback provided. The second hypothesis predicted that users would benefit less from the feedback that doesn't provide semantic information. The results were congruent with the hypothesis, although revealing an important role for spatial awareness. Masterblind can be an usable, enjoyable and a challenging experience for blind users as long as it provides semantically significant feedback.

KEYWORDS

User Experience Design; User and Cognitive models; Interface Design Games/Play

1. INTRODUCTION

A computer game adaptation of the board game Mastermind [1] was designed and prototyped to address the difficulties in visual interfaces blind users may have - Masterblind. There are several variations of the game, but the original concept is based on having a player generating/choosing a secret key of four coloured pieces out of a set of eight different colours - with or without repetitions of the same colour - while the other player, in several rounds, tries to guess the correct secret key previously generated. At each round the second player tests a combination of coloured pieces and according to the feedback given by the first player, he tries to deduce the key by presenting new combinations. The feedback provided by the first player consists in informing the second player of how many pieces are the correct colours in the correct position, and how many pieces are the correct colours but in the wrong position. The game ends when the key is discovered or the number of maximum attempts is reached. The main design problem was to understand how the original concept of Mastermind that relies so much on visual information could be adapted to a computer game for blind users, without any visual output. Three main aspects of the role of visual information were identified and hypothesized to have a significant role on the mechanics of the original game:

1) the distinctive capacity for the user to clearly identify each element of the secret key;

2) accurate but at the same time, vague feedback that provides just enough information for the player to derive the correct solution without losing the puzzling element that is essential for these kind of games;

3) accessibility of information about the previous plays to minimize repeated answers in the following attempts.

To address these aspects, several design choices were made. Following the direction of S. Targett et al. [2] using audio feedback and simplifying the game mechanics has driven those choices. First, to keep the balance between enjoyability and the challenge that one derives from a puzzle game such as this one, the number of possible elements for the secret keys were reduced from eight to only four elements and repetitions were excluded. This way, due to the secret key also having only four elements total and the repetitions no longer being allowed, one could eliminate the need for excessive feedback and consequent confusion, as the possible elements to choose for the secret key and that same secret key are both limited to four elements, it is already implied that the player is using the correct elements, reducing the feedback to only informing the player about how many elements are in the correct position. Then, the role of colour in the original game was replaced by using real physical objects - through Makey Makey [3] a circuit board that connects any conductive physical object to a computer by replacing the keyboard and mouse click signals with touch on real objects - and a distinctive sound, elicited when the player touched the object (and repeated in a sequential order at the end of each round) was associated with each one of the objects. Through this step the distinctive aspect of the elements was improved and the availability of information about the last play was reinforced by repetition and auditory memory. Finally, verbal feedback about the number of right positions in each round provided enough information for trying new combinations and derive the secret key, without reducing the challenge of the task. Still, the availability of information about previous plays needed to be further addressed. Possible trajectories were adding more features to the prototype (decreasing its simplicity) or improving the ability of the content to be remembered. Research has shown that blind people seem to be more efficient in remembering routines and patterns [4] and have more efficient auditory short-term and long-term memory [5] - although there are differences between congenital and non-congenital blindness in the accuracy and fidelity in memory tests[6]. But what kind of sounds would work better to help users recall the last sequence? In designing auditory cues in a user interface a distinction is made between auditory icons, earcons and speech [7]. An auditory icon is a brief sound that is used to represent a specific event, object, function, or action. They are essentially emulations or caricatures of naturally occurring sounds in everyday life taking advantage of the user's prior knowledge and natural auditory associations between sounds and their results [7, 8]. They can represent directly or indirectly, either by using the sound made by the target event, or by substituting a surrogate for the target - requiring additional learning to develop the relationship between the sound and a specific event [7]. Earcons are brief, nonverbal, distinctive audio sounds used to represent a specific event, usually abstract, synthetic, and mostly musical tones or sound patterns that can be used in structured combinations. Since they don't deliver any natural representational value they require more learning than direct auditory icons [7]. Since with Makey Makey the player can choose any four everyday objects of his choice (as long as they are conductive), it was not possible to refer the objects by their names (speech) or a direct auditory representation (auditory icon) of each object a player may choose. The research [9] suggests that although more realistic sounds, such as auditory icons reveal greater functional utility, there may be a preference for abstract musical sounds. Therefore we sought to find a compromise between the realism and the abstraction of the designed sounds, in order to provide further meaning to the user, exploring different levels of meaning either in the relationship between the sounds, or in the semantic and naturalistic relation that the sounds have in relation to the learning process of the users. Three alternatives for auditory feedback were designed and three different prototypes corresponding to those alternatives were used to test their efficiency. One alternative associates to each object a note of the pentatonic scale, considering the ease in creating recognizable melodies with different combinations of the notes of this scale provides additional melodic information over tonic sounds, introducing a second level of meaning that might strengthen memorization. Other alternative links voices of animals (cow, rooster, cat, sheep) reinforcing the recalling power through association with realistic sounds that are clearly identifiable to users and through conceptual immersion on the animal topic. The last one uses the sounds of vowels ("a", "e", "i", "o"), using basic speech sounds with a long history of learning and semantic and sequential value - providing an order familiar to most users -, that may benefit memorizing strategies. The main hypothesis of the present study predicts that blind users will consciously benefit from the auditory feedback provided and use it to better recall previous sequences. The second hypothesis predicts that, although users may find it more enjoyable, they will benefit less from the feedback that doesn't provide semantic or conceptual information. The prototypes were developed with the Scratch tool [10], a programming platform, developed for children, that allows simple and easy programming through direct manipulation of blocks and visual elements.

2. DATASET

2.1 Sample

The study took place over a period of two months at the headquarters of Acapo Coimbra carried out by students of Master Human Computer Interaction (HCI) of IPC Coimbra. We performed a set of nine individual sessions with blind volunteers, divided between 5 males and 4 females with ages ranging from 21 to 66 years old, education levels between the 4th grade and post-graduation, and a diverse background of job occupations. Although only approximately half of the volunteers had smartphones, we found that almost all of them were already familiarized with a computer, whether it be in work related tasks or leisure. It's also noteworthy mentioning that most of them were not used to play video games, playing more palpable and physical games instead, like cards, dominoes and various board games.

2.2 Methodology

Each session took around 30 minutes and were employed different qualitative research methods:
1) a semistructured survey (Initial interview); 2) a set of three usability tests ; 3) three retrospective think aloud (one after each test) ; 4) a questionnaire which was rated through a Likert scale [11] (a tool used in which participants are asked to respond to statements on a scale ranging from "strongly agree" to "strongly disagree").

2.2.1 Initial Interview

We started with a semi-structured interview where we collected data on the following topics:
- Demographic data; - Education; - Occupation; - Computer usage frequency; - Smartphone usage; - Games and computer games habits.

2.2.2 Usability Tests

Before starting the usability tests we introduced the game prototype to each participant so they could have a first contact with it and clearly understand the rules of the game. We tested three different versions of the game in which the order of the tests was randomized for every participant. Each version consisted in ten rounds in which the user could try to guess the correct key. The different versions differed on the feedback that was transmitted to the player about the outcome of each round of the game, one had a pentatonic scale, the other had animal sounds(a rooster, a cat, a sheep and a cow), and the last one had spoken vowels ("a", "e", "i","o").

2.2.3 Retrospective Think Aloud

At the end of each test the participants were asked to explain their reasoning in the game in order to guess the correct key. Think aloud methods are often used when trying to detect usability problems. The most successful form of think aloud to use together with a system is a retrospective think aloud methodology (RTA), which means that participants verbalize their thoughts after completing a task or a set of tasks. RTA allows the participant to complete a task on their own and in silence.

2.2.4 Questionnaire

At the end of the series of tests, participants were asked to answer a questionnaire based on a Likert scale, in order to gather feedback about the comparative efficiency of the different approaches.The scale has five-level

Likert item, that means: 1) Strongly disagree; 2) Disagree; 3) Neither agree nor disagree; 4) Agree; 5) Strongly agree. In the questionnaire, 8 questions (statements) were considered for evaluation by the users:

Q1 - It was easy to remember the previous combinations when I heard the pentatonic scale.
Q2 - Listening to the spoken vowels helped me more than listening to the pentatonic scale.
Q3 - It was difficult to remember the previous combinations when I heard the animal sounds.
Q4 - It couldn't guide myself by the sounds.
Q5 - Listening to the pentatonic scale helped me more than listening to animal sounds.
Q6 - It was easier to remember the previous combinations when I heard the spoken vowels.
Q7. – Listening to the animal sounds helped me more than listening to the spoken vowels.
Q8 - The sounds only hindered me

3. RESULTS AND DISCUSSION

Results show that the users were overall more successful with the prototype using animal sounds and sounds of vowels than the prototype with pentatonic notes as feedback. The figure 1 presents the number of users that successfully identified the correct key for each version of the prototype: pentatonic scale (22%), the spoken vowels (44%) and the animal sounds (56%). Note that the spoken vowels as well as pentatonic scale versions of the prototype present a small accuracy, (less than 50%).

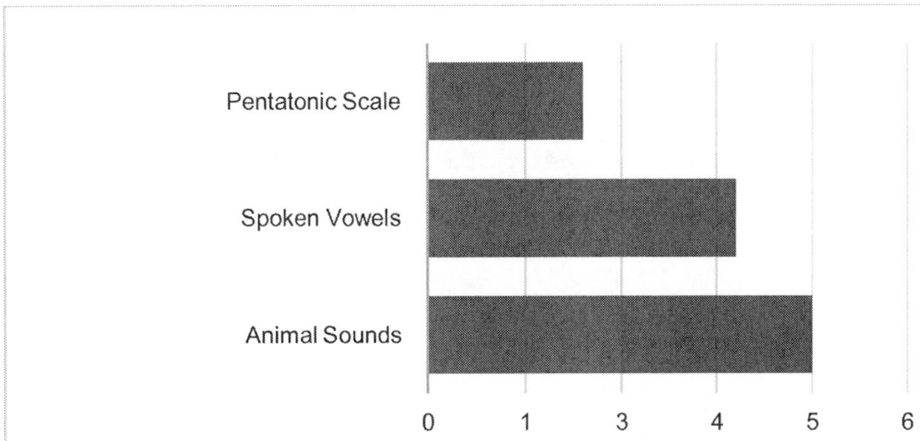

Figure 1. Number of users that successfully identified the correct key for each version of the prototype

Figure 2 refers to the number of unsuccessful tries (in 10) for each version of the prototype, by user. Results show that the spoken vowels version presents in average (5.25) less tries for the user to be successful, with the version where users were more successful – animal sounds – requiring in average a greater amount of unsuccessful tries (5.6) and the pentatonic scale version, requiring less tries (4) for the only two users that complete it successfully.

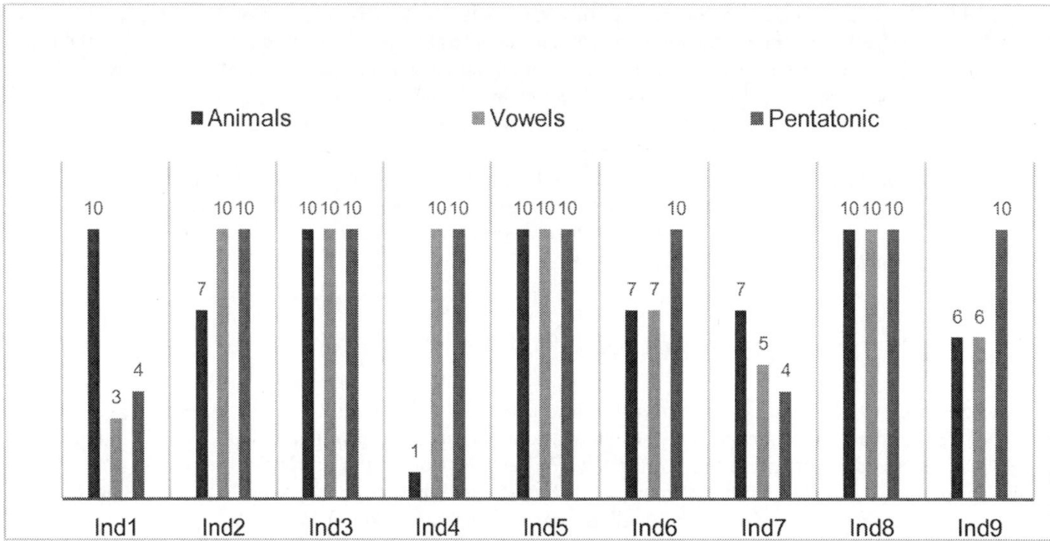

Figure 2. Number of unsuccessful tries for each version of the prototype, by user

The think-aloud was fruitful to understand the importance of auditory stimuli or other strategic references for memorizing sequences. Figure 3 shows that users describe paying attention to sounds, alone or in combination with spatial awareness, only in the versions with animal voices or with vowels; in the pentatonic notes version the users describe consciously ignoring the sounds.

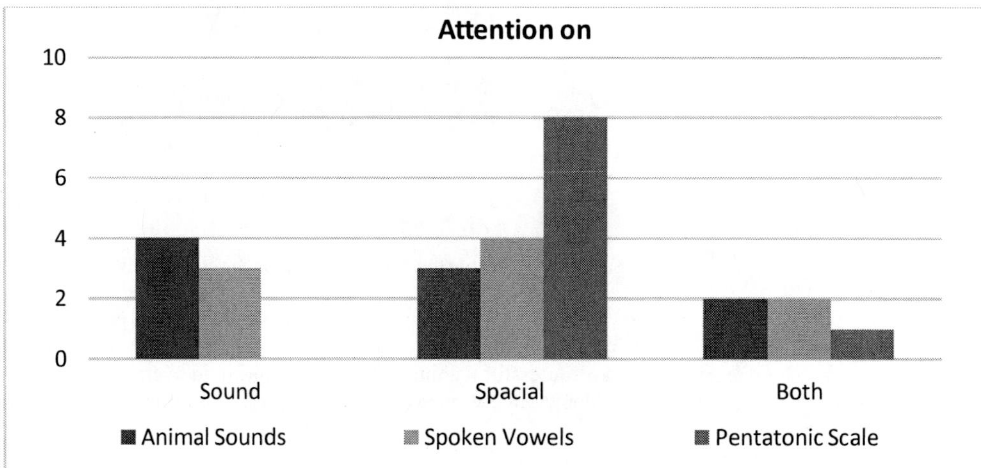

Figure 3. Version Attention

In the end of the tests, as explained in the last section, a questionnaire was done to better understand the use rand their interaction with the system. In table 1, the average of classification by all participants is presented for each question (Q1 – Q8). The results are consistent. The animal sounds are presented as the better alternative compared with both the vowels sounds version and the pentatonic notes version - which, comparatively, is the worst alternative. Both think-aloud and questionnaires results indicate that auditory feedback was not the only variable, and often not the most important, for recalling previous sequences. Spatial awareness of the objects seems to play an important role in this process.

Tabela 1. Classification Results – Average of Likert Scale

	Classification		*Classification*
Q1	3	Q5	3
Q2	4	Q6	4
Q3	2	Q7	4
Q4	3	Q8	2

4. CONCLUSIONS

In order to understand what kind of sounds would work better to help users recall the last sequence, three types of auditory feedback were designed. The main hypothesis predicted that blind users would consciously benefit from the auditory feedback provided and use it to better recall previous sequences. Although users describe having used more often spatial awareness as a strategy to recall previous sequences, they were actually more successful when they paid attention to sounds, alone or in combination with spatial awareness. The less they used auditory feedback the less successful they were. The second hypothesis may provide an explanation for the differences in users behaviour regarding attention to auditory feedback. Predicting that users would benefit less from the feedback that doesn't provide semantic information, was an assumption made on familiarity with the sounds (animal sounds, vowels) and the very structure of semantic memory. A sound like pentatonic notes that are less distinct, less familiar and is semantically irrelevant to the user, provide less power to the recalling process of previous sequences. Therefore, Masterblind can be an usable experience to blind people, as long as it uses semantically significant auditory feedback. Overall, the study offers evidence that an adaptation of a board game, such as Mastermind, that relies mostly in visual information can be successfully adapted to blind users and still provide a challenging and enjoyable experience - even with users that have little to no experience in computer games.

ACKNOWLEDGMENT

We would like to thank Dr. José Mário Albino of the Blind and Partially Sighted Association of Portugal (ACAPO - Coimbra) and Dr. Luís Barata of the University of Coimbra, for humbling providing research subjects. This work is support by Fundação Ciência e tecnologia (FCT) with the Grant ref. SFRH/BPD/101112/2014 to Ana Rita Assunção Teixeira

REFERENCES

[1] "Mastermind | toys for kids | hasbro games."http://www.hasbro. com/en-ca/product/mastermind: 93765D16-6D40-1014-8BF0-9EFBF894F9D4.

[2] S. Targett and M. Fernström, "Audio games: Fun for all? all for fun?," International Conference on Auditory Display, Boston, MA, USA, 2003.

[3] "Makey makey | buy direct (official site)." http://www.makeymakey.com.

[4] G. P. T. O. Noa Raz, Ella Striem and E. Zohary, "Superior serial memory in the blind: a case of cognitive compensatory adjustment," Biology, 17(13),pp. 1129–1133, 2007.

[5] K. Hötting and B. Röder, "Auditory and auditorytactile processing in congenitally blind humans," Hearing research 258.1, pp. 165–174, 2009.

[6] M. J. P. Achille Pasqualottoa, Jade S.Y. Lama, "Congenital blindness improves semantic and episodic memory," Behavioural brain research, 244, pp. 162– 165, 2013.

[7] W. Staab, "Auditory Icons, Earcons, and Speech", Wayne's World, 2014. [Online]. Available: http://hearinghealthmatters.org/waynesworld/2014/auditory-icons-earcons-speech/. [Accessed: 26- Jan- 2016].

[8] Rafa Absar and Catherine Guastavino, "Usability of non-speech sounds in user interfaces" in Proceedings of the 14th International Conference on Auditory Display, (Paris, France), pp. 24-27, 2008.

[9] Cynthia A. Sikora, Linda Roberts and La Tondra Murray, "Musical vs. real world feedback signals," in CHI '94: Proceedings of the SIGCHI conference on Human Factors in computing systems (Denver, CO, USA), pp. 220-221, ACM Press, 1995.

[10] MIT, "Scratch - imagine, program, share.." https: //scratch.mit.edu.

[11] Likert, R. (1932). A Technique for the Measurement of Attitudes. *Archives of Psychology*, 140, 1–55.

GNOME TRADER: A LOCATION-BASED AUGMENTED REALITY TRADING GAME

Fabio Zünd[1], Miriam Tschanen[1], Marcel Lancelle[2], Maria Olivares[3], Mattia Ryffel[3], Alessia Marra[3], Milan Bombsch[2], Markus Gross[2] and Robert W. Sumner[3]
[1] *ETH Zurich, Stampfenbachstr. 48, 8006 Zürich, Switzerland*
[2] *ETH Zurich,Universitatsstr. 6, 8092 Zürich, Switzerland*
[3] *Disney Research Zurich, Stampfenbachsstr. 48, 8006 Zürich, Switzerland*

ABSTRACT

We explore a location-based game concept that encourages real-world interactions and gamifies daily commuting activities. Enhanced with augmented reality technology, we create an immersive, pervasive trading game called *Gnome Trader*, where the player engages with the game by physically traveling to predefined locations in the city and trading resources with virtual gnomes. As the virtual market is a crucial component of the game, we take special care to analyze various economic game mechanics. We explore the parameter space of different economic models using a simulation of the virtual economy. We evaluate the overall gameplay as well as the technical functionality through several play tests.

KEYWORDS

Location-based gaming, Augmented reality, Virtual economy

1. INTRODUCTION

Through their unique combination of visual, narrative, auditory, and interactive elements, video games provide an engaging medium of expression within our society. The proliferation of mobile devices that combine computation and graphics processing with video and GPS sensors holds great potential to enhance gaming. Furthermore, augmented reality (AR) provides the ability to blend virtual and real-world experiences so that location-aware games extend past our televisions, weaving the magic of gameplay into cultural locations such as the cities in which we live. In this way, games become an augmented version of real settings, bridging between imaginative worlds and the reality around us.

In this article, we describe the design, testing, simulation, and implementation of an online multiplayer location-based AR game called *Gnome Trader*. In Gnome Trader, newspaper boxes throughout the country of Switzerland are augmented with virtual gnome characters who trade resources—nuts and peas—with players. Gnomes inhabit the boxes and vary their resource prices according to supply and demand. The core game mechanic is based on players increasing their wealth by buying and selling resources at different locations for different prices, allowing them to make a profit and to purchase upgrades. The use of augmented reality enforces the impression that a gnome is physically located in a particular box at a particular location, and thus can have a unique price compared to gnomes located elsewhere.

Although Gnome Trader follows core game design principles (Fullerton 2008) with a focus on being fun and entertaining, it has a deeper component that connects to serious gaming. At its heart, Gnome Trader represents a virtual economy. The prices of nuts and peas evolve depending on location-based transactions. Since the game is designed for large-scale deployment, it holds a unique promise to validate different economic models and better understand how the forces of supply and demand interact with pricing policies and player actions. By experimenting with the game economy, we hope to gain valuable insights about real-world economic challenges.

2. RELATED WORK

Creating a stable virtual economic model is a non-trivial process because the distribution and temporal progression of prices can greatly affect gameplay in unforeseen ways. In fact, constructing balanced economies is an ongoing topic in the gaming industry. Market crashes or hyperinflation are common ailments that can afflict even blockbuster productions, such as Diablo 3 (Earle 2013). Research related to game economies has been conducted with the focus on online trading games or massively multiplayer online games (MMOs), such as Eve Online or Everquest (Reeder et al. 2008, Castronova et al. 2009). However, virtual markets in online games often rely heavily on free trading between players and the ability to exchange in-game currency or goods for real money (Yamaguchi 2004, Debeauvais et al. 2012).

Research in the context of virtual economies often refers to agent-based modeling, an approach that consists of computational objects that interact according to predetermined rules. This approach allows one to consider richer environments with more complex behavioral perspectives and dynamic market prices. Agent-based modeling has been employed for the financial sector by modeling asset prices (Rekik, Hachicha & Boujelbene 2014), for food consumption (Deguchi et al. 2001), and for the Swiss wood market (Kostadinov et al. 2014). Most of these agent-based simulations attempt to mimic real-world markets as closely as possible, which differs from our goal of exploring the virtual market of a trading game in a more open-ended fashion. In Gnome Trader, our simulation models two core components. First, the simulation controls gnomes that represent non-player characters and do not exhibit individual needs. Second, it models player agents whose sole goal is to accumulate in-game currency by trading resources. The level of control over prices in our virtual trading game is unique and is not necessarily comparable to models of real markets. Therefore, special care must be given to the economic model used in the game design of Gnome Trader. We describe our exploration of dynamic and spatially varying pricing models that reflect the emergent behavior of real markets.

Location-based games received much attention in the past years, as demonstrated by games such as Ingress[1] and Geocaching[2]. AR applications on mobile devices benefit from versatile and intuitive interaction mechanisms and create a strong connection to the physical world. AR has been widely used, for instance, to enhance creative play and interactions (Zünd et al. 2014, Zünd et al. 2015) such as coloring books (Magnenat et al. 2015) and interactive narratives (Kapadia et al. 2015). Combining location-based technologies with AR enables a host of novel and highly immersive experiences.

3. GAME DESIGN

In Gnome Trader, the player embodies a virtual trader, equipped with a bag to carry resources and gold pieces. The goal of the player is to travel within the country and trade resources at specific locations to make a profit. Each newspaper box across Switzerland represents a registered trading location. The logo of the newspaper box acts as an AR marker. Combined with the mobile device's GPS location, our software can uniquely identify every box. We choose this marker and GPS setup as it obviates the costly task of physically altering the boxes in order to add QR codes, near-filed communication beacons, or other disambiguation technologies. Upon arriving at a newspaper box, the player opens the game app and points the smartphone's integrated camera at the box's logo. A virtual gnome with a trading interface appears on the screen, integrated into the video, to give the impression that the gnome is physically located inside the box. Figure 1 illustrates the Gnome Trader gameplay using screenshots from our prototype implementation.

[1] https://www.ingress.com/

[2] https://www.geocaching.com/

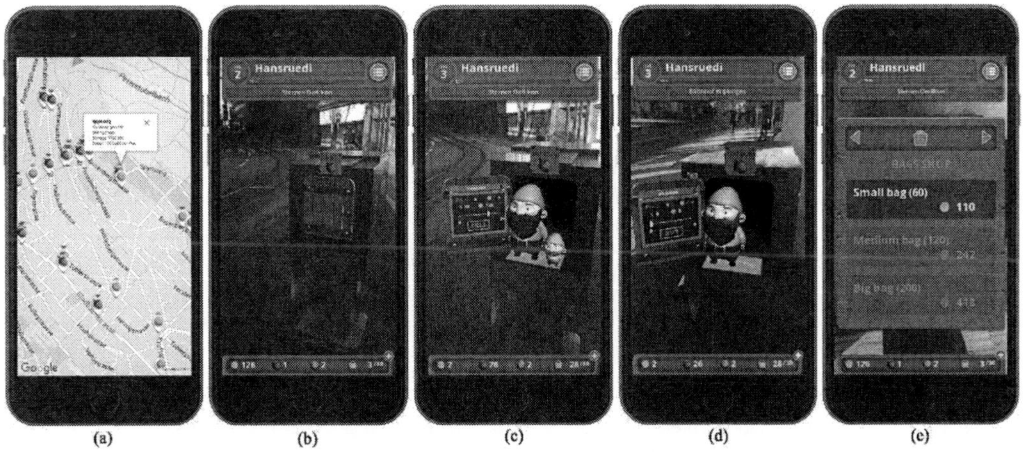

Figure 1. Screenshots of the prototype game. (a) The game map indicating trading locations. (b) A player approaches a trading location; the gnome's door is superimposed onto the newspaper box using AR. (c) A gnome family waiting to purchase nuts from the player; they offer 6 gold pieces per nut. (d) A gardener gnome offering nuts to the player at a price of 5 gold pieces per nut. (e) The bag shop menu; the player has enough money to unlock the next larger bag

Four types of trading locations exist: each newspaper box either contains a gardener gnome selling peas or nuts or a gnome family buying peas or nuts. Gardener gnomes produce resources at a constant rate until their storage is full. Analogously, family gnomes consume resources at a constant rate until their storage is empty. A crowdsourced approach is employed for adding new trading locations to the game. After the marker on an unknown newspaper box has been recognized by the game client of sufficiently many different players, a new trading location is inserted at that position in the city. Thus, the population of gnomes grows as players from new regions join the game.

The price of each resource is dynamically calculated by an economic model. We implemented two economic models, both of which are described in Section 3.1. Generally, a player can buy resources for a low price from a producer gnome with high storage and sell resources for a high price to a consumer gnome with low storage. For simplicity, in the current prototype, players cannot trade directly with each other. Their interaction is limited to the computer-controlled gnomes.

The player can access a city map depicting all gnome locations and information about their resources. This feature encourages the player to find an appropriate gnome to sell the currently carried resources at a higher price than purchased. The resource carrying capacity of the player is limited by the size of a resource bag. With enough gold, the player can purchase larger bags to carry more resources, therefore increasing trading efficiency. Thus, with increased wealth, the player can buy more resources to make an even higher profit.

The player can compare his or her performance to the other players on a global leaderboard, providing motivation to compete and continue playing. The total number of traded resources and gold is summed up for each player and displayed as a score.

3.1 Economic Models

A controllable and sustainable economic model is key to the success of the game as it defines how prices evolve over time and adapt to the behavior of the players. The goal of the economic model is to create a stable supply and demand behavior for the gnomes. Gnomes who are visited frequently by players should raise their prices, while gnomes who are rarely visited should lower their prices until a minimum price is reached. This behavior models a gnome's desire to maximize profit, while also introducing competition to the market. If an individual gnome's selling price is higher than those in the vicinity, players will buy elsewhere, forcing the gnome to lower prices. Such pricing models open up fascinating possibilities for gameplay. However, they are very hard to configure in a way that achieves a well-balanced market. We developed two specific models, inspired by existing work (Smith 1994, Davis & Williams 1986), that model the effects of asymmetric supply and demand configurations on prices converging toward a competitive equilibrium.

3.1.1 Model A: Production-Consumption

In the Production-Consumption model, each gnome continuously produces or consumes its resources at a fixed rate until the storage is full or empty, respectively. The resource price p is directly calculated from the storage ratio $r = \frac{S_{cur}}{S_{max}}$, where S_{cur} is the number of resources currently in storage and S_{max} is the storage size.

In a fixed interval, each gnome updates its price

$$p = w \cdot v(r) + k,$$
$$v(r) = \begin{cases} 2(r-1), & r < 0.5 \\ 1.5 - r, & otherwise \end{cases},$$

where w is the real world market influence described in Section 3.1.3, which is a constant scaling factor across all trading locations, and k is a randomization term that varies the price. The randomization term adds a certain amount of chance to the game, which increases suspense for the players. In the prototype, k was defined such that it decreases or increases the price up to ten percent. The price modifier term $v(r)$ doubles the price if the storage is empty and halves the price if the storage is full. A producer gnome with low storage is considered successful and should increase its price to make more profit. Analogously, a consumer gnome with a low storage will starve soon and should increase the price it is willing to pay.

3.1.2 Model B: History-Based

In the History-Based model, gnomes keep track of their trading success over time and adjust prices according to trends. A trading history logs how many resources were sold and purchased over the last couple of days. At each update step, the current earnings are compared to the history and evaluated for performance. If a producer gnome is successful, that is, if it was able to sell more resources than before, the selling price is increased. If the gnome sold less, the price is reduced. A consumer gnome is considered successful if it traded many resources recently, in which case it tries to lower the buying price, otherwise it is increased. Producer and consumer prices at time t are calculated as

$$p_{prod}^{t} = p_{prod}^{t-1} + m\left(\sum_{i=0}^{d-1} n_s^{t-i} / \sum_{i=1}^{d} n_s^{t-i} - 1\right) + (w^t - w^{t-1})$$
$$p_{cons}^{t} = p_{cons}^{t-1} + m\left(\sum_{i=0}^{d-1} n_b^{t-i} / \sum_{i=1}^{d} n_b^{t-i} - 1\right) + (w^t - w^{t-1}),$$

where the parameters n_s^t and n_b^t denote the amount of resources sold or bought by the gnome at time t, d controls the history depth, and m is a scalar model parameter used to weight the history influence. The term w is the real market influence described in Section 3.1.3. An important difference to the Production-Consumption model is that in this model gnomes have access to an unlimited number of resources.

3.1.3 Real World Economy Influence

To create a more realistic playing experience, the game's virtual economy is loosely tied to the real world economy. This feature gives the player a feeling of immersion and suspense as he or she can utilize real world measurements and estimates of the economy to make decisions in the game. This connection is created by introducing a gnome market index term w, which is calculated from a real market index, such as Dow Jones, NASDAQ, or Nikkei. As a result, fluctuations in the real market index are mirrored in the virtual market and visible in the individual gnome's price calculations. We calculate the gnome market index term

$$w^t = 3 + 1.9\,\mathrm{atan}\left(0.005(I^t - I_{AVG60}^t)\right)$$

for a time t by scaling the real market index I and removing low frequencies. The term I_{AVG60}^t denotes the 60-

day moving average of *I*. In our prototype, the Swiss Market Index (SMI) was employed for *I*. Specific values for the equation were found empirically.

3.2 Implementation

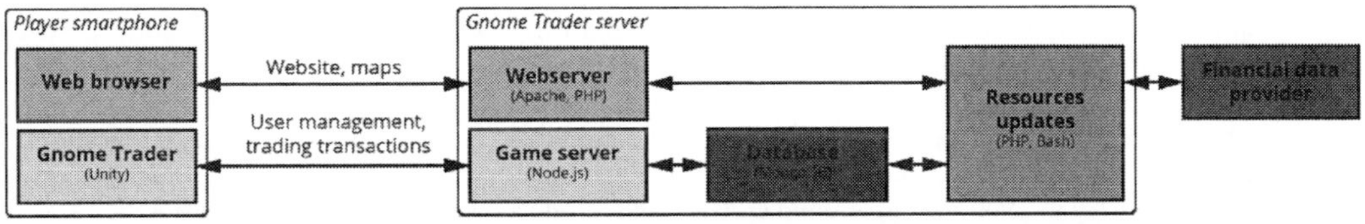

Figure 2. Gnome Trader client-server architecture overview. The game server provides user and trading location data to the Unity-based game client app. The game map, provided by a webserver, is viewed on any browser. Regular resource update and maintenance tasks are performed directly on the database. Financial data is retrieved from an external data provider

Figure 2 depicts the client-server architecture. The game client is implemented using the Unity[3] game engine, relying on the Vuforia SDK[4] for AR processing. A real-time websocket communication architecture based on socket.io[5] is employed to pass messages between the Unity client and a node.js[6] based server application. The server application stores user data, transaction data, and trading location data in a MongoDB[7] database. Maintenance scripts perform updates on the database at regular time intervals to, for example, recalculate prices and distribute resources. The game map is made accessible to the players on a website running on Apache[8]. The Google Maps API[9] allows our system to overlay gnome locations, their prices, and storage levels over the city street map. Financial data is retrieved from Quandl[10].

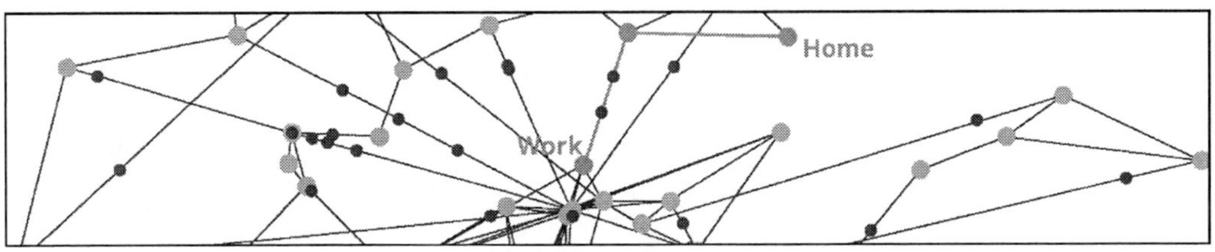

Figure 3. Part of a randomly generated city map with 40 player agents (red dots) and 40 gnomes (green nodes). An example agent's daily commute path from home to work is highlighted in orange

4. SIMULATION

It is crucial to be able to analyze potential pricing schemes of a trading game in a controlled manner before launch to reduce the risk of problematic behaviors such as massive inflation or market crashes. For this purpose, we propose an agent-based framework that simulates the virtual economy of Gnome Trader. The simulator uses a simplified model of the game. Players cannot buy upgrades or spend money in any way other than buying resources. There is only one type of resource to trade. The city map is generated at random, using an algorithm that is inspired by scale-free graphs (Li et al. 2005) and exhibits similar properties. Part of an example generated city map is depicted in Figure 3. The simulator was implemented using MASON[11], an agent-based modeling toolkit for Java.

[3] https://unity3d.com/
[4] https://developer.vuforia.com/
[5] http://socket.io/
[6] https://nodejs.org/
[7] https://www.mongodb.org/
[8] http://www.apache.org/
[9] http://developers.google.com/
[10] https://www.quandl.com/
[11] https://cs.gmu.edu/~eclab/projects/mason/

4.1 Player Behavior Model

Players are represented by agents in the simulator. The model distinguishes player movement and trading behavior and assumes the two to be independent. Agents never move to a gnome for the explicit purpose of making an advantageous trade. The reasoning for this choice is that traveling takes real effort. Thus, players are unlikely to go out of their way just to play the game. Instead, they will go about their business as usual, and only stop to play when a convenient opportunity presents itself. Because of this assumption, the agent behavior model used for the simulation tries to mimic the movement patterns of average people going about their daily lives in an urban environment. Players are assumed to commute between two fixed locations once per day, such as going to school or work. Agents can trade with gnomes they visit during their daily commute. They try to maximize profits by conservatively selecting the best trading opportunities along that path. Agents only sell when there is no better offer along their path. They also avoid selling a resource for less than it was bought, which is represented by the resistance price. The resistance price decays slowly over time to avoid locking agents out of trading indefinitely. Agents buy when a producer's price is lowest and there is a guaranteed profit to be made elsewhere by selling the resource for more money. The last condition prevents player agents from buying up worthless resources simply because they are cheap.

4.2 Results

Both economic models described in Section 3.1 were simulated under various configurations to explore the parameter spaces. The real world influence and the randomization term were omitted for the simulation, to observe the properties of the economic model without the interference of these added effects.

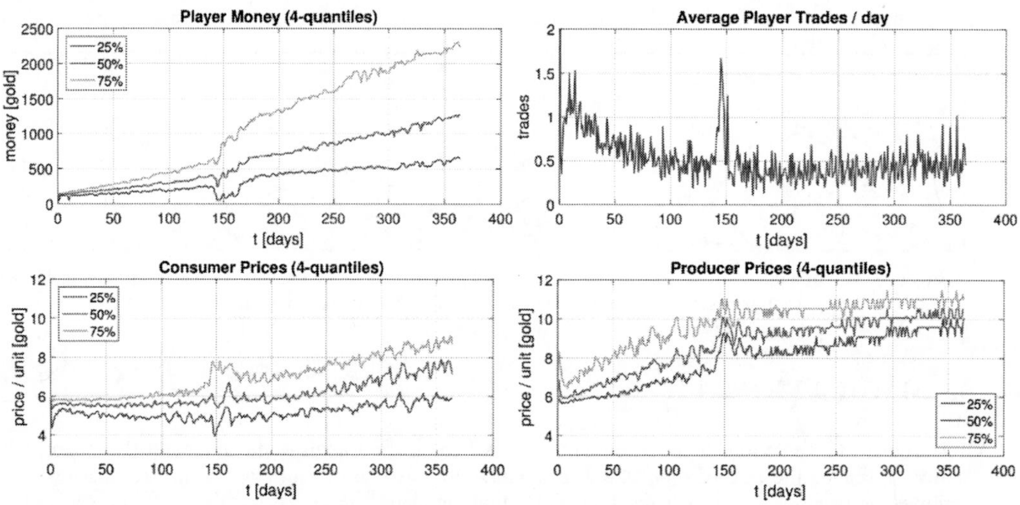

Figure 4. Simulation output of an undersupply scenario in the Production-Consumption economic model. The city contains 102 consumer gnomes and 98 producer gnomes. The market index is fixed at w = 6.0 and gnomes have a maximum capacity of 500 units. Production and consumption rates are at 20 units per day

4.2.1 Model A: Production-Consumption

The behavior of the Production-Consumption model depends on the ratio of consumer and producer gnomes as well as their production and consumption rates. If the parameters are chosen such that the inflow of resources into the system equals the outflow, then the economy is stable and prices fluctuate around a constant value. However, by upsetting this balance we can simulate a variety of interesting real market phenomenon, such as shortages and oversupply. For example, Figure 4 shows the output of a scenario with a slightly higher number of consumer gnomes than producer gnomes. This imbalance results in an undersupply of resources that causes the producer prices to rise continuously. The shortage causes consumer prices to spike after about 140 days. Player agents recognize the opportunity for profit, as evidenced by the subsequent increase in trading activity. Player wealth drops momentarily due to the investment. Prices fluctuate for a few days before the simulation continues normally.

The Production-Consumption model can be fine-tuned dynamically and offers developers a high level of control over the market behavior. The ability to reproduce real world phenomenon makes it an interesting choice for a game economy.

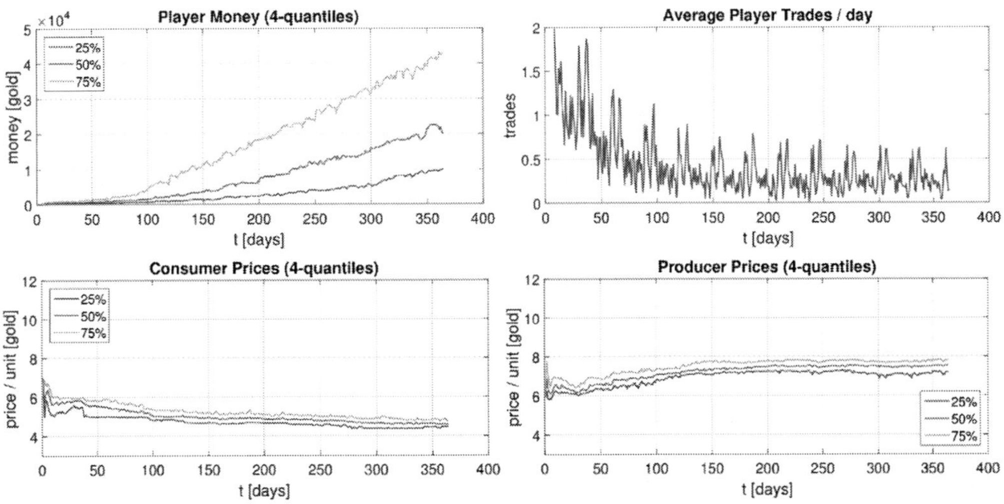

Figure 5. Simulation output with the History-Based economic model. Gnomes store trade histories for 30 simulation days and the multiplier is set to m = 2.0

4.2.2 Model B: History-Based

Figure 5 shows a simulation run of the same scenario using the History-Based economic model. The imbalance between consumers and producers has no apparent effect on this economic model, because its prices are only dependent on the sales and purchase volumes, not on the absolute amount of resources in the system. As such, it is more robust to variations in population sizes, but also easier to influence by certain player strategies. While the unlimited supply and demand for resources causes players to gain wealth at a much faster pace than in the Production-Consumption model, this phenomenon can be accounted for by balancing the initial prices accordingly.

5. PLAYTESTING

We tested the game prototype to evaluate the technical functionality and the appeal of gameplay. Following the agile development concept, we started with tests early during the development and finally conducted two more formal playtesting sessions.

In the first playtesting session 8 participants (5 male and 3 female, aged 17 to 26 years) played the prototype in Zurich, Switzerland. Each participant was engaged in the game for 2 hours in total over the course of a week. Afterwards, the participant's feedback was collected with a questionnaire. Most users needed some time to appreciate the concept of traveling physically to successfully play the game. While the participants did not lose interest in the game during that week, some mentioned that without any changes it may become less interesting to continue playing. The limited accuracy and robustness of the measured GPS location sometimes led to inconsistent trading location information, which negatively influenced the gameplay. Some participants also suggested that direct trading between players would be desirable.

A second playtesting session was conducted in Barcelona, Spain, with 19 participants over the course of an afternoon. The game was played again successfully and additional insights could be gained through a questionnaire. To generate a single figure that would encapsulate the player's satisfaction with the game, the Net Promoter Score was used. The average results for the score were very positive, standing at 73.5%. After playing, 79% of the participants indicated that they would play the game a few times per week or more. Feedback from the participants included that the AR approach requires good lighting conditions, which can be problematic at night time. Participants also mentioned that the high battery consumption should be addressed.

6. CONCLUSION

In this paper, we demonstrated a game prototype for a city-wide trading game. AR and real world market influence contribute to a rich and immersive gaming experience. Our simulator showed that the Consumption-Production economy model is well suited for implementation because it can be fine-tuned as required and reproduces the phenomenon of real markets. Alternatively, the History-Based economy model is more robust to variations in player and gnome populations but, at the same time, is also vulnerable to certain player strategies. We conclude from two play testing sessions that the game concept is functional and well received.

REFERENCES

Castronova, E., et al. (2009). As real as real? Macroeconomic behavior in a large-scale virtual world. *New Media & Society*, 11(5):685–707.

Davis, D. & Williams, A. (1986). The effects of rent asymmetries in posted offer market. *Journal Of Economic Behavior & Organization*, 7:303–316.

Debeauvais, T., et al. (2012). 10,000 gold for 20 dollars: An exploratory study of world of warcraft gold buyers. In *Proceedings of the International Conference on the Foundations of Digital Games*, FDG '12, pages 105–112. ACM, New York, NY, USA.

Deguchi, H., et al. (2001). *New Frontiers in Artificial Intelligence: Joint JSAI 2001 Workshop Post-Proceedings*, chapter Virtual Economy Simulation and Gaming – An Agent Based Approach, pages 218–226. Springer Berlin Heidelberg, Berlin, Heidelberg.

Earle, P. C. (2013). A virtual weimar: Hyperinflation in a video game world. https://mises.org/library/virtual-weimar-hyperinflation-video-game-world. Fullerton, T. (2008). Game Design Workshop: A Playcentric Approach to Creating Innovative Games. Taylor& Francis.

Kapadia, M., et al. (2015). Computer-assisted authoring of interactive narratives. In *Proceedings of the 19th Symposium on Interactive 3D Graphics and Games*, i3D '15, pages 85–92. ACM, New York, NY, USA.

Kostadinov, F., et al. (2014). Simulation of a swiss wood fuel and round wood market: An explorative study in agent-based modeling. *Forest Policy and Economics*, pages 105–118.

Li, L., et al. (2005). Towards a theory of scale-free graphs: Definition, properties, and implications. *Internet Mathematics*, 2(4):431–523.

Magnenat, S., etal. (2015). Live texturing of augmented reality characters from colored drawings. Visualization and Computer Graphics, IEEE Transactions on, 21(11):1201–1210.

Reeder, J., et al. (2008). Intelligent trading agents for massively multi-player game economies. In AIIDE.

Rekik, Y. M., Hachicha, W., & Boujelbene, Y. (2014). Agent-based modeling and investors' behavior explanation of asset price dynamics on artificial financial markets. *Procedia Economics and Finance*, 13:30 –46.

Smith, V. (1994). Economics in the laboratory. *The Journal of Economic Perspectives*, 8(1):113–131.

Yamaguchi, H. (2004). An analysis of virtual currencies in online games. *SSRN Electronic Journal.*

Zünd, F., et al. (2014). Influence of animated reality mixing techniques on user experience. In *Proceedings of the Seventh International Conference on Motion in Games*, MIG '14, pages 125–132. ACM, New York, NY, USA.

Zünd, F., et al. (2015). Augmented creativity: Bridging the real and virtual worlds to enhance creative play. In *SIGGRAPH Asia 2015 Mobile Graphics and Interactive Applications*, SA '15, pages 21:1–21:7. ACM, New York, NY, USA.

WHO'S IN MY GAME?: OTHER PLAYERS IN THE SINGLE-PLAYER *SPACECHEM*

Nicolás López Coombs
Utrecht University, De Hermelijn 41, 3972TS Driebergen-Rijsenburg, Netherlands

ABSTRACT

In this paper, I analyze the win screen in the puzzle game SpaceChem (Zachtronics 2011a), notable for the three data visualizations it uses in place of a traditional leaderboard. Through this case study, I aim to problematize taken-for-granted use of both data visualization and social networking features. I perform a visual analysis informed by affordance theory to identify the kind of behavior encouraged or discouraged by these elements as well as a prominent "Record Solution" button which allows sharing player solutions via YouTube. I find that these elements complicate the division between the diegetic and non-diegetic as they invite a player outside the game and onto another platform. Significantly, ambiguity between the world of a particular game and the data-gathering, networked systems they are part of is not unique to SpaceChem but rather part of a growing proportion of the games we engage in, be it through achievement systems or social networks.

KEYWORDS

Affordances, Intrinsic Motivation, Extrinsic Motivation, Data Visualization, YouTube

1. INTRODUCTION

Zachtronics' SpaceChem (2011a) is a puzzle game where the player works as a "reactor engineer" designing factories that "transform raw materials into valuable chemical products" (Zachtronics 2015). Players beat the game by providing one of the elusive yet seemingly endless possible solutions to each puzzle. Upon each level's completion, the player is presented with data visualizations of how other players' performance compares to theirs. Yet rather than a traditional leaderboard or high scores table, three bar graphs are shown, one measuring the number of cycles the in-game program requires to produce the 'chemical products', a second measuring the number of symbols the player used to build their factories and a third showing the number of different factories ('reactors') used to complete the challenge.

Most games make it clear from the outset what players are expected to do through game descriptions like this one from Candy Crush Jelly Saga[1]: "Take on this delightful Saga alone or play with friends to see who can get the highest score!" Yet SpaceChem never specifies whether ideal player performance involves a minimum of cycles, reactors or symbols, nor does it provide any standard score bar, thereby leaving one unsure how to interpret one's placement on the player performance graphs. When first confronted with these histograms, I was perplexed myself. I wondered why after having reached my objective of completing the puzzle, the game compared my performance to the gamut of other players who had, up until that point, been invisible to me. If the game was guiding me towards SpaceChem excellence, then why present me with three different graphs, each of which suggesting a different way to play? Perhaps there was no intended function for the graphs and they were just incidental by-products of data collection; once one has the data, it seems only natural that something be done with it.

These questions are not just significant for this case. Though data visualization has its roots in cartography and statistics, "graphic portrayal of quantitative information" (Friendly 2009, 1) continues to spread into other fields (ibid., 39). It's easy to understand why; studies show we consume information presented in a visual format more easily (Burn-Murdoch 2013). Social media has gone from

1 King. 2016. "Candy Crush Jelly Saga." iTunes. January 6. https://itunes.apple.com/gb/app/candy-crush-jelly-saga/id1047246341?mt=8&v0=WWW-EUUK-ITSTOP100-FREEAPPS&l=en&ign-mpt=uo%3D4.

text- to image-focused as users have embraced visual communication: "Pictures have become one of our default modes of sorting and understanding the vast amounts of information we're exposed to every day" (Walter 2012).

Yet the same simplicity and directness that make images convenient are what make visualizations dangerous. The fact that data visualizations often go viral despite flaws in methodology and source data led one journalist to write the strongly titled "Why you should never trust a data visualization" (Burn-Murdoch 2013). And the problem extends beyond the unedited world of social media. Even the venerable New York Times has been criticized for "[misusing] design…to tell a biased story" (Flagg & Syed, 2015).

The question remains, why would this be significant to a player? SpaceChem is not a journalistic setting, so what would be the possible negative outcome? Contemporary gamers who play on social media and mobile devices, who live-stream their gameplay on Twitch and who may not in fact own the games they paid for and have on their computer[2] have a significantly different experience than those of twenty, ten or even a few years ago. With these changes, game makers have had to develop new ways to monetize their product, many of which are not apparent to users. Methods such as "coercive monetization", which relies on fooling a player into making purchases, or "progress gates", which require a player to pay to advance within the game, use psychology to take advantage of player's desire to complete a game to make a profit in underhanded ways (Shokrizade 2013). As Tim Fields (2014) writes in his book, *Mobile & Social Game Design: Monetization Methods and Mechanics,* game makers "need [their] users to come back for more, as often as possible, and preferably with friends" (125). Given the prevalence of such strategies (ibid., 24), it becomes relevant to every player to consider the ways their game might be manipulating them and to what end.

With that in mind, my intent in this paper is to focus not on what data these visualizations communicate, but rather on how they affect the player's experience through my research question: What implications does the SpaceChem win screen have for the rest of the game? Further questions include: What are the affordances of the visualizations and the other elements of the win screen, most notably a YouTube button? What kind of behavior do they encourage or discourage? How do they compare to a traditional leaderboard?

1.1 Theoretical Framework and Methodology

In order to understand the effects the win screen has on game experience, I need to establish context. By performing a textual analysis of official materials offered by the developer, including game rules, game description, the Zachtronics blog and in-game narrative, I will show how the gameplay is depicted by the developer and therefore, how a player is likely to interpret their mission in SpaceChem. I will be searching these materials for anything that might help explain the role of the win screen's different elements, specifically items related to competition, player improvement and socializing.

Then I will go on to do a visual analysis of the win screen, drawing from affordance theory to identify the ways the win screen fulfills or diverges from the official game depiction seen in my first section. As defined by Norman, "Affordances reflect the possible relationships among actors and objects: they are properties of the world" (1999, 42). Using this concept to focus primarily on two elements, the histograms and the YouTube button, I will illustrate how the win screen encourages or discourages certain behaviors.

Medler's "Player Dossiers: Analyzing Gameplay Data as a Reward" explores player dossiers, which are statistical and visual presentations of past gameplay that offer "ways for players to connect to one another using online social networking features" (2011). He proposes that these systems offer both social rewards and the ability to "gain insights from their recorded gameplay" (np). While there are clear differences between the data profile a player dossier provides and the simplified data visualizations in SpaceChem, they both afford certain functions socially and for player improvement. Of even more interest will be a reflection on the ways the YouTube feature allows creation of another kind of social profile.

Not unrelated to the topic of player dossiers, Jakobsson's (2011) description of achievement systems as an "invisible MMO that all Xbox Live members participate in" highlights how game experience is informed by exterior data elements, whether they are achievements built into gaming platforms or visualizations that incorporate a player's performance into those of a broader community's. When Jakobsson talks about all Xbox players 'participating' in an achievement system, however, the meaning is quite different from that of the player participating in the game that they sat down and booted up. As Mirko Tobias Schäfer (2008, 85)

2 Walker, J., 2012. Thought: Do We Own Our Steam Games? *Rock Paper Shotgun*.

describes in his book *Bastard Culture*, participation can be both *explicit* or *implicit*, and the former "does not necessarily require a conscious activity of cultural production" and is "the result of software design that focuses on user actions." With that understanding, SpaceChem players implicitly participate in the visualization that results from their user-generated content just as Xbox players implicitly participate in the 'invisible MMO.' This design prompts some Xbox players to "feel trapped in a deterministic system that dictates ways of playing the games that they do not enjoy" (Jakobsson 2011). While I do not aim to know if SpaceChem players share these frustrations, research into achievement systems provides a useful framework for understanding the affordances of such implicit participatory systems and the motivations they offer.

All players are, of course, not created equal. While much game research focuses on the game itself as an artifact, Berry et al. (2013, 165) insist on the significance of the player's actions and experience *with* the game. If one is to understand how the data visualizations and YouTube feature in SpaceChem affect player experience, it is important to have an idea of how different individuals play games and what player types SpaceChem's features might appeal to. As Berry et al. write, "given players don't play at everything and tend to orient themselves towards the activities that are the most meaningful to them – which vary among players" (ibid., 167). They go on to divide these decisions on three axes, "competitive or casual, fandom or not fandom, dueling (PvP) or coping with adversity (PvE)" (ibid.).

Finally, I will conclude by outlining the implications of these different elements, not only for SpaceChem players but for other games as well.

2. ANALYSIS

2.1 Official Depictions

How does the player come to understand their task in SpaceChem? Do other game materials from the creator emphasize competition with other players or perfecting strategy? I will look at four different sources to find out: an official instructional video, the official website, the developer's blog and the in-game narrative.

After starting the game, the player is shown a YouTube video titled: "SpaceChem: A Brief Introduction" in which SpaceChem is described as "a game about ingenuity, open-ended puzzles and fake chemistry" (Zachtronics 2011a). It instructs a player to "take these" (indicating the atoms on the left) and "make these" (indicating the molecules on the right) (ibid.). It goes on to describe the mechanics of (un)bonding, grabbing, moving, rotating and dropping atoms (ibid.). Beyond that, it offers no further instruction.

SpaceChem's official site describes the game as "an obscenely addictive, design-based puzzle game about building machines and fighting monsters in the name of science!" (Zachtronics 2015). It goes on to detail the gameplay as follows: "Construct elaborate factories to transform raw materials into valuable chemical products! Streamline your designs to meet production quotas and survive encounters with the sinister threats that plague SpaceChem" (ibid.) From both the official video and website, the gameplay is framed as an uncomplicated and open puzzle game. Neither indicate any social elements or competition. As seen above, win conditions remain vague: "meet production quotas" (ibid.) or "make these" (Zachtronics 2011a).

Zachtronics' SpaceChem blog does not offer any clarification of general winning conditions either. However, the lack of a standardized play score metric was acknowledged in one blog post, though indirectly. This post offered players a contest composed of three different challenges, "each with their own rules" (Zachtronics 2012b). Success was measured according to speed, number of cycles and number of symbols (ibid.) A different post addressing the production of the "marvelous score graphs" stated that "score data is such an integral part of the SpaceChem gameplay experience" (Zachtronics 2011b) though why or for what purpose it might be used remained unsaid.

Within the game itself, there is a rather developed 12,000-word narrative, though it is not firmly integrated into the gameplay. Players are offered chapters sequentially as they begin each new level, yet the story remains separate, not only because it is only shown to players if they choose to click on the "Story" tab but also because it is presented in a textual format distinct from play. It provides some background detail for the player's role in the game: S/he works for SpaceChem, "the largest chemical engineering and manufacturing company in the universe" (Barth, H., 2012). It mostly details their day-to-day as a new employee at the company, though it also explains how various chemical and nuclear accidents create the giant monsters that serve as the bosses for each planet. The only suggestion that could be interpreted as indicating other players is in the second chapter, “A Brief History of SpaceChem” where the company is said to “currently employ over 200,000 individuals” (ibid.). It does not elaborate in any way that might provide roles for the other players represented in the histograms, nor an explanation for why their progress would be compared with the player's. (For example, the player could be competing with other engineers on different planets for engineer of the month.)

None of the official materials for the game provide any clarification as to how a player should play and beat the game beyond merely solving the puzzles. Unlike in the Candy Crush Jelly Saga example from the introduction, no concept of a score is introduced, nor is the player encouraged to beat their friends. Players are merely offered the freedom to input whatever solutions meet the requirements of the particular level. However, as we shall see further on, this does not mean that the game is not competitive or asocial.

2.2 Win Screen Analysis

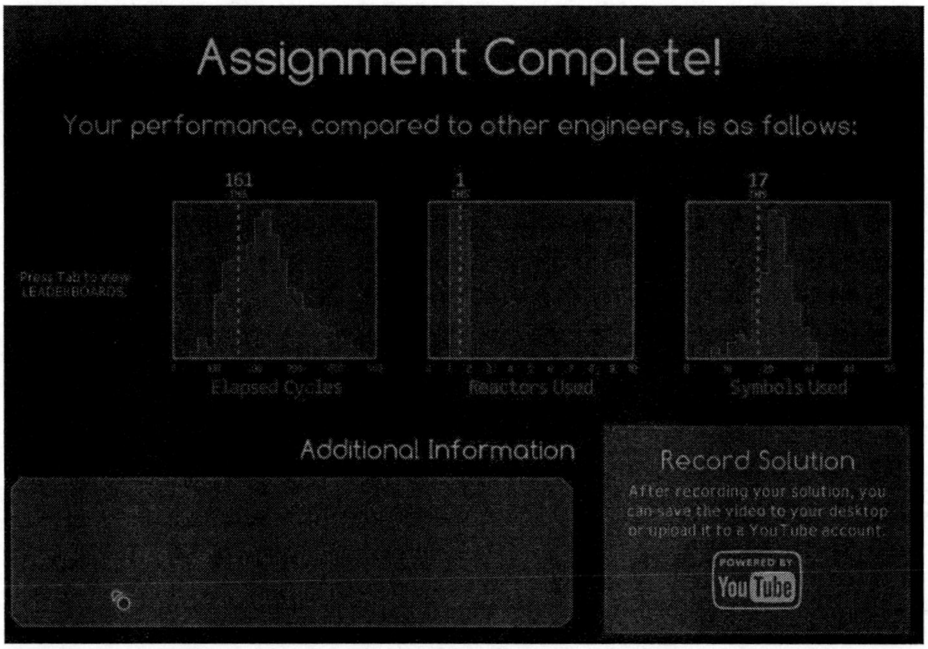

Figure 1. Screenshot of the SpaceChem win screen

Upon completing a level, the player is presented with the win screen (See Figure 1) that is the focus of this paper. Through a visual analysis, we will see how its affordances relate to and conflict with the depictions we have already seen.

At the top of the black win screen it says “Assignment Complete!”, a typical congratulation similar to those found in other games, such as Angry Birds[3] (“Level Cleared”) or Kingdom Rush[4] (“Victory”). The next line says “Your performance, compared to other engineers, is as follows.” You'll note that this is the first indication that there are other individuals playing the game. This changes the role of the aforementioned 200,000 engineers from in-game scenery to fellow players that one competes with, most suggested by the use of the word “compared”.

Below that text are three histograms in the center of the screen which are marked, from left to right, as “Elapsed Cycles,” “Reactors Used” and “Symbols Used”. To the left of these graphs “Press Tab to view LEADERBOARDS” is written. At the bottom left is a box for Additional Information (which is left blank in

3 Rovio Mobile, 2009. *Angry Birds*, Chillingo.
4 Armor Games, 2011. *Kingdom Rush*, Ironhide Game Studio.

the screenshots I have) while at the bottom right there is another box with the title "Record Solution" which allows the player to make a video of their gameplay to either download or directly upload to YouTube.

The "Assignment Complete!" text, while clearly the starting point for the reader, is not the focus of the screen. The set of three visualizations are the largest visible element and hold the center position. Though a traditional leaderboard (or high score table) is available, it is not shown automatically and is only indicated by discrete text off to the side, which, unlike the "Additional Information" or "Record Solution" is not placed within a distinguishing box. Furthermore, players cannot click through to the leaderboards (as they can for recording a solution), they must press the TAB key, making the leaderboards less convenient. The "Record Solution" box draws much more attention to itself with its larger size, brighter text color and distinctive YouTube logo. The "Record Solution" text is also the largest on the screen after "Assignment Complete!"

I therefore interpret the win screen to have the following primary functions: One, to congratulate the player. Two, to present the player with the data visualizations in order to encourage replay. And three, to motivate the player to record their solution and upload it to YouTube. While leaderboards are available to players, their significance is markedly downplayed by inconvenient access and inconspicuousness. In fact, in a PostMortem with gaming site Gamasutra, developer Zach Barth directly addressed his favoring of histograms over leaderboards, stating that leaderboards incentivize cheating and "For most players, the **only** thing a global leaderboard manages to tell you is that you suck" (Barth, Z. 2012, emphasis original).

The first of these three functions, congratulating the player, is quite typical and does not warrant extensive analysis. Researchers far more knowledgeable on the subject than I have shown that because humans react to praise and criticism from computers in much the same way they do with other humans, encouragement from the game is a common way to motivate players to continue playing.[5]

The second function requires more investigation. Why is it important to share this data with the player? And why present it in three different visualizations? As seen in the quotation above, Barth was clearly disenchanted with the traditional leaderboard system, although the histograms make use of similar exterior data recordings to compare player performance. As he writes in that same postmortem, the histograms quickly and legibly allow a player to position themself among "the aggregate" (2012). Barth goes on to say that most players will find out that "their solution is terrible" but respond by "replay[ing] the puzzle to improve their score" (ibid.). His interpretation of the player corresponds to the type described as "competitive" by Berry et al.: "The players...who spend a significant amount of time playing, and have achieved the most difficult tasks. They are deeply involved in the gameplay. They try to achieve the topmost goals" (2013, 171). I therefore propose that the histograms afford a comparison with other players that in turn encourages replay, at least for those players whose play style is 'competitive'.

The final function, recording to video, extends the aims of the second: using the 'aggregate' to encourage continued engagement with the game. It urges the player to make a video of their successful solution for a personal record or to share with others. While it does not explicitly encourage sharing, the inclusion of an upload to YouTube feature and the prominence of the YouTube logo make that implication clear. YouTube's slogan until 2011(the year of SpaceChem's release) was, after all, "Broadcast Yourself" (Tufnell 2013). More specifically, makers of Let's Play videos, wherein gamers provide audio commentary in a video of their gameplay, have attracted millions of subscribers to devoted YouTube channels (Glas 2015, 81). With a burgeoning social market for videos of gameplay, the obvious motivation for offering this feature is to encourage players to put their solutions online where they will be shared with others. While this practice does offer SpaceChem some amount of free publicity, I believe its significance lies more firmly in the social aspect. By uploading this video to YouTube, a player makes the SpaceChem community a part of their social network. Perhaps after uploading their video they will choose to look at some of the many other solutions to the same level. Other players may comment on his/her solution or s/he may choose to comment on one of theirs. Or they may choose to do none of those things, instead uploading the video and returning to the game (or even turning off the computer.) In any case, even before uploading, the player was made aware of that community thanks to the in-game, attention-drawing YouTube button. Whether or not they choose to look at the other videos, they will infer that videos exist which offer other solutions to the puzzle they just

5 See Bracken, C.C., Jeffres, L.W. & Neuendorf, K.A., 2004. Criticism or praise? The impact of verbal versus text-only computer feedback on social presence, intrinsic motivation, and recall. *Cyberpsychology & behavior,* Vol. 7, No. 3, pp. 349–357 and Wang, H. & Sun, C.-T., 2011. Game reward systems: gaming experiences and social meanings. *Proceedings of the 5th Digital Games Research Association*, pp.14–17.

completed, thus challenging them to, as Barth said earlier, "replay the puzzle to improve their score" (Barth, Z. 2012).

As previously mentioned, research from Berry, et al. (2013) shows us that all players are not created equal. While some think of the 'gamer' as a particular type, it is rather a term that encompasses individuals with all kinds of different play styles and preferences, not only in terms of what games they choose to play but also in how they play them, despite the fact that any particular game "favours certain styles over others by setting up systems of rewards only for some actions" (ibid., 175). This variety of play styles is often invisible to the players themselves until they are made aware of these differences by engaging with other players outside of gameplay via "guild forums, performance measurement websites and software, films on YouTube, etc." (ibid., 8). Such 'extracurricular' engagement with game culture was historically separate from the game itself. Yet in SpaceChem (among others), despite the lack of game communities, competitions, ways to identify other players (since the histograms do not show names or gamer tags), or other opportunities for interaction, users are directly confronted with the exterior gaming community.

This brings us back to Jakobsson's (2011) notion of the *Xbox Live Massively Multiplayer Online Game (XLMMO).* His characterization of the Xbox Live Achievement system (comparable to similar systems on Steam or Playstation) frames it as an overarching meta-game in which one progresses by completion of achievements in individual Xbox Live games. Achievements are often entirely separate from the goals needed to beat the game; for example, in Heavy Rain[6], the goal of the game is to save a child, yet there is an achievement completed when you let the child die. Thus completing an entire retail game does not mean that one has necessarily completed all the possible Xbox Live achievements for that game. In the eyes of many researchers, the achievement system thus provides "extrinsic motivators" (Jakobsson 2011). Similarly, the data visualizations, with their alternative ways to play the level create new motivations to play the level again.

Yet are these intrinsic or extrinsic motivators? Jakobsson's concept of intrinsic motivator is one that "emerges from interest and enjoyment in the task itself" (2011). Another way to look at it in a game context is to ask whether or not the player completes the task for a high score or achievement or if they do it because they are having fun. I would suggest that the visualizations in SpaceChem cannot be firmly placed on one side or the other. They certainly have extrinsic elements in that they compare a player to his/her fellows, but there is not a clear extrinsic reward for replaying the level, no high score or achievement. There is no profile where their performance is recorded for other players to see.

By contrast, within the *XLMMO*, the player develops a "game identity" which comes to represent "the social (gaming) capital that the player has built within the community" (ibid.). Medler's writing on player dossiers comes to similar conclusions, whereby the dossier positions a player within the community (Medler 2011). In SpaceChem, while there is no in-game analog for a player dossier, the player *is* encouraged to take their game activity to YouTube. Since YouTube is a social network, it is in many ways built on the same kind of identity-linked profile system as player dossiers. Yet instead of their profile "visually combining achievement data from a number of gaming platforms" (Medler 2011), users are socially defined by the gameplay videos they upload. Unlike the data visualizations, however, these videos are not visible in-game. These videos, like Medler's player dossiers, remain external to the game.

The fact that SpaceChem is a one-player game does not preclude it from having sociality. Take as example the reader of a novel who joins a book club. The group does not change the individual nature of reading but rather creates a social space to reflect on that experience. Another example might be the water cooler discussion of the Downton Abbey episode you watched on your own the night before. To use Schäfer's (2008) terminology, engaging with colleagues over Downton Abbey would be an example of socially-motivated "explicit participation" (85). Inclusion in a community in SpaceChem as a player represented on a histogram is unintentional and therefore "implicit participation" (ibid.). So what of recording and sharing your performance on YouTube? I would argue that this is somewhere in-between the two, as a player may very well choose to upload their performance without engaging with the other community members. They are clearly participating in terms of creating content, yet they are not necessarily interacting further with other members. The issue is further clouded by the ease with which SpaceChem allows a user to record their gameplay; the lower the barrier to entry, the less explicit the participation.

One might question the likelihood of a player making the effort to record and share their performance on YouTube without bothering to engage further, yet research from Ducheneaut et al. complicates that

6 Quantic Dream, 2010. *Heavy Rain*, Sony Computer Entertainment.

understanding of sociality in gaming. Their research into World of Warcraft found that large numbers of players, while opting not to play cooperatively with other players still preferred the game to a single-player alternative due to other social features: "The other players have important roles beyond providing direct support and camaraderie in the context of quest groups: they also provide an *audience,* a sense of *social presence,* and a *spectacle*" (2006, 7).

Therefore, video-making may for some players be merely about providing *themselves* with an audience. As Glas writes, "The way [Let's Play] creators play and react to games might just say something about their imagined ideal *player* (rather than spectator)" (2013, 84). So if the histograms provide additional motivation to players with competitive play styles, the YouTube feature does the same for the players interested in the social aspects of gaming, even if those social aspects are merely entail having an audience.

3. CONCLUSION

In beginning this research, I expected to conclude with a decisive function for the data visualizations and YouTube button on the SpaceChem win screen, something along the lines of it providing extrinsic motivation that pushes the player to longer engagement. Looking back, however, it does not seem to be that simple or clear cut.

The visualizations certainly complicate a user's sense of progress. The game's lack of clarity as to what ideal performance entails and the visualizations, by highlighting three separate metrics, further confuse the issue while potentially accomplishing the same results as achievement systems. Barth insists that providing these visualizations instead of a discouraging leaderboard motivates players to challenge themselves to do better. I would go a step further and suggest that these histograms, along with the YouTube feature, encourage a sense of player community by drawing the player's attention to other players. However, I think an equally plausible (but more cynical) interpretation would be that the visualizations encourage players to replay the same level with the intention of getting into the 'high score' group of all three histograms, thereby getting thrice the play value from a single puzzle. The problem with this interpretation is that it requires a categorization of the histograms as providing extrinsic motivation, which I find to be an oversimplification. I think both interpretations hold some truth and neither the whole story.

The YouTube button actually draws the player out of the game in order to share solutions with others. Yet it also motivates the player to later return by making them aware of the multiplicity of possible solutions, which in turn highlight the deficiencies of the player's performance. This aligns with the creator's proposed motive for the set of data visualizations: to highlight how a user can improve without being discouraging. In essence, the community of players are encouraged to themselves generate a help manual for the very difficult game. Such a tool allows players who have been stymied by a particular level to move on, while at the same time offering players the potential to improve their own proficiency, so they might be more successful in the next stage. Most of all, however, it allows players of this single-person game to gain an audience beyond their anonymized performance on the data visualizations.

The common thread to both these elements is that they take a single-player puzzle game and, having downplayed its official leaderboard, increase its duration by making users visible to one another. And while leaderboards offer the opportunity for formalized recognition of skill, SpaceChem players must use YouTube to broadcast their abilities. Most significantly, however, there is no simple opt-out for players. (Manual override is possible by, for instance, disconnecting from the Internet before playing.) Achievement systems remain outside most games and notifications can typically be disabled, allowing players to ignore these non-diegetic elements. SpaceChem players, however, have no such option. By incorporating achievement-like features into the data visualizations in its win screen, SpaceChem has blurred the line between the diegetic and non-diegetic, a phenomena I predict will only continue through increasing integration of games into other achievement, data and social systems.

It is always problematic to attempt to identify the motivations of gamemakers, who function within a space of conflicting artistic, commercial and pragmatic obligations. Regardless of the intentions the Zach Barth held in creating SpaceChem the way he did with its data visualization and YouTube functions, in the end it is only the game experience itself that matters. SpaceChem's unusual features provide an opportunity to reflect on the ways that games, for better or worse, motivate players towards certain behavior. As the gaming industry involves alongside social media, such reflections will only become more valuable.

3.1 Further Research

Though my work has provided certain insights, it could be improved by further analysis beyond the scope of this paper. Ethnographic research involving interviews with players and YouTube video makers would be useful to see how the player responds to these features. Nevertheless, I believe this article effectively calls attention to features which may easily have gone unquestioned, despite having a significant effect on the behavior and game-playing experience of the player.

REFERENCES

Barth, H., 2012. Zachtronics | Spoiler alert! Available at: http://www.zachtronics.com/spoiler-alert/ [Accessed January 10, 2016].

Barth, Z., 2012. Postmortem: Zachtronics Industries' SpaceChem. *Gamasutra*. Available at: http://www.gamasutra.com/view/feature/172250/postmortem_zachtronics_.php?print=1.

Berry, V. et al, 2013. Playing Styles. The Differentiation of Practices in Online Videogames. Bourdieu and Data Analysis: Methodological Principles and Practice, pp.165–180.

Burn-Murdoch, J., 2013. Why you should never trust a data visualisation. *The Guardian*. Available at: http://www.theguardian.com/news/datablog/2013/jul/24/why-you-should-never-trust-a-data-visualisation [Accessed January 28, 2016].

Ducheneaut, N. et al., 2006. Alone together?: exploring the social dynamics of massively multiplayer online games. In *Proceedings of the SIGCHI conference on Human Factors in computing systems*. ACM, pp. 407–416. Available at: http://dl.acm.org.proxy.library.uu.nl/citation.cfm?id=1124834 [Accessed January 28, 2016].

Fields, T., 2014. *Mobile & Social Game Design: Monetization Methods and Mechanics, Second Edition*, CRC Press.

Flagg, A. & Syed, M., 2015. A lesson from the New York Times on how to mislead with numbers. *Mondoweiss*. Available at: http://mondoweiss.net/2015/04/lesson-mislead-numbers [Accessed January 28, 2016].

Friendly, M., 2009. Milestones in the history of thematic cartography, statistical graphics, and data visualization. Available at: http://www.math.usu.edu/~symanzik/teaching/2009_stat6560/Downloads/Friendly_milestone.pdf [Accessed January 28, 2016].

Glas, R., 2013. Vicarious play: engaging the viewer in let's Play videos. *Empedocles: European Journal for the Philosophy of Communication*, 5(1-2), pp.81–86.

Jakobsson, M., 2011. The Achievement Machine: Understanding Xbox 360 Achievements in Gaming Practices. *Game Studies*, 11(1). Available at: http://gamestudies.org/1101/articles/jakobsson [Accessed December 4, 2015].

Medler, B., 2011. Player Dossiers: Analyzing Gameplay Data as a Reward. *Game Studies*, 11(1). Available at: http://gamestudies.org/1101/articles/medler [Accessed December 4, 2015].

Norman, D.A., 1999. Affordance, conventions, and design. *Interactions*, 6(3), pp.38–43.

Schäfer, M.T., 2008. *Bastard Culture! User participation and the extension of the cultural industries*, Utrecht University. Available at: http://dspace.library.uu.nl/handle/1874/33564 [Accessed January 28, 2016].

Shokrizade, R., 2013. The Top F2P Monetization Tricks. *Gamasutra Blogs*. Available at: http://www.gamasutra.com/blogs/RaminShokrizade/20130626/194933/The_Top_F2P_Monetization_Tricks.php.

Tufnell, N., The rise and fall of YouTube's celebrity pioneers (Wired UK). Wired UK. Available at: http://www.wired.co.uk/news/archive/2013-11/27/youtube-community [Accessed January 10, 2016].

Viegas, F.B. et al., 2007. ManyEyes: a Site for Visualization at Internet Scale. *IEEE Transactions on Visualization and Computer Graphics*, 13(6), pp.1121–1128.

Walter, E., 2012. The Rise Of Visual Social Media. Fast Company. Available at: http://www.fastcompany.com/3000794/rise-visual-social-media [Accessed January 28, 2016].

Zachtronics, 2011a. Spacechem, Zachtronics.

Zachtronics, 2011b. Zachtronics | SpaceChem: An Average Solution. Available at: http://www.zachtronics.com/spacechem-an-average-solution/ [Accessed January 10, 2016].

Zachtronics, 2012a. Zachtronics | SpaceChem PAX Challenge. Available at: http://www.zachtronics.com/spacechem-pax-challenge/ [Accessed January 10, 2016].

Zachtronics, 2012b. Zachtronics | SpaceChem: Statistics time! Available at: http://www.zachtronics.com/spacechem-statistics-time/ [Accessed December 4, 2015].

Zachtronics, 2015. Zachtronics | SpaceChem. Available at: http://www.zachtronics.com/spacechem/ [Accessed December 4, 2015].

A SOFTWARE FRAMEWORK FOR THE DEVELOPMENT OF PROJECTION-BASED AUGMENTED REALITY SYSTEMS

Marc Sunet[1], Marc Comino[1], Dimosthenis Karatzas[2], Antoni Chica[3] and Pere-Pau Vázquez[3]
[1] *ViRVIG Group – UPC, C/ Jordi Girona, 1-3, Barcelona*
[2] *Centre Visió per Computador, Edifici O, 08193, Bellaterra*
[3] *ViRVIG Group – UPC, C/ Jordi Girona, 1-3, Barcelona*

ABSTRACT

Despite the large amount of methods and applications of augmented reality, there is little homogenization on the software platforms that support them. An exception may be the low level control software that is provided by some high profile vendors such as Qualcomm and Metaio. However, these provide fine grain modules for e.g. element tracking. We are more concerned on the application framework, that includes the control of the devices working together for the development of the AR experience. In this paper we present a software framework that can be used for the development of AR applications based on camera-projector pairs, that is suitable for both fixed, and nomadic setups.

KEYWORDS

Augmented Reality, Modular design, Software framework.

1. INTRODUCTION

Augmented reality (AR) is a growing field that entered mainstream mainly thanks to the ubiquity of mobile devices. However, relying on the use of a mobile device for AR puts some limitations on the features that such a system may provide. Projection-based augmented reality, on the other hand, permits setups that let the user free hands to perform all sorts of interactions, such as virtually writing on physical documents. We are concerned on the development of systems for Human-Computer Interaction (HCI), and we will show examples of applications that provide different types of interaction using this approach. Among the different possible projection-based AR systems, we are more interested in fixed or nomadic setups. A key advantage is that since fixed setups do not require that the user moves cameras or projectors, such systems are easier to calibrate and less prone to accidents. Nomadic solutions [Huber et al. 2012] are in between fixed systems and mobile projected user interfaces [Huber, 2014]. They use pico-projectors that are placed on a fixed position for the duration of the experience. Therefore, they share the advantage of fixed systems in terms of usage: once set up, the user may have her hands free, which provides more flexibility for the interaction. On the other hand, like with mobile projected user interfaces, these are harder to calibrate. We will demonstrate our framework on a nomadic and a fixed setup.

Most setups use special purpose libraries and programs that have been developed hardware-dependent. This hinders the reproduction of an equivalent system in a different place if any of the hardware components are changed (e.g. substituting a projector because larger resolution or brightness is required).

To address this problem, we have developed a device independent, modular software framework, that abstracts the hardware layers into modules, and facilitates the substitution of the any module (camera, projector, input device) with little effort. The system also abstracts the capture and visualization modules. This way, the input can be addressed by naked hand gestures, or with other input devices, and the output can be carried out by simply drawing images or text, or with a more complex set of widgets able to simulate a full-featured virtual desktop. The key modules of our system are: *Hardware Abstraction Layers, Data Abstraction Layer, Communication Protocol, Visualization Module, Interaction Module, and Application Logic*. These components are sufficient to implement a vast amount of different setups, and most of the configurations can be achieved with little changes. Some applications will require extra modules, as we will see later when we describe some application examples. In the following, we will describe the different parts of the system, the two different setups we built based on this framework, and demonstrate its utility using an augmented document demo application to play music.

2. OVERVIEW OF THE SYSTEM AND RELATED WORK

The field of augmented reality is continuously evolving. With the explosion of mobile devices, augmented reality has gone mainstream, with users of all backgrounds using it for a wide variety of uses such as maps navigation, museum guides, and a bunch of professional applications. Most systems are commonly implemented as see-through systems. This imposes the limitation of requiring a device to be placed between the user and the reality, and sometimes its manipulation is cumbersome or poses limitations on the user freedom. On the other hand, projector-based augmented reality, does not let the user freely change its location, but it may essentially free her hands so that a wider set of interactions may be available (e.g. the Sprout PC [Hewlett-Packard, 2015] by HP). Despite the great variety of such systems, software is far from standardized. Many examples are proprietary, and others are just research-based demonstrations, with the focus placed on the interaction or visualization features, more than the software architecture that makes them possible.

Other previous research has focused on similar problems with a lower degree of generalization, such as in the case of the CAMPAR framework [Sielhorst et al., 2006] tailored to the operating room, with a special emphasis on the synchronization of devices. The approach by Kolomenski [Kolomenski 2013] is similar to ours in the devices used (camera, projector, IR pens…), like other systems [Linder and Maes, 2010, Mistry and Maes, 2009, Weiley and Adcock, 2013], but here we concentrate on the software modularization part. We do not focus on robot-operated systems (i. e. [Tsuji et al., 2013, Bernier et al., 2012]), since our approach is intended to be closer to a nomadic system. We also focus on projected-based AR instead of see-through approaches [Spindler et al., 2012], or systems that require external worn devices [Kim, 2012], since the environments we are interested on (e. g. public libraries), require freedom and little number of external devices. Freehand interaction promotes experimentation, and facilitates user rotation. Moreover, the lack of mobile parts improves the durability of the setups.

Our system consists on a set of decentralized modules that communicate to each other with the use of a communications system (see Figure 1-right). In this system, several channels are open, and the modules can freely register to receive the messages of the different kinds of information.

- Hardware abstraction layers: A set of modules are used to hide the nitty gritty details of the hardware specific components from the rest of the system. They thus allow the substitution of a camera or projector element without affecting the rest of the system (Figure 1-left, bottom modules).
- Communication protocol: Passing message system that the different modules connect to. It allows is easily parallelization, with different modules on different platforms (computers, mobiles, servers) in a transparent way. Figure 1-right shows and example of massage passing.
- Interaction module: The interaction module tracks the user input and issues messages corresponding to the different interactions that are detected (Figure 1-left, second row).
- Visualization module: This system is in charge of the rendering of the different elements to be visualized (Figure 1-left, second row).
- Data abstraction layer: It is in charge of the input and output of the data that has to be red/written from/to disk (see Figure 1-left, top left module). In many cases this module will be a simple one, but in some others, it might imply working against a more complex database system.
- Application logic: This component is the one that defines the current running application. Again, the communication with the other components is handled via messaging (Figure 1-left, top right module).

Apart from the fixed modules, which are common for most applications, other, extra modules can be implemented. Most of these will be application-specific, and we will not deal with them in this paper. We only mention them here for completeness, and they may appear in some examples later.

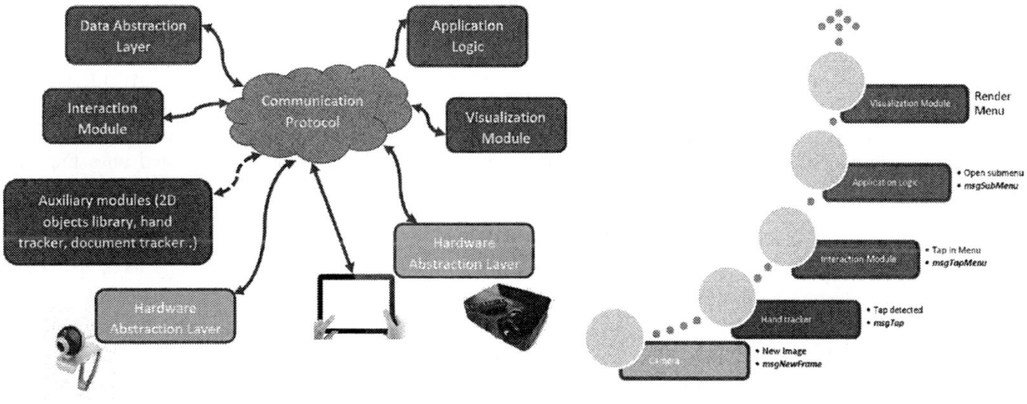

Figure 1. Architecture of our framework

The architecture of modules is shown in left scheme. Right image shows a full example of message passing throughout the system. Upon a hand gesture by the user, a tap, the system generates a submenu. The different modules issue messages into the system and the application logic decides the actions (e.g. opening a submenu) also through message passing.

2.1 Developed Modules

For the realization of our system, we developed the following modules: Projector HAL, Camera HAL, Application Logic, Communications Module, Interaction Module, Visualization Module, and the Data Abstraction Layer.

The Hardware Abstraction Layers are pretty simple, they abstract the access to images in the case of the camera, and the projection in the case of the projector. The camera images are queued in a buffer, and the interested modules can read them. The Application Logic is different in each case. However, since it makes strong use of the other modules, it commonly requires few lines of code. The Communications Module is the skeleton that vertebrates the whole system. All the information that is captured or generated is put into the communication system, and the modules that require it, register to the convenient channels. It has been implemented using Google Protobuffers [Google Developers, 2015] over a ZeroMQ [iMatrix Corporation 2012] transport protocol. Protocol Buffers are a language and platform-neutral system for serializing structured data. They are also extensible, which makes them quite useful in many communication systems. ZeroMQ is a messaging transport protocol is a transport layer protocol for exchanging messages between two peers over a connected transport layer such as TCP. In our system, all the modules that may generate data or commands puts messages into a channel, and the modules that wish to read this information only have to register to those channels. This way we achieve a hardly hierarchical structure that is easy to maintain and whose modules can be replaced simply.

We can see a working example of this protocol in a subset of the modules in Figure 1-right. In this example we show how a tap in a menu can be interpreted by our system and generate a submenu. The top-left image is a clipped version of the whole system, where only the modules intervening in the tap processing and reaction are shown. The bottom right part, encodes the different modules with the same colors to facilitate the reading. First, the camera generates a new frame where the hand is tapping on a concrete region of the working space. The camera HAL, as expected, generates a message with the image as the contents. The hand tracking auxiliary module reads the image and detects a tap. This tap is then passed to the system through another message (*msgTap*). The interaction module receives this message and passes the information to the application logic, which is aware of the elements that have been rendered (this can be achieved directly or through previous check with the visualization module). Then, the application logic decides that a new submenu must be opened, and passes this information to the visualization module as a new message that carries out a command, *msgSubMenu*.

For the sake of the reader, we have avoided a thorough description on the parameters and the current format that each message may carry, but there are easy to imagine.

The Interaction Module is the one in charge of getting the input from the user and convert this input into commands or information that is broadcast to the interested modules. We have implemented it in two different flavors: hand-based gestures, and IR-pen gestures. In Section 5 we provide more details on the interaction modules. The Visualization Module renders all the objects that are projected onto the working area. We have created a lightweight UI library built on top of SFML graphics tool [Gomila, 2015]. SFML is a multi-framework library that provides a simple interface to various multimedia components of the operative system. The principal feature of the UI we have developed is that it allows the 3D rendering of 2D widgets in order to correct the projection deformation induced by an arbitrarily-tilted projector. Moreover, it also serves as a pipe between the gesture module and the application, namely it detects on which widgets the gestures are performed and forwards this information. Finally, an image-based positioning algorithm has been implemented in order to avoid widgets from leaving the workspace when the object from which they are hanging is moved. Adjusting a resolution parameter finer positioning can be achieved at the expense of an increased processing time.

The *backoffice* system, Data Abstraction Layer, deals with persistent data. In one of the use cases we developed, for example, we dealt with documentary information. As a result, a database was required, in this case we used an Oracle database of documents with hand generated annotations. The result of the interaction with the application also generated a set of new annotations. These were also stored along the database. This required a module to handle this data. All of this can be abstracted from the application, and in some particular cases, where the data lacks the generalization of the framework we propose, may require slightly more effort, but most common data will be treated simply by a generic data abstraction module.

These developed modules are common to all applications and only little modifications to to some of the systems may be required if we change the input or output devices. In our case, we did not have to change anything for the transition of our nomadic system to the fixed system.

Each application will use all of the previous modules, but the *Application Logic* is dependent on the application to be developed. Therefore, it will be different for every application, but the other components can be simply used as is. Together with these modules, we found that other components can be commonly required in many scenarios, these are enumerated here:

- Rendering subsystem: For the visualization part, several strategies can be used, in our case, we developed a library of visual objects and a library of visual feedback elements.
- Document tracker: When the application scenario is intended to simulate a virtual desk, the tracking of documents becomes a must. Therefore, this module may be of great utility.

Some of the scenarios we worked with throughout the development of the project dealt with documents. In some cases, the scenario consisted in augmenting the document, by adding some information on demand, and in some other cases, the document was used as input (for identifying or capturing images, etc.). In all these cases, apart from the concrete software for capturing or identifying elements, there is the need of tracking the document in the scene. Therefore, a simple document tracker was implemented and used to provide information both for the input (e.g. capturing information) and output (e.g. projecting extended information onto the document) systems.

2.2 Interaction

The interaction with our system can be carried out using two different techniques: hand-based, and with IR-pens. The most important advantage of the hand-based interaction is the lack of external elements. However, the most important limitation, is the hand segmentation. Since each user may have a different skin color, and the illumination conditions change along the day, the hand interaction lacks some degree of robustness. This is especially true, and may be a problem, for nomadic systems. Unfortunately, since in most places, we are not able to control the illumination totally, this may become a problem, although not as severe, for fixed systems. Ideal conditions should ensure the light is constant along the day, which is not common in most places.

On the contrary, the IR-pens require a third camera with its extra calibration stage. This is an extra element (though still maintaining a low cost at the hardware part). However, they present less problems when interacting because with the IR signal, the system is less dependent on illumination condition changes.

Moreover, the calibration stage is quite simple since it does not suffer the illumination changes and therefore is quite straightforward.

In any case, our system has the gestures implemented in the interaction module, and they are independent on the way they are captured. That is, the same gesture can be performed by a hand or by an IR-Pen, in our case, since these two trackers were implemented, but it would be easy to perform equivalent gestures with other external devices such as the MYO Armband or the Leap Motion, the only issue is the concrete gesture tracker, but the interaction module remains the same.

In order to properly determine the gestures, and to maintain uniformity, the gestures are performed in three stages, as shown in Figure 2:

Initialization: The gesture is detected and identified. Initial visualization cues are provided.

Updating: Gesture is performed by the user. Visual cues identify and communicate the gesture to the user.

Finish: Gesture finishes. If an action is linked to the gesture, it is triggered.

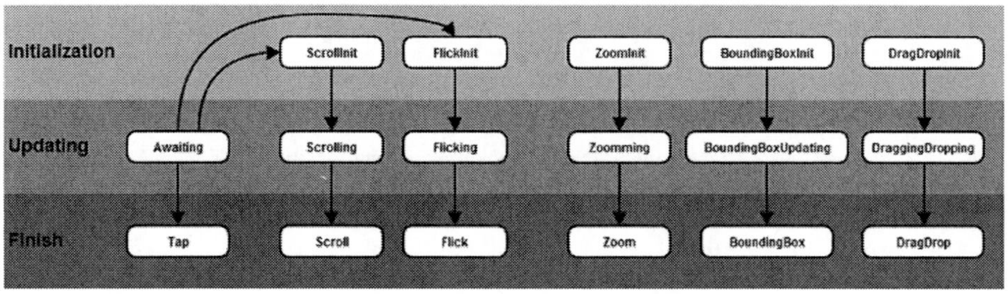

Figure 2. The different stages of the gestures that can be determined by our system

Note that the figure determines a state machine that is updated throughout the gesture tracking. Each of the boxes correspond to messages issued by gesture tracker to the system. Therefore, the interested modules can read them and act accordingly. In our case, the Visualization Module is aware of the gestures being carried out and generates the appropriate visual cues to inform the user that a certain gesture is being detected and where.

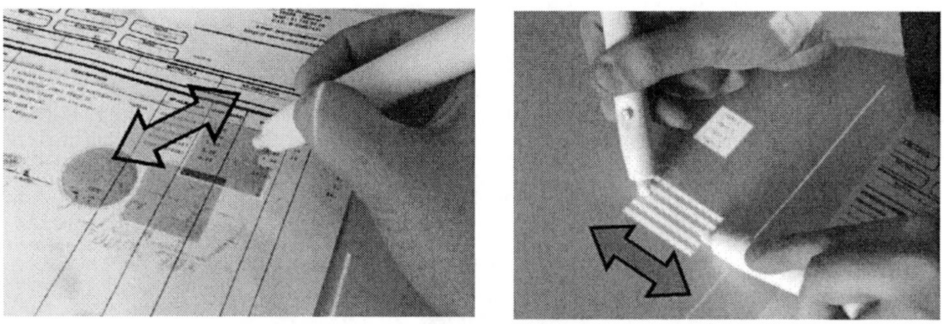

Figure 3. Interaction with the IR-pen system with one and two pens respectively

For many of the gestures, especially when they last long, the visualization system will provide some visual cue to help the user understand that the gesture has been determined. The different visual cues may go from projecting the input point as a circle, to more elaborated effects such as marking a certain button or menu entry as selected. Since in our case we have implemented a set of widgets that cover the main elements of a virtual desktop, many of these visual cues are implemented as different states of the widgets (e.g. selected vs non-selected). Other effects are simply provided with the interaction of the widgets. For example, when performing a drag-and-drop operation, the element is moved as the user drags its virtual position. This is shown for instance in Figure 3-left. In the first case, a drag-and-drop operation (indicated by arrows on the left) is being carried out by the user. The visual cue that communicates the behavior is the actual translation of the rectangle in purple. We can also perform other two-hands operations such as scaling, as shown in

Figure 3-right. The displacement of the pens is also indicated here with the blue arrow, and the user will see an effective incremental resizing of the object while the gesture is not finished.

The gesture management module has been implemented agnostic of the interaction element. We have designed a set of one-hand or two-hand gestures that include simple taps, swipes, and so on, that can be implemented both by hand or IR-pen. In both cases, the user can work with one hand/pen or with two, and the detected gestures are equivalent for the hand and the pen. The different gestures that are detected when operating with a single hand (tap, scroll, flick, and drag-and-drop) are shown in Figure 4 (4 leftmost gestures). Zoom and resize are easier using two input points. We detect them with the use of two hands (Figure 4 – rightmost images). Input position is determined by detecting a contact between the index and the thumb.

Figure 4. The one-hand gestures that can be detected by our system: tap, slide, flick, and rotate

3. EXAMPLE SETUPS

We have developed two different setups, a nomadic and a fixed system. With the aid of the previously described modules, few extra packages were required.

The nomadic system, was intended to show the capabilities of a projection-based augmented reality system paired with a camera and with hand or IR-pen interaction. The main features of the system were the portability and the flexibility in mount therefore, several aspects had to be implemented in an adaptive way, which greatly increases the difficulty of the software development. These, were the main decisions we had to take:

- Hardware: The hardware, if the system has to be moved, must be light and easy to mount. We chose a small Logitech C615 and a pico-projector from MicroVision, the MicroVision Showwx (an always-in-focus projector), together with an articulated arm that had a heavy basis to be stable on the table.
- Calibration: The calibration system may not rely on fixed environment, so several elements such as illumination, background, and so on, must be taken into account in case the system moves.

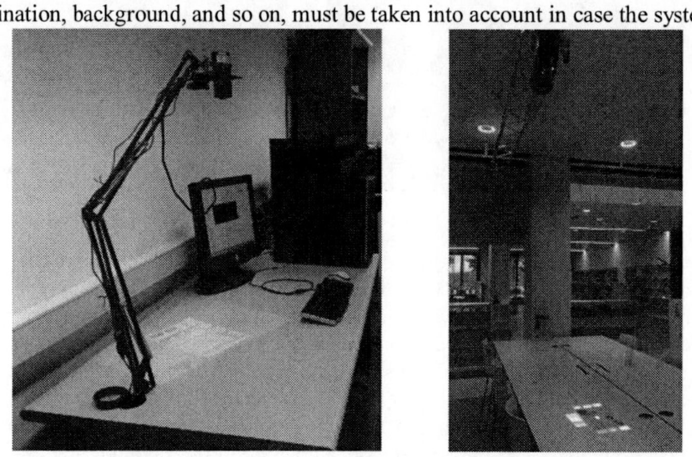

Figure 5. The initial setup of the nomadic system and fixed setup (right) built in a public library

The fixed setup has the projector/camera pair fixed in a structure that is attached to the ceiling. This way, the users have free space around them to experiment and freely perform gestures to interact with the application.

The selected hardware with the initial nomadic setup is shown in Figure 6-left. A second version, with a more professional look, was also created with the use of a shell printed using a 3D printer. After a thorough analysis of capabilities of the different devices in the market, in terms of quality, image resolution, distance of projection/capture, and so on. The selected set is affordable and easy to transport. Its total cost was less than $500. For the PC, we used a commodity portable device (less than $1000), with no special features, since the computational requirements of whole system are low. The body of the system consisted on a modified lamp arm and a couple of plastic pieces printed on a 3D printer to fit the camera and projector.

The *calibration* was a second, important issue. Since the nomadic system can be built in different places, we need a calibration process that is able to adapt to different lighting conditions. There are two different aspects (that involve many variables) that may be taken into account when calibrating such a system: a) Illumination: Conditions may change between different places, so the calibration system must be as robust as possible to lighting changes, and b) working area conditions: The size, color, and orientation of the working area may change due to physical limitations. Although no large room is necessary to fit all the elements, the available space may change from place to place. The calibration can be started as required, since it also uses the same messaging system to communicate the different found matrices, and it uses a background subtraction to increase robustness. The general process follows these steps:

1. Detect the homography between projector and camera
2. Estimate camera parameters.
3. Detect the orientation and size of the valid working area.
4. Calculate the remaining homographies with the working area.
5. (Optional) Calibrate other external gesturing elements, e.g. IR-pen.
6. (Optional) Set-up other input devices, e.g. tablet, that requires some communication set-up.
7. Communicate the homographies.

The calibration stage involves several steps: The first step, where the projector-camera homography is calculated, is achieved by projecting three rectangles with the projector. These three rectangles have different RGB colors and are read by the camera. Then, from these rectangles, the camera parameters are estimated by detecting the rectangles' corners. Next, we use an auxiliary document inside the working area to determine its orientation and size. We determine the maximum valid working space by fitting the largest rectangle in the limits of the camera viewing space and projector space. Once we have the homographies, they are broadcast to the whole system, so that all modules, can read them. From now on, all the communication referring to projected virtual elements, is be carried out in working space. The visualization system is in charge of positioning the elements properly, and automatically repositioning them to avoid occlusions when necessary.

The fixed system is composed by a Basler ac2500-14gc camera and a projector InFocus IN 3138HDA, which provides HD projection with 4000 ANSI lumen. Moreover, this system also uses an IR camera, which is basically a very similar camera, a Basler ac2500-14gm with an IR longpass filter (850nm, M27×0,5mm) for the IR Pens. The devices here, in contrast with the nomadic system, can be of higher quality, and the distance of the projector to the surface is of 2.2m, and the area of projection is about 1.1m wide (16:9). The main difference of the fixed system with the nomadic one is the intended use. The objective in this one is to have a living lab in a public library where the users may experiment with projected augmented reality technologies. More specifically, the users will be, mainly, children, and therefore, we have developed a set of small toy applications to be used by the children. In Figure 6-right we can see how the fixed system looks. The fixed system uses the same, previously enumerated software packages to perform all the tasks. The only difference with the previous system is that the projectors and cameras have a larger resolution and can be placed at a larger distance, so that we can build a fixed system that is less prone to accidents.

One of the toy applications we have developed is a music player. In this application, the user shows a music score that the system is able to detect and interpret. The user only has to select the note, and the system plays it. The system can also change the instrument that plays the music by letting the user choosing among a set of predefined instruments. Everything happens in a very user-friendly way, by providing most of the options as icons the users may select. We can see an example of this application in Figure 6, where the projected elements such as the piano tiles or the instrument icons are all interaction widgets. The system tracks the document position, so if it changes, the widgets are automatically rearranged accordingly. The user can choose the instrument, play a note, or play the whole song.

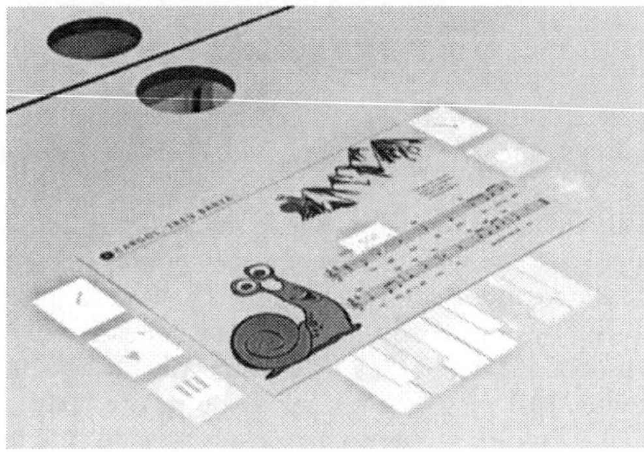

Figure 6. The music toy application where children can play with different instruments

4. CONCLUSIONS AND FUTURE WORK

In this paper we have presented a software framework tailored for the rapid development of augmented reality setups that are based on the projector-camera pair. The system is highly distributed and all components execute individually and communicate through a communication system based on Google Protocol buffers over a ZeroMQ transport layer. All the modules communicate using a protocol defined by the Communications Module that is the center of all the system. We can even attach external devices (e.g. a tablet) to the communications system. The development of a simple application with our new framework can take as few as a week if no other hardware elements have to be added. It consists basically on reprogramming the *Application Logic* module to fulfill the users' needs. Besides the general modules, we have also implemented other modules for document tracking, widget rendering, and so on, that are easily integrated and can be shared by other modules. In future we want to continue developing the system, but concentrating on new features that may be driven by new example applications, or new input devices.

The authors acknowledge the project support for the project by TIN2014-52211-C2-1-R by the Spanish Ministerio de Economía y Competitividad with EU FEDER funds.

REFERENCES

Bernier, E., et al. 2012. The MobilAR Robot, Ubiquitous, Unobtrusive, Augmented Reality Device. *Biennial Conference on Engineering Systems Design and Analysis. American Society of Mechanical Engineers*, 375–381.

iMatix Corporation. 2007-2012. ZeroMQ Message Transport Protocol. *http://rfc.zeromq.org/spec:23,* checked June 2015.

Google Developers. 2015. Protocol Buffers, *https://developers.google.com/protocol- buffers/*, checked June 2015.

Gomila, L.. 2015. Simple and Fast Multimedia Library.. *http://www.sfml-dev.org/*, checked June 2015.

Hewlett-Packard. 2015. Sprout Official Page. *http://sprout.hp.com/us/en/,* last checked June 2015.

Huber, J., 2014. A Research Overview of Mobile Projected User Interfaces. *Informatik-Spektrum*, 37, 5, pp. 464–473.

Huber, J. et al., 2012. LightBeam: Nomadic Pico Projector Interaction with Real World Objects. *CHI '12 Extended Abstracts on Human Factors in Computing Systems*. ACM, New York, NY, USA, pp. 2513–2518.

Kim, D. 2012. Digits: freehand 3D interactions anywhere using a wrist-worn gloveless sensor. *ACM symposium on User interface software and technology*. ACM, pp. 167–176.

Kolomenski, A., 2013. Realization of a spatial augmented reality system– A digital whiteboard using a Kinect sensor and a PC projector. *Ph.D. Dissertation*. Texas A&M University.

Linder, N. and Maes, P., 2010. LuminAR: portable robotic augmented reality interface design and prototype. In *Adjunct proceedings of the 23nd annual ACM symposium on User interface software and technology*. ACM, pp. 395–396.

Mistry, P. and Maes, P., 2009. SixthSense: a wearable gestural interface. *ACM SIGGRAPH ASIA 2009 Sketches*. ACM, 11.

Sielhorst, T. et al., 2006. Campar: A software framework guaranteeing quality for medical augmented reality. *International Journal of Computer Assisted Radiology and Surgery*, 1 (2006), 29.

Spindler, M., et al., 2012. Towards spatially aware tangible displays for the masses. *Workshop on Designing Collaborative Interactive Spaces for e-Creativity, e-Science and e-Learning at AVI*, Vol. 12.

Tsuji, K. et al., 2013. Robust projection method for a mobile robot with a camera and a projector based on a structured-environment approach-Experiments of the modified method considering a distance between a marker and a robot. *Robot Motion and Control (RoMoCo), 9th Workshop on IEEE*, pp. 36–41.

Weiley, V. and Adcock, M., 2013. Drawing in the Lamposcope. *ACM Conference on Creativity & Cognition*. ACM, pp. 382–383.

COMPARING MESHES - A VOLUME BASED APPROACH

Ralph Erdt and Peter Dannenmann
Hochschule RheinMain
University of Applied Sciences, Department of Engineering
Am Brückweg 26, 65428 Rüsselsheim, Germany

ABSTRACT

Two new emerging technologies will greatly influence industrial production processes in the future: 3D printers and 3D cameras. These technologies already work together in small scale production processes. We expect that in future industrial mass-production processes they will work together in the same way. An object generated by a 3D printer is based on a CAD model. However, as in every physical process, the 3D printer's product does not really reproduce the CAD model since there are production errors and production tolerances. Therefore, the product has to be checked whether it meets the desired quality standards. In case of some 3D structure this means that the product's surface resembles the CAD model close enough or, to be more precise, that the distance between the product's surface and the surface of the CAD model is smaller than some defined maximum deviation. 3D cameras provide means to scan an object's surface easily. They compute a cloud of points that resemble the scanned object's surface and in a second step they reproduce the scanned object's surface by triangulating the point cloud. For comparing the CAD and scanned surface, at the moment the normal distance of the single points to the CAD surface is computed. In this paper we will introduce a better possibility for comparing scanned and CAD surface: We will introduce a volume based approach. By calculating the volume between two meshes and normalizing it with respect to the surface area, we introduce a method of computing a measure for the scanned object's surface quality that is independent of the density of the points of the scanned surface.

KEYWORDS

CAD Data, Optical Measurement Techniques, Offset Computation

1. INTRODUCTION

In today's production processes, the first step of producing some structure is to generate a CAD model of it. When the CAD model is ready and it meets the desired specifications, the structure is produced. However, during the production process problems may occur. Therefore, after production, it has to be tested whether the produced structure also meets the desired specifications and whether the structure's surface does not deviate too much from the desired shape.

There are several possibilities to test whether the production process successfully reproduced the correct shape of some structure. At the beginning of industrial production processes, the correct shape of produced surfaces was measured using gauges (Deutsches Institut für Normung e.V., 1995). Later Coordinate Measurement Machines were used to measure the coordinates of some specified points on the surface (Richard et. al., 1999, Hansen et. al., 2006). Currently, 3D scanners are the most modern devices to measure surfaces (Ghazali et.al., 2011). In order to evaluate some produced structure, it is scanned by a 3D scanner and the surface reconstructed from the 3D scan is compared to the CAD model. However, this method of comparing the produced part with the CAD model has got some disadvantages: The main disadvantage is that typically the comparison only takes place at the single points of the scanned surface and that only these points' distance to the CAD model's surface is computed (Vera et.al., 2013). This method does not take into account the density of the measured points. Therefore, the influence of one point (whether it is a point that is related to a larger area or whether it is a point that is surrounded by other points) is not taken into account by traditional methods.

In order to overcome such drawbacks we present a new approach for calculating distances between two meshes: We propose to use a volume based approach. Instead of merely calculating the distance of measured points to the surface of the CAD model we calculate the volumes between two adjacent triangles of the meshes of the measured surface and the CAD model and normalize them with respect to the CAD-model's surface area.

The remainder of this paper is structured as follows: In the section "Algorithm" we explain the algorithm we developed step by step. Based on this description, we discuss some disadvantages of our algorithm and how they can be overcome. After this conclusion we present some ideas for future work.

2. ALGORITHM

In this section we will describe the algorithm to perform the volume based comparison of two triangle meshes.

2.1 Definitions

We are comparing two meshes M_1 and M_2 which both are described by an array of triangles T_{Mi}. Every triangle in turn is defined by three points (a; b; c). We denote the single triangles within M_1 by $t_{1,i}$ and triangles within M_2 by $t_{2,i}$.

In order for the algorithm described below to work correctly, the meshes have to be aligned e.g. using some best-fit-algorithm.

2.2 Basic Idea

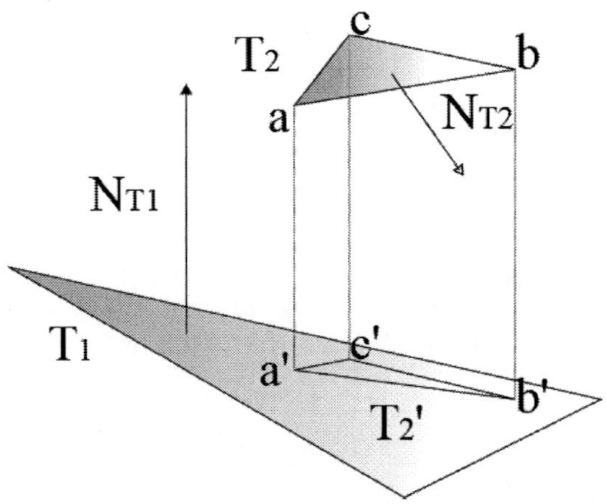

Figure 1. Graphical representation of calculating volumes between two triangles

The basic idea behind the algorithm described in this paper is to calculate the volume between every triangle of T_{M1} and T_{M2} or, to be more precise the volume between every triangle of T_{M2} and its projection of the respective triangles of T_{M1}: For every triangle $t_{1,i}$ of mesh one T_{M1}: compute the projection of every triangle $t_{2,i}$ of mesh two T_{M2} along the surface normal of $t_{1,i}$ onto $t_{1,i}$. Then calculate the volume between $t_{2,i}$ and its projection onto $t_{1,i}$. Sum all the volumes for all projections of triangles $t_{2,i}$ that do not have an empty intersection with triangle $t_{1,i}$.

However we have to mention, that a mesh can have multiple layers or just a front and a back face. So we cannot just project every triangle $t_{2,i}$ onto $t_{1,i}$. First we have to check whether there is another triangle $t_{2,j}$ whose projection onto $t_{1,i}$ has go a non-empty intersection with the projection of $t_{2,i}$ and which is nearer to $t_{1,i}$. We choose the nearest triangle of T_{M2} since we assume the nearest surface to be the one that is intended to match the surface of the CAD model. Since that distance computation is only needed to determine which triangle is nearer we do not need a precise volume-computation. Therefore, the distance between the triangles of T_{M1} and T_{M2} in this part of the algorithm only is determined as the mean value of the point distances between the edges of $t_{2,i}$ and $t_{1,i}$.

$\sum_{Distance} = 0$
for all t_1 : T_{M1} **do**
    for all t_2 : T_{M2} **do**
        GOON ← true
        for all t_{1b} : T_{M1} **do**
            if $|t_1 - t_2| > |t_{1b} - t_2|$ **then**
                GOON ← false
            end if
        end for
        if GOON **then**
            $\sum_{Distance} \leftarrow \sum_{Distance} + \text{calcVolume}(t_1,t_2)$
        end if
    end for
end for

2.3 Calculating the Volume between Two Triangles

In this section we will describe how to calculate the volume between two triangles. First we show an easy case to introduce in the problem. After that, we will discuss the generalisation.

Basic calculation:
Two triangles in 3D space are generally askew like shown in Figure 1: In this figure there are two triangles: T_1 and T_2. The triangle T_2' is the projection of triangle T_2 onto triangle T_1. The points a; b; c are the points of the triangle T_2. The points a'; b'; c' are the points of the projected triangle T_2'. This triangle is the projection of T_2 along $\overrightarrow{N_{T_1}}$ the surface normal of T_1

The volume searched for is the volume of the prism between the points a; b; c and a'; b'; c'. To calculate this volume, we have to compute the projected points a', b', c' (see e.g. Akenine-Möller, 2010).

When we have computed the coordinates of the projected points, the volume is easily calculated: This volume is computed as the product of the prism's base area (i.e. the area of the projected triangle T_2') and its "height":

$$V = h * b$$

The "height" of the prism is given by the distance of m', the circumcenter of T_2' and its projection onto T_2. This distance is equivalent to the weighted average of the distances |a-a'|, |b-b'|, and |c-c'| according to the barycentric coordinates of the circumcenter of T_2'. These barycentric coordinates of m' are calculated as:

$$(\alpha,\beta,\gamma) = \left(\frac{|m'-c'|\times|m'-b'|}{|c'-a'|\times|b'-a'|},\frac{|m'-c'|\times|m'-a'|}{|c'-a'|\times|b'-a'|},\frac{|m'-a'|\times|m'-b'|}{|c'-a'|\times|b'-a'|}\right)$$

Then the prism's height is computed by

$$h = \alpha * |a'-a| + \beta * |b'-b| + \gamma * |c'-c|$$

The prism's base area is given by the area of the projected triangle T_2':

$$b = \sqrt{s*(s-|b'-a'|)*(s-|c'-a'|)*(s-|c'-b'|)}$$

$$\text{given that } s = \frac{|b'-a'|+|c'-a'|+|c'-b'|}{2}$$

Generalization:

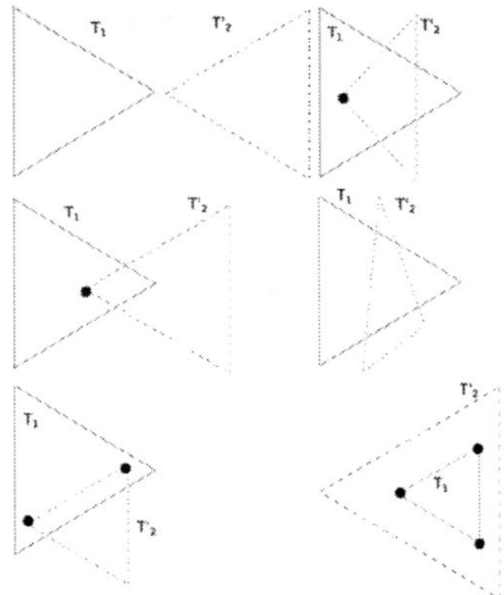

Figure 2. Possible correlations between a triangle and a projected triangle

The calculation shown above is the calculation for the best case: T_2 is completely contained in T_1. However, there are other possible cases, as shown in Figure 2 an described below:

1) T_2 completely outside of T_1
2) One point of T_2 inside of T_1
3) Two points of T_2 inside of T_1
4) One point of T_2 inside of T_1, but the other points of T_2 are outside at different sides of the triangle T_1
5) No point of T_2 inside of T_1, but the triangles overlap completely
6) T_1 complete inside of T_2

Obviously there are a few more combinations, namely the symmetric ones of the cases shown above: n points of T_1 are lying inside of T_2 and the other overlapping variations.

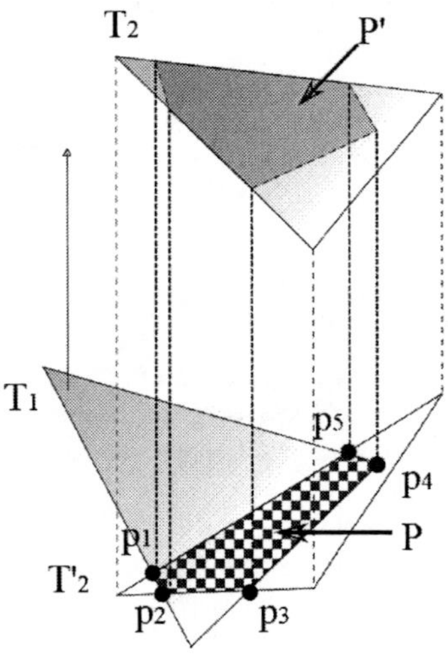

Figure 3. Example of a projected polygon in general

With these possibilities the resulting volume is more complex than the prism calculated in the section "Basic calculation". Figure 3 shows an example of such a complex volume. In this figure the volume between the polygons P and P' is the shared volume of the triangles T_1 and T_2

To calculate the volume in such cases, we first need to figure out the polygon P (in Figure 3 marked with black dots).

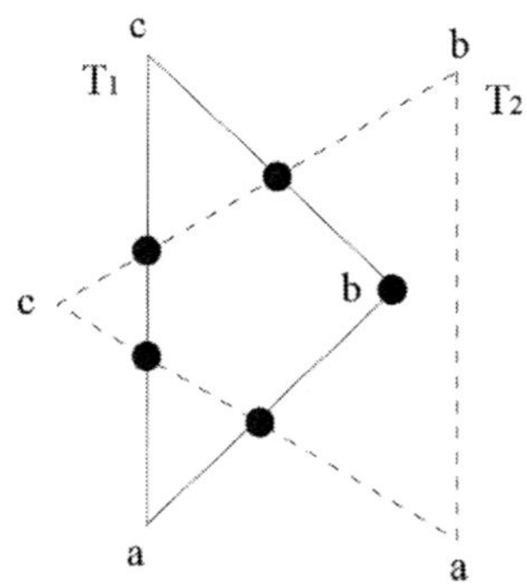

Figure 4. Intersection points between two triangles

In Figure 4 we show a sketch for the needed points:

- Intersection points of the edges of both triangles
- Triangle points located in the other triangle

For getting the intersection points $\{p_1, p_2, .., p_n\}$, we just need to check every edge of T_1 for an intersection with every edge of triangle T_2'. If we find an intersection we just have to add the resulting point to a list:

We define "×" as "cross":
Define: × (*edge*; *edge*) : *point* **as** intersection point (or nothing, if there is not an intersection point)

The pseudocode is the following:

```
for all e1 ← edges T1 do
        for all e2 ← edges T'2 do
                addList(e1 × e2)
        end for
end for
```

As described before, we also need the triangle points located in the other triangle (as seen in Figure 4). To do this, just iterate over all the points and check them:

We define "Θ" as "inside":
Define: Θ (*point*; *triangle*) : *bool* **as** "true", if the point is inside a triangle (or touches it)

The pseudocode is the following

```
for all p ← points T1 do
        if p Θ T2' then
                addList(p)
        end if
end for
for all p ← points T2' do
        if p Θ T1 then
                addList(p)
        end if
end for
```

As result we get a list of points $\{p_1; p_2; ..., p_n\}$. The size of this list can get these numbers:

- 0: There is no intersection: volume = 0
- 1-2: the triangles touch each other without overlapping: volume = 0
- 3-6: the triangles overlap. Take the next steps (even if the count is 3: Possibly some point has been "back projected". Therefore we cannot go the easy way and use the algorithm described in section "Basic calculation" directly.)
- other: The algorithm is not designed to generate more than six points. If this case occurs anyway then some error has occurred during the calculation.

For the calculation, we also need the distance between the points in this generated list and the original triangle T_2 (as shown in Figure 3). To do this, we just have to "back-project" the points $\{p_1, p_2, .., p_n\}$ onto the triangle T_2 and get the points $\{p_1'; p_2'; .., p_n'\}$. The needed distances are the distances between the points p_x and p_x'.

However, we do not have a volume formula for polygons. So we have to split the points to subdivide the problem into "easy" sub problems: With three points, we can use the algorithm described in section "Basic calculation". On the other hand, we cannot use any three points we want. We have to split up the polygon into triangles into such a way that the sum of all triangles represents the polygon and that on the other hand the triangles do not overlap. For achieving this, we chose the structure of a triangle fan to represent the polygon as a set of triangles. In order to convert the polygon into a triangle fan, the polygon's vertices have to be ordered in such way, that they describe a convex polygon. This can be done by a bounding box algorithm (see e.g. (Jarvis, 1973) for a suitable algorithm).

Now finally we get all the needed points (see Figure 3) in the correct order and can calculate the volume by subdivision: a triangle in "P" is always given by two neighbouring points and the first point, resulting in a triangle fan as described above:

The pseudocode is the following:

```
volume = 0
for all x ← 3 ... #points do
        volume += calcVolume(points[1]; points[x - 1]; points[x]; points'[1]; points'[x - 1]; points'[x])
end for
```

2.4 Using the Calculated Volume to Assess the Quality of a Mesh

Using the volume calculation as described above we calculate the complete volume between two meshes. This is enough to make some general statement about the similarity of two meshes: If the volume is near zero, the meshes are very similar.

However, this statement is only useful, if the meshes are equally big. If, e.g. one mesh covers a much smaller area than the other one, the statement is worthless. So we have to perform another step: We need to calculate the ratio to which the meshes cover each other. To perform this, we need to sum up the areas of the projected triangles of M_2 (like T_2' in Figure 1). This area then can be compared to the sum of the areas of all triangles of M_1.

For a detailed analysis (like e.g. a pseudo color view) the computed volume related to each triangle of M_1 has to be considered. Keep in mind that not every triangle in M_1 needs to be covered by triangles of M_2 by 100%. To normalise the volume related to these triangles, we suggest dividing the calculated volume by the coverage ratio of the triangle to get a normalized volume.

3. CONCLUSION AND FUTURE WORK

We used the presented algorithm to assess the production quality of structures within a manufacturing context. We compared meshes that were generated by a 3D measuring device to meshes representing an ideal geometry. The presented algorithm yielded very promising results; we were able to determine areas of the produced structures that showed deviations from the desired geometry very well (see Figure 5)

Figure 5. Screenshot of our application to determine differences between measured and reference structure

In applying the algorithm, however, we detected one drawback: In section 2.3 we describe, that we need the intersection-points of two overlapping triangles in a correct order. Our first approach to solve this task is shown in the algorithm presented below. We assumed that this algorithm computes the intersection-points in the correct order:

Require: triangle *T* consist of three edges *a*; *b*; *c*
Require: every edge *{a, b, c}* consist of points *x*; *y* | *x*: startpoint; *y*: endpoint
Require: $a_y = b_x$; $b_y = c_x$; $c_y = a_x$
Require: × and Θ are used as defined above

```
for all e1 : edges T1 do
        if e1 Θ T2' then
                add e1
        end if
        for all e2 : edges T2' do
                if (e1 × e2) then // When crossing exists
                        add e1 × e2
                        if e2 Θ T1 then
                                add e2
                        end if
                end if
        end for
end for
```

Considering Figure 4 (and many others) the algorithm seems to work. However, in Figure 6 you see an example of a possible combination, in which the algorithm did not work: When using the algorithm, the point order is wrong (as shown in the figure). In this case, the points have to be reordered.

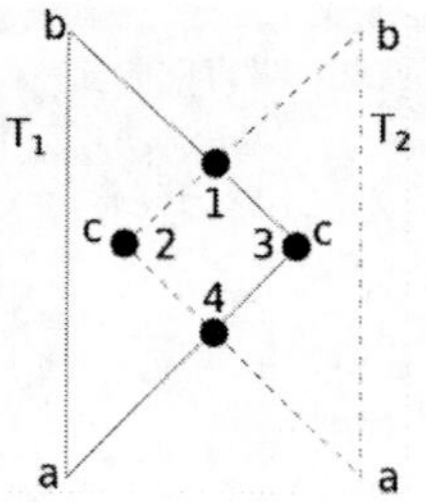

Figure 6. Demonstration of the point order when use the algorithm described

Therefore it is better just to collect the points in general as described by the pseudocode in section 2.3. Then they can be put into the correct order afterwards by applying some convex hull algorithm as also described in that section.

As seen in the description of our algorithm in section 2.3, it has got a complexity of $O(n^3)$. This is not too bad, but with high numbers of triangles (which is more than possible) the algorithm gets slow. So we suggest a few optimizations as future work to speed up the algorithm:

- We suggest introducing a "maximum distance" between triangles to be considered for intersection computation. Triangles farther apart than this maximum distance would not be considered for the calculation.
- In addition to this, a partitioning of the mesh is advised to massively reduce the number of triangles in the working set.
- We also advise to compare the surface-normals of the triangles of the two meshes. If the faces of the considered triangles on the mesh of the reference- and the measured geometry differ more than a given value Δ, they are not considered as related triangles.

Besides improving the algorithm itself, we are also planning to integrate the presented algorithm into an industrial environment. This includes the management of the measurement data generated by the 3D optical measurement device as well as an automated supervision of the comparison results. Such an automated supervision will enable the final software system to find positions where the produced structure fails to meet the defined tolerances automatically.

ACKNOWLEDGEMENT

This paper describes a part of a project funded by the German Federal Ministry for Economic Affairs and Energy within the framework "Zentrales Innovationsprogramm Mittelstand" (ZIM) under the funding code KF2604104LP3.

REFERENCES

T. Akenine-Möller, T., Haines, E., and Hoffman, N., 2010. *Real-time rendering*, 3rd ed. Peters, Wellesley, MA

Deutsches Institut für Normung e.V., 1995. *DIN 1319 "Grundlagen der Messtechnik.* Berlin.

R. Ghazali, Ahmad Eziwan Enche Sukri, Abd Rahman Abd Latif, Abd Rauf Abd Rasam, Z. A. Latif, A. M. Samad, 2011, Evaluating the relationship between scanning resolution of laser scanner with the accuracy of the 3D model constructed, *Proceedings of IEEE International Conference on Control System, Computing and Engineering (ICCSCE)*, Penang, Malaysia, pp. 590 – 595

Hansen H.N., Carneiro K., Haitjema H., De Chiffre L., 2006. "Dimensional Micro and Nano Metrology". *CIRP Annals,* 55-2, 721-743

Jarvis, R., 1973, "On the Identification of the Convex Hull of a Finite Set of Points in the Plane," *Information Processing Letters* 2, pp. 18–22, 1973.

Richard, C., Helps, G., Hawks, V. D., 1999, Instrumentation technologies for improving manufacturing quality, *Proceedings of Electrical Insulation Conference and Electrical Manufacturing & Coil Winding Conference*, Cincinnati, OH, USA, pp. 567 - 571

Sergio Vera, Debora Gil , Agnés Borràs, Marius George Linguraru, Miguel Angel González Ballester, 2013, Geometric steerable medial maps, *Machine Vision and Applications*, Volume 24, Issue 6, pp 1255-1266

ENHANCED MAGNIFICATION FOR REDUCED MOVEMENT IN VIRTUAL REALITY ENVIRONMENTS

Eva Monclús, Isabel Navazo and Pere-Pau Vázquez
ViRVIG Group – UPC, Barcelona

ABSTRACT

Although Virtual Reality (VR) environments have seen slower adoption rates than expected among the medical community, throughout the last years, several new techniques and devices (e.g. Oculus Rift) have been developed that might boost the popularity of VR. However, the use of 3D environments is not exempt of some shortcomings, such as the difficulties of adaption to 3D, that sometimes produces motion sickness, or the increase in effort the user has to undergo when interacting with a 3D system, as compared to using a simple mouse on a desktop. Our proposal is tailored to focus on the second problem. More concretely, we propose a magnification technique that is able to reduce the movements required to explore a concrete part of a volumetric dataset as compared to other zooming techniques. Our technique, builds the zooming result in the same virtual position of the initial interaction while still maintaining a contextual view on the region of interest and its surroundings. This way, the user reduces the amount of movements required to explore a model and efficiency is increased. An informal user study was carried out that confirmed our hypotheses.

KEYWORDS

Virtual reality, 3D interaction, Volume Rendering, Magnification

1. INTRODUCTION

Virtual environments have been a very active research field since the nineties. However, despite the improvements in medical visualization techniques, and its decrease in price, it is still very difficult to see such tools in medical centers. Even 3D inspection of medical models has still a relative small room as compared to other, typical 2D image analysis for diagnosis and surgery training or planning. This does not mean that 3D is not used at all. On the contrary, we see, day to day, success cases that show how 3D rendering of medical models is used for concrete diagnostic problems or surgery planning. Unfortunately, these techniques are still not commonplace. The use of 3D environments is challenged by other elements, such as the need of special setups (that may include large rooms, some technologically advanced elements, and so on). Compared to 3D rendering on a desktop, that can be achieved with most commodity GPUs, this is still a qualitative step to be overcome. A typical inspection scenario in a 3D environment involves the use of a 3D pointing device to move, rotate, zoom in and out, or select. These tasks require time and effort, since the 3D pointing device must be moved in the air, which requires a very different class of movements than the common mouse point and click. One of the big advantages of mouse pointers is that the arm can rest on the same surface the mouse is placed, which sensitively reduces fatigue, and improves precision at the same time. Therefore, the use of a 3D pointing device may require larger movements and is affected with precision problems (such as the Heisenberg effect on selection [Bowman, D.A., et al. 2002]) if no particular care is posed.

Our objective in this paper is to address the potential fatigue problem by reducing the amount of movements required by the user in a concrete task: the magnification of a region of interest. Commonly, this is achieved by dragging the model closer to the user, or by using some metaphor such as the Magic Lenses [Brown and Hua, 2006]. In the first case, a relatively large amount of movement is required. This causes the lost of the context due to the clipping of the rest of the model against the limits of the screen. In the second case, the user is required to maintain the pointing position and the typical hand shaking may difficult the inspection. Moreover, if the selected view is fixed until new interaction, the context is also lost as in the previous case.

We present here a new technique tailored to enhance the magnification procedures in Virtual Reality Environments (in our case we use a 2.7x2m PowerWall screen). It is shown in Figure 1.

The advantages of our technique are twofold:

a) Users are able to obtain a magnified view with minimal effort and,
b) Interactive exploration of the zoomed view, while preserving the context in a secondary view.

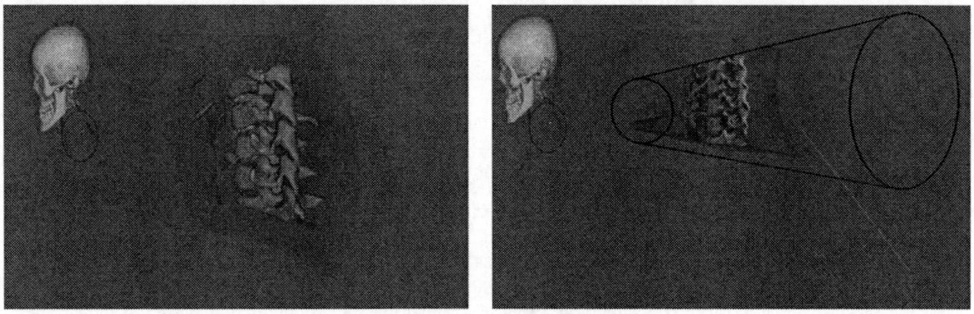

Figure 1. Enhancement magnification

In order to reduce user arm movement, the technique generates a cylinder around the pointing ray that is then used to extrude a volume and magnify it with a single click. The volume comes closer to the user and thus ample arm movements are avoided.

As we will show in the following sections, this approach reduces the amount of movements, while preserving the context of the zooming place and achieves a high frame rate.

2. RELATED WORK

There are two different areas that overlap in our work: 3D interaction, and enhanced visualization of volume models in virtual reality.

Although not many, some 3D interaction techniques have addressed the creation of tools for the interaction with volumetric models in Virtual Reality environments.

[Hinckley et al., 1994] proposed a 3D user interface for pre-operative neurosurgical planning based on the physical manipulation of familiar real-world objects (head, cutting-plane and stylus-shaped props) in free space to access and manipulate a virtual model. [Preim et al., 2002] and [Rossling et al., 2010] propose a set of tools for measurements of distances, angles, or volumes in Virtual Reality setups, although working with triangle-based models. [Reitinger et al., 2006] presented a 3D measurement toolkit developed for liver surgery especially tailored for a VR platform. Their measurements include distance, volume, and angles. Their evaluation indicated that VR-based measurement tools have a sufficient benefit compared to 2D desktop-based systems in terms of task completion time. In terms of accuracy, slightly better results in most of the tasks were achieved. In this approach, anatomical structures models (liver, vessels...) are computed through segmentation from CT scans and they are represented by opaque triangle meshes where the user may select points by using a virtual pencil. [Hagerdorn et al., 2007] proposed a set of tools for performing measurements in a virtual reality visualization environment. A 3D Rubberbanding line for selecting *free* points in the scene is proposed. They use clipping planes for accessing interior parts of the volume dataset. Their scene is also composed by triangle meshes. Finally, another work also tailored to reduce the user movements in VR environments is due to [Monclús et al. 2013]. This is a data-guided interaction metaphor for the efficient and accurate anchor point selection in medical models. Our objective here is also movement reduction, but, instead of addressing the problem of anchor point selection, we focus on magnification exploration.

Several methods have been proposed for advanced volumetric medical data inspection. The interested reader may refer to the recent survey by [Tominski et al., 2014]. We can group them in: *Cut-away views*, *Focus+context* visualization, *Lens and distortion*, and *Advanced transfer functions*.

In the Lens and Distortion approaches, the general motif is a virtual lens that is placed in front of the volume, between the user and the region of interest. Throughout the virtual lens, the rendered image is different to the usual render. Though this may have several forms, the initial approach was tailored to simulate a real lens. As a consequence, the information is magnified and distorted [Bier et al.,1993] so that the user may see with a higher detail the region of interest. Later on, [Zhou et al., 2003] use a sphere as a focal region. [Wang et al. 2005] extend the metaphor by allowing the user to determine a focus point and modify lens parameters and render the views with a GPU-based raycasting implementation [Hadwiger et al., 2006]. [Viega et al.,1996] also use a 3D volumetric lens, but the models are not volumetric data sets. [Svakhine et al., 2005] use a magic-sphere metaphor for establishing the focal region and combine different rendering techniques in order to improve the amount of information shown to the user.

Most of these previous methods are designed for desktop, not Virtual Reality environments, and therefore do not deal with the 3D interaction. Some notable exceptions may be [Brown and Hua, 2006], who propose a platform for augmented virtual reality that displays the focus view in a separate display that acts as a window in the virtual or real world. [Coffey et al., 2011] propose a technique for exploring volumetric models using the World in Miniature metaphor by the use of a multitouch surface and a stereo wall. Finally, [Monclús et al., 2009] developed a pointing technique that renders the inner part of the 3D model while still preserving a high amount of contextual information by the combination of two different transfer functions and a pointing device that behaves as a lantern.

Perhaps the most related approach to our system is the one by [Taerum et al., 2006]. The authors focus on obtaining a magnification close up with context. However, they concentrate in the visualization technique and we deal with more interaction-related issues. Moreover, their work has been also developed for desktop, and we focus on VR environments, so some of our objectives are out of their scope. In our case, we zoom-in by moving the magnified view to the user and moving apart the original model. Additionally, we let the user to freely inspect the extracted region. The way we let the user interact with the magnified view *à la exploded views* paradigm. These techniques let the user separate the volume in different parts [McGuffin et al., 2003, Bruckner and Gröeller, 2006] or peel away regions of the volume [Birkeland and Viola, 2009]. These techniques facilitate the inspection by providing individual manipulation of the separated regions. However, unlike ours, they are not for VR and do not focus on zooming. Thus, they are not intended for fatigue reduction, and and only facilitate inspection of magnified regions with other zooming metaphors.

Finally, our magnification view could be considered similar in spirit to the Exo-Vis widgets by [Tory and Swindels, 2003]. However, these do not deal with the 3D interaction process since they do not work on a VR setup, and our objective is to provide, not only a closer look on the geometry, but also the possibility of exploring the whole 3D extruded region. As said, since most of these techniques have been developed for desktop setups, they are not directly applicable to VR environments.

3. ENHANCED MAGNIFICATION

In this Section we present our approximation to minimal effort model magnification. The magnification process runs in four steps (depicted in Figure 2):

1. Initial navigation (1): we explore the volume using a typical GPU-raycasting with an input device.
2. Selection of the magnification region (2a & 2b) with the use of a virtual cylinder and interactive extrusion and magnification of the selected region is carried out.
3. Exploration of the magnification region (3), by showing the whole 3D region bound by the cylinder.
4. Switch back to the initial navigation mode (1).

As said, the first stage is simply a 3D rendering of the volume dataset using a Direct Volume Rendering (DVR) algorithm based on raycasting [Hadwiger et al., 2006]. So at this stage, the user may freely rotate and pan the model using a 3D pointer (a Wanda device). To facilitate eventual zooming, we include a visual cue that indicates the region to be magnified by using the metaphor proposed in [Monclús et al., 2009], which was dubbed *Virtual Magic Lantern* (VML). This technique is intended to provide the visualization of inner information while maintaining context. In order to do so, the authors perform a ray casting that renders differently (e. g. with different transfer functions) the inner and outer part of a cone cast by the user with a pointing device. This facilitates context preserving, since both the inner and outer parts are represented in the main view. We apply a simplified version of this technique, since it provides an intuitive cue that illustrates the region that is going to be magnified. For this purpose, instead of using a transfer function that makes the interior of the region of interest invisible, we simple apply a transfer function with a color change, as shown in Figure 3 (left). The size of the Volume of Interest (VOI) can be changed interactively by using a joystick sported by the Wanda device. In this way, an accurate selection of the desired VOI can be achieved.

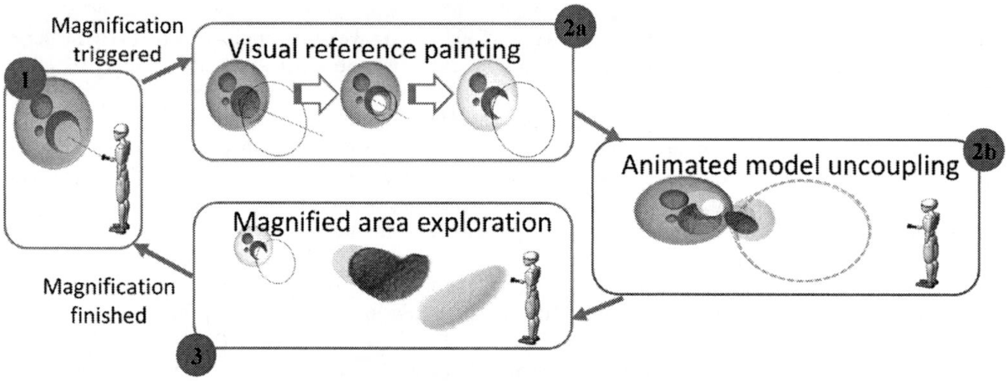

Figure 2. Overall magnification process

The magnification process runs in four stages. In the first stage, while the user is exploring the volume dataset, a circular visual cue is provided which indicates the region of interest that would be selected. Pressing a button of the input device, the magnification process starts. In the second stage, first the magnification region is gradually rendered using a wireframe representation of a cylinder. Subsequently, the extruded cylinder is progressively moved towards the viewer and at the same time, the rest of the model is moved away from the user; providing in this way an animation of the uncoupling of the model. The third stage permits the exploration of the magnified region. The magnification finishes once the user presses again the same button. At this time an animation is performed which switches back to the initial navigation mode.

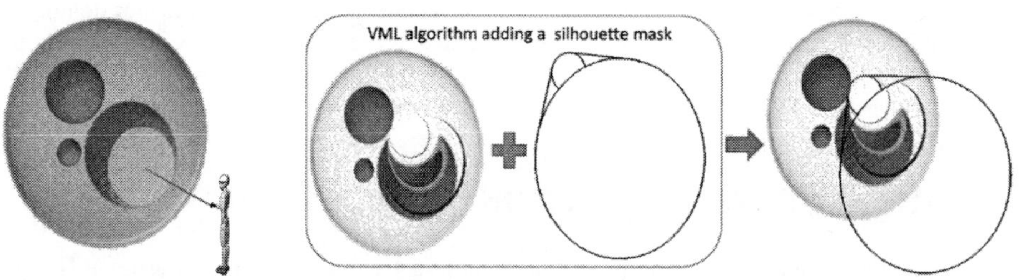

Figure 3. The visual indication of the Volume of Interest previous to the selection (left) helps the user pointing to the region of interest and having a precise idea on which area will be magnified. Right image shows the selection procedure that extracts a cylindrical region using a version of the Virtual Magic Lantern metaphor

The second stage consists in the effective selection of the magnification region. With a click on a button of the Wanda device, the magnification starts. Since the region we are going to move closer to the user is a 3D bounded volume, we show the extent of the volume by drawing the cylinder that bounds the selected region, over the volume. This is painted progressively by using a mask of the volume that is generated offscreen. Once the bounding cylinder has finished drawing onto the geometry, we extract the magnified region from the rest of the volume. The effect in our render is that we extrude a cylinder (the magnified region) from the rest of the volume (the context). Then, in order to make a gradual change to the exploration of the magnified region, the extruded cylinder is progressively moved towards the viewer. At the same time, the context, that is, the rest of the model (where the extruded volume is illustrated with a hole) is also moved away from the user, in a gentle way, to guarantee the continuity. Thus, the impression is that both parts are uncoupled and separated.

The rendering of the context (the rest of the model with a hole) is carried out by adapting the Virtual Magic Lantern [Monclús et al., 2009] technique to our problem. In this case, the interior part is rendered with a transfer function that removes the data interior to the cylinder, as shown in Figure 3-right. In order to better communicate the extent of the removed region, we also add the edges of the cylinder in a different color.

The third stage provides the exploration of the magnified region. In this case, the zoom, not only contains what the user was seeing in front of her, but consists of the whole 3D region bound by the cylinder used to select the VOI (see Figure 4). The details on how this is implemented in the context of volume rendering is explained in Section 4.

If the user wants to analyze other parts inside the Volume of Interest, it is also possible. Since the cylinder has moved towards the user, little or no movements are required to analyze the VOI from a close position, as shown in our user study. Rendering such complex interaction is challenged by the demanding GPU required by VR environments, where two views (one for each eye) is required. This requires some optimizations (see the following section) to guarantee realtime framerates while inspecting the extruded region.

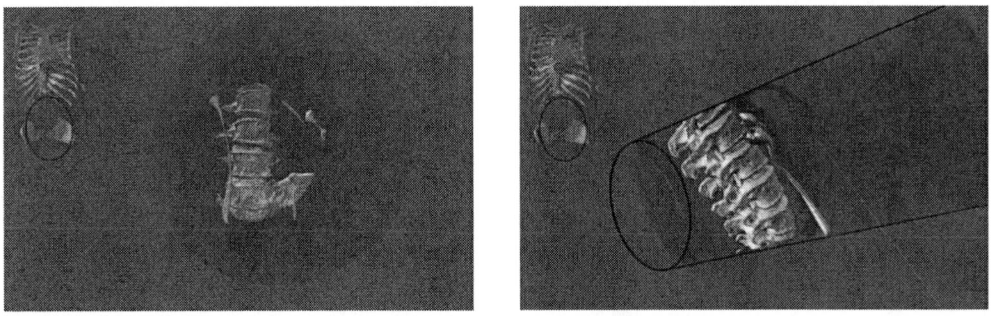

Figure 4. Inspecting the magnified 3D region. Further than simply looking at a larger version of the magnified zone, the user can freely inspect the whole 3D cylindrical region of the model

The fourth stage is triggered when the user again clicks the interaction button. In this stage, the two parts of the model are coupled together again. In order to perform this, the transformations that have been made to the magnified portion of the model are undone, and then, a soft coupling is achieved by moving back the extruded region and the remainder of the volume to the same original 3D position.

4. IMPLEMENTATION

Our rendering method uses state of the art GPU-based raycasting of volume models [Hadwiger et al., 2006]. This technique may achieve realtime framerates in desktop GPUs, though some care has to be taken when porting it to VR environments, since in this case, two views have to be created, one for each eye.

In a much shortened description, the raycasting algorithm performs these three typical steps:

1. Render the back faces of the bounding box of the volume dataset and code the outgoing points of the rays in its color. Store the result as a texture.
2. Render the front faces of the bounding box of the volume dataset and code the ingoing points of the rays in its color. Store the result as a texture.
3. Execute a GPU-based volume raycasting using the ingoing and outgoing positions indicated by the previously computed textures.

The initial exploration of the model in the first stage uses the conventional ray casting algorithm with our implementation of the VML technique for each eye, since it still achieves realtime framerates in our VR setup.

For the advanced magnification technique, we need to modify completely the first and second step of the classical algorithm and perform an additional test in the third step. Typically, volume datasets are modeled as rectangular 3D textures. A naïve approach would require decoupling the two parts to render in two different 3D textures, but doing so interactively is costly. We solve this limitation in realtime by changing how the shaders render the model, since the only transformation required is a set of affine transformations. So, in order to render the inner part of the volume, we use a 3D cylinder as an auxiliary structure, and analyze the rays that traverse the volume and classify the sampling points against the cylinder. This process is depicted in Figure 6. So, first of all, in order to determine the ingoing and outgoing points, it is necessary to calculate the transformation that brings the cylinder geometry to its initial position. This is achieved by applying an affine transformation to the vertices' positions at the vertex shader (see Figure 6, transformation 1). Since the intersection of the geometry of the cylinder with the volume dataset may be partially outside, we have to guarantee that we have correct positions even for the outside part of the cylinder. To solve this little inconvenient, the bounding box of the volume dataset is enlarged since all the cylinder geometry is included (see Figure 6, transformation 2). To provide the magnification effect, the VOI (expressed by the cylinder) is automatically brought closer to the user and its size is increased.

After calculating the in and out positions, step 3 is executed. The GPU-based raycasting algorithm is modified slightly. More concretely, we have to ensure that the sampled rays only correspond to the ones belonging to the extruded interior part of the cylinder. We guarantee this by discarding the part of the ray that is outside the volume dataset. This process is illustrated in the *Volume RayCasting* block of Figure 5, where the texture coordinates that fall outside of the volume dataset are painted in red.

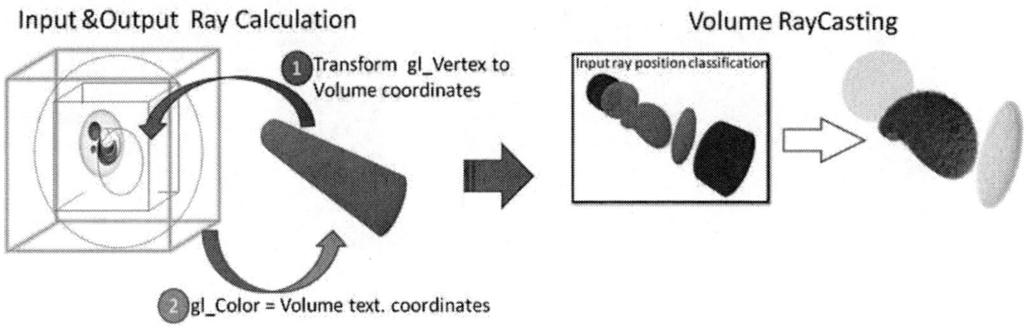

Figure 5. Rendering the extruded region

The implementation of the enhanced magnification rendering consists of modifying the GPU raycasting algorithm [Hadwiger et al., 2006]. The virtual cylinder is used to classify the regions of the volume that have been extruded, facilitating the in and out positions of the rays for the extruded region we have to render.

Finally, the interaction with the extruded region, while keeping the context of the model, would imply 4 rendering steps in order to have the stereo views for both (the VOI and the volume model with the context), in our VR environment. To guarantee realtime, we perform another optimization trick. Instead of rendering the context (i.e. the rest of the model with the hole, as depicted in Figure 5) each frame, we use the simile of a poster (generated with a single offscreen step), which contains the image corresponding to the projection at the very moment of the selection process.

5. USER STUDY

In order to evaluate how the system works and whether the users find it useful, we have performed an informal user study with five participants. The study gathered both qualitative and quantitative data.

In the study the users had to use the typical zoom by dragging the volume or our enhanced magnification technique to locate some elements that were placed in a model. The tasks consisted in asking the user to count the number of objects that were placed at different cavities of a head, such as the nose or the ear. The elements were small enough to force the users to zoom in apart from rotating the model in order to find them. In Figure 6 we show an example of the model before and after of the manipulation that reveals the elements. Throughout the experiment, we measured the distance covered by the movement of the arm throughout the manipulation, the distance covered by the head of the users, and the time devoted to the completion of the tasks. The experiment was carried out in a 2.7x2m PowerWall. Users were tracked using an Intersense IS-900 tracking system consisting on a Head Tracker and a MiniTrax Wanda. Before performing the tasks, the users were asked to do a small training in order to understand how both zooming techniques work, and to make sure they understood the objectives of the tasks. After the experiment, the users were asked to complete a small test where they had to answer, in a Likert scale from 1 to 7, where 7 was the maximum value, whether they found the magnification techniques suitable for solving the problems they were asked to.

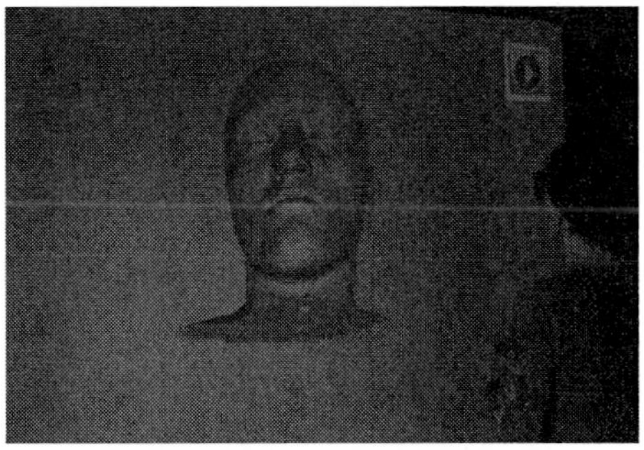

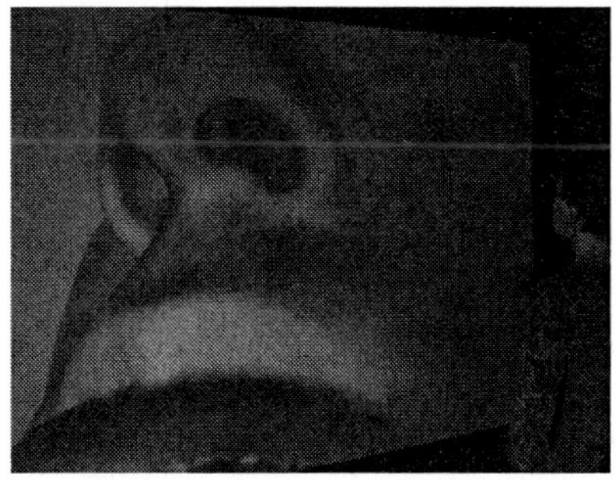

Figure 6. Left image shows the initial configuration of the first task: counting the number of markers inside the nose I order to find those, the users had to rotate the model and get close enough to the cavity, as shown in the right image

The results of the experiment found that with our new technique, the amount of displacement the users had to do is reduced by more than a half, and the time devoted to the task solving is around 60% than when using the conventional zooming method.

Table 1. Results of the experiment. The first row measures the total amount of distance that the arm had to move to perform the tasks. The second row presents the total movement the user did during the experiment (measured as the displacements done by the user's head. Finally, the last row shows the total time. Clearly, our approach requires much less effort than the classical magnification in 3D environments, and thus is likely less fatiguing

	Optimized Magnification	Classical zooming
Total Arm Movement (avg)	2.14 m (stdev. 0.92)	4.72 m (stdev. 0.92)
Total User Movement (avg)	0.595 m (stdev. 0.22)	1.287 m (stdev. 0.45)
Total Time (avg)	25.49 s (stdev. 5.1)	38.48 s (stdev. 10.5)

The post-hoc questionnaires also showed higher preference for the optimized magnification tool over the classical zooming. In a Likert scale from 1 to 7, where 7 is the best score, our method had an average of 6.4 (stdev. 0.55) points while the classical zoom had a 3.8 (stdev. 0.84) score.

6. CONCLUSIONS AND FUTURE WORK

We have presented a new interaction metaphor that allows the user to perform smart zooms in VR environments. Our technique has two important advantages:

- The zoom is achieved with minimal interaction. The usual systems let the user to move the model close, and this, in a VR setup usually requires a set of long movements with the arm. With the proposed metaphor, only pointing and with only one click is needed to obtain the zoom in a gentle fashion.
- The magnified region can be inspected while still preserving the context. Other systems, such as the lens-based methods, overlap the magnification to the rest of the model, and thus, the context of the interaction region is occluded. With our approach, the context is always present on the screen.

Furthermore, we let the user to interact with the whole 3D extracted region which facilitates the inspection of complex and cluttered models.

Overall, the technique reduces the ample movements often required to obtain a magnification of the model. Our informal user study showed our hypothesis is plausible as it showed far smaller amount of displacements to perform the same tasks using our method than with classical magnification interaction. We want to improve the framerates for complex models, as stage 2 still reduces framerates in the animation. However, this is a common problem for VR setups when dealing with volumetric models, since raycasting is very GPU-intense, and image-resolution dependent, and in VR we need to generate two different views, one for each eye. Our magnification technique is faster than normal zooming for the VOI inspection because we cut away the rendered volume with the screen region actually used to the magnification. We also plan to make a larger user study including physicians, although for the set of users we tested, the results are clearly promising.

The authors **acknowledge** the support for the project by TIN2014-52211-C2-1-R by the Spanish Ministerio de Economía y Competitividad with EU FEDER funds.

REFERENCES

Bier, E. A. et al., 1993 Toolglass and magic lenses: the see-through interface. *SIGGRAPH'93: Annual conference on Computer graphics and interactive techniques*, pages 73–80, New York, USA. ACM.

Birkeland, A. and Viola, I. 2009, View-dependent peel-away visualization for volumetric data. *Proceedings of the Spring Conference on Computer Graphics*, pages 133–139. Springer, 2009.

Bowman, D.A., et al. 2002 Novel uses of pinch gloves for virtual environment interaction techniques. *IEEE Virtual Reality*, 6:122–129.

Brown L. D., and Hua, H., 2006. Magic lenses for augmented virtual environments. *IEEE Computer Graphics and Applications*, 26(4):64–73.

Bruckner, S., and Gröller, M.E. 2006. Exploded views for volume data. *IEEE Transactions on Visualization and Computer Graphics*, 12(5):1077– 1084, 9.

Coffey, D., et al. 2012, Interactive slice WIM: Navigating and interrogating volume data sets using a multisurface, multitouch VR interface. IEEE Transactions on Visualization and Computer Graphics, 18(10):1614–1626.

Hadwiger, M., et al., 2006. *Real-time Volume Graphics.* A. K. Peters, Ltd., Natick, MA, USA.

Hagedorn, J., et al. 2007. Measurement tools for the immersive visualization environment: Steps toward the virtual laboratory. *Journal of Research of the National Institute of Standards and Technology*, 112(5):257–270.

Hinckley, K., et al. 1994. A three-dimensional user interface for neurosurgical visualization. In *the SPIE Conference on Medical Imaging*, pages 126–136. SPIE.

McGuffin, M. J., et al. 2003. Using deformations for browsing volumetric data. In *Proceedings of IEEE Visualization 2003*, pages 401–408. IEEE.

Monclús, E., et al., 2009 The Virtual Magic Lantern: an interaction metaphor for enhanced medical data inspection. *Virtual Reality Systems and Tools*, pages 119–122. ACM.

Monclús, E., et al., 2013. DAAPMed: A dataaware anchor point selection tool for medical models in vr environments. In *International Joint Conference on Computer Vision, Imaging and Computer Graphics Theory and Applications*, pages 308–317, 2013.

Preim, B., et al., 2002. Integration of measurement tools in medical 3d visualizations. *Proceedings of IEEE Visualization '02*, pages 21–28. IEEE Computer Society, 2002.

Reitinger, B. 2006. Spatialan alysis tools for virtual reality-based surgical planning. *3D User Interfaces*, 0:37–44,.

Rössling I., et al., 2010. Fast and flexible distance measures for treatment planning. *International Journal of Computer Assisted Radiology and Surgery*, 5:633–646, 2010.

Svakhine, N., et al. 2005. Illustration motifs for effective medical volume illustration. *IEEE Computer Graphics and Applications*, 25(3):31–39.

Taerum, T., et al., 2006. Real-time super resolution contextual close-up of clinical volumetric data. *EuroVis*, pages 347–354. Eurographics Association, 2006.

Tominski, C., et al., 2014, A Survey on Interactive Lenses in Visualization. *EuroVis State-of-the-Art Reports*, Eurographics Association, 2014.

M. Tory and C. Swindells, 2003. Comparing exovis, orientation icon, and in-place 3D visualization techniques. *In Graphics Interface*, pages 57– 64, 2003.

Viega, J., et al.1996. 3D magic lenses. *In Proceedings of the 9th Annual ACM Symposium on User Interface Software and Technology*, pages 51–58, New York, NY, USA. ACM.

Wang, L., et al., 2005. The magic volume lens: An interactive focus+context technique for volume rendering. *Proceedings IEEE Visualization*, 0:47, 2005.

Zhou, J., et al., 2002. Focal region-guided feature based volume rendering. *International Symposium on 3D Data Processing Visualization and Transmission*, pages 87–90, Los Alamitos, CA, USA, 2002. IEEE Computer Society.

VERTEX CORRESPONDENCE CONTROLLED BY GRADIENTS: CARTOON ANIMATION APPLICATIONS

Vladimir Savchenko[1] and Maria Savchenko[2]
[1]*Faculty of Computer and Information Sciences, Hosei University*
3-7-2 Kajino-cho, Koganei-shi, Tokyo184-8584, Japan
[2]*Graduate School of Advanced Mathematical Sciences, Meiji University*
4-21-1 Nakano, Nakano-ku, Tokyo 164-8525, Japan

ABSTRACT

One of the objectives in cartoon style animation is to produce inbetweening cartoon frames preserving artistic and stylistic characteristics. In computer animation various types of interpolation are used to generate key frames. The idea of retargeting or cloning artist expressions for facial animation is widely used in areas like movies, games, broadcasting, and cartoon animation. We suggest a simple retargeting technique to generate cartoon animations by using a geometry mapping.

KEYWORDS

Mapping, homotopy map, radial basis functions

1. INTRODUCTION

One of the objectives in cartoon style animation is to produce inbetweening cartoon frames preserving artistic and stylistic characteristics. In computer animation various types of interpolation are used to generate key frames. The idea of retargeting or cloning artist expressions for facial animation is widely used in areas like movies, games, broadcasting, and cartoon animation. In this paper we give a brief overview of the common methods related to producing lips cartoon animations and afterwards we suggest a simple technique to generate such animations. This technique allows producing a geometry mapping according to shapes generated, for instance, by artists. Let us notice that cartoon lips in many cases are drastically different from live actor lips.

Realistic facial animation is a problem of a great interest and recently has been discussed in many papers. Widely used approach to solve the retargeting problem is based on using MockUp technology for an expression mapping. However, due to an anthropomorphic principle the target face must be human-like in order to convey acting to a human audience.

Animated cartoons methods are well discussed in Michelsen (2009). The paper overviews the oldest form of animated cartoons, the traditional animation and the computerized technology of animation. Hand drawing naturally requires long period of production and big consumption expense. Michelsen notices that "the traditional hand drawn frame-by-frame films are being substituted by computerized cartoons. Hopefully companies will not close their hand drawing departments as some have done and simply focus on CGI. A mixture of both is essential." Moreover, despite the fact that anime like animation is extremely popular now for many people it is ostentatious and symbolic meaning cannot be earned from animation, see Cho (2001). One can notice that in Japanese anime character's mouth commonly moves up and down and appears to be looping. Authors of (Buck et al., 2001) mention that we as observers expect absolute fidelity of photorealistic video. To attain different animation styles authors propose to use a library of various hand-drawn faces that allows users to pick and choose then style according to their preferences. On spirit, our work is similar to paper (Buck et al., 2001). Although facial features can be tracked by motion capture techniques to produce performance-driven animation. Based on using a library of various lips configurations drawn by artists or inherited from old animations, our technique can be used as a supplement for hand drawing cartoon animation methods and even for anime like animations.

This paper aims at developing trajectories joining starting and destination arbitrary but not self-intersecting curves to continuously deform one curve into another. To the best of our knowledge, no previous work has proposed this approach. To illustrate applicability of the proposed technique we produce a lip animation without the prior knowledge of the facial geometry of an actor and animated character. We consider the case where curves are embedded in the plane. Nevertheless, the technique can be extended to the case where possible surface area swept by a homotopy between 3D curves.

Problem description:

- Defining a geometry mapping, that is determine which *points* in the target correspond to *vertices* in the source model is difficult for sufficiently different starting and destination contour configurations.
- Different number of vertices or connectivity to establish target/source correspondences.
- The boundary of starting and destination curves specifies neither the topology nor the geometry or physical/anatomical constrains of the warped models.
- Scaling of the models.
- A basic principle that the source and target movements should be similar is used.
- Let us notice that the natural way to produce desirable warping between starting and destination shapes, in fact, is based on the idea of achieving the similarity of curves. However, there are no standard measurements for similarity between two point sets.

The main features of the proposed algorithm:

- Finding a homotopy map: linear warping between implicitly defined geometry objects is used.
- Warping vectors similarities: deviations between points of starting and destination curves are used for achieving shapes of the animated contour.
- Alignment: to produce contour deformation of a target curve transformations based on radial basis functions (RBFs) are applied.

Papers that we considered to be relevant to the problem of cartoon animation let us come to conclusion that there are two dominant directions: diphone- and triphone-based methods for producing high-quality lip syncing and a so-called expression cloning providing transfer vertex motion vectors from a source to target face model. The methods have merits and drawbacks, for instance, lip syncing is well suited for professional animators, expression cloning uses sufficiently complex dense surface correspondences algorithms. In (Efrat et al., 2002), authors remark that there are many qualities that are desirable in a good morphing scheme:

- Starting and destination curves are usually connected and simple, all intermediate shapes should also be connected and simple.
- The morphing should transform a connected portion of starting to a connected portion of destination curve.

It is also useful for the transformation to treat curves as near-rigid objects and to avoid superfluous deformations during the morphing.

De Juan and Bodenheimer (2006) are using non-rigid elastic deformation of the images and RBFs to generate an inbetween of two key images. The approach requires the shapes to properly aligned. Our system addresses to finding retargeting correspondences automatically and requires little user guidance - a simple one parameter user interface allows the user to automatically produce target frame deformations.

2. RELATED WORK

This section briefly reviews the state-of-the-art techniques on performance-driven facial animation, deformable registration methods, tracking facial features, and lip syncing.

Image registration whose task is to find a transformation field that relates points in the source image to their corresponding points in the target image is a very important subject that has been widely applied in medical research, see (Sotiras et al., 2013). In the paper main emphasis is given to techniques applied to medical images. Authors give an extensive overview (more than 400 references) of deformable registration methods, putting emphasis on the most recent advances in the domain. Authors of the paper (Efrat et al., 2002) note that there are two common ways used in the literature to specify morphing schemes. The first approach uses zero sets of implicit functions to represent the morphing. Interpolating between (the zero sets of) these functions produces the morphing. However, implicit models are known to exhibit certain shortcomings. They have the drawback that intermediate shapes are not guaranteed to be simple. Moreover, so called ghost objects can be generated. Second one is based on an optimal morphing between simple polylines. An algorithm proposed by Bespamyatnikh (2002) is based on using the geodesic shortest path between polygonal points. Nevertheless, despite the starting and destination curves being implicit and not user-controllable as noticed in (Efrat et al., 2002), our main premise is that the implicit nature of intermediate curves and even surfaces allows constructing trajectories between simple polygons for sufficiently uncomplicated curves representing human and cartoon lips. Different requirements on the morphing scheme give an uncountable number of different morphing schemes, as it was noticed in (Efrat et al., 2002). From our point of view it also looks reasonable, to apply the RBFs technique for producing image transformations. Actually, this technique is based on the idea of bending energy minimization to treat curves as near-rigid objects for synchronizing, say, an artist`s lip and a character's mouth movements naturally along animation. The animator creating multiple images does not need any specific rules to generate the data needed for synchronizing the lip and mouth movements of an actor. For sticking starting and cartoons image, a simple placement, for example, relative to the barycenter of images is produced, and after that the method proposed uses only one scaling parameter defining the amplitude of character's lip motion (magnitude adjustment). The direction adjustment is produced automatically according to the coordinates on starting and destination curves. Let us also notice that there is an analogy between the method presented in Bespamyatnikh (2002) and our approach. At least for a surface of revolution about a z-vertical line gradient flows generate the geodesic shortest path. However, an example in Bespamyatnikh (2002) illustrating the problem of continuously morphing one simple polyline into another, such that every point p of the initial polyline moves to a point q of the final polyline using the geodesic shortest path from p to q, seems to show that the proposed algorithm does not solve the problem of one-to-one correspondence of contour points.

Success of solving a retargeting problem in the expression mapping drastically depends on accurately tracking facial features. There are many works related to developing robust methods of tracking facial features, in particular, lip contours. See, for instance, (Tian et al., 2000) where a multistate mouth model and combining lip color, shape and motion information are discussed. Accurately and robustly tracking lip motion in image sequences is difficult because lips are highly deformable; they vary in shape and color. Synchronizing the lip and mouth movements naturally along with animation is discussed in (Xu et al., 2013). The paper presents a simple, portable and editable lip synchronization method that works for multiple languages, requires no machine learning, can be constructed by a skilled animator, runs in real-time, and can be personalized for each character. The retargeting problem is formulated as a Poisson equation in (Seol et al., 2012). Specified (e.g., neutral) expressions at the beginning and end of the animation as well as any user specified constraints in the middle of the animation serve as boundary conditions. A Bayesian formulation is then employed to produce target animation.

A new muscle-based facial animation technique that uses the actuation basis, a set of 3D facial shapes corresponding to the full actuation of individual muscles was presented in (Choe and Ko, 2001). Instead of completely relying on a mathematical method, the system lets artists manually sculpt (the initial draft of) the basic elements, so that more a predictable deformation of the face can be attained.

Animation technique based on morphing between a set of base shapes was firstly proposed in (Alexa et al., 2000). The paper (Baxter et.al, 2009) presents a novel approach to the creation of varied animations from a small set of simple 2D input shapes. The method includes three steps: (1) establish correspondences between shape boundaries; (2) simplify these boundaries while keeping their correspondences and ensuring the original shapes are properly embedded and (3) triangulate the interiors compatibly. Paper (Sumner et al., 2005) proposes a mesh kinematics approach. The method allows the user to directly position any subset of mesh vertices and produces a meaningful deformation automatically. Complex pose changes can be accomplished intuitively by manipulating only a few vertices. However, similar to the method of Baxter et al. the user sets a first correspondence point to initialize the algorithm that is the creation of this mapping is made with a tool that automatically computes the triangle correspondence from a small set of m user selected marker points. The matching approaches aim to assign every point of starting shape to its corresponding point in destination shape. Nevertheless, simplification of boundary points is applied.

An approach of finding a set of matching portions of two quadrilateral meshes as large as possible is discussed in (Eppstein et al., 2009). Actually, in the paper we follow this strategy. Results of finding curve to curve point correspondences depend on the starting point; trajectories defining the transformation flow from one image domain to another and vice versa are not identical, as shown in Figure 1. It leads to the strategy finding as large a set as possible of matching points of two curves for tracking features of base forms by union of trajectories obtained by traveling from one to second base form and vice versa.

3. ALGORITHM

Automated correspondence selection is based on the use of an implicitly defined geometry object. There are several kinds of implicit surfaces, but in general implicit surfaces can be represented by a function f: $\mathbf{R}^3 \rightarrow \mathbf{R}^3$ which takes a point $\boldsymbol{p} \in \mathbf{R}^3$ and returns the field value $f(\boldsymbol{p})$ of that point.

3.1 Defining an Interpolating Implicit Surface

Different techniques for constructing an implicit object were proposed in literature. For instance, an arbitrary 2D polygon (convex or concave) can be represented by a real function taking zero value at polygon edges. In this case, the polygon-to-function conversion algorithm provides an exact polygon boundary description as the zero set of a real function; see Peterson (1984). In (Turk and Brien, 2002) authors examine three ways to define an interpolating implicit surface. Common to all three approaches, is the specification of zero-valued constraints through which the surface must pass. The paper (Savchenko et.al.,1995) presents an approach used in this work to the reconstruction of geometric models from given sets of points using volume splines. It results in the representation of a solid by the inequality $f(\boldsymbol{p}) \geq 0$. The volume spline is based on using RBFs (see section related to space mapping) for interpolation of scalar function values of a chosen "carrier" solid. The particular case where a surface is reconstructed from cross-sections is also proposed in this work. The general idea of the approach is to introduce a *carrier solid* with a defining function f_c and to construct a volume spline U interpolating values of the function in the points $\boldsymbol{p}_i$. The algebraic difference between U and f_c describes the reconstructed solid.

To reconstruct an object from contours, RBF interpolation of contour points is applied to each cross-section, using two dimensional "carrier" and spline functions of two variables U(x,y). Suppose the resultant functions $f_1(x,y)$ and $f_2(x,y)$ represent cross-sections belonging to the planes z_1 and respectively z_2. Intuitively, it is clear that transition and scaling between the cross-sectional shapes can be defined using interpolation or a homotopy map

$$f(x,y,z) = (1- g(z))f_1(x,y) + g(z)f_2(x,y), \qquad (1)$$

where $g(z_1) = 0$ and $g(z_2) = 1$. Note that this method produces a connected surface if the areas $f_1(x,y) \geq 0$ and $f_2(x,y) \geq 0$ have nonempty intersection. To construct $f_1(x,y)$ and $f_2(x,y)$ a thin–plate interpolation is used, see below.

Metamorphosis (or shape morphing) is an operation on two geometric objects resulting in a new object with intermediate shape. If z is interpreted as a time variable, this mapping describes a time-dependent metamorphosis of one shape to another.

3.2 Computing a Mapping between Shapes

In this work, homotopy map (1) is used for producing correspondent vectors to provide space deformation of target shapes. We are using points located in the direction of steepest *ascent* that is gradients of the function (1) to establish one-to-one correspondence between contours points are used, see Figure 1.

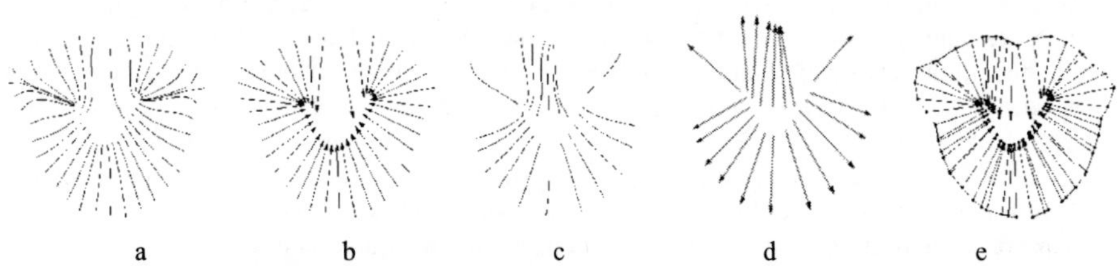

Figure 1. Illustration of one-to-one mapping of contours points. Trajectories connecting starting and destination points (a) and correspondent map (b) for left image domain to second and vice versa (c) and (d). (e) Union of maps

In Figure 1 (a and c), a set of points defined by the homotopy map (1) is being created according to gradients of the function defined for the current time step. To find the intersection of a ray l, $l = 1,2,3, \ldots, N$, where N is a number of points on the initial S model, with target surface W the implicit surface defined by function (1) in points along the current ray is evaluated. There are several techniques to find intersections with implicit surfaces. Ray Marching, see, for instance Bloomenthal (1994), is implemented. In our implementation, simple ray interval analysis defined by number of intervals T is used. In our experiments, for all examples we assign number of intervals $T = 70$. When Ray Marching fails to find the first intersection with the length equal 3 times the average distances between contour points we simply skip this ray.

The goal of the next step is to bring two models (initial and destination) into point's correspondence. It is done almost as it was discussed above. The result is shown in Figure 2(a). In this step we don't use tracing from destination object. Once the two models are brought into points correspondence, the deformation vectors (offsets from the initial or rest expression) shown in Figure 2(b) can be calculated (transferred). Transferring a motion vector can then be done by changing local coordinate systems. The motion can also be locally scaled by using the ratio of locally defined bounding boxes in the two models.

(a) (b)

Figure 2. A correspondence map for initial to second model (a). The deformation vectors (b)

3.3 Applying Space Mapping Technique

Space mapping in $\mathbf{R}^n$ defines a relationship between each pair of points in the original and deformed objects. Let an n-dimensional region $\Omega \subset \mathbf{R}^n$ of an arbitrary configuration be given, and let Ω contains a set of arbitrary control points $\{\boldsymbol{q_i} = (q_1^i, q_2^i, \ldots, q_n^i) : i=1,2, \ldots, N\}$ for a non-deformed object, and $\{\boldsymbol{d_i} = (d_1^i, d_2^i, \ldots, d_n^i) : i=1,2, \ldots, N\}$ for the deformed object. $N = k + p$, where k is the number of points in the target object, p is the number of the boundary constrains. It is assumed that the points $\boldsymbol{q_i}$ and $\boldsymbol{d_i}$ are distinct. The goal of the construction of the deformed object is to find a smooth mapping function that approximately describes the spatial transformation applied to the target shape. The inverse mapping function that is needed to warp an image is given in the form: $\boldsymbol{q_i} = \boldsymbol{f}(\boldsymbol{d_i}) + \boldsymbol{d_i}$, where the components of the vector $\boldsymbol{f}(\boldsymbol{d_i})$ are splines interpolating displacements of initial points $\boldsymbol{q_i}$, see Figure 2. Vectors (black color) show the starting points q_i and destination points d_i defining the constraints h_i (see below).

We consider a mapping function as a thin–plate interpolation, see, for instance Buhmann (2003). A volume spline $f(P)$ having values h_i at N points P_i is the function

$$f(P) = \sum_{j=1}^{N} \xi_j \phi(|P - Pj|) + \mathrm{p}(P), \quad (2)$$

where $p = v_0 + v_1 x + v_2 y$ is a degree-one polynomial. To solve for the weights ξ_j we have to satisfy the constraints h_i by substituting the right part of Equation (2), which gives

$$h_i = \sum_{j=1}^{N} \xi_j \phi(|P_i - P_j|) + p(P_i),$$

Solving for the weights ξ_j and v_0, v_1, v_2, it follows that in the most common case there is a double bordered matrix **T** which consists of three blocks, square sub-matrices **A** and **D** of size $N \times N$ and 3×3 respectively (for 2D case), and **B** which is not necessarily square and has the size $N \times 3$. Notice, that once we have the QR decomposition of **T**, we solve with two right-hand sides to obtain h-values for x, y-directional transformations applied to the image points.

4. IMPLEMENTATION AND EXAMPLES

The ultimate goal for research in facial modeling and animation is designing a system that operates in real time. We have implemented our algorithm, using C++ and CUDA. The GPU is efficiently used for rendering warped images. Simple geometry distribution of image points produces a considerable speed up. Although some of techniques to find intersections with implicit surfaces can drastically reduce the total time of finding gradients flows, for instance, using Lipschitz conditions, the most effective and natural way to speed up Ray Marching is to use parallel processing. To find good design solutions to speed up calculations by using GPU for calculating homotopy trajectories seems a problem which does not have a solution because of limited number of the initial and destination points of curves; maximum number of corresponding points did not exceed one hundred. In our software implementation, a combination of a multi core processor system (OpenMP for C) and GPUs is used.

For testing the method proposed we were generating 400x400 pixel images on GPU: GeForce GT 540M. Production of 21 animation frames (some of them shown in Figures 2 and 3) by using lips points corresponding to the 8 frames shown in Figure 5 mounted approximately to 6 seconds on the 8 cores of an Intel Core i7 Quad computer.

Figure 3. Set of frames based on generic image *"Cartoon Dog With Measuring Tape." Image courtesy of Mister GC at FreeDigitalPhotos.net*

Figure 4. Set of frames based on generic image "*Photographer.*" *Image courtesy of ratch0013 at FreeDigitalPhotos.net*

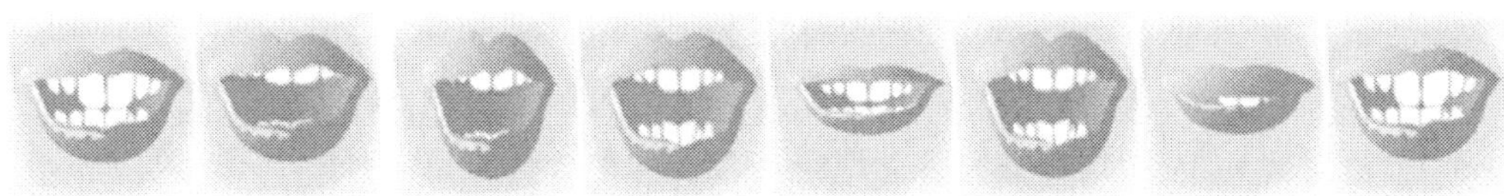

Figure 5. Talking lips from http://animatedgif.net/lipsmouth/dctalking_e0.gif

5. CONCLUSION

The paper presents a simple technique for developing correspondence maps. We give examples of using such maps in the cartoon animation for lip motion cloning.

We believe the proposed approach would primarily help novice animators to quickly produce realistic lip animations, and also enable reusing of well-known or classic animations for newly generated imagery.

For practical applications of the algorithm, an additional procedure to take care of the special case of the lip contact line lips has to be implemented in future.

REFERENCES

Michelsen, E.R, 2009. Animated cartoons, from the old to the new: evolution for the past 100 years. Reykjavik University, Iceland, http://olafurandri.com/nyti/papers2009/AnimatedCartoons.pdf

Cho, J., 2001. Research on Animation Lip synchronization technology, A study on application and development of domestic animation lip synchronization. *Int. Journal of Asia Digital art & Design*, pp. 87-92. http://www.adada.info/journals/no1703_01.pdf

Buck, I. et al., 2000. Performance-Driven Hand-Drawn Animation. *In NPAR 2000 : First International Symposium on Non Photorealistic Animation and Rendering,* pp. 101-108.

Efrat, A. et al., 2002. *New Similarity Measures between Polylines with Applications to Morphing and Polygon Sweeping*, *Discrete and Computational Geometry*, 28, pp. 535–569.

De Juan C.N. and Bodenheimer B., 2006. Re-using traditional animation: Methods for semi-automatic segmentation and inbetweening. *In Proceedings of Simposium on Computer Animation 2006*, pp. 223-232.

Sotiras, A. et al., 2013. Deformable Medical Image Registration: A Survey, *IEEE Trans Med Imaging,* 32(7), pp. 1153-1190.

Bespamyatnikh, S., 2002. An optimal morphing between polylines. *Int. J. Comput. Geom. Appls.*,Vol. 12(3), pp. 217-228.

Tian, Y. et al, 2000. Robust Lip Tracking by Combining Shape, Color and Motion. *Proceeding of the 4th Asian Conference on Computer Vision (ACCV'00)*, pp.1040-1045.

Xu, Y. et al., 2013. A Simple Method for High Quality Artist-Driven Lip Syncing, I3D '13, *Proceedings of the ACM SIGGRAPH Symposium on Interactive 3D Graphics and Games*, pp. 181-181.

Seol, Y. et al., 2012. Spacetime Expression Cloning for Blendshapes. *ACM Transactions on Graphics*, Vol. 31, No. 2, Article 14.

Choe.B. and Ko,H., 2001. Analysis and Synthesis of Facial Expressions with Hand-Generated Muscle Actuation Basis. *Proceedings of Computer Animation* 2001, pp. 12–19.

Alexa, M. et al., 2000. As-rigid-as-possible shape interpolation. *In SIGGRAPH '00: Proceedings of the 27th annual conference on Computer graphics and interactive techniques*, New York, NY, USA pp. 157–164.

Baxter, W, et al., 2009., N-way morphing for 2D animation, Computer Animation and Virtual Worlds 2009; 20: 79–87 Published online 3 June in Wiley InterScience , (www.interscience.wiley.com) DOI: 10.1002/cav.310

Sumner R. et al., 2005. Mesh-Based Inverse Kinematics. *SIGGRAPH 2005, ACM Trans. Graph 24,3,*pp.488-495.

Eppstein D. et al., 2009. Approximate topological matching of quad meshes. Published online: 16 April 2009, Springer-Verlag.

Peterson D., 1984. Halfspace representation of extrusions, solids of revolution, and pyramids. *SANDIA Report SAND84-0572,* Albuquerque, NM: Sandia National Laboratories.

Turk, G. and O'Brien, J.F., 2002. Modelling with Implicit Surfaces that Interpolate. *ACM Transactions on Graphics,* Vol. 21, No. 4, October 2002, pp. 855–873.

Savchenko, V.V. et al., 1995. Function Representation of Solids Reconstructed from Scattered Surface Points and Contours. *Computer Graphics Forum,* Volume 14, (1995) number 4, pp. 181-188.

Bloomenthal, J., 1997, *Introduction to Implicit Surfaces,* Morgan Kaufmann, *ISBN 1-55860-233-X.* Edited by Jules Bloomenthal With Chandrajit Bajaj, Jim Blinn, Marie-Paule Cani-Gascuel, Alyn Rockwood, Brian Wyvill, and Geoff Wyvill

Buhmann, M.D, 2003. *Radial Basis Functions: Theory and Implementation.* Cambridge University Press.

The OpenMP® API specification for parallel programming. http://openmp.org/wp/

PSEUDO-DENSE OPTICAL FLOW BASED ON PUZZLED IMAGES

Olivier Demuynck
Spain

ABSTRACT

A novel image segmenting method is proposed in this paper. This segmenting method based on region growing returns images further entitled puzzled images. Based on puzzled image, a new pseudo-dense optical flow method is presented and discussed. Additionally, an optical flow cumulative function, assisted by a Least Square based iterative error filtering method, is presented and proposed for background detection and/or 3D background estimation.

KEYWORDS

Image segmentation, optical flow

1. INTRODUCTION

Optical flow is usually needed in many dynamical computer vision applications, mainly for tracking purpose, considering static or moving camera. State of the art methods are already achieving very interesting experimental or simulated results. Nevertheless robustness usually implies a high computational cost that cannot be assumed by many applications where dense optical flow is required. Additionally, after an extensive review of the state of the art, it seems that natural scene dense optical flow is still an important challenge. The following discussion tends to ease the understanding of the chosen strategy for the developed method by limiting the citations to the most relevant optical flow processing proposals.

An interesting method is depicted in [1]. This method relies on [2]. Lucas Kanade Feature Tracker method [2] assume that, considering a practically fast enough frame rate, an image region of a given frame can be found in the next frame according to a mathematical expression which includes a displacement vector and an affine transform (in a same period of time, [3] proposed an optical flow evaluation method). In [1] Bouguet's arguments, focusing on accuracy and robustness, contrast the interest of using small or large integration windows, respectively for patches occlusion and lightning purpose. Thus, the proposed algorithm uses a pyramidal implementation of this method that start from a very low resolution image up to the original frame size. This iterative technique thus approximately extracts the displacement vector and affine transform, which are further progressively refined. Finally, experiments introduce additional multiplicative and additive value to respectively adapt the contrast and brightness, resulting in a more robust tracking in terms of illumination variations. Practically, for time processing restriction and relevance of the selected regions, this method usually uses previously processed keypoints.

The method depicted in [4] assumes the neighbor of a given point in an image can be approximated to a quadratic polynomial function. It considers a global displacement, which can be mathematically solved in such quadratic polynomial expression. This work is developed using synthetic video sequences. Experiments can thus return a quantitative evaluation of the method, and any illumination variation is thus isolated. Nevertheless, some synthetic video sequences, for texture positioning reason can actually affect the global result. This method, concerning processing time, allows practically a dense optical flow evaluation.

[5] and [6] present a very similar quality result. In [5], additionally with the complex neural implemented mechanisms (that implies memory limitations), the good synthetic video sequence based result of the proposed method is shown to be very approximated in natural scenes. In [6], the intention of progressively processing natural scene is exposed. Indeed, combining a complex hardware set (UV lightening system, 8MPixel frames, and computer assisted scene motion control) some "stop motion" style video sequences

have been grabbed. As mentioned in the paper, even if those sequences are more realistic than synthetic video sequences, it stills some laboratory scene.

[7] and [8] present others different methods improving some particular aspects ([7] orient the study on optical flow discontinuity issue). Finally, and omitting all the evident machine vision applications that could benefit with an efficient optical flow estimation, experiments such the one proposed in [9], where the optical flow in movies sequences is analyzed in order to further find relation with brain areas activity, demonstrate a wider field of applications interest.

The proposed approach, titled pseudo-dense optical flow based on puzzled images, and further described in this paper, is based on the first method [1]. Nevertheless, in spite of selecting some keypoints, the intension is to implement a pseudo-dense optical flow for real scene applications. The particle pseudo is used in order to emphasis the divergence between the common meaning of the word dense, and its combination with the optical flow process. Indeed, and even if tracking methods could be used in order to temporally fix any occluded information in a scene, a dense optical flow would basically require a static observation of a static scene, that actually would result in an inexistent optical flow. The term pseudo-dense optical flow thus implies that the frame to frame occlusions will cause partial lacks of information. The main idea of this method focuses on the detection of the previously mentioned patches. A new segmentation method, resulting in a puzzled image, has thus been developed. Each puzzle piece, corresponding to an image patch, could present different speeds and orientations in successive frames. Finally, optical flow process requires a previous experimental study between camera motion, scene elements range of speed, and frame rate. Indeed, in order reach robust processed information, a significant enough displacement is required. Nevertheless, optical flow methods would frequently return an erroneous result considering a too large displacement between two successive frames.

The method is described as follow: A first section presents the method for the patches segmentation. This new method, based on region growing technique, which uses the colour information (intensity in case of grayscale image), is further entitled puzzled image. A second section depicts the global pseudo-dense optical flow algorithm. A third section presents an optional optical flow cumulative method, assisted by a least square based iterative error filtering, oriented to background segmentation. In a fourth section, this least square based iterative error filtering is depicted. A fifth section presents some results and processing time, allowing a discussion in a last conclusion section.

2. PUZZLED IMAGE

The puzzling step returns a group of indexed regions (puzzle pieces) covering the all input image, segmented according to their colour information (intensity, in case of grayscale image). Many image processing techniques could achieve building this puzzled image: Region growing, Maximally Stable Extremal Region (MSER), downsampling, etc. The puzzled image presented for method illustration is produced by an edges limited region growing (see Figure 1). Note that, even if it could offer some advantages, the listed MSER based method would further result in a more complex managing technique, due to the multiple, and overlapped, regions options at a given image location.

Note that, this process is relatively slow, and for time processing restriction purpose, the input image is limited to contain a maximum of 10850 pixels. Finally, as can be observed in Figure 1, each segmented region is painted using its own mean colour value (intensity in case of grayscale images).

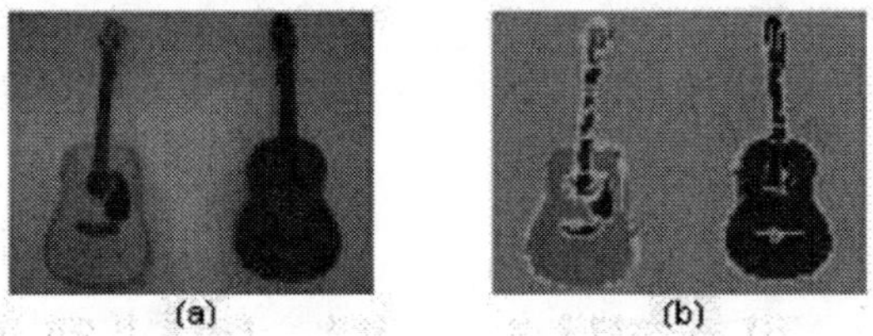

Figure 1. Illustration of puzzled image method. (a) the input image, and (b) the puzzled image

3. PSEUDO-DENSE OPTICAL FLOW PROCESS

For each pixel coordinate of the resized input image, the optical flow is processed using the Bouguet's method [1]. Then, a clustering function processes, for each puzzle piece, the orientation and magnitude. The orientation and magnitude are obtained by an iterative process (similar to the statistical error filtering method depicted in Section 4) that successively computes the mean value, the standard deviation, and filter the outliers according to those two values. This iterative process refines the mean orientation and magnitude values until a maximum number of iteration or a precision threshold is reached.

In Figure 2, the pseudo-dense optical flow is illustrated. Note that the images are strongly blurred because the video was grabbed with a mobile phone camera (original frame size 1280x720).

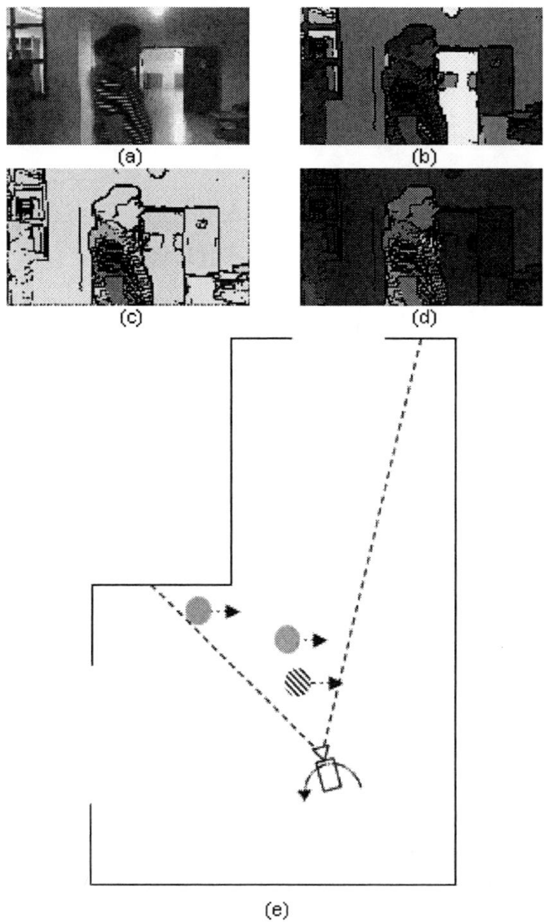

Figure 2. Illustration of the pseudo-dense optical flow process. (a) the input image, (b) the puzzled image, (c) the optical flow orientation painted according to Hue colour circle, (d) the optical flow magnitude, and (e) this illustration frame situation

In order to ease the method illustration interpretation presented in Figure 2, Figure 3 presents the Hue colour circle used for orientation painting (image (c) in Figure 2), which, even in grayscale printing presentation, allows intuitively to verify that the centered person indeed depicts a left to right displacement, as it is presented in the scheme (e) of Figure 2. The optical flow magnitude (image (d) in Figure 2) is additionally extended to the [0, 255] range for observation purpose.

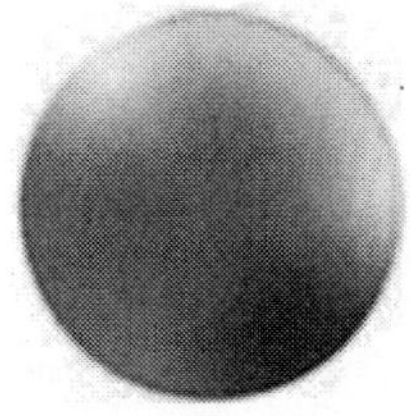

Figure 3. Hue colour circle used for optical flow orientation painting

Since orientations associated with a low magnitude value are usually corrupted, a minimum magnitude threshold can be used for optical flow filtering (this threshold should be experimentally set according to the image acquisition system hardware). In Figure 2, the mobile phone camera moved fast enough, between the two concerned frames, for the background optical flow to also be properly estimated. For many applications, particularly in case of static camera, the use of a magnitude threshold would return the required optical flow information. Nevertheless, considering the background information could be necessary in moving camera applications, cumulative optical flow information has also been implemented in order to extract a consistent background optical flow.

4. OPTICAL FLOW CUMULATING PROCESS

The optical flow cumulative information process assumes first that the background to be represented by the biggest puzzle piece. Once the number of frame and respective optical flow information is registered, the process applies a regular points spreading grid on the current puzzled image. The points grid found inside the background region are searched back in all the previous frames according to the registered optical flow information, and are cumulated. The information is then filtered by a Least Square based iterative error filtering process (further detailed in section 5) to return a unique value of background orientation and magnitude. Note that this filtering method is used assuming that the transformation between the two considered frames combines exclusively a translation and a rotation (focal variations caused by auto focus functionality, usually implemented on mobile devices, would corrupt the proposed mathematical solution).

The rotation and translation information are then used to properly present the two N frames interval distant frames in a direct horizontal correspondence. The background is finally extended to others puzzle pieces by processing the disparity map (method inspired by [10]) using the original sized frames, as it is illustrated in Figure 4. Depending on the video quality, the observed scene could thus benefit with a third dimension for any posterior analysis purpose.

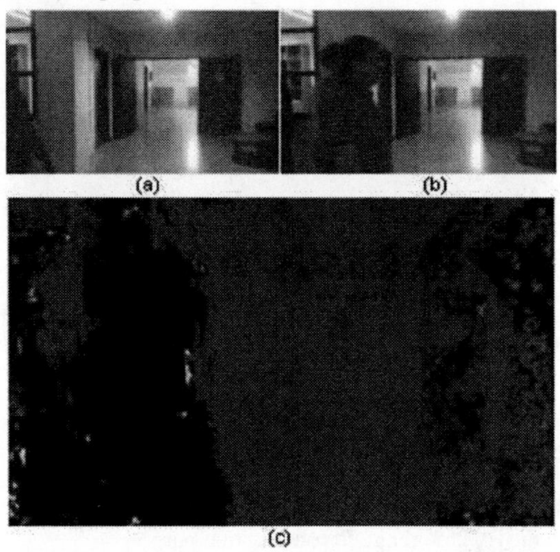

Figure 4. Illustration of the disparity based background extraction. (a) the N^{n} previous frame, (b) the current frame, and (c) the disparity map

As can be observed in image (c) of Figure 4, the background segmentation is still quite noisy. Nevertheless the foreground for distance range purpose cannot be correctly processed and thus is automatically segmented. Depending on the observation situation, this process could thus, at least theoretically, be more efficient than basic optical flow segmentation where a temporally static foreground element could not be detected.

The considered video in this study is grabbed in almost constant speed motion and direction. Once the frame buffer is containing the required number of frames, the optical flow cumulative process is launched. Nevertheless, the disparity map is only processed when the translation vector magnitude reaches a number of pixels threshold (that should be set according to the image acquisition system hardware) in order to generate a relevant enough disparity map. An improvement of this method, in case the camera motion could include accelerations and/or orientation variations, should not be based on a number of cumulated frames (set as an input parameter), but should process this disparity map information anytime the cumulated translation vector magnitude is relevant enough. In spite of basically assuming the background as belonging systematically to the biggest puzzle piece, a processed information feedback could allow an efficient selection of the deepest puzzle pieces as part of it.

5. LEAST SQUARE BASED ITERATIVE ERROR FILTERING

This filtering method assumes that a set of point's correspondences contains a majority of inliers. Considering the transformation, between the two considered frames (camera positions), a combination of translation and rotation, the system of equations is given by the expression (1).

$$R.Pi + T = Pi' \tag{1}$$

Where R and T are respectively the rotation and translation matrices, and Pi and Pi' are the ith pair of corresponding points.

R and T are respectively given by the expressions (2) and (3).

$$R = \begin{pmatrix} \cos\theta & -\sin\theta \\ \sin\theta & \cos\theta \end{pmatrix} \tag{2}$$

$$T = \begin{pmatrix} Tx \\ Ty \end{pmatrix} \tag{3}$$

The linear equation system can thus be written as in the expressions (4), where n is the number of pairs of corresponding points (required to be higher than two for solving purpose).

$$\begin{pmatrix} \cos\theta & -\sin\theta & Tx \\ \sin\theta & \cos\theta & Ty \end{pmatrix} . \begin{pmatrix} x1 & \dots & xi & \dots & xn \\ y1 & \dots & yi & \dots & yn \\ 1 & \dots & 1 & \dots & 1 \end{pmatrix} = \begin{pmatrix} x1' & \dots & xi' & \dots & xn' \\ y1' & \dots & yi' & \dots & yn' \end{pmatrix} \tag{4}$$

Expression (4) can also be generically presented in the expression (5) form.

$$W.A = B \tag{5}$$

And the least square solution of expression (5) is then given by the formula in expression (6).

$$W = B.((A^T.A)^{-1}.A^T)^T \tag{6}$$

Once processed the solution according to expression (6), the corresponding points *Pi''* are then computed according to the expression (7), that actually refers to expression (4). Corresponding points *Pi''* are thus the ones that best fit with the least square processed solution.

$$\begin{pmatrix} \cos\theta & -\sin\theta & Tx \\ \sin\theta & \cos\theta & Ty \end{pmatrix} \cdot \begin{pmatrix} x1 & \dots & xi & \dots & xn \\ y1 & \dots & yi & \dots & yn \\ 1 & \dots & 1 & \dots & 1 \end{pmatrix} = \begin{pmatrix} x1'' & \dots & xi'' & \dots & xn'' \\ y1'' & \dots & yi'' & \dots & yn'' \end{pmatrix} \tag{7}$$

The Euclidian distance error between each *Pi'* and *Pi''* pair of points is then computed according to expression (8).

$$dist(Pi', Pi'') = \sqrt{(xi' - xi'')^2 + (yi' - yi'')^2} \tag{8}$$

Those error distances are then filtered by an iterative statistical process. This process computes the mean value *M* of a given set of error distances (first iteration includes the whole set of corresponding points), it computes the standard deviation *StD*, and conserves the error distances included in the range [*M-StD*, *M+StD*]. By reducing the set of error distances, this method selects thus the best point's correspondences. The process finishes anytime it reaches a precision threshold *T* ($\Delta M \leq T$), a maximum number of iterations, or because the set of error distances is not consistent enough.

This error distances filtering process allows the corresponding *Pi* and *Pi'* pair of points to be filtered, and the least square method is launched on the reduced point's correspondences set in order to refine the solution.

6. RESULTS

Running on a 2.8 GHz processor, and 3,50GB RAM, the time processing are approximately the following: 1) input image resizing (original size: 1280x720): 0.3 ms, 2) image puzzling process: 40 ms, 3) puzzle pieces mean color painting: 20 ms, 4) pseudo dense optical flow process: 40 ms, 5) puzzle pieces optical flow process: 20 ms, and optionally 5) optical flow cumulative: 0.2 ms, 6) disparity based background detection: 2.2 s. Excepted for image resizing step, all those processing times vary according to number of puzzle pieces. Considering a 150 frames video sequence, in a scene where 8 peoples are walking, time processing per frame is found around 0.1 seconds (and keeps less than 2.5 seconds when optical flow cumulative function and disparity map are processed). Since complexity of an observed scene could strongly vary depending on the observation conditions and application, and that processing time would mainly vary according to that scene complexity, it is preferred not to present a more precise time processing result.

The resulting pseudo-dense optical flow has not been quantitatively evaluated since grabbed videos where unsupervised. Nevertheless, it can be observed that almost rigid neighbouring puzzle pieces are conserving an almost similar orientation and magnitude, which tends to demonstrate the efficiency of the method.

Those results could be somehow affected by the video quality, grabbed for a mobile device, which result strongly blurred. The contour definition being affected and neighboring colours smoothed the puzzling image step is not optimum. Nevertheless, it further slightly corrects this phenomenon.

The resulting cumulative pseudo-dense optical flow process is also demonstrating the efficiency of the method, since disparity map process requires a high precision left/right image positioning in order to achieve an interpretable resulting image. Additionally, and according to the previously mentioned hardware used for the video recording, the blurring effect is strongly affecting the disparity map process. Indeed, a webcam test has also been performed, where images are just slightly better in term of smoothing effect (but is still mainly affected by rolling shutter and brightness auto-adjustment). The disparity map, in that case, is clearly extracting different depth of the observed objects.

7. CONCLUSIONS

In this paper, a novel approach for pseudo-dense optical flow estimation is presented. It is shown that the precision of this process can also allow processing a disparity map, which usually requires a high positioning precision. Thus the proposed method tries to solve some current challenges in terms of scene motion segmentation and/or reconstruction in natural scene.

Additionally, the use of puzzled images (a new image segmentation method presented in this study) have been also found interesting for object detection, where neighbouring puzzle pieces can be combined and compared with a reference object contour. This object detection functionality would ideally combine with this pseudo-dense optical flow method.

ACKNOWLEDGEMENT

The implementation of the method uses the OpenCV library, which community is acknowledged here.

REFERENCES

[1] Bouguet, 2000, Pyramidal Implementation of the affine Lucas Kanade Feature Tracker Description of the algorithm, *Intel Corporation, Microprocessor Research Labs, Technical Report.*

[2] Lucas, and Kanade, 1981, An Iterative Image Registration Technique with an Application to Stereo Vision, *Proceeding International Joint Conference on Artificial Intelligence (IJCAI)*, pp.674-679.

[3] Barron, Fleet, and Beauchemin, 1994, Performance of Optical Flow Techniques, *International Journal of Computer Vision*, 12:1, 43-77.

[4] Farneback, 2003, Two-Frame Motion Estimation Based on Polynomial Expansion, *Image Analysis*, 2749:363-370.

[5] Bayerl, and Neumann, 2007, A Fast Biologically Inspired Algorithm for Recurrent Motion Estimation, *IEEE Transactions on Pattern Analysis and Machine Intelligence*, Vol. 29, No. 2.

[6] Backer, Scharstein, Lewis, Roth, Black, and Szeliski, 2009, A Database and Evaluation Methodology for Optical Flow, *Microsoft Research Technical Report.*

[7] Alvarez Leon, Esclarin Monreal, Lefebure, and Sanchez Perez, 1999, A PDE model for computing the optical flow, *Proceeding XVI Congreso de Ecuaciones Differenciales y Applicaciones*, pp. 1349-1356.

[8] Aubert, Deriche, and KornProbst, 1999, Computing Optical Flow via Variational Techniques, *SIAM Journal on Applied Mathematics*, Vol. 60, No. 1, pp. 156-182.

[9] Bartels, Zeki, and Logothetis, 2008, Natural Vision Reveals Regional Specialization to Local Motion and to Contrast-Invariant, Global Flow in the Human Brain, *Cerebral Cortex*, Vol.. 18, pp. 705-717.

[10] Heiko Hirschmuller, 2008, Stereo Processing by Semiglobal Matching and Mutual Information, *IEEE Transactions on Pattern Analysis and Machine Intelligence*, Vol. 30, No. 2, pp. 328-341.

ULTRA-LOW-LATENCY AUTOMATIC ENDOSCOPIC IMAGE ORIENTATION STABILISATION

Wiebe Van Ranst, Toon Goedemé and Joost Vennekens
EAVISE Research Group, KU Leuven
Jan Pieter De Nayerlaan 5, Sint-Katelijne-Waver, Belgium

ABSTRACT

Minimally invasive surgery often makes use of endoscopes with an angled lens. When using such an endoscope, the on-screen image tends to rotate wildly, which may confuse the surgeon. A low-impact way of solving this problem is by using computer vision techniques to track the rotation of the incoming footage and then counterrotating the image. Such an approach has already been proposed in the literature, but it has never been examined whether it is possible to integrate such an algorithm into a state-of-the-art Digital Operating Room environment, where minimal latency is required. In this paper, we compare three different ways of implementing a counterrotation algorithm on the hardware that is available in the NUCLeUS Digital Operating Room of the company eSaturnus.

KEYWORDS

Endoscopy, Image stabilisation, Ultra-low-latency

1. INTRODUCTION

Minimally invasive surgery is a type of surgery where small incisions are made in order to operate at a remote location in the patient's body. These incisions make room for the required instruments, as well as an endoscope which acts as the surgeon's eyes during the procedure. The endoscope is commonly equipped with an angled lens (typically set at 30 degrees, see figure 1), in order to enable the surgeon to get a broader view. Moreover, this also makes it possible to look behind objects by turning the endoscope, thus revealing perspectives which would be concealed with a normal endoscope. While this extra information provides a significant benefit to the surgeon, the angled lens is also a source of confusion and disorientation, since the act of rotating the endoscope also rotates the on-screen image (Breedvel, 1997). For certain kinds of procedures, this confusion can be avoided by placing a small amount of water into, e.g., the abdominal cavity in order to provide the surgeon with a reference "horizon". In situations where this is not possible, the

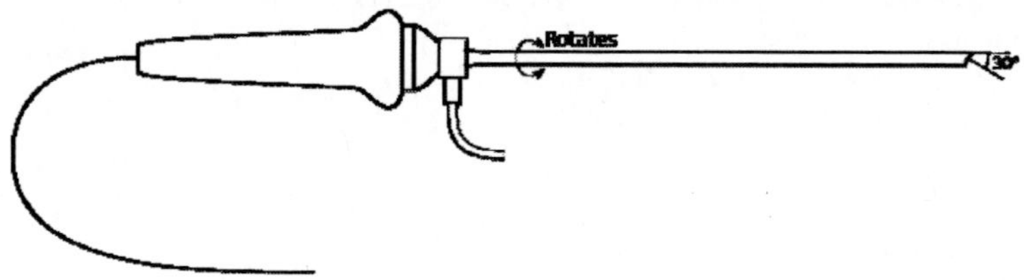

Figure 1. The endoscope lens rotates freely on the camera attachment

surgeon may choose to use an endoscope that allows its lens to be rotated independently of the endoscope itself (see figure 1). A downside of this solution, however, is that the movement required to turn only the lens while keeping the endoscope steady is quite cumbersome and often requires both hands of the operator, while also restricting camera movement.

A more promising approach is to solve this problem by postprocessing the video footage coming from the endoscope. Such postprocessing may consist of automatically counter-rotating the output of the endoscope, or of drawing a virtual "horizon" on screen, which informs the surgeon of the current rotation of the image.

In both cases, the core problem is that of determining the current rotation angle. Generally speaking, there are two ways of doing this: either by using some kind of hardware gravity sensor (Höller et al., 2009), or by using the images captured by the endoscope. While the use of a gravity sensor has the advantage of being drift free, an obvious disadvantage is that it requires a special endoscope equipped with such a sensor. In addition, gravity sensor endoscopes do not work if they are held above the patient, looking down.

By contrast, the image-based approach has the advantage that counter-rotation can be implemented entirely in software. Indeed, by tracking the translation between consecutive frames of the video feed, the orientation of the video can be automatically determined. Such an approach has already been investigated (Moll et al., 2009), but—to the best of our knowledge—it has never been implemented in a system used for live surgery. One of the main problems that need to be tackled in order to make this possible is that the video feed needs to be rendered at minimum latency. Indeed, for the hand-eye coordination of the surgeon, latency is a crucial parameter (Rayman et al., 2005). A recent study found that a latency above 130ms has detrimental effects on surgeon's performance (Kumcu et al., 2013).

The company eSATURNUS has developed a state-of-the-art digital operating room environment, called NUCLeUS™, which operates at extremely low latency: it streams 1080p60 video with a latency of <16ms, i.e., less than one frame. In this paper, we investigate how a video-based rotation tracking algorithm can be successfully integrated in this system. To do this, we have to tackle the unique challenge of combining high-framerate, high-resolution images with the requirement of ultra-low latency. We investigate the implementation of the algorithm on embedded hardware as a method for coping with these challenges.

This research has resulted in the development of a prototype, that can be seen in action at: http://www.youtube.com/watch?v=2tMk0u0yWc0.

The remainder of this paper is organized as follows. In section 0, we lay out the algorithm we used for our implementation, while section 0 explains how the algorithm is implemented on resource constrained hardware. Finally, section 0 discusses results in terms of performance and accuracy.

2. ROTATION COMPENSATION

The requirement for ultra-low latency forces us to consider a relatively simple approach to computing the rotation of the video. For this reason, we avoid feature matching techniques, such as SIFT (Lowe, 1999) or SURF (Bay et al., 2006), and have chosen to use a tracking algorithm instead.

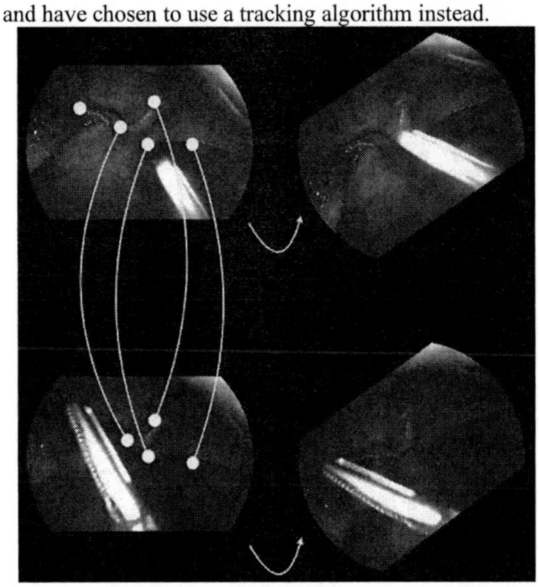

Figure 2. The tracking approach

The general idea of such a tracking approach is illustrated in figure 2. The left-hand side of this figure shows two consecutive frames of the incoming video. A number of distinctive points in the image (also called "corners") are extracted and these are then tracked across subsequent frames. From the movement of the corners from one frame to the next, the rotation angle between the two frames can be calculated. This angle can then be used to rotate the frame back to the reference orientation. The resulting "straight" frames are shown on the right-hand side of this figure.

To implement this approach, we have chosen to use a KLT tracker (Lucas and Kanade, 1981; Tomasi and Kanade, 1991). Our general approach is as follows. Processing starts when the operator enables the rotation compensation. This is done by pressing a button on the endoscope, while holding it level. At that point, the system takes the most recent frame of the stream and applies the corner detection algorithm. Once the corners have been extracted, the system can start tracking them through the next frames. However, over the course of the video, the system may lose track of some of the original corners. Once the number of tracked corners drops below a certain threshold, the corner detection algorithm is again applied and the process continues. We now discuss each of these components in more detail.

2.1 Detecting Corners

To detect corners in the endoscopy images, we use Harris corners (Harris and Stephens, 1988), which are known to produce good results for video footage in which there are small changes between consecutive frames (Schmid et al., 2000). We have also tried Shi and Tomasi's "Good features to track" (Shi and Tomasi, 1994), and found that they produce almost identical results on typical endoscopy footage (see figure 3). As suggested in the OpenCV manual, we track only corners that have a "quality level" of at least 0.01. On average, this results in about 170 corners being tracked.

2.2 Tracking

We use a pyramidal implementation of the KLT tracker as described in (Bouguet, 2001). The implementation makes use of a scale space pyramid built on top of the original image. Each new layer is constructed by

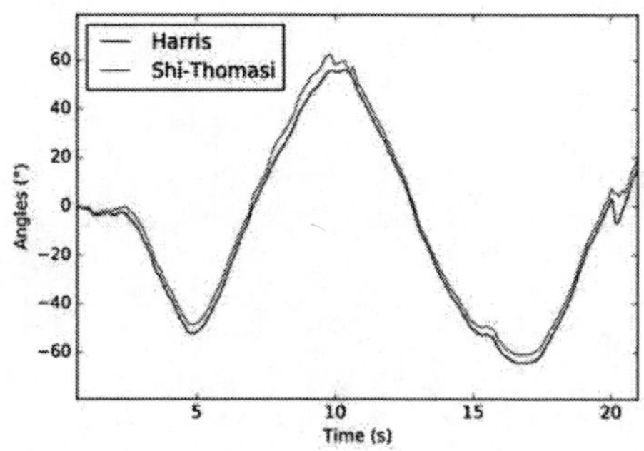

Figure 3. Harris vs. Shi-Tomasi

downscaling the previous layer by some constant factor. Feature tracking then commences at the top—i.e., lowest resolution—layer. These rough results are then gradually refined by descending in the pyramid.

2.3 Calculate Transformation

In this step, two point clouds—one from the previous frame and one from the current frame—are compared to each other in order to calculate the transformation between two frames. We calculate the homography between both clouds using OpenCV's RANSAC (Fischler and Bolles, 1981) implementation.

2.4 Interpolation of Estimated Angle

The Kalman filter assumes that the change in rotation angle is constant over time and so it predicts the angle α_t at time point t by the following linear model:

$$\begin{bmatrix}\alpha_{t+1}\\ \dot{\alpha}_{t+1}\end{bmatrix} = \begin{bmatrix}1 & \delta_t\\ 0 & 1\end{bmatrix}\begin{bmatrix}\alpha_t\\ \dot{\alpha}_t\end{bmatrix}$$

Here, δ_t is the time elapsed between time points t and $t+1$ (because the angle computation might have to skip frames, δ_t may not be constant).

After making the new prediction α_{t+1}, the Kalman model is then updated using a weighted average of α_{t+1} and the new measurement, i.e., the angle that was computed by the KLT tracker (the observation vector contains only the new angle). The weights depend on a process covariance matrix Q and a measurement covariance matrix R. We have empirically determined the values $Q = \begin{bmatrix}1 & 0\\ 0 & 77\end{bmatrix}$ and $R = \begin{bmatrix}1 & 0\\ 0 & 1\end{bmatrix}$ for these matrices. The high value for velocity in the process covariance matrix indicates that, the predicted velocity is often off by a large margin, when the surgeon makes sudden movements.

When frames have to be dropped, the Kalman filter may start to drift away from the real rotation angle. This can happen in particular when there are sudden camera movements that violate the Kalman filter's assumption of a constant α_t . In such a case, the Kalman filter may have to perform a large correction when a new angle finally does arrive. This can give a jerky effect in the video. Therefore, we pass the resulting angle to a moving average filter which further smooths out the jerkiness. This filter keeps track of the last n samples (in our case, $n=10$) and is updated at a constant interval. Our implementation does this in a separate thread. The output of the moving average filter is used as the final result.

3. IMPLEMENTATION

The general architecture of the NUCLeUS Digital Operating Room is shown in figure 4. Video is captured by the source module, which transmits a direct, full HD feed to the receiver module, which decodes this feed and displays it on screen. There is also a secondary, lower-resolution SD feed, which can be used for other purposes, e.g., it can be streamed over the internet to medical staff follow the procedure from a remote location.

This architecture provides us with different options for implementing the tracking algorithm:

- REC: The computation of the angle happens entirely on the receiver module.
- R&S: The KLT tracker runs on the source module, while the Kalman and moving average filters run on the receiver.
- SRV: The angle computation happens on the separate compute server.

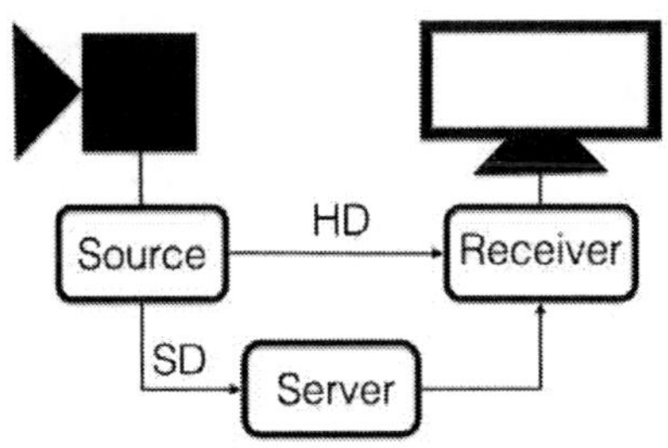

Figure 4. System architecture

We describe each option in more detail below.

3.1 Using only the Receiver Module (REC)

The receiver module contains a quad core processer and a Vivante GC2000 GPU, which supports the Embedded Profile (EP) of the OpenCL standard (Maghazeh et al., 2013). The REC approach uses this GPU to run the KLT tracker. When a new frame comes in, it is first downscaled to a resolution of 800x448px and then copied to GPU memory space. The GPU then calculates each level of the image pyramid of the frame, as well as its derivatives in both x and y directions, using the Scharr operator (Scharr, 2007). In all cases, a single work item is launched for every pixel in the output image.

Once the image pyramid is computed, the actual tracking starts. We launch one workitem for each corner in the previous frame. On a typical desktop GPU, this would use only a fraction of the available compute units. However, since the Vivante GC2000 GPU only has four compute units, this parallelization strategy is able to keep the available hardware occupied. Inside the kernel, the displacement of each feature is calculated using the KL tracking algorithm.

Finally, we transfer the updated locations of the corners back to the CPU and use OpenCV to calculate the transformation between the current and previous point cloud. We then apply the Kalman and moving average filter.

3.2 Using both the Receiver and the Source Module (R&S)

This variant splits the computation over the receiver and source module: the source calculates the rotation angle and the receiver applies the Kalman and moving average filter. One advantage of using the source module to calculate the rotation angle is that we can make use of the already downscaled secondary video stream that is available on this module, while in the REC approach, the full HD stream still has to be downscaled on the receiver. Because the source module does not have a GPU, this implementation uses the OpenCV CPU version of the KLT algorithm instead of our own OpenCL EP implementation. The resulting angle is transmitted to the receiver module as part of the header of the image that is sent, so no additional communication delay is incurred.

3.3 Compute Server (SRV)

This approach performs the tracking on the separate desktop machine that gets the secondary SD feed. The resulting angle is sent to the receiver module, which uses it to rotate its direct HD feed and then renders the results it on-screen.

Because the angle and HD image arrive through different paths, they need not be synchronized: the receiver always uses the most recent angle it has received to rotate the most recent image. Because of this, the angle computation cannot increase the latency with which the video feed is rendered. If the angle computation is too slow, this will have as its only effect that the rotation will use an angle that is slightly off. The Kalman filter on the receiver module can compensate for this effect, while the additional moving average filter avoids jerkiness upon receiving a delayed angle.

If the compute server is powerful enough to keep up with the framerate, however, then no interpolation of the angle is necessary. In this case, the Kalman filter just smooths out sudden movements, at the expense of causing the rotation angle to lag slightly behind.

4. RESULTS

In this section we evaluate our different implementations in terms of both performance and accuracy.

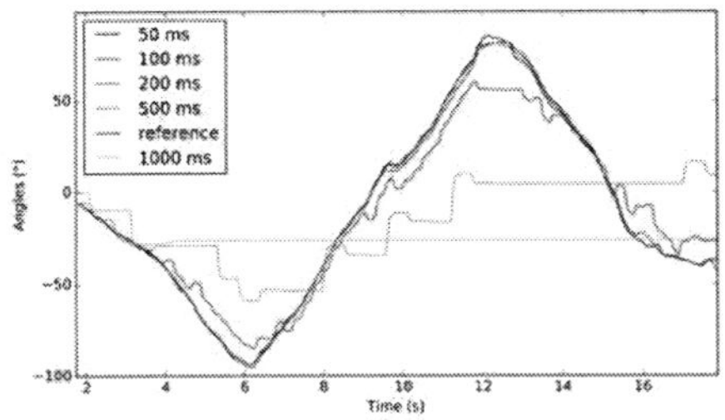

Figure 5. Angles at different update rates

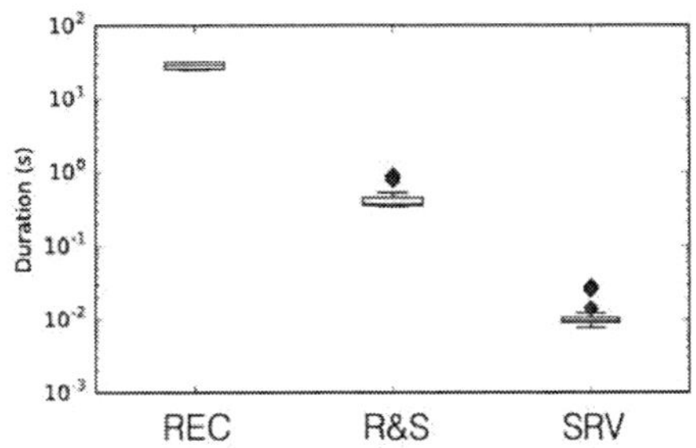

Figure 6. Runtime comparison

If the computation of the rotation angle cannot be performed fast enough to keep up with the framerate of the video, our approach is to drop frames from the angle computation. In this way, we avoid increasing the latency with which the video is rendered, but this obviously comes at the cost of lowering the accuracy of the computed angle. Figure 5 examines the effect of increasing the interval between two angle computations on the accuracy of the angle. The baseline corresponds to computing an angle for each frame of the 30fps video. We can therefore achieve the baseline by computing each angle within 33ms. As the time needed for each frame increases, we have to drop more frames and the accuracy deteriorates. As figure 6 shows, we can go as low as 5fps and still have a reasonable approximation of the baseline.

Figure 6 shows the performance of our algorithm on the different system configurations discussed in section 0, measured over 40 trials.

The REC approach is infeasible, as it takes an average of almost 28s per frame. The Vivante GPU that is available on this module is therefore clearly not powerful enough to perform the required computation.

Shifting the computation of the rotation angle to the source module (R&S) provides a significant improvement. This is due to the fact that the source module's CPU (an Intel atom Z530) is more powerful than the processors that are available on the receiver, as well as the fact that we avoid having to downscale the video twice. However, the average computation time of 0.43s means that we could still only compute 2 angles per second. As we can see from figure 5, this is an unacceptably poor approximation of the real rotation angle. Moreover, the worst execution time for this approach was substantially slower (0.89s) than the average. Therefore, this approach has to be ruled out.

We can conclude that the approach with a separate compute server (Intel Xeon E5-2630 in our tests) is most feasible in this case. While the downside of this approach is obvious—i.e., the need for additional hardware—the gain in runtime outweighs the cost for this latency-sensitive application. Indeed, with an average runtime of 11ms and a worst runtime of 28ms, this solution is able to keep track with the 30fps framerate of the video. Taking also into account the network transfer of the low-resolution image feed to this compute server and the communication of the angle from the server to the receiver, the latency with which the computed angle arrives at the receiver module is approximately between 50 and 100ms. This slight lag in rotation angle is not noticeable in practice.

As discussed before, the video itself is rendered from the direct HD feed, so angle computation does not affect its latency at all. However, the GPU that is available on the receiver module of NUCLeUS cannot actually counterrotate the HD video in 60fps. One solution is to work with 1280x720@30fps video instead. The other is to simply render the incoming HD feed as is, but to impose a "horizon" on it that informs the surgeon of the current rotation. We have implemented both approaches.

5. CONCLUSION

To cope with the disorientation arising from the use of angled endoscopes, we have developed an orientation stabilisation method, based on the KLT tracker (Lucas and Kanade, 1981; Tomasi and Kanade, 1991), and examined how to integrate this into the NUCLeUS Digital Operating Room. This state-of-the-art system aims at providing an ultra-low-latency solution, which is important since research suggests that latency is a key parameter for surgeon's performance. The aim of this paper is therefore to investigate methods of integrating orientation stabilisation into this system without adversely affecting this latency.

We have developed two embedded implementations of the KLT tracker: an OpenCL EP implementation running on the GPU in the receiver module and an implementation running mainly on the CPU in the source module. Our experimental results demonstrate that neither of these implementations is fast enough to allow a reasonable approximation of the rotation angle. However, the IP-based architecture of NUCLeUS also allows a third option, namely that of running the bulk of the computation on a separate desktop machine. This options allows the latency with which the video is rendered to remain unchanged, while the rotation angle that is computed never lags more than a few frames behind.

ACKNOWLEDGMENT

This work is supported and partially carried out at eSATURNUS nv. This work was supported by IWT Flanders via the Hippocrates project.

REFERENCES

Bay, H., Tuytelaars, T., Van Gool, L., 2006. Surf: Speeded up robust features, in: Computer vision–ECCV 2006. Springer, pp. 404–417.

Bouguet, J.-Y., 2001. Pyramidal implementation of the affine Lucas Kanade feature tracker. Intel Corp. 5, 1–10.

Fischler, M.A., Bolles, R.C., 1981. Random sample consensus: a paradigm for model fitting with applications to image analysis and automated cartography. Commun. ACM 24, 381–395.

Harris, C., Stephens, M., 1988. A combined corner and edge detector., in: Alvey Vision Conference. Citeseer, p. 50.

Höller, K., Penne, J., Schneider, A., Jahn, J., Boronat, J.G., Wittenberg, T., Feu\s sner, H., Hornegger, J., 2009. Endoscopic orientation correction, in: Medical Image Computing and Computer-Assisted Intervention–MICCAI 2009. Springer, pp. 459–466.

Kumcu, A., Elprama, S., Vermeulen, L., Duysburgh, P., Platisa, L., Van Nieuwenhove, Y., Van De Winkel, N., Jacobs, A., Van Looy, J., Philips, W., 2013. Effect of video latency on performance and subjective experience in laparoscopic surgery, in: 15th Medical Image Perception Society Conference, Abstracts. pp. 59–59.

Lowe, D.G., 1999. Object recognition from local scale-invariant features, in: Computer Vision, 1999. The Proceedings of the Seventh IEEE International Conference on. IEEE, pp. 1150–1157.

Lucas, B.D., Kanade, T., 1981. An Iterative Image Registration Technique with an Application to Stereo Vision, in: IJCAI. pp. 674–679.

Maghazeh, A., Bordoloi, U.D., Eles, P., Peng, Z., 2013. General purpose computing on low-power embedded GPUs: Has it come of age?, in: Embedded Computer Systems: Architectures, Modeling, and Simulation (SAMOS XIII).

Moll, M., Koninckx, T., Van Gool, L., Koninckx, P., 2009. Unrotating images in laparoscopy with an application for 30° laparoscopes, in: 4th European Conference of the International Federation for Medical and Biological Engineering.

Rayman, R., Primak, S., Patel, R., Moallem, M., Morady, R., Tavakoli, M., Subotic, V., Galbraith, N., Wynsberghe, A. van, Croome, K., 2005. Effects of Latency on Telesurgery: An Experimental Study, in: Medical Image Computing and Computer-Assisted Intervention (MICCAI), Lecture Notes in Computer Science.

Scharr, H., 2007. Optimal filters for extended optical flow. Springer.

Schmid, C., Mohr, R., Bauckhage, C., 2000. Evaluation of Interest Point Detectors. Int. J. Comput. Vis. 37.

Shi, J., Tomasi, C., 1994. Good features to track, in: Computer Vision and Pattern Recognition (CVPR). IEEE, pp. 593–600.

Tomasi, C., Kanade, T., 1991. Detection and Tracking of Point Features. Carnegie Mellon University.

International Conferences Interfaces and Human Computer Interaction 2016,
Game and Entertainment Technologies 2016 and
Computer Graphics, Visualization, Computer Vision and Image Processing 2016

THE MOBILE ROBOT NAVIGATION METHOD BASED ON ONBOARD SENSORS AND CAMERA DATA FUSION

Vladimir Filaretov[1], Aleksandr Novitsky[2] and Dmirty Yukhimets[2]
[1]*Far Eastern Federal University,*
[2]*Institute of Automation and Control Processes FEB RAS,*
Vladivostok, Russia

ABSTRACT

In this paper, we propose a method of constructing a mobile robot (MR) navigation system (NS) based on fusion of data obtained from onboard sensors and video camera with use of extended Kalman filter (EKF), which allows significantly improve the accuracy of MR navigation in conditions where global positioning systems are not available or have a greater error. The budgetary webcam which, at the expense of the low price, allows to reduce the cost of system in general acts as the video data obtaining device. The method proposed consists of two steps. The first step is obtaining MR movement and orientation data based on video processing. A second step is the fusion of said navigation data and data obtained from the MR onboard sensors.

KEYWORDS

Mobile robot, Navigation system, Image Processing, Visual odometry, Kalman filter, Data fusion

1. INTRODUCTION

Currently, the use of mobile robotics in various areas of life (industry, services, home area, entertainment) is expanding rapidly. At the same time problem of MR cost reduction, ensuring their autonomous work and, in some cases, group interaction come to the forefront. One of the most important condition for the successful solution of these problems is the implementation of high-precision NS that provides formation of information about MR movement position and orientation parameters. The major problems in the creation of these systems are very noisy data obtained from the navigation sensors, errors accumulation in case of inertial navigation systems usage, the complexity of global navigation systems usage in enclosed spaces, etc. The use of expensive navigation sensors installed on MR board is not always a solution of this problem, as often their price is too high, compared with the final cost of the work performed by cheaper MR that require operator presence.

The problem of increase in accuracy of the MR NS is often solved by using of the approaches based on Kalman filters (KF) as these filters are capable to suppress noise and to restore dynamic object state vector components, which are not measurable on the current control system sampling step. An example of creation of wheeled MR NS based on fusion of local and global NS data obtaining with various frequency considered in paper [12]. The approach of wheeled MR local NS construction based on nonlinear KF taking into account MR wheel slippage is considered in paper [1]. In paper [7] analytical expressions for definition of aircraft orientation based on measurement of his angular speeds and linear accelerations are presented. Often for fusion of data arriving from onboard sensors of various mobile robots the approaches based on a method of the smallest squares are used [8].

Nevertheless, despite rather high efficiency of the known methods of data fusion, all of them have the low accuracy in the absence of the data obtained from global positioning systems. One of the most perspective methods of the specified problem solution is use of the visual data obtained from onboard video camera, which acts as an additional source of navigation information.

It should be noted that the navigation based on the use of video data is already used for realization of NS of various types of MR rather widely, for example, as described in [3,4,10,11]. At the same time these methods possess lacks which are caused by MR uneven movement, lack of control points, color artifacts, video frame overbright and blur, etc.

The approach that allows us significantly increase the accuracy of the MR NS is the fusion of the data obtaining from inertial navigation sensors and video camera. As onboard sensors and video data provide different MR movement parameters, or duplicate them, use them together for realization of the MR NS allows to provide the higher NS accuracy, than we can get using onboard sensors or a video camera separately.

In paper [11] the method of creation of the wheeled MR NS based on fusion of the data obtaining from onboard sensors and a video camera proposed. However this method demands information of exact positioning of a video camera concerning a MR movement surface, and can be applied only to the wheel MR moving on a flat surface that significantly reduces application area of this method.

Thus, in this paper the problem of creation of approach to development of universal NS of various types MR based on a fusion of the data obtained from navigation sensors and a video camera is solved. This method allows to obtain more accurate MR movements navigation data, in comparison with the traditional approaches based on use or inertial, or visual navigation.

2. DESCRIPTION OF THE VISUAL ODOMETRY METHOD

For realization of the MR NS it is necessary to determine MR shifts by axes of coordinates of absolute coordinate system (CS) based on processing of the video data obtained from MR on board video camera. It allows to correct the data obtained from inertial navigation sensors without use of global navigation systems or expensive systems of local navigation, for example, of submersibles hydroacoustic navigation systems.

For this purpose we develop an algorithm which includes the following consistently carried out stages:

1. Video camera calibration that performed for elimination of lenses distortions. With any standard way we calculate internal parameters of a video camera which then are used for comparison of pixel coordinates of points on images with actual coordinates in absolute CS.

2. Distortions correction of on the current frame, using the video camera parameters calculated on previous step.

3. Feature detection on the current frame of a video stream (fig. 1a, red circles), using a Shi-Tomasi corner detection method [13] and a binary mask from last iteration. This eliminates various illumination influence as the geometrical features contained in the image, which poorly depend on frame brightness change, are used.

4. Calculation of an optical flow for the found features (fig. 1a, blue lines between red and green circles), using the iterative Lucas-Kanade [9] method with pyramids [15]. At this step, there is a comparison of the identified feature points and definition of identical points on the current and previous frames. This comparison allows to calculate shifts of the identified feature points. From the viewpoint of calculation this is the most difficult step.

5. Vector field analysis on existence of errors of tracking, including moving objects. At this step we exclude feature points which belong to the moving objects in the view area of a video camera and which can negatively influence determination of MR movement parameters.

6. Creation of a binary mask (fig. 1b) based on obtained correspondences for prevention of new feature points detection around current ones. Radius of the vicinity is selected empirically and depends on parameters of step 3. Thus on the following frame of a video stream we detect new features only on those fragments of a frame which become covered by white part of a mask.

7. Calculation of the MR movement increments by averaging of movements of all feature points pairs on the current and previous frame:

$$d_x = \frac{\sum_{k=0}^{n-1}(p_{1xk} - p_{0xk})}{n},$$
$$d_y = \frac{\sum_{k=0}^{n-1}(p_{1yk} - p_{0yk})}{n}, \tag{1}$$

where d_x and d_y are the MR movement increments on X and Y axes respectively, p_1 and p_0 are the pair of found features, n is the number of the found feature points pairs.

8. Construction "left" and "right" (fig. 1a, blue and yellow lines respectively) perpendiculars from features on the current frame of a video stream. Perpendiculars are created to the lines connecting pairs of feature points:

$$\alpha = \arctan\left(\frac{p_{1yk} - p_{0yk}}{p_{1xk} - p_{0xk}}\right),$$
$$ort_{Lxk} = p_{1xk} - s \cdot \sin(\alpha),$$
$$ort_{Lyk} = p_{1yk} + s \cdot \cos(\alpha),$$
$$ort_{Rxk} = p_{1xk} + s \cdot \sin(\alpha),$$
$$ort_{Ryk} = p_{1yk} - s \cdot \cos(\alpha), \tag{2}$$

where (ort_{Lxk}, ort_{Lyk}) and (ort_{Rxk}, ort_{Ryk}) are the coordinates of points which the "left" and "right" perpendiculars created from a point p_{1xk} passes through, s is the scale coefficient for easy display of perpendiculars on a frame.

9. Calculation of perpendiculars intersection points, for further calculation of the average center of these points (fig. 1a. big red dot):

$$r_x = 2 \cdot \frac{\sum_{i=0}^{n-2}\sum_{j=i+1}^{n-1} \frac{(ort_{Lxi} \cdot ort_{Ryi} - ort_{Lyi} \cdot ort_{Rxi})(ort_{Lxj} - ort_{Rxj}) - (ort_{Lxi} - ort_{Rxi})(ort_{Lxj} \cdot ort_{Ryj} - ort_{Lyj} \cdot ort_{Rxj})}{(ort_{Lxi} - ort_{Rxi})(ort_{Lyj} - ort_{Ryj}) - (ort_{Lyi} - ort_{Ryi})(ort_{Lxj} - ort_{Rxj})}}{n \cdot (n-1)},$$
$$r_y = 2 \cdot \frac{\sum_{i=0}^{n-2}\sum_{j=i+1}^{n-1} \frac{(ort_{Lxi} \cdot ort_{Ryi} - ort_{Lyi} \cdot ort_{Rxi})(ort_{Lyj} - ort_{Ryj}) - (ort_{Lyi} - ort_{Ryi})(ort_{Lxj} \cdot ort_{Ryj} - ort_{Lyj} \cdot ort_{Rxj})}{(ort_{Lxi} - ort_{Rxi})(ort_{Lyj} - ort_{Ryj}) - (ort_{Lyi} - ort_{Ryi})(ort_{Lxj} - ort_{Rxj})}}{n \cdot (n-1)}, \tag{3}$$

where (r_x, r_y) – average center of perpendiculars intersection points.

10. Yaw angle increment calculation based on movement of all feature points against the found center:

$$\alpha = \frac{\sum_{k=0}^{n-1}\left(\arctan\left(\frac{p_{1yk} - r_y}{p_{1xk} - r_x}\right) - \arctan\left(\frac{p_{0yk} - r_y}{p_{0xk} - r_x}\right)\right)}{n}. \tag{4}$$

11. Updating of MR position information in absolute CS based on the increments calculated.

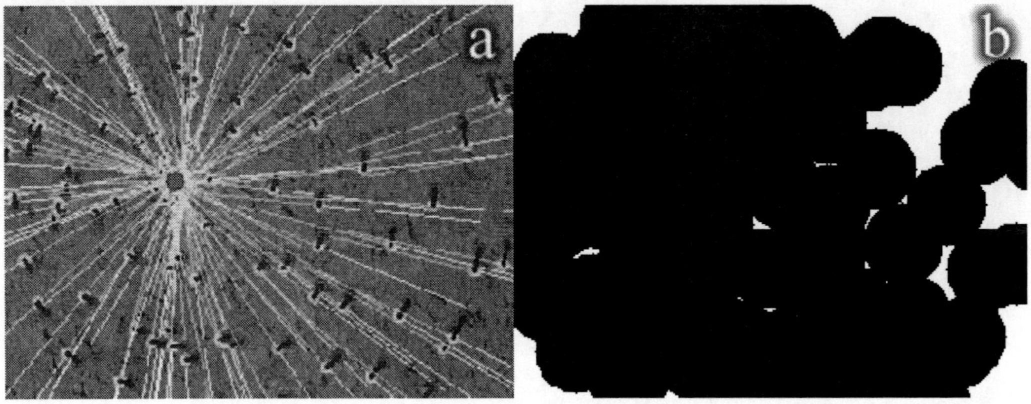

Figure 1. The processed frame from a video camera (a), a binary mask (b)

In the presented algorithm step 1 is carried out only once during configuration of system for calculation of specific video camera lenses distortions parameters, and steps 2 – 11 are carried out for each frame of a video stream all the algorithm work time. Thus, at each iteration the algorithm allows to calculate MR linear coordinates increments in absolute CS and a yaw angle, which are then used to ensure the data fusion.

3. DATA FUSION

After obtaining navigation information based on the data from MR video cameras we fuse it with the data obtained from the MR onboard navigation sensors. This data fusion is proposed to be carried out by means of the KF [5, 6], which is used to solve such problems. Important advantage of KF is also it's ability to suppress noise of sensors.

When using KF the kinematic model of object of management (2) needs to be presented in the form:

$$\mathbf{x}_{k+1} = f(\mathbf{x}_k, \xi_k),\\ \mathbf{z}_k = h(\mathbf{x}_k, \mathbf{v}_k), \tag{5}$$

where $\mathbf{x} \in R^n$ – system state vector, $\xi_k \in R^n$ – normal random process that describes the modeling errors with zero mean and covariance matrix $\mathbf{Q}$, $\mathbf{z}_k \in R^l$ – measurement vector, $\mathbf{v}_k$ – white Gaussian measurement noise with zero mean and covariance matrix $\mathbf{R} \in R^{l \times l}$.

Since the model of wheeled MR is non-linear, it is advisable to use EKF [5, 6], which provides a linearization of the model (5) in the vicinity of the point $(\mathbf{x}_k, \mathbf{z}_k)$ by decomposing the non-linear functions $f(\cdot)$ and $h(\cdot)$ in Taylor series. The expressions, which implements EKF, are as follows:

$$\widetilde{\mathbf{x}}_{k+1} = f(\mathbf{x}_k),\ \widetilde{\mathbf{P}}_{k+1} = \mathbf{A}_k \cdot \mathbf{P}_k \cdot \mathbf{A}_k{}^T + \mathbf{Q},\ \mathbf{K}_k = \frac{\mathbf{P}_k \cdot \mathbf{H}_k}{\mathbf{H}_k \cdot \mathbf{P}_\mathbf{k} \cdot (\mathbf{H}_k)^T + \mathbf{R}},\\ \mathbf{x}_{k+1} = \widetilde{\mathbf{x}}_{k+1} + \mathbf{K}_k \cdot (\mathbf{z}_{k+1} - h(\widetilde{\mathbf{x}}_{k+1})),\ \mathbf{P}_{k+1} = (\mathbf{I} - \mathbf{K}_k \mathbf{H}_k)\widetilde{\mathbf{P}}_{k+1}, \tag{6}$$

where $\mathbf{A}_k = \dfrac{\partial f(\mathbf{x}_k, \xi_k)}{\partial \mathbf{x}}$, $\mathbf{H}_k = \dfrac{\partial h(\mathbf{x}_k, \mathbf{v}_k)}{\partial \mathbf{x}}$, $\mathbf{P}$ - covariance matrix of the state error vector.

For the kinematic model of the MR horizontal plane motion state and measurement vectors, as well as the matrix of the linearized model will look like the following:

$$\mathbf{x}_{k+1} = \begin{bmatrix} \omega_{k+1} \\ \upsilon_{k+1} \\ \varphi_{k+1} \\ x_{k+1} \\ y_{k+1} \end{bmatrix} = \begin{bmatrix} R\dfrac{\omega_{Rk} - \omega_{Lk}}{L} \\ R\dfrac{\omega_{Rk} + \omega_{Lk}}{2} \\ \varphi_k + \omega_k h \\ x_k + \upsilon_k \cos(\varphi_k) h \\ y_k + \upsilon_k \sin(\varphi_k) h \end{bmatrix}, \ \mathbf{A}_k = \begin{bmatrix} 0 & 0 & 0 & 0 & 0 \\ 0 & 0 & 0 & 0 & 0 \\ h & 0 & 1 & 0 & 0 \\ 0 & \cos(\varphi_k)h & -\upsilon_k \sin(\varphi_k)h & 1 & 1 \\ 0 & \sin(\varphi_k)h & \upsilon_k \cos(\varphi_k)h & 1 & 1 \end{bmatrix},$$

$$\mathbf{z}_k = \left[\omega_{ENCk}, v_{ENCk}, \varphi_{ENCk}, x_{ENCk}, y_{ENCk}, \varphi_{IMUk}, x_{IMUk}, y_{IMUk}, \varphi_{CAMk}, x_{CAMk}, y_{CAMk}\right]^T, \quad (7)$$

$$,\mathbf{H}_k = \begin{bmatrix} 0 & 0 & h & 0 & 0 \\ 0 & 0 & 0 & \cos(\varphi_k)h & \sin(\varphi_k)h \\ 0 & 0 & 1 & -\upsilon_k \sin(\varphi_k)h & \upsilon_k \cos(\varphi_k)h \\ 0 & 0 & 0 & 1 & 0 \\ 0 & 0 & 0 & 0 & 1 \\ 0 & 0 & 1 & -\upsilon_k \sin(\varphi_k)h & \upsilon_k \cos(\varphi_k)h \\ 0 & 0 & 0 & 1 & 0 \\ 0 & 0 & 0 & 0 & 1 \\ 0 & 0 & 1 & -\upsilon_k \sin(\varphi_k)h & \upsilon_k \cos(\varphi_k)h \\ 0 & 0 & 0 & 1 & 0 \\ 0 & 0 & 0 & 0 & 1 \end{bmatrix},$$

where ENC, IMU and CAM indices correspond to the data computed with information obtained from the encoder [2], angular velocity sensors and video camera respectively.

The main advantage of this approach is the ability to create local navigation system providing for the MR complex trajectories movement using relatively inexpensive hardware.

4. SIMULATION RESULTS

To determine the performance and efficiency of the created algorithm of a fusion of data obtaining from onboard navigation sensors and video cameras modeling of it's work has been carried out. During research of this algorithm two-wheeled MR Pioneer P3-DX (fig. 2) created in the environment of simulation of V-REP PRO of EDU [14] has been used. The robot has been equipped with the following sensors: angular velocity sensor measuring angle relative to the vertical axis; accelerometers measuring accelerations on X and Y axes in the related CS, a video camera. This set of sensors for data fusion allows to use MR movement model in the horizontal plane (see expressions (8)).

Figure 2. MP Pioneer P3-DX, created in the simulation environment V-REP PRO EDU

Results of the experiments made at various movement trajectories are shown in figures 3 (a - f). In figures 3 (a, c, e) we introduced the following notation:

- (dotted line) real trajectory of the MR movement;
- (continuous line with the turned triangular markers) trajectory based on video data obtained from onboard video camera;
- (continuous line with triangular markers) the trajectory based on data obtained from the MR onboard sensors;
- (continuous line with round markers) the trajectory computed with use of the proposed data fusion algorithm.

In figures 3 (b, d, f) is shown a course MR corner on k step. Here:

- (dotted line) real MR course angle;
- (thin dashed line) course angle based on video data obtained from onboard dash video camera;
- (continuous line) course angle based on data obtained from the MR onboard sensors;
- (thick dashed line) course angle computed with use of the proposed data fusion algorithm.

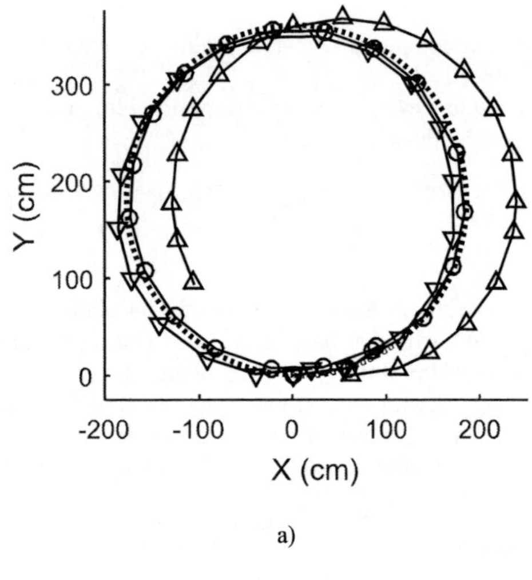

a)

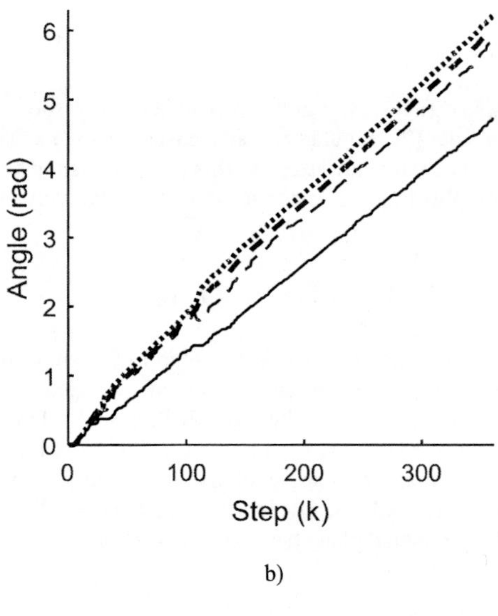

b)

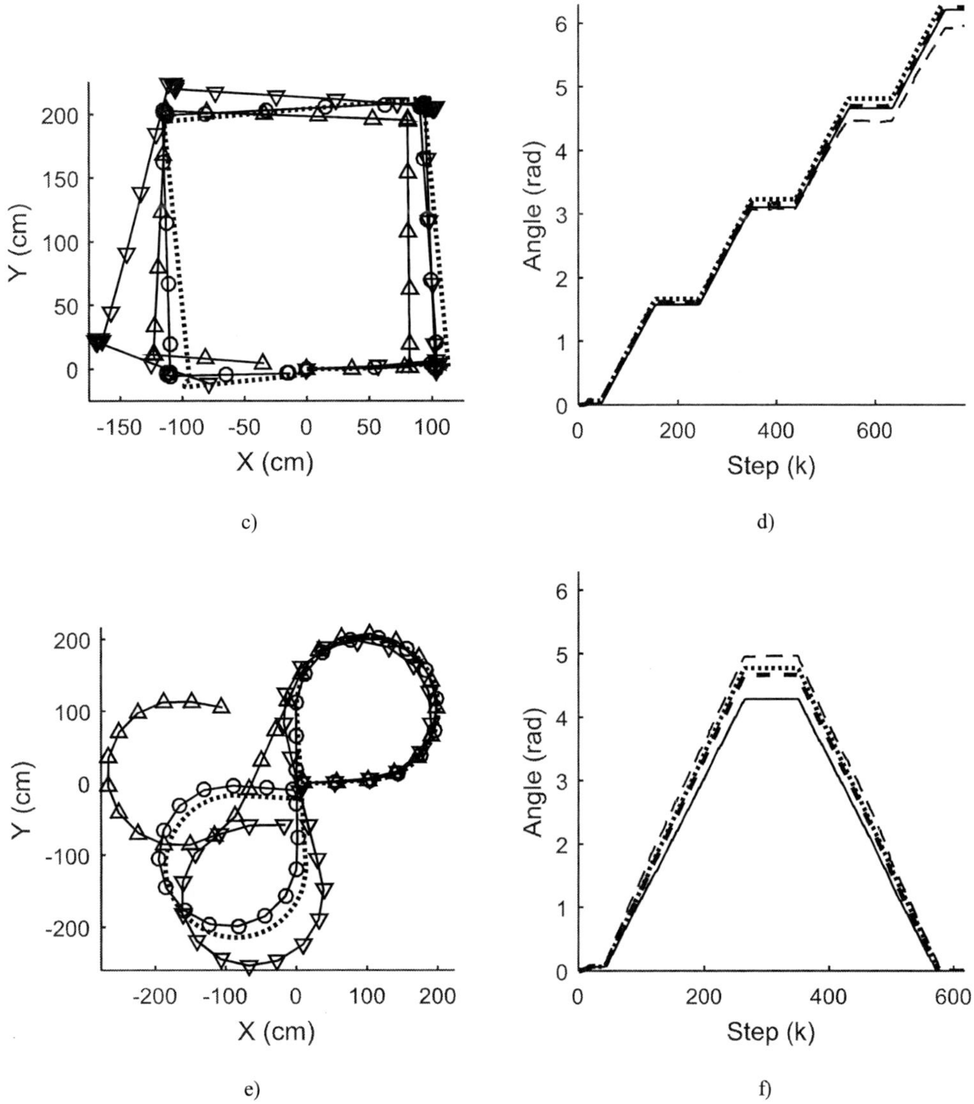

Figure 3. The experimental results of the proposed data fusion algorithm

It is obvious that using only onboard sensors or only a video camera as the MR NS doesn't yield satisfactory results. At the same, error in robot position determining using only onboard sensors up to 100 cm and error in robot orientation is up to 1.5 rad. When using the camera error in robot position up to 50 cm and error in robot orientation is up to 0.45 rad. By using the proposed method of signals fusion received simultaneously from navigation sensors, and from the MR camera allowed to determine the robot coordinates with high accuracy. The maximum deviation of the MR actual trajectory does not exceed 15 cm and orientation error is up to 0.2 rad, but in some sections position and orientation errors were reduced to 5cm and to 0.08 rad respectively.

Thus, the results of preliminary studies fully confirmed the efficiency and effectiveness of the method of fusion of data obtained from MR onboard sensors and cameras.

5. CONCLUSION

In this paper, we propose a method for determining the MR coordinates, based on fusion of data obtained with various onboard sensors and video camera. This method uses the EKF, which allows working with non-linear models. The results of the experiments have shown efficiency and effectiveness of this method and MR on-board sensors and video camera data fusion algorithm.

ACKNOWLEDGEMENT

The work done in this paper was supported by the Russian Science Foundation (project №14-19-00081).

REFERENCES

[1] Anjum, M. et al, 2010. Sensor Data Fusion using Unscented Kalman Filter for Accurate Localization of Mobile Robots. *Proc. of International Conference on Control, Automation and Systems*, Gyeonggi-do, Korea, pp. 947-952.

[2] Bartenev, V. et al, 2011. A mathematical model of the motion of the mobile robot with two independent driving wheels on a horizontal plane. *News of the Samara Scientific Center of the Russian Academy of Sciences*, vol. 13, No. 4, pp. 288-293.

[3] Brinkworth, R. and O'Carroll, D., 2009. Robust Models for Optic Flow Coding in Natural Scenes Inspired by Insect Biology. *PLOS Computation Biology*, Vol. 5, No. 11, pp. 1-8.

[4] Dille, M. et al, 2010. Outdoor Downward-facing Optical Flow Odometry with Commodity Sensors. *Field and Service Robotics: Springer Tracts in Advanced Robotics*, Vol. 62, pp. 183-193

[5] Haykin, S., 2001. *Kalman filtering and neural networks*. John Wiley and Sons, New York, USA, p. 298.

[6] Julier, S. and Uhlmann J., 1997. A new extension of the Kalman filter to nonlinear systems. *Proceedings of AeroSense: The 11th International Symposium on Aerospace: Defence Sensing, Simulation and Controls*. Orlando, Florida, USA, pp. 182-193.

[7] Kizimov, A. et al, 2011. UAV inertial strapdown attitude and heading reference system. Sensors and Systems Journal, No. 4, pp. 37-42.

[8] Li, R. et al, 2000. Unified optimal linear estimation fusion. *Proceedings of International Conference on Information Fusion*. Paris, France, pp. 486-492.

[9] Lucas, B. and Kanade, T., 1981. An Iterative Image Registration Technique with an Application to Stereo Vision. *Proceedings of Imaging Understanding Workshop*. San Francisco, California, USA, pp. 121-130.

[10] Maimone, M. et al, 2007. Two Years of Visual Odometry on the Mars Exploration Rovers. *Journal of Field Robotics, Special Issue on Space Robotics*, Vol. 24, No. 3, pp. 169-186.

[11] Novitsky, A. and Yukhimets, D., 2015. The navigation method of wheeled mobile robot based on data fusion obtained from onboard sensors and camera. *Proceedings of International Conference on Control, Automation and Systems*. Busan, Korea, pp. 574-579.

[12] Pavlovsky, V. et al, 2011. Mobile Robot Navigation System Based on Beacons and VideoMarkers. *Mechatronics, Automation and Control*, No. 10, pp. 66-71.

[13] Shi, J. and Tomasi, C., 1994. Good Features to Track. *Proceedings of the IEEE Conference on Computer Vision and Pattern Recognition*. Seattle, WA, pp. 593-600.

[14] V-REP simulator (http://www.coppeliarobotics.com).

[15] Yves, B., 1999. Pyramidal Implementation of the Lucas Kanade Feature Tracker. *Microsoft Research Labs, Tech. Rep.*

A COMPARATIVE STUDY OF COMPUTERIZED APPROACHES FOR TYPE P63 OVARIAN TISSUES USING HISTOPATHOLOGY DIGITIZED COLOR IMAGES

T M Shahriar Sazzad[1], Leisa Armstrong[1] and Amiya Kumar Tripathy[1, 2]
[1]*Edith Cowan University, WA, Australia*
[2]*Don Bosco Institute of Technology, Mumbai, India*

ABSTRACT

Computer based histopathology tissue analysis especially human ovarian reproductive tissue analysis is an important laboratory routine analysis for reproductive tissue identification. This allows experts to provide necessary treatment for women who face conceiving complications. Existing scanning modalities are not optimal to analyze human ovarian reproductive tissues as they mostly analyze grayscale images which do not provide satisfactory results. In this situation manual microscopic analysis is the best practice for the experts. The problem associated in manual analysis is this process is time consuming and inconsistent in experts experimental result. To minimize the labor cost, effort and time it is essential to design a computer based analysis approach which can automatically identify the ovarian reproductive tissues. In this paper analysis and comparison of existing fully automated approaches on type P63 ovarian tissue images using digitized histopathology images has been highlighted. This paper proposes a more suitable automated approach for type P63 digitized color images in comparison to manual microscopic identification approach based on accuracy. A comparison of various existing automated approaches with manual identification results by experts indicates excellent performance of the automated approach.

KEYWORDS

P63, image artifacts, cluster, classification, identification.

1. INTRODUCTION

At present there are various types of pathology diagnosis scanners available to analyze various types of tissues (Kiruthika & Ramya, 2014). These modern digital scanners are useful to assist pathology experts to perform their laboratory routine task quickly and with less effort. In comparison to all existing pathology digitized scanners ultrasound remains one of the most popular techniques to pathology experts as it is cheaper, portable and less risky to patients (Kiruthika & Ramya, 2014). Although ultrasound is popular and widely used scanner in the pathology laboratory, its limitation is that it can only process grayscale images and smaller tissues (Skodras et al., 2009). In addition, research work by (Kiruthika & Ramya, 2014) mentioned that analysis of medical images using ultrasound scanners requires highly skilled professionals. Considering the above mentioned limitations, in the pathology laboratory manual microscopic analysis is considered as a more viable option to analyze different types of tissues (Kiruthika & Ramya, 2014).

At present manual microscopic biopsy slide analysis of human ovarian reproductive tissues is considered as "gold standard" for general clinical analysis (Kelsey, Caserta, Castillo, Wallace, & Gonzálvez, 2010). While microscopic tissue analysis remains the "gold standard", problems arise as this process is time consuming, prone to error, with inconsistencies owing to intra and inter observation variability (Muskhelishvili, Wingard, & Latendresse, 2005). This is due to the fact that multiple experts are essential to identify regions of interest (ROIs) in the same slide and at least two experts are necessary for validation. To overcome time and effort associated with manual process computer based analysis approach could be a viable option (Lamprecht, Sabatini, & Carpenter, 2007; Muskhelishvili et al., 2005).

Various types of biopsy slides can be found for regular clinical tissue analysis in the pathology laboratory. These include H&E (Haematoxylin and Eosin), Ki-67 (Protein 67), PCNA (Proliferating Cell Nuclear Antigen) and P63 (Protein 63 with counter and non-counter stain) under various magnifications. Generally most tissues are colorless and are hard to distinguish between various tissues (Magee et al., 2009). To overcome the issues mentioned by (Magee et al., 2009) experts use dyes or colored organic substances during slide preparation to change the tissue color which assist experts to analyze various tissues efficiently. Haematoxylin and Eosin (H&E) are commonly used slide in the pathology laboratory mentioned by (Picut et al., 2008). However; H&E color images acquired from H&E biopsy slides contains a great variety of intensity variations (Muskhelishvili et al., 2005). This intensity variation limits to indentify smaller tissues accurately especially ovarian reproductive tissue using H&E digitized images (Bolon et al., 1997).

Color digitized images of PCNA slides are more suitable in comparison to H&E (Picut et al., 2008). Research study by (Kelsey et al., 2010) incorporated type PCNA digitized color images acquired from human ovarian reproductive tissues and mentioned that type PCNA performs better identification result in compare to H&E. They also mentioned that stain type P63 would be another suitable option in compare to type H&E and PCNA for ovarian reproductive tissue identification.

An example of type P63 counter-stained and non-counter-stained digitized images acquired from P63 ovarian tissue biopsy slides is shown in Figure 1 with marked (reproductive tissues) images.

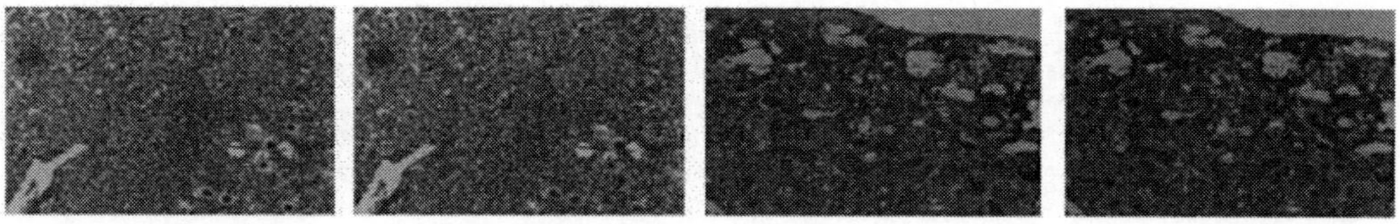

(a) (b) (c) (d)

Figure 1. (a) is a type P63 counter-stained image and (c) is a type P63 (both 100x magnification) non-counter-stained image. (b) is a marked image of (a) where red circles were identified ovarian nucleus by 2 experts in the laboratory. (d) is a marked image of (c) where red circles were marked by 2 experts and blue circles were marked by at-least 1 expert

2. RELATED WORK

Research work by (Picut et al., 2008; Skodras et al., 2009) mentioned that most existing research works are semi-automated approach rather than an automated and are related to ovine and rat ovarian tissue analysis. Existing available automated approaches are not related to ovarian reproductive tissue analysis but for cancer cell or tumor cell analysis (Picut et al., 2008; Skodras et al., 2009). At present only a few automated research works have been carried out using human ovarian tissues which include analysis of PCNA digitized color images by (Kelsey et al., 2010), P63 non-counter stained digitized color images by (Sazzad, Armstrong, & Tripathy, 2015) and P63 counter stained digitized color images by (Sazzad, Armstrong, & Tripathy, 2016). Research study of (Kelsey et al., 2010) may not be a suitable automated approach due to the fact that conventional threshold based approach was considered and for each new batch of images manual calibration of processing parameters is an essential requirement. Research works of (Sazzad et al., 2015, 2016) are automated approaches where type P63 non-counter and counter stained color digitized images were considered. In addition, no calibration of processing parameter is required for each new batch of images and the accuracy rate is acceptable by the laboratory experts. Comparative study for the proposed automated approaches of (Sazzad et al., 2015, 2016) would be a viable choice for this research study.

Research work of (Sazzad et al., 2015) mentioned that experts in the laboratory mainly consider microscopic magnification for visualization which leads an easy analysis during microscopic analysis. In relation to resolution and contrast optical microscopic magnifications for digitized color images are generally not perfect (Claxton, Fellers, & Davidson, 2006) as it causes intensity variations. For computerized image analysis perspective resolution is considered as an important factor instead of microscopic magnification (Claxton et al., 2006; Lodish, 2008). In addition, using color chemicals during slide preparation cause intensity variations due to the fact that different tissues consume color chemicals differently (Magee et al., 2009). In comparison with P63 non-counter stained biopsy slides extra color chemicals are used to prepare type P63 counter stained biopsy slides. This extra color helps experts to distinguish and enhances various tissues (i.e. red, pink and orange) (Kelsey et al., 2010). Color chemicals are helpful for biopsy microscopic analysis but limits computerize image processing as digitized images acquired from biopsy slides contains intensity variations (Magee et al., 2009). Intensity variation cause improper segmentation and leads to a faulty identification (Eramian, Adams, & Pierson, 2007). For a better segmentation is it necessary to minimize intensity variations at the beginning (Li & Nishikawa, 2015).

At present none of the existing approaches (Kelsey et al., 2010; Landini & Othman, 2003; Picut et al., 2008; Sertel, Catalyurek, Shimada, & Guican, 2009; Skodras et al., 2009) except (Sazzad et al., 2015, 2016) have considered correcting image artifact issues due to the fact that for most existing approaches grayscale images were considered during segmentation. For grayscale images it is not necessary to consider image artifacts issues (Magee et al., 2009). It is a hard task to analyze and process smaller tissue using grayscale images in compare to color images and ovarian tissues are typically smaller in comparison to other tissues and vary in shape, size and color (Magee et al., 2009). The limitations associated with grayscale image processing lacks to analyze type P63 digitized ovarian reproductive tissue color images.

3. PROPOSED WORK

This research study incorporated both type P63 non-counter and counter stained digitized color images acquired from pathology biopsy slides. To work with both digitized color images existing automated approaches were reviewed. Detailed working flowchart of this proposed research study is shown in Figure.2.

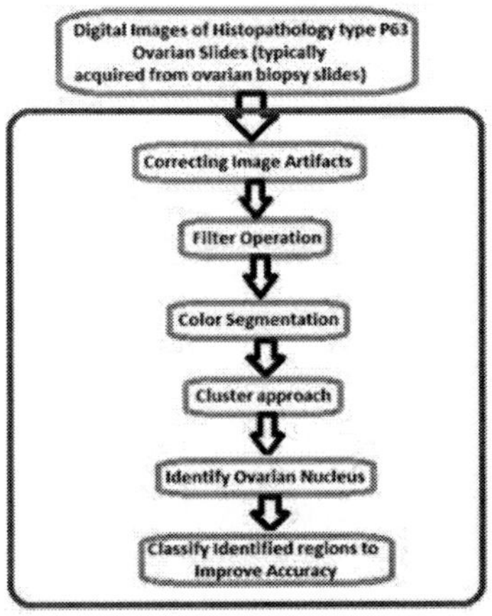

Figure 2. Block diagram for automated identification process

3.1 Correcting Image Artifacts

One of the popular approaches to correct image artifacts is Gaussian low-pass filter approach (Leong, Brady, & McGee, 2003). Research work of (Sazzad et al., 2015) indicated that the results found after correcting image artifacts using Gaussian low-pass filter was not satisfactory. Research work of (Sazzad et al., 2015) proposed that morphological operation using cell diameter would be a viable option which shown to provide satisfactory results. A slight modification was made by (Sazzad et al., 2016) for the proposed morphological approach of (Sazzad et al., 2015) which also shown to provide satisfactory results.

This research study incorporated both proposed approaches (Sazzad et al., 2015, 2016) to minimize image artifacts issues. Comparative results of two different proposed approaches are shown in Figure 3.

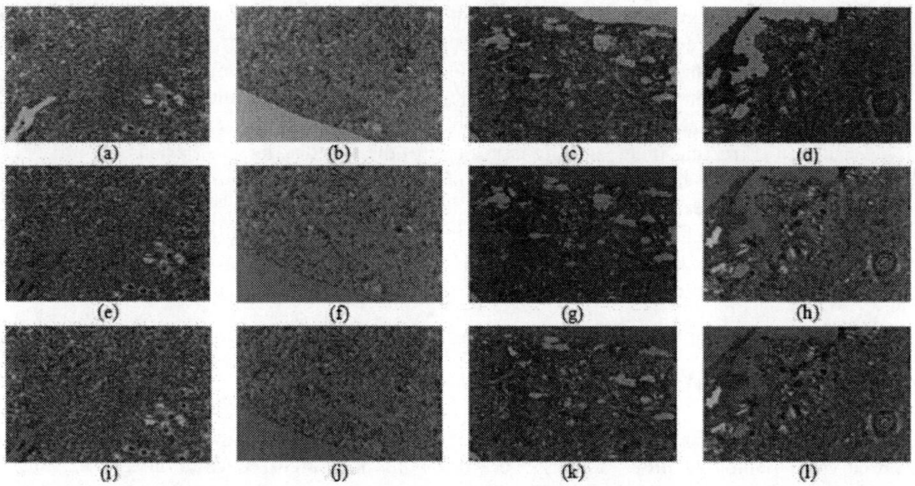

Figure 3. (a) and (b) are P63 counter stained images with different contrast. (c) and (d) are P63 non-counter stained images with different contrast. (e), (f), (g) and (h) are the corrected images using morphological operation where cell diameter was directly incorporated as SE (Sazzad et al., 2015). (i), (j), (k) and (l) are corrected image using morphological operation where FWHM was incorporated to compute SE (Sazzad et al., 2016)

3.2 Filter Operation

Median or mean filter was incorporated by (Bapure, 2012; Kelsey et al., 2010; Landini & Othman, 2003; Picut et al., 2008; Sertel et al., 2009; Skodras et al., 2009) to eliminate image noises. Median filter has the capability to filter noises better in comparison to mean filter (Arias-Castro & Donoho, 2009). Median filter was unable to provide satisfactory results mentioned by (Sazzad et al., 2015) due to the fact that it may cause blurred effect. To overcome the issues associated with median filter research work of (Sazzad et al., 2015) proposed pixel based mean shift filter. The proposed approach is a modification of the proposed approach of (Comaniciu & Meer, 2002) which has shown to provide satisfactory results in comparison to a median filter approach. This research study incorporated pixel based mean shift filter approach as a filter operation for this research study's test images. Filtered results of are shown in Figure 4.

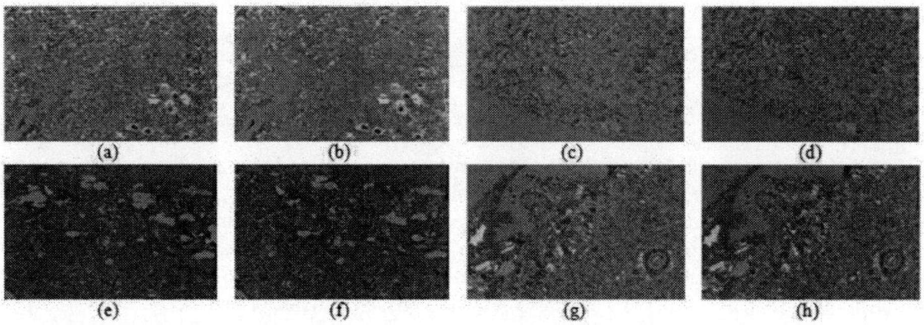

Figure 4. (a), (b), (c), (d), (e), (f), (g) and (h) are filtered images using pixel based mean shift filter (Sazzad et al., 2015)

3.3 Color Segmentation

Conventional threshold based and watershed based approaches were incorporated by (Bapure, 2012; Kelsey et al., 2010; Landini & Othman, 2003; Picut et al., 2008; Sertel et al., 2009; Skodras et al., 2009) for segmentation. Threshold based and watershed based approaches are generally suitable for gray-scale images rather than color images which are not appropriate for color image segmentation (Magee et al., 2009).

For color images processing mean shift (Comaniciu & Meer, 2002) or region fusion (Nock & Nielsen, 2004) approaches could be suitable. Mean shift is a time consuming approach (Wu, Zhao, Luo, & Shi, 2015). Region fusion is more viable in comparison to mean shift approach as it requires less processing time (Nock & Nielsen, 2004). The limitation of region fusion approach is that it needs a processing parameter in between 0-10 whereas cell diameter for 100x magnification in bigger than 30. To overcome the issues associated with region fusion approach (Nock & Nielsen, 2004) modification is made by (Sazzad et al., 2015) which has shown to provide satisfactory results. A comparative result mentioned by (Sazzad et al., 2015) indicated that region fusion approach performs better than mean shift approach. A further modification was carried out by (Sazzad et al., 2016) which has also shown to provide satisfactory results. This research study incorporated both modified region fusion based segmentation approaches proposed by (Sazzad et al., 2015, 2016). Comparative results of two different approaches are shown in Figure 5.

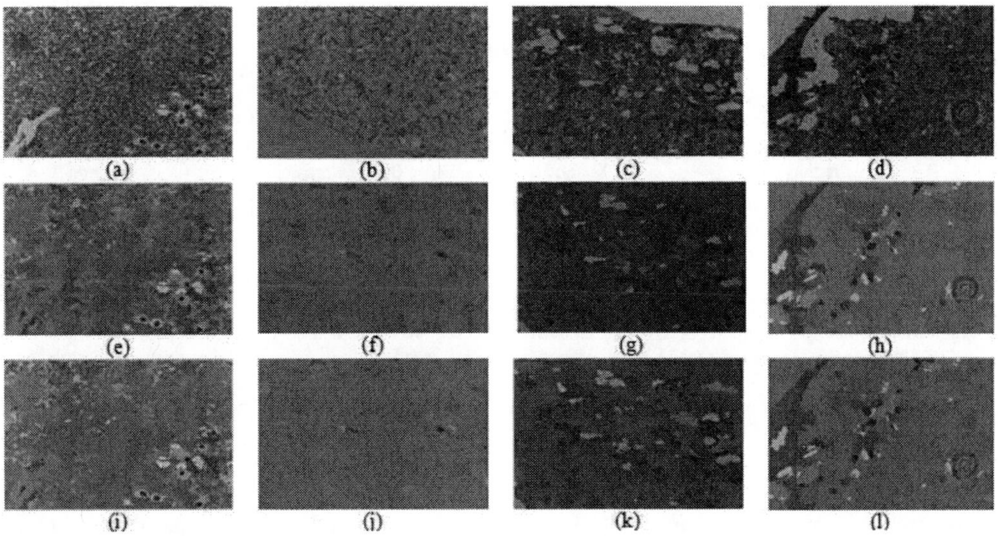

Figure 5. (a), (b), (c) and (d) are research study test images. (e),(f),(g) and (h) indicates segmented images using proposed approach of (Sazzad et al., 2015). (i),(j),(k) and (l) indicates segmented images using proposed approach of (Sazzad et al., 2016)

3.4 Cluster Approach

For color image processing it is essential to cluster the segmented regions for efficient identification (Cheng, Jiang, Sun, & Wang, 2001). None of the existing approaches (Bapure, 2012; Kelsey et al., 2010; Landini & Othman, 2003; Picut et al., 2008; Sertel et al., 2009; Skodras et al., 2009) have considered any available cluster based approaches. An exception to this is the work of (Sazzad et al., 2015) where mean shift cluster based approach proposed by (Fukunaga & Hostetler, 1975) was incorporated with a modication for the selection of data points. Modification was carried out by (Sazzad et al., 2015) and was incorporated by (Sazzad et al., 2016) which has shown to provide satisfactory results. This research study incorporated modified mean-shift cluster approach proposed by (Sazzad et al., 2015).

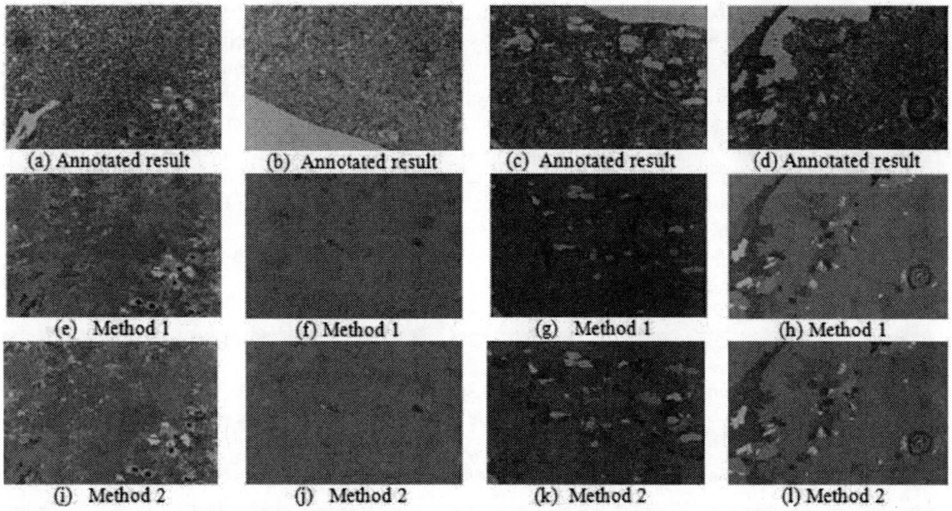

Figure 6. (a), (b), (c) and (d) indicates experts identified marked results where red marked regions were confirmed by 2 experts and blue marked regions were confirmed by at-least one expert as nucleus. For image (a) Method 1 (image (e)) and method 2 (image (i)) found 5 regions correctly. For image (b) method 1 (image (f)) and method 2 (image (j)) found 1 region correctly. For image (c) method 1 (image (g)) has found 13 regions where 11 regions were marked by experts in red circle in image and 2 regions were marked as blue. For image (c) method 2 (image (k)) found 14 regions where 11 regions were marked by experts in red circle in image and 3 regions were marked as blue. For image (d) method 1(image (h)) found 9 regions where 5 regions were marked by experts in red circle in image and 4 regions were marked as blue. For image (d) method 2 (image (l)) found 9 regions where 5 regions were marked by experts in red circle in image and 4 regions were marked as blue. No missed region neither false region detected by any methods for any of the test images

3.5 Identify Ovarian Nucleus

Research work by (Gurcan et al., 2009) mentioned that features of digitized histopathology images can be categorized as object level features and spatial features. Based on the region of interests essential features needs to be selected (Gurcan et al., 2009). All existing computerized approaches (Bapure, 2012; Kelsey et al., 2010; Landini & Othman, 2003; Picut et al., 2008; Sazzad et al., 2015; Sertel et al., 2009; Skodras et al., 2009) have incorporated necessary features to identify the ROIs. This research study incorporated the algorithm proposed by (Sazzad et al., 2015). Figure 6 indicates the identified results of 2 different methods.

3.6 Classify Identified Regions to Improve Accuracy

Due to different shape, size and color issues associated with ovarian reproductive tissues it may be possible for the identification algorithm to identify some false regions (not ovarian reproductive tissues). Therefore; it is necessary to separate the false regions from ovarian reproductive tissues to increase the accuracy rate. None of the existing approaches (Bapure, 2012; Kelsey et al., 2010; Landini & Othman, 2003; Picut et al., 2008; Sertel et al., 2009; Skodras et al., 2009) except the work of (Sazzad et al., 2016) considered classification approach. This research study used the classification approaches used in (Sazzad et al., 2016). Table 1 indicates the classification accuracy for both type P63 counter and non-counter stained images.

4. EXPERIMENTAL RESULTS

Existing computerized approaches were considered in this study to review the identification result based on accuracy. Comparative result of different approaches including approximate average processing time, precision and recall are shown in Table 2 where C refers to counter-stained and NC refers to non-counter stained type P63.

5. DISCUSSION AND CONCLUSION

This paper has reviewed all existing computerized approaches where ovarian reproductive tissues were analyzed using digitized ovarian images acquired from various types of biopsy slides which include type PCNA and P63 counter and non-counter stain. This research study mainly focused on two fully automated approaches (Sazzad et al., 2015, 2016) due to the fact that these approaches are fully automated and no processing parameter are necessary for each a new set of images. Other automated human reproductive tissue analysis process by (Kelsey et al., 2010) was also reviewed in this research study to compare the accuracy shown in Table 2. Laboratory experts considers ±10% error rates for a computerized approach (Kelsey et al., 2010). Comparative results in Table 2 indicate that research work of (Sazzad et al., 2015, 2016) provides a significant accuracy rate of over 95% in compare to the proposed approach of (Kelsey et al., 2010) which is under 90%.

In compare to type P63 counter stained images P63 non-counter stained images requires less average processing time. In addition to that P63 non- counter stained biopsy slide preparation is cost effective in compare to counter stained biopsy slides. If processing time and cost is considered then type P63 non-counter stained digitized color images acquired from biopsy slides could be a more appropriate choice. The accuracy rate for both type P63 has shown to provide almost similar accuracy rate in compare to manual microscopic analysis.

This research study review results indicates that any type of P63 color digitized images can be analyzed using either method 1 (Sazzad et al., 2015) or using method 2 (Sazzad et al., 2016). It will be entirely laboratory experts' choice to choose a suitable biopsy slide for ovarian reproductive tissue analysis.

This study is novel due to the fact that this is the first published study where a complete review of existing automated approaches were conducted using type P63 counter and non-counter stained color images. In addition to that a significant amount of images were tested considering human ovarian reproductive tissues. Research work of (Kelsey et al., 2010) used type PCNA where only a few number of images were considered. It is not essential to be a laboratory expert to analyze ovarian reproductive tissues using the proposed approaches but only requires knowing the image magnification. A general computer with 1.9 GHz processor was used in this study to process all the test images where 500 x 500 image windows were used.

Table 1. Comparative results of 3 different classifiers (type P63 Counter (C) and Non-Counter (NC) stained images)

Name	150 images were used (50 in each group)			Accuracy	
	Group 1	Group 2	Group 3		
SVM	Training	Test	Test	95 (C) / 96 (NC)	96 (C) / 96 (NC)
	Test	Training	Test	97 (C) / 96 (NC)	
	Test	Test	Training	96 (C) / 96 (NC)	
K-NN	Training	Test	Test	93 (C) / 95 (NC)	93 (C) / 93 (NC)
	Test	Training	Test	94 (C) / 93 (NC)	
	Test	Test	Training	92 (C) / 91 (NC)	
P-NN	Training	Test	Test	92 (C) / 90 (NC)	92 (C) / 92 (NC)
	Test	Training	Test	93 /(C) 93 (NC)	
	Test	Test	Training	91 (C) / 93 (NC)	

Table 2. Comparative results of different existing approaches

Number of test images (304)	avg. processing time (sec)		Precision	Recall
Method 1(Sazzad et al., 2015)	C	22.47	0.95	0.96
	NC	22.03	0.95	0.97
Method 2(Sazzad et al., 2016)	C	22.74	0.96	0.95
	NC	22.21	0.96	0.96
Automated approach(Kelsey et al., 2010)	C	24.37	0.84	0.85
	NC	24.01	0.86	0.88

ACKNOWLEDGEMENT AND FUTURE WORK

The authors would like to thank Assistant Professor and head of the department (Pathology) Doctor S.I. Talukder (MBBS, M.Phil (Pathology), Shaheed Sayed Nazrul Islam Medical College, Kishoreganj, Bangladesh) for providing the test images, marked images and necessary feature information. In future this research study will consider both type PCNA and type P63 images for a comparative study.

REFERENCES

Arias-Castro, E., & Donoho, D. L. (2009). Does median filtering truly preserve edges better than linear filtering? *The Annals of Statistics*, 1172-1206.

Bapure, K. (2012). Automated Image Analysis for Nuclear Morphometry Using H&E and Feulgen Stains in Prostate Biopsies.

Bolon, B., Bucci, T. J., Warbritton, A. R., Chen, J. J., Mattison, D. R., & Heindel, J. J. (1997). Differential follicle counts as a screen for chemically induced ovarian toxicity in mice: results from continuous breeding bioassays. *Toxicological Sciences, 39*(1), 1-10.

Cheng, H.-D., Jiang, X., Sun, Y., & Wang, J. (2001). Color image segmentation: advances and prospects. *Pattern Recognition, 34*(12), 2259-2281.

Claxton, N. S., Fellers, T. J., & Davidson, M. W. (2006). Laser scanning confocal microscopy. *Department of Optical Microscopy and Digital Imaging, Florida State University, Tallahassee, http://www.olympusconfocal. com/theory/LSCMIntro. pdf.*

Comaniciu, D., & Meer, P. (2002). Mean shift: A robust approach toward feature space analysis. *Pattern Analysis and Machine Intelligence, IEEE Transactions on, 24*(5), 603-619.

Eramian, M. G., Adams, G. P., & Pierson, R. A. (2007). Enhancing ultrasound texture differences for developing an in vivo'virtual histology'approach to bovine ovarian imaging. *Reproduction, Fertility and Development, 19*(8), 910-924.

Fukunaga, K., & Hostetler, L. D. (1975). The estimation of the gradient of a density function, with applications in pattern recognition. *Information Theory, IEEE Transactions on, 21*(1), 32-40.

Gurcan, M. N., Boucheron, L. E., Can, A., Madabhushi, A., Rajpoot, N. M., & Yener, B. (2009). Histopathological image analysis: A review. *Biomedical Engineering, IEEE Reviews in, 2*, 147-171.

Kelsey, T. W., Caserta, B., Castillo, L., Wallace, W. H. B., & Gonzálvez, F. C. (2010). Proliferating cell nuclear antigen (PCNA) allows the automatic identification of follicles in microscopic images of human ovarian tissue. *arXiv preprint arXiv:1008.3798*.

Kiruthika, V., & Ramya, M. (2014). *Automatic Segmentation of Ovarian Follicle Using K-Means Clustering.* Paper presented at the Signal and Image Processing (ICSIP), 2014 Fifth International Conference on.

Lamprecht, M. R., Sabatini, D. M., & Carpenter, A. E. (2007). CellProfiler™: free, versatile software for automated biological image analysis. *Biotechniques, 42*(1), 71.

Landini, G., & Othman, I. (2003). Estimation of tissue layer level by sequential morphological reconstruction. *Journal of microscopy, 209*(2), 118-125.

Leong, F. W., Brady, M., & McGee, J. O. D. (2003). Correction of uneven illumination (vignetting) in digital microscopy images. *Journal of clinical pathology, 56*(8), 619-621.

Li, Q., & Nishikawa, R. M. (2015). *Computer-Aided Detection and Diagnosis in Medical Imaging*: Taylor & Francis.

Lodish, H. (2008). *Molecular cell biology*: Macmillan.

Magee, D., Treanor, D., Crellin, D., Shires, M., Smith, K., Mohee, K., & Quirke, P. (2009). Colour normalisation in digital histopathology images.

Muskhelishvili, L., Wingard, S. K., & Latendresse, J. R. (2005). Proliferating cell nuclear antigen—a marker for ovarian follicle counts. *Toxicologic pathology, 33*(3), 365-368.

Nock, R., & Nielsen, F. (2004). Statistical region merging. *Pattern Analysis and Machine Intelligence, IEEE Transactions on, 26*(11), 1452-1458.

Picut, C. A., Swanson, C. L., Scully, K. L., Roseman, V. C., Parker, R. F., & Remick, A. K. (2008). Ovarian follicle counts using proliferating cell nuclear antigen (PCNA) and semi-automated image analysis in rats. *Toxicologic pathology, 36*(5), 674-679.

Sazzad, T., Armstrong, L., & Tripathy, A. (2015). *An Automated Detection Process to Detect Ovarian Tissues Using Type P63 Digitized Color Images.* Paper presented at the Tools with Artificial Intelligence (ICTAI), 2015 IEEE 27th International Conference on.

Sazzad, T., Armstrong, L., & Tripathy, A. (2016). *An Automated Approach to Detect Human Ovarian Tissues Using Type P63 Counter stained Histopathology Digitized Color Images* Paper presented at the IEEE-EMBS International Conference on Biomedical and Health Informatics (BHI).

Sertel, O., Catalyurek, U. V., Shimada, H., & Guican, M. (2009). *Computer-aided prognosis of neuroblastoma: Detection of mitosis and karyorrhexis cells in digitized histological images.* Paper presented at the Engineering in Medicine and Biology Society, 2009. EMBC 2009. Annual International Conference of the IEEE.

Skodras, A., Giannarou, S., Fenwick, M., Franks, S., Stark, J., & Hardy, K. (2009). *Object recognition in the ovary: quantification of oocytes from microscopic images.* Paper presented at the Digital Signal Processing, 2009 16th International Conference on.

Wu, G., Zhao, X., Luo, S., & Shi, H. (2015). Histological image segmentation using fast mean shift clustering method. *Biomedical engineering online, 14*(1), 24.

ACCURATE BACKGROUND POINTS DETECTION FOR ACTION RECOGNITION IN PRACTICAL VIDEO DATASETS

Yu Xiang[1], Yoshihiro Okada[1,2] and Kosuke Kaneko[3]
[1]*Graduate School of Information Science and Electrical Engineering,*
[2]*Innovation Center for Educational Resource of Kyushu University Library, Kyushu University*
[3]*Cyber Security Center, Kyushu University*
Motooka 744, Nishi-ku, Fukuoka, 813-0395, Japan

ABSTRACT

This paper treats the action recognition of moving objects such as humans in practical video-bases of unconstrained videos. For that, the motion of background image pixels, caused by the camera motion, in video frames of a scene strongly affects the accuracy. Removing such background moving influence is a challenging problem. State-of-the-art human action recognition approaches adopted human detection to exclude background or directly use some largest motion pattern clusters as candidate background pixels. In this paper, the authors propose a new background estimation method according to background nature. This method could estimate moving background pixels or camera motion from the selected background pixels. Compared with foreground pixels, background pixels have a high diversity and small average distances to the several borders of a video frame. Those are important criteria to estimate background pixels. The proposed approach is based on the long term analysis of point motion trajectories which are more suitable for video image processing. Experimental results show that the proposed approach achieves a very competitive background extraction performance for practical video-bases.

KEYWORDS

Action recognition, Motion trajectory, Background detection, Diversity, Border distance

1. INTRODUCTION

Human action recognition has become significant research topics in the field of image and video analysis. Recent research focuses on practical datasets of real videos. These video datasets are different from previous man-made datasets, such KTH [1], etc. They are collected from movies [2] [3], TV [4], web videos [5], etc. The action recognition on these practical video datasets is more and more difficult. Many descriptors are computed to capture the appearance, motion information. Currently, the motion boundary histograms (MBH) [6] [7] give the best robustness for the camera motion. In another word, they could implicitly reduce the influence of moving background pixels caused by the camera motion. However, from the research of Wang, et al [8], we know that we could still benefit from explicit camera motion estimation. The moving background caused by the camera motion generates irrelevant trajectories which influence the trajectories of the moving object of interest. If we could estimate the motion of background, we could improve the performance of optical flow based motion descriptors. But when estimating trajectories for the action recognition, very few approaches consider the camera motion. Jain et al. adopted decomposing visual motion into dominant and residual motions, both in the extraction of the space-time trajectories and for the computation of descriptors [9]. Wu et al. [10] propose a low-rank optimization to decompose trajectories into camera-induced and object-induced components. Park et al. [11] perform weak stabilization by factoring out camera motion and coarse object motion while preserving non-rigid motions that work as useful cues for action recognition and pose estimation in videos. Uemura et al. [12] combine local features based on the estimation of dominant homography with image segmentation to estimate the dominant camera motion, and separate the local motions characterizing the actions from the dominant camera motion. Vig et al. [13] use saliency-mapping algorithms to prune background features. This improves the action recognition accuracy.

Jiang et al. [14] [15] generate different motion components by clustering points trajectories and considering the top three large components as the candidate background. Based on the average velocity of the three components, they can correct the trajectory descriptors. The dense temporal trajectories [16] [17] [18] [19] proposed by Wang et al. have been proved effective for human action recognition to these practical video datasets. Because the sampling points come from the whole region of a video frame, reducing the influence of moving background is very important. In their research, they use a state-of-the-art human detector [20] to find a human in a video image, and then, they could focus their processing on moving human region. In this paper, we aim at solving the background motion estimation. Since moving background is caused by the camera motion, considering that all the background points have the same motion pattern is reasonable. So, for background motion estimation, calculating the average velocity of partial background is the same as the whole background. The idea is easy to understand but very important for our research. It requires us to concern the accuracy of extracted background points instead of the integrity of extracted background. This is different from traditional foreground and background segmentation methods. Current object segmentation is based on optical flow [21] and super pixel segmentation [22] [23]. In this paper, we propose an algorithm to find the background points as accurate as possible. We use object segmentation method, motion trajectory segmentation [24] to complete the initial segmentation. This segmentation method uses a long term point trajectory analysis to do the initial segmentation and uses the super pixel to improve the segmentation. This long-term analysis could perform good results in the motion consistent segmentations. Although super pixel estimation is usually time-consuming, we do not need to extract the accurate whole background, so we just use the result, some segmentation components, from the long term point trajectory analysis. The result is shown in figure 1. Different color indicates different motion segmentation. By comparing the input frame with its segmentation result, human could guess intuitively the red component is background. For helping a computer to obtain this conclusion automatically, we propose several analysis principles based on background natures. This is first contribution of our research. In addition, because we give up the super pixel, you could see the red component not only include the background but also some parts of the boxer. If we directly use the red component to estimate the background motion, the result is not effective. So, we propose an optimization method to ensure the points we finally extract are the background points. This is another contribution of our research.

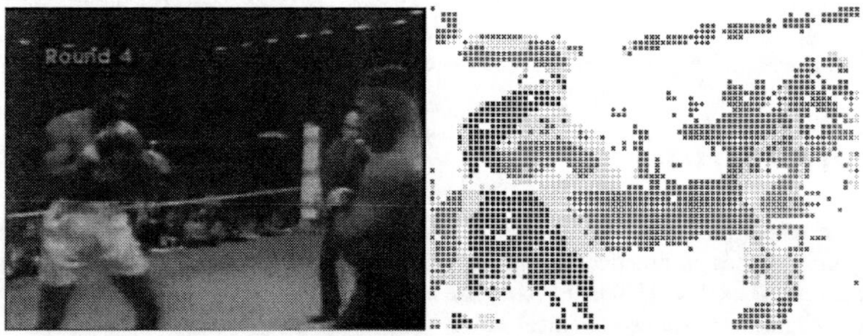

Figure 1. A video frame and its segmentation result by long term point trajectory analysis

The rest of this paper is structured as follows. Section 2 briefly introduces the motion trajectory segmentation. Section 3 elaborates the proposed approach and Section 4 presents experimental validations. Finally, we conclude the paper in Section 5.

2. MOTION TRAJECTORY SEGMENTATION

Our research is based on the motion trajectory segmentation by Keuper, et al [24]. The long-term motion of tracked points is described by a spatiotemporal curve called a motion trajectory [25] generated by the large displacement optical flow [26]. The motion trajectory segmentation analyzes the motion trajectory by minimum cost multi-cut problem. The minimum cost problem is to decompose a graph $G = (V, E)$ into an optimal number of segments such that the overall cost in terms of edge weights is minimized. The input consists of a weighted, undirected graph $G = (V, E)$ with a non-negative weight c_e for every edge $e \in E$, and a set of terminal pairs $\{(s_1,t_1),(s_2,t_2),...,(s_k,t_k)\}$. A multi-cut is a set of edges that are disconnected to each of the terminal pairs. Formally, a set $E' \subseteq E$ is a multi-cut if for all $i = 1,2,...,k$, there is no path between s_i and t_i in the graph $(V, E \backslash E')$. The cost of a multi-cut E' is given by $\text{cost}(E') = \sum_{e \in E'} c_e$. Thus, the minimum multi-cut problem (or multi-cut for short) is to find a multi-cut $\text{cost}(E')$. To formulate grouping as minimum cost multi-cut problem, Keuper et al. build a graph G such that every point trajectory is represented by a vertex $v \in V$ as shown in figure 2. If every vertex is connected by an edge $e \in E$ to its nearest neighbors, all solutions to the MC problem yield a segment into connected components. The weights of the edges $e \in E$ define how two trajectories are similar or dissimilar. The details could be found in [24].

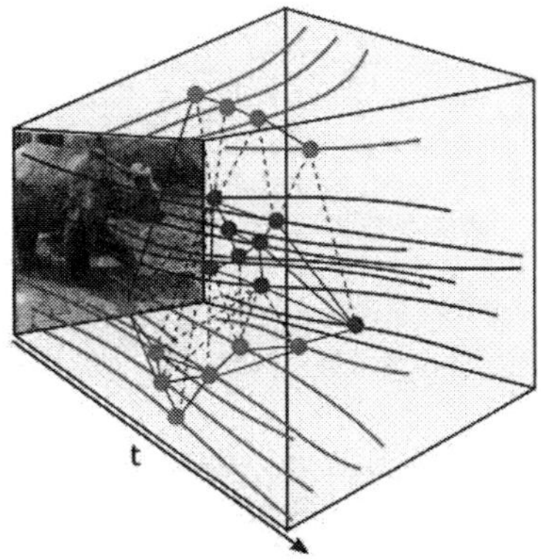

Figure 2. Long-term point trajectories represented by nodes in the graph $G = (V, E)$ those are connected with edges e ∈ E to trajectories with some temporal overlap but can also be connected over time. Here, a segment can either be represented as a node labeling (displayed in colors) or a consistent edge labeling (solid line ≅ 0, dashed line ≅1)

3. BACKGROUND POINTS EXTRACTION AND OPTIMIZATION

The Motion Trajectory Segmentation clusters those pixels into different components. Now what we need to do is to distinguish which component is the background. As previously mentioned, we select the background based on the nature of background in real videos. We introduce the details of the selection procedure here.

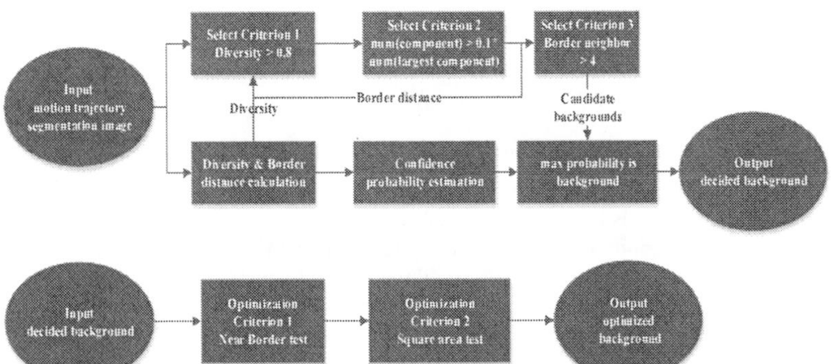

Figure 3. Framework of background extraction and optimization

Figure 3 is the framework of whole algorithm. The whole procedure mainly includes two parts, background selection and background optimization. As mentioned before, if we do not consider the super pixel segmentation and we just use the motion trajectory based segmentation result as the input of our research, the input segmentation will not be very good. So, after selecting the background component, optimization is necessary. The optimization could remove some points that not belong to the real background. In the following, we will introduce the details of background extraction and background optimization.

3.1 Background Extraction

The background extraction mainly includes two judgement parameters and three candidate background judgement criterions. One parameter is diversity. This parameter is used to evaluate the concentrative degree of some components. Evidently, the background component is discrete and the foreground component is concentrative. In this paper, we propose a method quantify the degree. The large number means discrete and small number means concentrative. The diversity will be used as criterion 1 and in background confidence probability estimation. Another parameter is border distance. This parameter evaluates far and near degree from components to borders. This parameter is also used in confidence probability estimation, and some middle results will be used as criterion 3. We will introduce the details of diversity and border distance, and those criterions relative to them.

3.1.1 Diversity

The idea of diversity comes from the definition of color spatial distribution (CSD) [27]. But there some differences between diversity and CSD due to the different research target and object. Firstly, although their research target is a single image, our research processes video frames. Secondly, although their research objective is to find salient parts, which are usually foreground in videos, but our research objective is to select the background component. Thirdly, before the processing, each pixel in a video frame has been classified into an explicit component indicated by one human-defined color, but in their research, these pixels just have probability calculated by Gaussian Mixture Models (GMM) to each color really existing in an image. These differences make the different calculation procedure. We define the diversity as:

$$Div(C) = Div_h(C) + Div_v(C) \tag{1}$$

$Div_h(C)$ and $Div_v(C)$ are respectively the diversity of pixel x in horizontal direction and vertical direction. The definition of horizontal direction is:

$$Div_h(C) = \frac{1}{|X|_C} \sum_x p(C \mid I_x) * |x_h - M_h(C)|^2 \tag{2}$$

$$M_h(C) = \frac{1}{|X|_C} \sum_x p(C \mid I_x) * x_h \tag{3}$$

Here, x_h is the x-coordinate of the pixel x, and $|X|_C = \sum_x p(C \mid I_x)$. $p(C \mid I_x)$ is the probability of each pixel x belonging to a certain component C. Instead of using Gaussian Mixture Models (GMM) to estimate the probability of each pixel belonging to the component, we use the motion trajectory analysis described in Section 2 to cluster pixels into some components for a video frame and indicate each component with one color. So, for each pixel, the probability belonging to a certain component is just 0 or 1. In addition, as mentioned above, we focus on the background selection, not foreground. So, the existence of pixels far from the component center is important evidence for the background. However, due to the error during the motion trajectory segmentation, there will be some pixels in the component are outliers, that is, although some pixels are far from the component center, they do not belong to this component. So, instead of perceptual judgement, we need a quantization for the diversity. Because the existence of outliers, instead of using all the pixels in the components, we just use the partial pixels with the highest diversity. This partial processing is proved to be important; otherwise, some foreground components will have higher diversity than background, because those pixels in the background near from the component center will decrease the diversity. According to these analyses, the diversity of some components is:

$$Div_{w\%}(C) = w\%(Div(C)) \qquad (4)$$

where $w\%$ represents the pixels having w% largest diversity in component C. We use 10% in this research. Finally, the diversity of C is:

$$Div_{normal}(C) = \frac{Div_{w\%}(C) - \min(Div)}{\max(Div) - \min(Div)} \qquad (5)$$

where the Div_{normal} means the diversity set of all the components. Diversities are normalized into [0, 1] for all the components before combining them in Equation (8). As mentioned above, the parameter diversity will be used in the candidate background selection criterion. Obviously, in most cases the pixels in the background component distribute in the whole frame, the background component has the large diversity. So we use the parameter to do the initial selection. If the diversity of some components is larger than some thresholding, we classify the components into background candidates. This is the criterion 1. Here we set the thresholding 0.8 in criterion 1. The value 0.8 comes from experiments based on current popular and challenging datasets for the motion recognition.

3.1.2 Border Distance

Generally, only the background has the large diversity, in these cases, the diversity could be enough to distinguish the background component from all the components. But real videos have complicated scenes, so we could see that in the motion trajectory segmentation [24], not only the background has the large diversity, but sometimes there are another one or two components have the large diversity. So besides the diversity, another parameter is necessary. Compared to the foreground, background usually has more pixels near to the frame borders. So, we consider the use of average distances from these pixels to borders as another judgement parameter. We respectively define distances from a point to a top border, a bottom border, a left border and a right border as P_t, P_d, P_l, P_r. The border distance of a point is the minimum distance among these four distances, $P_{dis} = \min\{P_t, P_d, P_l, P_r\}$. Similarly to the diversity estimation, not all the points are effective, only pixels close to the borders are effective. So we only use some nearest points to calculate the average border distance. The equation of border distance is:

$$Dis(C) = ((\sum_{w\%smallest(C)} P_{dis})) / \sum_{C} w\% \qquad (6)$$

where w% represents the nearest points what we extract. Similarly to the parameter diversity, border distances are also normalized into [0, 1] for all the components before combining them in Equation (8).

$$Dis(C)_{normal} = (Dis(C) - Dis_{\min}) / (Dis_{\max} - Dis_{\min}) \qquad (7)$$

The disadvantage of this procedure is that in some situations, some foreground components also have very small border distances, for example, the moment human or the shot of an object moves into or moves out. But in these situations, the regions they occupy are small. Besides the reason caused by these actual situations, over-segmentation also happens in the motion trajectory segmentation. The over-segmentation often happens in foreground components, and even if sometimes happens in background components, it generally segments into very small parts from whole background components. It barely influences the recognition to the rest background component. For treating these actual cases, we consider that the very small component is not the background component. Considering the videos with different resolution, we could not use an absolute quantity as the definition of a small component. For each video frame, we find the largest component, and consider those components smaller than the 10% of largest component not to be background. This is the criterion 2. Another easily thought thing is that at that moment, the moving objects are just near to minor borders. We divide four borders into eight parts from the middle of horizontal and vertical direction. As figure 4 shows, the four borders have been divided into eight parts, a, b, c, d, e, f, g, h. Through experiments, we find that the eight parts are enough, and more parts can't improve the accuracy of background points extracting greatly. When we calculate the distance P_{dis} for every pixel, we also record which part is nearest to the pixel. So, to any component we could know how many parts occur in our record.

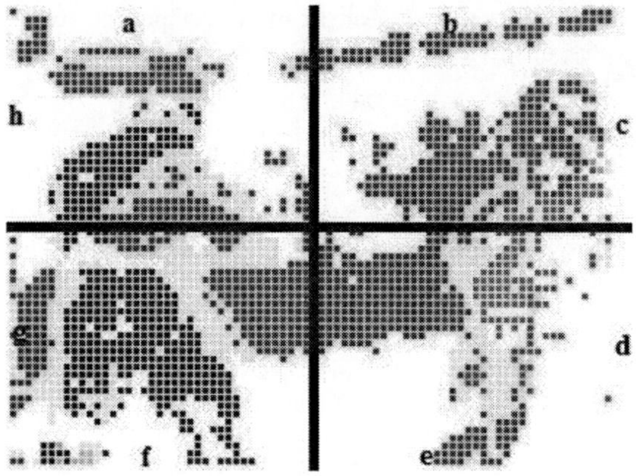

Figure 4. Eight border representation

If the number of recorded parts is larger than 4, we consider that this component is background. This is the criterion 3.

3.1.3 Selection

Until now, we have introduced two selection parameters and the relevant principles to these two parameters for selecting the candidate backgrounds. Now, we need to use these two parameters to determine finally background from candidate backgrounds. We combine two parameters as Equation (8):

$$P_{select} = Weight_{dis} * (1 - Dis(C)_{normal}) + Weight_{div} * Div(C)_{normal} \tag{8}$$

where the $Weight_{dis}$ is the weight of a border distance and the $Weight_{div}$ is the weight of diversity. Because large diversity value could indicate background in the most situations, the border distance only is the auxiliary judgement parameter. In addition, the large diversity and a small border distance mean high probability being background, so we need to subtract the border distance by 1. The finally selected background is the candidate background with the max P_{select} .

3.2 Background Optimization

As mentioned above, our research objective is to select the background as accurate as possible not as whole as possible. In another word, we hope the points in selected background components really belong to this component. Moreover, if the Motion Trajectory Segmentation [24] removes the improvement step for the super pixel segmentation, the research could not segment foregrounds and background appropriately. But we hope to remove the improvement step for the super pixel segmentation because this step is time-consuming. So, if our background selection algorithm is based on bad segmentation, the selected background component will be bad. This could be seen clearly in figure 5. So, an optimization is necessary. Considering our research target, we introduce a simple and effective algorithm. There are two primary optimization principles:

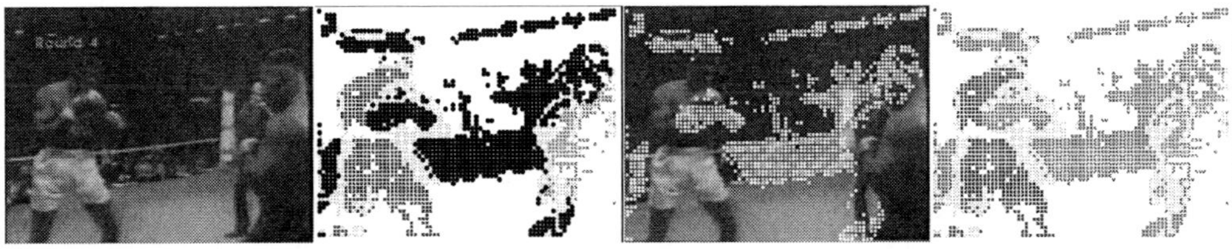

Figure 5. The fourth image is the motion trajectory segmentation result. Obviously, the red component occupies the human part. So, if we do not employ another optimization, the background we extract will cover the human part

1: The points near to border have high probability being background points.

2: The points near to foreground pixels have high probability being foreground points.

According to the two principles, we propose the algorithm as follows:

Input: point p in the selected background component, a frame width and a frame height.

(1) Border Select Box:

$Bou_{width} = Frame_{width}/40$, $Bou_{height} = Frame_{height}/40$

$Point > Bou_{width}$, $Point < (Frame_{width} - Bou_{width})$,

$Point > Bou_{height}$, $Point < (Frame_{height} - Bou_{height})$

Point Judgement Box:

$Rec_{width} = Frame_{width}/20$, $Rec_{height} = Frame_{height}/20$

For point p, the point judgement box is centered as p, width is Rec_{width}, height is Rec_{height}.

(2) If point p is out of Border Select Box

point p is the background point.

else if there are no foreground points in Point Judgement Box of p

point p belongs to the background component.

else

point p probably do not belong to the background component. So remove this point from the selected background component.

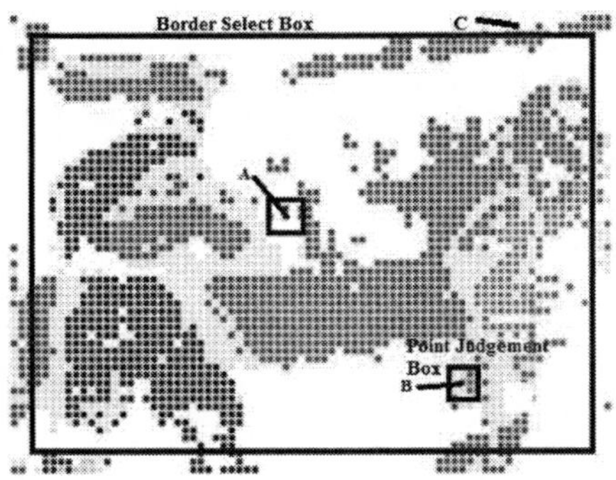

Figure 6. Optimization illustration. In this frame, the point C is out of the Border Select Box, so it could be held in the background component, the red component. There is no foreground point in Point Judgement Box of point A, so point A could be held in the background component. There are pink foreground points in Point Judgement Box of point B, so point B should be removed from the background component

As figure 6 shows, point C is out of the Border Select Box, so we confirm that point C is the background point. Point A and point B are in the Border Select Box, we need further analysis. Obviously, there are some foreground points in the Point Judgement Box of B, but there is no foreground point in the Point Judgement Box of A, so we consider that point A really belongs to the selected background component, and remove point B from the selected background component.

4. EXPERIMENT

To the best of our knowledge, we are the first one only concern the accuracy of extracting background point. Be different with other background segmentation researches, they concern both the accuracy and integrity of extracted background point. It means that we will remove candidate background points easier, not worry if delete real background points. But this is considered in traditional background segmentation. So it is unfair to compare the accuracy of extracting background point between our research and traditional background segmentation. Of course, it is also inappropriate to compare the integrity point between our research and traditional background segmentation. As mentioned above, we test our algorithm using some challenging datasets of real videos: Hollywood2 dataset [3], Stanford Olympic Sports dataset [28], HMDB51 dataset [29], and UCF101 dataset [30]. According to the experiments, we found that setting $Weight_{div}$ as 0.8, $Weight_{dis}$ as 0.2 could obtain best segmentation results over these dataset. Many videos in these datasets contain camera motion, viewpoint transformation and zoom. These influence the extraction result of background pixels.

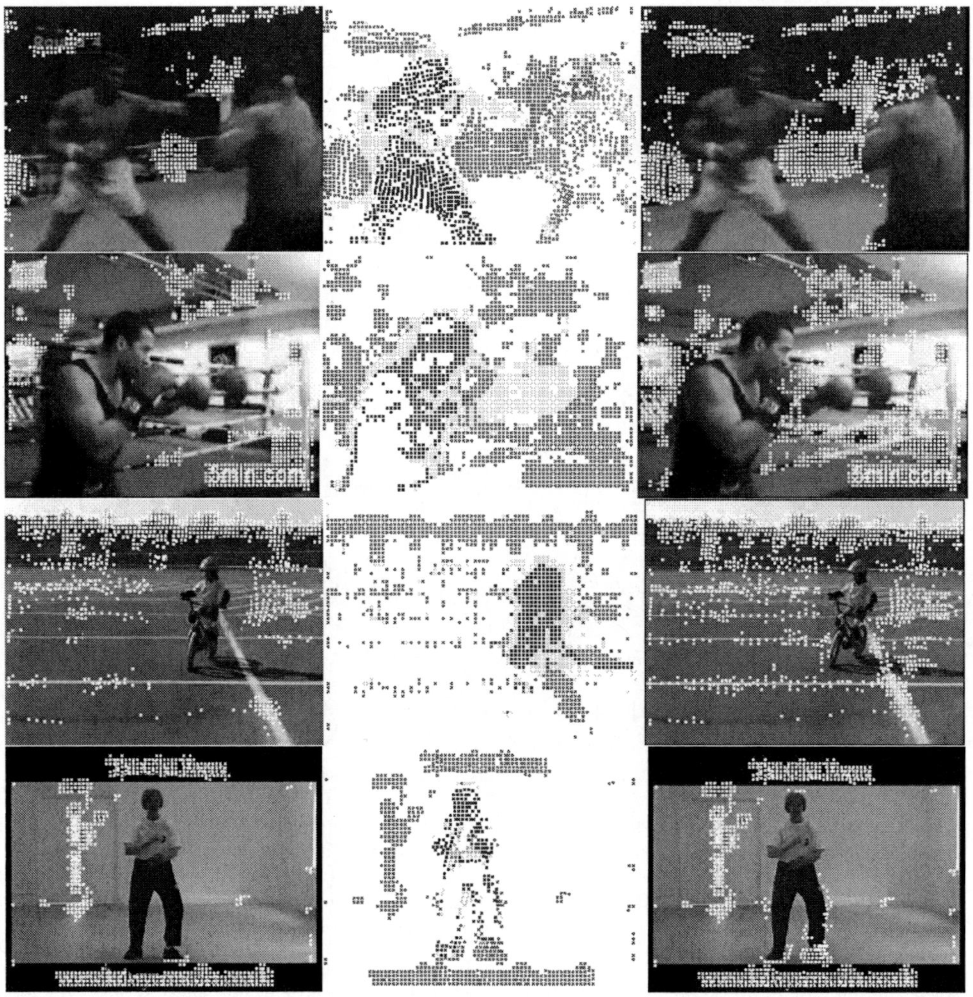

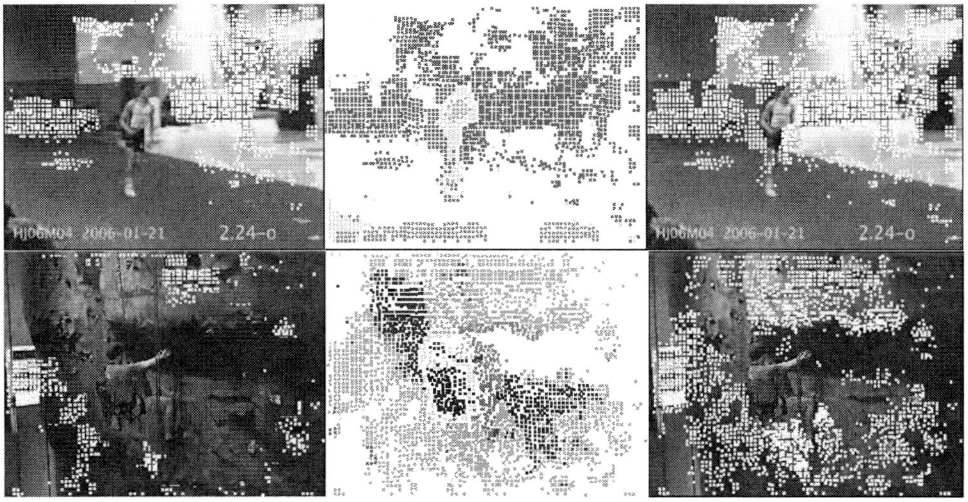

Figure 7. Experimental results of different scene videos

Figure 7 gives some examples from these datasets. These videos contain complicated hinge motions. Some motions are fast, like the punch and the jump. Some motions are very slow, like Tai Chi video. The background of Tai Chi video is static. The others have the camera moving. The videos of climbing and jump have the viewpoint transformation. Also, the video of climbing has the viewpoint zoom. Although there are so many different situations in our test videos, the proposed algorithm could finally extract accurate background pixels. Each row is an example of one frame. The left column is the frame with background pixels after optimization, the middle column is the segmentation by motion trajectory analysis [24], and the right column is the frame with background pixels before optimization. As mentioned above, the whole background extraction is not necessary. What we need is the accuracy of background pixels. It is clear that the background pixels in the left column nearly do not overlay the foreground, and the background pixels in the right column often overlay foreground. The reason causing this case is that the segmentation could not segment different object accurately. After all, the motion trajectory analysis based segmentation is to distinguish different motion not object and just the intermediate result. Since we give up the super pixel based segmentation optimization, the optimization in this paper is necessary. But from the biking example we find that sometimes the optimization is unnecessary. In these cases, the motion trajectory analysis based segmentation is consistent with object segmentation. This may be the fault of our algorithm, but in most cases, optimization is necessary.

Table 1. Video segmentation time, background point extraction time for above six videos and the average time for each frame of every videos

	Punch race 121 frames	Punch Training 231 frames	Biking 150 frames	Tai Chi 170 frames	High Jump 74 frames	Climbing 300 frames
Segmentation time	8min 2s	26min 3s	9min 30s	8min 10s	4min 20s	16min 40s
Video processing time	1.909 s	4.864 s	1.608 s	1.953 s	2.112 s	5.574 s
Average time per each frame	15.77 ms	21.05 ms	10.72 ms	11.48 ms	28.54 ms	18.58 ms

5. CONCLUSION

From the experimental results, we could see clearly that the proposed algorithm is stable and effective. The algorithm does not need any restriction to process a video, like the content type of a scene and the resolution. All the videos are practically useful ones. In addition, our algorithm does not require that the moving object should be a human because the algorithm is based on the background characteristic, not the human characteristic. Although there are so many advantages of this algorithm, the regret is that the algorithm is no real time on a personal computer as calculation times are shown in Table 1. To run the algorithm in real time, we need a high performance computer like a server machine consisting of multi-core processors. The algorithm could be used in applications needing background motion removal, for example, human action recognition.

REFERENCES

[1] C. Schuldt et al, 2004. Recognizing human actions: A local SVM approach. *International Conference on Proceedings of the Pattern Recognition*. Washington. DC, USA, pp. 32-36.

[2] I. Laptev et al, 2008. Learning realistic human actions from movies. IEEE Conference on Computer Vision and Pattern Recognition. Anchorage, AK, pp. 1-8.

[3] M. Marszałek et al, 2009. Actions in context. International Conference on Proceedings of the Pattern Recognition. Miami, FL, pp. 2929-2936.

[4] A. Patron-Perez et al, 2012. Structured learning of human interactions in TV shows. In IEEE Transactions on Pattern Analysis and Machine Intelligence, Vol. 34, No. 12, pp. 2441-2453.

[5] K. Chatfield et al, 2011. The devil is in the details: an evaluation of recent feature encoding methods. The 22nd British Machine Vision Conference. Dundee, United Kingdom, pp. 76.1-76.12.

[6] N. Dalal et al, 2006. Human detection using oriented histograms of flow and appearance. Proceedings of the 9th European conference on Computer Vision. Graz, Austria, pp. 428-441.

[7] V. Kantorov and I. Laptev, 2014. Efficient Feature Extraction, Encoding, and Classification for Action Recognition. IEEE Conference on Computer Vision and Pattern Recognition. Columbus, OH, pp. 2593 – 2600.

[8] H. Wang and C. Schmid, 2013. Action Recognition with Improved Trajectories. 2013 IEEE International Conference on Computer Vision. Sydney, Australia, pp. 3551-3558.

[9] M. Jain et al, 2013. Better exploiting motion for better action recognition. IEEE Conference on Computer Vision and Pattern Recognition. Portland, OR, pp. 2555-2562.

[10] S. Wu et al, 2011. Action recognition in videos acquired by a moving camera using motion decomposition of Lagrangian particle trajectories. 2011 International Conference on Computer Vision. Barcelona, pp. 1419-1426.

[11] D. Park et al, 2013. Exploring weak stabilization for motion feature extraction. IEEE Conference on Computer Vision and Pattern Recognition. Portland, OR, pp. 2882-2889.

[12] H. Uemura et al, 2008. Feature tracking and motion compensation for action recognition. The 19th British Machine Vision Conference, Leeds, United Kingdom, pp. 30.1-30.10.

[13] E. Vig et al, 2012. Space-variant descriptor sampling for action recognition based on saliency and eye movements. Proceedings of the 12th European conference on Computer Vision. Firenze, Italy, pp. 84-97.

[14] Y. G. Jiang et al, 2012. Trajectory based modeling of human actions with motion reference points. Proceedings of the 12th European conference on Computer Vision. Firenze, Italy, pp. 425-438.

[15] Y. G. Jiang et al, 2015. Human Action Recognition in Unconstrained Videos by Explicit Motion Modeling. In IEEE Transactions on Image Processing, Vol. 24, No. 11, pp. 3781-3795.

[16] H. Wang et al, 2011. Action recognition by dense trajectories. IEEE Conference on Computer Vision and Pattern Recognition. Barcelona, Spain, pp. 3169-3176.

[17] H. Wang and C. Schmid, 2013. Action Recognition with Improved Trajectories. 2013 IEEE International Conference on Computer Vision. Sydney, Australia, pp. 3551-3558.

[18] H. Wang et al, 2013. Dense trajectories and motion boundary descriptors for action recognition. In International Journal of Computer Vision, Vol. 103, No. 1, pp. 60-79.

[19] H. Wang et al, 2015. A Robust and Efficient Video Representation for Action Recognition. Online Available: http://arxiv.org/abs/1504.05524.

[20] A. Prest et al, 2012. Weakly supervised learning of interactions between humans and objects. In IEEE Transactions on Pattern Analysis and Machine Intelligence, Vol. 34, No. 3, pp. 601–614.

[21] A. Papazoglou et al, 2013. Fast Object Segmentation in Unconstrained Video. 2013 IEEE International Conference on Computer Vision. Sydney, Australia, pp. 1777-1784.

[22] B. Andres et al, 2011. Probabilistic image segmentation with closedness constraints. 2011 International Conference on Computer Vision. Barcelona, pp. 2611-2618.

[23] B. Andres et al, 2012. Globally optimal closed-surface segmentation for connectomics. Proceedings of the 12th European conference on Computer Vision. Firenze, Italy, pp. 778-791.

[24] M. Keuper et al, 2015. Motion Trajectory Segmentation via Minimum Cost Multicuts. 2015 IEEE International Conference on Computer Vision. Santiago, Chile, pp. 3271-3279.

[25] P. Ochs et al, 2014. Segmentation of moving objects by long term video analysis. In IEEE Transactions on Pattern Analysis and Machine Intelligence, Vol. 36, No. 6, pp. 1187-1200.

[26] T. Brox and J. Malik, et al, 2011. Large displacement optical flow: descriptor matching in variational motion estimation. In IEEE Transactions on Pattern Analysis and Machine Intelligence, Vol. 33, No. 3, pp. 500-513.

[27] M. M. Cheng et al, 2013. Efficient Salient Region Detection with Soft Image Abstraction. 2013 IEEE International Conference on Computer Vision. Sydney, Australia, pp. 1529-1536.

[28] J. C. Niebles et al, 2010. Modeling temporal structure of decomposable motion segments for activity classification. The 11th European Conference on Computer Vision. Crete, Greece, pp. 392-405.

[29] H. Kuehne et al, 2011. HMDB: A large video database for human motion recognition. 2011 International Conference on Computer Vision. Barcelona, pp. 2556-2563.

[30] K. Soomro et al, 2012. UCF101: A dataset of 101 human actions classes from videos in the wild. Online Available: http://arxiv.org/abs/1212.0402.

HIGH SPEED EDGE DETECTION IMPLEMENTATION USING COMPRESSOR CELLS OVER RSDA

Ahmed Abouelfarag, Marwa El-Shenawy and Esraa Khatab
Department of Computer Engineering
Arab Academy for Science, Technology and Maritime Transport

ABSTRACT

Recently. Computer vision is playing an important role in many essential applications, such as medical image analysis, visual surveillance, etc. Many of these applications are subject to a "real-time constraint", therefore it requires a fast and reliable computation system. Edge detection is the approach used most frequently for segmenting images based on changes in intensity, it extracts important structural information needed for high-level functionality and reduces the amount of data that needs to be processed. There are various kernels employed to achieve edge detection, such as Sobel, Robert, and Prewitt, upon which, the most commonly used is Sobel. This paper introduces a novel type of operator cells on the Reconfigurable Static Data-flow Architecture (RSDA), which is a scalable architecture optimized for the computation of image and video. This enhancement shows significant improvement, as it decreases the computational 26%, compared to using the conventional adder cells, and also decreases the LUTs and hardware resources of the architecture. A comparison between the conventional adders and different types of compressors has been exploited based on results from simulation on Isim simulator and a flooring plan using PlanAhead tool.

KEYWORDS

Data-flow architecture; real-time computation; computer vision.

1. INTRODUCTION

When building any system, the main objective is to achieve its required functionality with the highest achievable performance levels. However, there is no optimal solution; therefore any solution is a trade-off between power, time, silicon area, accuracy and many other less critical factors. Recently, computing algorithms have no longer been able to boost performance by continuously escalating the clock speed of the processors they run on. This prompted using processors with thousands of cores on them, which were principally designed for highly parallel operations.

Stream processing, especially video processing, requires high computational demands, along with the requirements of low power and low cost. In the recent years, many approaches have been devoted to develop architectures that could tackle these demands. Application-Specific Integrated Circuits (ASICs) yield the best performance regarding the computational throughput at low power consumption, on the other hand ASICs lack flexibility and also require high development time [1]. The next thought would be the general purpose Digital Signal Processors (DSPs), which grant proficient programmability. However, the higher the complexity of the system, the worse its performance gets [2].

In the recent years, GPUs have taken over the field of multimedia processing due to its massively parallel architecture [3], but at the same time, GPUs are not able to exploit low-level parallelism and they also occupy bigger silicon area compared to ASICs.

During the early stages of image processing, many image features must be identified in order to evaluate and estimate the structure of objects in images [4]. Edges are one of the important features as most objects' information are enclosed by their edges. An edge in an image can be identified as the sudden changes in intensities of the neighboring pixels. There are various edge detection techniques which differ in the complexity and accuracy. Techniques that use larger convolution kernels give better results, but on the same time they are computationally more complex [5].

A Reconfigurable Static Data Flow hardware Architecture (RSDA) for video/image processing has been introduced in [6]. It utilizes a large number of simple arithmetic and logic operators to form a highly parallel engine, in addition to finite state machine controllers in order to control the data-floe pipelines.

This paper outlines an enhancing operator cell that can be used in the RSDA, it makes use of compressor cells instead of using the conventional adders. The basis of this enhancement in the architecture is the Sobel edge kernels as they are the most suitable kernels due to their separability and lack of multiplications; in Sobel, multiplication delays can be avoided because multiplications by 0 or 1 are not considered multiplications, and also multiplication by 2 is a 1-bit shift that needs only one clock cycle [7]. Therefore, the main enhancement would be in improving the performance of the addition operations.

2. DWARF SELECTION

The Berkeley Dwarves are defined as "algorithmic methods that capture a pattern of computation and communication" which "present a method for capturing the common requirements of classes of applications while being reasonably divorced from individual implementations [8].

The most compatible dwarf with video/image processing is dense linear algebra, which exploits vector-vector, matrix-matrix, and matrix-vector operations. Any frame/image is considered a 2D-array on which we could do many different operations such as: pre-processing, segmentation, and feature extraction where the same operation is performed on most pixels. Real-time processing requires doing this dozens of times per second, which leaves only a few nanoseconds to process each individual pixel [9].

3. APPLICATION SELECTION

Any video is composed of successive sequence of frames that are played straightly after each other with a certain frame rate (frames per second "fps"). Eventually, in order not to increase time latency, a system must be developed which can perform data stream processing without going through a costly storage operation during its critical processing path. Accordingly, frames must be processed "in-stream" as they fly-by [9]. The architectural features that should be met are explained below:

- Single Instruction Multiple Data (SIMD): It encompasses broadcasting an individual instruction to multiple processors, which concurrently executes the instruction on different partitions of the data at the same time, thus allowing a bigger number of computations to be performed in a shorter time. SIMD also plays an important role in speeding up vector operations. That's why SIMD is thought of as a method to exploit Data-Level Parallelism (DLP).
- Very Long Instruction Word (VLIW): It speeds up high-level operations by providing the ability to perform multiple instructions in one cycle all at one time. This allows the instructions to be software-pipelined by the programmer. It must be put into consideration that for the VLIW to work properly, data operated on must have no dependencies among them. VLIW exploits Instruction Level Parallelism (ILP).
- Efficient memory subsystem: If there doesn't exist an efficient way of transferring the data streams between the system components, any other speeding-up techniques would be completely wasted. DMA is the known technique employed to transfer data within the system components without being a burden on the CPU.

4. BACKGROUND

4.1 Edge Detection

Edge detection is a primary operation in image processing and computer vision, especially in object detection applications. Edge detection aims at identifying the points of sharp changes in brightness or, in other words, the points having discontinuities [5].

Edge detection is normally performed using 2-D convolutions. Intensity values of edge pixels is evaluated by calculating the dot-product of the convolution kernel with the corresponding area of the image. There are various edge detection techniques such as Sobel and Canny edge detection methods. Canny detector has many advantages as it enhances signal-to-noise ratio of images and has a smoothing effect. On the other hand, Sobel operator is simple, les time consuming and also easier to implement. In this paper, Sobel edge detection technique is exploited, as it is more suitable for real-time video processing which requires high-speed operations to be performed. The Sobel operator has a two 3X3 kernels, as shown in Figure 1.

$$G_x = \begin{bmatrix} -1 & -2 & -1 \\ 0 & 0 & 0 \\ 1 & 2 & 1 \end{bmatrix} \qquad G_y = \begin{bmatrix} -1 & 0 & 1 \\ -2 & 0 & 2 \\ -1 & 0 & 1 \end{bmatrix}$$

Figure 1. Sobel Kernels

These kernels are applied separately to the image and produce separate horizontal and vertical gradients (Gx and Gy). Next, Gx and Gy can be combined together to calculate the magnitude of the gradient using the equation below:

$$G = \sqrt{G_x{}^2 + G_y{}^2}$$

Typically the magnitude could be calculated using:

$$|G| = |G_x| + |G_y|$$

4.2 Computation Patterns

Real-time video processing is intensely important in applications such as robotics and human interface applications where the processing capabilities are limited or devoted to many tasks. Parallel processing approaches allow the architectures to operate at moderate speeds, while still realizing the same task as a single, much powerful and expensive chip [10, 11].

Mapping an algorithm onto a parallel architectural platform requires the usage of a parallel programming model, which exploits the concurrency and synchronization of the parallel components within the application.

The finest grain of parallelism could be exploited in Task-based models such as Intel's Threaded Building Blocks (TBBs) and NVIDIA's Compute Unified Device Architecture (CUDA). Using the suitable programming model, the application is divided into small separate tasks, then the task system performs scheduling while assuring the proper behavior towards dependencies and achieving a maximum throughput.

4.2.1 Multi-Core and Many-Core Technologies

The semi-conductor industry has witnessed a significant shift from increasing clock speeds to increasing the number of cores. For instance, Intel's Core i7 processors have 4 çores with 140 single precision GFLOPS and a peak off-chip memory bandwidth of 32 GB/sec.

Many-core systems such as the GPUs developed by NVIDIA, Intel and AMD utilize more than tens of cores which deliver massive gain in the computational potentials. Table 1 shows a brief comparison between the performance criteria of GPUs and multi-core architectures [12].

Table 1. GPUs vs. Multi-cores

	GPU	Multi-core
Power Consumption	High	Medium
Clock Speed	Medium	High
Ease of Programming	Medium	Low
Speed Gain	High	Medium
Floating-point Precision	Single/double	Single/double

4.2.2 Digital Signal Processors

DSPs are well known for achieving high performance with lower usage and relatively smaller silicon area. Recently, modifications have been made on DSPs to make them able to perform repetitive operations [13]. Their highly parallel architecture with diverse functional units made them suitable for video/image processing. DSPs have been used in dual-core processor system-on-chips for customer electronic devices such as PDAs, portable media players, etc.

4.2.3 Field Programmable Gate Arrays

FPGAs are arrays of reconfigurable logic blocks with a network of programmable interconnections. Currently, it has been the focus of many research fields to improve their capabilities in the future generations [14]. FPGAs' main advantage is that it allows full or partial reconfiguration. FPGAs combine ASICs speed and flexibility with a shorter time to make.

4.2.4 RSDA

RSDA is based on the static data-flow model and the re-configurability of the hardware used. The main contribution was that RSDA uses reconfigurable hardwired connection and hardware shaking. RSDA is easy to program and has highly parallel capabilities. The architecture is composed of data-flow clusters which have a large number of arithmetic and logic operators, and a finite state machine controller. The conceptual architecture of the RSDA is shown in Figure 2.

There are several types of operator cells used to perform different operations. One type of operator cells performs arithmetic operations such as addition, subtraction, negation, absolute; another type of cells performs various types of comparisons. RSDA has the performance of RTL-based implementation, but with a little higher power consumption and a higher number of logic elements. On the other hand, RSDA has better programmability.

Implementing Sobel edge detection method using RSDA would need a mapping computation shown in Figure 3.

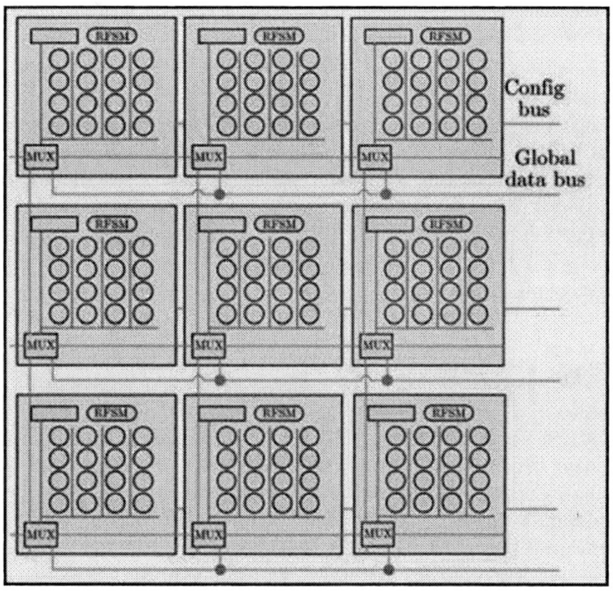

Figure 2. RSDA Clusters

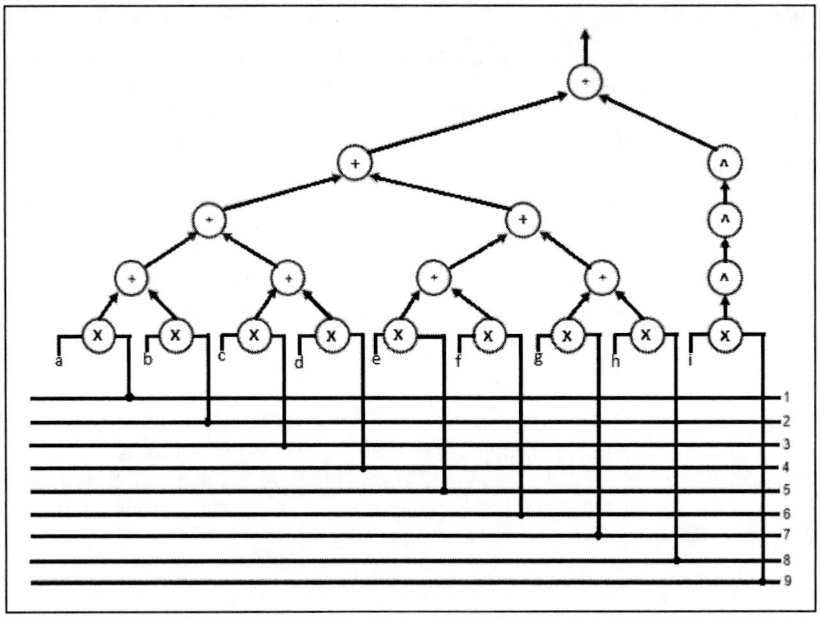

Figure 3. Computation mapping using ripple carry adders

In Figure 3, the numbers on the right represent the numbering of the image pixels that will be operated, and the letters from 'a' to 'i' are corresponding to the values in the Sobel kernels shown in Figure 1, and numbers as follows:

a	b	c
d	e	f
g	h	i

After multiplying each pixel to its corresponding value in the kernel, all the values need to be added together afterwards. Using the operator cells in the RSDA, only two numbers would be added at a time. In this paper an enhanced operator cell is introduced that will speed up the addition processes and improve resources usage. In Sobel technique, multiplications are not considered a burden because its kernels only has the values 0,1, and 2. Multiplication by 0 and 1 are not considered an operation while multiplication by 2 can be performed by a logical 1-bit shift operation. Therefore, the main concern in this paper is to enhance the addition-responsible operator cells.

5. PROPOSED MODEL

This paper introduces a novel operator cell to the RSDA architecture which makes use of compressors. Compressors are logic circuits that can add multiple bits at a time and that is why it is called "Column Compressors". Compressors significantly enhance the carry propagation delays [14]. Compressors are a basic component for multipliers and large-input adders, therefore it will obtain higher performance levels when used while implementing the Sobel edge detection technique. There are various compressor cells 3-to-2, 4-to-2, 5-to-2 and 9-to-2. It compresses multiple input bits that need to be added to two outputs, that's why it is called a compressor.

Using the conventional ripple carry adders will add each two values together. Therefore, multiple adders will be used. The main disadvantage of ripple carry adders is that they produce high carry propagation delays. When analyzing the timing constraints using Xilinx, the time taken to add two 8-bit numbers was 9.774 nanoseconds, which is considered a very high delay for real-time applications. This delay is due to the carry propagation delay. Figure 4 shows how the 8-bit addition operations are dependent on each other.

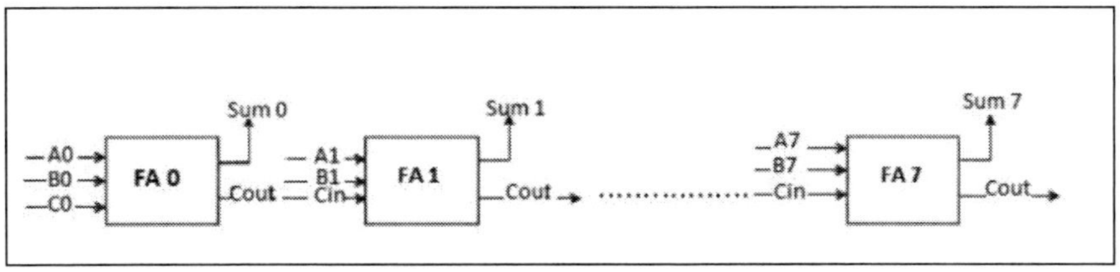

Figure 4. 8-bit addition using full adders

5.1 3:2 Compressors

The mapping computation of Sobel edge detection technique using 3:2 compressors is shown in Figure 5. Four 3:2 compressor operator cells are utilized, each cell is composed of 8 compressors in order to add 8-bit numbers. The delay of 3:2 was found to be much less than that of the ripple carry adders adding the 8 bits. For adding nine values, addition will be performed on two levels with each level having a delay of 5.144 nanoseconds. Therefore, the addition delay for the two stages would be 10.288 nanoseconds.

Table 2 shows the details of the estimated resources required related to the FPGA board Spartan 1800A.

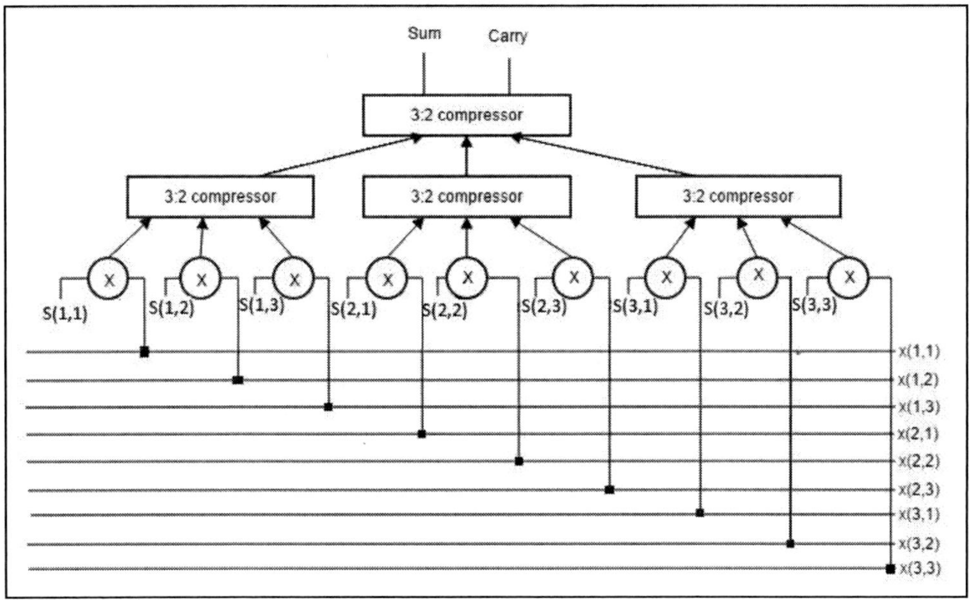

Figure 5. Computation Mapping of Sobel using 3:2 Compressors

Table 2. Resources required when 3:2 compressors used

Site type	Required
LUTs	160
SLICEL	40
SLICEM	40

5.2 4:2 Compressors

Using 4:2 compressors will enable the architecture to add more numbers per cell, but on the other hand it will increase the delay, due to carry dependencies and it will also need two-level addition to be able to add nine numbers, as shown in Figure 6.

When introducing the 4:2 compressor cells to the architecture, a pass through cell will be used (annotated by a '^') which passes data to the next level. The addition level using the 4:2 compressor cells produced a delay of 5.806 nanoseconds in addition to the delay of the next stage of the 3:2 compressor cells.

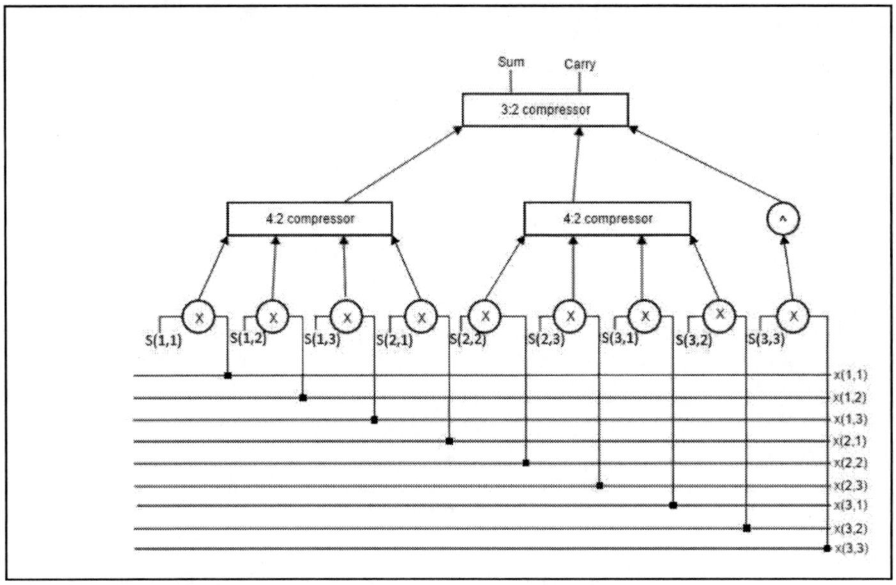

Figure 6. Computation mapping of Sobel when using 4:2 compressors

5.3 9:2 Compressors

As shown in Figure 7, when using 9:2 compressor cells, addition could be done on one stage. But, each compressor cell would produce a relatively high delay. Using eight 9:2 compressor cells would be produce a delay of 10.478 nanoseconds. Table 3 illustrates the resource estimation of 8 units of 9:2 compressor cells.

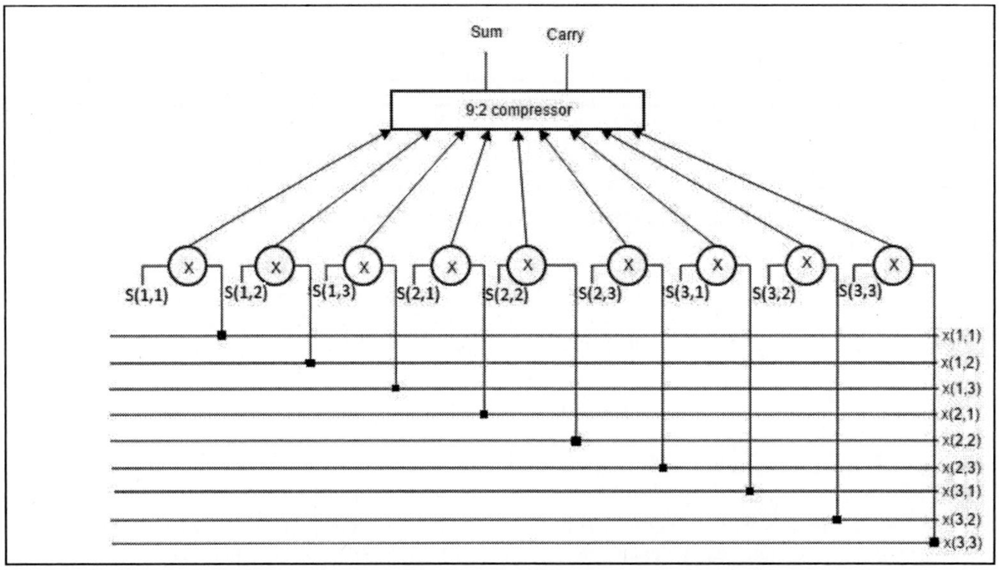

Figure 7. Computation mapping of Sobel when using 9:2 compressors

Table 3. Resources required when 9:2 compressors are used

Site type	Required
LUTs	280
SLICEL	72
SLICEM	72

6. RESULTS AND ANALYSIS

This paper presents a novel operator cell to the RSDA to enhance the performance of multi-bit numbers addition techniques, Sobel edge detection was taken as a test case in this paper. In Sobel edge detection technique two main operations are involved: multiplication and addition. Multiplications are not considered as burden because the only values in the Sobel kernels are 0, 1, and 2; multiplication by 0 and 1 doesn't need a multiplier cell, and multiplying by 2 can be performed by a 1-bit shift. Therefore, enhancing the addition operation will cause a significant enhancement in the performance level of Sobel edge detection. The introduced operator cell replaces the ADD operator cell which is used to add two values together, with a novel operator cell that is composed of multiple compressors. Each compressor cell consists of k compressors responsible for adding k-bit numbers with reduced delays.

Various types of compressors have been tested when adding nine 8-bit numbers. Tests were performed using the Isim simulator on Xilinx. The PlanAhead tool was also used to estimate the usage of resources. Simulations were done on FPGA Spartan board 1800A. Table 4 exploits a comparison of time delays when using the conventional adder cells and the different types of compressor cells.

Table 4. Time delay Comparison

Operator cell used	Time delay
Ripple Carry Adder	39.096 ns
3:2 compressors	10.288 ns
4:2 compressors	10.95 ns
9:2 compressors	10.478 ns

7. CONCLUSION AND FUTURE WORK

In this research, a novel operator cell based on compressors is introduced. Delay enhancement is achieved when using 3:2 compressors that could be used to add nine 8-bit values together, it will yield the least delay compared to the other compressor cells and also the ripple carry adder cells. When using the ripple carry adder, each addition stage would cost 9.774 nanoseconds. As shown in Figure 3, four addition stages are needed, which produces a total of 39.096 nanoseconds delay, while using 3:2 compressor cells as shown in Figure 5, it only needed two addition stages with each stage producing a delay of 5.144 nanoseconds, and a total of 10.288 nanoseconds.

This improved behavior was confirmed with experimental results that have shown a 26% increase in speed. Future work will focus on further improvements of the operator cells of the RSDA, such as decreasing power consumption and reducing resources consumption. More improvements could be done in order to enhance the performance of the operator cells when values consist of more than 8 bits.

REFERENCES

[1] Saponara, Michele Casula, and Luca Fanicci. "ASIP-Based Reconfigurable Architectures For Power-Efficient And Real-Time Image/Video Processing". Journal of Real-Time Image Processing 3.3 (2008): 201-216. Web. 13 Mar. 2016.

[2] Kumar, Vivek et al. "Heterogeneous Work-Stealing Across CPU And DSP Cores". 2015 IEEE High Performance Extreme Computing Conference (HPEC) (2015): n. pag. Web. 13 Mar. 2016.

[3] Mccool, Michael. "Signal Processing And General-Purpose Computing And GPUs [Exploratory DSP]". IEEE Signal Process. Mag. 24.3 (2007): 109-114. Web.

[4] Ramesh Jain, Rangachar Kasturi, and Brian G. Schunck. Machine Vision. New York: McGraw-Hill,1995.

[5] P. Sujatha and K. Sudha, "Performance Analysis of Different Edge Detection Techniques for Image Segmentation", Indian Journal of Science and Technology. Vol. 8, no. 14, 2015.

[6] Z. Liu, T. Li and J. Han, " A novel reconfigurable data-flow architecture for real time video processing", Journal of Shanghai Jiaotong University (Science), vol. 18, no. 3, pp. 348-359, 2013.

[7] J. Schiel and A. Bainbridge-Smith, "Efficient Edge Detection on Low Cost FPGAs", 2015.

[8] "The Landscape of Parallel Computing Research: A View from Berkeley", 2006.

[9] C. Johnston, K. Gribbon, and D. Bailey, "Implementing image processing algorithms on FPGAs," in Proc. Elev. Electron. New Zeal. Conf. ENZCon'04, 2004, pp. 118-123.

[10] Lin, Dennis et al. "The Parallelization Of Video Processing". IEEE Signal Process. Mag. 26.6 (2009): 103-112. Web. 13 Mar. 2016.

[11] Dennis Lin, Xiaohuang Huang, Quang Nguyen, Joshua Blackburn, Christopher Rodrigues, Thomas Huang, Minh N. Do, Sanjay J. Patel, and Wen-Mei W. Hwu, "The Parallelization of Video Processing", IEEE Signal Processing Magazine, November 2009.

[12] C. Blair, "Real-time video scene analysis with heterogeneous processors", May 2014.

[13] C. Narendra and K. Kumar, "Low power compressor based MAC architecture for DSP applications", 2015 IEEE International Conference on Signal Processing, Informatics, Communication and Energy Systems (SPICES), 2015.

[14] D. Jones, A. Powell, C. Bouganis and P. Cheung, " GPU versusFPGA for High Productivity Computing", 2010 International Conference on Field Programmable Logic and Applications, 2010.

A NEW RADIAL BASIS FUNCTION APPROXIMATION WITH REPRODUCTION

Zuzana Majdisova and Vaclav Skala
Faculty of Applied Sciences, University of West Bohemia
Univerzitni 8, CZ 30614 Plzen, Czech Republic

ABSTRACT

Approximation of scattered geometric data is often a task in many engineering problems. The Radial Basis Function (RBF) approximation is appropriate for large scattered (unordered) datasets in d-dimensional space. This method is useful for a higher dimension $d \geq 2$, because the other methods require a conversion of a scattered dataset to a semi-regular mesh using some tessellation techniques, which is computationally expensive. The RBF approximation is non-separable, as it is based on a distance of two points. It leads to a solution of overdetermined Linear System of Equations (LSE).

In this paper a new RBF approximation method is derived and presented. The presented approach is applicable for d-dimensional cases in general.

KEYWORDS

Radial basis function; RBF; approximation; optimization problem; linear reproduction

1. INTRODUCTION

Radial Basis Functions (RBFs) are widely used across many fields solving technical and non-technical problems. The RBF method was originally introduced by [Hardy, R.L., 1971] and it is an effective tool for solving partial differential equations in engineering and sciences. Moreover, RBF applications can be found in neural networks, fuzzy systems, pattern recognition, data visualization, medical applications, surface reconstruction [Carr, J.C. et al, 2001], [Turk, G. and O'Brien, J.F., 2002], [Pan, R. and Skala, V., 2011a], [Pan, R. and Skala, V., 2011b], [Skala, V. et al, 2013], [Skala, V. et al, 2014], reconstruction of corrupted images [Uhlir, K. and Skala, V., 2005], [Zapletal, J. et al, 2009], etc. The RBF approximation technique is really meshless and is based on collocation in a set of scattered nodes. This method is independent with respect to the dimension of the space. The computational cost of RBF approximation increases nonlinearly with the number of points in the given dataset and linearly with the dimensionality of data.

There are two main groups of basis functions: global RBFs (e.g. [Duchon, J., 1977], [Schagen, I.P, 1979]) and Compactly Supported RBFs (CS-RBFs) [Wendland, H., 2006]. Fitting scattered data with CS-RBFs leads to a simpler and faster computation, because the system of linear equations has a sparse matrix. However, approximation using CS-RBFs is sensitive to the density of approximated scattered data and to the choice of a "shape" parameter. Global RBFs lead to a linear system of equations with a dense matrix and their usage is based on sophisticated techniques such as the fast multipole method [Darve, E., 2000]. Global RBFs are useful in repairing incomplete datasets and they are significantly less sensitive to the density of approximated data.

2. ORIGINAL APPROACH

The original approach of RBF approximation with linear reproduction was introduced by [Fasshauer, G.E., 2007] (Chapter 19.4). Let us briefly summarize the properties of this approach in this section.

The goal of this approach is to approximate a given dataset of N points by a function:

$$f(\boldsymbol{x}) = \sum_{j=1}^{M} c_j\, \phi(\|\boldsymbol{x} - \boldsymbol{\xi}_j\|) + P_1(\boldsymbol{x}), \tag{1}$$

where the approximating function $f(\boldsymbol{x})$ is represented as a sum of M RBFs, each associated with a different reference point $\boldsymbol{\xi}_j$, and weighted by an appropriate coefficient c_j, and $P_1(\boldsymbol{x}) = \boldsymbol{a}^T \boldsymbol{x} + a_0$ is a linear polynomial. This linear polynomial should theoretically solve problems with stability and solvability. Now, it is necessary to determine the vector of weights $\boldsymbol{c} = (c_1, \dots, c_M)^T$and coefficients of the linear polynomial. This is achieved by solving an overdetermined linear system of equations (LSE):

$$\boldsymbol{h}_i = f(\boldsymbol{x}_i) = \sum_{j=1}^{M} c_j\, \phi(\|\boldsymbol{x}_i - \boldsymbol{\xi}_j\|) + P_1(\boldsymbol{x}_i) = \sum_{j=1}^{M} c_j\, \phi_{ij} + P_1(\boldsymbol{x}_i), \qquad i = 1, \dots, N, \tag{2}$$

where $\boldsymbol{x}_i$ is point from the given dataset and is associated with scalar value h_i. Moreover, additional conditions are applied:

$$\sum_{i=1}^{M} c_i = 0\,, \qquad \sum_{i=1}^{M} c_i \boldsymbol{\xi}_i = \boldsymbol{0}. \tag{3}$$

It can be seen that for d-dimensional space a linear system of $(N + d + 1)$ equations in $(M + d + 1)$ variables has to be solved, where N is the number of points in the given dataset, M is the number of reference points and d is the dimensionality of the data.

For $d = 2$, vectors $\boldsymbol{x}_i$, $\boldsymbol{\xi}_j$ and $\boldsymbol{a}$ are given as $\boldsymbol{x}_i = (x_i, y_i)^T$, $\boldsymbol{\xi}_j = (\xi_j, \eta_j)^T$ and $\boldsymbol{a} = (a_x, a_y)^T$. Thus, for E^2 and the given dataset we can write this LSE in the following matrix form:

$$\begin{pmatrix} \boldsymbol{A} & \boldsymbol{P} \\ \boldsymbol{\Xi} & \boldsymbol{0} \end{pmatrix} \begin{pmatrix} \boldsymbol{c} \\ \boldsymbol{a} \\ a_0 \end{pmatrix} = \begin{pmatrix} \boldsymbol{h} \\ \boldsymbol{0} \end{pmatrix} \tag{4}$$

This system is overdetermined ($M \ll N$) and can be solved by the least squares method as:

$$\begin{pmatrix} \boldsymbol{A}^T\boldsymbol{A} + \boldsymbol{\Xi}^T\boldsymbol{\Xi} & \boldsymbol{A}^T\boldsymbol{P} \\ \boldsymbol{P}^T\boldsymbol{A} & \boldsymbol{P}^T\boldsymbol{P} \end{pmatrix} \begin{pmatrix} \boldsymbol{c} \\ \boldsymbol{a} \\ a_0 \end{pmatrix} = \begin{pmatrix} \boldsymbol{A}^T\boldsymbol{h} \\ \boldsymbol{P}^T\boldsymbol{h} \end{pmatrix} \tag{5}$$

where

$$\boldsymbol{A}^T\boldsymbol{A} + \boldsymbol{\Xi}^T\boldsymbol{\Xi} = \begin{pmatrix} \sum_{i=1}^{N} \phi_{i1}\phi_{i1} + \xi_1^2 + \eta_1^2 + 1 & \cdots & \sum_{i=1}^{N} \phi_{i1}\phi_{iM} + \xi_1\xi_M + \eta_1\eta_M + 1 \\ \vdots & \ddots & \vdots \\ \sum_{i=1}^{N} \phi_{iM}\phi_{i1} + \xi_M\xi_1 + \eta_M\eta_1 + 1 & \cdots & \sum_{i=1}^{N} \phi_{iM}\phi_{iM} + \xi_M^2 + \eta_M^2 + 1 \end{pmatrix},$$

$$\boldsymbol{P}^T\boldsymbol{A} = (\boldsymbol{A}^T\boldsymbol{P})^T = \begin{pmatrix} \sum_{i=1}^{N} x_i\phi_{i1} & \cdots & \sum_{i=1}^{N} x_i\phi_{iM} \\ \sum_{i=1}^{N} y_i\phi_{i1} & \cdots & \sum_{i=1}^{N} y_i\phi_{iM} \\ \sum_{i=1}^{N} \phi_{i1} & \cdots & \sum_{i=1}^{N} \phi_{iM} \end{pmatrix}, \qquad \boldsymbol{P}^T\boldsymbol{P} = \begin{pmatrix} \sum_{i=1}^{N} x_i^2 & \sum_{i=1}^{N} x_i y_i & \sum_{i=1}^{N} x_i \\ \sum_{i=1}^{N} y_i x_i & \sum_{i=1}^{N} y_i^2 & \sum_{i=1}^{N} y_i \\ \sum_{i=1}^{N} x_i & \sum_{i=1}^{N} y_i & \sum_{i=1}^{N} 1 \end{pmatrix},$$

$$\boldsymbol{A}^T\boldsymbol{h} = \left(\sum_{i=1}^{N} \phi_{i1} h_i \;\; \cdots \;\; \sum_{i=1}^{N} \phi_{iM} h_i\right)^T, \qquad \boldsymbol{P}^T\boldsymbol{h} = \left(\sum_{i=1}^{N} x_i h_i \;\; \sum_{i=1}^{N} y_i h_i \;\; \sum_{i=1}^{N} h_i\right)^T.$$

It should be noted that additional conditions (3) introduce inconsistency to the least squares method. Specifically, the inconsistency is caused by adding the term $\boldsymbol{\Xi}^T\boldsymbol{\Xi}$ to $\boldsymbol{A}^T\boldsymbol{A}$. Therefore, the described RBF approximation with linear reproduction is inconveniently formulated, as it mixes variables which have a different physical meaning. Thus, another approach is proposed in the following section.

3. PROPOSED APPROACH

Let us consider that we have an unordered dataset $\{\boldsymbol{x}_i\}_1^N$ in E^2. However, note that this approach is generally applicable for d-dimensional space. Further, each point $\boldsymbol{x}_i$ from the dataset is associated with vector $\boldsymbol{h}_i \in E^p$ of given values, where p is the dimension of the vector, or a scalar value $h_i \in E^1$. For an explanation of the RBF approximation, let us consider the case in which each point $\boldsymbol{x}_i$ is associated with a scalar value h_i, e.g. a 2 ½D surface. Let us introduce a set of new reference points $\{\boldsymbol{\xi}_j\}_1^M$, see Figure 1.

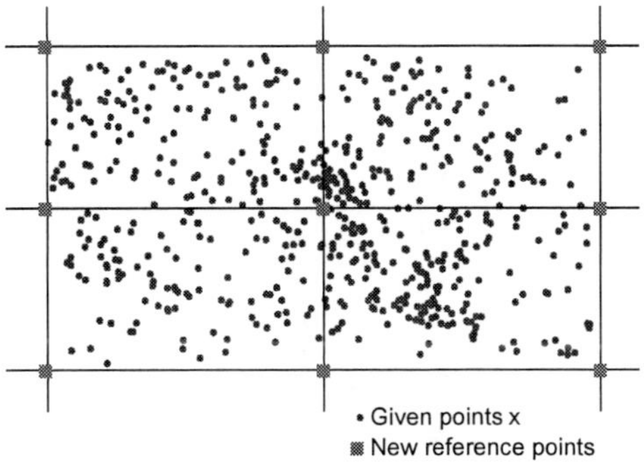

Figure 1. RBF approximation and reduction of points

It should be noted that these reference points may not necessarily be in a uniform grid. It is appropriate that their placements reflect the given surface behavior (e.g. the terrain profile, etc.) as well as possible. The number of added reference points $\boldsymbol{\xi}_j$ is M, where $M \ll N$. The RBF approximation is based on computing the distance of the given point $\boldsymbol{x}_i$ of the given dataset and the reference point $\boldsymbol{\xi}_j$ of the new reference points.

The approximated value can be expressed as:

$$f(\boldsymbol{x}) = \sum_{j=1}^{M} c_j \, \phi(\|\boldsymbol{x} - \boldsymbol{\xi}_j\|) \; + \; P_1(\boldsymbol{x}), \tag{6}$$

where the approximating function $f(\boldsymbol{x})$ is represented as a sum of M RBFs, each associated with a different reference point $\boldsymbol{\xi}_j$, and weighted by an appropriate coefficient c_j, and $P_1(\boldsymbol{x}) = \boldsymbol{a}^T \boldsymbol{x} + a_0$ is a linear polynomial. This linear polynomial should theoretically solve problems with stability and solvability.

It can be seen that for E^2 and the given dataset we get the following overdetermined LSE:

$$\boldsymbol{Ac} + \boldsymbol{Pk} = \boldsymbol{h}, \tag{7}$$

where $A_{ij} = \phi(\|\boldsymbol{x}_i - \boldsymbol{\xi}_j\|)$ is the entry of the matrix in the i-th row and j-th column, $\boldsymbol{c} = (c_1, \dots, c_M)^T$ is the vector of weights, $\boldsymbol{P}_i = (\boldsymbol{x}_i^T, 1)$ is the vector, $\boldsymbol{k} = (\boldsymbol{a}^T, a_0)^T$ is the vector of coefficients for the linear polynomial and $\boldsymbol{h} = (h_1, \dots, h_N)^T$ is the vector of values in the given points.

The error is then defined as:

$$R = \|\boldsymbol{Ac} + \boldsymbol{Pk} - \boldsymbol{h}\|, \tag{8}$$

then

$$R^2 = (\boldsymbol{Ac} + \boldsymbol{Pk} - \boldsymbol{h})^T(\boldsymbol{Ac} + \boldsymbol{Pk} - \boldsymbol{h}). \tag{9}$$

Our goal is to minimize the square of error, i.e. to find the minimum of R^2 (9). This minimum is obtained by differentiating equation (9) with respect to $\boldsymbol{c}$ and $\boldsymbol{k}$ and finding the zeros of those derivatives. This leads to equations:

$$\begin{aligned} \frac{\partial R^2}{\partial \boldsymbol{c}} &= 2(\boldsymbol{A}^T\boldsymbol{Ac} + \boldsymbol{A}^T\boldsymbol{Pk} - \boldsymbol{A}^T\boldsymbol{h}) = \boldsymbol{0}, \\ \frac{\partial R^2}{\partial \boldsymbol{k}} &= 2(\boldsymbol{P}^T\boldsymbol{Ac} + \boldsymbol{P}^T\boldsymbol{Pk} - \boldsymbol{P}^T\boldsymbol{h}) = \boldsymbol{0}, \end{aligned} \tag{10}$$

which leads to a system of linear equations:

$$\begin{pmatrix} \boldsymbol{A}^T\boldsymbol{A} & \boldsymbol{A}^T\boldsymbol{P} \\ \boldsymbol{P}^T\boldsymbol{A} & \boldsymbol{P}^T\boldsymbol{P} \end{pmatrix} \begin{pmatrix} \boldsymbol{c} \\ \boldsymbol{k} \end{pmatrix} = \begin{pmatrix} \boldsymbol{A}^T\boldsymbol{h} \\ \boldsymbol{P}^T\boldsymbol{h} \end{pmatrix}, \tag{11}$$

i.e.

$$\boldsymbol{B\lambda} = \boldsymbol{f}. \tag{12}$$

The matrix $\boldsymbol{B}$ is a $(M+3) \times (M+3)$ symmetric positively semidefinite matrix. Equation (11) can be expressed in the form:

$$\begin{pmatrix} \sum_{i=1}^{N}\phi_{i1}\phi_{i1} & \cdots & \sum_{i=1}^{N}\phi_{i1}\phi_{iM} & \sum_{i=1}^{N}\phi_{i1}x_i & \sum_{i=1}^{N}\phi_{i1}y_i & \sum_{i=1}^{N}\phi_{i1} \\ \vdots & \ddots & \vdots & \vdots & \vdots & \vdots \\ \sum_{i=1}^{N}\phi_{iM}\phi_{i1} & \cdots & \sum_{i=1}^{N}\phi_{iM}\phi_{iM} & \sum_{i=1}^{N}\phi_{iM}x_i & \sum_{i=1}^{N}\phi_{iM}y_i & \sum_{i=1}^{N}\phi_{iM} \\ \sum_{i=1}^{N}x_i\phi_{i1} & \cdots & \sum_{i=1}^{N}x_i\phi_{iM} & \sum_{i=1}^{N}x_i^2 & \sum_{i=1}^{N}x_iy_i & \sum_{i=1}^{N}x_i \\ \sum_{i=1}^{N}y_i\phi_{i1} & \cdots & \sum_{i=1}^{N}y_i\phi_{iM} & \sum_{i=1}^{N}y_ix_i & \sum_{i=1}^{N}y_i^2 & \sum_{i=1}^{N}y_i \\ \sum_{i=1}^{N}\phi_{i1} & \cdots & \sum_{i=1}^{N}\phi_{iM} & \sum_{i=1}^{N}x_i & \sum_{i=1}^{N}y_i & \sum_{i=1}^{N}1 \end{pmatrix} \begin{pmatrix} c_1 \\ \vdots \\ c_M \\ a_x \\ a_y \\ a_0 \end{pmatrix} = \begin{pmatrix} \sum_{i=1}^{N}\phi_{i1}h_i \\ \vdots \\ \sum_{i=1}^{N}\phi_{iM}h_i \\ \sum_{i=1}^{N}x_ih_i \\ \sum_{i=1}^{N}y_ih_i \\ \sum_{i=1}^{N}h_i \end{pmatrix}. \tag{13}$$

where $\phi_{ij} = \phi(\|\boldsymbol{x}_i - \boldsymbol{\xi}_j\|)$, point $\boldsymbol{x}_i = (x_i, y_i)^T$ and vector $\boldsymbol{a} = (a_x, a_y)^T$. It can be seen that this approach eliminates the inconsistency introduced in Section 2.

4. EXPERIMENTAL RESULTS

Both presented approaches of the RBF approximation have been compared for a dataset with a Halton distribution of points [Fasshauer, G.E., 2007] (Appendix A.1). Moreover, each point from this dataset is associated with a function value at this point. For this purpose, different functions have been used for experiments. Results for two such functions are presented here. The first is a $2D$ sinc function, see Figure 2 (left), and the second is Franke's function, see Figure 2 (right).

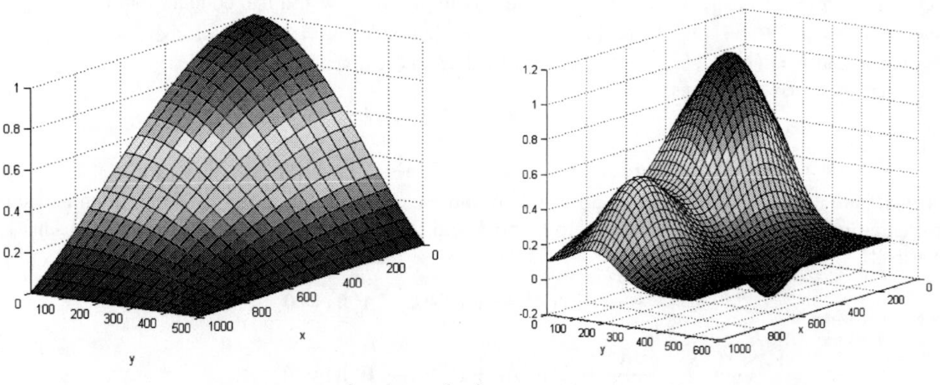

Figure 2. $2D$ sinc function defined as $\operatorname{sinc}\left(\frac{\pi x}{1000}\right)\operatorname{sinc}\left(\frac{\pi y}{500}\right)$, whose domain is restricted to $[0,1000] \times [0,500]$ (left) and Franke's function (right)

In addition, three different global radial basis functions with shape parameter α, see Table 1, have been used for testing. Also different sets of reference points have been used for experiments.

Table 1. Used global RBFs

RBF	$\phi(r)$
Gauss function	$e^{-(\alpha r)^2}$
Inverse Quadric (IQ)	$\frac{1}{1+(\alpha r)^2}$
Thin-Plate Spline (TPS)	$(\alpha r)^2 \log(\alpha r)$

These sets of reference points have different types of distributions. The presented types of distribution are the Halton distribution [Fasshauer, G.E., 2007] (Appendix A.1), see Figure 3 (left), an epsilon distribution, which is based on a random drift of points on a regular grid, see Figure 3 (right), and points on a regular grid.

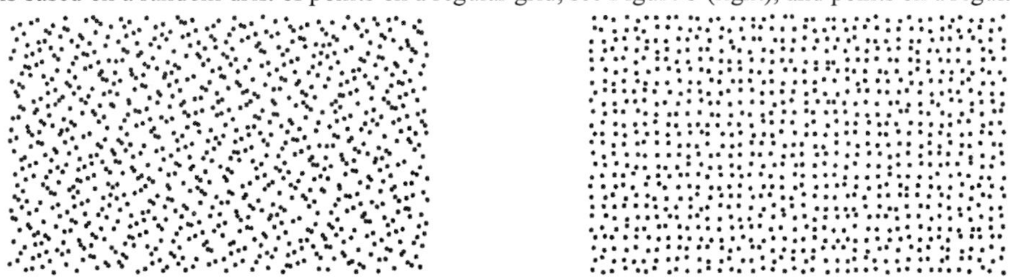

Figure 3. Halton points in E^2 (left) and epsilon points in E^2 (right). Number of points is 10^3 in both cases

4.1 Examples of RBF Approximation Results

An example of RBF approximation of 1089 Halton data points sampled from a $2D$ sinc function, for a Halton set of reference points which consists of 81 points, using both approaches is shown in Figure 4. The graphs are false-colored according to the magnitude of the error.

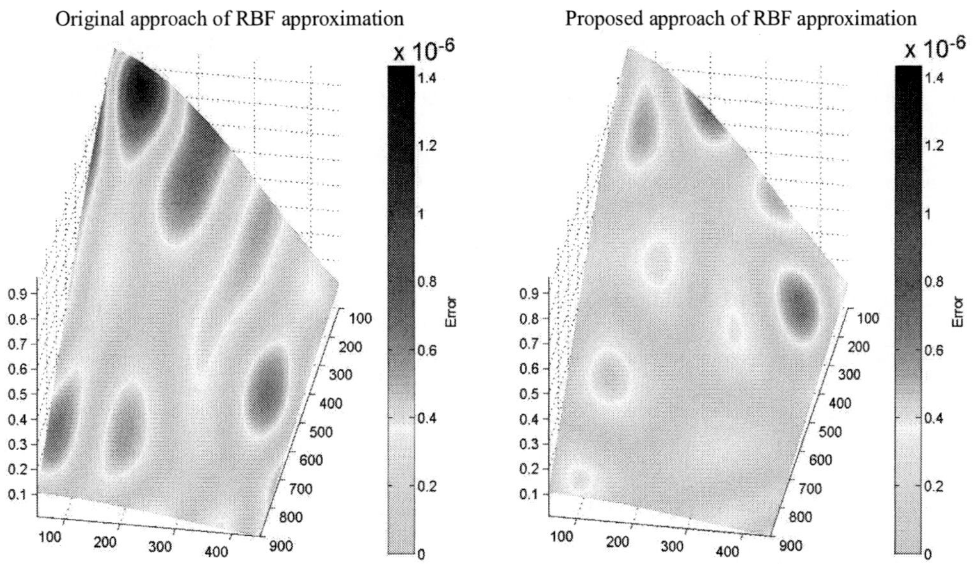

Figure 4. Approximation of 1089 data points sampled from a $2D$ sinc function, i.e. $\text{sinc}\left(\frac{\pi x}{1000}\right)\text{sinc}\left(\frac{\pi y}{500}\right)$, where $(x, y) \in [0,1000] \times [0,500]$, with 81 Halton-spaced Gaussian functions with $\alpha = 0.001$,false-colored by magnitude of error

A further example of RBF approximation of 4225 Halton data points sampled from a Franke's function and for a set of reference points which consists of 289 points on a regular grid, using both approaches is shown in Figure 5. The graphs are again false-colored by magnitude of error.

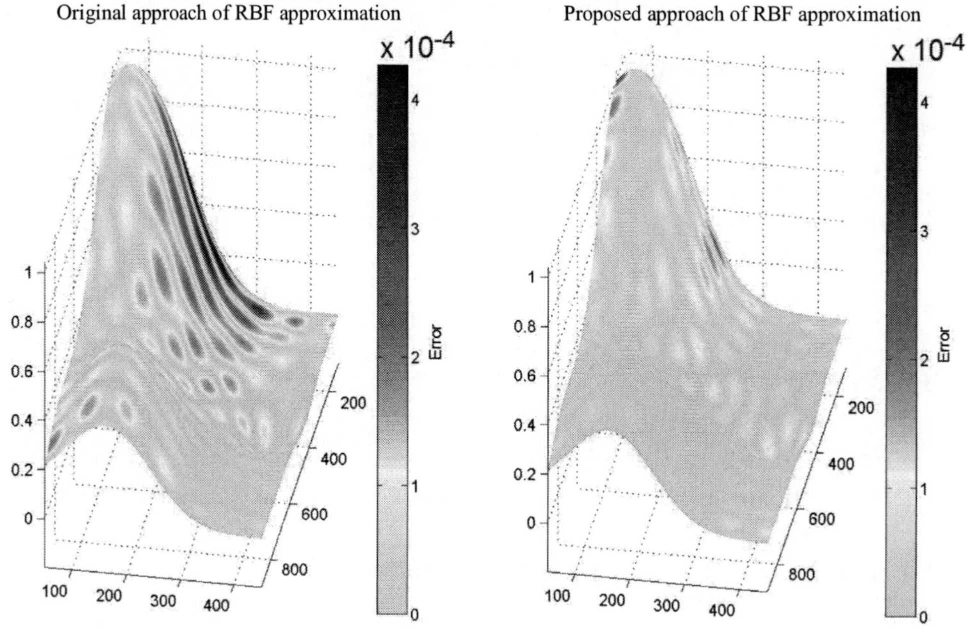

Figure 5. Approximation of 4225 data points sampled from a Franke's function with 289 regularly spaced IQ with $\alpha = 0.005$, false-colored by magnitude of error

It can be seen that the original RBF approximation with a linear reproduction returns a worse result in terms of the error in comparison with the proposed RBF approximation with a linear reproduction. Moreover, we can see from Figure 4 and Figure 5 that for the presented cases the maximum magnitude of error for the original approach is approximately two times greater than the maximum magnitude of error for the proposed approach.

There remains the question of how the RBF approximation depends on the shape parameter α selection. Many papers have been published about choosing optimal shape parameter α, e.g. [Franke, R., 1982], [Rippa, S., 1999], [Fasshauer, G.E. and Zhang, J.G., 2007], [Scheuerer, M., 2011]. In the following section, a comparison depending on the choice of shape parameter α is performed.

4.2 Comparison of Methods

In this section, the original approach and the proposed approach, which were presented in Section 2 and Section 3, are compared. Figure 6 presents the ratio of mean error of the original RBF approximation with the linear reproduction to the mean error of the proposed RBF approximation with the linear reproduction, i.e.:

$$ratio = \frac{mean\ error_{original}}{mean\ error_{proposed}}, \tag{14}$$

for a dataset which consists of 1089 Halton points in the range $[0,1000] \times [0,500]$, sampled from a $2D$ sinc function. The set of reference points contains 81 points with different behavior of the distribution, and for different global RBFs. Graphs in Figure 6 represent the experimentally obtained ratio according to the shape parameter α of the used RBFs.

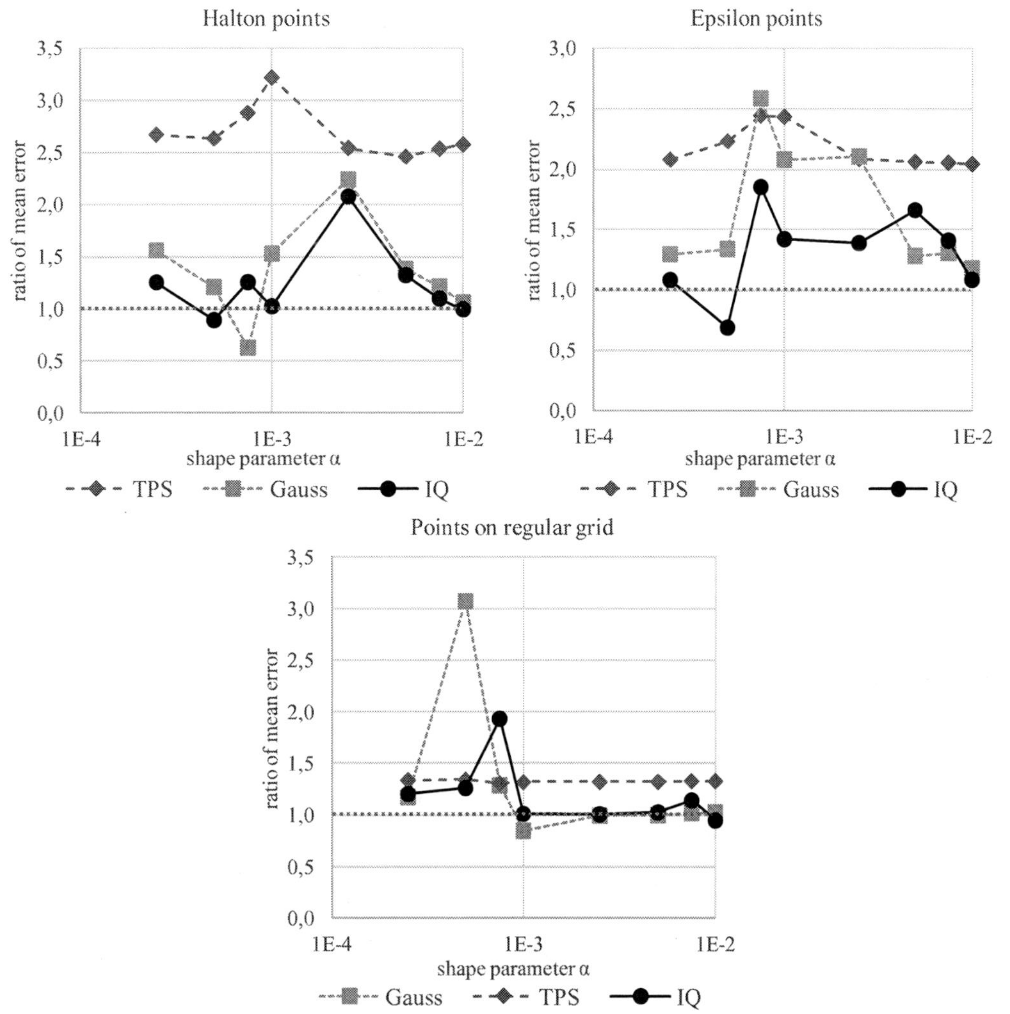

Figure 6. The ratio of mean error of the original approach to the mean error of the proposed approach of RBF approximation of 1089 data points sampled from a $2D$ sinc function with 81 reference points for different RBFs and different shape parameters. The used sets of reference points are: Halton points (top left), Epsilon points (top right) and points on a regular grid (bottom)

We can see that for the TPS, the mean errors of the proposed approach are significantly smaller than those of the original approach (ratio is greater than one). Furthermore, this ratio is not significantly different for the different shape parameters α. For the Gaussian function and epsilon reference points, the proposed RBF approximation gives better results than the original approach in terms of the mean error. In the remaining cases, with five exceptions, the proposed approach is also better.

The experiments prove that the proposed approach to RBF approximation is correct and gives better and more stable results than the original approach [Fasshauer, G.E., 2007].

5. CONCLUSION

This paper presents a new formulation for RBF approximation with a linear reproduction. The proposed approach eliminates inconsistency, which occurs in the original RBF approximation with a linear reproduction. This inconsistency is caused by adding additional conditions to the polynomial part. The experiments made prove that the proposed approach gives significantly better results than the original method in terms of accuracy. The presented approach is easily extendable for general polynomial reproduction and for higher dimensionality.

In future work, application of the proposed approach is to be performed on large real datasets and the performance can be further measured.

ACKNOWLEDGEMENT

The authors would like to thank their colleagues at the University of West Bohemia, Plzen, for their discussions and suggestions, and also anonymous reviewers for the valuable comments and suggestions they provided. The research was supported by MSMT CR projects LH12181 and SGS 2016-013.

REFERENCES

Carr, J.C. et al, 2001. Reconstruction and representation of 3D objects with radial basis functions. *Proceedings of the 28th Annual Conference on Computer Graphics and Interactive Techniques, SIGGRAPH 2001*, Los Angeles, California, USA, pp. 67-76.

Darve, E., 2000. The Fast Multipole Method: Numerical Implementation. *In Journal of Computational Physics*, Vol. 160, No. 1, pp. 195-240.

Duchon, J., 1977. Splines Minimizing Rotation-invariant Semi-norms in Sobolev Spaces. *In Constructive theory of functions of several variables*, pp. 85-100.

Fasshauer, G.E., 2007. *Meshfree Approximation Methods with MATLAB*. World Scientific Publishing Co., River Edge, NJ, USA.

Fasshauer, G.E. and Zhang, J.G., 2007. On choosing optimal shape parameters for RBF approximation. *In Numeric Algorithms*, Vol. 45, pp. 345-368.

Franke, R., 1982. Scattered data interpolation: tests of some methods. *In Mathematical Computing*, Vol. 38, pp. 181-200.

Hardy, R.L., 1971. Multiquadratic Equations of Topography and Other Irregular Surfaces. *In Journal of Geophysical Research*, Vol. 76, No. 8, pp. 1905-1915.

Pan, R. and Skala, V., 2011a. Continuous Global Optimization in Surface Reconstruction from an Oriented Point Cloud. *In Computer-Aided Design*, Vol. 43, No. 8, pp. 896-901.

Pan, R. and Skala, V., 2011b. A Two-level Approach to Implicit Surface Modeling with Compactly Supported Radial Basis Functions. *In Eng. Comput. (Lond.)*, Vol. 27, No. 3, pp. 299-307.

Rippa, S., 1999. An algorithm for selecting a good value for the parameter c in radial basis function interpolation. *In Adv. Comput. Math.*, Vol. 11, pp. 193-210.

Schagen, I.P, 1979. Interpolation in Two Dimensions - a New Technique. *In IMA Journal of Applied Mathematics*, Vol. 23, No. 1, pp. 53-59.

Scheuerer, M., 2011. An alternative procedure for selecting a good value for the parameter c in RBF-interpolation. *In Adv. Comput. Math.*, Vol. 34, pp. 105-126.

Skala, V. et al, 2013. Simple 3D Surface Reconstruction Using Flatbed Scanner and 3D Print. *SIGGRAPH Asia 2013, Poster Proceedings.* Hong Kong, China, p. 7.

Skala, V. et al, 2014. Making 3D Replicas Using a Flatbed Scanner and a 3D Printer. *Computational Science and Its Applications - ICCSA 2014 - 14th International Conference, Proceedings, Part VI.* Guimarães, Portugal, pp. 76-86.

Turk, G. and O'Brien, J.F., 2002. Modelling with implicit surfaces that interpolate. *In ACM Trans. Graph.*, Vol. 21, No. 4, pp. 855-873.

Uhlir, K. and Skala, V., 2005. Reconstruction of Damaged Images Using Radial Basis Functions. *Proceedings of EUSIPCO.* Antalya, Turkey, p. 160.

Wendland, H., 2006. Computational Aspects of Radial Basis Function Approximation. *In Studies in Computational Mathematics*, Vol. 12, pp. 231-256.

Zapletal, J. et al, 2009. RBF-based Image Restoration Utilizing Auxiliary Points. *Proceedings of the 2009 Computer Graphics International Conference.* Victoria, British Columbia, Canada, pp. 39-43.

INTERACTIVE VISUALIZATION OF MASSIVE 3D POINT CLOUDS

Jörg Futterlieb, Christian Teutsch and Dirk Berndt
Fraunhofer Institute for Factory Operation and Automation IFF
Measurement and Testing Technology
Sandtorstr. 22, 39106 Magdeburg, Germany

ABSTRACT

We present a technique for rendering and processing massive point clouds from 3D scanners on a standard computer system where the data size exceeds the RAM and VRAM. We utilize the capabilities of modern GPU hardware to achieve interactive framerates and a smooth visualization. These techniques enhance existing large data visualization techniques, like Level of Detail and deferred rendering approaches to handle large and unstructured 3d scan data. The data size is only limited by the hard disk memory available. We verify the methods developed at the example of different data sets with up to one billion 3D points.

KEYWORDS

3D Point clouds, Level of Detail, Deferred rendering, Out-of-core

1. INTRODUCTION

Non-contact optical methods of 3D digitization have replaced conventional methods in many applications. Regardless of the varying 3D measuring principles - many millions of measured 3D data are generated within a few seconds. This data delivers a description of a digitized component's surface topography. 3D scanning has a wide distribution in different industrial applications, e.g. in quality assurance or reverse engineering. Even whole environments from buildings to large industrial plants are digitized which results in a massive amount of 3D points that need to be processed and visualized.

The rapidly developing market of 3D sensors provides high-speed light-section scanners for industrial measurement applications that produce 3D scanlines of 1000 points with a frequency of 1000 Hz. So it takes just a second to generate a million 3D points. Even consumer products like a Microsoft Kinect generate more than 300.000 points per scan. Especially terrestrial laser scanners (TLS) and time of flight (TOF) cameras show a rapid development with regards to acquisition speed and scan data resolution.

Very often several scans from different places or viewing directions are aligned and merged together to produce a connected and comprehensive 3D representation. Finally we have to deal with hundreds of millions and up to a few billions of 3D points with many gigabytes of data which makes the fast processing and rendering of the 3D data a challenging task. In this work we are facing this problem with efficient methods for 3D data management and processing while keeping a special focus on massive 3D data visualization approaches based on deferred rendering methods using standard computer systems.

Large 3D data visualization is an active research area with several strategies and methods presented in the last years. We discuss previous and related work in section 2. In section 3 we present our approach for the interactive visualization of massive 3D point clouds, including the used hierarchical data structures, enhanced Level of Detail (LOD) algorithms and the (deferred) rendering pipeline. Section 4 discusses experimental results achieved with our implementation. Section 5 concludes and summarizes this work.

2. RELATED WORK

The interactive visualization of massive 3D point clouds has three major topics that we need to consider. At first structuring the raw 3D point cloud data is discussed because it needs to balance efficient data storage and fast data access for the 3D search & query algorithms. In order to provide a real-time interaction Level of Detail techniques for reducing the point cloud complexity are considered as the second task. Lastly, we consider approaches for the smooth and appealing visualization with latest deferred rendering methods.

Structuring the raw 3D point data is an integral component of our visualization framework, because the selection of visible points and the access to certain detail levels requires efficient spatial neighborhood queries. For the visualization of large volume data variants of Octrees are typically used (Wenzel, 2014; Wimmer & Scheiblauer, 2006), because they subdivide the entire space into regularly sized cells and voxels which can be addressed and accessed easily. They have proven to perform well for real-time 3D collision detection (Weller et al., 2013). Due to the regular subdivision scheme the efficiency of Octrees strongly depends on the distribution of data within the volume considered. 3D point clouds from optical (laser) scanners are representing an object's surface but not a volume, and additionally, these point clouds are often composed of partly overlaying scans which results in an inconstant point density. Thus, more flexible spatial data structures like AABB-trees and the variants of kd-trees (Richter et al., 2015; Goswami et al., 2012) are more suitable for our task. Kd-trees already show a high performance for 3D point clouds, e.g. for point cloud registration and pre-processing like smoothing, thinning and segmentation (Teutsch, 2007). Data storage and stream-wise processing of the huge point cloud is often done by well-known memory mapping techniques (Rusinkiewicz & Levoy, 2000; Dementiev et al., 2005). Additionally, there are Big Data storage schemes, where the data is stored and processed on a distributed filesystem (Boehm, 2014).

The second task is the application of Level of Detail (LOD) techniques. These methods generate down-sampled representations of the original (huge) data set in order to compute a resolution which depends on the distance between the virtual camera and the 3d data. The LOD may be discrete or hierarchical. The discrete methods provide various models in different resolutions that represent the same object, which are computed in advance. They are typically used for the LOD of polygonal meshes (Ribelles et al., 2010). On the other hand hierarchical methods encode the detail levels in a tree structure, where the tree layers provide representative points for specific volume clusters (Richter et al., 2015; Goswami et al., 2012).

The third task, the rendering part, is done by using pure point primitives or subsets of points which are approximated by another primitive e.g. the QSplat approach (Rusinkiewicz & Levoy, 2000). Botsch et al. (2005) gives an overview on point-based rendering techniques. They also discussing a GPU-accelerated approach with Deferred Shading, a render pipeline we further extend within this paper. Classic culling techniques like Frustum Culling, Backface Culling (Rusinkiewicz & Levoy, 2000), which are mostly known from polygonal meshes, are also appropriate for point clouds. Since most approaches focus on rendering just one data set, we also describe a method to handle and visualize many data sets simultaneously. Therefore, we introduce a scheduling mechanism which always ensures framerates required for interactive visualization. The overall performance and the interactive visualization are driven by a deferred rendering approach (Ferko, 2012), which reduces the amount of data to be rendered in one rendering call in contrast to classical fixed-pipeline techniques.

3. MASSIVE 3D DATA RENDERING

The choice of our data structure is determined by a trade-off between two objectives. On the one hand, we would like to use bounding volumes for the LOD approach that need only a few bytes to store them, and that enable fast visibility tests and distance computations. On the other hand, we want the bounding volumes fit the corresponding 3D point cloud data tightly. Thus, we decided to use a variant of a kd-tree as a common spatial 3D structure both for processing and visualization of the point clouds. In each level of the tree hierarchy the splitting planes provide the required bounding boxes. We benefit from the fact that the kd-tree is always balanced and that it encodes the required detail levels in its hierarchy with an even, regular distribution. Although the build time for a kd-tree is higher that e.g. for an octree, neighborhood search queries are processed in less time on average (Wenzel, 2014; Teutsch, 2007). The data storage and access to the massive amount of data is done via file mapping methods provided by the filesystem, which is comparable to the approach Richter et al. (2015). Our kd-tree build routine takes care that neighboring points in deep hierarchies are stored close to each other.

Our approach renders pure point primitives instead of approximating subsets by some primitives (like in the QSplat approach from Rusinkiewicz & Levoy, 2000). This is important for the later data analysis steps, where we need to ensure that all visible data is real scan data and not an approximation.

In the following we describe the data structures and algorithms for handling and rendering the point cloud data. The concept is divided into three sections, the Level of Detail techniques to select visible points from the data set, the pipeline for rendering the point data and lastly the scheduling of multiple point clouds.

3.1 Level of Detail Techniques

In order to guarantee a smooth and interactive visualization we need to adaptively select a subset of the whole point cloud for two reasons. At first the entire data set does not fit into the main memory (RAM) or the graphics memory (VRAM). Thus we need to load from the hard disk only that amount of points that is currently visible for the user. Secondly we further reduce the amount of visible points because it cannot be larger than the total number of pixel of the screen (~ 2M for a HD screen with 1920x1080 pixels). The less we load from the filesystem the faster the visualization will be since we wanted to achieve a real-time rendering and a smooth interaction with at least 60 frames per second.

Our rendering concept starts with a low resolution overview point set (2M points), which is statically stored in the VRAM and always ensures that data is visible between detail level switches. The transition between detail levels itself is smoothed by applying the deferred rendering approaches in the later steps. Depending on the distance of the virtual camera to the 3d data and the size of the viewing volume we dynamically extract a number of points from the detail levels of the kd-tree.

3.1.1 Extracting Levels of Detail

Since kd-trees recursively split the 3D volume into clusters of nearly the same point count, we take the corresponding and required detail levels directly from the tree hierarchy. The detail level count equals the tree depth, which is the logarithm of the point count. The amount of overview points is controlled to guarantee a framerate of at least 60 Hz. The tree level for the overview point cloud is computed by the following formula:

$$Treelevel_{Overview} = \log_2(\mathrm{N}_{\mathrm{OverviewPoints}})$$

We define the number of overview points as maximum value. The computed tree level is rounded to the next lower integer value.

The frustum queried is partitioned into successive axis-aligned bounding boxes for a fast point query from the kd-tree. A test for a point inside an axis-aligned bounding box is much cheaper than testing against six frustum planes, but viewing aslope along coordinate axes and especially in perspective projection the bounding box of the frustum also covers a large non-visible volume. We prevent that by dividing into smaller and disjoint axis-aligned boxes. Furthermore if the user is primarily interested in a detailed view of the camera-near points, the details are cached and rendered from near-to-far to show interesting details faster. Figure 1 shows this box-based partition steps.

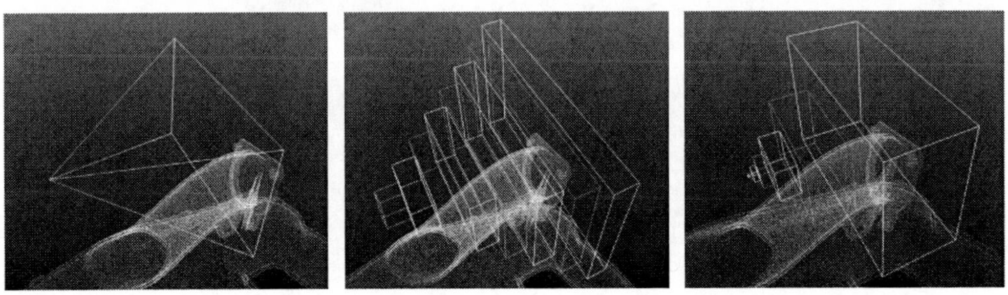

Figure 1. Illustration of a perspective frustum (left) and the frustum partition into axis-aligned boxes (middle and right), which are used for queuing data from the kd-tree. The middle image shows a partition with constant box depth (green marks the camera nearest box) and the right image shows an exponentially increasing box depth

A smaller axis-aligned box can still include several millions of points. Therefore we use the overview data to determine an adequate tree level for data queueing with the following function:

$$Treelevel_{Details} = Treelevel_{Overview} + \log_2(\frac{N_{IP}}{N_{OPIF}}),\ with\ N_{IP} > N_{OPIF} > 0.$$

The tree level for queueing the detailed point data depends on the ratio of the overview points already inside the frustum (N_{OPIF}) and the number of points to find (equals number of image pixels N_{IP}). When zooming into the point cloud, fewer overview points are inside the frustum and thus the tree level will be increased and more detailed data of the specific view volume is queued. In contrast to the overview point cloud, we do not take all points from the computed tree level. Depending on the tree depth, there may be several hundred million points in a tree level. We use the axis-aligned boxes computed previously to query the detailed point data from the tree. The tree is recursively traversed from the root node and if the computed tree level is reached, the respective points are rendered and a deeper tree traversal is canceled. This way of tree traversal only addresses the subset of the potentially visible points in a tree level.

In addition to the classical frustum culling we apply a detail culling that uses the current detail volume. If all points of this volume, respective subtree, would be mapped onto the same pixel the kd-tree traversal is stopped.

3.1.2 Caching and Blending LOD levels

Caching and rendering of a detailed view may take some seconds depending on the entire data set size. Thus we display intermediary results, generated at discrete time intervals, e.g. every second. For a smooth LOD transition we additionally apply an image-based blending that significantly reduces unwanted popup effects between different LOD resolutions. The detailed view is also cached on the GPU by using a Compute Shader (see section 3.2). This enables us to permanently show this view when moving the camera – only additional details are then blend into the existing view.

3.2 Deferred Rendering Methods

For rendering the point clouds we use a Deferred Rendering Pipeline (Pintus, 2011). Instead of rendering directly to the framebuffer we utilize a multi-pass approach consisting of a geometry pass followed by a lighting pass. In the first pass point attributes (position, normal vector, depth and color) are rendered into buffers (so called multiple render targets (MRTs)). These MRTs are separate texture buffers for each point attribute (see figure 2). The lighting pass computes the shading for each visible pixel *deferred* in a shader program while rendering the scene into the framebuffer (we use a full screen quad).

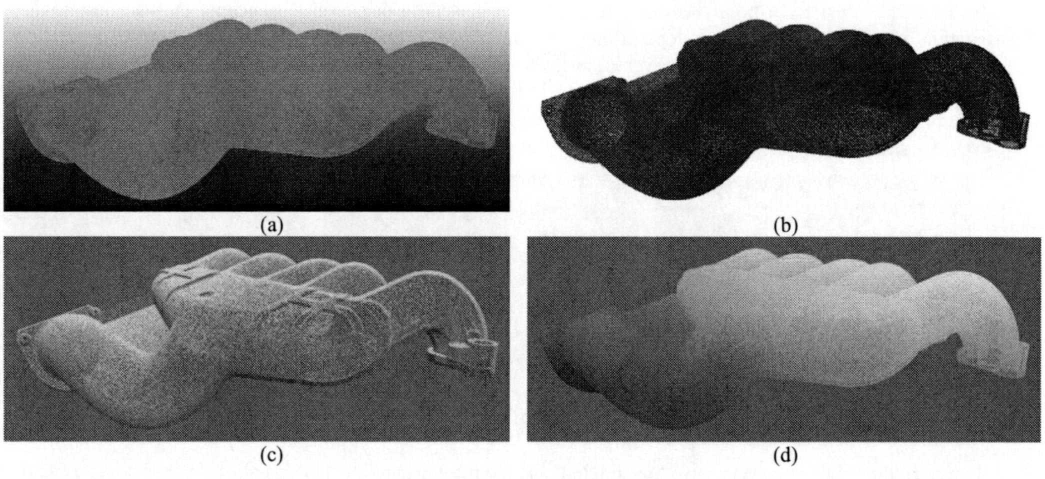

Figure 2. Multiple Render Target of the Deferred Rendering Pipeline containing a color buffer (a), depth buffer (b), normal buffer (c) and a position buffer (d)

In our visualization approach we enhance this procedure by applying the following steps iteratively:

1. Extract a subset of points from the kd-tree that is located inside the viewing frustum (we use 100.000 points in a local point buffer for each iteration).
2. Render the points into the MRTs, where the point attributes are stored in separated texture buffers. Within each iteration we only complement already existing information in the texture buffers (details are accumulated, see section 3.2.1).
3. Render a full screen quad to the framebuffer and apply the shading.
4. If all detailed point data is extracted then rendering is finished, otherwise continue again with step 1.

In order to achieve a good ratio of detail degree and processing time we extract points from a specific tree level only (corresponding to the number of screen pixels, see 3.1.1.). Otherwise, we traverse the entire tree via breadth-first search if we prefer to generate a full detailed image, which has longer processing times.

This rendering method improves the LOD performance by at least 30 percent, because the CPU does no time-delaying depth test and sends selected and probably visible points directly to the GPU which performs the Z-test extremely fast. This strategy reduces the work load of the CPU (for preselection of visible points) and utilizes the high bandwidth to the GPU and finally shortens the loading time of a detail level.

3.2.1 Detail Accumulation

If the camera is not moving, the render target will not be cleared and the cached detailed point data is rendered iteratively into the existing image (see a scheme of the pipeline in figure 3). The possibly visible points are cached stepwise from the kd-tree via breadth-first search and are then rendered.

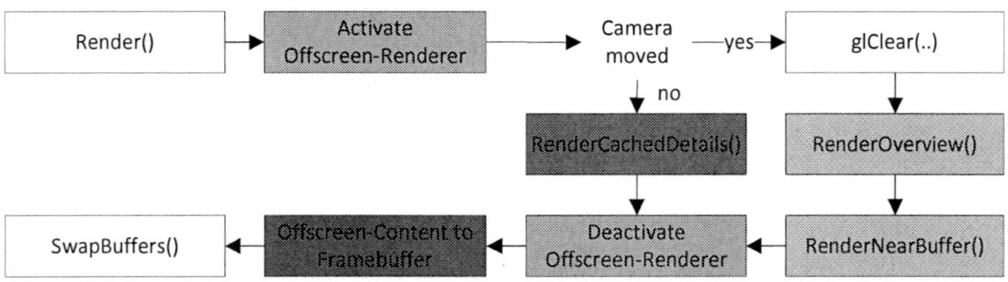

Figure 3. Scheme of the detail accumulation pipeline. All point data is rendered into an offscreen render target (green). If the camera has moved since last frame, the render target is cleared and the overview points as well as the cached detailed points from last frame are rendered (orange). If the camera stands still, only cached detailed points are added (red). Finally the content of the render target is rendered to the framebuffer for displaying the image on screen (blue)

This deferred detail accumulation pipeline allows a fully detailed view of the scene, even on low spec computer systems (OpenGL 2.X). When the camera position and orientation is constant between frames, no geometry is rendered twice, which results in high framerates. Figure 4 shows the detail accumulation from overview point cloud to full detailed point cloud.

Figure 4. Detail accumulation for 650M points: Overview data is always rendered (left). If the camera is not moved, details are accumulated (middle and right image) whereat the transition is blended smoothly at constant time intervals

3.2.2 Image-based LOD-Blending

We extended the rendering pipeline with two more render targets. Points from the kd-tree are rendered into the first target (which is never displayed on screen). The second and the third render target are shown on screen and are implementing a double buffer strategy. At discrete time intervals (e.g. 1 second) the images from the first render target are copied to the second or third render target. The visible change of the detail level is achieved via a continuous toggling and blending of the image from the second and third render target. This enables a computationally cheap and smooth LOD transition.

The detailed view is always inside the first render target. To render this data, when the camera is moving, the vertex/color/normal data is copied from the images of the Multiple Render Targets into a Vertex Buffer Object via a Compute Shader (OpenGL 4.3). Caching and rendering of the last near detailed view is done completely on the GPU.

3.3 Scheduling the Rendering of Multiple Data Sets

In our application we handle multiple point clouds with a scheduler mechanism. The scheduler provides a point stash for the overview point cloud, which is separated in N sections for N point clouds. The scheduler also provides a thread pool. The threads are processing tasks for data visualization by considering and scheduling the resource usage (free physical memory, disk usage) of each task. We split the operations for data processing and visualization into six major tasks. The first task indexes the file and quickly generates an overview. The next task computes the leafs and the nodes of the kd-tree. Afterwards, a task recomputes the overview point cloud based on the kd-tree. Overview recomputation is also done, when a new point cloud was loaded, or if a point cloud was removed from the scene. A subsequent task is queuing and rendering the detailed point cloud data. Finally there are two tasks for storing and loading a kd-tree from a file. Figure 5 shows the components of the scheduling concept.

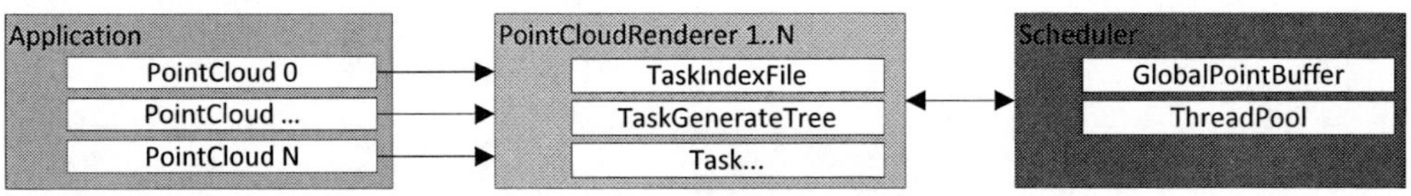

Figure 5. Each point cloud is handled by an instance of a PointCloudRenderer. Each PointCloudRenderer registers to a scheduler, which provides a global point buffer and a thread pool, which processes the tasks of each PointCloudRenderer in an ordered way due to resource usage (e.g. Hard disk I/O)

4. RESULTS AND DISCUSSION

We tested our implementation on a standard pc system, which contains an Intel i5-4670 processor, 8 GB RAM, a Nvidia GeForce GTX 760 graphics card and an Intel SSD with 180 GB. All test point clouds are stored in an Ascii-Format, where each line contains 3 floats for the position and three integers for the color of a point. We used data sets with up to 1 billion points (figure 6) for our evaluation.

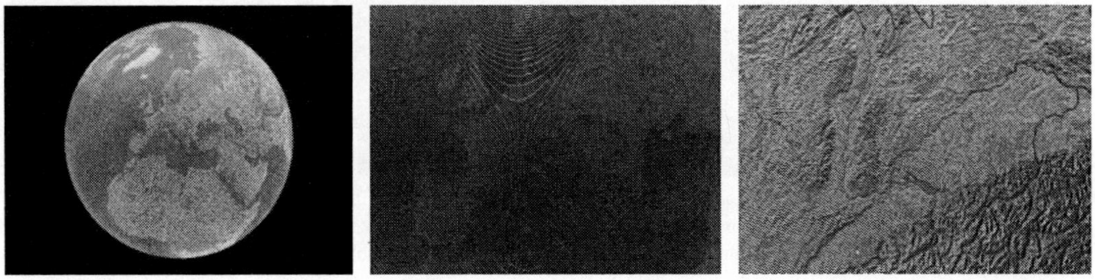

Figure 6. From left to right: Zoom into a 3D point cloud of earth data with 1 billion points (file size is 42.2 GB)

The rendered overview in each test case has 8 million points. When moving the camera, we always achieve a high interactive framerate with at least 150 fps at a 1920 x 1080 pixel resolution. We achieve up to 4000 fps, when the camera stands still, since detailed points are only added and are not rendered multiple times. This results in a very low input lag as one would expect from computer games. Nevertheless, the process of successively extracting all the points which are currently visible typically takes less than a second and depends on the file I/O performance of the system. In order to steadily provide feedback to the user we show intermediate results at discrete time intervals (with a smooth transition via image-based blending). Table 1 shows the processing time for individual steps of multiple test cases.

In addition, our detail accumulation technique is not limited to render static scenes. Via Compute Shader or a Shading Language it would be possible to mix the images with a dynamic scene (e.g. live sensor data).

Table 1. Processing times for example point clouds. Data set 1, 2 and 3 are single point clouds. Data set 4 is the data set 1 divided into 8 parts with nearly same point size (to evaluate the scheduling mechanism for multiple point clouds). Data set 5 is the divided data set 2. The tree building time is much lower in the divided data sets, due to the scheduling system. The time for the visible full detailed view depends on the view position and ranges from milliseconds to seconds. In typical viewing scenarios the full detailed view is available in less than a second. The last row of the table shows the maximum time measured from multiple different viewpoints

	Data set 1	Data set 2	Data set 3	Data set 4	Data set 5
Points	65m	233m	1bn	8 x 8m	8 x 29m
File size	2.6 GB	9.9 GB	42.2 GB	8 x 0.3 GB	8 x 1.2 GB
Index xyzc-file (total)	7.96 sec	29.91 sec	126.72 sec	7.90 sec	32.07 sec
Build kd-tree (total)	23.69 sec	260.90 sec	1691.31 sec	18.77 sec	78.19 sec
Detailed view (max)	6.02 sec	15.11 sec	46.71 sec	4.11 sec	14.95 sec

5. SUMMARY

In this paper we have presented techniques for the LOD rendering of massive 3D point clouds with up to a billion of 3D points utilizing an out of core data storage. In addition to improved technologies for structuring the raw data by using trees and memory mapping techniques for accessing massive data sets, we provided enhancements to existing LOD techniques. We extended the Deferred Rendering Pipeline to accumulate details and blend the LOD levels via image-based blending. Furthermore we introduced a scheduling system to handle and render multiple point clouds with interactive framerates. The techniques proposed extend existing approaches for the visualization of large volume data and large polygonal data to unstructured raw point data from optical 3D scanners. At the example of real test data sets we have shown that the implementation enables a fast and smooth exploration of massive point clouds on a standard computer system with interactive framerates.

REFERENCES

Wenzel, K. et al., 2014. Filtering of Point Clouds from Photogrammetric Surface Reconstruction. In *ISPRS – International Archives of the Photogrammetry, Remote Sensing and Spatial Information Sciences, Volume XL-5*, pp. 615-620

Wimmer, M., Scheiblauer, C., 2006. Instant Points: Fast Rendering of Unprocessed Point Clouds. In *Proceedings of the 3rd Eurographics / IEEE VGTC Conference on Point-Based Graphics*, pp. 129-136

Richter, R. et al., 2015. Out-of-core Visualization of Classified 3D Point Clouds. In *3D Geoinformation Science - The Selected Papers of the 3D GeoInfo 2014*, Springer International Publishing, pp. 227-242

Goswami, P. et al., 2012. An efficient multiresolution framework for high quality interactive rendering of massive point clouds using multi-way kd-trees. In *The Visual Computer Volume 29, Issue 1*, pp. 69-83

Rusinkiewicz, S., Levoy, M., 2000. QSplat: A Multiresolution Point Rendering System for Large Meshes. In *Proceedings of the 27th Annual Conference on Computer Graphics and Interactive Techniques*, pp. 343-352

Dementiev, R. et al., 2005. STXXL: Standard Template Library for XXL Data Sets. In *Algorithms - ESA 2005*, Springer Berlin Heidelberg, pp. 640-651

Boehm, J., 2014. File-centric Organization of large LiDAR Point Clouds in a Big Data context. In *Workshop on processing large geospatial data*, Cardiff, UK

Botsch, M. et al., 2005. High-Quality Surface Splatting on Todays GPUs. In *Proceedings of the Second Eurographics / IEEE VGTC Conference on Point-Based Graphics*, pp. 17-24

Pintus, R. et al., 2011. Real-time Rendering of Massive Unstructured Raw Point Clouds Using Screen-space Operators. In *Proc. of the 12th International Conference on Virtual Reality, Archaeology and Cultural Heritage*, pp. 105-112

Teutsch, C., 2007. Model-based Analysis and Evaluation of Point Sets from Optical 3D Laser Scanners. Shaker Verlag GmbH, Germany

Weller R., et al., 2013. Parallel collision detection in constant time. In *Virtual Reality Interactions and Physical Simulations (VRIPhys),* Lille, France, Eurographics Association, pp. 61-70

Ribelles, J., et al., 2010. An Improved Discrete Level of Detail Model Through an Incremental Representation. In *EG UK Theory and Practice of Computer Graphics*, pp. 59-66

Ferko, M., 2012. *Real-time Lighting Effects Using Deferred Shading: Creating a System for Real-time Rendering Without Relying on Pre-computation.* Lap Lambert Academic Publishing

International Conferences Interfaces and Human Computer Interaction 2016,
Game and Entertainment Technologies 2016 and
Computer Graphics, Visualization, Computer Vision and Image Processing 2016

DETECTING AND EXTRACTING SCENE TEXT IN DIGITAL IMAGES VIA SRC

Jun He, Bo Sun*, Yang Wu, Xiaoming Zhu and Yungang Wei
College of Information Science and Technology, Beijing Normal University
Xinjiekouwai Street No. 19, Beijing, China, 100875
(*Address all correspondence to: Bo Sun, Fax: 86-01058800315)

ABSTRACT

This paper proposes a new approach to detect the scene text in digital images more precisely and efficiently. The proposed approach includes image filtering, edge extraction, morphologic processing and SRC method. The experimental results demonstrate that our approach is effective and efficient for the scene text extraction and our accuracy and recall rate are all promising.

KEYWORDS

Scene Text, Text Region Detection, Sparse Representation, SRC

1. INTRODUCTION

Although the increasing matureness on optical character recognition (OCR) technology, recognizing scan text has been unable to meet the needs of our daily life. As a kind of high level semantic information, scene text is an auxiliary illustration to image content [1]. In recent decade, more and more people utilize mobile phones to shoot pictures everywhere and every time. So how to correctly recognize the scene text has become a new challenge to the traditional OCR technology [2][3][4][5]. Conventional OCR technology includes two steps: text detection and text recognition. At present, the development of scene text recognition has reached a bottleneck. In order to overcome this problem, the scholars pay more attentions to scene text detection for reducing the candidate blocks of OCR [6]. Unlike scan text, scene text is more complex and random. The objective factors of influencing the scene text detection often relate to illumination, scale, perspective, fuzzy, etc., some of which are shown in Figure 1.

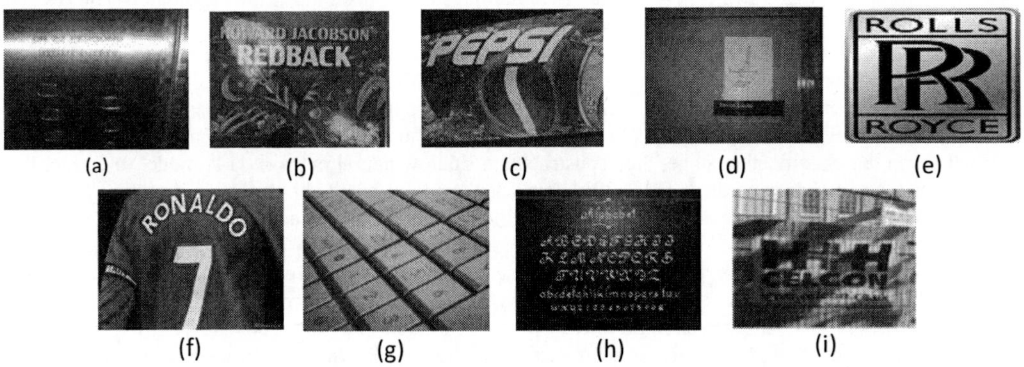

Figure 1. Typical difficulties in scene text detection
(a) Uneven Illumination, (b) Different Size, (c) Perspective Transformation, (d) Transparent Letters, (e) Overlap, (f) Winding Arrangement, (g) Fuzzy, (h) Word Art, (i) Shelter

According to different features (such as color, density, edge, corner, texture and stroke) of scene text regions, there are usually 6 methods, which are shown as follows.

(1) The method based on connected region analysis. It first utilizes the color or gray feature describing the differences between foreground and background. Then it connects the small connected regions to the large ones gradually by region clustering analysis, color quantization or histogram segmentation methods [7].

(2) The method based on edge feature extraction. It takes the advantages of the image edge with mathematical morphology processing operators and heuristic rules.

(3) The method based on corner feature extraction. It constructs a corner feature operator by the abundant image corner information and uses clustering and filtering methods to obtain scene text output. Figure 2 shows the Harris corner of scene text images.

Figure 2. Harris Corner of Scene Text Image

(4) The method based on stroke density. It constructs a stroke filter to obtain the feature blocks in scene text regions. Figure 3 shows different stroke density of the same scene text.

Figure 3. Different stroke density of the same scene text

(5) The method based on texture analysis: It utilize the textural difference between foreground and background to obtain the textural feature by wavelet transform, FFT, Gabor filtering, spatial variance and then eliminate the image noises to obtain scene text regions.

(6) The method based on machine learning: Scene text detection is a two classification via machine learning method. It needs to construct a sample library and build a classifier by ANN [25], SVM [26][27], MLP [28], etc. After classifier training, it can distinguish the candidate scene text blocks with other feature analysis methods.

ICDAR (International Conference on Document Analysis and Recognition) is the most influential academic conference in this field so far. In ICPR 2014, Microsoft Research Asia published their latest research achievements in this field. They used a CER (contrasting extremal region) [8] method as an improved method based on ER [9][12] method and MSER (maximally stable extremal region) [10][11][13] method. In the classification stage, they constructed a shallow neural network [14] model to extract the text areas in connected regions. In ICDAR-2013 test set, their final result shows 92.1% detection accuracy and 92.3% recall rate. Compared with the previous methods, their algorithm achieves great improvement in this field.

While in our latest research [15], we have used the SRC (sparse representation based classification) method to detect and extract text regions from a video. Unlike with Microsoft, we use the edge extraction operator [16][17][18], the morphologic close operator (dilation and corrosion) [19][20] and the connected region analysis method [21][22] to extract the candidate text blocks. In processing stage, we utilize SRC [23] as the classification model. In experiments, it has gained 95.4% text accuracy and 90.2% non-text accuracy. However, its partial-text accuracy is only 76.2%. Therefore, further study is preceded.

In this paper, we adopt ICDAR-2013 data set as our experimental data set and construct a partial-text classifier by SRC specially. Compared with [15], we build an image filter before using edge extraction operator in pre-processing stage and construct a Gaussian pyramid [24] in SRC processing stage. The experimental result shows the accuracy of partial-text detection is improved better and we have a promising recall rate. The remainder of this paper is organized as follows. Section 2 gives a detailed description on our work. The experimental results are presented in Section 3 and we summarize this paper in Section 4.

2. PROPOSED METHOD

2.1 Pre-Processing

Generally, the existing scene text detection methods can be roughly divided into three categories: sliding window based method, connected component based method and hybrid method. In our latest research, we first analyzed the connected component in pre-processing stage to obtain candidate text areas, then dealt with the test signals by sliding window with a step of 3 pixels, 5 pixels or 7 pixels.

However, considering the relationship between two neighboring frames, the noise often exists in the same regions of continuous frames, which has not be considered in [15]. While in this paper, since the ICDAR data set is of static images, before the edge extraction, we use image filtering to clear the noises in images. Averaging filtering [29], median filtering [30][31] and Gaussian filtering [32][33] are three most popular methods in denoising (Others are minimum variance filtering [34], Gabor filtering [35], etc.) and they have their own characteristics as following. Averaging filtering, as a simple method, can smooth the image and the speed is fast, but it cannot remove the noise completely. Median filtering is a common nonlinear filtering method, which can deal with smooth impulse noise very well and protect the sharp edge of images. However, it is necessary to introduce directional information when filtering the strong directional text images. That is we should take advantage of the text orientation to guide median filtering. Gaussian filtering is a linear smooth filtering method. It can eliminate Gaussian noise by the weighted average of a whole image. Processing each pixel in an image with a template, the value of the center pixel is replaced by the weighted average gray value of the neighborhood pixels in the template. Traditional Gaussian filter template is shown as Figure 4. Gaussian filter template is more popular, because the pixel with greater influence has greater weight. So the image edge details are robust to blur with the weight value inversely proportional to the distance to the center point. The efficiency is directly proportional to the template dimension, and then we finally use a 3*3 normalized matrix as the template.

0.0037	0.0147	0.0256	0.0147	0.0037
0.0147	0.0586	0.0952	0.0586	0.0147
0.0256	0.0952	0.1502	0.0952	0.0256
0.0147	0.0586	0.0952	0.0586	0.0147
0.0037	0.0147	0.0256	0.0147	0.0037

5*5

0.0625	0.1250	0.0625
0.1250	0.2500	0.1250
0.0625	0.1250	0.0625

3*3

Figure 4. Two conventional Gaussian filter templates

It's known that the edge extraction operator and the morphologic operator are essentially like a high frequency filter. While a Gaussian filter is low-frequency passing, it can reduce a large number of high frequency noises by blurring the image. So before edge-extraction, we utilize a Gaussian filter to erase high frequency noises. Then, some small objects merged with background, while the scene text area is fuzzy and easy to be extracted. The experimental result shows that Gaussian filter is better than others.

After filtering, we may get a color image with less Gauss noise. Considering most of the features only concentrated in few ROI (regions of interest), we use edge-operators to obtain ROI for reducing the redundant information in OCR. The state-of-art operators applied in edge detection include Sobel, Roberts, Canny, Prewitt, Laplace, Compass, etc., with which we can get many small gaps and isolated points. These gaps are some fractured text strokes, which can be decreased with morphological methods and the difference between scene text and background can be increased meanwhile. Common morphological operators are dilation, erosion, open, close. Figure 5 shows the schematic diagrams of the method of dilation and erosion. Figure 6 shows the schematic diagram of the method of open and close. In order to further eliminate the wrong candidates, we use horizontal projection and vertical projection to the binary image after morphological processing by a reasonable threshold. From Figure 7, we find that the different connected blocks in a binary image can be labeled out by the method of connected component analysis. In it, different colors represent different connected blocks. It seems that those blocks usually include 3 types: scene text blocks, background blocks and partial-text blocks, which can be segmented from the original frame as candidates in processing stage.

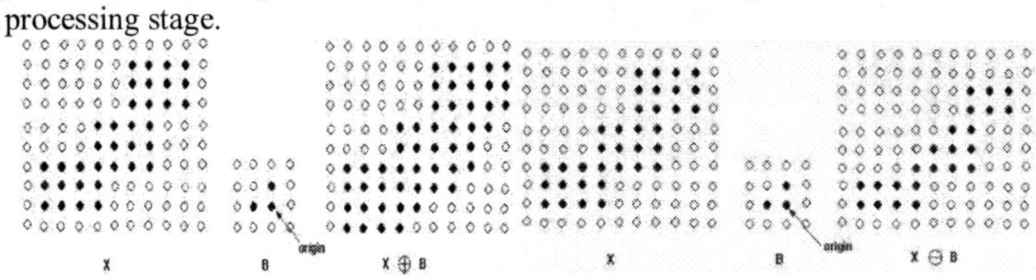

Figure 5. Schematic Diagram of Dilation (Left) and Erosion (Right)

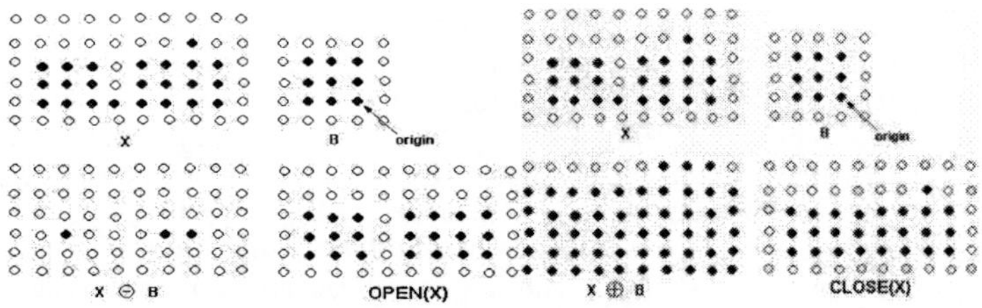

Figure 6. Schematic Diagram of Open and Close

Figure 7. Component Analysis for a Binary Text Image

2.2 Processing

Likewise, we have made modification and improvements in processing stage based on the latest research[15]. Firstly, the text dictionary is modified with the English character for the ICDAR-2013 data set. We use ICDAR-2013 "Robust OCR Trial Train" data set as the sources of the training samples. In SRC method, the larger amount of information contained in the dictionary, the higher classification accuracy. Therefore, for a scene text dictionary, we take full account of the sizes, fonts, types, colors, thickness, arrangements, brightness of text blocks (shown as Figure 8), and apply the Gaussian pyramid [36]. Building a Gaussian pyramid mainly contains two steps: processing each level image by a Gaussian filter and sampling each level image as next level image. In Figure 9, the biggest character of 'i' is the original, which is taken as level 0 in a Gaussian pyramid. Then, with Gaussian filtering, the interlaced sampling result is as level 1, and with the same operation level 2, 3 will be available. We utilize all level images in a Gaussian pyramid as the sample atoms of scene text dictionary. Compared with the method of height normalization[15], the experimental result shows that this method has better robustness and higher accuracy. Then we use a 9 * 9 sliding window to segment the pyramid images for some sliding blocks, which will be normalized as scene dictionary atoms. To improve the robustness to the offset, each Gaussian pyramid image is slide with a step of 2, 3, 5, 7 pixels. To improve the robustness to brightness mutation, the normalization is applied in a whole image [Figure 10]. After training text dictionary by K-SVD [37], we achieve an over-complete text dictionary. Similarly, in order to overcome the low accuracy of partial-text in [15], we specially construct a partial-text dictionary in the same way. The training samples are shown in Figure 11.

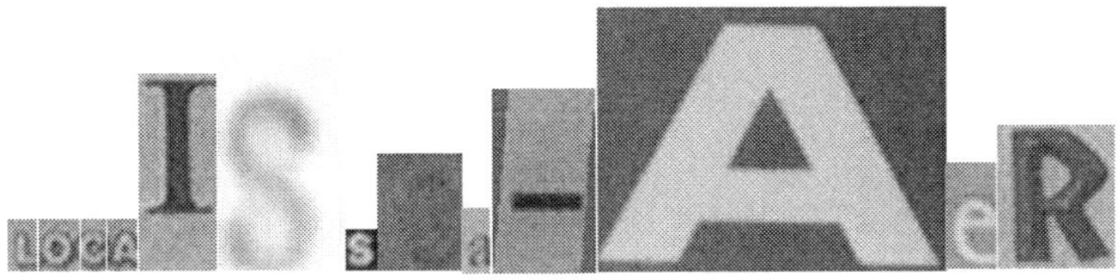

Figure 8. Characters of Training Set

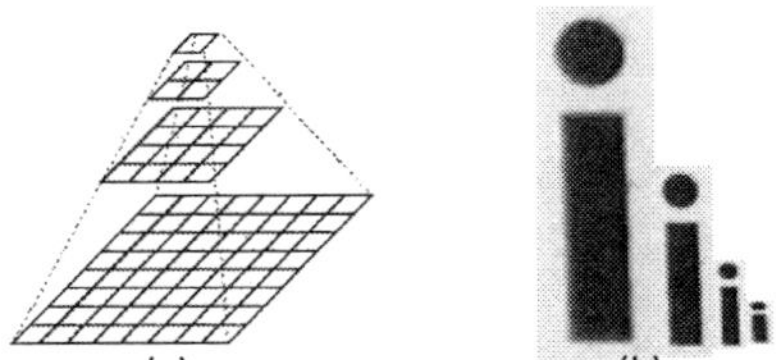

Figure 9. Gaussian Pyramid
(a) A Model of 4-level Gaussian Pyramid; (b)An character example

Figure 10. Original Image (Left), Offsets (Middle) and Brightness Mutation (Right)

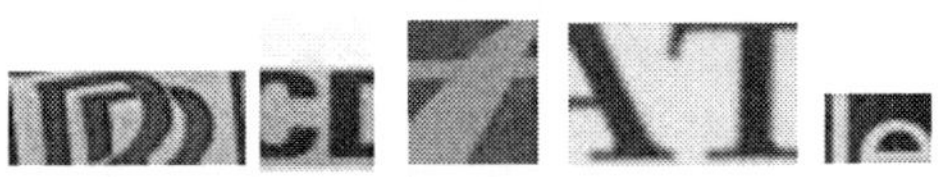

Figure 11. Training Samples of Partial-Text

Next comes the classification stage. In it, we no longer judge the final classification results based on a single residual, because the premise is that the test signal must belong to any class of the dictionary, The premise is not always accorded with, in which SRC coefficients will be distributed evenly in every class of dictionaries. Thus, we analyze the distribution of non-0 elements in sparse representation coefficients to prevent it. Figure 12 compares two types of sparse degree and it is inversely proportional to the distribution density of non-0 sparse coefficients.

We segment all candidate blocks in pre-processing stage by a 9 * 9 sliding window and normalize them same with dictionary atoms. Sparse representation optimization problem is a NP-hard problem for a redundant dictionary. Therefore, we utilize OMP (orthogonal matching pursuit) method to solve it. As an improvement for MP, OMP has faster convergence rate and optimized iteration results. Each testing sample is represented by three dictionaries, and three groups of sparse coefficients are got. As result, we get a judgment by the coefficient sparsity, that is, the testing sample will belong to the class of atoms with sparser coefficients. Finally, we analyze the statistic results in same candidate and finally classify it via voting with the threshold 50%.

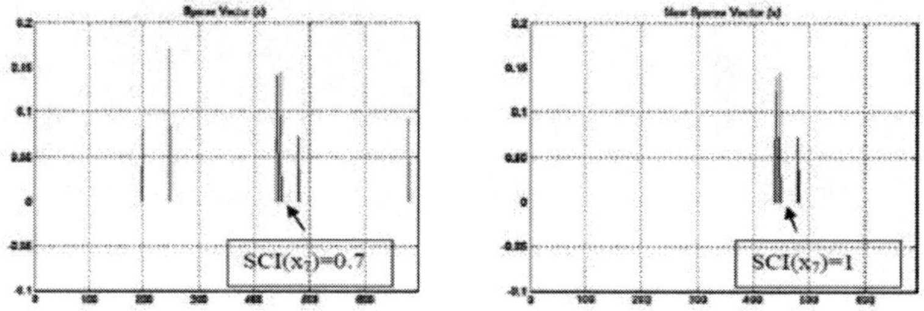

Figure 12. Comparison of two sparse coefficients distribution

3. EXPERIMENTAL RESULTS

In our experiments, we adopt ICDAR-2013 data set as our experimental data source. Our experimental environment is as follows: Windows 64 bit operating system, Intel(R) Core(TM) i7-3630QM CPU, 8GB RAM, NVIDIA GeForce GT 650M display adapter.

We rebuild the scene text dictionary and partial-text dictionary and they are showed below [Figure 12] and we still use the previous background dictionary. In order to improve the robustness of scene text size and thickness, we construct a Gaussian pyramid for training samples as the source of dictionary atoms. In Figure 13, each atom in the dictionary is an 81 * 1 vector which is the column quantization of 9 * 9 sliding block and each dictionary is an 81 * 2048 matrix.

Figure 13. Scene Text Dictionary (Left) and Partial-Text Dictionary (Right)

We use three filtering operators in the original test image and Figure 14 shows the experimental results. The results shows Gaussian filter can reserve better scene text details with a same denoising rate. We also improve the conventional 3 * 3 Gaussian Filtering template [Figure 4] and it is showed in Figure 15. Figure 16 shows different Gaussian filtering threshold has different denoising efficiency and it is inversely proportional to the definition of scene text image. We finally use 0.5 as our experimental threshold. After Gaussian denoising, we use 6 edge operators to extract the image edge and Figure 17 is the results of edge feature extraction. Figure 18 is the results of morphologic operation and Figure 19 is the results of connected region analysis after projection. In Figure 20, different connected regions represent different candidate blocks. We slide the candidates and achieve the test signals by column quantization and normalization same with dictionary atoms. Then we classify the signals by SRC with 10 iterative OMP [38] numbers and we choose 100 scene text images, 100 background images and 100 partial-text images as our test set. The final results are shown in Table.1 and our scene text recall rate is 86.7%.

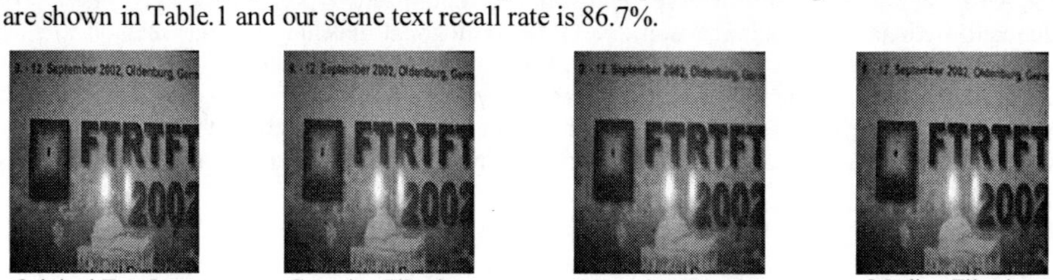

Original Test Image | Gaussian Filtering | Averaging Filtering | Median Filtering

Figure 14. Three Experimental Filtering Results

0.0113	0.0838	0.0113
0.0838	0.6193	0.0838
0.0113	0.0838	0.0113

0.1111	0.1111	0.1111
0.1111	0.1111	0.1111
0.1111	0.1111	0.1111

Figure 15. Our Gaussian Filter Template (Left) and Averaging Filter Template (Right)

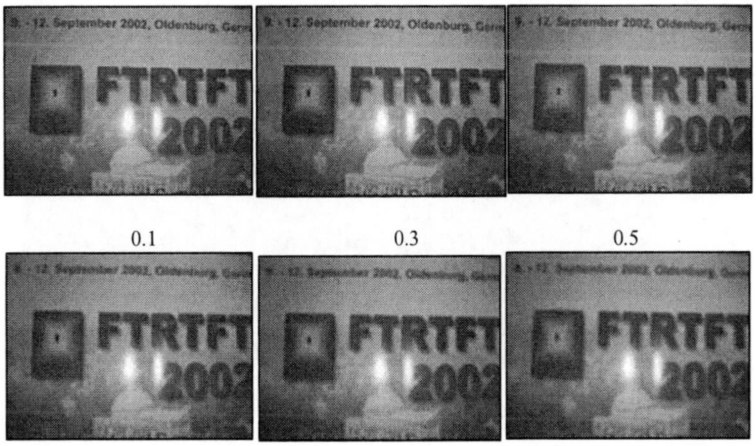

0.1 0.3 0.5

0.7 1.0 3.0

Figure 16. Results of Different Gaussian Filtering Parameters

Sobel Canny Laplace

Prewitt Roberts Compass

Figure 17. Edge feature extraction

Erosion Dilation Close

Figure 18. Morphologic processing

Figure 19. Connected region analysis of close (Left) and dilation (Right)

Figure 20. Experimental candidates after connected region analysis

Table 1. Final classifying results

	Scene Text	Background	Partial-Text
Judging Text	91	5	11
Judging Background	2	81	4
Judging Partial-Text	7	14	85
Correct rate	91%	81%	85%

4. CONCLUSION

In this paper, we propose a new approach to detect and extract scene text more precisely and efficiently. Our method includes pre-processing stage and processing stage. The aim of preprocessing stage is to reduce the redundant image information and obtain fewer candidates. In processing stage, we use SRC method to construct classifier and our training text samples and test text samples are all from ICDAR-2013 data set. In our experiments, we can not only do well with text size and thickness because of Gaussian pyramid but also improve the robustness of brightness because of gray normalization. We also take advantage of sparse residuals and the distribution of sparse coefficients to detect the validity of test signals. The experimental result shows that our method is promising. However, in our experiments, all thresholds are all based on experience and we plan to construct an adaptive threshold method to overcome this problem in future.

ACKNOWLEDGEMENT

This work is supported by the National Natural Science Foundation of China (Grant No.61501035), the Fundamental Research Funds for the Central Universities of China (2014KJJCA15), and the National Education Science Twelfth Five-Year Plan Key Issues of the Ministry of Education (DCA140229).

REFERENCES

[1] Ye Q, Huang Q, Gao W, et al. Fast and robust text detection in images and video frames[J]. *Image and Vision Computing*, 2005, 23(6): 565-576.

[2] Qi W, Gu L, Jiang H, et al. Integrating visual, audio and text analysis for news video[C]//*Image Processing*, 2000. Proceedings. 2000 International Conference on. IEEE, 2000, 3: 520-523.

[3] Hahn S H, Lee J H, Kim J H. A study on utilizing OCR technology in building text database[C]//Database and Expert Systems Applications, 1999. *Proceedings. Tenth International Workshop on. IEEE*, 1999: 582-586.

[4] Sharma O P, Ghose M K, Shah K B, et al. Recent trends and tools for feature extraction in OCR technology[J]. *International Journal of Soft Computing and Engineering* (IJSCE), 2013, 2.

[5] Yang H, Siebert M, Luhne P, et al. Lecture video indexing and analysis using video ocr technology[C]//*Signal-Image Technology and Internet-Based Systems* (SITIS), *2011 Seventh International Conference on*. IEEE, 2011: 54-61.

[6] Kim W, Kim C. A new approach for overlay text detection and extraction from complex video scene[J]. *Image Processing, IEEE Transactions on*, 2009, 18(2): 401-411.

[7] Kauchali S, Rooney W C, Biegler L T. Linear programming formulations for attainable region analysis[J]. *Chemical Engineering Science*, 2002, volume 57(11):2015-2028(14).

[8] Sun L, Huo Q. Character candidate generation using contrasting extremal regions for extracting text from scene images[R]. *MSRA Internal Technical Memo*, 2012.

[9] Pizer S M, Koenderink J J, Lifshitz L M, et al. An image description for object definition, based on extremal regions in the stack[C]//*Information processing in medical imaging*. Springer Netherlands, 1986: 24-37.

[10] Donoser M, Bischof H. Efficient maximally stable extremal region (MSER) tracking[C]//*Computer Vision and Pattern Recognition, 2006 IEEE Computer Society Conference on*. IEEE, 2006, 1: 553-560.

[11] Matas J, Chum O, Urban M, et al. Robust wide-baseline stereo from maximally stable extremal regions[J]. *Image and vision computing*, 2004, 22(10): 761-767.

[12] Lifshitz L M, Pizer S M. A multiresolution hierarchical approach to image segmentation based on intensity extrema[C]//*Information Processing in Medical Imaging*. Springer US, 1988: 107-130.

[13] Liu T, Chen J, Wang C. Improved Maximally Stable Extremal Region detector in color images[C]// *Information and Automation (ICIA), 2010 IEEE International Conference on*. IEEE, 2010.

[14] Nayak P C, Rao Y R S, Sudheer K P. Groundwater level forecasting in a shallow aquifer using artificial neural network approach[J]. *Water Resources Management*, 2006, 20(1): 77-90.

[15] Bo Sun, Yang Wu, Feng Xu. Detecting and extracting text in video via sparse representation based classification method[C]. *Lecture Notes in Electrical Engineering*, volume 339, 2015, 351-358.

[16] Shiozaki A. Edge extraction using entropy operator[J]. *Computer Vision Graphics & Image Processing*, 1986, 36(86):1–9.

[17] Russo F, Ramponi G. Edge extraction by FIRE operators[J]. *Proceedings of Third IEEE International Conference on Fuzzy Systems*, 1994, 1:249 - 253.

[18] Feng L, Suen C Y, Tang Y Y, et al. EDGE EXTRACTION OF IMAGES BY RECONSTRUCTION USING WAVELET DECOMPOSITION DETAILS AT DIFFERENT RESOLUTION LEVELS[J]. *International Journal of Pattern Recognition & Artificial Intelligence*, 2000, 14(6):779-793.

[19] Jiang M, Yuan D. A multi-grade mean morphologic edge detection[J]. *Journal of Shandong University*, 2003, 2:1079 - 1082.

[20] Wang S. Ship Wake Detection in SAR Images Based on Radon Transformation and Morphologic Image Processing[J]. *Journal of Remote Sensing*, 2001.

[21] Kauchali S, Rooney W C, Biegler L T. Linear programming formulations for attainable region analysis[J]. *Chemical Engineering Science*, 2002, volume 57(11):2015-2028(14).

[22] Studholme C, Hill D L G, Hawkes D J. Incorporating connected region labelling into automated image registration using mutual information[J]. *Mathematical Methods in Biomedical Image Analysis Proceedings of the Workshop on*, 1996:23 - 31.

[23] Wright J, Yang A Y, Ganesh A, et al. Robust Face Recognition via Sparse Representation[J]. *IEEE Trans Pattern Anal Mach Intell*, 2008, 31(2):210 - 227.

[24] Won Park J, Harper D T. An efficient memory system for the SIMD construction of a Gaussian pyramid[J]. *IEEE Transactions on Parallel & Distributed Systems*, 1996, 7(8):855-860.

[25] Baxt W G. Use of an artificial neural network for the diagnosis of myocardial infarction.[J]. *Annals of Internal Medicine*, 1991, 115(11).

[26] Joachims T. Making Large-Scale SVM Learning Practical. MIT-Press[J]. *Technical Reports*, 1999.

[27] Duan K B, Rajapakse J C, Wang H, et al. Multiple Svm-Rfe For Gene Selection In Cancer Classification With Expression Data[J]. *IEEE Trans Nanobiosci*, 2005, 4(3):228--234.

[28] Arber S. MLP-Deficient Mice Exhibit a Disruption of Cardiac Cytoarchitectural Organization, Dilated Cardiomyopathy, and Heart Failure[J]. *Cell*, 1997, 88(3):393–403.

[29] Alriksson P, Rantzer A. Distributed Kalman Filtering Using Weighted Averaging[J]. *Proceedings of International Symposium on Mathematical Theory of Networks & Systems Kyoto*, 2006.

[30] Yong H L, Kassam S A. Generalized median filtering and related nonlinear filtering techniques[J]. *IEEE Transactions on Acoustics Speech & Signal Processing*, 1985, 33(3):672 - 683.

[31] Huang T, Yang G, Tang G. A fast two-dimensional median filtering algorithm[J]. *Acoustics Speech & Signal Processing IEEE Transactions on*, 1979, 27.

[32] Shin D H, Park R H, Yang S, et al. Block-based noise estimation using adaptive Gaussian filtering[J]. *IEEE Transactions on Consumer Electronics*, 2005, 51(1):218 - 226.

[33] Tan S, Johnston D A. Performance Of Three Recursive Algorithms For Fast Space-Variant Gaussian Filtering[J]. *Real-Time Imaging*, 2003, 9(3):215-228.

[34] Shaked U, De Souza C E. Robust Minimum Variance Filtering[J]. *IEEE Transactions on Signal Processing*, 1995, 43(11):2474-2483.

[35] Young I T, Vliet L J V, Ginkel M V. Recursive Gabor Filtering[J]. *IEEE Transactions on Signal Processing*, 2000, 3(11):3342.

[36] Won Park J, Harper D T. An efficient memory system for the SIMD construction of a Gaussian pyramid[J]. *IEEE Transactions on Parallel & Distributed Systems*, 1996, 7(8):855-860.

[37] Zhang Q, Li B. Discriminative K-SVD for dictionary learning in face recognition.[C]// *Proceedings / CVPR, IEEE Computer Society Conference on Computer Vision and Pattern Recognition. IEEE Computer Society Conference on Computer Vision and Pattern Recognition*. 2010:2691 - 2698.

[38] Tropp J A, Gilbert A C. Signal recovery from random measurements via Orthogonal Matching Pursuit[J]. *Information Theory IEEE Transactions on, 2007*, 53(12):4655--4666.

Short Papers

THE MULTIMODAL EDGE OF HUMAN AEROBOTIC INTERACTION

Ayodeji Opeyemi Abioye[1], Stephen D. Prior[2], Glyn T. Thomas[3] and Peter Saddington[4]
[1]Doctoral Research Student
[2]Reader in Unmanned Air Vehicles
[3]Lecturer & Researcher in Aerodynamics & Flight Mechanics
Aeronautics, Astronautics and Computational Engineering
Faculty of Engineering and the Environment, University of Southampton, UK
[4]Principal Engineer
Tekever Ltd, Southampton, UK

ABSTRACT

This paper presents the idea of a multimodal human aerobotic interaction. An overview of the aerobotic system and its application is given. The joystick-based controller interface and its limitations is discussed. Two techniques are suggested as emerging alternatives to the joystick-based controller interface used in human aerobotic interaction. The first technique is a multimodal combination of speech, gaze, gesture, and other non-verbal cues already used in regular human-human interaction. The second is telepathic interaction via brain computer interfaces. The potential limitations of these alternatives is highlighted, and the considerations for further works are presented.

KEYWORDS

Aerobots, Gesture, Interface, Control, HCI, Multimodal.

1. INTRODUCTION

Although, the most prevalent Human Computer Interaction (HCI) technology for the control of aerobots is the joystick-type controller, other forms of interaction such as gesture and mind control are gaining wide interests. This paper investigates these alternative interfaces, suggests a comparison criteria, highlights some of their limitations, and emphasizes efforts that could suggest a breakthrough in aerobotic interaction.

2. RESEARCH BACKGROUND - AEROBOTS

Robots have been designed to reduce human workload, risk, cost, and human fatigue driven errors. Crucial in achieving this objective is making the interaction effective, efficient, and natural; perhaps by interacting via multiple modalities of contact, dialogue, and gestures (Fong & Nourbakhsh 2000). According to Green et al. (2007) "It is clear that people use speech, gesture, gaze and non-verbal cues to communicate in the clearest possible fashion." And perhaps because human robot interaction is essential for human robot collaboration, it might be necessary to develop systems that could adopt some of this natural human-human interaction techniques. The essence of human robot collaboration is probably the fact that robots can complement the human effort by optimizing problem solving techniques, performing tasks faster, and in many cases with greater dexterity.

2.1 Aerobots - a Flying Robot Manipulator

Aerobots, which is derived from 'AERial rOBOTs', can be considered as small unmanned multi-rotor aircraft systems with actuators to perform tasks analogous to fixed industrial robot manipulators. Aerobots can be considered as robot manipulators with an in-built ability to hover or fly, while still being able to perform the primary objective for which they were built, while being either at rest or in a dynamic motion. An aerobot may perform payload pickup while hovering or at rest, and potentially perform photography tasks while in a state of a slow dynamic motion.

Aerobots could be very useful in performing tasks such as: working in human hazardous or radioactive environment; search and rescue missions; military intelligence, surveillance, and reconnaissance (ISR) missions; logistics and transportation as in the DHL and Amazon examples; space exploration missions, such as the Mars rover; and videography, photography, and cinemography. In fact, aerobots are not just flying robots but flying robots that have a purpose to their flights.

However, the precision and accuracy of aerobots is poor compared to most industrial robot manipulators due to the inherent aerodynamic complexity of flying in 3-dimensional space. Other complexities could arise due to the continuously changing references, changing dynamic environmental conditions, un-location to a fixed origin, and slow sensor response. Although the effectiveness, efficiency, and precision of aerobots may not compare to the performance of the industrial fixed robot arm manipulators in many areas, there exists a plethora of tasks for which the aerobots are more suitable. The efforts of HCI researchers in the areas of hover and stabilization, sense and avoid, indoor navigation, autonomy, interaction interfaces to name a few, are further contributing to the overall performance of this system.

2.2 Human Aerobot Interaction

Human Aerobot Interaction (HAI) could be considered as part of Human Computer Interaction (HCI), which is more closely aligned with Human Machine Interaction (HMI) and Human Robotic Interaction (HRI). Research into human computer interfaces often encompasses the interaction between humans and machines, HMI, and the interaction between humans and several robotics systems, HRI (Myers 1998). This is due to the fact that these machines or robotic systems rely on computers for their operations. Therefore, any research involving human interaction with their computer systems, would eventually define their overall performance and interactions with humans, especially considering the fact that humans interact with them via their in-built computer systems, and these computers in turn control these machines or robotics systems in accordance with the human's control intents.

3. INVESTIGATION AND RESULT

3.1 The Joystick-Type Controller Dilemma

Typically the interaction between humans and aerobots, fundamentally consists of a radio controlled (RC) joystick transmitter controller, augmented with toggle switches, push buttons, and variable potentiometer, for improved control functionality as shown in Figure 1 (HobbyKing & Turnigy 2015).

Although most UAV operators eventually adapt to the operation of this joystick-type controller, and become very skillful, getting used to it as a compound impulse response or reflex action; it is still not natural. Briskly flicking both the left and right thumb, placed on the left and right joystick respectively, to maintain horizontal level balance, within fractions of a second, continuously keeping you fully engaged, for the whole flying duration, just to maintain balance and control, is definitely not natural.

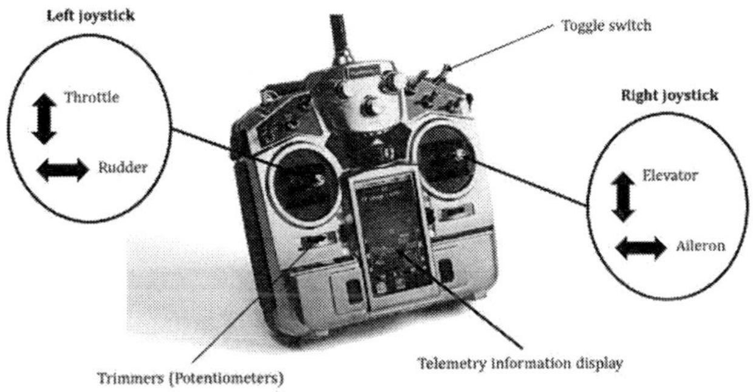

Figure 1. 10-channel Turnigy TGY-i10 (mode 2) telemetry RC controller

In addition to operating the left and right joysticks, the operator might be required to operate switches to perform some other functions such as payload drop or snapshot from an on-board camera, at some specified time, altitude, distance, space, and location. Simultaneously executing these could potentially feel unnatural.

In addition to this, the joystick-type controller is not intuitive enough. It is fine when a quadcopter is facing forwards but when it faces backwards or any of the sides, control becomes complicated. The human operator's and aerobot's orientation of forwards are no longer aligned. Several hours of training may be required to learn to adapt and compensate appropriately for such disorientation. An intuitive interface would probably compensate for this disorientation without transferring such overload to the human operator.

Also, due to the control overload on a small unmanned multi-rotor aircraft's operator, the situational awareness of the operator is reduced; making it impossible to simultaneously control multiple aircraft. According to Cavett et al. (2007), "because of the limitations of human cognitive skills, judgment, decision-making, and tactical understanding in the use of Unmanned Aerial Vehicles (UAV), there is a need to redesign the current human-computer interface (HCI) [referring to the joystick-type controller] to improve the interaction and communication links between operators and the UAVs..."

3.2 HHI-Like Aerobotic Control Interface

Unlike the joystick-based human-aerobot interaction, the human-human interaction has naturally evolved over several hundred years to include advanced speech and concept expression, as well as non-verbal forms of communications, such as gestures and gazes (Green et al. 2007; Sharma et al. 1998) as shown in Figure 2.

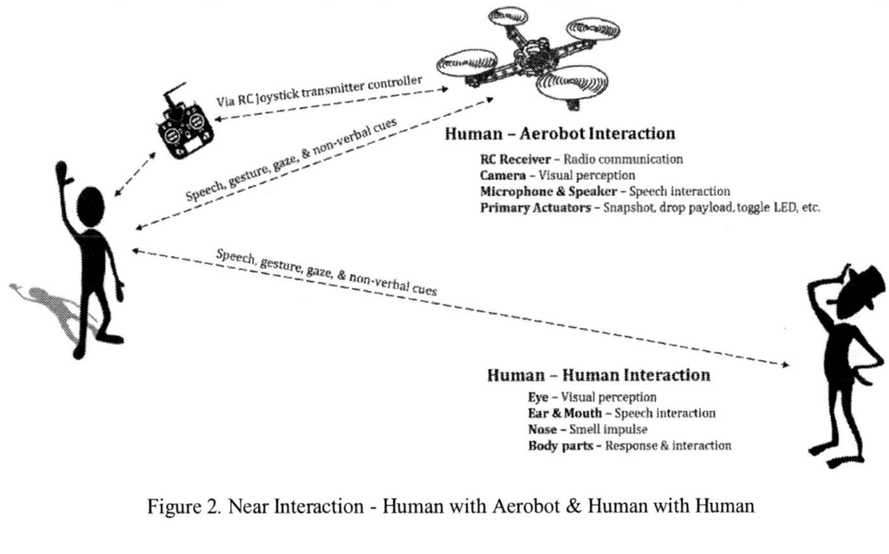

Figure 2. Near Interaction - Human with Aerobot & Human with Human

The natural human to human interaction often occurs within the context of a very small geographical area, hence the term 'near-interaction.' The idea of near-interaction is used to indicate the limit of up to a few hundred metres. If the human is too far away, it would be difficult to be heard; and also difficult to be seen when much farther away. Hence it might be difficult, if not impossible, to interact via speech, gaze, gesture, and other non-verbal methods, naturally. But this range limitation is also applicable to the human aerobotic interaction, as it becomes difficult for the on-board camera to successfully identify the human, for the microphone to detect the human voice amid several other environmental noise sources, for the human to hear the quadcopter talk through the on-board speaker, or for the human to keep sight of the aerobot at much longer distance (perhaps a few kilometers). At this stage, other technologies would probably need to be adopted, like using long-range high-mast antenna for ground surface communication or satellite communication, for both the human-human and the human-aerobot interaction.

In Figure 2, a hand gesture interaction was initiated which could suggest a human-human or human-aerobot interaction. Some notable human-aerobot hand gesture interaction research includes the application of the data glove such as the AcceleGlove (Hernandez Jose et al. 2002) and Magic glove (Chaomin et al. 2012), Magnetic hand tracking (Ma et al. 2010), Apple Watch (Reuters 2015), and the Myo armband device (Thalmic Labs 2013; Nagar & Xu 2015).

Gaze or eye tracking is a technique that seeks to determine the direction the eye is focused; perhaps, via the relative motion of the eye with respect to the head's position (Renitto & Thomas 2014). Electrooculography (EOG) techniques could be used to approach this from a biomedical point of view.

Perhaps the development of HHI-like aerobotic interaction would require a multimodal approach as suggested by Sharma et al. (1998). This is probably possible due to the advancement in computing power and signal processing technologies. But the complications associated with the integration of individual HCI interfaces (sensor fusion) would need to be addressed.

3.3 Brain Control Interfaces - Telepathic Interaction

The advancement in the development of brain computer interfaces (BCI), can be attributed to the understanding of the human neurology and the advancement in biomedical signal processing. These interfaces now find applications in various robotic systems. Telepathy is not necessarily a human-human interaction modality. Unlike the regular human interaction methods of speech and visual gesture that haves a "feel it and it happens" or "feel it as it happens" sensation, telepathic interaction emphasizes a "think it and it happens" interaction. In natural gesture interaction, machines are taught to interact via natural human methods. However, in mind control interaction, the machines are being equipped to interact with humans in a way that humans do not normally interact with each other, a way that is beyond the normal human-human interaction capability. Humans skillful in the art of manipulating other humans via induction, deception, and psychological means such as the psychic, medium, or paranormal extrasensory perception or the sixth sense, may argue otherwise.

A challenge that the BCI system faces, even though it is still under development, is security. The mere thoughts of the human vulnerability to telepathic credit card hack elicits a fearful response and natural reluctance to the adoption of such technology (as a defensive strategy) until security of such systems can be guaranteed (Martinovic et al. 2012). This means security is put in the forefront of this development rather than taking a back seat as is often the case with new technologies. While this may suggest the possibility of absolute transparency in interaction, the breach of privacy and human right could be called to question.

3.4 Performance Metrics

A major consideration in the development of any system is how to measure the system's performance. According to Lindquist (1985), the effort-to-learn and the effort-to-use contributes to the usability of HCIs. The similarity of the developed interface to other known interfaces, the knowledge of similar interfaces, and the complexity of the developed interface, contributes to the effort-to-learn and usability of the developed system. Another performance metric of interest is probably a comparison of the interface's functionality with alternative existing interfaces. In this case, a comparison of the interface precision, accuracy, efficiency and effectiveness could be carried out. A performance benchmark could be drawn around the most generally accepted HCI interface such as the joystick-type controller for the case of new aerobots control interfaces.

Generally, a good interface design improves the overall user experience, makes interaction enjoyable, intuitive, easy to learn, and is functionally effective with accepted level of precision and accuracy. As implied from Chao (2009), a good HCI is not about the human adapting to the limitation of the computer (as used to be the case), but about the computer adapting to the human's natural tendencies and expectations.

3.5 Challenging Development

Some of the challenges associated with the development of aerobotic control interfaces includes technological constraint, ethics, regulations and control, security, safety and privacy, inherent complexity, and dynamics. The interface can only be as good as its supporting, fundamental, and underlying technology. Many new interfaces being proposed depends on technologies still in their nascent stages; such as the case of using the Apple Watch in an aerobotic interaction (Reuters 2015).

Besides the aerobots primary function (search, surveillance, or picking up objects with an installed robotic arm), there exists a secondary but fundamental task of remaining aerial (in flight, having a sense of location in 3-dimensional aerial space, avoiding collision, and navigating through static and dynamic objects). In addition, the dynamic complexity associated with such supposedly-basic operation is further complicated by an infinite aerial location possibility, coupled with dynamically changing environmental properties. This complexity is further compounded when interacting with dynamic objects (Byung-Woo et al. 1999)

3.6 Research Resilience

Despite the existence of these developmental challenges, HCI researchers have remained resilient, pushing against the odds, and extending the edge of human machine interaction experience. Soto-Gerrero & Ramrez-Torres (2013) demonstrated visual gesture interaction on a Parrot AR drone via an android-based mobile phone platform. Lafleur et al. (2013) demonstrated BCI (telepathic mind) control of a quadcopter in three-dimensional space. The works of Milanova and Qing (Milanova & Sirakov 2008; Qing et al. 2008) suggests the possibility of emotional gesture interactions with aerobots. They independently investigated systems to recognise expressions of joy, distress, surprise, interest, frustration, anger, disgust, fear, and a neutral expression among several human observable facial expressions. Researchers have even made it possible for aerobots to collaborate with human actors as shown in a Shakespeare's play, "A Midsummer Night's Dream" (Murphy et al. 2011). With the continued resilience of HCI researchers, a breakthrough in human aerobotic interaction will probably occur very soon.

4. CONCLUSION

In this paper, the idea of a multimodal human aerobotic interaction was presented. An attempt was made to describe the aerobotic system as a flying robot with, potentially, more complicated applications than is often considered. The human aerobotic interaction, which is generally performed via a joystick-type controller interface was investigated and the limitations of this interface, presented. This resulted in the discussion of a more intuitive interaction, emulating the human-human interaction methods, which combines speech, gaze, gesture, and other non-verbal cues. The challenges of developing such a system and how to measure its performance were also discussed. Besides this HHI-like multimodal interaction, another method was also discussed - a telepathic interaction via a brain computer interface, which is considered to be beyond the normal human-human interaction.

4.1 Further Works

The next phase of this work will investigate the complexity associated with developing a HHI-like multimodal human aerobotic interface. The follow-on from this will be to integrate a novel technological principle in the development of such a multimodal system that will combine one or more of speech, gesture, gaze, and other non-verbal cues.

REFERENCES

Journal

Byung-Woo, M. et al., 1999. Visual recognition of static/dynamic gesture: gesture-driven editing system. *Journal of Visual Languages and Computing*, 10(3), pp.291–309.

Green, S. et al., 2007. Human Robot Collaboration: an Augmented Reality Approach a Literature Review and Analysis. *Mechatronics*, 5(1), pp.1–10.

Lafleur, K. et al., 2013. Quadcopter control in three-dimensional space using a noninvasive motor imagery-based brain-computer interface. *Journal of Neural Engineering*, 10(4).

Lindquist, T.E., 1985. ASSESSING THE USABILITY OF HUMAN-COMPUTER INTERFACES. *IEEE Software*, 2(1), pp.74–82.

Martinovic, I. et al., 2012. On the Feasibility of Side-Channel Attacks with Brain-Computer Interfaces. *Usenixorg*, pp.1–16.

Murphy, R. et al., 2011. A Midsummer Night's Dream (with flying robots). *Autonomous Robots*, 30(2), pp.143–156.

Myers, B.A., 1998. A Brief History of Human Computer Interaction Technology. *ACM Interactions*, 5(December), pp.44–54.

Renitto, J.E. & Thomas, N.K., 2014. A Survey on Gesture Recognition Technology. *international Journal for Technological Research in Engineering*, 1(10), pp.1058–1060.

Conference paper or contributed volume

Cavett, D. et al., 2007. Human-computer interface for control of unmanned aerial vehicles. In *2007 IEEE Systems and Information Engineering Design Symposium, SIEDS, April 27, 2007 - April 27, 2007*. Charlottesville, VA, United states: Inst. of Elec. and Elec. Eng. Computer Society.

Chao, G., 2009. Human-computer interaction: Process and principles of human-computer interface design. In *2009 International Conference on Computer and Automation Engineering, ICCAE 2009, March 8, 2009 - March 10, 2009*. Bangkok, Thailand: Inst. of Elec. and Elec. Eng. Computer Society, pp. 230–233.

Chaomin, L. et al., 2012. The magic glove: A gesture-based remote controller for intelligent mobile robots. *Proceedings of the SPIE - The International Society for Optical Engineering*, 8301, p.83010M (11 pp.)–83010M (11 pp.).

Fong, T. & Nourbakhsh, I., 2000. Interaction challenges in human-robot space exploration. In *Proceedings of the Fourth International Conference and Exposition on Robotics for Challenging Situations and Environments*. pp. 340–346.

Hernandez Jose, L., Kyriakopoulos, N. & Lindeman, R., 2002. The AcceleGlove a Hole-Hand Input Device for Virtual Reality. *ACM SIGGRAPH Conference Abstracts and Applications*, p.259.

Ma, Y. et al., 2010. Magnetic hand tracking for human-computer interface. In *14th Biennial IEEE Conference on Electromagnetic Field Computation, CEFC2010, May 9, 2010 - May 12, 2010*. Chicago, IL, United states: IEEE Computer Society, p. IEEE Magnetics Society.

Milanova, M. & Sirakov, N., 2008. Recognition of emotional states in natural human-computer interaction. In *8th IEEE International Symposium on Signal Processing and Information Technology, ISSPIT 2008, December 16, 2008 - December 19, 2008*. Sarajevo, Bosnia and herzegovina: Inst. of Elec. and Elec. Eng. Computer Society, pp. 186–191.

Nagar, A. & Xu, Z., 2015. Gesture control by wrist surface electromyography. In *2015 IEEE International Conference on Pervasive Computing and Communication Workshops*. pp. 556–561.

Qing, C. et al., 2008. Hand-Gesture and Facial-Expression Human-Computer Interfaces for Intelligent Space Application. In *Medical Measurements and Applications, 2008. MeMeA 2008. IEEE International Workshop on*. pp. 1–6.

Sharma, R., Pavlovic, V.I. & Huang, T.S., 1998. Toward multimodal human-computer interface. *Proceedings of the IEEE*, 86(5 pt 1), pp.853–869.

Soto-Gerrero, D. & Ramrez-Torres, J.G., 2013. A human-machine interface with unmanned aerial vehicles. In *Electrical Engineering, Computing Science and Automatic Control (CCE), 2013 10th International Conference*. Mexico City: IEEE, pp. 307 – 312.

Other Sources

HobbyKing & Turnigy, 2015. Turnigy TGY-i10 10ch 2.4GHz Digital Proportional RC System with Telemetry (Mode 2). Available at: http://www.hobbyking.com/hobbyking/store/__58455__Turnigy_TGY_i10_10ch_ch_2_4GHz_Digital_Proportional_RC_System_with_Telemetry_Mode_2_.html [Accessed February 8, 2016].

Reuters, 2015. Using The Force? No, it's an Apple Watch flying this drone. *Tech Innovation and Intellectual Property*, pp.1–3. Available at: http://www.reuters.com/article/us-apple-watch-drone-idUSKBN0UE14Q20160101 [Accessed January 21, 2016].

Thalmic Labs, 2013. Homepage - Gesture Control Has Arrived. , pp.1–5. Available at: https://www.myo.com/ [Accessed January 19, 2016].

International Conferences Interfaces and Human Computer Interaction 2016,
Game and Entertainment Technologies 2016 and
Computer Graphics, Visualization, Computer Vision and Image Processing 2016

TECHNOLOGY IN THE CLASSROOM: A PILOT TEST WITH A HUMANOID ROBOT

Kaberi Naznin, Dr. Vivienne Farrell, Dr. Karola von Baggo and Dr. Clinton Woodward
Swinburne University of Technology PO Box 218 Hawthorn, Victoria 3122, Australia

ABSTRACT

Integrating new technology into the classroom is an evolutionary process. In this paper, we will present the progress of our work in developing an approach to integrate a humanoid NAO robot into learning environments in a manner that encourages and engages learners to actively reflect on the learning activity. Initially interviews with primary school teachers were conducted in Bangladesh and Australia to enable an understanding of their attitudes, expectations and acceptance to the use of new technology. The results of the interviews with the primary school teachers were analysed and formed the basis of the requirements for an observational study on integrating an emerging technology into primary school student education. We developed a lesson plan using a humanoid robot and pilot tested it with ten primary school students. We discovered that our lesson plan did appear to encourage discovery and reflective learning. However, it also needs to consider compulsory curriculum requirements and available technical assistance and is likely to most benefit senior primary school aged students. This pilot study will form the basis of further study.

KEYWORDS

Integrating emerging technology and Humanoid robot learning to program

1. INTRODUCTION

Integrating technology into the classroom can have a positive influence on a student's learning outcome, and support their cognitive development in various ways (Clements & Sarama 2002). Teachers can create an environment where students can learn by doing, enabling students to understand difficult concepts using technology (Mouza 2005). Far too often the use of the technology fails to meet the needs of either the teacher or the students and end up a wasted purchase and misspent precious time.

The introduction of classroom technology can be the source of frustration if not enough consideration is given to the needs, wants and capabilities of the teachers and students. Issues such as; how to select a suitable technology (Simon & Nemeth 2012); how to use to technology to meet the needs of the curriculum; what is the appropriate age of students to match a particular technology (Clements & Sarama 2002; Mouza 2005); how to determine the necessary abilities of the teachers and their available time to spend on the technology (Clements & Sarama 2002); how will the students use respond to the technology, what are the possible learning benefits of students by technology-enhanced activities? (Clarke and Zagarell 2012; Mouza 2005) This research attempts to determine if there are ways to reduce the technology failure lessons that so readily occur (Simon & Nemeth 2012)? In this study, we set out to discover the priorities for teachers when considering the integration of an emerging technology into their classroom. From this information we designed a short lesson plan that would be easily employed and enabled us to refine the necessary relevant student needs and skills of our target group. The emerging technology selected was a humanoid robot (NAO) as it was still unfamiliar to our cohort of teachers and students.

This paper initially describes the interviews that were held with primary school teachers. The expectations and requirements for teachers are initially discussed. Based on the teachers' feedback, we then discuss the pilot study lesson plan design to be undertaken with primary aged children. The implementation, results and refinement process are presented and then discussed. This is followed by a conclusion and further work.

2. INTERVIEWS WITH TEACHERS

A Semi- structured Interview (Lazar, Feng & Hochheiser 2010) with eleven primary school teachers was conducted in Australia and Bangladesh to assist in developing an understanding of their attitudes and acceptance to the use of emerging technology in the classroom. The interviews assisted us in gaining a better understanding of what support teachers felt they required for integrating new technology and how they could use it in the classroom. Participation in the interview was voluntary, and participants' data was de-identified. The interviews were conducted in schools, to enable observation of the physical and technical context. Teachers were scheduled for approximately one-hour interviews.

There were two parts of conducting interviews. In part 1, we prepared background questions that related to their teaching experience, and their use of technology both in and out of the classroom. The part 1 questions were sent to teachers one week before the intended interview. Part 2: Teachers were then shown a video about the capabilities of a humanoid robot in the classroom and asked to reflect on its use in the classroom. Audio recordings were taken from the interviews with the consent of the participants. We used participants' codes instead of participants' names; for Australian teachers, A1, A2, A3,.., A6, and B1, B2,....B5 for Bangladeshi teachers.

2.1 Results and Discussion of Interviews

In this section, we will discuss the requirements that were collected during interviews with teachers. Here, we only discuss the results of Part 2 interviews that lead us to the design of the pilot study.

MUST FIT IN WITH CURRICULUM

All teachers identified that fitting into the curriculum was essential as time constraints did not allow for further extensions of activities.

Further all teachers were able to identify how a humanoid robot could fit to the current curriculum activities. Science, math, and work requiring inquiry where students would be able to program it to assist were identified (A1, A5 and A6).

For future curriculum all Australian and most of the Bangladeshi teachers suggested how students could use this robot to learn programming, and identified the benefits students could gain using the robot. Programming was identified as an emerging curriculum requirement that required skills and knowledge that are not currently held by all teachers.

Programming skills: "Simple programming on how the actual robot works. For example, lots of students would be interested in how he/she knows how say works, how it moves, back and forth with the robot. Mini project how the robot works" (A2).

ACT AS A TEACHING ASSISTANT

The robot could repeat the instructions if students could not understand, that would be good rather than a teacher explaining again and again (A6).

OFFER ALTERNATIVE TEACHING METHODS:

"Sometimes teachers could teach something one way, but there are three, or four different ways. If teachers have a robot, they could do all different ways using the robot. Okay, this is one way, have a go. Here is a different way, now having a go and here is the 3rd different way. Now they can work out which one is best for them" (A2).

SUITABLE AGE GROUP OF STUDENTS

Some teachers thought that the older students in the primary school would definitely love this humanoid robot (A3, A4, A5 and A6). Teachers were unsure if the robot would be suitable for younger primary children. It was thought they may not have the necessary skills or may even be fearful.

IN A GROUP, OR INDIVIDUALLY

Most of the teachers suggested that they considered that the robot would be most useful in small groups (A3, A4, A6) or group situations (A2, A3, B1, B4) or groups as a rotation (A2, A3).

STUDENT OWNERSHIP OF THEIR LEARNING

"The students creating on their own instead of being led by the teacher. Here is something teachers want to do, students able to take ownership to take actions" (A1).

BENEFITS FOR STUDENT LEARNING

"Technology, when used in the right context with the right pedagogy, enables powerful learning. It can connect students to a global audience and harness their creativity, empowering them to create" (A6). It engages students and provides for differences in learning styles. It can be interactive. It can be colorful and interesting. It can present information but in a different way. It can provide drill and practice for students (A6, A1).

STUDENT MOTIVATION

A variety of students would be motivated and find benefits from this robot: students who need the next step, or a little bit more of a challenge, but do not like to keep going on with their work perhaps need some inspiration something else to develop their learning, students who cannot sit for a long time, this robot would work better for them (A3).

TECHNICAL SUPPORT

All teachers identified that they need technical support while using this robot. Teachers shared with us some of their frustration stories for the integration of brand new technology.

"Teachers used interactive whiteboards in the past, again many technical difficulties, without adequate support provided. This, of course, discouraged teachers to use these technologies"(A2).

Teachers were concerned that they would find they were ill prepared to use the technology in the class, which would ruin any further use of the robot.

Learner: Teachers would like to be a learner first to know everything that it could do, how it could work, what are the projects we could do, and how someone else could use it (A1, A3).

Professional training: A4, A3 and A6 would like to receive the PD (professional development) training required to use this technology, holding, touching, and spending enough time for trial and error. Available time to learn the technology and create new learning material was considered as a serious concern for the uptake of a new technology.

Summary of teacher interviews

Most of the teachers discussed the positive benefit of using the humanoid robot with the students. They would have the opportunity to deliver curriculum relevant material in novel ways. All types of students will be engaged, and learning outcome of students would be improved if teachers could use this technology in the right context with the right pedagogy.

From the teacher's responses we have designed our pilot observational study for primary school children with the humanoid robot. It is not reasonable to meet all of the requests of the teachers in a single lesson plan therefor priority is given to the most tenable requirements.

Curriculum requirement: Learning the basic concept of programming, i.e. sequencing.

- Group size: individual, small groups of 2 and 3 will be trialed to determine optimal group size.
- Age Groups: Grade 2 through to grade 6 will be trialed to determine required basic literacy and cognitive skills and reaction to the robot.
- Student direction: Students will follow structured introduction then take ownership of furthering their own direction and learning.
- Teacher training and preparation: This has been kept to a minimum by using pre-programmed routines and allowing students to undertake discovery learning.

3. OBSERVATIONAL STUDY WITH STUDENTS

The purpose of this study is to refine the criteria of the lesson plan activities, target age group, group or individual activity, learning environment and students learning outcome. HCI (Human Computer Interaction) observational method (Lazar, Feng & Hochheiser 2010) was used where primary aged students participated in learning the concept of programming using a humanoid robot. The internal-external observation was considered during testing (Miyake, Miyagawa & Tamura1998) where the observer encouraged students to talk during the free play activity but did not take part in the activity itself; the facilitator directed them in some points.

Initially ten primary students participated in this study and we considered it as pilot testing to assist in refining the study for future investigation. Students worked in a small group in the usability lab, and the facilitator was available for support and monitoring. Initial surveys were undertaken to determine the children demographics and previous use and exposure to computers. The duration of a session was approximately one and half-hours. Both Qualitative and Quantitative data has been collected during this study. There were five stages of this study.

Stage 1: the facilitator demonstrated the robot's pre-programmed actions such as walking, talking, sitting, waving. A demonstration followed on how to use the choreographe library, drag and drop boxes, and compile and output.

Figure 1. a. The humanoid robot can walk. b. The robot cannot run. c. Students were working with cards to make their own sequence (Stage 2)

Stage 2: The facilitator provided the students with cards that contained different actions that the humanoid robot can and cannot do. Students were asked to identify the actions the robot can do and the use the cards to create their own sequence of actions, which are shown in Figure 1.

Stage 3: Students explored by themselves how the NAO robot Choreograph works, which are shown in Figure 2. Students then attempted to use choreograph drag and drop to act out the sequence of actions created in stage 2. During this stage, students were encouraged to talk about their thoughts and reasons for undertaking various paths and activities.

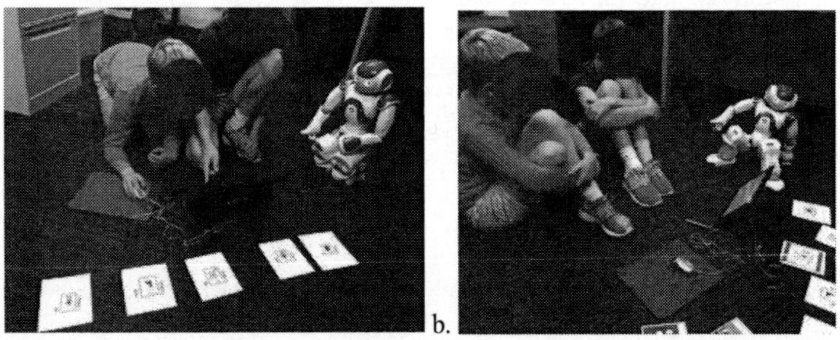

Figure 2. a. Students were working with the choreographe, and b. the robot performed based on students program using choreographe (Stage 3)

Stage 4: Students were given free playtime with the robot to see if they reused any gained knowledge.

Stages 5: At the end, the facilitator discussed with the students, their favorite moments, important events, exciting activities and challenges during testing.

Results and discussion of the pilot study

The pilot study included 10 students who were tested in the groups.

PREFERRED STUDENT AGE GROUP

Young students were very excited with the robot that they were not interested how the robot works. They had difficulties to the use of choreographe such as finding actions from the library and linking boxes to generate a sequence. It was found that the younger students lost attention in the final free playtime. Later year students were (individually /group) engaged and keen to learn how the robot works.

GROUP WORK

Students worked well in groups sharing their knowledge and resources. We found that groups of three students were too noisy to enable each member to hear the ideas of the quieter members, and they had a problem with the sharing resources and ideas. Where students worked in pairs there was more opportunity for all students to have equal access and present their ideas. Both groups of 2 and 3 were more encouraging and less concerned to try new activities than the individual.

TECHNICAL SUPPORT

Even with the most basic of activities, i.e. using only pre-programmed actions, the facilitator found technical issues during the demonstration with the robot in that it did not play all of its actions which it needed to be performed. The facilitator considered the situation of a teacher and needed to be comfortable with this robot first by effective training and time allowance, and several trials and errors testing before the demonstration.

STUDENTS' OWNERSHIP

Students took ownership of their work and explored with the choreographe (stage 3) rather than facilitator led activities. Students were able to use their previous activities to explore further sequences and question what else could be done using the robot.

STUDENTS LEARNING OUTCOME

Students worked in a group and every time they created a new sequence of actions using the choreographe. They learnt the concept of sequencing. They explored their knowledge with the choreographe and they had found more actions and parameters then the facilitator demonstrated to them.

4. CONCLUSION

The integration of any new technology requires extensive planning and organisation. It is evident from the teacher interviews that the teacher's focus is to ensure that the time invested on any new technology will result in a positive learning experience that meets curriculum requirements.

The pilot study found that children of grades 5 and 6 were more suited to the level of basic cognitive skills required and worked better in groups of 2 rather than 3 or individually. The children took ownership of their learning and were self motivated during the free play. It was not evident whether this would enable students to move to the next level of learning to program. It was evident that the teacher's concern of the need for training and technical support is well founded and should be of paramount importance even where the activities are as basic as this study.

This paper has identified how primary school teachers can integrate a humanoid robot into their classroom among suitable age group students and to examine the impact of such integration on student learning. Finally, this paper will be helpful for the teachers finding meaningful ways of using the humanoid robot with students in the classroom while avoiding potential risks. Students gained hands-on experiences using the humanoid robot to make the robot speak and move. The humanoid robot has the potential to influence of student learning where students can learn, create, understand, and explore with the robot; but it can only do so in the hands of skilled teachers. The limitations of this research, teachers were not involved during observational study and it was not conducted in classroom. It is intended to undertake further study in the classroom with the teacher facilitating for more reliable information.

REFERENCES

Clarke, G. and Zagarell, J, 2012. Technology in the Classroom: Teachers and Technology: A Technological Divide: Childhood Education 88.2:136-139.

Clements, D.H.and Sarama, J, 2002. The Role of Technology in Early Childhood Learning. Teaching Children Mathematics 8.6: 340.

Lazar, J., Feng, J.H. and Hochheiser, H, 2010. Research Methods in Human-Computer Interaction. John Wiley & Sons.

Miyake, Y., Miyagawa, T. and Tamura, Y, 1998. Internal Observation and Mutual Adaptation in Human Robot Cooperation. Systems, Man, and Cybernetic. 1998 IEEE International Conference on. Vol. 4. IEEE, 1998.

Mouza, C, 2005. Using Technology to Enhance Early Childhood Learning: The 100 Days of School Project. Educational Research and Evaluation, 11(6), pp.513-528.

Simon, F. and Nemeth, K, 2012. Digital Decisions: Choosing the Right Technology Tools for Early Childhood Education. Chicago: Gryphon House.

MUSICAL OBJECT

Francisco Lopes, Tiago Cruz and F. Amílcar Cardoso
CISUC, Department of Informatics Engineering, University of Coimbra, Coimbra, Portugal

ABSTRACT

Music is a powerful medium for expressing emotions and feelings acquired during childhood; we are used to improvise rhythms and melodies, memorize and imagine harmonies and even full songs.
However, due to the complexity involved in the personal expression through an instrument, it becomes necessary not only to completely master it, but also understand the theoretical concepts that dictate the rules to which melodies must obey.
Assuming that most people with little or no musical knowledge whatsoever can create melodies using only their voice, this project's aim is to identify and promote these intuitions using the design of an interactive system. Ultimately, it will become possible to convey melodic ideas by changing the way an instrument's perception is later conducted and thus offering the possibility of musical expression to anyone.

KEYWORDS

Music, Expression, Intuition, Interaction Design, Musical Instrument, Electronics

1. INTRODUCTION

The interpretative face of musical experience is not as simple and fluid as the purely hearing side. Everyone can enjoy music, but for one to be able to express itself fluently with a melodic instrument, one must learn the principles governing the musical theory: the set of rules that must be followed so that they can combine sounds that result in enjoyable compositions, instead of chaos.

The aim of this project is to overcome this barrier using the users intuition. For example, even having no musical training, one is capable of recognizing musical aspects as "higher" or "lower" tones as well as volume and rhythm changes. Most of us can, with our voices, sing numerous songs. Some better than others are able to improvise melodies and follow instruments without being aware of every note and how many tones go up or down.

The digital world has been finding increasingly powerful answers for those who want to express themselves musically, but still a gap remains between the interactive applications that allow the composition of musical excerpts with some complexity and the control of its execution, in a creative and intuitive way to people with basic musical knowledge.

This project consists in the design of an electronic musical instrument that can be played by anyone. It aims to develop an interactive system that changes the way its users interact with the music and, above all, that is likely to be a medium of musical expression easy to understand and operate.

2. BODY OF PAPER

This design is based on the conceiving of an electronic musical instrument. A research was carried on projects related either by responding to the same problem or by presenting innovative interaction methods, that must be analyzed to better understand what may or may not be used and the improvements that can be made in this area.

The methods and tools were chosen accordingly and defined the entire process of the object conception.

2.1 Related Projects

In every exploratory process there is influence from several works as its final characteristics are only accomplished through a lot of experimentation. In this section follows a presentation of works worth highlighting, which influenced decisions made in this project's design, either by guiding or solving conception issues.

Trombone-Propelled Electronics it's an interesting work by Nicholas Collins (1991) as it results from an exploration process improvised with objects already owned by the author. Starting with a slider trombone, the author proceeded to attach a controller with sixteen keys each with a different sound manipulation effect. In the mouth piece a breath controller was used to generate the sound and the slider's movement controls the selected effect. This was made possible by coupling to it the end of a dog leash that goes through a knob that changes the value of the effect.

The Hands by Michel Waisvisz (1984), consists of a set of two ergonomically shaped plates with sensors, potentiometers and switches to be strapped to the user's hands (Waisvisz, 1985). The analogue information provided by the sensors is then translated to MIDI Standard. Although today this is a common practice, this was the first experimental interface to apply it. This instrument detects finger and hand movement and it's meant to be played like an "air accordion". The interfaced worked really well and Waisvisz improved it and used it in live performances until his later years.

Double Slide Controller by Tomás Henriques (2009) is in the middle of the aforementioned projects. As Collins, Henriques was also based in the trombone's interface, although it doesn't contain any of its parts. Comparable to The Hands, it also benefits from two hand actuated controllers which are part of two sliders, instead of only one, doubling its controls as Henriques aims to go beyond the simulation of the original instrument sound and interface. It uses a breath controller to trigger the sounds and the gesture driven interface allows the manipulation of several sound aspects.

AlphaSphere by Adam Place, Liam Lacey and Tom Mitchell (2013), was conceived to explore electronic sound characteristics and was later adopted as an instrument by organizing its sounds in scales matching the steel pan's tuning system. The object consists of a series of silicon-based membranes, disposed in a dome, which activate a sound when touched and distort it when some pressure is applied. This appealing and easy to use and understand interface was the project's true innovation leading to the instrument success and later its commercialization.

These devices were deemed relevant as they follow the same approach, which proved itself efficient: they were all inspired in existing instruments. Using different types of electronic controllers and sensors they simulate its acoustic counterpart's interface to control the production of sounds.

Recently there have been several projects that follow a different approach, the "gamification" of musical creation, designing software based products that allow the user to compose music by layers.

Some examples are the Reactable (2003) – a sensitive horizontal screen that recognizes a set of objects which the user alights in it, allowing the continuous shaping of the composition –, NodeBeat (2013) – a project similar to the previous one, developed as a mobile application instead, with a menu for the available "objects" – and Incredibox (2009) – a web application that portraits an "a capella" group of up to seven individuals whom you may assign a sound from a predetermined list.

These projects work with the same principles: the user must add modules to a continuous loop that can be a new sound or a modification of an existing sound. This method threats the musical generation as a performance and allows the creation of complex musical compositions. On the other and, it fails in delivering real time control of the whole generation as the user focuses in a single layer at a time while the others keep playing the same loop.

2.2 Methods

After specific research on different projects that would, in some way, respond to the stated problem, it was decided that the best option would be to build a physical interface. This approach was deemed ideal for this project as it grants a more natural and familiar way of playing music.

Allowing the user to control the outcome instantaneously and providing physical feedback of each value that is being controlled, it's possible to reach two important objectives from an instrument player perspective: to shape the melodies as desired in real time and to play along other instruments.

The interface was to be made of electronic sensors that should measure the various types of interaction, Arduino came up as a solution to the interpretation of the signals and Processing for the refining of data and its routing to a MIDI synthesizer, which is in charge of the sound generation.

2.3 Progress Documentation

Taking into account the various tools involved in the development of this project and the need to study them in parallel, the progress description is divided into different fields of study.

Considering the author himself is included in both the target audience and in the project's development, it's important to underline that many of the decisions involving changes in the product usability had a strong influence from his own experience.

Bearing this in mind, it is very possible for the execution of usability tests to furthermore motivate unique changes in this area in order to help establish the ultimate effectiveness allowing for the project to meet its objective.

2.3.1 Sound and Music Theory

The development of a system that produces sounds with distinct attributes requires a full understanding of what can in fact be controlled.

Sound is the auditory sensation triggered by propagating mechanical vibration oscillations, which take the name of sound waves and can be represented by their frequency (repetition of the wave at a given time), amplitude (measured in decibels, which gives us the feeling of volume) and periodicity (which can be either a simple wave or simply a wave pattern that keeps being repeated).

The music itself, in addition to a set of sounds, is represented by their arrangement. We therefore have the pitch (frequency), the intensity (amplitude) and timbre (periodicity) as well as the scale and duration of the sounds, which concern the sound configuration in terms of pitch values and time, respectively.

2.3.2 Electronic Sensors

Taking into account these sound variables, a number of electronic sensors were studied in order to select which would integrate the interface in the most intuitive and familiar way to the user.

Portraying most wind instruments, the airflow was determined as one of the key competitors in the interaction method for controlling the intensity of sound. This type of interaction isn't the one more suitable when it comes to getting specific results but in this case the relevance is in the control of the dynamics and the perceived differences between the values as opposed to the exact volume that you are playing at any given time.

After some tests in different types of sensors, a barometric pressure sensor was picked as the most adequate. The specific model is the Freescale Semiconductor Company's MPXV4006, used in medical devices to carefully measure the pressure exerted by the user's breath.

As for the pitch of the notes, the decision to grant control to hand and finger movement was quite immediate, as it is a characteristic that must be capable of being controlled quickly and accurately. It is envisioned that there would be a dedicated key for each finger so that a comprehensive training and development of dexterity wit the instrument would not be needed.

In addition to the activation of a tone, it was implied from the beginning that it would be possible to control, small variances in frequency effects such as "vibrato" and "pitchbend", frequently used in string instruments. For this purpose, it was decided that force sensors (force sensitive resistors) would be used to not only to detect touch, but also to measure the finger movement through the use of springs on top of the sensor.

Finally, it would be necessary to go through a scale so that the experience would not to be reduced to the small number of notes offered by the previous interface. It was decided to devote one hand to that purpose and the other to control the position on the scale, like some existing musical instruments, as is the case the guitar or the theremin.

This would require a controller with several buttons that could be used with one hand and, after testing several options, the Nunchuk joystick Nintendo Wii turned out to be the winning candidate due to its simplicity, comfortability and easy communication through Arduino.

2.3.3 Processing Sound and Music

After the interface was designed, it became necessary to design an application that could receive the values obtained by the sensors and translate them into MIDI messages that would later be sent to a synthesizer. In addition to the findings obtained during the idealization of the physical interface, some decisions were made before initiating this stage of the development.

Distinctions between the tone pitches are accomplished through four touch sensors, controlled by the fingers on one hand. The force exerted on each sensor controls small changes in the pitch of each tone. The shift in scale, changing the tone to be activated for each sensor, is made with the other hand through the Nunchuk. Similarly to wind instruments, intensity control is all about the user's breath. The timbre of the sound selection and the definition of the scale on which it intends to play are previously made in the developed application. Finally the duration is controlled implicitly: for a note to be activated it must be assigned a tone and intensity, and its duration results from the combination of the breath and touch controls.

To assign the tones for each touch sensor, a decision was made to group the notes in chords. Each song follows a scale and has a chord progression that grants it the notion of structure. By grouping the tones that could be played in chords it ensures that the notes you play are in harmony and allows for the control of this structure, without the user having to think of the relationship between the notes themselves.

The visual clues that allow for the use of this system are represented in a graphical interface, where you can view the options for the joystick. Along with the synthesizer, these components form the visual component of the application. SimpleSynth was the chosen software the development of this project, but it works with any synthesizer software that can use a MIDI virtual port as a source.

2.3.4 Materialization

The embodiment of this project is a process of trial and error as well as ne tuning, as most constructions of new interfaces are. Assuming this enterprise is a work in progress, we present the current state of the solutions.

In regards to the breathing component interface, it was necessary to build a system that would be connected to the sensor to forward the airflow from the mouth of the user. To this end, parts of irrigation systems revealed to be quite the answer. A valve that regulates the amount of air escaping the system before reaching the sensor was later included. The last-mentioned would customize the pressure required to reach minimum and maximum values in the sensor.

As for the touch interface, the solution is to use four springs placed inside small cylinders, combined with force sensors located at the one end and solid discs in the other, where pressure is exerted with the finger.

Arduino is the controller which binds together all of the sensors, including the chosen joystick. It receives their signals and directs them to the Processing application.

At the moment, the interaction with the designed touch sensors is not completely satisfactory due to the high stiffness of the springs, resulting in an uncomfortable placement of the hand. Enhancements are being made in order to use lighter and smaller springs, like the ones used in trumpet construction.

3. CONCLUSION

All things considered, it can be said this tool allows the user to express himself by generating sounds without the need of knowing this particular object nor concepts of music theory. As in almost everything, some practice will surely improve the results meaning the user can reproduce more accurately what's in his mind, but the familiarization time is very low - when compared with a conventional musical instrument - due to the simplicity of the interaction set.

On the other hand, for a user who masters musical theory this instrument can reveal itself to be very limiting for it has a distinct set of rules that dictate the tones that can be played. However, one can furthermore make changes to overcome this aspect, through exploring new, different of sensor interpretation. For example, changing the current control system of the pitch - which is very similar to the guitar - to the type of treatment used in most wind instruments, in which each combination of keystrokes has a different tone, one can play specifically desired notes.

Additionally, one might add sensors or external devices that allow the control of existing aspects in other musical instruments (which require a higher level of technique and coordination). Such an example would be for instance, the pedals of a piano, which allow more control of the duration of the notes.

As for the actual object in development, it is expected to be submitted to usability tests in real contexts thus allowing for both the error correction and identification of aspects that may be additionally improved.

It is to be an instrument that serves both musical expression and creative operation. Conclusively, an instrument also suitable to use in concerts or any other performance activities, solo or accompanied by many other instruments.

The expected product is only a suggested solution to the problem and, while being able to be used by anyone, it may very well be the driving force for others to take on their own vision on the matter, ultimately aimed at bridging the initially identified gaps.

REFERENCES

Aldwell, Edward et al, 2011. *Harmony & Voice Leading*. Schirmer, Boston, Massachusetts, USA.

Saffer, Dan, 2010. *Designing for Interaction, Second Edition: Creating Innovative Applications and Devices*. New Riders, Berkeley, California, USA.

Waisvisz, Michel, 1985. *THE HANDS, a set of MIDI-controllers*. Proceedings of the international computer music conference. Simon Frasier University, Canada, pp. 313-318.

Collins, Nicholas, 1991. *Low Brass: The Evolution of Trombone-Propelled Electronics*. LEONARDO MUSIC JOURNAL, Vol. 1, No. 1, pp. 41-44.

Henriques, Tomás, 2009. *Double Slide Controller*. Proceedings of the international conference on new interfaces for musical expression. Pittsburgh, USA, pp. 260-261.

Place, Adam et al, 2014. *AlphaSphere - from Prototype to Product*. Proceedings of the international conference on new interfaces for musical expression. Goldsmiths, London, pp. 399-402.

GOBBO - AN ALTERNATIVE COMMUNICATION TOOL TO STUDENTS OF APAE WITH CEREBRAL PALSY

Maria Renata M. Gobbo[1], Cinthyan Renata Sachs C. de Barbosa[1], Thiago Adriano Coleti[2] and Fabio de Sordi Junior[2]
[1]*Universidade Estadual de Londrina, Brazil*
[2]*Universidade Estadual do Norte do Paraná, Brazil*

ABSTRACT

This paper presents the process of developing an alternative communication tool to support the communication of people with cerebral palsy. This tool was developed aiming at improving the communication of cerebral palsy children allowing them to communicate with others through the selection of icons and images in an interface and for each item selected the software provides a synthesized sound related to its function. Thus, we developed such software using Android architecture, Portuguese language and intuitive figures in order to improve the communication of children. The software was tested in a Brazilian school that provides services for children with special needs. As a result, the software was considered effective for the task because the children could use the software. Some improvements were detected and should be developed in a future release.

KEYWORDS

Cerebral palsy.Alternative communication.Speech disorders.Accessibility.Handicap Applications.

1. INTRODUCTION

Communication is not only extremely important for people's cognitive development, but also for their socialization. When people present certain kind of verbal communication lack, we might hold alternative communication devices, which are able to support them, therefore, they are able to receive and transmit messages to others. People with cerebral palsy may struggle when communicating, not only the speaker, but also the listener. Data estimates that about 45% of children with cerebral palsy being 8 to 13 years old encounter difficulties towards speaking and communicating. Due to motor disabilities expressed from the language, the gesture legibility may be compromised, as well as the writing capacity when using a pen or a computer (Pennington, 2008).

The interaction with the world is very important to the intellectual and social growth and due to the communication disorders, people with cerebral palsy tend to have passive communication. To these people, communication could be performed through distinct ways as tools, which bring alternative communication (Geytenbeek, *et al.*, 2015; Pennington *et al.* ,2013).

Alternative communication refers to any tool or system of communication, which supports voice or writing, including gestures, manual signs (hand forms, body positioning, facial expressions, etc.) and symbols. Symbols could include prints, photographs and orthography (Prince, Clarke, 2012).

Such symbols are organized in low and high technology, according to Prince and Clarke (2012), communication helpers of high technology are electronic devices, which hold spoken voice. Helpers of low technology are books or graphs of images, photographs and symbols based on paper and words.

The alternative communication is indicated to people with communication problems and could be the only way in which such individuals can communicate ideas (Pennington, 2008).

From the aforementioned premise, it was possible to analyze the real limitations of people with cerebral palsy and also to verify all their motor and communication disabilities, either verbal or not. In such cases, the use of an alternative communication is indicated. The alternative could be built over computers, so that people are able to diminish or even surpass communication barriers (Miranda, Gomes, 2004). Thanks to the advent of technology, we are equipped with devices that are touch-sensitive. Such resource allows that, with some touch on the screen, a person with move restrictions could communicate to others. For that achievement, an alternative communication tool was developed. The tool runs on Android, which should be utilized on a tablet, aiming at supporting and aid people with cerebral palsy carrying speech restrictions.

Posteriorly, this tool was evaluated in a real environment (APAE - Association of Parents and Friends of Exceptional Children, of Bandeirantes, Paraná), involving students and teachers, aiming at investigating pros and cons of the tools, as well as its communication efficiency to the target audience.

2. TOOL DEVELOPMENT

An alternative communication tool was created, offering communication assistance focusing on people who presented difficulties of speech or muteness. Thus, people were able to send and receive messages one another and interact with the world more concretely.

After a few meetings with teachers, pedagogues and physiotherapists about the development of the present tools, about 100 images were chosen, separated in 4 main categories and more 5 sub-categories. The main categories, which can be observed in Figure 1, are: School, Pain, Bathroom and Break. Such categories are available on the home screen of the application. In this screen there are also two figures being "Yes" or "No". Using these two last figures students could easily answer direct questions.

The category "pain" was chosen as people with cerebral palsy could endure pain caused by muscle atrophy due to the motor disability, caused by the paralysis. The figures within this category are: leg, foot, back, arm, mouth, eye, hand, ear, head and tooth. In order to create this category, meetings with physiotherapists were performed, thus, it was possible to recognize the place where these children mostly felt pain (Gobbo, 2015).The category "bathroom" is present in the application to assist students with physical needs. This category guarantees greater security to people, once they are able to express their physical needs at the moment.

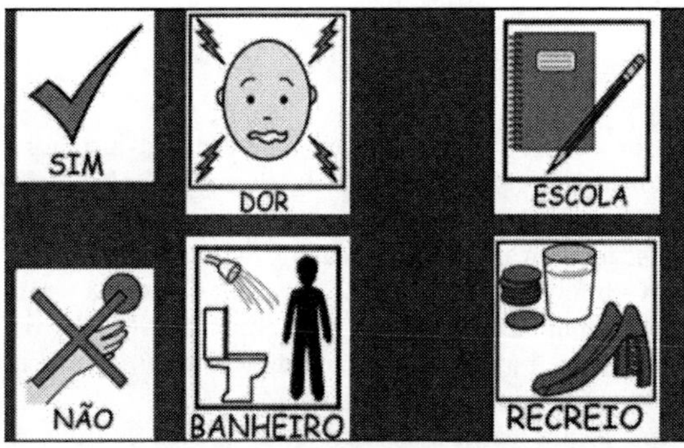

Figure 1. Home screen of the application

Figure 2. “School” category screen

The category "break" is a way to encourage students to socialize during their break. The category "school" is dedicated to activities performed within APAE and it is divided in subcategories: the subcategory "Portuguese", which presents the alphabet, the subcategory "math", which is showing numbers, the subcategory "arts", which presents the main activities developed during class, the subcategory "physiotherapy" takes into account exercises that commonly are performed with these patient students. The application also takes into account a subcategory that contains images to their interaction with other students inside the classroom as could be observed in Figure 2.

In order to reach the results present in this work, it was necessary to perform research on cerebral palsy, characteristics and particularities of the disease aiming at understanding, in fact, the real situation of our target audience so the application can assist them regardless their limitations.

To the development of the tool, in addition to the contribution of the teachers, certain existing alternative communication tools were analyzed. It was done in order to obtain a base of their main functionalities and then be implemented within the application developed from this work.

All images present in the developed application were chosen by professionals responsible by children with cerebral palsy, along with the developer of the application. It was taken into account students' day-to-day and probable interactions with thirds.

2.1 Validation Along With Teachers

SUS is a usability scale for simple systems, which measures effectiveness, efficiency and satisfaction of the user. Brooke proposed this scale in 1986 and it is so far used. In this scale we may find a questionnaire containing 10 questions with 5 answer options each, where the evaluator could agree or disagree with the questions. It was developed in order to extract particular impressions of the users, based on their experience towards what is being evaluated (BROOKE, 1996).

The SUS scale was used in order to evaluate the tool from the teachers' point of view. They answered to 10 questions based on the SUS scale and therefore the system's usability was verified. In addition to the questions which made part of the SUS scale, in order to obtain a technical evaluation, other three types of open questions were applied: **1) Applications' pros; 2) Applications' cons; 3) What is missing in the application.**

The questionnaire was answered by APAE's teachers, audiologists and also by physiotherapists. From the analyses over the obtained answers, it was possible to execute improvements on the application, such as: creation of categories of alphabetization with numerals and the alphabet, buttons that return from categories, creation of a category to the physiotherapy sessions.

For the validation of the GOBBO application in conjunction with the student, it was created a questionnaire followed by the same scheme of the SUS' usability scale. The teacher who followed the student whilst the use of GOBBO, once student with paralysis presented certain motor limitations and could not answer the questionnaire alone answered the questionnaire.

In the questionnaire one may find four questions, which analyze how the student behaves towards GOBBO. The questions are:

- Frequency of the application's use: represents how much the student has utilized the application.
- Ease of use: aims at analyzing whether the student has succeeded in easily utilizing the application or the student has found difficulties.
- Reliability when using the application: aims at analyzing whether the student trusts the application or the student is afraid of utilizing the application;
- Correct completion: analyzes whether the student succeeded in communicating as he or she expected.

In order to perform the validation with the student, firstly, the student went through a user experience process with duration of 8 hours inside the educational environment. According to the observations made during the training, the biggest difficulties took place during the first day, once the student presented a motor limitation greater than expected and thus, the student could not click on the desired figure. Therefore, the student ended up frustrated by not being able to use the app due to the lack of coordination and performance.

In the end of the eight hours which were divided in four days, it was applied a questionnaire, the four questions were analyzed in three different levels, as the application has symbols which are easier to find and others that require screen navigation.

The first level presents the figures that are in the application's home screen, where the main categories are: School, Pain, Bathroom and Break, thus, the student were not required to navigate to any other screen. The second level required navigation inside the categories in order to find the image, for instance, the person who aims at going to the bathroom and brushing her teeth, in case she is not on the home screen of the category "Bathroom" she should navigate to the third screen which would function as the third level, namely, she would need to navigate through the subcategories in order to find the desired symbols.

The student's teacher answered the questionnaire, once she knows better his limitations and thus, she would be able to answer more accurately the questionnaire.

2.2 Validation Results

The questionnaire presented in this work was applied to 10 people: 2 physiotherapists, 1 audiologist, 1 pedagogue and 6 special education teachers. The first analysis was a technical analysis performed through an open questionnaire, and the other analysis regarded usability, performed through the SUS's questionnaire.

2.2.1 Technical Analysis with Teachers

As stated earlier, the technical analysis was comprised by an open questionnaire containing three questions, in which we were able to analyze pros and cons and the points missing in the application.

Analysis the answers the following points were found:

- **Positive points (pros):**

Coherent drawings followed by the action; assists in the communication; well elaborated content; could be used in order to assist the communication to children with other diseases such as autism and stroke; objective and simple layout; assists in the interaction of the children in the classroom.

- **Cons:**

"Yes" and "No" symbols should use the positive and negative sign; home screen containing too much information.

- **What is missing in the application:**

Lack of numerals; lack of alphabet; return button in the categories and subcategories; the creation of a subcategory in the category "School" with the physiotherapy activity.

Once the analysis was concluded, it was performed a re-adaptation of the system with all observations pointed out in the open questionnaire. We noticed that the lack of a return button for the categories and subcategories, for the physiotherapy category, which is also a constant activity within the school and the lack of numerals and alphabet. Although the application is focused on the communication and not on the education itself, the teachers' desire to work with the application GOBBO was taken into account.

2.2.2 Usability Analysis with the Teachers

Firstly, the analysis was performed from the respondent average. After that, the SUS scale was scored, which reached 84,5 points. According to Brooke (1996), in order to interpret the score, we may take into account the average score that should be kept always above 70 points.

2.2.3 Result Analysis with the Students

In order to validate the application with the student, we applied a questionnaire with 4 questions. The tests were performed with a 12-year-old child with ataxic cerebral palsy, presenting a severe frame of motor coordination lack in the low members and a moderated lack of motor coordination in the superior members.

In the first level test, the student demonstrated great facility when using the application. The student didn't hesitate in using the GOBBO application and was able to touch on the screen every time he was asked for.

Five diverse questions were chosen where the answer could be whether yes or no. The student answered all questions correctly, demonstrating great facility and reliability while using the application. The same happened when the student was asked to try the "break" category, where, on the first attempt, it worked.

In the second level test, the student also had great performance. He was able to return to the home screen and navigate access once more the category "break" and touch the symbol "eat". In this case, he had to navigate between two screens and did not make any mistakes. The student was also asked to find the symbol "take a bath", where in the first attempt he presented difficulties, once his hand was touching the tablet and afterwards another category was being touched. However, in the second attempt, he was able to find the requested symbol.

In the third level test, he struggled a bit, as he would have to navigate through three different screens. The same happened in the second level, as the student's hand was touching the tablet before the touch of his fingers, which resulted in opening a different screen.

The experience was considered valid by the teachers, physiotherapists and audiologists, once that the student was able to perform most part of the proposed activity.

Teachers stated that the application assisted the student not only in the communication, but also guaranteeing an stimulation for using the language, where the application was reproducing via sound the words that the symbols represented, as well as stimulated the cognitive sense of the student, as he had to memorize and find out where each symbol was placed and stimulated the student in the motor part, once the student had to make more precise movements in order to be able to touch in the application symbols.

3. CONCLUSION

The issue arisen by this work led us to the development of an alternative communication system, developed on Android, which suits children with cerebral palsy. The focus of the current work has to do with its usage within the child's education context, always aiming at the child's interaction inside a classroom, not only involving the teacher but also the other students.

During the validation of the application, we noticed that the GOBBO application was well accepted not only by teachers, but also by students, which could be observed from the SUS score that was 84,5%, and also due to the open questions where teachers could write freely pros and cons, where we could notice the pros surpass the cons. The acceptability of the application by the teachers could be observed as well through their informal statements, as they showed themselves interested in using the application.

Certain future improvements could be found through the applications' validation. For instance, adding more activities regarding to the day-to-day life of the child, therefore, they are able to utilize them in the familiar context. As a consequence, the communication would be extended outside schools. However, such improvements should be planned carefully, once the unplanned increasing of the quantity of figures could affect the navigation between the screens, then, mitigating one of the main qualities of GOBBO: the navigation simplicity.

REFERENCES

Brooke, J. (1996). SUS-A quick and dirty usability scale. Usability evaluation in industry. Vol. 189, No. 194, pp. 4-7.

Geytenbeek, Joke J.; Oostrom, Kim J.; Harlaar, Laaurike; Becher, Jules G.; Knol, Dirk L., Barkhof, Frederick; Pinto, Pedro S.; Vermeulen, R. Jeroen, 2015. Language comprehension in nonspeaking children with severe cerebral palsy: Neuroanatomical substrate?,*European Journal of Paediatric Neurology,* Vol. 19, pp. 510-520.

Gobbo, M. R. M.; Coleti, T. A. ;Sordi Jr, F, 2015. Proposta de umaFerramenta de ComunicaçãoAlternativa para Alunos da APAE com Paralisia Cerebral..*In: SimpósioBrasileiro de FatoresHumanosemSistemasComputacionais*, Salvador. Proceedings of IHC-15.Vol. 1. pp. 462-465.

Miranda, cristian l.; Ivone C. D., Gomes, 2004.*Contribuições da comunicaçãoalternativa de baixatecnologiaemparalisia cerebral semcomunicação oral: relato de caso.* Rev CEFAC, Vol. 6, No. 3, pp. 247-52.

Pennington, Lindsay, 2008. *Cerebral palsy and communication, Paediatrics and Child Health*, Vol. 18. pp. 405-409.

Pennington, Lindsay. Virella, Daniel. Mjopen, Tone. et al., 2013 Development of The Viking Speech Scale to classify the speech of children with cerebral palsy. *Research in developmental disabilities*, Vol. 34, No. 10, pp. 3202-3210.

Price, Katie. Clarke, Michael, 2012. Augmentative and alternative communication for children with cerebral palsy, *Paediatrics and Child Health*, Vol. 22, pp. 367-37.

Schlosser, Ralf W.; Sigafoos, Jeff, 2006. Intervenções de comunicaçãoaumentativa e alternativa para pessoas com deficiências de desenvolvimento:.*Revisãonarrativa de estudosexperimentais de casoúnicocomparativos Research in deficiências de desenvolvimento.* Vol. 27, No. 1, pp. 1-29.

DESIGNING APPLICATIONS FOR INTELLECTUAL DISABILITY USERS TO TEACH INDEPENDENCE SKILLS

Marian McDonnell and Colette Verdes
Institute of Art Design & Technologies
Kill Avenue, Dun Laoghaire, Co. Dublin, Ireland

ABSTRACT

Research in the area of designing instructional technologies for teaching independent living skills for the intellectual disability (ID) population is limited. This present case study evaluating an eLearning application called Let's Go for ID users to aid independent travel aims to add to the research in the area. Semi-structured interviews were carried out with nine instructors. The qualitative method of thematic analysis was used to analyse themes and provided valuable data on the evaluation of the application. Findings highlighted areas that need improvement under the themes: images/colour, navigation, audio, symbols and alerts wording. Age appropriateness of images is possibly a new finding in this limited area as the topic has not appeared in the extensive literature that was analysed. Instructors were of the opinion that this application is a useful learning tool for ID users.

KEYWORDS

Intellectual disability, Assistive technology, Human computer interaction, Interface design, Independent travel

1. INTRODUCTION

1.1 Intellectual Disability and Instructional Technologies

ID is a neurodevelopmental disorder characterised by impairments in both intellectual and adaptive functioning (American Psychiatric Association, 2013). The three main areas affected include the conceptual, social and practical domain.

In recent years, mobile technologies complete with eLearning applications have become a popular tool in aiding those with ID. These include devices such as the iPod touch, iPad, tablets and smartphones. Mobile technologies can increase quality of life and independence in those with ID (Rodríguez, Strnadová, & Cumming, 2015). Advantages are portability, user friendliness as well as allowing for accessibility features. The devices have a large number of applications that can facilitate individuals with ID in areas of communication and life skills and are also relatively inexpensive long term. In addition, these devices are less stigmatising (Mechling, 2011). Bouck (2012) surveyed a group of individuals with ID and found that 97% of them were dependant on a caregiver for daily assistance. This shows the importance of assistive technologies, to help people become more independent and less reliant on caregivers.

1.2 Indirect Studies with Carers and Parents

HCI research often involves the intended users in research and usability studies. However, accessibility to this population can be difficult for researchers. Sears and Hansa (2011) state that it is difficult to recruit users with disabilities. The use of non-representative users can lead to inaccurate conclusions about mobile technologies effectiveness. Other issues in HCI research include small number of participants and lack of control groups.

A number of studies Weafer (2010); Dawe (2006); Dawe (2007) including ones on aphasia, autism, and locked in syndrome have used carers and relatives as an indirect means of carrying out the research and this is viewed as adequate. Results of a survey by Feng et al (2008) reflected the parents' perception of the children with Down Syndrome computer capabilities. Similarly, this present study will collect data on the instructors' perception of the specific design needs in applications for users with ID.

1.3 Interface Design Recommendations

Designing for those with ID can be challenging for several reasons. As mentioned earlier, some research does not include the intended user with an ID and also user testing does not occur. In addition, there is a lack of design principles when developing applications, as "one size does not fit all!". ID accessibility can call Universal Design into questioning – as it is not possible to design a product for all especially in the broad area of ID (Kennedy, Evans & Thomas, 2010). The Inclusive New Media Design (INMD) project described by Kennedy et al. (2010) used Participatory Design (PD) to bring 29 ID individuals together with 31 web designers. This resulted in the formation of UI (Universal Interface) design principles for ID. Principles included the use of pictures for information but also repetition of that information in text, simple navigations with few choices, providing interaction and feedback. Other recommendations were made for ID mobile design by Dekelver et al (2015) and included the use of a consistent menu, high contrast between background and text, warnings and personalisation of UI through the menu.

Modelling and visualising information are also listed as important in HCI as well as developing sites to fit all screen sizes (Jaimes, Sebe & Gatica-Perez, 2006). Mechling, (2007) suggested audio prompts an important to include when designing AT to help people with ID in starting and carrying out everyday duties. Reading and spelling can be problematic for this user group and eradicating the need for these is helpful. In the design of interfaces for Down syndrome users, everything must be easily seen and simple to understand. Anything hidden or pull down menus are difficult to find. Auto complete boxes are useful generally and particularly useful for this population (Kumin et al., 2012).

1.4 The Present Study

This present case study of evaluating an eLearning application for ID users to aid independent travel aims to add to the research in the area. This study aim's to evaluate the instructors' perception of the Let's Go application in training ID adults to travel independently. Let's Go is being designed and developed at the researchers' Institute. Evaluation of Let's Go aims to fill a gap in the literature in making recommendations for the interface design of applications towards independence for those with ID. The study aims to discover if instructors consider the multimedia eLearning application Let's Go suitably designed for learners with ID.

2. METHOD

2.1 Qualitative Thematic Analysis

Thematic analysis can be defined as "a method for identifying, analysing and reporting patterns (themes) within data" (Braun & Clarke, 2006). Many different forms of qualitative research can be used including thematic analysis, discourse analysis, grounded theory and "giving voice". Thematic analysis was used by Weafer (2010) to discover the views of people with cognitive impairments, their parents and trainers on independent living. Results indicated the desires and difficulties of the participants with regard to independent living. Therefore thematic analysis can give valuable information on life experiences and hence was chosen as the best method for this study.

2.2 Semi-structured Interviews

Focus groups and interviews, structured and semi structured, are used in Qualitative Thematic Analysis. Focus groups benefit from data produced through interaction between participants (Kitzinger, 1995). Focus groups were not suitable in this process as the research intended to analyse the interaction between the participant and the application. Interactions between participants were not helpful in answering the research question. Therefore, interviews were deemed as suitable for this purpose. Valuable data can be collected from an interview that is successfully planned (Qu & Dumay 2011). Interviews can be carried out in a structured, un-structured or semi-structured manner. Semi-structured has the advantage of appearing more casual and the participant may be more comfortable (Robson, 2006). It allows the researcher to ask specific questions that will generate data on the instructor's perception of the application as well as open ended questions that will provide rich data on the instructors' thoughts. For this reason, this method was selected for the present study.

2.3 Participants

Purposeful sampling was used to recruit nine instructors from Carmona House Services, Glenageary, Co. Dublin. This method of sampling is used to identify and select participants with the ability to provide valuable information for the research topic (Palinkas et al., 2013). Due to ethical issues it was deemed unsuitable to test the application with the users. The instructors were chosen as testers due to their in-depth knowledge and experience of working with the user population. All participants were female and ranged in age from 23 – 45. The participants had worked as instructors with special needs for between 2 months and 10 years. Qualitative research uses a small number of participants. Large numbers are not required as the results are not generalised to the population.

2.4 Materials

The following materials were used: a computer, pen, participants Information Letter, Participant Consent Form, Participant Consent Form for Quotes, Demographic Questionnaire, Interview Schedule, Adapted System Usability Scale (SUS) ,Participant De-brief Form. The SUS has a reasonable reliability with a minimum Cronbach's Alpha of 0.85 (Bangor, Kortum, & Miller, 2008). The scale contains 10 questions measured on a 5 point Likert scale from strongly disagree to strongly agree. The SUS is short and easy to understand for individuals not familiar with technical terminology (Fritz, Balhorn, Riek, Breil, & Dugas, 2012).

2.5 Procedure

Three interview sessions were held at three different Carmona House Services training facilities. This is the place where training would be carried out by the participants therefore giving ecological value to the study. Ecological validity refers to the degree to which the everyday experiences of participants is represented in the data collected (Stone, Shiffman, Atienza & Nebeling, 2007). Dates and times suitable to both instructors and the researcher were agreed. Instructors were given an information sheet explaining what the study was about and what their participation involved. A consent form was then read and signed along with a consent form for quotes. Prior to using the application, instructors completed a demographic questionnaire. Interview questions were then administered to discover how satisfactory users found the Let's Go application. Instructors then evaluated the Let's Go application on a 5 point Likert scale from strongly agree to strongly disagree. The last document instructors completed was an adapted version of the SUS.

Interviews took from 20 minutes to half an hour to complete. The nature of the participant's job is very time consuming and demanding. Therefore, the interviews were kept as short as possible. Finally, instructors were given a de-brief, informed of the ability to withdraw from the study if requested and thanked for their participation.

3. RESULTS

Results of the adapted System Usability Scale (SUS) indicated that overall, instructors were satisfied with the usability of the application. Valuable information, gathered through interview, was thematically analysed, providing a rich insight into the suitability of the application. Results from the Let's Go questionnaire showed instructors perceived users would have the most difficulty with, ease of reading, clarity of the application and noticing important features.

4. DISCUSSION

This is a pioneering study in this area as there is limited research and there is a lack of suitable eLearning and mobile applications to evaluate. The study gives a detailed analysis of the instructor's perception of the Let's Go application. Thematic analysis provided a manner of analysing the data resulting in an informative description of how the instructors perceived the Let's Go application. Findings were in line with the literature with the exception of age appropriateness of photographs, which could possibly be a new finding adding to the literature in the area. In relation to video modelling, the data indicated that it works well when teaching. Modelling and visualising were listed as important when designing multi modal interfaces (Jaimes et al., 2006).

The method of the present study had some limitations. A small number of participants undertook the study leading to only qualitative methods of analysis being used. Using a larger sample and quantitative analysis could give more a greater evaluation of the application. Data collected represented the instructor's perception of the user's opinion rather than the view of the actual user. Users with ID were not recruited for ethical reasons, concurring with Sears et al. (2011) who state that recruiting users with ID was problematic. The view of the user may differ. Therefore, research including the user is necessary to ensure a more appropriate evaluation. Instructors had difficulty with the drag and drop even though this was highlighted as beneficial in training on Independent Travel Assistance (Krug, 2005)

Future research should test the application with the actual users getting information direct from the source rather than perceived view from the instructors. The user group may not be able to communicate ideas on the usability of the application as clearly as the instructors were. Therefore the qualitative method may not be useful for this type of testing. Quantitative methods may be more suitable.

Carmien et al. (2005) reported preparing users to travel independently was costly, tedious and laborious. Results indicated that the Let's Go application would be useful as an eLearning application, helping to reduce time and cost of paper training for this user group.

ACKNOWLEDGEMENT

Without the help and collaboration of the management and staff in Carmona Services, South Dublin, this research project would not have been possible. The researchers thank Day Services Co-coordinator Audrey Carroll and her staff Amanda Mulroy and Jenna Parsons for their commitment, time and effort.

REFERENCES

American Psychiatric Association. 2013. *Diagnostic and statistical manual of mental disorders* (5th ed.). Arlington, VA: American Psychiatric Publishing

Bangor, A., Kortum, P. T. and Miller, J. T. 2008. An empirical evaluation of the system usability scale. *Intl. Journal of Human–Computer Interaction,* 24(6), pp 574-594.

Bouck, E. C. 2012. Secondary students with moderate/severe intellectual disability: Considerations of curriculum and post-school outcomes from the National Longitudinal Transition Study-2. *Journal of Intellectual Disability Research*, 56(12), pp 1175-1186.

Braun, V.,Clarke, V. 2006. Using thematic analysis in psychology. *Qualitative Research Psychology*, 3(2), pp 77-101.

Carmien, S., Dawe, M. and Fischer, G. et al. 2005. Socio-technical environments supporting people with cognitive disabilities using public transportation. *ACM Transactions on Computer Human Interaction* 12(2), pp 233-262.

Dawe, M. 2006.: How young adults with cognitive disabilities and their families adopt assistive technologies. In *Proceedings of the SIGCHI conference on Human Factors in computing systems.* pp. 1143-1152. ACM.

Dawe, M. 2007. Understanding mobile phone requirements for young adults with cognitive disabilities. In *Proceedings of the 9th international ACM SIGACCESS conference on Computers and accessibility.* pp. 179-186. ACM.

Dekelver, J., Kultsova, M., and Shabalina, O. et al. 2015. Design of Mobile Applications for People with Intellectual Disabilities. In *Creativity in Intelligent Technologies and Data Science*, pp. 823-836. Springer International Publishing.

Feng, J., Lazar, J. Kumin, L. et al. 2008. Computer usage by young individuals with Down syndrome: an exploratory study.In *Proceedings of the 10th international ACM SIGACCESS conference on Computers and accessibility* pp. 35-42. ACM.

Fritz, F., Balhorn, S. et al. 2012.Qualitative and quantitative evaluation of EHR-integrated mobile patient questionnaires regarding usability and cost-efficiency. *International journal of Medical Informatics*, 81(5), pp 303-313.

Jaimes, A., Sebe, N., and Gatica-Perez, D. 2006. Human-centered computing: a multimedia perspective. In *Proceedings of the 14th annual ACM International Conference on Multimedia* (pp. 855-864). ACM.

Kennedy, H., Evans, S., and Thomas, S. 2010. Can the Web Be Made Accessible for People with Intellectual Disabilities? The Information Society, 27(1), pp 29-39.

Kitzinger, J. 1995. Qualitative research. Introducing focus groups. *BMJ: British Medical Journal,* 311(7000), pp 299.

Krug, S. 2005. *Don't make me think: A common sense approach to web usability.* Pearson Education India.

Kumin, L., Lazar, J., and Feng, J. H. 2012. Expanding job options: Potential computer-related employment for adults with Down syndrome. *ACM SIGACCESS Accessibility and Computing*, (103), pp 14-23.

Kumin, L., Lazar, J. and Feng, J. 2012. A usability evaluation of workplace related tasks on a multi-touch tablet computer by adults with Down syndrome. *Journal of Usability Studies*, 7(4), pp 118-142.

Mechling, L. C. 2007. Assistive technology as a self-management tool for prompting students with intellectual disabilities to initiate and complete daily tasks: A literature review. *Education and Training in Developmental Disabilities*, pp 252-269.

Mechling, L. C. 2011. Review of twenty-first century portable electronic devices for persons with moderate intellectual disabilities and autism spectrum disorders. *Education and Training in Autism and Developmental Disabilities*, 46, pp 479–498.

Palinkas, L. A., Horwitz, S. M., and Green, C. A. 2013. Purposeful sampling for qualitative data collection and analysis in mixed method implementation research. *Administration and Policy in Mental Health and Mental Health Services Research,* pp 1-12.

Qu, S. Q., and Dumay, J. 2011. The qualitative research interview. Qualitative Research in Accounting & Management, 8(3), pp 238-264.

Robson 2007 *How to do a research project: a guide for undergraduate students*. Oxford, UK: Blackwell Publishing.

Rodríguez, C. D., Strnadová, I., and Cumming, T. M. 2015. Implementing iPad and Mobile Technologies for Students with ID. Recent *Advances in Assistive Technologies to Support Children with Developmental Disorders*, 27.

Sears, A., and Hanson, V. 2012. Representing users in accessibility research. ACM Transactions on Accessible Computing (TACCESS), 4(2), pp1-6.

Stone AA, Shiffman S, and Atienza AA, 2007 *The science of real-time data capture: self reports in health research*. Oxford: Oxford University Press

Weafer, J. A. 2010 Independent and Community Living-the views of people with disabilities families and frontline staff. *Focus Group Consultation Report*

VIRTUAL-REALITY BASED LEISURE EXPERIENCE OF NINTENDO WII FOR ELDERLY

Muge Akyildiz Munusturlar and Suleyman Munusturlar
Anadolu University, Faculty of Sport Sciences, Eskisehir, Turkey

ABSTRACT

However, there have been very few studies on examining whether video games might provide leisure experience and on the experiences gathering from playing video games as a leisure pursuit. The use of Nintendo Wii has become common in rehabilitation particularly in older population, where the term "Wiihabilitation" has been set out (Wollersheim et al., 2010, p.: 86). As the purpose of this study was to discover and understand the dimensions of leisure experience of elders' leisure playing Wii games as a leisure activity, a qualitative research design was adopted. Purposive sampling method was adopted in this study. The sample was composed of 13 older people who were the participants of the Municipality in Eskisehir-Turkey. The intervention took 40 minutes per a session, two times in a week for 6 weeks. Participants played all four games in each session for ten minutes. According to the results of the interviews, three themes were uncovered related to leisure experience gained through Wii game exercises. For labeling the emerged themes, the recent leisure experience literature was frequently consulted. These three preliminary themes are labeled as social experience, physical experience and relaxation.

KEYWORDS

Leisure, Nintendo Wii, Experience

1. INTRODUCTION

The research on the effects of videogames was discovered that there are negative consequences of playing videogames such as addiction, isolation, and aggressiveness. But recently, in the literature it has claimed that there are also therapeutic benefits of using videogames which are specially and innovatively designed rather than those that are commercially available (Griffiths, 2003). They have been used as a method of rehabilitation or therapy in many different groups (Griffiths, 2003) such as disabled students (Pearson and Bailey, 2007), patients or people with several disorders (Kim et al., 2015; Paavola et al., 2013), people with multiple sclerosis (Nilsagard et al., 2012; Plow and Finlayson, 2011; Prosperini et al., 2014), older adults (Bainbridge et al., 2011; Chen et al., 2012; Chesler et al., 2015; Gardner, 2011; Wollersheim et al., 2010), adolescents with autism (Getchell et al., 2012), children with migraine without aura (Esposito et al., 2013), children with down syndrome (Aliber, 2015; Rahman and Rahman, 2010), and injured young athletes (Vernadakis et al., 2013).

The results suggested that therapeutic use of video games can increase physical strength and balance, decrease pain, improve quality of life, help to release aggression, increase problem solving ability, provide to develop social and communication skills and enhance motivation to participate physical exercises.

However, there have been very few studies on examining whether video games might provide leisure experience and on the experiences gathering from playing video games as a leisure pursuit. The use of Nintendo Wii has become common in rehabilitation particularly in older population, where the term "Wiihabilitation" has been set out (Wollersheim et al., 2010, p.: 86). Therefore, the main aim of this study is to identify the dimensions of the leisure experience in older population who are playing Nintendo Wii Console games in their leisure.

2. METHOD

As the purpose of this study was to discover and understand the dimensions of leisure experience of elders' leisure playing Wii games as a leisure activity, a qualitative research design was adopted. Purposive sampling method was adopted in this study. The sample was composed of older people who were the participants of the Municipality in Eskisehir-Turkey. An information pack was given to the participants of the Municipality and 13 participants who were interested in participating were recruited in the study. Participants were excluded if they had epilepsy, a pace-maker or serious health condition and under the age of 60. The Nintendo Wii game intervention consisted the use of two Nintendo Wii Console games and two Nintendo Wii Fit Console games; tennis, dance, soccer heading and penguin slide were the games chosen for this study. The intervention took 40 minutes per a session, two times in a week for 6 weeks. Participants played all four games in each session for ten minutes.

In-depth interviews were conducted with 13 older people after the Nintendo Wii game intervention. The interviews were recorded and transcribed verbatim by the researchers and themes emerged from interviews have been determined. Data analysis process consisted listening to each audiotaped interviews and reread transcripts three times and coding independently to verify coding and to ensure data quality and reliability. A total of 13 interviews were held.

Table 1. The key questions of the interviews

1. How did you feel while you were playing the games?
2. Did you feel flow while you were playing? Please explain.
3. How did you feel when you win or lost the game?
4. What kind of experiences did you gain?
5. How do you explain your experiences to your friends?
6. Which game did you like best and why?
7. What do you think about the benefits/harms of playing Wii?

3. FINDINGS

The demographic characteristics of the sample was shown in Table 2. According to the results of the interviews, three themes were uncovered related to leisure experience gained through Wii game exercises. For labeling the emerged themes, the recent leisure experience literature was frequently consulted. These three preliminary themes are labeled as social experience, physical experience and relaxation.

Table 2. Summary of the participants' demographic backgrounds

Name	Age	Occupation	Gender
Esma	60	Teacher/Retired	Female
Fatma	60	Housewife	Female
Hayriye	60	Housewife	Female
Vildan	61	Housewife	Female
Gülçin	63	Nurse/Retired	Female
Müyesser	63	Laborer/Retired	Female
Emine	64	Teacher/Retired	Female
Sebahat	65	Public Official/Retired	Female
Hilmi	60	Teacher/Retired	Male
Ali	61	Lawyer/Retired	Male
Ahmet	61	Tailor/Retired	Male
Ramazan	61	Hairdresser	Male
Tayfun	64	Public Official/Retired	Male

3.1 Social Experience

Playing games has an important effect on shaping the socialization. Social experience were mentioned mostly by the interviewers as Wollersheim et al. (2010) suggested in their study. Interviewers have associated Wii games with friendship, interaction and helping each other. Below are some opinions about this theme;

"We were not very closely before the Wii group, but now after the Wii sessions, we are going out, speaking more, supporting each other, having dinner, and of course laughing…" (Müyesser).

"I don't like talking too much, but between the games we are asking questions each other about the score or about the game. And we are competing each other like who will be the first, so it provides us keeping the conversation and happy" (Ali).

3.2 Physical Experience

The Wii was reported by the participants to be physically beneficial and healthy. It was found that Wii intervention had been effective to be physically active and in improving balance and strength as was evidenced in the following quotes from the interviews;

"In my free time I usually do home-based activities such as watching TV, cooking, reading newspaper or going to the friends' house etc., but playing Wii made me feel active and energetic, now I am feeling happy because I am really feeling that I am doing something good for my body and mind…" (Gülçin).

"…I was feeling tired even when I was doing houseworks or doing my laundry. But now I am feeling that I am doing every work faster, so Wii groups helped me to be physically active…So I can say that playing Wii in leisure improves balance, and makes the body stronger" (Tayfun).

3.3 Relaxation

It was also found that participants gained relaxation experience while playing Wii. The interviewers reported that playing Wii made them spiritually nourished and relaxed. This result was clearly reflected in the data provided by the interviewers;

"I found playing Wii is very relaxing. It was impossible for me to leave home because I have three kids, and it is very luxury for me to go to the gym or participating in any kind of sports. But Wii is easy to buy, easy to use…So playing Wii will be my best option to spend my leisure and to relax" (Hayriye).

4. RESULTS AND DISCUSSION

Overall, a total of three themes social experience, physical experience and relaxation emerged in this study. The present study makes two major contributions to the literature related leisure experience. Firstly, this particular kind of leisure activity –Nintendo Wii Console games- in the context of leisure experience has not been studied before. Secondly, in Turkey there exist relatively little research on both leisure experience for the older population and the effects of playing Nintendo Wii on leisure experience. Therefore, the results of this study lend some support to the literature in Turkey.

REFERENCES

Bainbridge, E., Bevans, S., Keeley, B., Oriel, K. (2011). "The effects of the Nintendo Wii Fit on community-dwelling older adults with perceived balance deficits: A pilot study", Physical & Occupational Therapy in Geriatrics, 29(2), 126-135.

Chesler, J., McLaren, S., Klein, B., Watson, S. (2015). "The effects of playing Nintendo Wii on depression, sense of belonging and social support in Australian aged care residents: A protocol study of a mixed methods intervention trial", BMC Geriatrics, 15 (106), 1-9.

Esposito, M., Ruberto, M., Gimigliano, F., Marotta, R., Gallai, B., Parisi, L., Lavano, S.M., Roccella, M., Carotenuto, M. (2013). "Effectiveness and safety of Nintendo Wii Fit Plus training in children with migraine without aura: A preliminary study", Neuropsychiatric Disease and Treatment, 9, 1803-1810.

Gardner, B. (2011). "Effectiveness of the Nintendo Wii Fit games on the balance of a community-dwelling older adult in Eastern North Carolina", Master Thesis, The Faculty of the Department of Occupational Therapy, East Carolina University.

Getchell, N., Miccinello, D., Blom, M., Morris, L., Szaroleta, M. (2012). "Comparing energy expenditure in adolescents with and without autism while playing Nintendo Wii games", Games for Health Journal, 1(1), 58-61.

Griffiths, M. (2003). "The therapeutic use of video games in childhood and adolescence", Clinical Child Psychologhy and Psychiatry, 8, 547-554.

Kim, K.J., Jun, H.J., Heo, M. (2015). "Effects of Nintendo Wii Plus training on ankle strength with functional ankle instability", Journal of Phys. Ther. Sci., 27, 3381-3385.

Nilsagard, Y., Forsberg, A.S., Koch, L.V. (2012) "Balance exercise for persons with multiple sclerosis using Wii games: A randomized, controlled multi-centre study", Multiple Sclerosis Journal, 19(2), 209-216.

Pearson, E., Bailey, C. (2007). "Evaluating the potential of the Nintendo Wii to support disabled students in education", Proceedings ascilite Singapore.

Plow, M., Finlayson, M. (2011). "Potential benefits of Nintendo Wii Fit among people with multiple sclerosis", Int J MS Care, 13, 21-30.

Prosperini, L., Fanelll, F., Petsas, N., Sbardella, E., Tona, F., Raz, E., Fortuna, D., De Angelis, F., Pozzilli, C., Pantano, P. (2014). "Multiple sclerosis: Changes in microarchitecture of white matter tracts after training with a video game balance board", Radiology, 273(2), 529-538.

Wollersheim, D., Merkes, M., Shields, N., Liamputtong, P., Wallis, L., Reynolds, F., Koh, L. (2010). "Physical and psychosocial effects of Wii video game use among older women", Intenrational Journal of Emerging Technologies and Society, 8(2), 85-98.

THE VIRTUAL REALITY: INTERFACE WITH TECHNOLOGY, DIGITAL GAMES AND INDUSTRY

Pablo Gobira and Antônio Mozelli
Escola Guignard, Universidade do Estado de Minas Gerais (UEMG)
Rua Ascânio Burlamarque, 540 - Mangabeiras, Belo Horizonte/MG/Brazil, 30315-030

ABSTRACT

The article shows the evolution of virtual reality interfaces and technologies to the current moment and verifies what led them to an alleged decline in early 1990. Due to the development of the industry of digital games, new forms of interaction have being researched and presented to the public. It will also be shown the application of virtual reality in different contexts of digital games, in addition to reporting a brief experience of the research group in art, science and technology, Lab | Front (Laboratório de Poéticas Fronteiriças - CNPq/UEMG).

KEYWORDS

Virtual reality; interfaces; digital games

1. INTRODUCTION

This article presents a brief history of development and technological advances in virtual reality (VR) up to this moment which seems to be expanding. Due to advances in research and development of the game industry, virtual reality and its immersion technologies appear to be growing. In the 1990s, this technology promised to be a trend, but high production costs have limited their use and interest to only specific scientific communities.

Between 1990 and the middle of the first decade of this century, other forms of interaction and languages have been explored due to increasing Internet access and dissipation of data in virtual networks (Rocha, 2010). The interests in VR has decreased more and more, as well as the attention of researchers and scientific centers to handle the subject. However, it is important to emphasize that innovation efforts as well as the varied interests, not ceased altogether. This is something that this paper aims to demonstrate to the exposure of continuous events in a "story of the VR."

2. THE DEVELOPMENT OF INTERFACES: VIRTUAL REALITY IN EXPANSION

Attempts in history have already shown the man's interest in mastering virtual reality technologies. In the seventeenth century, the church used the projections of Athanasius Kircher made with the optical principle called *camera obscura*, an early example in history. Athanasius created the "live" view of hell that caused great astonishment and served for many Christians as a powerful argument against sin. He made the mental picture of hell and demons possible through the smoke employment, inclusion of strange insects, which seemed magnified monsters. He used the simulation to make a fictional world real. The image hitherto unseen by the faithful could have caused a sense of immersion in another reality. The space of the church was intended to provide the observer with knowledge of the possible, that is, the virtual existence of the infernal world (Giannetti, 2006, p. 150).

When virtual reality is thought, many authors refer to the development of stereoscopy and the first images in three dimensions, as well as others point to interfaced experiences out of the body. The principle of stereoscopy presents each eye an image corresponding to their point of view. Thus, it is possible to simulate the sensation of depth and relief, since human eyes are distant from each other by a few centimeters, it does not have the same view of the world (Arantes, 2005, p. 114).

For most authors, it was between the years 1950 and 1960 that the pioneers started the development of stereoscopic instruments for immersion and graphic simulation. It should highlight the Sensorama of Morton Heilig in 1950 as a kind of synesthetic theater. In it, an immersive booth, a vibrating seat, handlebars, a binocular display device, a set of fans, stereo speakers and a nasal device simulated the experience of driving a motorcycle in specific places of the United States (Rejane, 2001, p. 29).

In 1962 at MIT, Ivan Sutherland developed the direct manipulation program called Sketchpad. Using a pen, one could draw directly on the cathode ray tube and displaying the image in almost real time. This was a major breakthrough in computer graphics research at the time. Later, between 1966 and 1970, Sutherland developed the Head-Mounted Display, a version of a more advanced stereoscopic viewing helmet, allowing interaction with located infographic images before the viewer's eyes (Giannetti, 2006, p. 121).

In 1968, Sutherland published an article in Harvard University, called "The Head-Mounted Three Dimensional Display," in which it was described the development of a stereoscopic helmet traceable. The helmet had two mini CRT displays that projected images directly into the user's eyes and you could track the head movements through a mechanical and ultrasonic interface. Sutherland developments made a landmark in the history of VR, thereby establishing the concept of immersion.

The Augmented Reality (AR), so common today, was based on the creation of interactive helmet video, developed by engineers from Philco, along with interactive helmet for computer graphics Sutherland. They both had tracking technologies. A few decades after this, the use of video, tracking and computer graphics integrated - and interacting in real time - enabled the development of augmented reality applications. (Kirner, 2008)

In the mid-1970s, a number of artifacts began to be developed for the evolution of virtual reality. In 1977 the glove Dataglove was designed to contribute to the multisensory aspects of the VR being marketed only in 1985, by the company VPL Research. In 1981, the US Air Force created one Cockpit simulator for pilots where it was possible to use an optical sight helmet with increased vision and aircraft information, visual indication of missiles available for shooting. The helmet had an acrylic display and allowed to mix view of the scene overlaid with images generated by projection of a CRT display inside the helmet. This was one of the first augmented reality projects, it cost was in the range of millions of dollars.

In 1989 the Power glove was released for the Nintendo video game, developed by Mattel company, but was not successful in the video game industry being adapted for virtual reality systems based on computers like the firsts Personal Computers (PC).

The appearance of CAVEs (Cave Automatic Virtual Environment), a virtual reality system for projection on walls as an alternative to the use of helmets, was shown in SIGGRAPH'92 event in 1992, developed at the University of Illinois at Chicago, by Carolina Cruz -Neira. Since 1992 computer graphics companies such as Silicon Graphics Inc. and Sense8 Co. has begun producing tools and software for the development of applications in virtual reality.

Softwares as WorldToolKit and Iris Inventor use their own library of functions in C and C ++ for modeling and 3D visualization, making it possible to increase productivity and quality of applications. They also have provided the structural foundation of what would become the VRML (Virtual Reality Modeling Language). In the academic community, conferences and workshops they appeared to discuss the research frontiers in virtual reality and in the year 1995 the IEEE VR event was created by combining the VRAIS'93 and Research Frontiers in Virtual Reality IEEE Workshop conferences.

In 1999 the ARToolKit, a free software written in C that allowed tracking video, aroused worldwide interest in augmented reality area and there were several other free tools led to virtual reality applications and augmented reality with the growth of the Internet and applications native Web.

This historical presented aims to highlight the evolution and development of virtual reality to the current scenario, where the VR is in fact expanding. Below we will discuss if there was really a fall of VR started in the 1990s in relation to this contemporary expansion.

3. VIRTUAL REALITY: FROM FALL TO GROWTH?

According to the discussion held by Professor Mark Bolas (2011), from the Creative Technologies Institute of the University of Southern California (USC), there is a matter determined by the "hype". Hype is an English word which suggests the extreme promotion of an idea, person or product, as if coming into fashion. There was a hype around virtual reality in the 1990s and it turned out impossible to carry out their promises. This is a common phenomenon observed in the Gartner Hype Curve developed by Jeremy Kemp at Gartner Inc., an American company Research in Information Technology.

Since then, game developers have persisted in creating experiences with higher level of engagement. The scenarios and virtual worlds have magnificent ability to simulate details. The growth areas such as scientific visualization, has made advances in distribution of computing and network games like World of Warcraft and other Massively Multiplayer Online (MMO) and they also have contributed to the stability of virtual reality.

Besides technological developments, societies around the world are more comfortable with the idea of virtuality than in the 1990s. Most people have cell phones and use the Internet to communicate across applications, instant messaging and e-mails, watch movies in digital format, play online games and have accounts on social networks. It seems that society has never been more receptive and engaged with the virtual reality.

We act like that actually there was no fall in the growth of the VR. There was a timid industrial development in the use and applications of VR that almost could generate a break. The development was in those years, for the reasons given above, did not have such a big advertising as we are seeing in the context of games that, on other occasions, tried to include virtual reality without much success. This lower investment in the VR is reversed now, as we shall see.

4. VIRTUAL REALITY, GAMES AND INDUSTRY

When mobile devices such as cell phones, are used as binoculars interfaces for VR, they enable widespread access to such content. As example of these interfaces, companies like Google and Samsung have showed mid and low cost solutions for VR access.

In the year 2016, other binocular interfaces were also presented to the public during the famous American event - Consumer Technology Association (CES). The most anticipated, especially by the public of the games, were the virtual reality systems Oculus Rift, HTC Vive and Sony's design, Project Morpheus, which works with the PlayStation 4 console. These are robust interfaces that require higher graphical processing of its hardware. With the main focus on immersion in digital games, these interfaces allow greater interaction with the game's elements as they are equipped with sensors and joysticks integrated into the body immersion system. Another interface, in this case for augmented reality, is the product of Microsoft, HoloLens: a helmet with holographic projection system that combines virtual reality with the outside world, and allows viewing a mixed reality (Baig, 2016). Importantly, these more robust interfaces are also used for other virtual reality applications and experiments, expanding its use not only for the development of digital games.

The social network Facebook, which in 2014 bought the company that developed the Oculus Rift interface, affirmed that it wants to change the use of their social network by being able to share a more meaningful experience with its members (Schnipper, 2014).

Another trend is the possibility to follow the broadcast of television events such as basketball games as well as watching golf championships using virtual reality. The evolution of video cameras, that star to record 360° films and 3D, allows producers to reinvent ways to tell stories and generate new challenges for the cinematographic industry (Baig, 2016).

5. OTHER APPLICATIONS OF VIRTUAL REALITY

The realistic and immersive nature of virtual reality has allowed the user to play the role of another person. Psychologists in the Virtual Human Interaction Lab, Stanford University (USA), are conducting several projects using virtual reality in order to generate empathy in users. Through the capabilities of technology, students can see their appearance and behavior reflected in a virtual mirror as someone who is different and may experience a scenario from the perspective of either party of a social interaction.

Studies have been applying virtual reality to teach empathy towards people with disabilities, with different skin color, with different economic goals, and different age groups. Another project called "Sustainable Behavior" from the same laboratory at Stanford University, grant users to experience a dive in a filled coral life which may be over, if our behavior on pollution do not change. The laboratory also has a research project on a virtual learning environment, where the virtual environment allows greater focus and attention to the class goals.

Something similar to what is developed at Stanford has been held since 2009 by professor and researcher Mel Slater, Department of Computer Science at University College London, where he studied "the exploration of virtual reality in the study of moral judgment."

Another work that also aims to teach empathy to people is the work of student Yifei Chai, from Imperial College London has developed a virtual reality system in order to give users the feeling of being in someone else's body and also to be able to control it (Stuart, 2014).

Artists are proposing demonstrations and performances using virtual reality to show their work. An art installation, *The Machine to be Another*, allows the virtual exchange of genres among participants. It can use the body of another party through a system of cameras and glasses for VR. The concept of exchange and personification of virtual body, called digital embodiment (Munster, 2006), is widely used in virtual reality, especially in digital games. When taking on a character or avatar in a digital game the notion of itself is changed to a different notion of control.

Another artist, Thorston Wiedemann, tested his ability to stay on virtual reality for 48 hours in various virtual worlds in Games Science Center in Berlin (Germany) (Pangburn, 2016).

6. EXPERIENCE OF ART AND VIRTUAL REALITY

Through the work of the research group in art, science and technology, Lab|Front (Laboratório de Poéticas Fronteiriças - CNPq/UEMG) is intended to give a brief experience with virtual reality coming from a research project on curatorial and exhibition spaces with the presence of digital technology.

From that interest in digital technology, and the development project, the opportunity arose to investigate the use of virtual reality immersive technologies, generating research technological development and innovation that is beginning in 2016. The staff (Pablo Gobira, Antônio Mozelli and William Melo) is producing a virtual reality environment simulating the representation of the human body in transformation. Through the use of 3D computer modeling, one of the specific design goals was to create a similar form to the human body and allow the immersion of the interactor in that environment. However, the modeled forms simulate the body interator aging.

The first models in computer graphics were produced using three-dimensional modeling software Blender and carry out the application programming in Unity development environment. The first tests were performed with the stereoscopic kit Google cardboard and also the models of cell phones LG Nexus 5 and Samsung Galaxy S4 Mini with Android OS versions Jelly Bean and KitKat.

Through research and the design of the immersive virtual reality installation with intense exploitation of these technologies, it was possible to propose another experiment in virtual reality. We have created a virtual gallery that represents the Art Gallery of Guignard School (UEMG). The experiment of the gallery provided the realization of curating the performance of works resulting from the extension project "Sala de Estar".

To create the virtual gallery, it was necessary to model three-dimensional real space with reference to the floor plan of the Guignard School. Textures were created for the floor and walls of the gallery using photographic references of the actual location. After the construction of the 3D model of the gallery, several works by artists who participated in the project "Sala de Estar" were put virtually within the gallery space after scanning, according to the proposed arrangement in curatorial project. Programmatically, it was possible to create a virtual walkthrough in the installation cyberspace, where the user through head movements was possible to perform virtual navigation in the gallery.

As a result of the Virtual Gallery experiment, the exhibition "Saindo da sala" that has been exposed twice was created, one for the closure of the "Sala de Estar" project and another during the 17th Seminar of Research and Extension of UEMG.

7. CONCLUSION

Many uses seem to be possible with virtual reality interfaces, and it seems that some stability has been achieved due to industry advancements and the mass adoption of the technology. It is even possible that the hype described by Bolas (2011) may be in manifestation and that some of these interfaces, especially for digital games, are only attracting the attention of consumers eager for news. But it is no longer possible to disregard the other manifestations in addition to those of the games industry.

The prospects for the development and use of these interfaces are challenging, however, many applications have already become references. In technological development perspective, it is necessary to readjust the current models of design and interaction design for virtual environments. New elements have been added for immersion development. The possibility of navigation in a virtual environment differs from a multi-touch environment in 2 dimensions, for example (Malaika, 2015).

The possibility of embody other body types, digital/virtual embodiment, allows the user new ways of expression and control over virtualized object. Research on brain-computer interface lead the innovations of what can be the future of these interactions. One is the recent development NESD notice (Neural Engineering System Design) of the DARPA (Defense Advanced Research Projects Agency), a neural interface that can stream audio and video communication in the brain with the machine.

Technological advances in virtual reality interfaces in the XXI century are in fact taking place and converging with other findings. We have seen in this article that the industry, mainly digital games, has keeping great interest in developing products for the general public. We finally confirm that applications of VR to overcome the game field borders to other areas guarantee the continuity of studies not only on virtual reality or augmented reality, but to study the potential of different realities.

ACKNOWLEDGEMENT

We would like to thank: CNPq, FAPEMIG and PROPPG/UEMG for our research support; and the member of Lab|Front research group, Fernanda Corrêa, who contributed to the translation of this article.

REFERENCES

Arantes, Priscila, 2005. *Arte e Mídia*. Ed. Senac, São Paulo, Brazil.

Baig, Edward C., 2016. CES 2016 will be virtual reality showcase. *In USA Today*, 2 jan. 2016. Access: <http://www.usatoday.com/story/tech/columnist/baig/2015/12/31/ces-2016-virtual-reality-showcase/77564238/>

Bolas, Mark, 2011, Keynote remixed: what happened to virtual reality. *Proceedings of ISMAR*, 2011. Access: http://projects.ict.usc.edu/mxr/blog/keynote-remixed-what-happened-to-virtual-reality/

Giannetti, Claudia, 2006. *Estética Digital*. Sintopia da Arte, a Ciência e a Tecnologia. C/Arte, Belo Horizonte, 2006.

Heilig, Morton. Morton Heilig Website. Acess: <http://www.mortonheilig.com/InventorVR.html>

Kirner, C., 2008, Evolução da Realidade Virtual no Brasil. *Procedings of X Symposium on Virtual and Augmented Reality*. João Pessoa, Brazil, pp. 1-11.

Malaika, Yasser, 2015, Interaction Design in VR: The Rules Have Changed (Again). *Proceedings of Game Developers Conference Europe*, Cologne, Germany. Access: http://www.gdcvault.com/play/1022810/Interaction-Design-in-VR-The

Munster, Anna, 2006. *Materializing New Media*: Embodiment in Information Aesthetics. Dartmouth College Press, England.

Pangburn, DJ, 2016. This Guy Just Spent 48hours in virtual reality. *In The Creators Project*, 14 jan. 2016. Access: <http://thecreatorsproject.vice.com/blog/48-hours-in-vr>

Rejane C. A., Cantoni, 2001. *Realidade virtual*: uma história de imersão interativa. Programa de Pós-graduação em Comunicação e Semiótica da PUC-SP, São Paulo, Brazil.

Rocha, Cleomar, 2010, Três concepções de ciberespaço. *Proceedings of 9º Encontro Internacional de Arte e Tecnologia*. Brasília, Brazil.

Schnipper, Matthew, 2014. The Rise and Fall and Rise of Virtual Reality: coming Monday - An Oculus Rift in every home? *In The Verge*, 2014. Access: <http://www.theverge.com/a/virtual-reality/>

Stuart, Keith, 2014. What a virtual reality art show could say about the future of games. *In The Guardian*, 20 nov. 2014. Access: <http://www.theguardian.com/technology/2014/nov/20/virtual-reality-art-future-games>

KINECT BASED 3D VIDEO GENERATION

Liming Zhang[1], Jun Lan[1], Hanxiong Yin[1], Guibo Luo[2] and Yuesheng Zhu[2]
[1]*Faculty of Science and Technology, University of Macau, Avenida da Universidale, taipa, Macau, China*
[2]*Shenzhen Graduate School, Peking University, University Town, Nanshan District,Shenzhen 518055, P.R.China*

ABSTRACT

This paper presents a new approach on 2D to 3D video automatic conversion based on Kinect. There are mainly two contributions in our approach. First, the depth maps captured by Kinect are usually of poor quality. There are a lot of depth information missing regions. An improved energy function based Inpainting algorithm is proposed, which can help to recover the missed depth information smoothly. Then a new hole filling approach in depth image based rendering (DIBR) is proposed to synthesize the 3D images by using the corresponding color images and the repaired depth maps. Experiments are conducted on videos in different scenes. The results show the effectiveness in both the quality and the running time.

KEYWORDS

2D to 3D video conversion, Kinect, Depth map, Depth image based rendering (DIBR)

1. INTRODUCTION

With the development of the multimedia technology, 3-dimensional TV (3DTV) is becoming one of the main TV products in the market nowadays. 3DTV can provide a user 3D impression as if he is really over there, by displaying 3D images on the 3D display monitors of glasses/non-glasses types [12]. There are two disadvantages for 3DTV. One is that 3D display sets themselves are much more expensive than 2D ones are. The other is that 3D videos/movies are much more expensive and difficult to shoot than 2D ones are, as more advanced equipment and techniques are needed. Even though users choose to buy a 3DTV, they have to use it as a conventional TV in most of the time due to the lack of 3D video resources. In our daily life, 2-dimensional (2D) displays are still dominate, including conventional TV sets, computer monitors, mobile phones, etc. In this situation, developing a low cost and convenient technique to support easy shooting 3D video resources, meanwhile generated 3D videos can be watched on both 2D and 3D displays with glasses, will be of significance and practice for normal users in general entrainment and family video records.

This paper introduces a Kinect based 3D video generation technique. Kinect is a motion sensing input device by Microsoft for Xbox 360 with wide availability and low cost (www.xbox.com/en-US). It is originally designed to replace the game controller. It builds a revolutionary way for people to play games and change the way they experience the entertainment [14]. There are a number of Kinect based application developments reported in the literature and internet [6, 14], including object tracking and recognition, human activity analysis, hand gesture analysis and indoor 3D mapping [6], etc. The Kinect 3D related studies focus on the sparse feature matching, dense point matching [6], and graphic based 3D reconstruction [7].

There are two steps in converting 2D videos into 3D ones, including depth map generation and depth image based rendering (DIBR). Kinect provides a color camera and an infrared depth sensor that can capture the depth information of the video shot by the camera simultaneously. Its depth sensor is based on a projection of fixed pattern of infrared light. An offset infrared camera receives the projected infrared light and the built-in controller estimates the depth using the distortion of the pattern [10]. However, the captured depth maps are usually affected by the environment factors, such as the illumination, distance, occlusion etc., which cause the instability of the depth images both temporally and spatially (See Figure 2(b)). The captured depth map needs to be repaired first before DIBR.

There are also some literatures focusing on Kinect based 3D video generation [8, 9]. In both studies, a normal inpainting approach and median filter are used to repair the disocclusion areas. And both inpainting and median filter generate blurred edges on objects which usually decrease the effectiveness on 3D effects.

The main contributions of our approach are twofold. (I) A revised Inpainting algorithm is proposed to combine the color and texture information from the color image with the depth information from depth image together to repair the depth missing regions. A novel energy function is proposed to combine those information together. (II) An improved DIBR is introduced, which uses a novel hole filling technique. It can warp the 2D image into 3D one effectively and efficiently than other DIBR techniques do.

2. THE PRINCIPLE OF OUR PROPOSED APPROACH

2.1 Overview of the Proposed Approach

Our study aims at generating 3D video based on the 2D video and the corresponding depth map sequence captured by Kinect. The framework of the proposed approach is shown in Figure 1. There are two major steps. The first step focuses on depth map missing region repairing, and the second step is to apply the depth image-based rendering technique to convert the 2D video to 3D.

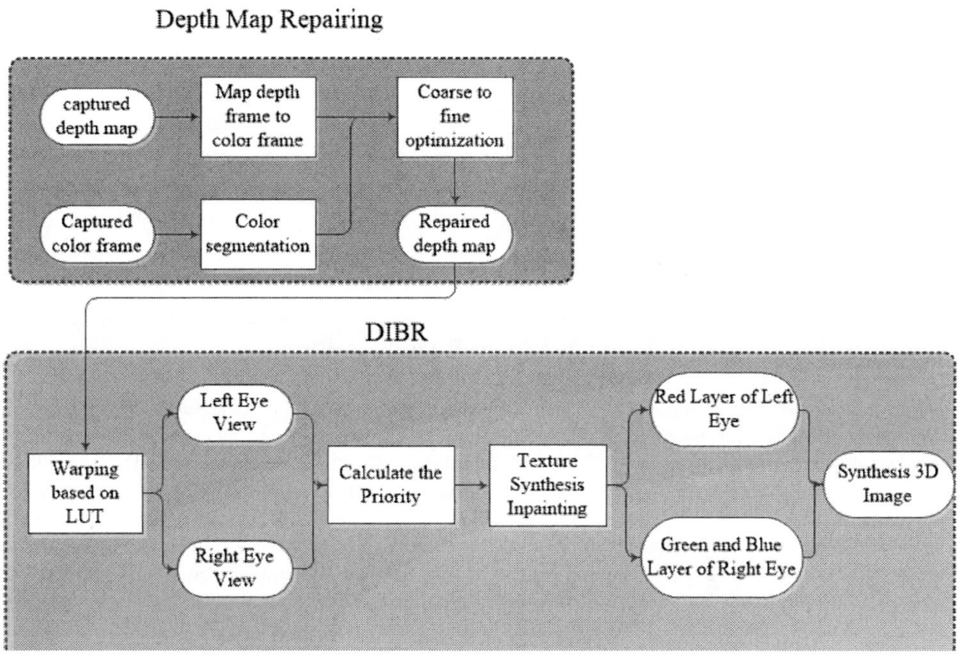

Figure 1. The framework of the proposed approach

2.2 Proposed Depth Map Repairing Technique

In depth map based 2D to 3D video generation, the final quality of 3D video highly depends on the quality of the depth map. However, the depth map captured by Kinect usually has a number of depth missing regions with different sizes. It cannot be used directly in 3D video generation.

Digital image inpainting is a popular algorithm to be used in filling the missing regions of an image from the surrounding areas using the color and texture information. Inpainting has been reported the effectiveness in the literature [1]. In our approach, Inpainting is used in depth map missing regions repairing. As the depth map is a gray level image without color and texture information, Inpainting algorithm is not effective by using only depth map. Figure 2(b) shows a depth map captured by Kinect. Due to the light reflection by the TV set, there is no depth information on TV set. Figure 2(c) shows the depth map after normal Inpainting repairing. We can see that the depth information in TV set is incorrect. To solve this problem and get a high quality depth map, we propose a depth map Inpainting algorithm. It first aligns the depth map and the corresponding color image together, then uses the following energy function for repairing [3, 11].

$$E(p) = \lambda_T T(p) + \lambda_{sc} S_c(p) + \lambda_{st} S_t(p), \quad (1)$$

where p represents the pixel we are processing, $T(p)$ is the distance between p and the neighbor, $S_c(p)$ and $S_t(p)$ are color and texture similarity functions, λ decides the contribution of each term.

The color and texture similarity functions imitate Gaussian function, which are calculated by (2) and (3), respectively.

$$S_c(p) = \frac{1}{|N(p)|} \sum_{q \in N(p)} \exp\left(-\frac{\|I(p) - I(q)\|^2}{2\sigma_{sc}^2}\right), \quad (2)$$

$$S_t(p) = \frac{1}{|N(p)|} \sum_{q \in N(p)} \exp\left(-\frac{\|LBP(p) - LBP(q)\|^2}{2\sigma_{st}^2}\right), \quad (3)$$

where $N(p)$ represents the neighborhoods of p, σ_{sc} and σ_{st} are constants. In (2), $I(.)$ is a vector contains R,G,B channels. *LBP* represents local binary pattern [5].

$$LBP(p) = \sum_{q=0}^{M-1} s(g_q - g_p)2^q, \quad s(x) = \begin{cases} 1 & if\ x \geq 0 \\ 0 & if\ x < 0 \end{cases}, \quad (4)$$

where g_p is the gray value of the central pixel, g_q is the value of its neighbors, M is the total number of involved neighbors. The pixel with minimum E is the point to be repaired. The final depth map after repairing is shown in Figure 2(d).

2.3 Proposed Improved Depth Image Based Rendering

Depth-image-based rendering (DIBR) is the process of synthesizing "virtual" left- and right-eye views of a scene from the original image and associated depth map [2]. One major problem of DIBR algorithm is due to the fact that areas, which are occluded in the original view, might become visible in any of the "virtual" left- and right-eye views. This event is usually referred to as *disocclusion* [4] and the corresponding regions are called holes. Figure 2(e) shows the situation of the disocclusion. There are some DIBR algorithms reported in the literature, including multi-directional extrapolation hole-filling method and gradient-based deformable template hole-filling method [13], etc. They are usually applied to the whole virtual view image directly to fill the holes. There are two disadvantages of them. The templates are usually complicated, which result in the high computational cost. In another aspect, if the holes were large, the middle pixels in the hole might cause errors.

In our approach, we propose a new hole filling algorithm. The algorithm for left-eye view hole filling is shown in Algorithm 1. The algorithm for right-eye view hole filling will be similar, except for the gradient search direction changed to up-right, right, and down-right. The reason is that the hole locations in different eye views are different.

The principle of the proposed algorithm is that the holes are filled twice. The first filling procedure is to search the gradient similar background neighbors to fill the hole and the searching only need to be done in three directions. After this procedure, the big holes become much smaller. The second filling procedure only need to compute the neighbor average to fill the rest holes. The algorithm reduces the computation cost dramatically, meanwhile the correct matching rates are increased. In the literature, it is reported that the fast DIBR is about 20 seconds, while our proposed approach only needs 1 second.

Algorithm 1. Hole filling algorithm for left-eye view

Input: left-eye view with holes

Output: left-eye view after hole filling

1. Procedure 1:Search the holes from left to right, top to bottom
2. In each hole, compare the gradients of both the pixels in hole and the neighbor background pixels in three direction: up-left, left, and down-left
3. Filling the pixel in the hole by the pixel with closest gradient
4. Procedure 2: Search the holes from left to right, top to bottom
5. Fill other pixels in hole by average of the pixel surroundings

Experiments has been conducted by a number of indoor scenes with different light conditions. The generated 3D videos are satisfied in general with only 1 minute delay. Figure 3 shows more hole filling results.

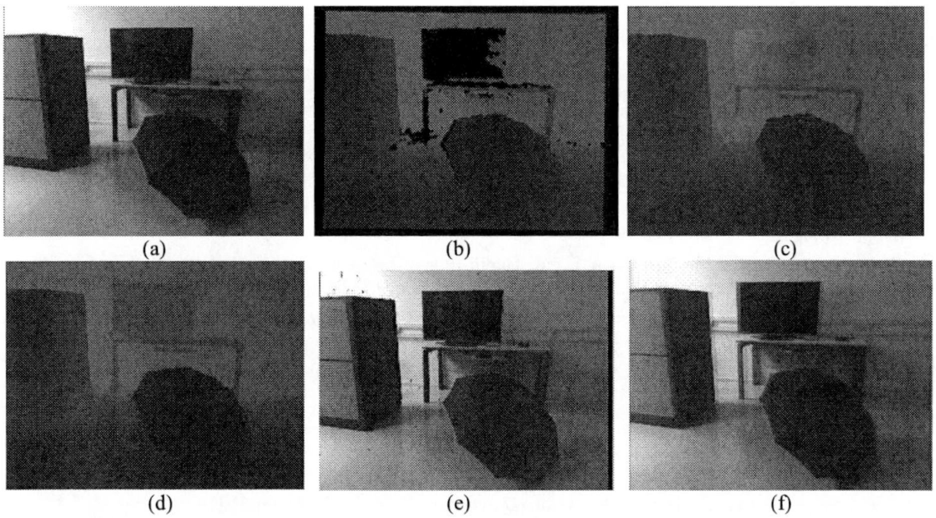

Figure 2. Kinect depth map based 2D to 3D image conversion process. (a) Image from Kinect RGB camera. (b) Image from Kinect depth sensor. Black regions are the areas losing the depth information. (c) Depth map after Inpainting repairing. (d) Depth map after proposed approach repairing. (e) Right view image after warping. (f) Final converted 3D image

(a) (b)

Figure 3. (a). Right view image after warping. (b). Right view image after

3. CONCLUSION

This paper presents a technique to generate 3D videos based on Kinect. The technique provide a low cost way for users to shoot 3D videos by themselves. The applications can be used as family 3D video records or game entrainment by 3D interface in the future.

ACKNOWLEDGEMENT

This work is supported by the Science and Technology Development Fund of Macao SAR FDCT 056/2012/A2 and MYRG 2014-00009-FST.

REFERENCES

[1]. Bertalmio, M., et al, 2000. Image inpainting. *Proceedings of ACM Conference Computer Graphics (SIGGRAPH)*, New Orleans, USA, pp.417-424.

[2]. Bleyer, M., et al, 2011. Object Stereo-Joint Stereo Matching and Object Segmentation. *Proceedings of 24th IEEE Conference on Computer Vision and Pattern Recognition*. Colorado Springs, USA.pp.3081-3088.

[3]. Cao, X., et al, 2011. Semi-Automatic 2D-to-3D Conversion Using Disparity Propagation. *IEEE Transactions on Broadcasting.* Vol.57, No.2, pp.491-499.

[4]. Fehn, C., 2003. A 3d-tv Approach Using Depth-Image-Based Rendering (DIBR). *Proceedings of The IASTED International Conference on Visualization, Imaging and Image Processing (VIIP 2003),* CA, USA, pp.482-487.

[5]. Guo, Z., et al, 2010. A Completed Modeling of Local Binary Pattern Operator for Texture Classification. *IEEE Transactions on Image Processin*g, Vol. 19, No. 6, pp. 1657-1663.

[6]. Han, J., et al, 2013. Enhanced Computer Vision with Microsoft Kinect Sensor: A Review. *IEEE Transactions on Cybernetics.* Vol. 43, No.5, pp. 1318-1334.

[7]. Izadi, S., et al, 2011. KinectFusion: Real-time 3D Reconstruction and Interaction Using a Moving Depth Camera. *Proceedings of ACM Symposium on User Interface Software and Technology*, Santa Barbara, CA, USA.

[8]. Joachimiaka, M., et al, 2013. Complete Processing Chain For 3D Video Generation Using Kinect Sensor. *Proceedings of International Conference on 3D Imaging (IC3D 2013)*, Liege, Belgium.

[9]. Lee, S., et al, 2011. Real-time stereo view generation using Kinect depth camera. *Proceedings of Asia Pacific Signal and Information Processing Association third Annual Summit and Conference (APSIPA ASC 2011)*, Xi'an, China.

[10].Matyunin, S., et al, 2011. Temporal Filtering for Depth Maps Generated by Kinect Depth Camera. In: 3DTV Conference: *Proceedings of The True Vision-Capture, Transmission and Display of 3D Video (3DTV-CON).* Antalya, Turkey, pp. 1-4.

[11].Miao, D., et al, 2012. Texture-assisted Kinect Depth Inpainting. Proceedings of *IEEE International Symposium on Circuits and Systems (ISCAS)*, pp. 604–607.

[12].Min, D., et al, 2009. 2D/3D Freeview Video Generation for 3DTV System. *Signal Processing: Image Communication.* Vol.24, pp.31–48.

[13].Xi, M., et al, 2013. Depth-image-based rendering with spatial and temporal texture synthesis for 3DTV. *EURASIP Journal on Image and Video Processing.* Vol. 9. DOI: 10.1186/1687-5281-2013-9.

[14].Zeng, W., 2012. Microsoft Kinect Sensor and Its Effect. *IEEE Multimedia Magazine*. vol. 19, no. 2, pp. 4-10.

CONTOUR SMOOTHING ALGORITHM BASED ON CONTOUR EXTREMES

Oleksandr V. Koriukalov and Vasyl M. Tereshchenko
Taras Shevchenko National University of Kyiv, 83000, Kyiv, Glushkova st., 4d, Ukraine

ABSTRACT

In this article we propose linear time algorithm for contour smoothing, based on finding extremes. First we find vertexes where contour convexity changes, than obtain local minimums, maximums and points of support, which should be used in resulting contour. The main goal of proposed approach is to compute accurate interior area of a bounding contour, it was successfully applied for recovering object contour after segmentation algorithms or human annotations, for contours noise reduction after jpeg compression.

KEYWORDS

Contour smoothing, recovering contour, contour noise reduction, extreme

1. INTRODUCTION

Contour smoothing is actual and well studied task of computer graphics. Algorithms from this scope should be applied for inverse digitization tasks, rendering, static imagery, photogrammetry, GIS, medical diagnostic systems, images segmentation tasks and other. Contour lines are very important features in the representation of quantitative relief over a wide range of scales. As scale is reduced, contour lines should be generalized. One of the generalization routines involves smoothing lineal features. Nevertheless, contour lines are a special class of lineal feature, as they represent a three-dimensional object.

As described at [1] in computer graphics black and white images are often represented as two dimensional array of pixels, so it is convenient to have possibility to manipulate such images via the contours, that describe black-white boundaries. Here we use simple polygon as image contour definition, and input parameter l, that specifies the threshold between normal and noisy contour structure. First we find vertexes, where contour convexity changes, than find extremes between those points, which should be used for building smoothed contour. The reminder of the article is organized as follows: in current section we provide existing approaches analysis, section 2 describes main algorithm and its applications, section 3 – conclusions.

Let us consider existing approaches for similar contour smoothing problems. Many contour smoothing algorithms are designed to solve digitized curve approximation problems. In article [1] fast linear-time algorithm for finding smooth polygonal approximation to a digitized contour was proposed. The polygonal contour has the minimum possible number of inflections and obeys a localized best-fit property. For computing contour inverted Bresenham's algorithm [3] is used. An efficient technique for piecewise cubic Bézier approximation of digitized curve was presented in [6]. We will describe this approach more detailed in one of the following paragraphs. Our technique is applicable for tasks from this scope.

Algorithm, presented in [10], smooths the contour line irregularities, that generate flat and erroneous triangles in a Delaunay triangulation, smoothing is achieved by moving only the sharp vertex toward the barycenter of the flat triangle. In [11] local regression lines are used for contour smoothing.

Smoothing splines is often used for finding smooth curved contour. Normalized uniform B-splines was used as basis functions for designing optimal smoothing spline curves in [4]. Assuming that the data for smoothing is obtained by sampling some curve with noises, an expression for optimal curves is derived when the number of data becomes infinity. It is then shown that, under certain condition, optimal smoothing splines converge to this curve as the number of data increases. In [5] presented an algorithm based on weighted smoothing splines for contour extraction from a triangular irregular network (TIN) structure based on sides.

The eclectic procedure for smoothing contour lines derived from TIN is presented in [9].

Bézier curves are another prevalent, widely used approach for smoothing contours. An efficient technique for piecewise cubic Bézier approximation of digitized curve was presented in [6]. An adaptive breakpoint detection method divides a digital curve into a number of segments and each segment is approximated by a cubic Bézier curve so that the approximation error is minimized. Initial approximated Bézier control points for each of the segments are obtained by reverse recursion of De Castaljau's algorithm [7]. Two methods, two-dimensional logarithmic search algorithm (TDLSA) and an evolutionary search algorithm (ESA), are introduced to find the best-fit Bézier control points. Similar technique is described in [8], first they also divide input curve into segments, applying cubic Bézier curves to each of them, then introduce new points for finding resulting contour.

Proposed in this article approach does not compute such smooth, accurate contour as splines or Bézier curves based approaches, it computes accurate interior area of a bounding contour, and user is provided opportunity to choose boundary type, depending on task specificity. Our algorithm is simple to implement, time and memory usage are linear.

2. MAIN ALGORITHM

We faced with necessity of special contour smoothing algorithm, while trying to implement certain contour classification approach. For more distinct classification we should have ability to remove local curve noise, to minimize its effect on classification result. In our tasks contour noises appeared as a result of inaccurate segmentation algorithms or human annotations, or after image's mask jpeg compression, so we often need to remove some small background parts near boundaries that does not belong to object. Therefore we needed algorithm for building bounding contour, based on the most locally internal vertexes of input contour. Proposed approach solves this task, moreover we have ability to choose as bounding contour most locally external vertexes and other variations.

Source contour is presented as a polygon. Algorithm has three input parameters, which should be selected depending on source data features:

l – maximum length of curve to replace, or maximum length of interval between the ends of the curve, or maximum contour's segments count; Optionally you can choose length in pixels, or as a percentage of the size. This parameter specifies the threshold between normal and noisy contour structure.

n – number of passages over contour vertexes. Depending on images algorithm should be launched more than one time. Usually maximum $n = 10$ required.

k – size of Gaussian blur.

First we propose to find vertexes, where contour convexity changes, than find extremes between those points, Figure 1.

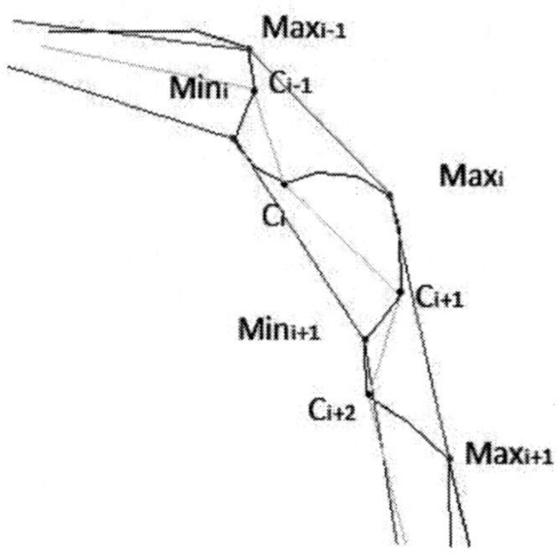

Figure 1

For finding vertexes where contour convexity changes C = {c_i}, next checking criteria proposed: the multiple of two vectors cross product should be less than zero(formula 1). In terms of mathematical analysis the second derivative of function, describing contour, should change sign in this point.

$$f''(x) = 0;\ ((xi - xi\text{-}1)*(yi+1 - yi) - (xi+1 - xi)*(yi - yi\text{-}1)) * \\ * ((x_{i+1} - x_i)*(y_{i+2} - y_{i+1}) - (x_{i+2} - x_{i+1})*(y_{i+1} - y_i)) < 0; \quad (1)$$

Then, viewing contour points in clockwise order we can find extremes E = {e_i}: e_i is the farthest point from segment connecting c_i and c_{i+1}; extremes on right side will be "minimums", on left size - "maximums".

On next step, depending on task specificity, we replace contour edges between minimums (optionally maximums, or c_i's) with straight line interval connecting minimums (optionally maximums, or c_i's). Minimums should be chosen for noise reduction, maximums or c_i's for tasks, where internal background pixels are acceptable. If the distance between minimums is bigger than *l*, replacement of segment does not provided.

Here we can use another approach for forming resulting contour, based on support lines [13] (the line which crosses contour in a single point, figure 2. left). To avoid situations when background parts lie inside of minimums based contour figure 2 right, C_{i+2} on fig. 1, in case when minimum is concave(segment, connecting minimums, crosses contour in more than one point, fig. 2 left) or convex(segment crosses contour in single point and line intersects contour in more the one point), we should use instead of it corresponding support vertex.

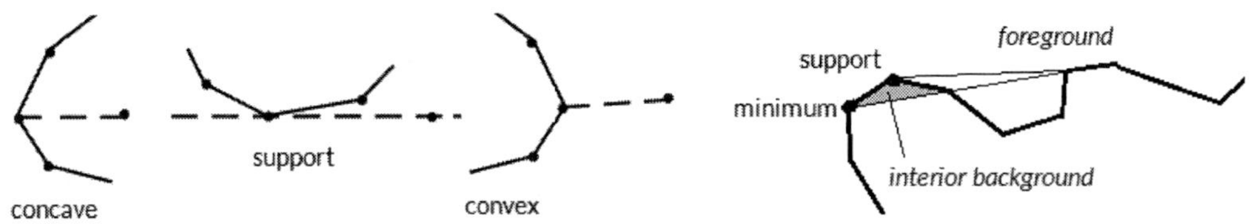

Figure 2. Point definitions

Now, we can repeat all steps from the beginning *n* times, or until algorithm wont find vertexes to replace. In the end we propose to smooth contour with *k* kernel size Gaussian blur [12].

2.1 The Complexity of Algorithm

Theorem 1. Proposed The algorithm requires O(n * m) run time and O(m) memory, where m is source contour vertexes count, n – number of passages over contour vertexes.

Proof. While finding C = {c_i}, on each step we watch every vertex one time, processing totally *m* steps – this requires O(*m*). Then, we find extremes and points of support, using in worst case linear time O(*m*). This procedure repeats *n* times, that is why total algorithm time complexity is O(*m***n*). We use O(*m*) memory for storing input contour. Than we need worst case O(*m*) memory for storing C = {c_i}, O(*m*) memory for extremes, and O(*m*) memory for points of support, that's why total memory complexity is O(*m*).

3. APPLICATION

We successfully applied this approach for recovering object contour after segmentation algorithms or human annotations, for contours noise reduction after jpeg compression. Some results are presented on Figure 3. For computing initial polygonal contour from black and white image we can use Canny edge detection algorithm [2]. This approach is applicable for inverse digitization tasks, described in [1], for finding distinct contour we can choose $Mid_i = (Min_i + Max_i) / 2$, as contour vertexes. Algorithm from article [1] can be called a particular case of our method.

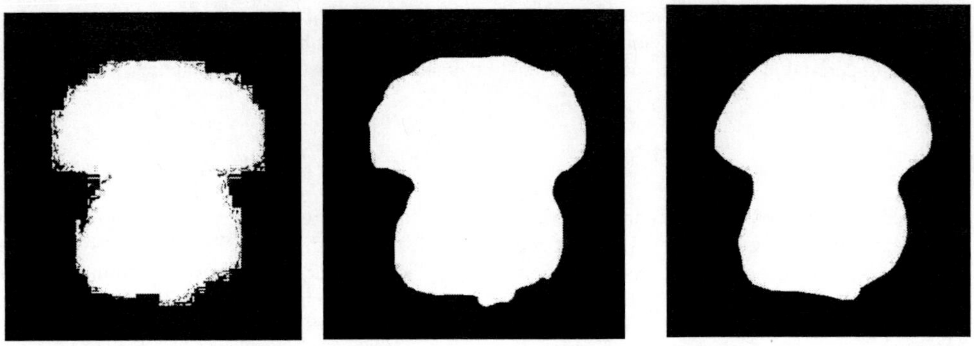

Figure 3. Minimums based contour: original image; smoothed image, l = 16 pixels; smoothed image, l = 30 pixels

4. CONCLUSION

In this paper, we proposed a linear time algorithm for contour smoothing, based on contour "extremes". Algorithm is simple to implement: first we find vertexes where contour convexity changes, than obtain local minimums, maximums or support points, which should be used in resulting contour. The main benefit of our approach is an opportunity to compute accurate interior area of a bounding contour, depending on task specificity, it does not compute such smooth, accurate contour as splines or Bézier curves based approaches. This can be achieved by building bounding contour, based on the most locally internal vertexes of input contour. Our approach should be applied for inverse digitization tasks, recovering object contour after segmentation algorithms or human annotations, for contours noise reduction after jpeg compression and other.

REFERENCES

1. John D Hobby, 1988, Smoothing digitized contours. *Nato ASI Series,* Vol. F40, Theoretical Foundations of Computer Graphics and CAD, Springer-Verlag Berlin Heidelberrg.
2. Canny Edge Detection, March 2009, *09gr820.*
3. Bresenham J. E., March 1965 , Algorithm for computer control of a digital plotter. *BM Systems Journal archive*, Volume 4 Issue 1, pp 25-30.
4. Hiroyuki Kano, Hiroyuki Fujioka, Magnus Egerstedt, Clyde F. Martin, 2005, Optimal smoothing spline curves and contour synthesis. *World Congress*, Volume 16, Part 1, pp 49.
5. Leonor Maria, Oliveira Malva, 2005, Contour Smoothing Based on Weighted Smoothing Splines. *Developments in Spatial Data Handling,* Departamento de Matematica, F.C.T.U.C., Apartado 3008, 3001 454 Coimbra, Portugal, pp 125-136.
6. Sarbajit Pala, Pankaj Gangulyb, P. K. Biswasc, October 2007, Cubic Bézier approximation of a digitized curve. *Journal Pattern Recognition archive*, Volume 40, Issue 10, pp 2730-2741.
7. Finding a Point on a Bézier Curve: De Casteljau's Algorithm. Available from:http://www.cs.mtu.edu/~shene/COURSES/cs3621/NOTES/spline/Bezier/de-casteljau.html
8. Shu Hongping, Wei Zhaoyu, 2012, Contour Smoothing Algorithm Based on Bezier Curves and Application. *Computational Intelligence and Communication Networks (CICN)*, 2012 Fourth International Conference, pp 283-285.
9. Albert H. J. Christensen, February 2001, Contour Smoothing by an Eclectic Procedure. *PE&RS*, Volume 67, Number 2, Photogrammetric engineering & remote sensing.
10. Jesus Irigoyen, Maria T. Martin Jaime Rodriguez, 2009, A Smoothing Algorithm for Contour Lines by Means of Triangulation. *The Cartographic Journal: The World of Mapping*, Volume 46, Issue 3, pp 262-267.
11. Smoothing 2D Contours Using Local Regression Lines. Available from: http://scripts.filehungry.com/product/tools_and_utilities/development_tools/smoothing_2d_contours_using_local_regression_lines/
12. Moo K. Chung, July 2012, Gaussian Kernel Smoothing.
13. F.P. Preparata and M.I. Shamos, 1985, Computational Geometry: An Introduction. *Springer-Verlag*, New York.

LOCAL THICKNESS COMPUTATION IN 3D MESHES AND 3D PRINTABILITY ASSESSMENT

Celestin Lanterne[1,2], Stefka Gueorguieva[1] and Pascal Desbarats[1]
[1]*University of Bordeaux, 351, Cours de la Libération, 33405 Talence*
[2]*FabZat, 120, Ave de Maréchal Leclerc, 33130 Bègles*

ABSTRACT

We present an approach to printability assessment of 3D meshes depending on shape's local thickness measure. We propose a method for detection of regions with critical thickness based on volume bracketing. Our method is conceived as a designer assistance tool and can be iterated until the structural soundness is achieved.

KEYWORDS

3D printing, structural analysis, model repair, polygonal mesh

1. INTRODUCTION

Digital object representations used as input data in rapid prototyping work flows should fulfill design and fabrication constraints that ensure the manufacturing of solid prototypes. These constraints can be analyzed in a twofold sense: as geometry and topology requirements related to the definition of an object with well identified interior and exterior volume, and structural weakness requirements related to the 3D printability assessment and the lack of critical features that can damage the integrity of the manufactured prototype.

There is a great variety of mesh repairing methods [21,2] that fix up errors in geometry and topology structure and transform input mesh into watertight manifold surface [9,7]. Unlike mesh repairing, printatiblity assessment is a more recent domain of investigations, growing considerably along with the ubiquitous 3D printing applications such as stress analyzing [18,24,15], heterogeneous material object fabrication [5], model balancing [17], printing of articulated models [8], partitioning into printable parts [14].

Structural weakness control is related to the 3D local thickness. In computational geometry, shape thickness is broadly used for surface shape extraction [6], reconstruction [1,16] and skeletonization [10,13,20,19]. Thickness control is the result of complex structural optimization computations [4] and the optimal shape is not manufacturable by standard rapid prototyping work flows.

The purpose of this paper is to present a simple and practical method for 3D printability assessment based on local thickness evaluation of meshes that include portions of not watertight surfaces often encountered in industrial applications. Depending on the critical threshold of manufacturability, surface wall thickness is corrected through an user interaction interface ameliorating the solidity of the prototype.

2. RELATED WORKS

Methods for local thickness estimation can be classified into two categories, surface-based and volume-based, depending on the local structure thickness in use. Following the surface-based approach, local thickness is defined for every point on the surface as a measure of the distance to the "opposite" surface. Jones et al. [12] , for example, propose a measure of the brain cortical thickness. The volume of the cortex is represented as the domain for the solution of the Laplace's equation ($\nabla^2\psi=0$) with boundary conditions at the gray-white junction and the gray-CSF junction. Normalized gradients of ψ define a vector field with vectors tangent to field lines connecting both boundaries. The cortical thickness for a given point of the cortex is defined as the path length along the field line that passes through the point and connects the opposite boundary. The key advantage of this definition is that thickness is uniquely defined for any point in the cortex.

The volume based approach can be illustrated by the method of Hildebrand et al. [11] that estimates local thickness by fitting maximal spheres to every point in the structure. The local thickness at a given point is defined as the diameter of the largest sphere which contains the point and which is completely inside the structure. The model-independence is the basic advantage of this method. It can easily quantify the variability of the thickness and facilitates remodeling undergoing structure. Unfortunately, there is a loss of reciprocity and uniqueness of thickness measure.

The above methods estimate local thickness independently of the downstream applications. Considering 3D printing technology in use, local thickness can be defined in a more technology dependent way. For layered manufacturing for example [3], selecting the build direction resolves some problems in local wall thickening of open contoured surfaces.

3. OUR APPROACH

We are interested in printability assessment of input model that is composed by different connected components, enclosing volumes or being flat, with possible encapsulations, intersections and missing boundaries. Shape thickness can be associated to the measure of the distance between component boundaries that define the limit between the empty space and the solid material. The basic idea is to use a ray tracing algorithm to compute the local thickness as the distance between the pair of "opposite" boundaries.

Algorithm 1: Local thickness computation in 3D Mesh
Input: Triangle mesh T
Output: $T[] = \{thickness_{fT}\}$, $\forall f_T, f_T \in T$, $thickness_{fT}$ measure of local thickness for f_T
begin
  for $\forall f_T, f_T \in T$ **do**
    Trace r_{fT} through the geocenter of f_T and opposite to the normal of f_T;
    for $\forall f, f \in T \wedge f \neq f_T$ **do**
      Compute $D_{fT}[f]$, $D_{fT}[f] = (inter_f, dist_f, orient_f)$;
      if $r_{ft} \cap f \neq 0$ **then**
        $inter_f$ = true ; $dist_f$ = the distance from the geocenter of f_T to f along r_{fT} ;
        $orient_f$ = -1 if r_{fT} has the same direction as the normal of f else $orient_f$ = 1 ;
      else
        $inter_f$ = false ; $dist_f = \infty$; $orient_f = \infty$;
      endif
    done
  Compute $T[f_T]$, $T[f_T]$ = **LTC**(f_T, D_{fT});
  done
end

Let T denotes the input model. For each face f_T, $f_T \in T$, a ray r_{fT} is traced through the geocenter and opposite to the face normal. Crossing points between the ray and the input model are computed. To each crossing point a bracket, left or right, is associated depending on whether the ray "enters" or "leaves" the model component according to the normal orientation of the intersected face. Thus, along the ray, a bracketing expression is constructed. We check for balanced brackets in this expression. Local thickness is defined as the distance between the crossing points corresponding to the first left bracket and the matching right bracket. We denote the above processing as a whole like "volume bracketing".

The Algorithm 1 iterates on each face of the input model in two steps. First, a preprocessing phase to compute information necessary to volume bracketing, and second, given by Algorithm 2, the construction and the evaluation of the volume bracketing expression.

```
Algorithm 2: LTC(f_T ,D_fT)
  Input: Face f_T , f_T ∈ T , D_fT[] = { (inter_f , dist_f , orient_f ) }, ∀ f, f ∈ T ∧ f ≠ f_T
  Output: thickness f_T
  begin
    Let IntExt = 1 and FindExt = false ;
    Sort D_fT[] in increasing order according to dist_f ;
    for all d ∈ D_fT[] do
      if d.inter_f == true then
        IntExt += d.orient_f ;
        if IntExt == 0 ∧ FindExt == false then
          FindExt = true ; thickness_fT = d.dist_f ;
        endif
      endif
    done
    if IntExt ≠ 0 then thicknessf_T = false; endif
  end
```

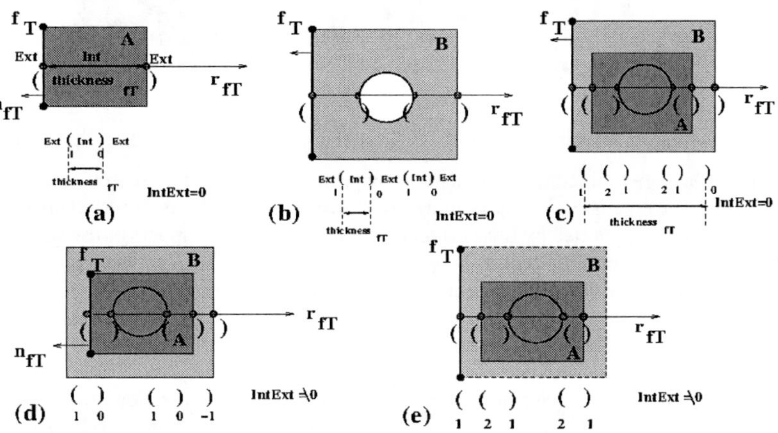

Figure 1. (a,b,c) Local thickness evaluation. (d) Evaluation failure for internal face f_T, , f_T, $\in \partial A \wedge f_T \in B$.(e) Evaluation failure for unbounded model

In Figure 1, a two dimensional case is illustrated. For the example Figure 1(a), the input is a component A with simple connected boundary ∂A. The ray r_{fT} crosses ∂A , in a single point. A left bracket is associated to the geocenter as long as r_{fT} "enters" into A, and a right bracket is associated to the intersection point, as long as r_{fT} "leaves" A. Checking for balance in the expression is simply associated to a counter ***IntExt***, incremented by one when crossing a left bracket, and decremented by one, when crossing a right bracket. At the geocenter, ***IntExt*** is initialized to one. The thickness is measured when ***IntExt*** is annulled for the first time. The scan of the crossing points continues all over the ray r_{fT} . The thickness calculation is valid only if at the end, ***IntExt=0***. A component with a hole is shown in Figure 1(b). When the initial face belongs to an internal shell, Figure 1(d), or in some cases when the input mesh includes missing boundaries, Figure 1(e), the algorithm fails. Cases when faces do not support a valid computation of the local thickness are left for post processing. Indeed, the computation failure indicates the presence of errors or biases in the input model that should be fixed before re-iterating the computation.

4. RESULTS

All prototypes are produced on a "Z-Corp" printer with a height of 7 cm. First, we illustrate an example of printability assessment based on Kate's model. The input mesh, shown in Figure 2(a), is a multi-shell model with intersections and flat surfaces. The evaluation of the local thickness is given in Figure 2(b) and the 3D printing is shown in Figure 2(c). It can be seen that regions with critical thickness, as the right hand and the belt, are detected by the volume bracketing algorithm. In the first case, the designer corrects the critical thickness by attaching the hand to the hip thus avoiding hand's break during printing. In the second case, the critical region is left unchanged that produces a crack in the prototype.

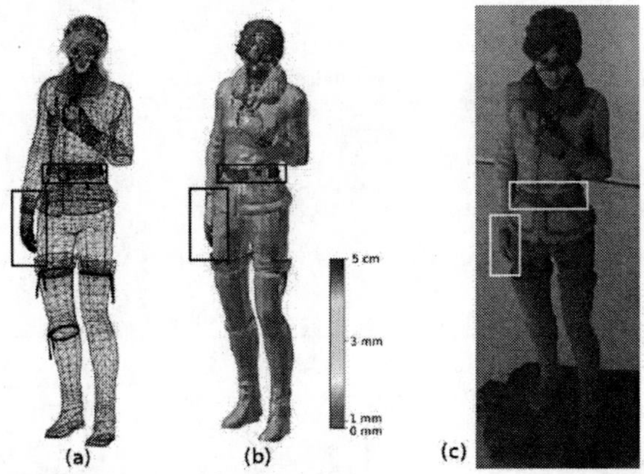

Figure 2. (a) Kate's mesh model (b) Local thickness evaluation (c) Kate's prototype

In Figure 3 we give thickness evaluation by volume bracketing on commonly used test models [15,18,22,23,24]. The results of the 3D printing are shown in Figure 4. As expected arms and legs of banana man break on printing as pointed by their critical local thickness. The support of the soccer cup is built in six strips. Despite of the critical thickness of each individual strip, the prototype preserves its integrity. In contrast, hanging ball does not contain regions with critical thickness but the gravity of the ball cut off the connection to the shelf. Lastly, the shell is of uniform thickness as does the corresponding prototype that remains in a single piece. These experiments show that volume bracketing provides correct evaluation of the local thickness. Our method supplies a simple and fast feedback on the printability of the input models but is less precise than structural analysis supported by multi-objective optimization and mechanics analysis. For example, in comparison with stress analysis of Stava et al. for the shell model shown in Figure 3(e), illustration issued from [18] Figure 5, volume bracketing produces uniform thickness and does not take into account structural weakness ought to gravity and stress. Besides the fact that there is good probability for prototype to break in regions with critical thickness, additional structural weakness constraints are needed to fully determine printability assessment.

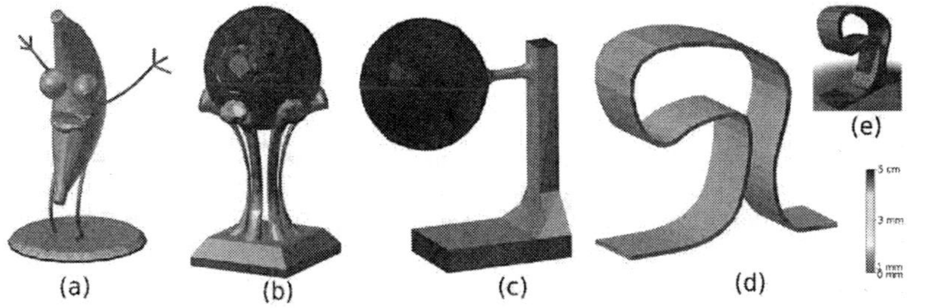

Figure 3. Local thickness evaluation (a) Banana man (b) Soccer cup (c) Hanging ball (d) Shell

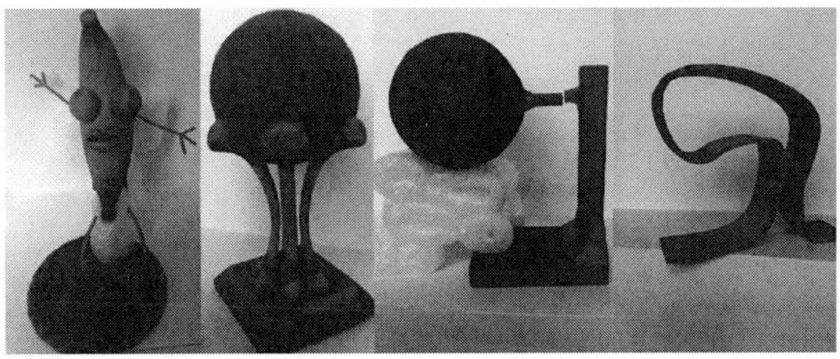

Figure 4. Prototypes of test models produced on a "Z-Corp" 3D printer

5. CONCLUSION

Printability assessment of mesh models is related to the structural soundness and weakness control on input date. In the present article, we propose a method for detection of regions with critical thickness based on volume bracketing. The method is used for local thickness evaluation of meshes with available face normal orientation. The elaborated method is implemented and experienced in an industrial 3D prototyping chain as an interactive designer assistance tool. The experimental results are economically viable in comparison with the classical work flows based on the watertight surface reconstruction as a preprocessing step that is time consuming, computationally expensive and possibly error-prone. The provided industrial feedback implies further case study for errors to be repaired before prototype manufacturing and deeper understanding of the physical constraints. Our goal is to reduce as much as possible interaction during mesh repairing while maintaining the initial designer concept.

ACKNOWLEDGEMENT

This work is supported by ANRT, the Association of National Research and Technology, The Industrial Agreements for Training through Research (CIFRE) grant, FabZat SAS Company. We thank F. Pitoun and D. Chevalier for triggering this research, providing us with 3D printing support.

REFERENCES

[1] Amenta, N. et al., 2001. The power crust, unions of balls, and the medial axis transform. *Comput. Geom.*, Vol. 19, No. 2-3, pp. 127-153.

[2] Attene, M. et al., 2013. Polygon mesh repairing: An application perspective. *ACM Comput. Surv.*, Vol. 45, No. 2, pp. 15.

[3] Alexander, P. and Dutta, D., 2000. Layered manufacturing of surfaces with open contours using localized wall thickening. *Computer-Aided Design*, Vol. 32, No. 3, pp. 175-189.

[4] Allaire,G. And Jouve, F., 2008. Minimum stress optimal design with level set method. *Engineering analysis with boundary elements*, Vol. 32, No. June, pp. 909-918.

[5] Bickel, B. et al., 2010. Design and fabrication of materials with desired deformation behavior. *ACM Trans. Graph.*, Vol. 29, No. 4, pp 63:1-63:10.

[6] Blum, H. and Nagel, R. N. ,1978. Shape description using weighted symmetric axis features. *Pattern Recognition,* Vol. 10, No. 3, pp. 167-180.

[7] Berger, M. and al., 2014. State of the art in surface reconstruction from point clouds. *Eurographics,* Strasbourg, France, pp. 161-185.

[8] Cali, J. and al., 2012. 3D-printing of non-assembly, articulated models. *ACM Trans. Graph,*, Vol. 31, No. 6, pp. :130:1-130:8

[9] Dey, T.K. and Goswami,S., 2003. Tight cocone: A water-tight surface reconstructor. J. *Comput. Inf. Sci. Eng.*, Vol. 3, No. 4, pp. :302—307.

[10] Dey, T.K. and Sun, J. , 2006. Defining and computing curve-skeletons with medial geodesic function. Proceedings *of the Fourth Eurographics Symposium on Geometry Processing*, Cagliari, Sardinia, Italy, pp. 143-152.

[11] Hildebrand, T. and Rüegsegger, P., 1997.A new method for the model-independent assessment of thickness in three-dimensional images. *Journal of Microscopy*, Vol. 185, No. 1, pp. 67-75.

[12] Jones, S.E. and al., 2000. Three-dimensional mapping of cortical thickness using Laplace's equation. *Human Brain Mapping*, Vol. 11, No. 1, 12-32.

[13] Ju, T. and al., 2007. Computing a family of skeletons of volumetric models for shape description. *Computer-Aided Design,* Vol. 39, No. 5, pp. 352-360.

[14] Luo, L. and al., 2012., Chopper: partitioning models into 3d-printable parts. ACM Trans. Graph., Vol. 31, No. 6, pp. :129:1-129.9.

[15] Lu, L. and al., 2014. Build-to-last: strength to weight 3d printed objects. *ACM Trans. Graph.*, Vol. 33, No. 4, pp. :97:1-97:10.

[16] Petitjean, S. and Boyer, E., 2001. Regular and non-regular point sets: Properties and reconstruction. *Comput. Geom.* Vol. 19, No. 2-3, pp. :101-126.

[17] Prévost, R. and al., 2013. Make it stand: balancing shapes for 3d fabrication. *ACM Trans. Graph*, Vol. 32, No. 4, pp. :81:1-81:10.

[18] Stava, O. and al., 2012. Stress relief: improving structural strength of 3D printable objects. *ACM Trans. Graph.*, Vol. 31, No. 4, pp.48:1-48:11.

[19] Sobiecki, A. and al., 2013. Qualitative comparison of contraction-based curve skeletonization methods. *Mathematical Morphology and Its Applications to Signal and Image Processing*, 11th International Symposium, Uppsala, Sweden, pp. 425-439.

[20] Telea, A. and Jalba, A., 2012. Computing curve skeletons from medial surfaces of 3d shapes. *Theory and Practice of Computer Graphics,* Rutherford, United Kingdom, pp. 99-106.

[21] Tu, J., 2009. Fixing geometric errors on polygonal models: A survey. *J. Comput. Sci. Technol.*, Vol. 24, No. 1, pp 19-29.

[22] Umetani, N. and Schmidt, R. , 2013. Cross-sectional structural analysis for 3d printing optimization. *SIGGRAPH Asia,* Hong Kong, China, November, pp. 19-22

[23] Wang, W. et al., 2013, Cost-effective printing of 3d objects with skin-frame structures. *ACM Trans. Graph.*, Vol. 32, No. 6, pp. 177:1-177:10.

[24] Zhou, Q. and al., 2013. Worst-case structural analysis. *ACM Trans. Gr.,* Vol. 34, No. 4, pp. 137:1-137:12.

AN SEMI-AUTOMATIC APPROACH FOR FAST STATISTICAL DATA EXTRACTION FROM AORTIC VALVE

Aleksandrs Sisojevs[1], Rihards Starinskis[2] and Pēteris Stradiņš[2]
[1]*Engineering Research institute "Ventspils International Radio Astronomy centre" of Ventspils University College*
101 Inženieru Str., Ventspils, LV-3601, Latvia
[2]*Riga Stradiņš University, 16 Dzirciema Str., Rīga, LV-1007, Latvia*

ABSTRACT

The statistical data of aortic valve is very important input information for medical diagnostics and anatomical pathology research. The approach for this data extraction is photo survey of aortic valve and next image processing. In this paper the authors have implemented different methods of pattern recognition for extracting the statistical data from photographic images. The modification of "k-Nearest Neighbors" method was proposed. The experimental results show the efficiency of the selected methods and proposed modification.

KEYWORDS

Aortic valve, calcification, pattern recognition, segmentation.

1. INTRODUCTION

Calcific aortic valve calcification (CAVS) is an active process that affects aortic leaflets middle layer with no effective medical therapy. To quantify calcification may predict mortality, morbidity and complication after cardiovascular surgery [1]. Also identification of calcification after cardiovascular surgery may help to understand the pathological process more accurate and detailed. The information of the calcification severity in the post-operative aortic valve may correlate with prosthetic valve calcification and patient reoperation. CAVS is major condition that cause the valve replacement in the developed world.

Without a doubt, a very important principle of diagnostics is the visualization of the aortic valve along with the analysis of echocardiogram's physiological parameters. The possibility to analyze the aortic valve on the macro and micro levels only appears when extracting the valve during the prosthetics of aortic during these two processes, it is possible to examine the valve and analyze the distribution of the pathological tissue. For these purposes, the Fix-Hodges method [5; 6] seems efficient, since we obtain specific data that can be used for defining the correlation between pathological tissue and echocardiogram's parameters.

The histological study shows the inflammation process in the aortic valve leaflets that characterized with extracellular matrix remodeling with increasing fibrosis, valve thickening, angioneogenesis (the normal valve is avascular structure) and calcium deposition. So impressive changes in microscopic level, cannot be hidden in the macroscopic level. Our aim was to identify and score pathological area in the postoperative aortic valve.

2. IMPLEMENTED METHODS AND PROPOSED MODIFICATION

In order to solve the task of image segmentation methods of object recognition (classification) are used in this work. This same approach in [19] was used. In this work, the objects of classification are sets of image pixels, described in the RGB color space. Two methods of object recognition were used: "Template Matching" and "k-Nearest Neighbors" method (or "Fix-Hodges method" [9; 10]). In this works the modification of "k-Nearest Neighbors" method is proposed. The method "Template Matching" [11;12], for our task is described in [19]. Method "k-Nearest Neighbors" or Fix-Hodges method [13; 14] is also a classification method, which in this work is used for the purposes of image segmentation. When using this method, a consecutive analysis is conducted for each image pixel, where the class affiliation for the pixel is unknown. To decrease the time segmentation in [20] was proposed modification of the "k-Nearest Neighbors" algorithm. The main idea of the proposed modification is a reduction of objects in the class *p*. The set of known objects class *p* is subdivided into several subclasses. Then, in each of the subclasses is computed template. A set of received templates of subclasses create a new class for use in the "k-Nearest Neighbors" algorithm. The implementation of the proposed modification consists of the follows steps of: assigning to objects of the test class an additional parameter *t* and the next division into subsets. Described parts can be implemented consistently throughout the following steps.

Step 1: in the test class are two of the object selected, the distance between which is the maximum. Let these points described as p_s and p_f.

Step 2: Translation of all objects of test class in a way that would point p_s coincided with the origin (the point (0, 0, 0)). Figure 1a illustrates this case.

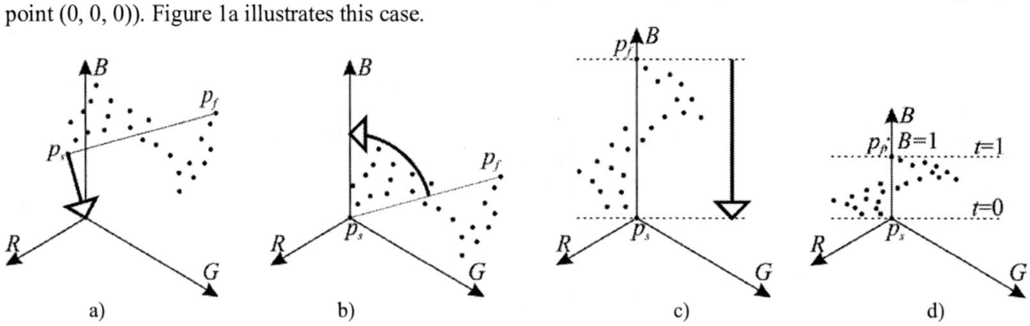

Figure 1. Transformations of Class p

Step 3: the rotation of the test object's class such that the line segment p_s - p_f would coincided with one of the coordinate axes. In the experimental part of this paper is applied to the rotation axis about coordinate *Ob*. In this case, the complex rotation by two simple rotation is implemented: first rotation is around the *Or* axis, and second rotation is around the *Ob* axis. Taking to considering, that the rotation about the O_g axis takes in negative direction. Figure 1b illustrates the rotation of Class *p*.

Step 4: The scaling of the test class by *Ob* axis. Fig.1c illustrates this case. The scaling result is normalization of test class axially *Ob* axes, coordinates *B* values in the objects of class are in the range [0.0; 10]. This case is shown in Figure 1d. Thus, it can assign the value of an additional parameter *t* for the test object class using condition:

$$t_i = p_{i,B}. \qquad (1)$$

Step 5: splitting a set of objects on a subset of the test class, as shown in Figure 2a.

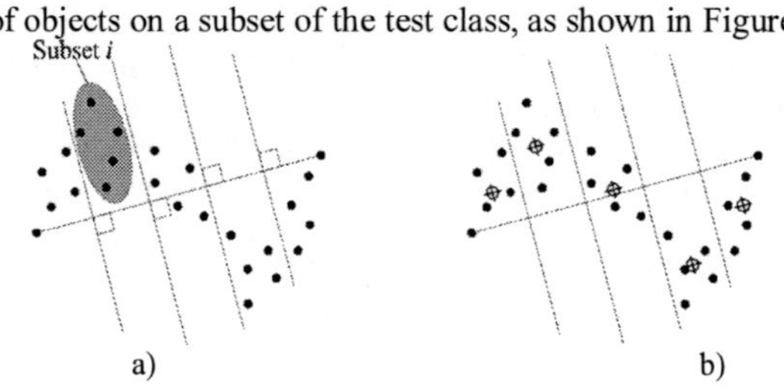

Figure 2. Class p splitting by subsets

For class *p* splitting into subsets the value of the parameter *t* is used:

$$N = \left\lfloor \frac{t_i}{S} \right\rfloor. \qquad (2)$$

where: *N* - No. of the subset to which it include the *i*-th object from the class *p*;
t_i - value of parameter t of *i*-th object in the class *p*;

S - number of subsets for which spitted test class p.

Step 6: calculating template values in each subset, as shown in Figure 2b.

Thus obtained new objects to create a class for use in the method "k-Nearest Neighbors".

3. EXPERIMENTAL RESULTS

In work [19] the input data were photo images of biopsy object. In this work were available objects biopsy - aortic valve obtained from surgical operations. These objects are kindly provided from Heart Surgery Center of Latvian Cardiology Center of Pauls Stradins Clinical University Hospital. So the first task of the experimental part of this work is the task of the photographic shooting.

In the experimental part of the work was applied biomedical object photo shoot to across the light. The Figure 3 shows the scheme of photo shooting. At the Figure 3 is: 1. photo camera; 2. glass bowl; 3. saline solution (*NaCl*); 4. biological object (aortic valve); 5. paper; 6. LED light source.

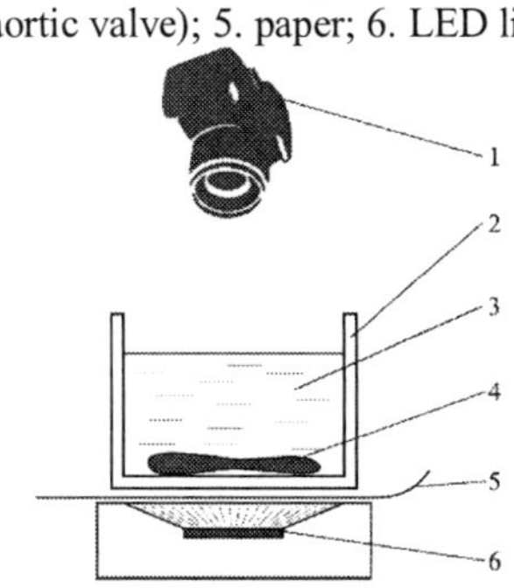

Figure 3. Photo shooting scheme

For statistical data was extracted from the photographic objects of pathological biopsy using the following input data:

- 7 aortic heart valve photographs;
- 7 template segmentation images;

The input images are shown in Figure 4a. In order for the methods "Template Matching" and "k-Nearest Neighbors" to work properly, it is necessary to use images of the start segments (segment map). An example of such a segment map for the input images is shown on Figure 4b.

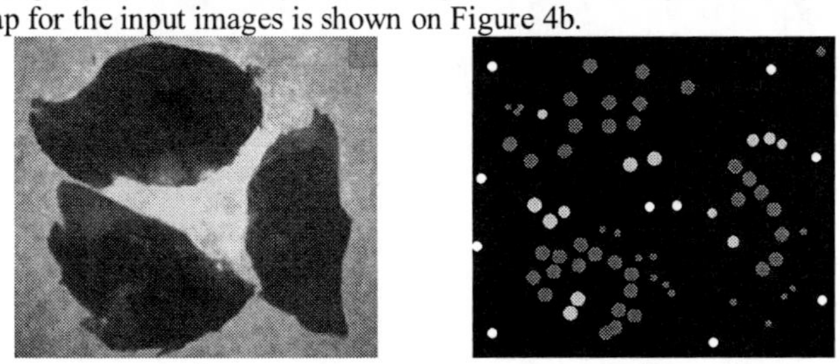

a) b)

Figure 4. The example of input images and start segment's images

The testing consists of two parts. First is the segmentation of the 6 input images based on the 6 segment maps (each input image has its own respective segment map). Each image was processed with three different segmentation methods: "Template Matching" method, unmodified "k Nearest-Neighbor" method and modified "k Nearest-Neighbor" method.

The second part of the testing consists of calculating the number pixels in the segmented regions of interest as well as the percentile correlation of these regions. In practice, two classes of segments were examined – the pathological tissue and the macroscopically unchanged tissue [19].

The first experiment was the segmentation of input images based on the segment map using the method "Template Matching". The segmentation time results are shown in Table 1, columns 4-6.

As seen from table 1 column 6, the use of modified "k-Nearest Neighbors" method gives a good result in terms of segmentation time (approximately 300 times faster than the unmodified method).

Table 1. Sample segmentation data and segmentation time data in experiments

Object	Sample segmentation		Segmentation time, min:sec.		
Nr.	Class 1, %	Class 2, %,	"Template Matching"	Unmodified "k Nearest-Neighbors"	Modified "k Nearest-Neighbors"
1	80,011	19,989	0,06	03:00,8	0,3
2	57,705	42,295	0,05	01:21,0	0,31
3	76,684	23,316	0,06	01:38,8	0,3
4	75,746	24,254	0,07	01:58,9	0,33
5	64,586	35,414	0,07	01:45,9	0,34
6	70,308	29,692	0,06	01:48,2	0,32
7	64,126	35,874	0,08	03:04,9	0,44

As seen from table 2, columns 2-4, the use of "Template Matching" method a not so good result in terms of precision (less than 5% difference) only in 1 out of 6 objects (16,7%).

The second experiment performed on the images was the segmentation of input images based on the segment map using the unmodified method "k-Nearest Neighbors". The input data is the same as in the first experiment. The statistical results for the third experiment are shown in table 2, columns 5-7. As seen from table 2, columns 5-7, the use of "k-Nearest Neighbors" method gives a good result in terms of precision (less than 5% difference) in 6 out of 7 objects (83,3%).

Table 2. Statistical data of segmentation in experiments

Object	Segmentation using the "Template Matching" method			Segmentation using unmodified "k Nearest-Neighbor" method			Segmentation using modified "k Nearest-Neighbor" method		
Nr.	Class 1, %	Class 2, %,	Δ, %	Class 1, %	Class 2, %,	Δ, %	Class 1, %	Class 2, %,	Δ, %
1	69,591	30,409	-10,42	76,931	23,069	-3,08	77,211	22,789	-2,8
2	48,213	51,787	-9,492	58,467	41,533	0,762	55,547	44,453	-2,158
3	66,451	33,549	-10,233	84,142	15,858	7,458	74,643	25,357	-2,041
4	62,367	37,633	-13,379	74,371	25,629	-1,375	75,02	24,98	-0,726
5	64,888	35,112	0,302	62,625	37,375	-1,961	63,554	36,446	-1,032
6	53,93	46,07	-16,378	70,191	29,809	-0,117	69,319	30,681	-0,989
7	61,81	38,19	-2,316	65,46	34,54	1,334	61,572	38,428	-2,554

The third experiment performed on the images was the segmentation of input images based on the segment map using the modified method "k-Nearest Neighbors". The input data is the same as in the first two experiment. The statistical results for the third experiment are shown in table 2, columns 8-10. As seen from columns 8-10 of table 2, the use of modified "k-Nearest Neighbors" method gives a best result in terms of precision (less than 5% difference) in 7 out of 7 objects (100%).

4. CONCLUSION

Several object recognition methods ("Template Matching" method and method of "k-Nearest Neighbors") were implemented in this work in order to solve the task of image semi-automatic segmentation.

After a series of experiments it was concluded that:

- the method of "k Nearest-Neighbors" provides a more precise result than the "Template matching" method;
- the modification of "k Nearest-Neighbors" methods gives better result by segmentation time.

It can also be noted that the method of "k-Nearest Neighbors" requires more time for full segmentation (up to 3 minutes) when compared to "Template Matching" method (up to 0,1 seconds).

The segmentation time by modified "k Nearest-Neighbors" methods is approximately equivalent of to "Template Matching" method (up to 0,6 seconds).

A manual method of segmentation was also applied in order to obtain the sample results for experiments.

ACKNOWLEDGEMENT

The research was supported by the National Research Programme "The next generation of information and communication technologies" (NexIT, Project 2).

REFERENCES

1. Pomerance A. Pathogenesis of aortic stenosis and its relation to age. Br Heart J 1972;34:569–74.
2. Three dimensional volume quantification of aortic valve calcification using multislice computed tomography G J Morgan-Hughes, P E Owens, C A Roobottom, A J Marshall Heart 2003;89:1191–1194
3. 2014 AHA/ACC Guideline for the Management of Patients With Valvular Heart Disease A Report of the American College of Cardiolog
4. The aortic valve calcium nodule score (AVCNS) independently predicts paravalvular regurgitation after transcatheter aortic valve replacement (TAVR) Lorenzo Azzalini, MD, Brian B. Ghoshhajra, MD, Sammy Elmariah, MD, Jonathan J. Passeri, MD, Ignacio Inglessis, MD, Igor F. Palacios, MD, Suhny Abbara, MD. Journal of Cardiovascular Computed Tomography Volume 8, Issue 2, March–April 2014, Pages 131–140
5. K.Akat, M.Borggrefe, J.J. Kaden Aortic valve calcification: basic science to clinical practice
6. J. D. Miller, R.M. Weiss, D.D. Heistad, Calcific Aortic Valve Stenosis: Methods, Models, and Mechanisms
7. M. Misfeld, H.-H Sievers, Heart valve macro- and microstructure University of Luebeck, Clinic of Cardiac and Thoracic Surgery, RatzeburgerAllee 160, 23538 Luebeck, Germany
8. Guidelines on the management of valvular heart disease (version 2012) The Joint Task Force on the Management of Valvular Heart Disease of the European Society of Cardiology (ESC) and the European Association for Cardio-Thoracic Surgery (EACTS)
9. E. Fix, J.L. Hodges, Discriminatory analysis, nonparametric discrimination: Consistency properties. Technical Report 4. - USAF School of Aviation Medicine, Randolph Field, Texas, 1951.
10. E. Fix, J.L. Hodges, Discriminatory analysis—nonparametric discrimination: small sample performance. Technical Report, - USAF, TX, 1952. (Reprinted as pp. 280–322 of Agrawala, 1977.)
11. R. O. Duda, P.E. Hart, D.G. Stork, Pattern Classification, 2nd Edition. Wiley-Interscience, 2000.
12. N.J. Nilsson, The Mathematical Foundations of Learning Machines. San Francisco: Morgan Kaufmann, 1990.
13. E.A. Patrick, Fundamentals of pattern recognition. Prentice-Hall, 1972.
14. T.M. Mitchell, Machine Learning, McGraw-Hill Science, 1997.
15. R. Starinskis, V. Groma, A. Sisojevs, Aortas vārstuļa stenozes morfoloģiskā un datorizētā attēlu analīze, RSU XIX Morfoloģisko zinātņu konferences referātu tezes. – Rīga: Rīgas Stradiņa universitāte, lpp. 38.-39., 2014.
16. D. Randall Wilson, T. R. Martinez, Improved Heterogeneous Distance Functions. Journal of Artificial Intelligence Research 6, pp. 1-34, 1997.
17. R.Euler, J.Sadek, The πs Go Full Circle. Mathematics Magazine, Vol.72, No.1, pp.59-63, 1999.
18. R. Jin, S. Wang, Y. Zhou, Regularized Distance Metric Learning: Theory and Algorithm. Advances in Neural Information Processing Systems 22, pp. 862-870, 2009.
19. A.Sisojevs, K.Bločko, R. Starinskis An Approach for Statistical Data Extraction from Photo Images of Pathological Biopsy Objects. RTU Journal, Technologies of Computer Control. Nr.15, 2014, 5.-13.lpp.
20. Sisojevs, A., Starinskis, R. An Approach for Fast Statistical Data Extraction from Biomedical Objects. . RTU Journal, Technologies of Computer Control. Nr.16, 2016, pp. 64.-71.

VISUAL DEFICIENCIES OF DIGITIZED ANALOG VIDEO - A STUDY OF A VIDEO HOME SYSTEM (VHS) ARCHIVE

Stefanie Müller and Maximilian Eibl
Technische Universität Chemnitz, Germany

ABSTRACT

This paper contemplates first considerations about categorizing typical issues concerning the visual quality in digitized analog video. The basis of our study is analog archive material produced in the early 1990ies by German local TV stations that is stored on (S)VHS tapes. These tapes are now being digitized, stored for archive purposes and optimized for further usage, e.g. in nowadays produced documentaries. The categorization of quality issues is the starting point for a profound image optimization.

KEYWORDS

Video Home System; Image Restoration; Video Archive; Image Enhancement; Cultural Heritage;

1. INTRODUCTION

The Video Home System VHS was introduced by JVC in 1976 with the release of the world's first VHS-based *VCR JVC HR-3300.* It rapidly became the standard tape format for amateur video. Especially during the 1980ies and the early 1990ies VHS was the most successful system despite others, like Video 2000, being technically more advanced.

After the Second World War the western allies installed the public broadcasting service in West Germany (GFR) based on the model of the BBC. In 1984 also private broadcasting services were allowed. After the reunification in 1990 especially in East Germany many local TV stations appeared. From today's perspective they profoundly documented the challenges and achievements the people in Eastern Germany had to face in these years being thrown from a socialist to a market-based system. Due to economic reasons these very small local TV stations used (S)VHS tapes for production as well as for storage.

Nevertheless, during the 1990ies VHS and it´s follower SVHS became replaced by digital formats. In 2008, *JVC* announced the end of production of (S)VHS video players and the german company *SK Holding* recently bought up the last available tapes, now branded as XLYNE [XLYNE 2015] and PLATINUM [PLATINUM 2015]. Due to the restricted life period, the recorded material is increasingly affected by defects or diminished quality by now. The older the tapes get, the more loss occurs. The old videos not only need to be digitized as soon as possible with the help of high quality video players, but also need a restoration in order to preserve the cultural heritage.

In this paper we report our experiences with local TV stations in Germany, which often could not afford to run a professional archive including long lasting technical equipment, ideal air conditioning and an adequate documentation and indexing. Quite frequently, tapes were not cataloged and were stored with no information about the content somewhere in simple cartons. The tapes have been since then without any consideration of archival standards – technically as well as documentary. We are trying to lift this treasure of documented history in order to save the archive footage and make it reusable for today´s video production requirements.

2. PRELIMINARY AND RELATED WORK

The technological base of our work is the software framework AMOPA (Automated Moving Picture Annotator), which we implemented in the course of several projects during the last years. AMOPA is able to detect shots (hard cuts as well as dissolves), and to identify similarities between shots (in order to realize a scene composition). It extracts several low level visual features, but also realizes the detection of several object classes like e. g. faces as well as the transcription of written text. [Ritter et al. 2011] Spoken language (English and German) can be identified and transcribed. [Herms et al. 2014] Thus, AMOPA is able to automatically create valuable metadata for any audiovisual media.

In order to automatically process media stored on tapes we constructed a digitization and annotation line which comprises (1) several different tape players for different tape types (VHS, Betacam, Hi-8, DV, etc.), (2) a small robot which fills and empties the players with tapes, (3) a digitizer for analog video, (4) a transcoder enabling us to use different codecs, (5) AMOPA for the automatic annotation, (6) a database for the storage of the media and its annotations, and (7) software and hardware for organizing the whole workflow. [Manthey et al. 2013] [Rickert et al. 2013] This automatic approach is finally enhanced by a set of tools for manual annotation.

During the last year we started to use this digitization and annotation line for processing (S)VHS-archives of 12 local TV stations. Until today some 200 3h- and 4h- tapes are processed. The material was produced between 1992 and 1994 showing indoor scenes (news presenter in the studio or interviews and events in other premises) and outdoor scenes (buildings, streets, soccer games, construction workers etc.). Some of the tapes had been stored under poor circumstances for the last two decades. The documentation of the content is very sketchy, sometimes only done by simply labeling tapes. Considering this archival practice we are happy that most of the tapes (>99%) are still playable.

Nevertheless, due to the age of the original material, image impairments like Chroma Shift, Color Loss or Image Ghosting occur increasingly. A shortcoming of our technology became obvious: Currently no image optimization has been implemented in the digitization line. In a pilot study, we did several experiences with software toolkits like AviSynth or Magix, but the results were not satisfactory. In terms of image enhancement quite a lot of common methods exist, e. g. in Image Forensics [Piva 2014]. Others are used in the field of medical image processing and are based on histogram equalization, e. g. [Kim 1997] or [Wan et al. 1999]. Yang et al. propose a video sequence noise reduction method based on motion complexity classification, which is able to quantify the spatial distortion and the type of distortion. [Yang 2009] Uma and Annadurai restore images affected by blur and random noise by using a multilayer morphpogical neural network [Uma et al. 2005]. A lot of books filled with mechanical descriptions of the former video equipment or the digitizing process itself can be found, but overall there is very little literature that deals with the detection and improvement of (S)VHS impairments. Le Dinh proposes an image enhancement method for S-VHS using a cascaded Neutral Network structure and a restored luminance signal. The results are more defined edges and details in chrominance. [Le Dinh et al. 2007] Steiner et al. describe a generic crowdsourcing framework with which digitized analog VHS artefacts such as noise or ghosting can be identified. [Steiner et al. 2013] Nevertheless, no overview of (S)VHS artefacts, defined in name and description exists.

A restoration of digitized video archives would have to handle a wide range of problems: Recoloring, Denoising, Data Recovery, Retargeting, Reframing, Upsizing or Upscaling to name just a few. Thus the next goal of our work is to develop techniques, which are able to define and optimize the image quality of (S)VHS material.

3. TYPES OF SHORTCOMINGS

Therefore, we identified upcoming challenges concerning the restoration and optimization of old video footage. Here, we focus on visual issues. Audio is disregarded in this study.

(1) (S)VHS is a technique for video amateurs and the producers of local TV were indeed amateurs in these days: It was rather a learning-by-doing process. Because of this lack of professionalism the footage is full of backlight shots, incorrect white balancing, vast zooming and so on. Due to the absence of the typical test pattern in front of every video, a correct adjustment of technical aspects like color fidelity is not possible.

(2) Today's viewing habits have changed dramatically. Consumers expect high resolution videos and saturated colors in a widescreen format. The European television standard has evolved from low resolution Standard Definition Television (SDTV: 720x576 lines, 4:3) to High Definition Television (HDTV: 1920x1080 pixel, 16:9), which could soon be replaced by the next generation of Ultra High Definition Television (UHDTV: 4096x3072 pixel, 16:9). A quite similar process happened to the analog storage media (S)VHS, which was replaced by the more advanced digital media (HD)DVD and BluRay. Even the manner of video editing (pace and style) has changed.

(3) Mathematical difficulties arise during the compression of analog to digital material. For example, PAL uses the color model YPbPr (analog) or rather YCbCr (digital): Basically, the color information is divided into the background brightness Y and the two chrominance components Pb or Cb and Pr or Cr. Rounding problems caused by A/D-conversion result in information loss during the quantization. Digital grain or macroblock artefacts arise by inadequate bitrate for compressing.

(4) Mechanical difficulties such as the condition of tapes and players must be taken into account. Normally, the expected lifetime of (S)VHS tapes ends after about 10 to 20 years depending on the quality of the tapes and the circumstances of its storage. High quality tapes stored under optimal conditions may have a lifetime of even more than 30 years. In the worst case the tape has become physically completely damaged and is not playable anymore. Playable tapes though encompass a huge range of visual impairments that were either caused by the analog (S)VHS format (tapes) or during the original recording (camera) or playback (players, cables). Moreover, some impairments appear on one player while they disappear on another. Therefore, the workflow of digitizing (S)VHS tapes needs to be analyzed, too. For following projects it is highly significant that we use all possible features a video player is offering in terms of image quality before digitizing starts. Professional devices (e.g. JVC players used in our digitization line) are equipped with a set of handy functionalities like tracking, edge correction, video stabilizer, picture sharpness, TBC and noise reduction. Besides, (S)VHS equipment is no longer available.

4. IDENTIFICATION OF IMPAIRMENTS

As a starting point, 81 hours of digitized tapes have been reviewed in a random sample study aiming to find and identify types of impairments. In the course of this survey and literature research we have detected about 48 different types of impairments representing a cross section of the footage that either occur occasionally or periodically. So far the most frequently occurring deficiencies are shown in figure 1: (1a) *Pinking or Greening:* Pink or green horizontal stripes appear at the upper part of the screen. This error is produced when footage was recorded on cheap VCR's or tapes and is triggered by misaligned video heads. (1b) *Color Loss:* One or more colors are temporarily lost. The video appears in the remaining color mix or in B/W. (1c) *Noise/Grain:* The video image is distorted by noise. Analog tape is a lossy format with native noise or grain. (1d) *Drop Outs:* If particles come off the tape, white or black lines become visible due to the data loss in one or more lines. (1e) *Head Switching Noise* can also occur during the switch of the VCR heads. The lower part of the video is distorted.

More over, one or more colors are shifted in vertical or horizontal direction (*Chroma Shift*). This is normally caused from degraded tapes (e.g. impreciseness, numerous copies of copies), polluted video heads, power problems of the VCR or the low bandwidth of the color information on (S)VHS (brightness: 3,0 MHz, color: 0,6 Hz). *Vertical Jitter* let the video irregularly and quickly bouncing up and down and is caused by corrupted timing of the tape. *Image Ghosting* weakly redoubles the content so that the same image appears slightly shifted near to the original. Usually, this error is caused by power issues or poor coaxial quality. During the occurrence of *Top-Screen-Tearing* the upper part of the video image is faulted as a result of timing errors on the analog tape inside the player. *Interlace Artefacts* appear as irregularly moving aliasing, which is caused by deinterlacing. Due to the mix of different programs recorded separately on one tape, all impairments occur in different manifestations. Furthermore, these deficiencies do not only appear singularly but also combined. Figure 2 shows a video sequence with multiple impairments occurring combined (here: Color Shift, Drop Outs, Jitter, Noise, Pinking/Greening).

Figure 1. Most frequently occurring image impairments

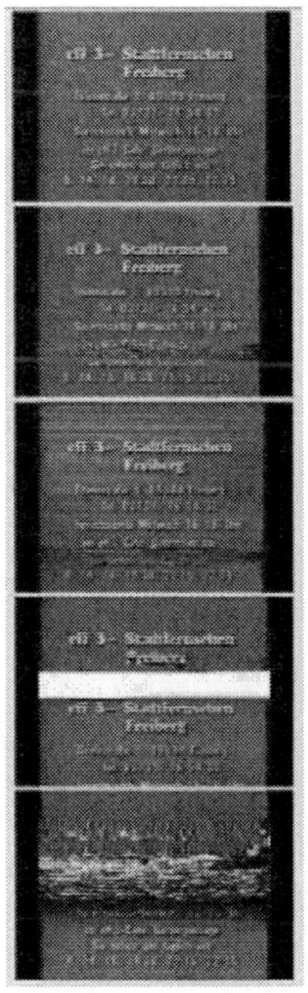

Figure 2. Combined progressing picture errors

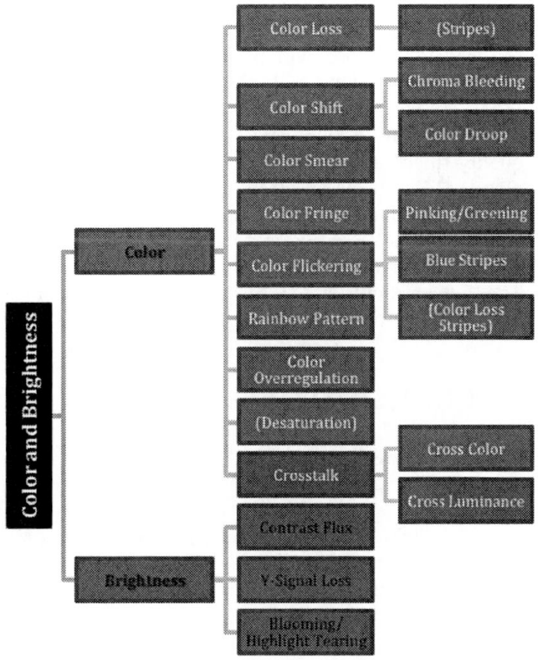

Figure 3. Excerpt of category overview. Here: Color and Brightness

5. FURTHER STEPS

The seen impairments were opposed to the literature to define name and description. The authors put up possible categories, which will be adjusted in a card sorting session and expert interviews. So far, the above mentioned errors can be divided into the sections *color and brightness* (see figure 3), *distortions*, *noise*, *sync* and *other* (yet not identified or categorized). The next step is the implementation of the categories and errors in order to execute a machine learning process using manually extracted images taken from 100 analyzed videos. To create a complete overview of the existence, characteristic and frequency of the occurring errors and their significance, all processed video footage is going to be automatically analyzed and evaluated. Conclusions about the quality of the available material can be drawn afterwards. Our final goal is the definition and implementation of a strategy for image enhancement for the (S)VHS videos. Here our thoughts are still in the beginning. Nevertheless, we want to illustrate shortly two of the possible starting points.

(1) The overall quality of video has evolved greatly since 1990. Therefore, it is important to upscale, recolor and retarget the video data in order to match today´s user expectations. Several approaches like pixel repetition, bicubic or bilinear interpolation are already part of commercial image processing software. Other approaches mostly rely on multi-image super-resolution or example-based super-resolution. Glasner et al. propose a combination of both methods and achieve super-resolution from as little as a single image without a database or prior example. "Our approach attempts to recover at each pixel its best possible resolution increase based on its patch redundancy within and across scales."[Glasner et al. 2009] Another approach is proposed by Freedman et al., who built a "single-image upscaling technique that extends existing example-based super-resolution frameworks." Their work is not based on external example patches, but they "extract patches from extremely localized regions in the input image.[...] The new filters are nearly biorthogonal and hence produce high-resolution images that are highly consistent with the input image without solving implicit back-projection equations." [Freedman et al. 2011] More feasible methods of recoloring, upsampling and retargeting will be examined in due time.

(2) A few studies need to be undertaken to underline the importance of this interdisciplinary research. Therefore, the producer as well as the consumer of video content plays a big role. First of all, local as well as national TV stations will fill out a questionnaire regarding their working and archiving methods. The outcome of this study will include the following: How do they handle the before mentioned impairments? What is their current procedure of combining (S)VHS material in Full HD productions and how time-consuming is this workflow? Another planned study takes the audience and their valuation of video quality (then and now) into account. How do you define and influence quality impression or viewing pleasure? Which impairments are the worst or which errors don´t attract attention at all? These and other questions will be asked during a survey with subjects viewing the before mentioned errors in different manifestations. Based on this ranking we will be able to decide which errors are the most important to fix. Another big role plays the existing editing software. Therefore, a study of their algorithms will be conducted. The outcome will be a comprehensive list containing general software informations, available features, a comparison of results and the used algorithms to fix image impairments.

6. CONCLUSION

In this paper we have described work-in-progress in the field of digitization of video archives. Our focus lies on (S)VHS archives of small local TV stations containing material from the early 1990ies. Based on some 200 tapes we began to identify and classify typical quality issues in the visual appearance of the material in order to obtain a clearly defined error space. Using standard technology to optimize the video turned out to be promising, but not satisfying. Currently, we are defining and implementing more enhanced methods of image enhancement specialized to our (S)VHS stock in order to preserve old footage and make it reusable for today´s requirements.

REFERENCES

Xlyne, 2015, http://xlyne.com

PLATINUM, 2015, http://www.go2sk.de/home.html?L=1

Ritter, M., Eibl, M., 2011, An Extensible Tool for the Annotation of Videos Using Segmentation and Tracking In Proc. *DUXU 2011 - Design, User Experience, and Usability*, LNCS 6769, Springer (2011), pages 295-304

Herms, R., Ritter, M., Wilhelm-Stein, Th. and Eibl, M., 2014, Improving Spoken Document Retrieval by Unsupervised Language Model Adaptation Using Utterance-Based Web Search, In Proc. *INTERSPEECH 2014*, pages 1430-1433

Manthey, R., Herms, R., Ritter, M., Storz, M. and Eibl, M., 2013m A Support Framework for Automated Video and Multimedia Workflows for Production and Archive, In Proc. *HCI International 2013*, LNCS 8018-III, Springer (2013), 336-341

Rickert, M., Eibl, M., 2013, Evaluation of Media Analysis and Information Retrieval Solutions for Audio-Visual Content through their Integration in Realistic Workflows of the Broadcast Industry. In Proc. *ACM RACS - Research in Adaptive and Convergent Systems*, ACM Press (2013), pages 118-121

Piva, A., 2013, An Overview on Image Forensics. *ISRN Signal Processing,* Volume 2013, Article ID 496701, 22 pages

Kim, Y., 1997, Contrast enhancement using brightness preserving bi-histogram equalization, *IEEE Trans. Consum Electron,* Volume 43/ 1, pages 1-8

Wan, Y., Chen, Q., Zhang, B.M., 1999, Image enhancement based on equal area dualistic sub-image histogram equalization method, *IEEE Trans. Consum. Electron*, Volume 45/1, pages 68 -75

Yang, C., 2009, Video Noise Reduction based on Motion Complexity Classification. *Asia-Pacific Conference on Computational Intelligence and Industrial Applications 2009. PACIIA 2009,* Volume 2, pages 176

S. Uma, Dr. S. Annadurai, 2005, Colour Image Restoration Using Morphological Neural Network, *ICGST International Journal on Graphics, Vision and Image Processing*, Volume 8, pages 53-30

Le Dinh, K., Le Dinh, C.T., 2007, Cascaded Neural Network-based S-VHS Restoration, *IEEE Transactions on Consumer Electronics*, Volume 53, pages 513-518

Steiner, T., van Hooland, S., Verborgh, R., Tennis, J., Van der Walle, R, 2013, Identifying VHS Recording Artifacts in the Age of Online Video Platforms, *ACM SIGIR 2013,* Volume 47, pages 31-37

Glasner, D., Bagon, S., Irani, M, 2009, Super-Resolution from a single image, *2009 IEEE 12th International Conference on Computer Vision,* pages *349-356*

Freedman, G., Raanan, F., 2011, Image and video upscaling from local self-examples. *ACM TOG – Transactions on Graphics,* ACM Journal (2011), no. 12

SOLVING THE TASK OF FACE RECOGNITION IN CASES OF INSUFFICIENT TRAINING SET

Olga Krutikova and Aleksandrs Glazs
Riga Technical University
Setas street 1, Riga, Latvia, LV-1084

ABSTRACT

This paper describes methods that are aimed to solve face recognition tasks with an insufficient training set. These methods include: creation of a 3D model of a head that is based on a basic training set - three images of faces (profile, half turn, full face), placing and analyzing control points on a model, calculating distances between points (the ones not used in the creation of a model), which is followed by face recognition. The created 3D model allows acquiring additional images of faces (at different angles), which significantly increases the results of recognition of unknown faces, as compared to only using the basic training set. The proposed methods were tested on various images of faces. The results have shown that these recognition methods can be used in cases, when the initial information about the shape of the face is insufficient, for example, in forensics.

KEYWORDS

Face recognition, 3D model, insufficient training set, control points.

1. INTRODUCTION

The problem of face recognition in images is an important aspect of computer vision. Faces are similar in their anatomical structure, but they differ significantly in shape. Solving this problem is important for various fields, especially in cases, where initial information is limited.

A large amount of face recognition 2D algorithms have been proposed. For example, in (Turk and Pentland, 1991) it was proposed to use eigenfaces to find and recognize faces in images. Face recognition techniques using linear/Fisher discriminant analysis (LDA) (Zhao, 1998) or support vector machines (Heisele, 2001) for the classification were also developed. The main disadvantage of the proposed methods is that they are very dependent on the turn angle of the head, lighting, and they also require a large training set.

Using a 3D model of a face/head allows to solve the main problem of 2D recognition: information about the shape of the face at different turn angles of the head. In (Zhao, 2000) a method was proposed that preprocessed 2D images to create a 3D model. This shape-from-shading (SFS)-based method used a depth map to generate synthetic frontal images. The Linear Discriminant Analysis (LDA) was applied to the synthetic images instead of the original images. A disadvantage of this method is the difficulty of calculating a mathematical model of lighting, it is also not always possible to accurately recreate the shape of the face, and the model might contain distortions and holes.

In (Huang, 2001), (Blanz, 2002), (Blanz and Romdhani, 2003) it was proposed to use a 3D morphable model. The main disadvantage of these methods is that they use a 3D scanner to create models, which is impossible if the initial data are simple 2D images.

In (Bronstein, A. M., Bronstein, M. M. and Kimmel, 2003) it was proposed to use photometric or stereo light to acquire information about the 3D structure. The range image and the texture of the face are acquired. Next, the range image is preprocessed by removing certain parts such as hair, which can complicate the recognition process. A canonical form of the facial surface is computed. The recognition itself is performed on the canonical surfaces. The disadvantage of this method is that several images of the face are taken in different lighting conditions and the 3D geometry is extracted by assuming a Lambertian reflection model. Also, the images are not always available in different lighting conditions and there are problems with calculating a reflection model.

Another method (Popatheodorou, 2004) uses Principal Component Analysis (PCA), which is widely used for 2D recognition and was modified for 3D recognition. They propose to extend the capabilities of the algorithm and combine color, depth map and color map (Tsalakanidou, 2003). However, the main disadvantages of the PCA method are strict requirements for the images of faces (distinct background, size, rotation of the head up to 30°). This approach also cannot be used if the training sample contains only several images.

In (Godil, Ressler, Grother, 2004), a scanned 3D models of a head are used to increase the training set. Stickers or anthropometry landmarks are placed on the person, before scanning. The seventy-three Anthropometry Landmarks were extracted from the scans. The performance of the system based on the 3D information was evaluated by comparing it to the one based on color map information using a PCA based method. The disadvantages of this method is that it uses scanners for creating 3D models and the model topology was rough in the face region. Also, the recognition algorithm requires a color map, which is unacceptable, if the images that are used for creating the models and are synthesized with the help of models are halftone.

In (Howland and Wang, 2006), it was proposed to use the PCA and then LDA methods, but their algorithm was tested on the images of faces, where the turn angle of the head varied only in the range of -30° to 30°.

In this paper, it is proposed to use a semi-automatic method for the creation of the 3D model of the head from 3 images of faces (Krutikova, 2013, 2014), in which an average 3D model of a head is adapted to a specific face by using control point that are placed on the images of the face, which allows to avoid using any additional equipment (3D scanner, stereo cameras) in creation of the models.

There are also many manual, semi-automatic and automatic face recognition algorithms (Scheenstra, 2005). Since the recognition process is complex and consists of many stages, the manual algorithms are too slow and are susceptible to operator error. In large data bases, the search for faces can take a considerable amount of time, which is not always acceptable. Automatic method requires minor interventions from the operator, but it is not always possible (lighting, turn of the head), since the control points may not be properly detected and would require additional configuration.

In this paper, a method of face recognition is proposed, which uses information that was acquired with the help of a 3D model of the head (Krutikova, 2013, 2014). Points that are placed on the base images, are transferred on to the model of the head, which allows to calculate the distances between the points at different turn angles of the head. Control points are also placed on the new image of the face and the face recognition is based on the calculated distances between the points.

2. PROPOSED METHODS

2.1 Method of Face Recognition Based on the Control Points

The proposed method allows recognizing a new image of a face based on the data that was acquired from the 3D model of the head, which is created for each class based on the images from the insufficient training set. To create the model, control points are placed on the images from the training set. The distances between the control points of each model of the head and the control points on the new image are then calculated. The sums of squared distances are calculated. The smallest sum of squared distances corresponds to the found face. The proposed method consists of several steps:

1. Creation of the 3D model of the head for each class using the training set (3 images – profile, half turn, full face,) (Krutikova, 2013, 2014). The recognition does not need textured models, it only uses the mesh, which contains all the necessary vertices of the model, which allows to reduce the consumption of resources and make loading and reading information from the model faster. For example, loading a model without textures takes (0.372 s), with textures (1.32 s).

The images from the insufficient training set with placed control points can be seen on Figure 1.1. The 3D model of the head (Figure 1.3) was created, using an 3D model of an average head (Figure 1.2), by adapting its vertices according to the placed control points.

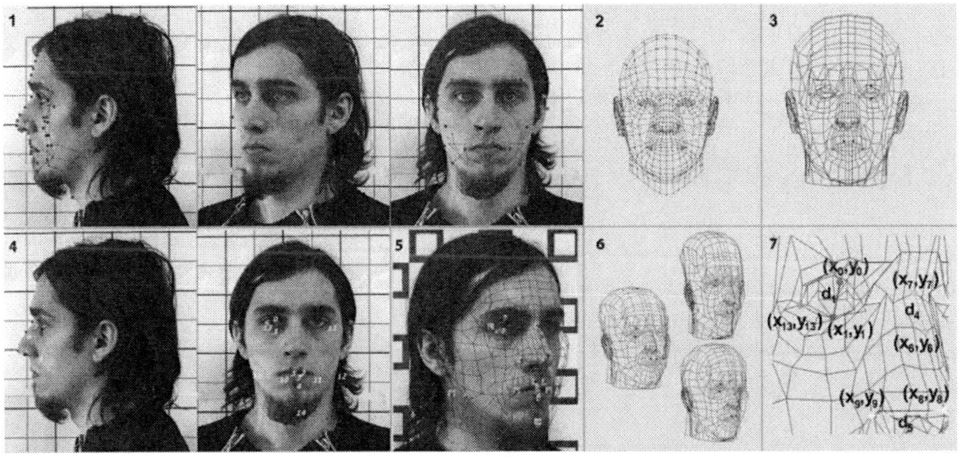

Figure 1. Creation of the 3D model of the head

2. The control points (Figure 1.4), which are used to calculate distances, are automatically transferred from the training set images on to the 3D model of the head and are marked in different colors (Figure 1.3, Figure 1.7).

3. Control points are placed on the new image of the face from the examination set (Figure 1.5).

4. Each 3D model j of the head is automatically positioned on the image of the face (if needed the model is scaled) and the model j is rotated to most resemble the rotation angle of the head on the image (or its closest angle) (see Figure 1.5, Figure 1.6).

5. The distances between the control points on all the head model images and the control points on the new face image are calculated.

5.1. To calculate distances between the control points on the 3D model, all control points are marked in pairs with different colors.

5.2 The image is scanned horizontally w and vertically h, until the intensity of red I_r, green I_g, and blue I_b channels is the same as the desired color.

5.3 The Euclidian distances k, $k \in [1:N]$ between the control points $p+1$ and p, for the image of the model j (Figure 2.6) can be determined as follows (see Formula 1) :

$$d_{j_k} = \begin{cases} \frac{1}{h}\left(y(p+1)_{k,j} - y(p)_{k,j}\right), k = 1,2 \\ \frac{1}{h}\sqrt{\left(x(p+1)_{k,j} - x(p)_{k,j}\right)^2 + \left(y(p+1)_{k,j} - y(p)_{k,j}\right)^2}, k \in [3:N] \end{cases} \quad (1)$$

The Euclidian distances for a new image of the face (Figure 1.7) can be determined similarly (see Formula 2):

$$d_{e_k} = \begin{cases} \frac{1}{h}\left(y(p+1)_{k,e} - y(p)_{k,e}\right), k = 1,2 \\ \frac{1}{H}\sqrt{\left(x(p+1)_{k,e} - x(p)_{k,e}\right)^2 + \left(y(p+1)_{k,e} - y(p)_{k,e}\right)^2}, k \in [3:N] \end{cases} \quad (2)$$

where $j \in [1:m]$ – model number, m – amount of models;
$k \in [1:N]$ – distance number, N – amount of distances;
$p \in [1:Q]$ – control point index, Q – amount of control points;
d_{j_k} – distance (with number k) between the control points of the model (j), pixels;
d_{e_k} – distance (with number k) between the control points of the new image (e), pixels;
x_{j_p}, y_{j_p}, – coordinates of the control point (p) of the model (j), pixels;

x_{e_p} , y_{j_p} – coordinates of the control point *(p)* of the new image *(e),* pixels;

h - height of the image of the model, pixels.

H - height of the new image of the face, pixels.

6. Sum of squares is calculated between certain distance numbers for the new image *e* and the image *j* that was acquired from the 3D model (see Formula 3).

$$d_j = \sum_{k=1}^{N} (d_{j_k} - d_{e_k})^2 \quad (3)$$

where *j*- class number, $j \in [1..m]$

d_j -sum of squares *(j)*

8. To recognize the face now it is necessary to solve the optimization task - find the minimal sum. The minimal sum of squares of distances is calculated and it is determined, whether the face belongs to any class j^*.

$$d_j \to \min_{j \in [1..m]} \Rightarrow j^*$$

3. EXPERIMENTS

The proposed method was tested on images from twelve classes (12 people) with 3 images (Figure 3. a) profile, b) half turn, c) profile) in each class that are used to create 3D models (Figure 3. d), e), f)). Images that were used to create the models and test the algorithm were taken using as -lens reflex digital camera Nikon D5200 24.1 MP CMOS Digital SLR with AF 70-300mm F/4-5.6 Tamron Tele-macro lens, with resolution 6000x4000 and stored using the .JPG format, and for model creation the image resolution was reduced to 1702x1200. For the examination set, the image resolution was further reduced to 762x861. The average time to create models (without placing the control points) -30 sec.

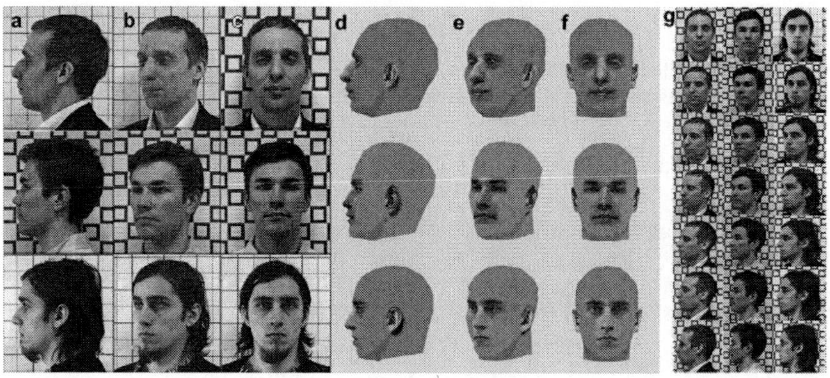

Figure 2. An example of initital data for 3 clases: a), b), c) training set, d), e), f) 3D models of each class, g) examination set

The proposed method was tested (Dell Inspiron 5710, Intel(R) Core(TM) i5-3210M CPU (2*2.5 GHz), Video card - NVIDIA GeForce GT 630M), using an examination set, which consisted of 84 images with various turn angles of the head that varied from -90 to 0 degrees with an interval of 15 degrees.

Control points were placed on each new image of the face and the distances were calculated, the sum of squares and minimal values were also calculated. The algorithm was tested using the extended training set (the model was used), and the base training set (without the model). When the algorithm was tested using the extended training set there were no mistakes. Table 1. shows the test result for the 1st experiment, where all calculated minimal values belong to the correct class.

Table 1. An example of recognition results for first image, when the extended training set was used

New image (e)	Model (j)	Rotation angle, degree						
		-90°	-75°	-60°	-45°	-30°	-15°	0°
1	1	0.57	1.125	2.171	0.693	0.025	0.237	0.145
	2	3.046	3.444	5.912	2.67	0.772	0.59	0.691
	3	3.449	4.233	7.687	4.146	0.578	0.749	0.559
	4	1.861	1.795	2.476	1.81	1.305	1.002	1.163
	5	1.576	2.952	5.271	1.379	0.746	0.478	0.518
	6	3.16	4.897	7.976	3.311	0.873	1.482	1.804
	7	3.88	3.416	2.424	1.466	1.49	1.332	1.383
	8	1.378	2.802	2.746	0.78	0.68	0.819	0.739
	9	2.066	2.499	4.644	2.275	0.596	3.164	2.762
	10	5.894	5.444	6.532	3.876	2.285	1.778	2.278
	11	3.551	4.648	8.748	4.105	0.765	0.794	0.714
	12	2.369	4.796	10.4	2.355	0.65	1.714	1.8

In Table 1. every image from the examination set has a corresponding rotation angle (from -90 to 0 degrees). The table shows the 1st block (experiment) that containins 12 rows, where each row describes a different model. The 1st block contains the distances of the examination face from the 1st class for all 12 models and the row with the minimal distances is highlighted. As can be seen in the table, for instant the 1st experiment consisted of recognizing faces that belong to the 1st class. In the 1st block the model, which corresponds to this class, was rotated so that it would most resemble the turn angle of the face on the image and then the distances were calculated using formulas 1,2,3. As can be seen in the Table 1, the 1st line of the 1st block contains the smallest sums of distances. The graphical representation of the 1st block of the table can be seen in Figure 3, where 12 classes are shown in different colors, at different rotation angles of the head (from -90 to 0 degrees), and the smallest values of the sum of squared distances correspond to the 1st class. The second block had similar results (recognizing faces that belong to the second class) etc.

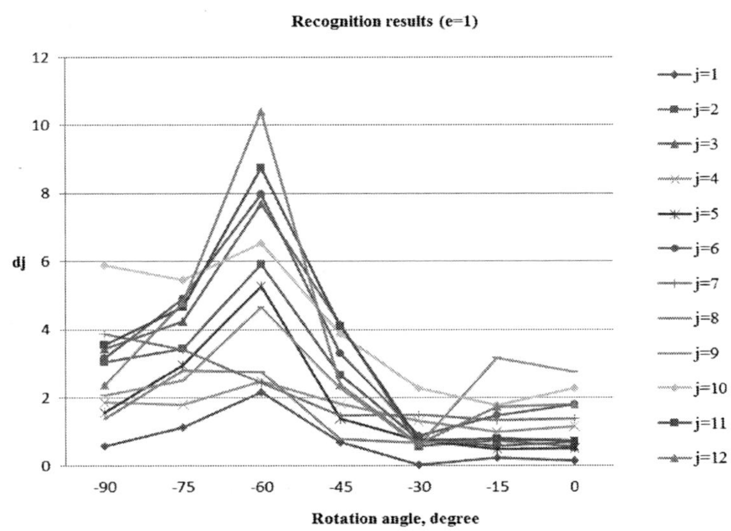

Figure 3. Recognition results for images e from the expanded training set that correspond to 1st class

In the case when the base training set (3 initial images) was used, the amount of errors for 49 images (7 classes) was 6, for (12 classes) 18.

4. CONCLUSION

In this paper, a method of face recognition is proposed, which uses information that was acquired with the help of a 3D model of the head and is aimed to solve face recognition tasks with an insufficient training set.

The created 3D model allows acquiring additional images of faces (at different angles), which significantly increases the results of recognition of unknown faces, as compared to only using the basic training set. The proposed methods were tested on various images of faces. As can be seen from the results, when the extended training set was used there were no mistakes.

The results have shown that these recognition methods can be used in cases, when the initial information about the shape of the face is insufficient, for example, in forensics.

REFERENCES

Blanz, V., Vetter, T. 2003. Face Recognition Based on Fitting a 3D Morphable Model. In *IEEE Transactions on Pattern Analysis and Machine Intelligence,* Vol. 25, No. 9, pp. 1063-1074.

Blanz, V., Romdhani, S., Vetter, T. 2002. Face Identification across different poses and illuminations with a 3D morphable model. *Proceedings of the IEEE International Automatic Face and Gesture Recognition.* Freiburg, Germany, pp. 192-197.

Bronstein, A. M., Bronstein. M. M., Kimmer, R. and Spira, A. 2003. 2003. 3D face recognition without facial surface reconstruction. *Center for Intelligent Systems Report CIS#2003-05, Technion-Israel Institute of Technology.*

Godil, A., Ressler, S., Grother, P. 2004. Face Recognition using 3D Face Shape and Color Map Information: Comparison and Combination, *Proceedings of SPIE, Vol 5404 Biometric Technology for Human Identification,* Orlando, FL, pp. 351-361.

Heisele, B., Ho, P., Poggio, T., 2001. Face recognition with support vector machines: Global versus component-based approach. Proceedings Eighth IEEE International Conference on Computer Vision. Vancouver, Canada, pp. 688–694.

Howland, P.; Wang, J.; Park, H. 2006. Solving the small sample size problem in face recognition using generalized discriminant analysis; Pattern Recognition, Volume 39, Issue 2, pp. 277-287

Huang, J., Heisele, B., and Blanz, V. 2001. Face recognition with support vector machines: global versus component-based approach. *Proceedings Eighth IEEE International Conference on Computer Vision.* Vancouver, Canada, pp. 688-694.

Krutikova, O., Glazs, A. 2013. Development of a New Method for Adapting a 3D Model from a Minimum Number of 2D Images. In *Technologies of Computer Control*, Vol.14, pp. 12-17.

Krutikova, O., Glazs, A. 2014. Increasing the Training Set in Face Recognition Tasks by Using a 3D Model of a Face. In *Technologies of Computer Control.* Vol.15, pp.14-19.

Popatheodorou, T., Rueckert, D. 2004. Evaluation of Automatic 3D Face Recognition Using Surface and Texture Registration, *Proceedings Sixth IEEE International Conference on Automatic Face and Gesture Recognition*, Seul, Korea, pp. 321-326.

Romdhani, S., Vetter, T. 2003. Efficient, Robust and Accurate Fitting of a 3D Morphable Model. *Proceedings Ninth IEEE International Conference on Computer Vision.* Nice, France, pp. 59-66.

Scheenstra, A., Ruifrok, A. and Velktkamp, R. C., 2005. *Proceedings of* 5th International Conference, AVBPA 2005, NY, USA, pp. 891-899.

Tsalakanidou, F., Tzocaras, D. and Strintzis, M. 2003. Use of Depth and Colour Eigenfaces for Face Recognition. *In Pattern Recognition Letters*, Vol. 24, pp. 1427-1435.

Turk, M.A., Pentland, A.P. 1991. Face Recognition Using Eigenfaces. *Proceedings of the IEEE Conference on Computer Vision and Pattern Recognition*, Maui, Hawaii, USA, pp. 586-591.

Zhao, W.Y, Chellappa, R., Krishnaswamy, A., 1998. Discriminant analysis of principal components for face recognition. Proceedings of the 3rd IEEE Internatational Conference on Automatic Face and Gesture Recognition. Nara, Japan, pp. 336–341.

Zhao, W.Y., Chellappa, R. 2000. SFS Based View Synthesis for Robust Face Recognition. Proceedings of the IEEE International Automatic Face and Gesture Recognition. Grenoble, France, pp. 285-292.

POINT CLOUD REGISTRATION WITH SURFACE DESCRIPTORS

Luis Gerardo de la Fraga and Daniel López-Escogido
CINVESTAV, Computer Science Department
Av. IPN. No. 2508, 07360 Mexico City

ABSTRACT

In computer vision a common problem is the registration of 3D data, which consists in to minimize the sum of squares of the distance between metrical marker correspondences. Commonly used marker correspondences are points, in two or more datasets. The most popular algorithm used to solve this problem is the Iterative Closest Point (ICP) due to its easy implementation and fast convergence. In this paper is introduced a methodology using some features of ICP and a general-use-optimizer like Levenberg-Marquardt. The proposed approach also uses vectors as surface descriptors, and those vectors are used to describe planes, cylinders, and cones, contained in synthetic and real shapes. Additionally in the sphere model is used its center point. Using this information, it is proposed the minimization of an objective function which gives more weight to the part of surface alignment. Experimental results show us that the registration using surface descriptors is more efficient, it can be solved both with fewer iterations and less execution time, than using only points.

KEYWORDS

Point cloud registration, surface registration, robust registration, surface descriptors, Levenberg-Marquardt.

1. INTRODUCTION

In the literature the problem of minimize the sum of the square of the distance between correspondences in a shape named model in a reference coordinate system, and a shape named data in a different reference coordinates system, through finding a quasi-optimal transformation matrix T, is known as pose estimation [3], registration [4], alignment [15], surface matching [1], among others. Several problems in computer vision involve the registration of datasets in 2D and 3D [2]. Registration task is relevant for the integration of range data and alignment of different scans, CAD, inverse engineering, pattern recognition, robot navigation, and other research and industrial areas.

Since the publication of the ICP algorithm by Besl and McKay [10] and independently by Zhang [17] several approaches have been raised (see surveys [4, 12]), one requirement to the fast ICP convergence is that the initial approximation needs to be reasonable good [15]. The registration problem involves first to find the points or features of correspondence between the two shapes, and then, based on these correspondences the estimation of the geometric registration is performed. Finding the correspondence is a problem itself [7], and the most common way to solve it with ICP is by finding the minimal Euclidean distance between markers. The other step in this algorithm is how to find the estimation of the transformation matrix; two common ways is using methods with quaternions [10, 17] and singular value decomposition (SVD) [7] and recently minimization of energy function by least-squares [2]. Mainly works treat with points and other works add information like tangent vectors [13], color, planes, quadrics, tessellations, among others [4, 12]. In this work is introduced a combination of minimization of an objective function with points information, adding surface descriptors, and the use of a use-general-optimizer like Levenberg-Marquardt (LM). The reason of this approach is because we are using cloud data points from scanned 3D surfaces, from those data points we fit surfaces to them, and therefore we have much more accuracy in the surface location than in the location of single points. Also, our work uses the fitted surfaces as high level descriptors instead of medium level descriptors used in [18].

This article is organized in six sections: In section 2 our problem definition is given; section 3 describes briefly the LM algorithm; in section 4 the implementation to solve our problem is described; in section 5 some experiments and results are explained. Finally in section 6 some conclusions of this work are given.

2. PROBLEM DESCRIPTION

In this paper we deal with the registration problem of two 3D shapes described by a set of points and a set of surface descriptors. For notation we use the shape named model denoted by the two sets: $\{m_i\}_{i=1}^{n}$ and $\{s_j\}_{j=1}^{k}$, where m_i are the elements in the set of points, and s_j are the elements in the surface descriptors, respectively. The shape data, denoted by the two sets: $\{d_i\}_{i=1}^{p}$ and $\{v_j\}_{j=1}^{q}$, where d_i are the elements in the set of points, and v_j are the elements of the surface descriptors, respectively. In this work is tackled the problem of finding a rigid transformation T that applied to the surface descriptors and points in shape data best fits to the shape model. A rigid transformation in 3D involves the application of a rotation matrix $R \in \mathrm{R}^{3\times3}$ and a vector $\mathbf{t} \in \mathrm{R}^3$ for the translation. The rotation matrix R can be described by the product of three matrices; it could be the rotations around three main axes, with the correspondent Euler's angles α, γ and β. We defined this rotation as $R = R_z(\alpha)R_y(\beta)R_z(\gamma)$, where R_y and R_z are defined as:

$$R_y(\beta) = \begin{bmatrix} \cos\beta & 0 & \sin\beta \\ 0 & 1 & 0 \\ -\sin\beta & 0 & \cos\beta \end{bmatrix}, \text{ and } R_z(\gamma) = \begin{bmatrix} \cos\gamma & -\sin\gamma & 0 \\ \sin\gamma & \cos\gamma & 0 \\ 0 & 0 & 1 \end{bmatrix}$$

Joining the rotation R and translation $\mathbf{t}$ parameters in the vector $\mathbf{a}=[\alpha, \beta, \gamma, t_x, t_y, t_z]$ the transformation T applied to a point $\mathbf{x}$ is defined by:

$$T(\mathbf{a};\mathbf{x})=R\mathbf{x}+\mathbf{t}$$

For a vector $\mathbf{v}$ the transformation is defined by:

$$T(\mathbf{a};\mathbf{v}) = R\mathbf{v}$$

To solve the registration problem first is necessary to know some correspondences between points in the *model* and the *data*, and with these correspondences the matching error between them is evaluated. To avoid a greedy searching in the 3D space commonly is used the well known *kd*-tree spatial clustering algorithm to find the closet point between *model* and *data* shapes, each point in model may have a correspondent point in data but only one, and the distance must meet to be under a tolerance τ. Even thought the problem could be solved using the correspondence between points, in this work we want to focus in the use of surface descriptors mainly planes, spheres, cylinders, and cones. A plane can be described by the equation:

$$ax + by + cz + d = 0 \quad (1)$$

The vector $\mathrm{n}=[a, b, c]^T$ is the normal vector that describes a family of planes for different values of d. A sphere can be defined by the equation (2):

$$(\mathbf{r} - \mathbf{r}_c)^T(\mathbf{r} - \mathbf{r}_c) = r^2 \quad (2)$$

where $\mathbf{r} = [x, y, z]^T$ is a point on the surface of the sphere, and $\mathbf{r}_c = [x, y, z]^T$ is the center of the sphere, and the scalar r is the sphere radius. Knowing the value of $\mathbf{r}_c$ and $\mathbf{r}$ is possible to draw any sphere in the 3D space. We use the cylinder and cone equations described in [9]. The cylinder surface can be described by a point $\mathbf{p}_0 = [x_0, y_0, z_0]^T$ on the cylinder main axis, and unitary vector $\mathbf{u}$ that gives direction of such main axis. In a similar form to the cylinder, the surface descriptor for a cone can be any point $\mathbf{p}_0$ on the main axis, and a unitary vector $\mathbf{u}$ signaling the direction of the main axis. In this work the inner product definition was used to evaluate orientation between vectors:

$$\mathbf{v} \cdot \mathbf{u} = \|\mathbf{v}\| \, \|\mathbf{u}\| \cos\theta \quad (3)$$

According to equation (3) two vectors are parallel or have the same orientation if the angle θ between them is 0 radians. To explode this fact, we add this feature to an objective function that takes into account errors between correspondence points and surfaces. Thus our error function is defined as:

$$E(\mathbf{a}) = \sum_{i=1}^{n}\left(\mathbf{m}_i - T(\mathbf{a}; \mathbf{d}_i)\right) + w\sum_{j=1}^{k} \arccos\left(\frac{s_j \cdot T(\mathbf{a}; \mathbf{v}_j)}{|s_j||T(\mathbf{a}; \mathbf{v}_j)|}\right) \quad (4)$$

and the estimated value for parameters in vector **a** is obtained by the minimization of:

$$\hat{\mathbf{a}} = \operatorname{argmin} E(\mathbf{a}) \quad (5)$$

3. LEVENBERG-MARQUARDT ALGORITHM

The Levenberg-Marquardt (LM) algorithm [5] is a well known method for solving non-linear least-squares problems including non-linear data-fitting problems in iterative way. LM involves the combination of the gradient descent and the Gauss-Newton methods, LM can find a solution, in many cases, even if it starts far of the global minimum. The main application of LM is the least-square curve fitting: given a set of observed data *d* and a set of independent values *m* the goal is to optimize the parameters $\mathbf{a}_i$ (i = 1,2,3,…,n=card(**a**)), of the curve *f(d,* **a***)* so that the sum of the squares errors is minimum:

$$E(\mathbf{a}) = \sum_{j=1}^{n} [m_j - f(d_i, \mathbf{a})]^2$$

4. IMPLEMENTATION FOR SOLVING 3D REGISTRATION

LM algorithm needs to estimate a matrix of derivatives respect each one of the parameters in **a** (Jacobian matrix **J**). This problem can be solved using the finite differences method, this approach is useful for functions or data where an exact derivative is not possible to compute, some researchers have given contributions for solving derivatives with finite differences in the context of numerical methods [14, 11, 6]. Our objective function to be optimized has been defined in equation (5); as part of the ICP algorithm we need a correspondence function ϕ, this function has an important role to the correct convergence of the algorithm; ϕ in our implementation finds the closest point between the set *model* and the set *data* using *kd*-trees. In order to set the correspondent vectors to register the shapes also is used a correspondence function ϕ_2 that evaluates the minimal angle between vectors using equation (3) and it sets the correspondences to be optimized. To initialize the algorithm we first translate the center of mass of the point cloud in the set *data* to center to the set *model*, then we apply the function ϕ and ϕ_2 to find the best correlation of points and vectors between these datasets, points and vectors without correspondence are removed from the optimization set used in LM. The vector **a** is defined and initialized as follows with $\alpha = \beta = \gamma = 0$ and **t** = centroid of set *model*. The implementation of the error evaluation function E, takes as input the *model* and *data* points and the parameters optimized by LM in each iteration, this function constructs the rotation *R* and the vector translation **t** taking the values of a and it applies the transformation to the *data* set and then it evaluates the differences between the correspondent points given by the function ϕ and returns a vector for each point in the form:

$$e_i = [x_i, y_i, z_i]^T$$

and for each vector correspondences is returned a vector with the errors:

$$e_j = [25\theta_j]$$

The final error vector is the concatenation of vectors e_i and e_j.

The value of the constant w in the equation (4) was defined experimentally equals to 25, and it was the value chosen for all our experiments. Implementation was performed using Python 2.7.6 with the package LMFIT [8], which implements the LM optimizer, with a computer with OS Windows 7, 64 bit processor Intel i5 @ 2.5GHz and 4GB RAM memory.

5. EXPERIMENTS AND RESULTS

In order to evaluate our registration approach three different experiments were executed. First experiment is depicted in figure 1. To the left, in figure 1, synthetic data was generated to produce a unitary cube, it is represented by its respective eight 3D points (each one in its eight vertexes), and three vectors that define the orientation of three of its faces. The patch for registration is a tetrahedron, which is defined by four 3D points and three vectors on only three of faces. The tetrahedron fourth face in this example is not need; it could be considered an interior face that is not used in the registration.

In the experimentation phase was selected for registration only one point of the tetrahedron which is equal to one cube vertex, and its associated three vectors of the faces that lie in that vertex. A vector only give us the orientation of one face (or plane) and it is still necessary to specify a point on the 3D objects to register to fix the position of the face. But remember here that our objects come from fitting their associated point clouds, then its orientation has a better estimation that any of their point locations.

Results of 31 executions of the registration are shown in Table 1. In each run, also a random rotation and translation around the model was performed. Figure 1 in the right is depicted the final registration.

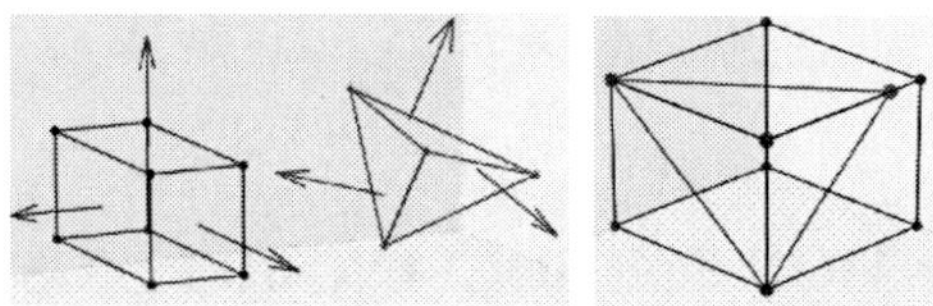

Figure 1. Left: Unitary cube used as *model* and tetrahedron the shape to be registered also, are depicted the vectors used for the registration. Right: Final registration using the proposed approach

Table 1. Statistical results after 31 executions using the data for the *model* and patch depicted in figure 2

	Iterations	Time [sec]	Error
Average	31.7	0.0085	4.24×10^{-8}
Max.	36	0.0099	1.31×10^{-7}
Min	29	0.0055	3.06×10^{-9}
Std. Dev.	3.19	0.0012	5.24×10^{-8}

Second experiment was performed with two different datasets. The point clouds were obtained using a high precision laser scanner installed in our laboratory. The object is a computer USB adapter, which was chosen because it is built with geometric primitives like planes and cylinders. The way to estimate the normal vectors for the planes and the director axis for the cylinders is the described in [9]; shape *model* contains 3,664 3D, and for this test two planes and three cylinders were fitted to this shape model. The shape *data* contains 5,461 3D points, and was fitted to it the same number of primitives: two planes and three cylinders. On both shapes was chosen a fixed point on one of the planes.

Average running time of registration using only the cloud point is 2.01 seconds (average of 15 executions). Statistical results after 31 executions are shown in table 2, results show us that average time for the execution takes only 0.1117 seconds, compared with a registration approach using only 3D points, our approach, using surface descriptors, can improve a lot the execution time.

Table 2. Statistical results after 31 executions using the data for the *model* and patch depicted in figure 2

	Iterations	Time [sec]	Error
Average	496.81	0.1117	3.28×10^{-2}
Max.	500	0.1473	3.31×10^{-2}
Min	492	0.1039	3.23×10^{-2}
Std. Dev.	2.89	0.0130	2.87×10^{-4}

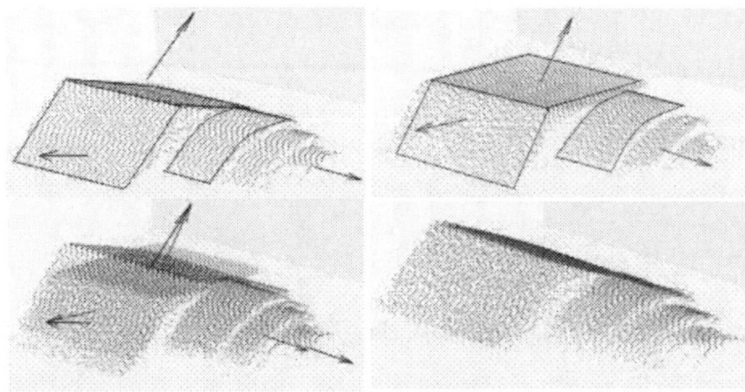

Figure 2. In these images are depicted shapes with two planes and three cylinders, vectors that describe the planes and the cylinder used in the registration are drawn with arrows. Up left: point cloud *model*. Up right: point cloud *data*. Dawn left initialization before registration process. Dawn right: final registration

Another third test was performed, but now with a shape scanned in two parts because it is so big to be scanned in a single pass. The registration is performed using only the surface descriptors of the 3D scene, *i,e.* two planes, one sphere, a cylinder, and a cone. But, remember that for the two spheres their fitted centers are their descriptors. Figure 3 to the left depicts the two scans of the mechanical tool, the *model* is in blue and the point cloud contains 16,048 vertexes, and the point cloud for patch in red contains 12,169 vertexes. In table 3 is shown the average of iterations, execution time, and error. Figure 3 to the right shows the final registration obtained with the proposed methodology.

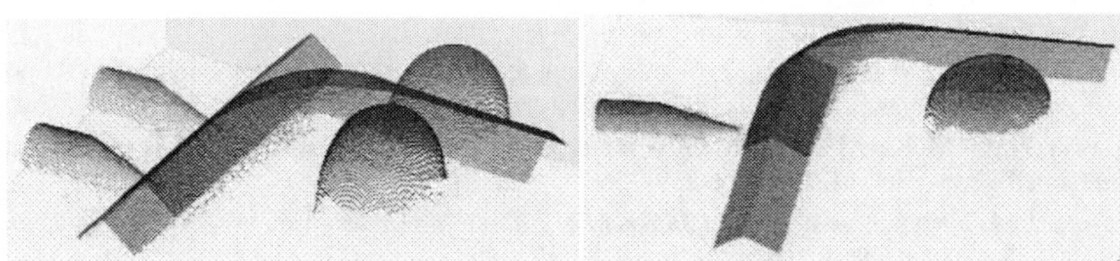

Figure 3. Left: Initialization for the shape registration. Registration is performed using only the surface descriptors for two planes, one cylinder, a cone; for the sphere was used its center as its descriptor. Right: Final shape registration for datasets using our proposed methodology

Table 3. Statistical results after 31 executions using the data for the model and patch depicted in figure 3

Iterations	Time [sec]	Error
462	0.1152	3.85×10^{-2}

6. CONCLUSIONS

In this work was introduced a methodology to resolve the registration problem using surface descriptors for plane, cylinder, and cone. Those surface descriptors are the normal vector for the plane, the main axis direction for both the cylinder and the cone. For the sphere we use its estimated center. The first stage of our proposed methodology is similar to the ICP algorithm: The selection of correspondence points between a model and patch to be registered, using *kd*-trees. The second stage is to use Levenberg-Marquardt, a general-use-optimizer. The objective function to minimize is the square of the sum of distances among the point correspondences, and also the sum of scalar products between the vectors that describe the surface descriptors. The scalar product estimates the alignment between the surface descriptors. We showed this proposed methodology with synthetic and real data. We obtained the real data with a 3D scanner. Experiments show us that the methodology proposed converges in few quantities of iterations with minimal error and fast execution time.

ACKNOWLEDGEMENT

This work has been partially supported by project Conacyt 168357.

REFERENCES

[1] A. Gruen and D. Akca, 2005, Least squares 3D surface and curve matching. *Journal of Photogrammetry and Remote Sensing*, Vol. 59, No. 3, pp 151-174.

[2] A. W. Fitzgibbon, 2003. Robust registration of 2D and 3D points set. *Image and Vision Computing*, Vol. 21, pp 1145-1153.

[3] C. Wohler, 2009. *3D Computer Vision: Efficient Methods and Applications*. Springer (X.media.publishing), isbn: 3642017312.

[4] J. Salvi. et al, 2007. A review of recent range image registration methods with accuracy evaluation. *Image and Vision Computing*, Vol. 25, No. 5, pp 578-596.

[5] J. J. Moré, 1977. *The Levenberg-Marquardt Algorithm: Implementation and Theory*, Numerical Analysis. G. A. Watson, Lecture Notes in Mathematics 630, Springer Verlag, pp 105-116.

[6] M. H. Chaudhry, 2008. *Open-Channel Flow*. Springer, On line ISBN: 978-0-387-68648-6.

[7] M. Greenspan and G. Godin, 2001. A nearest neighbor method for efficient ICP. *Proceedings. Third International Conference on 3-D Digital Imaging and Modeling*, pp 161-168.

[8] https://lmfit.github.io/lmfitpy/. Non-Linear Least-Square Minimization and Curve-Fitting for Python. Available online: Last date checked Feb 26th, 2016.

[9] D. López-Escogido and L.G. Fraga, 2014, Automatic extraction of geometric models from 3D point cloud datasets, *11th International Conference on Computing Science and Automatic Control (CCE),* pp 1-5

[10] P. J. Besl, N. D. McKay, 1992. A Method for Registration of 3-D Shapes. IEEE Trans. on Pattern Analysis and Machine Intelligence, Vol. 14, No. 2, pp 239-256.

[11] P. Olver, 2014. *Introduction to Partial Differential Equations. Undergraduate Texts in Mathematics*. Springer, On line ISBN: 978-3-319-02099-0.

[12] S. Rusinkiewicz, M. Levoy, 2001. Efficient Variants of the ICP Algorithm. *Int. Conference on 3D Digital Imaging and Modeling*, pp 145-152.

[13] T. Wu et al, 2010. Automatic 3D point clouds registration method. *Proceedings of SPIE* 7855, pp 785526.

[14] W. H. Press, et al, 2002. *Numerical Recipes in C: The Art of Scientific Computing*. Cambridge University Press, (2Nd Ed.) New York, USA.

[15] Y.F. Wu et al, 2015. A New Method for Registration of 3D Point Sets with Low Overlapping Ratios. *Conference on Computer Aided Tolerancing*, Vol. 27, pp 202-206.

[16] Z. Xie, S. Xu and X. Li, 2010. A high-accuracy method for fine registration of overlapping point clouds, *Image and Vision Computing*. Vol. 28, No. 4, pp 563-570.

[17] Z. Zhang, 1994. Iterative point matching for registration of free-form curves and surfaces. *International Journal of Computer Vision*, Vol. 13, No. 2, pp 119-152.

[18] S. Afaq, A. Shah, M. Bennamoun, and F. Boussaid, 2014, Performance Evaluation of 3D Local Surface Descriptors for Low and High Resolution Range Image Registration, *International Conference on Digital Image Computing: Techniques and Applications*, pp 1-7.

A MODERN VISUAL GRAPHIC SEARCH HOMEPAGE

Xin Bai, Dawn Wang and Huizhen Ji
The Microsoft Corporation
Redmond, WA 98052

ABSTRACT

Most current search homepages, like http://bing and http://google, are all text based. There is a text box for user to enter a search query string. In addition, it contains some menus and sub-menus on the interface, and they take time to find. Moreover, it is not the best fit on a mobile device with a touchscreen. And it is not fun. It was originally designed for a PC with a mouse click, and not for a mobile device with a touchscreen.

Visual graphic search homepage, which we present here, brings up a new search interface to display the query suggestions graphically. It primarily focuses on the customer experience, especially on a mobile device with a touchscreen. By using the graphic search homepage, the user will gain a streamlined search experience with a better performance.

KEYWORDS

Symmetric, spin, tile, visual graphic search, query suggestion, touchscreen

1. INTRODUCTION

People seldom search on a mobile phone because the current search homepages on a mobile phone are not user friendly.

Most of search homepages, like http://bing, http://google, and http://baidu, are all text based on both of a PC and a mobile device. The user goes to a textual box, enter a query string as a keyword(s), and start searching. It takes some effort for user to navigate around to compare the search results. By Intuition, this is not the best choice of search interface on a mobile device with a touchscreen, as a person needs to move finger around a textual box. In any case, it is not the most pleasant and efficient way for a user to search on a mobile device with a touchscreen. Eventually, the user may give up using today's search homepage on a mobile device with a touchscreen.

In order to draw the user back to the search homepage on a mobile device with a touchscreen, a precise influence to user's emotion becomes essential. We present here a search interface with a visual graphic design to try to tackle on the problem, as graphic communication quickly affects us both cognitively and emotionally. In addition, emotions play an essential role in decision-making [1].

In addition, per scientific study, human brain deciphers image elements simultaneously, while textual language is decoded in a linear, sequential manner taking more time to process. When it comes to quick, clear communication for customers, visual trumps text almost every time [1] [2].

Actually, the vast majority of what we communicated was not text based [3]. One instance is that textbooks have progressed from a majority of text to a majority of graphics [4].

In the design presented in this paper, a visual graphic user interface displays multiple sets of query suggestions. The user is able to preview and even compare the search results before one decides to dig into the search result detail. Besides the query suggestions starting with the search keyword(s), the reversed query suggestions can be retrieved and presented to the user as well. The visual graphic design provides a user-friendly interface, which is easily selected by a finger on a touchscreen mobile device.

Also, the graphical representation of the search interface is displayed on a display device, in which each display element could float individually. In this case, the size of each floating display element is changeable; and the background color of each floating element can be set to different ones as well.

2. BACKGROUND

As a user enters a query string into a search textual box, which is associated with a search engine, like http://bing, the user is often presented with one or more query suggestions. These are based on the query string or the characters of the query string that have been entered by the user. These query suggestions are often displayed to the user in a user interface element below the search box as a list and may be generated by the search engine based on a history of queries that have been received by the search engine from the user or other users. The user may then submit the original query that they entered to the search engine or may select one of the displayed query suggestions to submit to the search engine.

There are several drawbacks associated with present techniques for presenting query suggestions.

First, search engines typically limit the query suggestions that are presented to the user to some arbitrary number such as the top five, ten, or twenty.

Second, there is no way for the user to compare the search results that may be returned by the search engine with respect to each of the query suggestions.

Third, current techniques for presenting query suggestions are not optimized for touchscreens, such as those used on tablet computers and smart phones by using a finger or stylus.

Finally, search engines typically display the query suggestions that start with the search keyword(s) and present to the user. In addition, there is no way for the user to request reversed query suggestions that are initially presented to the user.

On the other hand, the visual graphic user interface for a search homepage presented here can display multiple sets of query suggestions. The end user is able to compare the search results by using hover-over. A set of reversed query suggestions can be retrieved and presented to the end user. Also, the graphic user interface is easily selected by a finger on a touchscreen device.

In the next three sections (3, 4, 5), a conceptual explanation to a design is introduced. Later on, in the section 6, as a proof of concept, a real design of a tile-like visual graphic user interface along with visual pictures is presented. Within the section, we explain each of the visual graphic user interface components as well as the associated actions.

3. MULTIPLE QUERY SUGGESTION SETS

In the design, a system for displaying graphical representations of query suggestions and for facilitating interaction with the graphical representations through a touchscreen or a regular screen is provided.

The system includes a computing device with a touchscreen or a regular screen, and a suggestion engine. The suggestion engine is adapted to display a user interface; receive a query through the user interface; receive a plurality of query suggestions; and each query suggestion is associated with a rank.

The system selects a first subset of the query suggestions according to the rank associated with each query suggestion and displays graphical representations in the user interface.

A clockwise spinning gesture is received through the user interface by the computing device. Based on the clockwise gesture, a subset of the query suggestions is selected by the computing device according to the rank associated with each query suggestion. The users rotate the graphic user interface to indicate that they would like to receive different set of query suggestions.

4. QUERY SUGGESTIONS COMPARISON

A user enters a query into an element of the visual graphic user interface. The query suggestions that are based on the query are displayed around the query in the user interface.

When the user holds or hovers a user input device over a particular element of the user interface, a pop-up window is displayed with the search results that are responsive to the query suggestion that is associated with the element, allowing the user to compare the query suggestions based on the search results.

5. COUNTER CLOCKWISE SPINNING

A counter clockwise gesture is received through the user interface by the computing device. Based on the counter clockwise gesture, a subset of the reversed query suggestions is selected by the computing device according to the rank associated with each reversed query suggestion.

Graphical representations of each reversed query suggestions are displayed in the user interface by the computing device. Each graphical representation is displayed in a position of the plurality of positions of the user interface based on the rank associated with the reversed query suggestion.

6. HEXAGON TILE DESIGN

Based on the principles described in the conceptual design in above three sections, we started to design a modern visual graphic search homepage in this section.

A symmetric visual graphic user interface should look more comfortable for end user. In addition, it is feasible to be spun with a finger on a device. Therefore, we decided to use a symmetric visual graphic interface with a couple of hexagon elements. Figure 1 below shows the visual graphic interface design.

The visual graphic interface looks like a tile, in which a couple of elements make of. Basically, it has a center element as well as a couple of surrounding elements. The tile element could be chosen as any shape, such as, a circle, a rectangle, a square, a hexagon, or any other shapes. Here, we chose hexagon as the basic element shape.

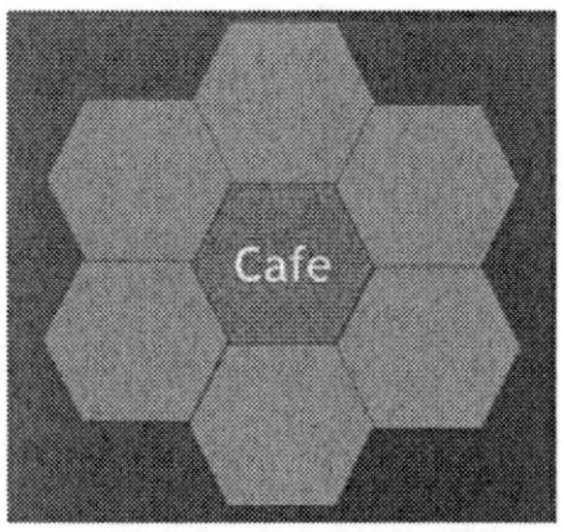

Figure 1. Visual graphic interface in a symmetric tile and hexagon element

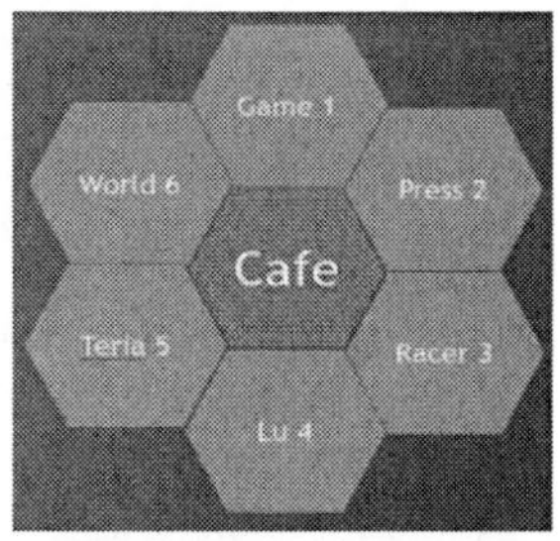

Figure 2. Populate surrounding elements with ranked query suggestions

The query keyword(s) for search can be entered in the centered element, for example, 'Café'. A keyboard will be popped up while a user clicks or taps on the center element for keying in the query string. Also, the user has an option to speak by voice to enter the query keyword(s). The query keyword(s) is then displayed in the center element of the symmetric visual graphic user interface.

As soon as the query keyword(s) is entered, it starts the search with a click or tap at the any location of device screen. And the surrounding hexagon elements will be populated with the ranked query suggestions. A sequential of numbers (like, 1, 2, 3, 4, 5, 6, etc.) are marked in the elements to indicate the item's rank or popularity.

Figure 2 shows the displayed search results in the surrounding elements after the user enters the keyword 'café' as query string for search at the center element of the tile. The printed names in the surrounding elements with a rank from 1 to 6 are retrieved and returned from a query suggestion engine.

When the first set of retrieved query suggestions in the elements surrounding the center element are not one's interest, a user is able to spin the symmetric graph with a finger or by clicking on a button, which results in a new set of query suggestions being populated in the surrounding elements. In this example, a clockwise spinning will result in retrieving and returning the next six query suggestions (7 to 12) as shown in Figure 3.

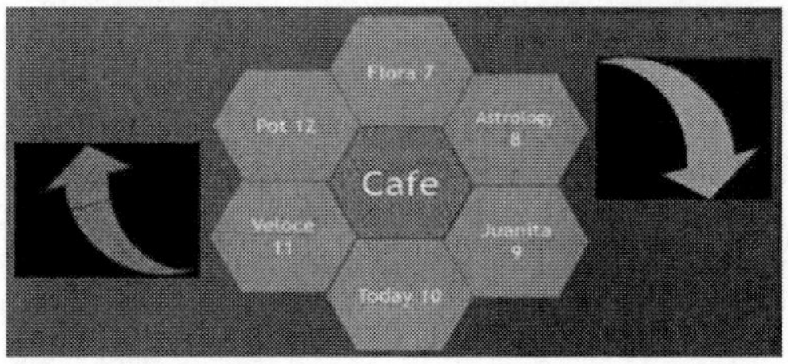

Figure 3. A Clockwise spinning retrieves and returns next set of query suggestions

Not only the query suggestions that start with the search keyword(s) can be retrieved, but also, the reversed query suggestions which only includes the search keyword(s) can be retrieved and returned. If a user does a counter-clockwise gesture to the graphic, it will actually retrieve and return a set of reversed query suggestions.

Figure 4 shows the results that are from a counter-clockwise spinning. Also, the tile background color can be changed to a different color to indicate it is the result from a counter-clockwise spinning. In this case, it is changed to dark brown color to differentiate the set of reversed query suggestions.

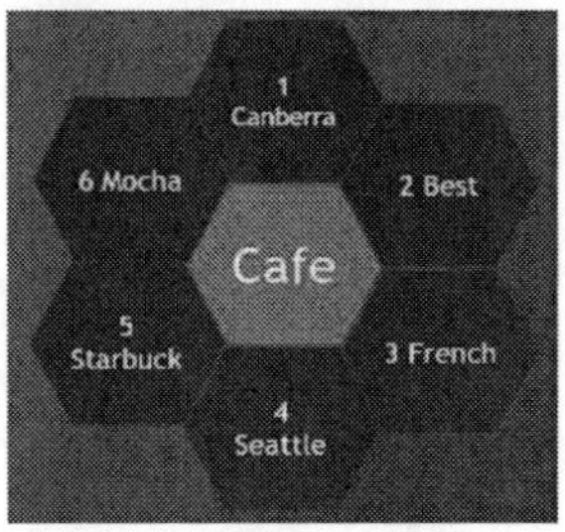

Figure 4. A counter-clockwise spinning retrieves and returns a set of reversed query suggestions

Figure 5. A hover-over onto a targeted element retrieves and returns search result with link description

When a user hovers over onto a targeted tile element, which represents a specific query suggestion, such as 'Starbuck', a window will be popped up. It displays the search result with a link description including some details as to the query suggestion. The user can hover over onto different elements to preview before starting the actual search. Continuously, if the user taps on the selected element, such as, 'Starbucks', it will trigger the search.

Figure 5 shows the targeted tile element highlighted in green ('Starbuck') and the popped-up window per a hover-over gesture.

When the user clicks or taps one of the surrounding elements, which one is interested in, a call is trigged and sent to the search engine. The search results are retrieved and returned to the user and displayed the same as today's look as shown in Figure 6.

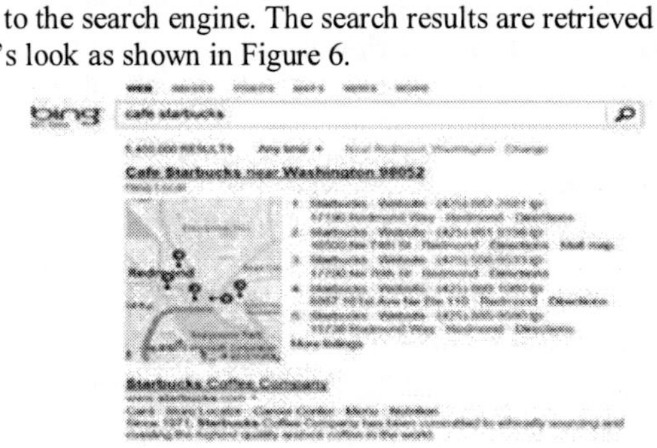

Figure 6. Today's look of search result

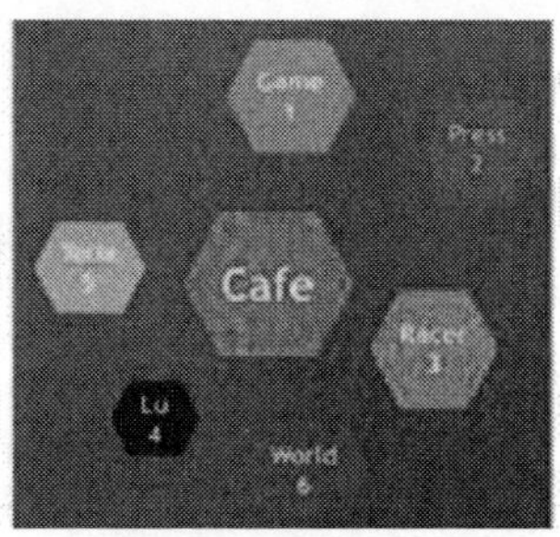

Figure 7. Floating elements with different sizes and background colors

Also, many rich design can be played around for the visual graphic search homepage. For example, the element size and its background color can be varied in the design. Furthermore, the elements themselves could be floated on the device screen so that it looks vibrant and fun. Figure 7 gives an example of floating elements with different size and background colors.

7. CONCLUSIONS

Per study, graphics expedite and increase our level of communication [4]. Pictures enhance or affect emotions and attitudes. Graphics engage our imagination and heighten our creative thinking by stimulating other areas of our brain [5]. That is why this proposed design on a visual graphic search homepage is originated.

A symmetric tile-like visual graphic user interface is composed of a number of elements of a specific shape with a centered element. The element can be in any graphic shapes, like a circle, a rectangle, a square, a hexagon, or any others. As an implementation, a hexagon is chosen as the basic graphic shape to construct the tile.

Multiple sets of query suggestions can be retrieved, returned, filled within the surrounding elements of the tile with a clock-wise gesture. In the meanwhile, a set of reversed query suggestion can be retrieved, returned, filled within the sounding elements of the tile as well. A hove-over gesture on a query suggestion element can help with the comparison of the search results before one submits it for search. Finally, there is a flexibility to design the shape, size, background color of a tile element to best fit the user's need.

The visual graphic search homepage is quicker and clearer way for user to start searching on a mobile device with a touchscreen. It is a modern alternative to today's plain textual search homepage. Many designs can be conducted and played around it, which fit the customer needs better.

Although the visual graphic interface best fits on a mobile device with a touchscreen, it can be implemented as a web homepage on a regular PC as well. Besides, it can be implemented either as a web homepage or a mobile application.

With increasing usage of mobile devices by user for a daily communication, the visual graphic design of the search homepage [6][7] will play a crucial role as an alternative interface to the user.

ACKNOWLEDGEMENTS

We would like to thank Mr. Chad Foster and Mr. Deepak Upadhyay from Microsoft, who have provided some valuable feedback.

REFERENCES

[1] Mike Parkinson,1991. *The Power of Visual Communication.* http://billiondollargraphics.com/infographics.html

[2] Stevenson Johnson, 2004, *Beauty and the Beastly PC, The Graphics on Your Screen Can Affect the Way You Feel—and Think,* Discover Volume 25: Number 5 (May 2004): 20-21.

[3] Duncan Davies, Diana Bathurst, and Robin Bathurst, 1990. *The Telling Image the Changing Balance between Pictures and Words in a Technological Age.* (Oxford: Clarendon Press, 1990).

[4] W.H. Levie and R. Lentz, 1982. *Effects of Text Illustrations: A Review of Research,* Educational Communications and Technology Journal 30 (4) (1982): 195-232.

[5] D. Bobrow and D. Norman, 1975, 1980. *Some Principles of Memory Schemata,* (in D. Bobrow and A.Collins [eds.]), Representation and Understanding: Studies in Cognitive Science (New York: Academic Press, 1975), 131-149 and D. Rumelhart, *Schemata: The Building Blocks of Cognition*, (in R.J. Spiro, B.C. Bruce and W.F. Brewer [eds.]), Theoretical Issues in Reading Comprehension (Hillsdale, New Jersey: Lawrence Erlbaum Associate, 1980), 33-58.

[6] Xin Bai, Dawn Wang, Huizhen Ji, 2015. *Displaying Graphical Representations of Query Suggestions* (Patent MS# 358483.01)"

[7] Robin Good, 2009, *Top Visual Search Engines: The Most Interesting Ways to Visually Explore Search Engine Results*, http://www.masternewmedia.org/top-visual-search-engines-the-most-interesting-ways-to-visually-explore-search-engine-results/

Reflection Papers

HUMAN ACTIVITY RECOGNITION IN AMBIENT ASSISTED LIVING FOR ALZHEIMER'S PATIENT: A REVIEW OF TRENDS AND CHALLENGES IN MALAYSIA

Nur Waheeda Basharudin and Ku Nurul Fazira Ku Azir
School of Computer and Communication Engineering
Universiti Malaysia Perlis,
Perlis, Malaysia.

ABSTRACT

Human activity recognition is one of the method to model human behaviors and activity patterns. The works have becoming a significant research interest in recent years for various applications such as for assisted living and healthcare. This paper will reviews some of the related works based on stochastic methods or well known as probabilistic method to classify human activities which are focusing on kitchen activity. However, many challenging issues need to be reviewed in order to design and implement these technologies. The main purpose of this review is to extensively identify the existing method and characterize the literature in a manner that brings key challenges of future probabilistic method to meet the demand of cultures and social of Alzheimer's patient in Malaysia.

KEYWORDS

Human activity recognition, ambient assisted living, activities of daily living, ambient intelligent

1. INTRODUCTION

Alzheimer is a common disease that is being diagnosis in dementia illnesses. Alzheimer's patient often experience difficulties in performing activities of daily livings (ADLs) due to their in capabilities of forgetting the locations of common items, experiencing confusion and memory loss. This will cause them having difficulties to live independently at their own home. In Malaysia, it is estimated that there are about 50,000 people with this disease (Anon n.d) and the figure is increasing each year. Unfortunately, Malaysia only had few non-governmental organizations (NGOs) care centers to provide services to the Alzheimer's patient and their care takers such as the Alzheimer's disease Foundation Malaysia (ADFM) that had established only three care centers. Dementia Society Perak and Johor Bahru Alzheimer Disease Association (JOBADA) are another two NGOs in Malaysia. The trends show that the patients are likely to stay at their home or with their family members which does require a lot of care and attention. A survey from Economic Plan Unit of Prime Minister's Department Malaysia also shown that only 20% of Malaysian have a high class income of RM5000 and above per month or EUR1100. This is another reason why not all family is affordable to send their family members who suffer from Alzheimer to the care center. Moreover, the awareness of the disease itself is very low in Malaysia, which may lead to an abuse case where the family members did not know how to treat Alzheimer's. Thus, a support is crucially needed not just from the family members and care takers, but also from the development of the technologies. Due to that reason, many works have been done to assist Alzheimer's patients in their daily activities such as live monitoring of patient's medical progress or lifestyle by embedded sensors or accelerometers thru Ambient Assisted Living (AAL) Environment. The AAL is an environment which is using Information and Communication Technologies (ICT) in a person's daily living and working environment to enable them to stay active longer, remain socially connected and live independently.

For that reason, it is essential to introduce the AAL into the Malaysian's environment, cultures and social lifestyle. However, there are few concerns and challenges of bringing up these technologies. . The acceptance of the technologies in assisting their daily life bring big issues as the questions will be 'how can these technologies can provide the best care compared to traditional way'? or 'how the technology can understand their needs by just monitoring their behavior'? Therefore, in this research we proposed a unique way of providing subtle or 'natural' way of interaction to in the AAL thru ambient display. Ambient display is a new approach to interfacing people with online digital information. Ambient displays present information within a space thru subtle changes in light, sound and movement which can be processed in the background of awareness. However, it is significantly necessary to revise some of the works related to human activity recognition in order to meet the goals of providing natural interaction through ambient displays.

2. HUMAN ACTIVITY RECOGNITION

"Human activity recognition" (HAR) is the most significant components in AAL environment (Rashidi & Mihailidis 2013). The objective of HAR is to recognize human activities in real life to meet the goals of context-aware computing. However, accurate activity recognition is challenging because human activities are complex and highly diverse. HAR has been implemented in a particular system to recognize behavior pattern of Alzheimer's patient in various intelligent environment (Rashidi & Mihailidis 2013). When attempting to recognize human activities, there is a need to determine the kinetic states of a person so that computer can efficiently recognize the activity. Depending on their complexity, human activities can be categorized into four different levels which are gestures, actions, interactions and group activities (Aggarwal & Ryoo, 2011).

Various number of research have been focusing on recognize of the activities. Some of the works are focusing on probabilistic model such as Hidden Markov Model (HMM) , Conditional Random Field (CRF) , Skip Chain Conditional Random Field (SCCRF) (Kim et al. 2010). The others probabilistic model are Dynamic Bayesian Network (DBN) (Sheng & Zhu 2012), Support Vector Machine and Hidden Markov Model (SVM&HMM) algorithm uses RGBD (Microsoft Kinect) (Zheng 2015), Deep Learning (DL) algorithm (Fang & Hu 2014), Independent Subspace Analysis (ISA) algorithm (Nguyen & Yoshitaka 2014), and Active Learning Based algorithm (Hoque & Stankovic 2012).

Meanwhile there are some other works that have been done on recognizing activities through camera (Lam et al. 2015), wearable inertial sensors (Oniga & Orha 2016), and recently through smart phones (Dernbach et al. 2012). Since human activities are complex, these activities may be decomposed into other simpler activities which are generally easier to identify. Usually, the detection of objects in a scene may react to a better understanding human activities as it provides useful information about the ongoing event. Therefore, there are two types of activities recognition which are vision-based and wearable sensor-based (Chen et al. 2012).

In this research, we are interested in recognizing human activities in the kitchen environment. There are several research that have been done to recognize the activities based on detecting and analyzing the sequence of objects that are being manipulated by users. Lei and Fox (2012) recognize kitchen activities through RGB-D (Kinect-style) cameras to identify hands and objects. Meanwhile, work of Smart Cueing Kitchen Cooking Assistant (Mahajan & Ding, 2014) and Anon (2013) recognize kitchen activities recognition based on the scene context. . There are also some researches that used RFID tagged and video data combined with Dynamic Bayesian Network model (Wu et al. 2007) applying motion detector with an easy filter algorithm (Yin & Bruckner 2011)to observe daily activities of the elderly. Kitchen AS-A-PAL had been designed based on tracking technology requirement using networks of PhidgetRFID readers (Surie et al. 2013).

3. CHALLENGES OF DESIGNING AFFECTIVE AAL

The development of full automated human activity recognition with low error is challenging not just due to the technical or hardware requirements, but is also influenced by social, cultures and habits of the patients. Therefore, building a visual model for learning and benchmark datasets of activity of Alzheimer's patients are very challenging. The exploration of how Alzheimer's patient interact with ubiquitous computing environment are difficult as they need to perceiving, learning and adapting to the digital environment. In addition, computer may have problems to identify nonverbal affective feedback from Alzheimer's patient in which their emotion such as sad, fear, disgust or happy are shown differently from a normal person. What are needed are patience and practice. This is because senior citizen often are not prepared with steadily stick at the task. The same thing might happen to Alzheimer's patients, as they may do something over and over like repeating an activity or undo something that has just been finished. Another challenge issue of deploying the AAL system for Alzheimer's patient is their acceptance toward the technology instead of the traditional computer environment. For example, elder people consistently describe phone as annoying and fiddly. Those who own them may seldom is use them, and often not touching them for days This should be advancing autonomously through technologies that require little or no effort from Alzheimer's patient, while user interface should be simple and understood by the patient. The design must includes the whole sections of the population for the benefits of technology. The most challenge issues for AAL is to understand Alzheimer's behaviors that could change at any time. One of the ways is by implementing ambient cues during cooking activities such as a red light which indicates a danger or hot burner. These ambient cues must also be fit into their understanding to receive and responds to the given cues. The biggest challenges is when there is any interruption during the activities. While the system may try to guide the patient to resume back their activities. Alzheimer's patient may have different level of consciousness and alertness. In addition, applying an algorithm in the system to recognize and predict patient's activities is quite tricky. To get an excellent recognition and prediction, we have to compare tasks and possibilities of the events happened correctly. The final step is to analyze the results so that it meets with user requirements. Usability and user experience can also be considered when designing AAL system especially in Malaysia. To overcome these issues, education for Malaysian on the importance of ambient technologies should be given. This includes the benefits of using it along with the collaboration with the government to provide advanced solution such as high speed communication lines and large storage cloud database.

4. CONCLUSION

It is important to note that Alzheimer's disease affects millions of people each year, and these numbers will continue to rise as the population increases. Alzheimer's disease has a financial impact and equally emotionally impact on caregivers and families of those who are afflicted. Therefore, it is hope that the current works and research of AAL systems can provide many opportunities to train Alzheimer's patient to be independent as well as for monitoring and improving their health conditions. Therefore, the advanced techniques of human activity recognition are required to unleash the full power of the AAL technologies. However, there are still many challenges that need to be understood especially in implementing these technologies in Malaysia.

ACKNOWLEDGEMENT

The research in this paper is supported by Fundamental Research Grant Scheme (FRGS) [Grant Number: 9003-00551]. The authors would like to express gratitude to Malaysia Ministry of Education (MOE) and Universiti Malaysia Perlis for the facilities provided.

REFERENCES

Anon, About Alzheimer's - ADFM. Available at: http://www.adfm.org.my/Home/about-alzheimer-s [Accessed March 14, 2016].

Chen, L. et al., 2012. Sensor-based activity recognition. *IEEE Transactions on Systems, Man and Cybernetics Part C: Applications and Reviews*, 42(6), pp.790–808.

Dernbach, S. et al., 2012. Simple and Complex Activity Recognition through Smart Phones. , pp.214–221.

Hoque, E. & Stankovic, J., 2012. AALO: Activity recognition in smart homes using Active Learning in the presence of Overlapped activities. *Proceedings of the 6th International Conference on Pervasive Computing Technologies for Healthcare*, pp.139–146.

Kim, E., Helal, S. & Cook, D., 2010. Human Activity Recognition and Pattern Discovery. *Training*, 9(1), pp.48–53.

Lam, K.-Y. et al., 2015. SmartMind: Activity Tracking and Monitoring for Patients with Alzheimer's Disease. *2015 IEEE 29th International Conference on Advanced Information Networking and Applications*, pp.453–460.

Oniga, S. & Orha, I., 2016. Wearable sensors network for activity recognition using inertial sensors Wearable sensors network for activity recognition using inertial sensors. , (March).

Rashidi, P. & Mihailidis, A., 2013. A survey on ambient-assisted living tools for older adults. *IEEE Journal of Biomedical and Health Informatics*, 17(3), pp.579–590.

Surie, D., Lindgren, H. & Qureshi, A., 2013. Kitchen AS-A-PAL : Exploring Smart Objects as Containers , Surfaces and Actuators. , pp.171–178.

Wu, J. et al., 2007. A Scalable Approach to Activity Recognition based on Object Use.

Yin, G. & Bruckner, D., 2011. Daily Activity Model for Ambient Assisted Living. , pp.197–204.

TACTILE MAPS AS TEACHING TOOL FOR THE SPATIAL PERCEPTION OF PEOPLE WITH VISUAL IMPAIRMENT

Fernanda Poletto Silva[1], Vânia Ribas Ulbricht[2] and Stephania Padovani[1]
[1]*University of Paraná, Department of Design and Engineering, Curitiba, Brazil*
[2]*University of Florianopolis, Department of Design and Engineering, Santa Catarina, Brazil*

ABSTRACT

The congenitally blind (born blind) make up a considerable percentage excluded in Brazilian education due to their condition. The lack of public policies for education makes it difficult to rise to the labor market and the communication between blind and sighted. To counter this problem, the related article is a theoretical approach to the tactile perception of the congenitally blind, through kinesthetic sensations or multisensory properties (surface and geometric). In addition, the graphic variables (line direction, connection points, holding the shape and texture elevation) assist in building codes for tactile recognition of three dimensional objects. The results indicate the insertion of graphic variables associated with the properties of tactile perception (temperature, hardness, texture, roughness, shape, size, weight, volume and density) as elements that facilitate the arrest and immediate identification information on a given object. Finally, it is concluded that the design of performance becomes relevant in the selection of graphic variables in tactile maps, for help in the tactile exploration (codes) of congenitally blind in trying to translate effectively the information contained in three-dimensional objects.

KEYWORDS

Congenital blind, three-dimensional object, spatial perception, tactile maps

1. INTRODUCTION

In Brazil, the Brazilian Institute of Geography and Statistics (IBGE, 2010) tell that 23.9% of the population possess types of deficiency in distinct degrees. In the population of the Paraná, about 26.155 they are characterized as blind congenital people. The data of the Ministry of the Education (2006) approach the blindness as a serious or total alteration of one or more elementary functions of the vision that affect the capacity to perceive color, size, distance, perspective, position or movement in a more or less including field. This can occur since the birth (congenital blindness), or later (adventitious blindness). Faé (2009) affirm that for the blind person is difficult executes the spatial orientation, reflecting the form as it understands and represents the space, in the three-dimensional object recognition. This article contributes in the use of the graphical variable associates with tactile perception in the three-dimensional object recognition for congenital blind people. The use of Maps tactile is important tool for teaching for the spatial perception. Therefore encourages the study of geometric shapes as cognitive organization process in the tactile perception of three-dimensional objects mediated by a teacher bringing the two worlds in sharing information. A template is a set of styles and page layout settings that determine the appearance of a document. This template matches the printer settings that will be used in the proceeding and the CD-Rom. Use of the template is mandatory. Clearly explain the nature of the problem, previous work, purpose, and contribution of the paper.

2. METHODOLOGICAL PROCEDURES

This article is primarily characterized by a brief review of the literature review consists of dissertations, theses, articles, journals and conference proceedings (COCHRANE, 2010) to list publications between the years 2010-2016 (English and Portuguese). In this collection, we obtained 10 relevant documents, of which 02 were excluded due to the restriction of the content and were found in databases: Capes, Scielo and Google

Scholar. Then broke for a brief exploratory field research with an exploratory interview, where you can apply the techniques structured interview with a group of people at his residence. The field research allowed to draw the audience profile: Total congenitally blind (born blind or lost his sight under five years old), between 18 to 40, with higher degree of education or incomplete, residents in the city of Curitiba – Paraná (Brazil) The selection of participants was through the stored visual memory of that target audience, a different perception of the world around him. Thus necessitating a consistent method with the perception of reality of individuals. Respondents blind them secondary school students, containing the necessary training to understand the content of mathematics and maturity to freely discuss about it. The names of the participants were identified as Group 1 residents Environment 1 and Group 2 residents Environment 2. Group 1 consists of four (4) congenitally blind, recommended by the Paraná Institute of the Blind (IPC), where three (3) born with disabilities and one (1) has acquired four years old. Group 2 has six (6) congenitally blind, recommended by the Inclusion Service and Assistance to Students with Special Educational Needs (SIANEE) where four (4) were born with disabilities and two (2) acquired less than three (3) years . Totaling ten (10) respondents according to table 1:

Table 1. Selection of participants (2016)

Group 1	**Sex**	**Age**	**Limitation Visual**	**Level of Education**
Participant A	Male	27 years	Born	Degree in Music
Participant B	Male	23 years	Born	Degree in Psychology
Participant C	Female	21 years	Since (4) years	Degree in Arts
Participant D	Male	28 years	Born	Degree in Psychology
Group 2	**Sex**	**Age**	**Limitação Visual**	**Level of Education**
Participant E	Male	32 years	Born	Graduate in Law
Participant F	Female	26 years	Since (3) years	Degree in Journalism
Participant G	Female	27 years	Nasceu	Degree in Psychology
Participant H	Male	40 years	Since (1) year	Degree in Psychology
Participant I	Female	22 years	Born	Degree in Ed. Physics
Participant J	Female	35 years	Born	Graduate in Politics

This proposal aims to understand how the tactile perception assists in the association process of everyday objects with educational objects geometry. The difficulty of the blind in both domestic environment was accentuated when asked to associate everyday objects with three-dimensional objects. The dynamics identified the physical, during the tactile perception of the blind, facilitating the manipulation of three-dimensional objects. The difficulty occurred with objects of complex aspect and the combination of two geometric shapes. Participants differentiated the everyday objects through the perception of properties: size, volume, weight, temperature, texture, roughness, hardness and Braille. The geometric property *"shape"*, highlighted in purple, is characterized as the closest of the concepts of geometry. While the surface properties (texture, roughness and temperature) are related to the proportion and object manipulation. The tactile stimulating aspects of the handling of the elements recognized by the blind. In the later stage, blind people should associate the everyday objects with geometric shapes. The Group 1 and 2 were able to relate the geometric shapes with flat figures. However the Group 1 selected the tee box, the mattress and the plastic cup and Group 2 the toothpaste box, jewelry, circular ornament sunflower and glass.

3. THREE-DIMENSIONAL OBJECT PERCEPTION FOR BLIND PEOPLE

Damásio (2005) defines the perception as process of organization and interpretation of sensorial data (sensations), for the development of the conscience of the environment that in the fence and of we ourselvesThe sensorial modalities are distinguished: for the vision, hear, touch, smell and taste" (Taylor, 2009 .p 181). Miller (2008) the presence and condition of the individual become excellent for the perception of the stimulation, given that the individual possess distinct types of perception that if adjust to the received information. However, the apprehended information assists in the organization of the representations of the world. The author classifies the perception, in distinct sensorial modalities such as:

a. **Visual perception:** perception of luminous rays for the visual system. They are characterized for the perception of the forms, space relations, colors, luminous intensity and movements.

b. **Hear perception:** perception of sounds, which if bases on the analysis of the perception of timbres, heights and frequencies, of the sonorous intensity, beyond the rhythmic perception, intensely related with the secular perception.
c. **Smell perception:** perception of odors for the nose, pertinent sensation for our palate, nominated during the feeding.
d. **Taste perception:** perception of flavors for the language, associate to the pleasure. As the Smell, it less represents one of the developed directions in the human beings.
e. **Tactile perception:** object perception and sensations through the skin. This type of perception allows to recognize the form, the size and the temperature of objects in contact with the skin beyond the positioning of the body as physical protection.
f. **Time perception:** perception of the time, production of rhythms, secular order and concurrence and this related with the auditory perception. The secular perception results of the combination of the directions and the potentialities of the brain.
g. **Space perception:** perception of the distances between objects and not identified by the agencies. It implies in the auditory, visual perception. Therefore when an object if approaches or if it moves away through the dimensions for the increase or reduction from the sound.

4. TACTILE MAPS FOR RECOGNIZING THREE-DIMENSIONAL SHAPES

According Loch (2008) conception of tactile maps, is equivalent to the conventional maps, that is, that there are two phases: the preparation and the use of them. Access to tactile maps, models and practical field activities allows students to train their perceptions from the other senses, especially when the process begins at the stage of schooling, providing a better understanding of the information available and facilitating the life of the person with Visual impairment (LOCH, 2008). According to Soler (1999), cited by Ventorini (2007), touch is the sense that the human brain offers a range of information types of external and internal means. However, identification of objects by touch is not achieved simply by touch and exploitation, it is necessary to develop a tactile sensitivity to see them and know them. So, blind people should be encouraged to develop tactile sensitivity from the beginning of medical diagnosis. As for the graphics, such as graphs and charts, make up significant to understand texts and data effectively and synthesized form. The mockup Geographic Tactile or Model Topographic Reduced Tactile is called as the partial or full three-dimensional representation of the Earth's surface textures, Braille texts, shapes, strong colors, sounds, or other tactile elements for the visually impaired get geographical information about the area studied (LABTATE, 2010). Therefore, the use of resources such as maps and models is significant in the teaching-learning process as it prioritizes the cognitive development of the student. The use of Tactile Cartography next topic is a direct contribution of this article

4.1 Tactile Cartography in the Education of Congenitally Blind

In Brazil, the production of tactile mapping is still precarious. Some research on tactile maps as were made at USP in the Department of Geography at USP - Teaching Laboratory and Didactic Material - LEMADI, where surveys are designed to the development, implementation and evaluation of tactile graphical representations for visually impaired students. Some institutes and individual support foundations with special needs linked to the Ministry of Education, as Benjamin Constant Institute (IBC) and Santa Catarina Foundation for Special Education (FCEE), and philanthropies like Dorina Foundation for the Blind, and Laramara - Brazilian Association of assistance to the Visually Impaired produce, adapt and distribute materials for educational activities and the daily life of blind or with low vision. Among such materials, are a few maps, generic and graphic floor plans. However, despite the efforts of these institutions in respect of tactile maps, it was not possible to achieve an efficient mapping pattern or enough for teaching and not meet demand at the level of Brazil. Tactile maps in the state of Santa Catarina are produced by FCEE, state government body that, among so many activities to support education of people with special needs, has been struggling to meet schools of public schools in relation to the maps for the teaching History and Geography. FCEE makes the transformation of maps of textbooks to tactile maps of textbooks in Braille. It was this advice which led to projects of tactile maps and the Tactile Cartography Laboratory and School of UFSC - LABTATE, created in 2006 in the Department of Geosciences (LOCH, 2008). Loch (2008) reports that for making tactile maps the cartographer must translate it and know how to do it (generalization) for different age groups, in addition to considering the notion of degree of cognitive and spatial development of the user, especially the blind person. The cartographer should still be aware of the technology available for such a task (breeding and reproduction) and the need to perform cognitive tests with congenitally blind, because most of the time what he considers good for tactile graphic translation is not considered for reading expected when the map is examined for its potential user. They are presented inprocedures or the most important factors to be considered in tactile mapping, as well as their manufacture, the two moments of the cartographic process: its production and use.

Procedure 1: Select the basic conventional maps

You need to choose the base and generalizing these maps to adapt them to the tactile mode. However, the generalization not due to scale reduction. The map should be rustic that allows the deployment of textures to the tactile reading the differentiation of lines, points and areas that compose it. Therefore, the mapping may be done expansions and deformations that would never be permitted in conventional mapping.

Procedure 2: Select the symbology and graphic variables

In cartographic tactile points, lines and / or areas of a tactile map stand out from the map of the supporting substrate like a relief tax on the flat base that contains the map, be it a paper, a plastic or metal plate or rubberized. Thereafter it can now be understood as differences in volume, which is difficult to construct for the majority of tactile maps production methods, since the heights and areas need to be easily touch sensitive steps.

Procedure 3: Use the tactile graphic variables on maps

tactile graphic variables in the construction of maps is necessary to take into account the cognitive actions derived from touch. In this context, haptic tactile graphic variables used in the maps can be correlated to the visual variables the specific considerations require tactile discrimination. The graphical touch point and the variable length linear deployment may be used in up to three different sizes as well as the blind has difficulties to detect differences or associations.

Procedure 4: Determining the layout and text

The layout and text on the map is important in tactile mapping as in conventional cartography as a map to be understood from the texts he brings in his body or in the legend. The geographical orientation (marking North direction) is very important to read the positioning of a tactile map on a small scale, as well as the graphic scale, which helps the blind person to imagine the dimensions or extensions in reality.

Procedure 5: Other important factors

Another important factor to be considered in the design of tactile maps refers to the amount of attributes or classes that a map can contain, when prepared with tactile variables. We studied the translation of visual components of maps: the frame, symbol, the place title, scale and legend.

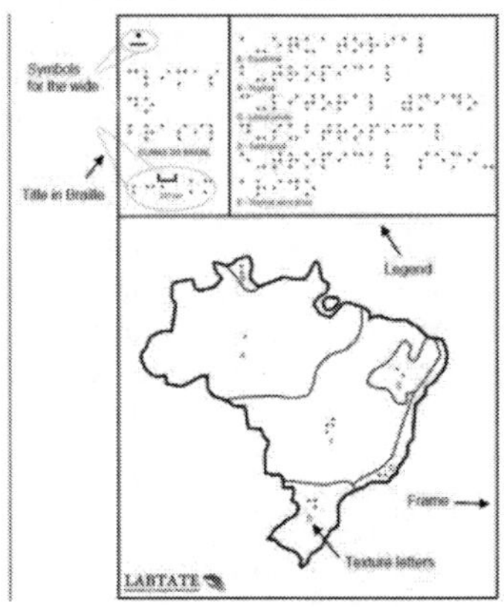

Figure 1. Selection of participants (2016)

5. CONCLUSION

The perception of congenital blind depends on the sensations in the process of the mental image formation, exclusively the touch. The mental image of the object is associated with the properties of tactile perception (temperature, texture, roughness, shape, size, weight and volume), with the full awareness that it is restricted to the hands. The Graphic variables with line orientation, union points, exploration of form, and the elevation of texture (thickness or height) become relevant in the physical aspects of the object to build tactile codes in recognition of three-dimensional objects. Besides the tactile aspects of three-dimensional objects allowed distinguish them from each other and identify effective graphic variables in the transmission of information. However, "shape" and "size", facilitate tactile perception in the recognition of sides, edges and internal elements composing each object. Therefore, the tactile perception is fragmented and abstract, restricted only for hand movement of the blind person through touch. However, the difficulty is the combination of the dimensions relating them to a "whole". Participants also reported not understand the concept of geometry. Blind fall under the use of models and adapted objects, as well as citing other different format materials that allow their identification. It was also necessary to reinforce the distinction between hub and square, sphere and circle to start the associations of objects. Therefore encourages the study of geometric shapes as cognitive organization process in the tactile perception of three-dimensional objects mediated by a teacher bringing the two worlds in sharing information.

REFERENCES

Abbagnano, N. 2007.Dicionário de Filosofia. São Paulo: WMF Martins Fontes.

Brasil. 2006. Ministério da Educação e do Desporto. MEC. Secretaria de Educação Fundamental. Secretaria de Educação Especial (SEESP). Política Nacional de Educação Especial na Perspectiva da Educação Inclusiva. MEC/SEESP. Home:http://portal.mec.gov.br/seesp/arquivos/pdf/politica.pdf> 22/08/2013.

Damásio, A.2005.O mistério da consciência: do corpo e das emoções ao conhecimento de si. 7. ed. São Paulo: Companhia das Letras.

FAÉ, M. 2009. Conteúdo para os alunos cegos.Home: <http://www.agb.org.br/XENPEG/artigos/GT/GT3/tc3%20%2849%29.pdf> 31/07/2014.

Gil, A.C. 2011. Métodos e técnicas de pesquisa social. 6. ed. São Paulo: Atlas.

Goodwin, A. W., Macefield, V. G., & Bisley, J. W. 1997. Encoding of object curvature by tactile afferents from human fingers. Journal of Neurophysiology,78, 2881-2888.

Instituto Brasileiro de Geografia e Estatística (IBGE). O Instituto Brasileiro de Geografia e Estatística. Home:http://www.ibge.gov.br/home/disseminacao/eventos/missao/instituicao>22/08/2014.

Kappers, A. M. L. 2007. Haptic spatial processing: Allocentric and egocentric reference frames. Canadian Journal of Experimental Psychology,61, 208-218.

Klatzky, R. L. 1998. Allocentric and egocentric spatial representations: Definitions, distinctions, and interconnections. In C. Freksa,

Klatzky, R. L., & Lederman, S. J. 2009. Object recognition by touch. In J. J. Rieser, D. Ashmead, F. Ebner, & A. Corn (Eds.), Blindness and brain plasticity in navigation and object perception(pp. 185-207).Mahwah, NJ: Erlbaum.

Lacey, S., Campbell, C., & Sathian, K. 2007.Vision and touch: Multiple or multisensory representations of objects? Perception, 36,1513-1521.

Lederman, S. J., & Klatzky, R. L. 2009. Human haptics. In L. R. Squire (Ed. in Chief), Encyclopedia of neuroscience(Vol. 5, pp. 11-18). San Diego: Academic Press.

Loch, Ruth E. N. 2008. Cartografia Tátil: mapas para deficientes visuais. Portal da Cartografia.Londrina, v.1, n.1, maio/ago., p. 35 – 58. Home: http://www.uel.br/revistas/uel/index.php/portalcartografia

Miller, J. C. 2008. Retention of high tactile acuity throughout the life span in blindness. Perception & Psychophysics, 70, 1471-1488.

Sanders, A. F. J., & Kappers, A. M. L. 2008. Curvature affects haptic length perception. Acta Psychologica,129, 340-351.

Sathian, K. (2003). Neural networks active during tactile form perception: Common and differential activity during macrospatial and microspatial tasks. International Journal of Psychophysiology,50, 41-49.

Soler. M.A 1999.Didática multissensorial de las ciencias:un nuevo método para alumnos ciegos, deficientes visuales, y también sin problemas de visión. Barcelona: Ediciones Paidós Ibérica.

Taylor, J. L. 2009. Proprioception. In L. R. Squire (Ed.), Encyclopedia of neuroscience (Vol. 7, pp. 1143-1149). Oxford: Academic Press.

Treisman, A. M., & Gelade, G. 2004. A feature-integration theory of attention. Cognitive Psychology,12, 97-136.

E-LEARNING MULTIMODAL SYSTEM FOR TEACHING AND LEARNING PROGRAMMING

Ana Rita Teixeira[1, 2], Anabela Gomes[3, 4] and João Orvalho[1]
[1]*Master in Human Computer Interaction (HCI), Polytechnic of Coimbra, ESEC. IEETA/UA, Rua Dom João III Solum, 3030-329 Coimbra, Portugal*
[2]*Institute of Electronics and Informatics Engineering of Aveiro – University of Aveiro Campus Universitário de Santiago, 3810-193 Aveiro - Portugal*
[3]*Engineering Institute of Polytechnic Institute of Coimbra Rua Pedro Nunes, Quinta da Nora, 3030-199 Coimbra, Portugal*
[4]*Centre for Informatics and Systems – University of Coimbra, Pólo II - Pinhal de Marrocos, 3030-290 Coimbra*

ABSTRACT

The high failure rates and abandonment are common in introductory programming courses in many higher education institutions worldwide. Different solutions have been proposed in literature trying to solve the problem but the situation remains virtually unchanged. Some members of this group also contributed with computer-based tools and different studies to understand and reduce this problem. Among the works carried out, the importance of investing in motivational aspects and the ability to solve problems is highlighted. This paper describes a new approach in order to contribute in solving this problem. The idea is to investigate the psychophysiological response of individuals during testing. The goal is to measure aspects of interest like the ability of abstraction, emotions, concentration, frustration, immersion, load/stress and cognitive level, in complex scenarios such as the resolution of programming problems. Thus, we intend to use new forms of interaction as Brain Computer Interfaces (BCI), eyetracking and other low-cost instruments (e.g.: BITalino) using body signals to extract information of interest. This information will be included in an e-learning system adapting its interface according to the users actions.

KEYWORDS

Brain Computer Interfaces; Human Computer Interaction; Neuropsychological Assessment; Cognitive Abilities; Programming Learning; Adaptive Systems

1. INTRODUCTION

High failure and dropout rates are common in introductory programming courses in many high education institutions worldwide [2, 3, 6, 7, 8]. This is a situation that affects mostly freshmen as those courses are usually placed at the beginning of the curricula [3]. Many causes for the learning difficulties have already been identified. [2, 7, 8]. Different solutions have been proposed in literature, but the situation remains mostly unchanged, as many students continue to struggle with basic programming. Our research group started its work in Computer Science Education Research with the development of some visualization tools intended to help students in their early programming stages [9]. Research in this field includes efforts in several areas, from psychological studies to computer-based tools. Our current research focuses on student understanding mainly the mental and conceptual models that students have about a particular subject matter and their conceptions and misconceptions about it.

The first phase of this work intends to acquire measurements on aspects of interest (emotions, concentration, frustration, load/stress, cognitive level) in complex scenarios such as solving programming problems. To this end we intend to use new forms of interaction such as Brain-Computer Interface (BCI) and other low-cost instruments (e. g.: BITalino) using body signals to extract information of interest. BCI research seeks to develop an alternative communication channel between humans and machines, which implies no muscular intervention in the communication process. These devices determine the intent of the user from scalp-recorded electrical brain signals (EEG - Electroencephalogram) or from electrodes surgically implanted on the cortical surface (ECoG- ElectroCorticoGraphy) or within the brain (neuronal action potentials or local field potentials) [1]. These signals are translated into commands that operate a computerized application. Despite advances in this research field the BCI systems are still presenting several challenges that can be resumed in: Usability, Accuracy and Speed. Many factors determine the performance of a BCI system, among them is the quality of the brain signals, the methods used to extract signal information and the output applications. A BCI device must take into account all of these factors to provide a reliable performance [5]. The traditional BCI system has two distinct stages. The first one is the training stage, where mutual adaptation of the BCI system and the user is performed. During this stage, the BCI parameters are tuned based on specific training scenarios. The second stage corresponds to the normal functioning of the BCI, termed as the on-line stage, where the BCI parameters are fixed. However the EEG signals are non-stationary, their statistics can suffer significant changes over time, and periodic calibration of the system may improve its reliability. In order to address these issues, the key characteristic of the BCI is its adaptability. The BCI system must be able to identify malfunctioning events (for example accumulation of errors in interpreting the user intentions) and provide a way to correct them [5]. A new adaptive BCI architecture is used which can switch back to the training stage in order to adapt the BCI parameters in malfunctioning situations. We intend to use this kind of BCI systems to build an adaptive e-learning system modifying its contents, navigation and interface according to the user needs. This project includes a body of research, development, implementation and testing translated into a set of steps described below.

1.1 Phase1 - Experimental Protocol Elaboration and Setup Assembly

Previous studies show that engineering students have great difficulties in solving problems. Mainly the difficulty in abstract thinking, necessary for learning programming. The Neuropsychological Assessment plays an important role in the diagnosis of problems at the level of development and learning. One of its prominent areas is the study of executive functions. The problem being investigated is the study of brain and body functions that may provide useful indicators (of cognitive, mental, emotional and other states). These could be used for the implementation of new strategies in order to minimize the difficulties presented by the students while programming. Thus, we intend to measure what is happening with the user and determine how specific parts of the brain or other body elements can measure different functions [1, 10]. This study involves the testing and studying of intended functions, in order to find patterns that measure the ability of individuals to formulate abstract principles, emotional states or other cognitive elements of interest based on the feedback received after each test. Another problem identified in previous studies is the lack of motivation that students show when having to learn to program. This phase includes the creation of a set of experimental protocols that will allow us to verify the learning performance and motivation of the users for programming learning. In a first approach we will consider several types of signal acquisition devices, with different types of nature, in order to acquire the maximum cognitive features possible. The signal acquisition devices used are: EEG signal acquisition devices, Video signal acquisition devices and software to obtain keyboard and mouse input data. EEG signal acquisition devices will allow extracting very important parameters such as excitement or frustration levels, attention, sleepy or stress conditions. Video information will allow us to detect facial expressions and eye tracking information useful to infer the level of attention and focus of the user. Keyboard and mouse input information give us details of the users input patterns.

1.2 Phase 2 - Signal Acquisition and Data Base Creation

In this phase, we aim to develop a number of individual tasks that involve cognitive abilities; which underlie the complex task of general computer programming. Programming involves attention, abstract reasoning, problem solving, decision making, and error monitoring, among others. Our aim is to make EEG recordings while participants are performing these tasks. The EEG will then be processed offline with various advanced signal-processing techniques in order to identify the psychophysiological signatures of these processes. These electrophysiological features of the EEG can be later used in a BCI to help monitor brain processes involved in computer programming. All tasks will be programmed using the experiment generator software E-Prime. We will use standard psychological tasks, which are known to involve the aforementioned cognitive abilities and to elicit specific event related potentials (ERPs), which, among other EEG features, can also be used to identify certain brain processes. At the end of this phase we intended to have a Database with the synchronization of the following signals: an EEG signal, a video signal and a Keyboard/mouse input data.

1.3 Phase 3 - Signal Analysis and Feature Extraction

The main goal of this phase is to develop techniques and methods of signal processing analysis. The implementation of a filtering routine for removing artifacts based on a signal processing methods in order to clear any previously collected EEG will be done. A standard technique based on Singular Spectrum Analysis (SSA) with zero delay will be used. The study of signal processing methodologies for the analysis of ERP signals in order to characterize them quantitatively and qualitatively will be done. Induced potentials represent transient components in the electroencephalogram generated by responses to a sensory stimulus. To make the evoked potential signal visible, a large number of single trial responses are needed to carry out an average of the set to obtain the activity associated with a given condition. Therefore, for the study of evoked potentials it is necessary to consider signals representing different levels of analysis: the single trial segment, the average set and the large average. Different signal processing techniques are used in this study. At the end of this phase we intended to have the EEG signal characterization. We also expected the interpretation of brain regions activated in EEG and possible patterns of distinct activation.

1.4 Phase 4 - Experimental Protocol Validation and the Signal Processing Methods

The main objective in this task is to develop an adaptive system based on BCI and HCI. BCI is used to provide information on the learning capabilities of the user. After we identify the different patterns that occur in the electrical brain activity on different learning performances we will use these patterns to build a learning system that will adapt to the abilities of the user. To build this system we will start to develop a typical BCI system that identifies the specific patterns discovered in the previous tasks. As outputs of the BCI we will provide ways to improve the learning abilities of the user, providing for instance tips on how to solve the problem. This BCI system will have the following structure:

- Signal acquisition: one of the main concerns in this project is to build a system that will be easy to use, however the typical EEG acquisition devices are non-portable and have long lasting setup time. We will test several EEG signal acquisition devices trying to find a good compromise between portability and signal quality. - Filtering: in this step we will use several methods like spatial filtering, surface Laplacian filtering, Common Average Reference, Kalman filtering among other methods that can be more suitable.
- Feature Extraction: as features we will use the results obtained in task 3.
- Feature Classification: in this phase we intent to classify the patterns in the several possible outputs. We can use methods like Linear Discriminant Analysis or Neural Networks to classify the data.

At the end of this phase it is expected to have a fully functional BCI system that can provide proper decisions in the different learning abilities that will be used.

1.5 Phase 5 - Development of an Adaptive System Based on BCI and HCI

The categorization of users will be used in an adaptive e-learning system [4]. This e-learning system will adapt to the user in different ways: depending on the cognitive state of frustration/satisfaction, the user's learning preferences, the available resources, among others, to provide the student with pleasant and adjusted experiences. This adaptation will include essentially two main modes of interaction: one involving the analysis of real- time user and other based on the stored profile of the user in question.

Therefore, the purpose of this phase is to do a literature review, design, specification and implementation of an adaptive e-learning system in terms of content and interaction forms. For the base e-learning system one considers the use of an LMS (Learning Management System) as Moodle. However, an adaptive feature implies the inclusion and integration of other modules. There will be an ITS module for the management of the learning scripts library and their relationship with students. A LM (Link Mining) module responsible for monitoring student behaviour during the use of the platform should also be planned.

This phase will involve the following tasks: - State of art survey and competitive analysis of the solution; - Collection, analysis and negotiation of requirements, development of SRS and the acceptance test plan; - Installation of Moodle platform; - Implementation of the front-end and back-office of the platform; - Implementation of the static and dynamic activities of the database; - Implementation of learning scripts that are the student's pedagogical itineraries; - Implementation of the dynamic generation and self assessment of student activities; - Implementation of feedback mechanisms/interaction appropriate to various user profiles; - Validation (test) and report. At the end of this phase an adaptive e-learning system with the features above-mentioned and its correspondent validation is expected.

2. CONCLUSION

Previous studies show that currently engineering students have great difficulties in solving problems. Highlighted is the difficulty in abstract thinking, necessary for learning programming. The Neuropsychological assessment plays an important role in the diagnosis and treatment of people with disorders at the level of development and learning. The problem being investigated is the study of brain and body functions that may provide indicators of cognitive, mental, emotional and other states. The idea is to obtain indicators that could be used as new strategies to minimize the difficulties presented by the students while programming. This study involves testing and study intended functions, in order to find patterns to measure the ability of individuals to formulate abstract principles, emotional states or other cognitive elements of interest based on the feedback received after each test item. Another problem identified in previous studies is the lack of motivation that students show when learning to program. So we intend to use new forms of interaction for the registration of EEG signals synchronized with the presentation of stimuli (visual or auditory) during the execution of tasks. These make possible the quantification of aspects of interest as immersion, motivation, attention load, cognitive effort, user abstraction capability, among others. One possibility is to use tests that measure the learning of concepts, thinking flexibility and ability to learn and apply new rules. The big idea of this study is to investigate, using the latest techniques of interaction, neurophysiological responses while conducting tests of interest. The initial scope of research is in the area of programming, in which the research team has invested, but the areas of application are vast, not only in education but also in the clinical area. These investigations will allow the acquisition of very important data in order to advance in the area of Computer Science Education Research. At the same time it will be possible to propose new forms of adaptive interaction allowing significant advances in the areas of Human Computer Interaction, with applications in education and later in clinical practice.

ACKNOWLEDGMENT

This work was supported by FCT Grant (Ref:SFRH/BPD/101112/2014) to Ana Rita Teixeira

REFERENCES

1. Acar, Z. and Makeig, S., 2013. Effect of forward model errors on EEG source localization. *In Brain Topography*, Vol. 26, No. 3, pp.378-396.
2. Bennedsen, J. and Caspersen, M. E., 2006. Abstraction ability as an indicator of success for learning object-oriented programming? *In SIGCSE Bulletin inroads*, Vol. 38, No 2, pp 39-43.
3. Carbone, A., Ceddia, J., Simon, D'Souza and Mason, R., 2013. Student Concerns in Introductory Programming Courses. *Proceedings of the fifteenth Australasian Computing Education conference*. Adelaide, Australia, pp. 41-50.
4. De Bra, P., Aroyo, L. and Chepegin, V., 2004. The Next Big Thing: Adaptive Web-Based Systems. *In Journal of Digital Information*. Vol. 5, No. 1, Art. No. 247.
5. Figueiredo, N., Silva, F., Georgieva, P., Milanova, M. and Mendi. E., 2015. *Towards an Adaptive Brain-Computer Interface – An Error Potential Approach*. Multimodal Pattern Recognition of Social Signals In Human-Computer-Interaction Lecture Notes in Computer Science. Springer, Stockholm, Sweden.
6. Fincher, S., and Petre, M., 2004. *Computer Science Education Research*. RoutledgeFalmer, Taylor & Francis Group, Oxford, UK.
7. Gomes, A. and Mendes, A. J., 2007. Learning to program - difficulties and solutions. *Proceedings of the International Conference on Engineering Education*. Coimbra, Portugal, (CD-ROM).
8. Jenkins, T., 2002. On the difficulty of learning to program. *Proceedings of the 3rd Annual LTSN_ICS Conference* Loughborough, United Kingdom, pp. 53-58.
9. Santos, A., Gomes, A. and Mendes, A. J., 2010. Integrating New Technologies and Existing Tools to Promote In *Programming Learning. Algorithms*, Vol. 3, No. 2, pp. 183-196.
10. Tomé, A. M., Teixeira, A. R., Figueiredo, N., Georgieva, P., Santos, I. M. and Lang, E. W., 2010. Clustering evoked potential signals using subspace methods. *Proceedings of Annual International Conference of the IEEE Engineering in Medicine and Biology Society*. San Diego, California, USA, pp. 3986–3989.

Posters

A LOGO DESIGN TOOL BASED ON PROCEDURAL MODELING OF DESIGN ELEMENTS

Hyoji Ha[1], Hyunwoo Han[1], Sungyun Bae[1] and Kyungwon Lee[2]
[1]*Life Media Interdisciplinary Program*
[2]*Department of Digital Media*
Ajou University, 206, World cup-ro, Yeongtong-gu, Suwon-si, Gyeonggi-do 443-749, Korea

ABSTRACT

A myriad of individuals and companies devote much effort to discover the right logo to represent their image, since it greatly affects the overall visual identity such as brand image, product design or promotion design. While it is not an easy task to create an appealing and competitive logo, growing needs for a new logo design tool proved its necessity. This study thereby seeks to develop process criteria based on the classified formative characteristics of a logo, and provide a tool that allows users to efficiently design a logo under certain procedural modeling. The logo design tool in this research is expected to reduce time to optimize a logo by enabling users to select the design elements at each step according to their preference.

KEYWORDS

Design elements, Symbol marks, Logo design process, Procedural modeling

1. INTRODUCTION

This study aims to apply a logo design tool based on the pre-identified design elements, and facilitate users to design a logo through procedural modeling. Criteria to classify the formative characteristics for a logo were provided with reference to Principles of form and Design, which we implemented to develop a logo design process. The paper further describes a process to create a logo as desired by the user, on the basis of a process developed in this study.

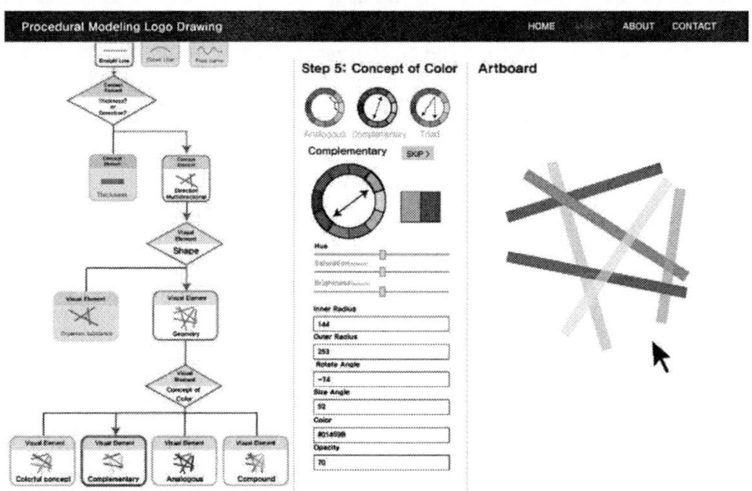

Figure 1. Implementation of the logo design tool suggested in this study; it assists efficient and optimized logo design based upon procedural modeling. This exhibition shows selecting 'concept of color – complementary' under visual element(http://202.30.24.169:3001/ci/procedural_modeling_logo_drawing)

2. MAIN PROPOSAL

2.1 Data Analysis Processing

In order to simplify the logo design process, we needed to establish several basic formative principles. We thereby outlined the fundamental elements of a logo design referring to the criteria suggested in Principles of form and Design. Modeling elements were labeled as Concept element, Visual element, Correlation element, and Interrelationships of Forms and their subordinate attributes, as illustrated in Table 1[1][2][3].

Table 1. Modeling element of the Logo Trends

Basic element	Attribute	
Concept element	**Point**	Natural point, Intersections, Vertex
	Line	Type(straight line, curve line, free curve), Speed, Thickness
	Surface	Type(square, rectangle, circle, triangle, polygon), Transformation, Perspective
	Volume	Corn form, cylinder, cube, sphere
Visual element	**Shape**	Natural object(organism substance, inorganic substance), Artificiality (geometry, artifact, typography)
	Concept of Color	Type(analogous, monochromatic, triad, complementary, compound, colorful concept)
	Texture	
Correlation element	**Rhythm**	
	Space	
	Weight	
	Composition	Direction(one direction, multi direction, rotation)
The Interrelationships of forms	**Detachment, Touching, Overlapping, Penetration, Union, Subtraction, Intersection, Coinciding**	

2.2 Logo Design Based on Procedural Modeling

In this chapter, we aim to explore the process of logo design based upon the formative criteria as defined in Table 1. It thus suggests an easy-to-use and intuitive design tool with a flowchart structure, named as 'procedural model', in order to effectively create a logo[4][5]. We will assume that the desired logo is composed of two arc-shaped geometric layers that are geometric with complementary colors, where the layers are rotating and overlapped. Designing a logo meeting such conditions under our logical progress is represented as Figure 2~Figure 4.

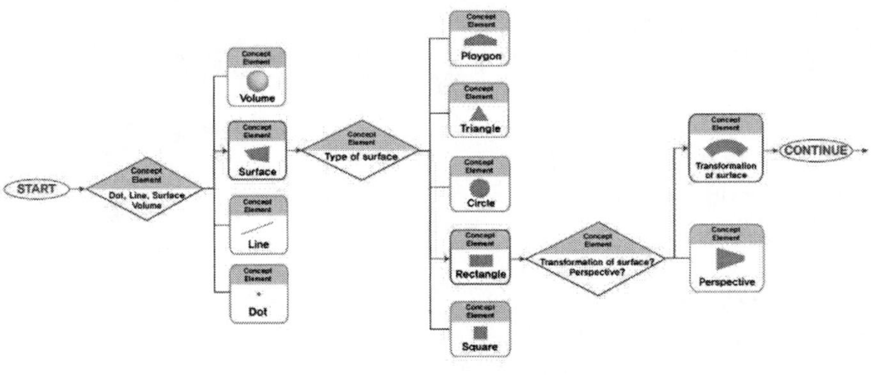

Figure 2. "Concept element" Logo design process in accordance with procedural modeling: A logo being created as presented with the red arrow

Upon initiating the design process, the first options include Point, Line, Surface, and Volume when selecting the concept element. Selecting Surface in order to create arcs will lead to choosing Type of Surface as subordinate attributes of Surface. Users will then be allowed to select Rectangle among Square, Rectangle, Circle, Triangle and Polygon, which is finalized after reshaping the arcs via Transformation of surface.

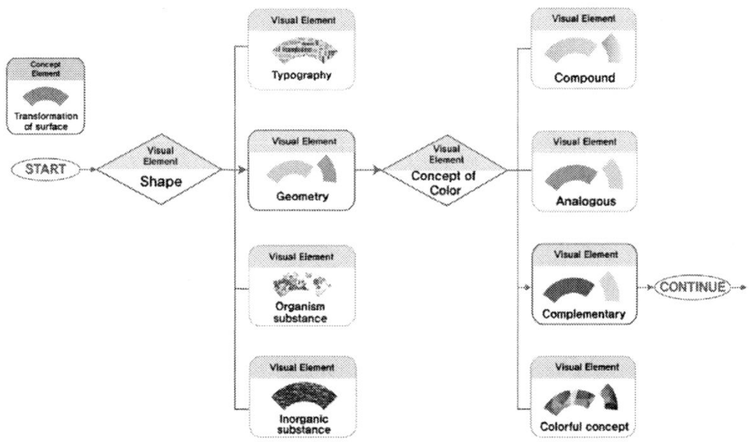

Figure 3. "Visual element" Logo design process in accordance with procedural modeling: A logo being created as presented with the red arrow

Next, Visual element, guides users to visualize the arc as the user intended, by adjusting Natural object and Artificiality. Selecting Geometry will bring about additional layers so as to form geometric patterns. Finally, in Concept of color, Complementary will be selected to represent complementary colors as desired in our example.

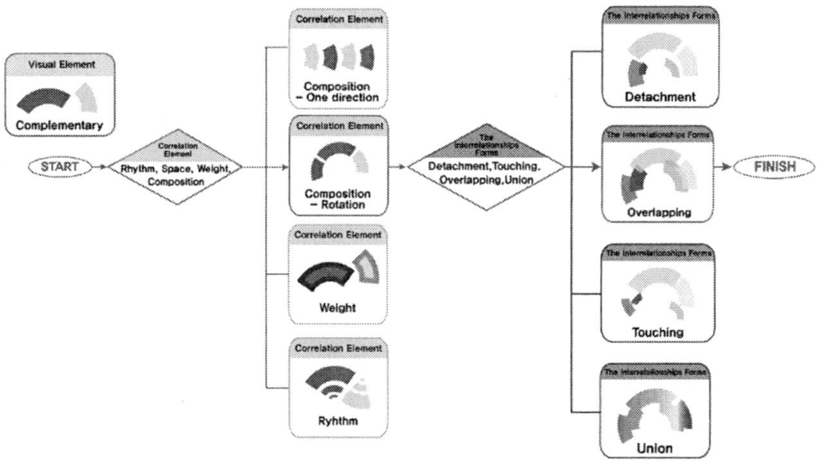

Figure 4. "Correlation element & The Interrelationships of forms" Logo design process in accordance with procedural modeling: A logo being created as presented with the red arrow

Eventually, in Correlation element, the user will select Rotation under Composition among Rhythm, Space, Weight and Composition to give a sense of rotation with the layer composition. This logo will be finalized when the layers are overlapped with each other after the user selects Overlapping under The Interrelationships of Forms.

The result of our framework is presented in Figure 1. It consists of four main fields; a logo design process flowchart, design element options upon following the procedure, Artboard where the actual logo is presented as being created, and the control board to adjust the details of a layer.

3. CONCLUSION

This study proposed a tool allowing users to easily create a logo under certain process based upon the formative characteristics of logo design. It can perform as a step-by-step guide to navigate the directions when designing a logo, and is also significant that this tool could effectively reduce the cost and time to create a logo. The study further aims to demonstrate a map reflecting the logo trend which can be associated with the logo design tool presented in this research, seeking a more efficient method to create a trendy logo.

ACKNOWLEDGEMENT

This research paper was published and supported under 2016 BK21 Program by Ajou University.

REFERENCES

Book

[1]Wucius,W, 1972. *Principles of Two-Dementional Design.* John Wiley & Sons Inc, New York, USA.

[2]Wucius,W, 1993. *Principles of Form and Design.* John Wiley & Sons Inc, New York, USA.

[3]Wucius,W, 1996. *Principles of Color Design.* John Wiley & Sons Inc, New York, USA.

Journal

[4]Lee K. et al, 2015. Development of Digital Tree Authoring Tool Based on Procedural Growth Model, *Korea Information Science Society*, Vol. 2015, No. 6,pp. 1327-1329.

Conference paper or contributed volume

[5]Schwarz, M. and Mueller, P., 2015. Advanced procedural modeling of architecture. *Proceedings of ACM Transactions on Graphics.* Los Angeles, USA, 107, pp. 1-12.

AN EYE TRACKER STUDY TO DETERMINE IF A CONSISTENT WEB PAGE LAYOUT IMPROVES USER PERFORMANCE

Gautham Mamidi and Ratvinder Grewal
Department of Mathematics and Computer Science
Laurentian University, Canada

ABSTRACT

This paper presents the results of a program that was written to convert a Web page to adhere to a consistent layout. Images and adverts are removed from the consistent layout. A usability test was conducted and eye tracking data was gathered. The results of experiment showed that users had different eye movements on Web pages depending on layout and design.

KEYWORDS

Eye-tracking, user performance, consistent layout

1. INTRODUCTION

Websites can be divided broadly into four genres: News, Shopping, Information, and Entertainment. News Websites have different categories of news, including international, national, regional, sports, financial, and breaking news. These Websites have the text, textual links, advertisements, photos, and videos. News Websites were chosen in my research but the findings can be extended to other genres of Websites.

User efficiency in finding information on Web pages is hindered due to differing Web page designs [1, 4], advert placement, and other image distractions especially when searching for information.

In this research we use a program to transform (see figure 1) in real-time the original Web page (referred to as the *original Web page*) to a Web page with simple and consistent design with colours, fonts, and link placement but no images nor advertisements (referred to as the *consistent Web page*). We compare and contrast the users' performance when doing search tasks using original Web pages and consistent Web pages.

Figure 1. A Web page is transformed to a generic layout

2. METHOD

The Boilerpipe API was chosen to extract content from a Web page and the HTML parser API was chosen to extract links from a Web page. Programming was done using Java J2EE Servlets, JSP, HTML, Java Script, and AJAX. The converted Web page runs on a Tomcat server.

A computer, mouse, and eye-tracker were used in a lab to conduct the counter-balanced experiment on 10 participants. Task O represents a task performed on an original Web page, and Task C represents a task performed on a consistent Web page. The eye-tracker captured data at 30Hz and recorded the participants' sciatic eye movement and gaze fixation. This experiment continues from previous work [2, 3] that measured the amount of time it took for users to navigate the Web page to click on a specified link.

The screen was divided into 16 quadrants of equal size depending on the size of the Web pages; referred to as viewing zones and numbered 1 to 16 (see figures 2 and 3). The Web pages were divided into objects of interest and these were named using alphabet letters. The objects of interest were blocks of links, content, images, and advertisements.

Figure 2. Zones and objects of interest on original Web page

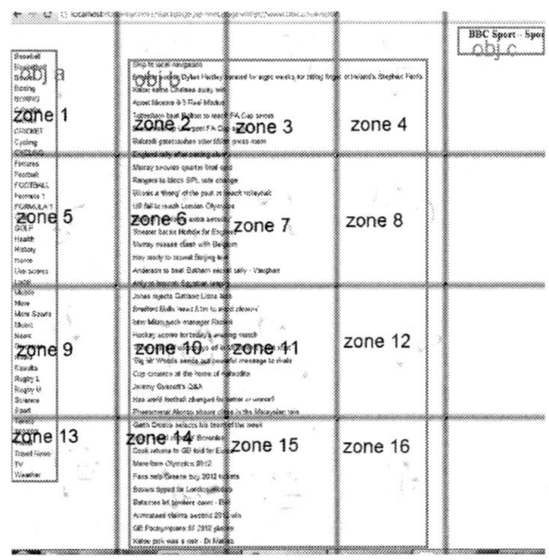

Figure 3. Zones and objects of interest on Consistent Web page

The first task involved searching for menu links: "sports" on Yahoo Web page (Task O3.1/C3.1); "sports" on BBC Web page; (Task O3.2/C3.3); "sports" on New York Times Web page (Task O3.3/C3.3); "sports" on MSN Web page (Task O3.4/C3.4).

The second task involved searching for content links: "Hockey scores for today" on Yahoo Web page (Task O3.11/C3.11); "Hockey scores for today" on BBC Web page (Task O3.12/C3.12); "Hockey scores for today" on New York Times Web page (Task O3.13/C3.13); "Hockey scores for today" on MSN Web page (Task O3.14/C3.14).

3. RESULTS

By analyzing the results it can be seen that the participants eye gaze start from the top left side when searching for menu links on the consistent Web page. The search for the content link also starts with the eye gaze at the top of the Web page. It was noted some participants started the scan bottom up. The search pattern formed a definitive relationship between layout and link placement.

As expected there was no definitive relationship in eye gaze for the original Web page. The view pattern during the search was different for all Web pages primarily due to the different objects of interest and layout. The viewing zones and objects of interest were determined if more than 80% of user population viewed them.

It was noted that participants viewed fewer zones when searching for menu links on the original Web page than searching for content links (see table 1).

Table 1. Original Web page menu link search patterns

Tasks	Link placement zones	Viewing zones	Viewed objects of interest
Task O3.1	1, 5, 9, 13	1, 5, 9, 13	b, c
Task O3.2	2, 3, 4	1, 2, 3, 5	a, b
Task O3.3	1, 5	1, 2, 5, 6, 10	a, b , c
Task O3.4	1, 2, 3, 4	1, 2, 3, 5	a, b, c

Table 2. Consistent Web page menu link search patterns

Tasks	Link placement zones	Viewing zones
Task C3.1	1, 5	2, 5
Task C3.2	1, 5, 9, 13	2, 5, 9
Task C3.3	1, 5, 9	5
Task C3.4	1, 5, 9, 13	5, 9, 13

In Task O3.1 the menu link was placed in zones 1, 5, 9, 13 and the viewing zones were the same whereas in Task O3.2 the menu link was placed in zones 2, 3, 4, however the participants did view other zones. It was observed that the participants view patterns were carried over from the previous task.

For the menu link search using the consistent Web page the viewing patterns were in fewer viewing zones probably because the placement of links was always in a similar spot (see table 2). From the results it was observed from Task C3.1 to Task C3.4 the participants showed a consistent search pattern.

4. CONCLUSION

The experiment tested if users perform better when using a consistent version of Web pages compared to the original version of the Web page. Tasks were developed for users to perform and performance was recorded based on time taken to complete each task. Results showed that a change in user performance from the original Web page to the consistent Web page.

The recording of eye gaze showed a correlation between eye gaze patterns and link placement. The consistent Web page link placement had a similar viewing patterns across tasks and participants whereas original Web page link placement had varying viewing patterns with no consistency. Results showed that participants viewed more areas on the screen when performing tasks on original version of Web page than on the consistent version of Web page.

REFERENCES

[1] Burke M. et al. High-Cost Banner Blindness: Ads Increase Perceived Workload, Hinder Visual Search, and Are Forgotten. ACM Transactions on Computer-Human Interaction, Vol. 12, No. 4, December 2005. 423–445.

[2] Mamidi, G., Grewal, R.S. Consistent vs. Inconsistent Layout on a Web Page: A User Performance Perspective. Proceeding of the IADIS International Conference WWW/Internet (ICWI 2013), October 22-25, 2013, Texas, USA.

[3] Mamidi, G., Grewal, R.S. The Transformation of Web Pages towards a Consistent Layout to Gauge the Change in User Performance. Proceedings of the International Conference on Modelling, Simulation and Visualization (MSV) Methods, July 22-25, 2013, Las Vegas, USA.

[4] Melody Y. Ivory, and Rodrick Megraw. Evolution of Website Design Patterns. ACM Transactions on Information Systems, Vol. 23, No. 4, October 2005. 463–497.

AN EXPLORATORY GAME BASED ON SEMANTICS TO IMPROVE HISTORY LEARNING

Omar Gustavo Bravo-Quezada[1], Martín López-Nores[2] and José Juan Pazos-Arias[2]
[1]*GIHP4C Research Group, Universidad Politécnica Salesiana*
Calle Vieja 12-30 y Elia Liut, Cuenca, Ecuador
[2]*AtlantTIC Research Center for Information and Communication Technologies*
Department of Telematics Engineering, University of Vigo
EE Telecomunicación, Campus Universitario s/n, Vigo, Spain

ABSTRACT

The teaching of History in primary and secondary education often attains low levels of learning and understanding. Building on the success of previous experiences in the area of serious games, we are investigating the potential of situational curiosity and serendipity to increase the retention of historical facts. We present a game designed to explore networks of relationships among the topics of upcoming classes and topics that may be of interest to their students in a given place and/or on a given date. The game is backed by an intelligent system that uses DBpedia and YAGO as the main sources of knowledge in the search for semantic links among concepts. The teachers are given tools to revise the meshes of concepts and relationships, to modify things and to introduce new relationships.

KEYWORDS

Serious games; semantics; graph visualization and manipulation

1. INTRODUCTION

Universities worldwide have long understood History as a huge mesh of interrelated facts and concepts, entwined with the development of all other areas of human knowledge. However, in primary and secondary schools (just like in most of the cultural media offering interpretation and dissemination to the wide public) History is commonly presented in a siloed, simplistic and localistic manner that promotes memorizing rather than understanding, does not account for cross-border cultural aspects and prevents history and culture from being viewed as a shared, global experience.

Proponents of new teaching methodologies often call to develop student-centered approaches to stimulate reflection and retention (Maloy & Laroche, 2010). Likewise, several works in the area of serious games for tactile and mobile devices (Backlund & Hendrix, 2013) have already attained very positive results in terms of learning and engagement. Following these references, we have been working to harness the potential of *digital storytelling* (Robin, 2008) through the technologies of the *Semantic Web*, aiming to develop a serious game that will allow the students to explore networks of relationships among the topics of upcoming classes and topics that may be of interest to them in certain locations and on certain date. The exploration of connections is intended to arise situational curiosity and serendipity, which are phenomena that cannot be furnished by textbooks.

Our game is backed by an intelligent system that looks for the most relevant concepts to link proactively (i.e. on behalf of the teachers), taking advantage of the availability of huge, open knowledge bases of interrelated facts on the Internet. Specifically, we have been using DBpedia (Auer et al., 2007) and YAGO (Suchanek, Kasneci & Weikum, 2007). The findings of the intelligent system are presented to the teachers through proper interfaces, so that they can revise the connections, discard the ones they find irrelevant/wrong and introduce new relationships, thus closing the loop by contributing to enrich the knowledge bases.

2. APPROACH

There are three basic stages in implementing the interactive experiences we propose:

- First, our intelligent system provides a graph of semantic connections among concepts representing the topics to develop in an upcoming class and others that may be of interest to the students in the foreseen context (locations and date).
- Second, teachers edit the graph to discard irrelevant/wrong connections or introduce new ones. They can also link multimedia contents from whichever sources to illustrate the concepts.
- Finally, when the time for the class comes, the students engage in a team competition to explore the graph of connections among concepts and browse the linked contents.

For the first stage, our intelligent system works with an ontology of significant dates ("*international days of*", "*commemorative dates*", "*national days of*", "*birth dates of*", ...) which, just like the topics of interest for the teachers, are linked to concepts from DBpedia and YAGO. We also seek to gather relevant contextual opportunities from hot topics in social networks, possibly related to news in the media and foreseeably lasting until the dates of the classes. Having that, a set of algorithms developed by ourselves as evolutions of those included in the RelFinder tool (Heim et al., 2009) start creating the graph of semantic connections by looking for connecting paths in more or less direct ways. On the day after a Champions League game between FC Bayern München and Atlético Madrid, a Physics class could be enriched with a story taking from Albert Einstein to Pep Guardiola through the following direct path: "*Albert Einstein*" → "*was born in*" → "*Ulm*" → "*is a city of*" → "*Germany*" → "*takes place in*" ← "*Bundesliga*" ← "*plays in*" ← "*FC Bayern München*" ← "*is trainer of*" ← "*Pep Guardiola*". This can readily promote the effect of situational curiosity, whereas the serendipity aspect would be furnished by more subtle (indirect) connections, like the fact that Einstein was a great supporter of the state of Israel and eleven Israelis were killed during the 1972 Olympic games in Munich.

In the second stage, teachers are given visualization tools (also inspired by RelFinder, though implemented in HTML5 using D3.js libraries[1]) to manipulate the graphs, adding or removing concepts, and attaching any kind of multimedia contents from Internet sites. In the preceding example, they could choose to display the property "*was born in*" outgoing from the node of "*Pep Guardiola*" to highlight one differential aspect between the two characters. The property "*worked as*" would link to separate concepts (say, e.g. "*scientist*" and "*football manager*") that do not belong to any connecting path either, but which are worth showing anyway. If the teachers want to use concepts that are not offered by the tool (because they are not captured in DBpedia or YAGO), they may enter them manually. We did this ourselves, for example, to capture the important historical fact that Einstein was one of the Jews who left Germany in 1933, together with Richard Kohn, who was the trainer of FC Bayern München at the time.

One important aid provided by the teachers' tools relates to the dynamics of the game. This is like "*filling in the gaps, with multiple choices given*", so that certain textual tags (corresponding to concepts or to semantic properties) are left blank, and the students have to decide which option, out of a set of five possibilities, is the right one. For example, the concept reached from "*Albert Einstein*" through the semantic property "*was born in*" could be filled with one option from the set "*Beijing*", "*Berlin*", "*Ulm*", "*Brasília*" or "*Princeton*". Knowing the domain of the "*was born in*" property, our semantics-based algorithms can suggest possible entries for the menu of choices, so that the teachers can select the most interesting ones to promote reflection, fun, surprise and other reactions, also bearing in mind the previous knowledge of the students (e.g. in advanced courses, the aforementioned menu could be changed to a more focused one, like "*Zurich*", "*Berlin*", "*Ulm*", "*Tel Aviv*" or "*Braunau am Inn*").

The game can be played individually or in teams, using computers or mobile devices. Since all the members of a team will be in the same place, they can collectively decide what is the next blank to fill in, discuss the choices (and reflect and laugh) orally, and then decide by voting on their devices. They can display the content attached to a node in the graph just by clicking/tapping on it. Wrong choices incur short time penalties. The teams get more or fewer points as per the order in which they fill in all the blanks. A global view of the progress of the game can be displayed on a collective screen.

---

[1] https://d3js.org/

3. ONGOING WORK

The goal of our research is to contribute to improving the learning experiences in primary and secondary education, linking whichever concepts through historical events and characters to highlight the transversal nature of History. We believe that the concept of our interactive and exploratory game, together with the assisting tools for teachers and the capability to transparently enrich a global knowledge base, can make a significant contribution to the current standards of teaching.

We plan to measure the educational value of our proposal with the collaboration of teachers and students through surveys and focus groups. To this aim, we have been in negotiations with educational institutions and companies interested in the concept, and the plan is to make the first real tests during the next academic year (2016-2017).

ACKNOWLEDGEMENT

The authors from the University of Vigo have been supported by the European Regional Development Fund (ERDF) and Xunta de Galicia under project CN 2012/260 "*Consolidation of Research Units: AtlantTIC*", and by the Ministerio de Educación y Ciencia (Gobierno de España) research project TIN2013-42774-R (partly financed with FEDER funds).

REFERENCES

Auer, S. Bizer, C., Kobilarov, G., Lehmann, J., Cyganiak, R. and Ives, Z., 2007. DBpedia: A nucleus for a Web of open data. *Proceedings of the 6th International Semantic Web Conference (ISWC)*. Busan, South Korea, pp. 722-735.

Backlund, P. and Hendrix, M., 2013. Educational games - Are they worth the effort? A literature survey of the effectiveness of serious games. *Proceedings of the 5th International Conference on Games and Virtual Worlds for Serious Applications (VS-GAMES)*. Bournemouth, United Kingdom, pp. 1-8.

Heim, P., Hellmann, S., Lehmann, J., Lohmann, S. and Stegemann, T., 2009. RelFinder: Revealing relationships in RDF knowledge bases. *Proceedings of the 4th International Conference on Semantic and Digital Media Technologies (SAMT)*. Graz, Austria, pp. 182-187.

Maloy, R.W. and Laroche, I., 2010. Student-centered teaching methods in the History classroom: Ideas, issues, and insights for new teachers. *In Social Studies Research and Practice*, Vol. 5, No. 2, pp 46-61.

Robin, B.R., 2008. Digital storytelling: A powerful technology tool for the 21st century classroom. *In Theory and Practice*, Vol. 47, No. 3, pp 220-228.

Suchanek, F.M., Kasneci, G. and Weikum, G., 2007. YAGO: A core of semantic knowledge. *Proceedings of the 16th International World Wide Web Conference (WWW)*. Banff, Canada, pp. 697-706.

THE RESEARCH ON ELECTRONIC COMPUTER GAMES AS A RECREATIONAL ACTIVITY IN TURKEY

Süleyman Munusturlar and Müge Akyildiz Munusturlar
Anadolu University, Faculty of Sport Sciences, Department of Recreation, Turkey

ABSTRACT

Entertainment games provide engaging activities and it would appear that far from waning, interest in games for leisure is still growing. The availability of new consoles, platforms and technologies for the delivery of games is an important factor in this continued growth. The aim of this study is to determine characteristic and habits of computer game players in Turkey. In line with this purpose following processes were followed and reported. Study group of the research is chosen by random sampling method through online questionary techniques from 69 women and 252 men, 321 people in total. Two different data collection tools were used in gathering research data. As a result of the study, most of the computer game players choses target shooting games and sportive, action, and fantasy games follow to target shooting games as popularity and more than half of players (%56) prefer to play multiplayer games than single player games. It is reported that players spend approximately 10,1 hours playing computer game per week.

KEYWORDS

Computer games, electronic leisure habits, electronic games

1. INTRODUCTION

Over the last 40 years computer games have increasingly replaced more traditional games as leisure activities and have had a trans- formational impact on how we spend our leisure time. Entertainment games provide engaging activities and it would appear that far from waning, interest in games for leisure is still growing. The availability of new consoles, platforms and technologies for the delivery of games is an important factor in this continued growth (Connolly, 2012). Playing digital games on a personal computer, a game console, a handheld device, or on the Internet is a relatively new, but massively popular form of mediated entertainment. In the public eye, games are generally constructed as the province of children, but one may wonder if this image is accurate (Williams, 2006).

Gardner (1991) claimed that the use of videogames provided excellent behavioral observation opportunities such as increasing repertoire of problem-solving strategies, eye–hand coordination, the satisfaction of cognitive activity in the involvement, release of aggression and control. Videogames can also influence the child's social integration. In a number of studies, it has been established that children behave more socially after playing videogames (van Schie & Wiegman, 1997).

Games and their outcomes and impacts have been analyzed along a number of dimensions and it is proposed that these classifications should help in developing a more organized framework for understanding games. In categorizing games it is useful to consider the primary function of the game, that is whether the game was developed initially as a game for entertainment, a game for learning or as a serious game. Digital commercial games (such as Mario Brothers and Grand Theft Auto) were developed primarily for fun, entertainment and recreation, while the main aims of games-based learning and serious games are learning and behaviour change. The terms serious games and games-based learning are sometimes used synonymously (Corti, 2006), although serious games have been developed for the broader purposes of training and behaviour change in business, industry, marketing, healthcare and government NGOs as well as in education (Sawyer & Smith, 2008). Sweetser & Wyeth (2005) claimed that understanding game usability has had priority over understanding game enjoyment, while Vorderer, Klimmt & Ritterfield (2004) have suggested that research has neglected to consider the nature of media enjoyment generally. A differentiation in genres is a convenient way to bring some order into the diversity of games. Game genre can be splited by the intention of the game as; action, adventure, animated tutorial, board game, fighting, generic games, generic online games, mobile device, N/A, platform, puzzle, racing game, role-playing, simulation, sports, strategy, virtual reality (Tan & Jansz, 2008; Holtz & Appel, 2011; Lucas & Sherry, 2004). The aim of this study is to determine characteristic and habits of computer game players in Turkey. In line with this purpose following processes were followed and reported.

2. METHOD

2.1 Study Group

Study group of the research is chosen by random sampling method through online questionary techniques from 69 women and 252 men, 321 people in total. In order to prepare the data set collected from 321 participants for statistical analyses, missing data and extreme values are excluded from data set and then the research continued with 300 participants.

2.2 Data Collection Tools

Two different data collection tools which was personal information form created so as to determine participants' demographic information and electronic game experience scale which was developed by researchers based on literature were used in gathering research data.

3. FINDINGS

Findings on computer game experiences of participants showed that most of participants plays serious computer games more than 5 years. This finding is followed by %10 less than 1 year, %3 between 1 and 2 years, %5 between 2 and 3 years, %8 between 2 and 3 years.

Findings on computer game time spending of participants showed that, %30 of participants less 1 hour, %18 of participants 1-2 hours, %17 of participants 2-3 hours, % 17 of participants 4-5 hours, %15 of participants more than 5 hours play computer games in a day. It has been seen that, %56 of participants play multiplayer, %44 of participants play single player games as serious computer game.

Game broadcasting and watching game broadcastings habits of participants were investigated. It is reported that %51 of participants play video games only, %39 of participants watching broadcasts of others, %1,8 of participants broadcasting their own game videos, %8 of participants not only watching broadcasts but also broadcasting their own videos in addition to playing computer games.

Game genre choices of participants were investigated. The most preferred game genre is shooting target games as %27,4 and the least preferred game genre is arcade games as %2,3. Other game genres are sorted by popularity in computer game players as; %16,1 fantasy games, %14,4 action and adventure games, %10,4 sport games, %7,4 strategy games, %6,7 Facebook games, %5 racing games, %3,7 role-playing games, %3,3 simulation games.

4. RESULTS AND DISCUSSION

As a result of the study, most of the computer game players choses target shooting games and sportive, action, and fantasy games follow to target shooting games as popularity. Lucas & Sherry (2004) reported that female players like the non-mental rotation games such as puzzle, arcade, quiz, board games etc., but conversely male players like mental rotation games such as fighting, shooting target, sports, racing etc. As an other result of the study, more than half of players (%56) prefer to play multiplayer games than single player games. Pena & Hancock (2006) stated that multiplayer games are getting be more popular for serious players because of including more cognitive effects such as aggression, social interaction, exposure etc., than single player games. Results of the study showed us that computer game players have an experiences more than 5 years mostly. Hsu & Lu (2004) reported that players game experiences as approximately 3 years. And computer games are played by females as 5.30 hours, by males as 14.8 hours per week. Approximately 10,1 hours playing computer game average per week is higher than results of some studies (Lucas & Sherry, 2004; Chou and Tsai, 2007; Eastin, 2006) in international literature. Results show that computer game players not only playing computer games but also broadcasting video games and watching broadcasts of other players.

REFERENCES

Connolly, T. M., Boyle, E.A., MacArthur, E., Hainey, T., Boyle, T.M. (2012). A systematic literature review of empirical evidence on computer games and serious games. Computers & Education 59 (2012) 661–686.

Chou, C., & Tsai, M.-J. (2007). Gender differences in Taiwan high school students' computer game playing. Computers in Human Behavior, 23, 812–824.

Corti, K. (2006). Games-based learning: a serious business application. PIXELearning Limited. Retrieved 29 November 2009 from. http://www.pixelearning.com/docs/games_based learning-pixelearning.pdf.

Eastin, M. S. (2006). Video game violence and the female game player- self- and opponent gender effects on presence and aggressive thoughts. Communication Research, 33(6), 448–466.

Gardner, J.E. (1991). Can the Mario Bros. help? Nintendo games as an adjunct in psychotherapy with children. *Psychotherapy, 28*, 667–670.

Holtz, P., & Appel, M. (2011). Internet use and video gaming predict problem behavior in early adolescence. Journal of Adolescence, 34, 49–58.

Lucas, K., & Sherry, J. L. (2004). Sex differences in video game play: a communication-based explanation. Communication Research, 31(5), 499–523.

Pena, J., & Hancock, J. (2006). An analysis of socioemotional and task communication in online mutiplayer video games. Communication Research, 33(1), 92–109.

Sawyer, B., & Smith. (October 2008). Keynote address. In The second European conference on games-based learning (pp. 16–17). Barcelona Spain: Universitat Oberta de Catalunya.

Sweetser, P., & Wyeth, P. (2005). GameFlow: a model for evaluating player enjoyment. ACM Computers in Entertainment, 3(3), 1–24.

Tan, E. S., & Jansz, J. (2008). The game experience. In H. N. Schifferstein & P. P. Hekkert (Eds.), Product experience (pp. 531–556). San Diego: Elsevier.

Van Schie, E. G. M., & Wiegman, O. (1997). Children and videogames: Leisure activities, aggression, social integration, and school performance. Journal of Applied Social Psychology, 27, 1175–1194.

Vorderer, P., Klimmt, C., & Ritterfield, U. (2004). Enjoyment: at the heart of media entertainment. Communication Theory, 14(4), 388–408.

Williams, D. (2006). A brief social history of game play. In: P. Vorderer and J. Bryant (Eds.) *Playing videogames*, pp. 197–212. Mahwah (NJ): Lawrence Erlbaum.

VECTOR FIELD RBF INTERPOLATION ON A SPHERE

Michal Smolik and Vaclav Skala
Faculty of Applied Sciences, University of West Bohemia, Univerzitni 8, CZ 30614 Plzen, Czech Republic

ABSTRACT

This paper presents a new approach for Radial Basis Function (RBF) interpolation on a sphere. Standard approaches use the Euclidian metrics for the distance calculation of two points. However, for interpolation on a sphere, more naturally is computation of the distance as the shortest distance over the surface on a sphere, i.e. spherical distance of two points is more natural for interpolation on a sphere. We present the results on synthetic and real wind vector datasets on a globe.

KEYWORDS

Vector field, Radial Basis Functions, interpolation on sphere, visualization, spherical distance.

1. INTRODUCTION

Interpolation is probably the most frequent operation used in computational methods. Several methods have been developed for data interpolation, but they expect some kind of data "ordering", which is quite prohibitive for the case of k-dimensional data interpolation because of the computational cost.

Interpolating scattered vector data on a surface becomes frequent in applied problem solutions [Turk, G., O'Brien, J.F., 2002]. When the underlying manifold is a sphere, there are applications to geodesy [Aguilar, F. J., et al, 2005], meteorology [Eldrandaly, K. A., Abu-Zaid, M. S., 2011], astrophysics, geophysics, geosciences [Flyer, N. et al, 2014], and other areas. Radial basis function interpolation on a sphere [Golitschek, M. V., Light, W. A., 2001], [Baxter, B. J., Hubbert, S., 2001] has the advantage of having a continuous interpolant all over the sphere, as there are no borders.

2. RADIAL BASIS FUNCTIONS ON A SPHERE

Radial basis functions (RBF) is a technique for scattered data interpolation [Pan, R. and Skala, V., 2011] and approximation [Fasshauer, G.E., 2007].

The RBF interpolation can be computed on a sphere and has some advantages. There are no non-physical boundaries, there are no problems with interpolation on the poles, there are no coordinate singularities and the maximal distance of any two points has an upper limit.

The calculation of the distance r between two points $\boldsymbol{x}_1$ and $\boldsymbol{x}_2$ on a sphere can be computed as the Euclidian distance between these two points. In cases where both points lie on a unit sphere, then $r \in \langle 0; 2 \rangle$.

Another possibility is to compute the distance as the shortest distance between two points $\boldsymbol{x}_1$ and $\boldsymbol{x}_2$ on the surface of a sphere, measured along the surface of the sphere. The distance is computed using

$$r = \|\boldsymbol{x}_1 - \boldsymbol{x}_2\|_{spherical} = \cos^{-1}(\boldsymbol{n}_1 \cdot \boldsymbol{n}_2)\,, \tag{1}$$

where $r \in \langle 0; \pi \rangle$ and

$$\boldsymbol{n}_1 = \boldsymbol{x}_1 / \|\boldsymbol{x}_1\| \qquad \boldsymbol{n}_2 = \boldsymbol{x}_2 / \|\boldsymbol{x}_2\|\,. \tag{2}$$

The distance r in (1) is measured in radians. When the sphere has a radius equal to one, the computed distance in radians is equal to the distance measured along the surface of the sphere.

The RBF interpolation on a sphere is computed using the same formula as standard RBF. The only difference compared to the standard equation for RBF interpolation is when computing the distance between two points, as both of these approaches can be used.

2.1 Example of Vector Field on Sphere on Synthetic Data

An example of a vector field on a sphere can be described analytically. This analytical description must fulfill one criteria, which is that this function is continuous all over the sphere. For this purpose, we can use goniometric functions that have a period equal to 2π, i.e.

$$\sin\alpha = \sin(\alpha + k \cdot 2\pi) \qquad \cos\alpha = \cos(\alpha + k \cdot 2\pi)\,, \tag{3}$$

where k is an integer, i.e. $k \in \mathbb{Z}$.

The first example of a vector field on a sphere is described using the following equations:

$$\begin{bmatrix} u \\ v \end{bmatrix} = \begin{bmatrix} \sin 4\delta \\ \cos 4\theta \end{bmatrix} \qquad \begin{bmatrix} u \\ v \end{bmatrix} = \begin{bmatrix} \sin 3\delta + \cos 4\delta \cdot \cos 3\delta \\ \cos 4\theta - \sin 4\theta \cdot \sin 3\delta \end{bmatrix}, \tag{4}$$

where δ is an azimuth angle, i.e. $\delta \in \langle -\pi; \pi \rangle$ and θ is a zenith angle, i.e. $\theta \in \langle 0; \pi \rangle$. Data $[u, v]^T$ represents the direction vector on the surface of the sphere at point $[P_x, P_y, P_z]^T$:

$$[P_x \quad P_y \quad P_z]^T = [\sin\theta\cos\delta \quad \sin\theta\sin\delta \quad \cos\theta]^T. \tag{5}$$

The vector fields (4) were discretized on uniformly distributed 10 000 points on the sphere and then interpolated using RBF on the sphere with CSRBF with a shape parameter equal to 1:

$$\varphi(r) = (1 - r)_+^4(4r + 1)\,. \tag{6}$$

The interpolation, when using (1) to compute the distance r for basis function $\varphi(r)$, can be seen in Figure 2(a, b). This visualization was created with ray-tracing and line integral convolution on the sphere.

To measure the quality of the interpolation, we can compute the mean error of speed and the mean error of angular displacement of vectors. The mean errors were computed for 10^6 randomly generated positions on the sphere. The results can be seen in Table 1. Note that both vectors $[u, v]^T$ in (4) are computed in $[ms^{-1}]$.

Table 1. Errors of RBF interpolated vector fields (4) on a sphere for both ways of computing distance between two points

		Speed error $[ms^{-1}]$	Angular displacement error $[rad]$
Euclidian distance	vector field (4 left)	$2.452 \cdot 10^{-4}$	$4.233 \cdot 10^{-4}$
	vector field (4 right)	$1.884 \cdot 10^{-3}$	$2.672 \cdot 10^{-3}$
Spherical distance	vector field (4 left)	$1.686 \cdot 10^{-4}$	$3.074 \cdot 10^{-4}$
	vector field (4 right)	$1.379 \cdot 10^{-3}$	$1.906 \cdot 10^{-3}$

It can be seen that the RBF interpolation when using spherical distance gives better results for both vector fields, i.e. more accurate speed and more accurate orientation at every location on the sphere on average, see Table 1. The RBF interpolation is less accurate for the vector field (4 right) than for the vector field (4 left). The reason is that the vector field (4 right) is significantly more complicated than (4 left). The distribution of speed errors and angular displacement errors is visualized in Figure 1. Histograms were created from 10^6 samples and data were grouped into 71 bins.

2.2 Real Example of Vector Field on Sphere on Experiment Data

Numerical forecasts can predict weather as well as wind velocity and direction. For this example, one such prediction of the wind vector field for the whole world was used. This data contains information about wind speed and wind direction every one degree in latitude and longitude. Therefore, the resolution of the numerically computed dataset is 360×180, which is 64 800 vectors in total.

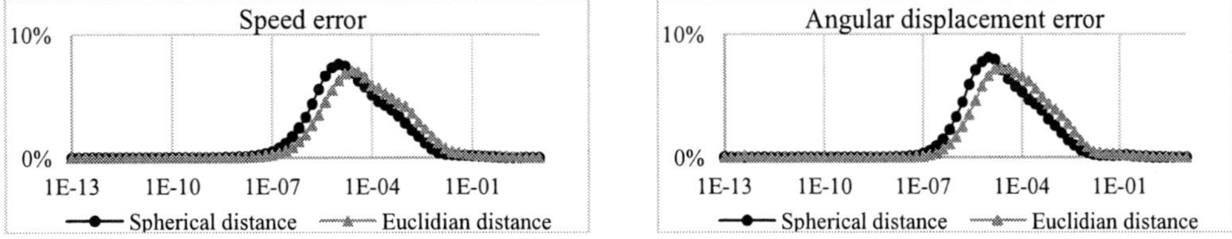

Figure 1. Histogram of speed error distribution (a) and displacement error distribution (b) for a vector field (4 left)

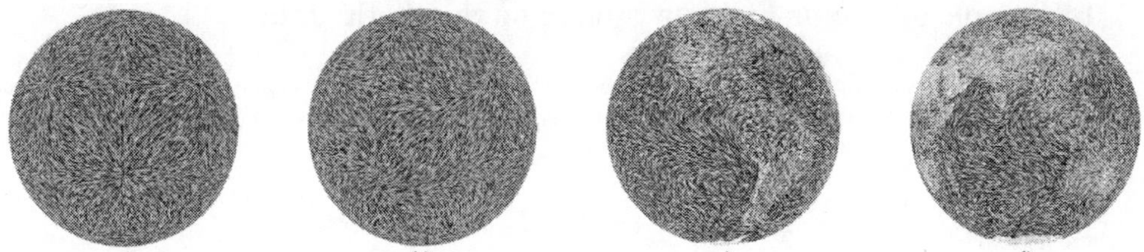
a) b) c) d)

Figure 2. Visualization of examples of vector fields. All vector fields were interpolated using RBF and visualized as LIC images on a sphere. Equations (4 left) (a) and (4 right) (b). Sources, resp. sinks, and saddles are clearly seen in both images . Both images (a, b) are visually identical to the ones with an original analytical description. Visualization of an RBF interpolated wind vector field from numerical simulation (c, d)

Some reduction of this dataset was done, as for the North or South Pole only one vector is needed and for near locations, the computed vectors can be reduced as well. After the reduction, there were 62 742 vectors. This wind data were interpolated using RBF with CSRBF (6) and shape parameter $\varepsilon = 1$. The RBF interpolation was used to create the visualization of wind vector field on the sphere, Figure 2(c, d).

3. CONCLUSION

Two approaches for interpolation on a sphere using Radial Basis Functions were presented. The new approach uses the spherical distance as the parameter for the radial basis function computation. The proposed approach gives better results for interpolation on a sphere in comparison to the original standard approach using the Euclidian distance. The proposed method was verified on synthetic analytical datasets and non-trivial real wind datasets of a weather forecast. In future, the proposed approach will be explored more deeply for t-varying datasets together with aspects of implementation for very large dataset processing.

ACKNOWLEDGEMENT

The authors would like to thank their colleagues at the University of West Bohemia, Plzen, for their discussions and suggestions, and anonymous reviewers for the valuable comments and suggestions they provided. The research was supported by MSMT CR projects LH12181 and SGS 2016-013.

REFERENCES

Aguilar, F. J., et al., 2005. Effects of terrain morphology, sampling density, and interpolation methods on grid DEM accuracy. *Photogrammetric Engineering & Remote Sensing*, Vol. 71, No. 7, pp.805-816.

Baxter, B. J., Hubbert, S., 2001. Radial basis functions for the sphere. *Recent Progress in Multivariate Approximation*, pp. 33-47, Birkhäuser Basel.

Eldrandaly, K. A., Abu-Zaid, M. S., 2011. Comparison of Six GIS-Based Spatial Interpolation Methods for Estimating Air Temperature in Western Saudi Arabia. *Journal of Environmental Informatics*, Vol. 18, No. 1.

Fasshauer, G.E., 2007. *Meshfree Approximation Methods with MATLAB*. World Scientific Publ. Co., Inc., NJ, USA.

Flyer, N. et al., 2014. Radial basis function-generated finite differences: A mesh-free method for computational geosciences. *Handbook of Geomathematics*. Springer, Berlin.

Golitschek, M. V., Light, W. A., 2001. Interpolation by polynomials and radial basis functions on spheres. *Constructive Approximation*, Vol. 17, No. 1, pp. 1-18.

Pan, R. and Skala, V., 2011. A Two-level Approach to Implicit Surface Modeling with Compactly Supported Radial Basis Functions. *In Eng. Comput. (Lond.)*, Vol. 27, No. 3, pp. 299-307.

Turk, G., O'Brien, J. F., 2002. Modelling with implicit surfaces that interpolate. *ACM Transactions on Graphics*, Vol. 21, No. 4, pp. 855-873.

Doctoral Consortium

SERIOUS GAMES AS A MEANS OF THE APPROXIMATION OF CULTURAL HERITAGE OF THE CZECH REPUBLIC

Lenka Chadimová
IRIT Université Toulouse III – Paul Sabatier, 118 Route de Narbonne, Toulouse, France
Faculty of Education, Univerzita Hradec Kralove, Rokitanského 62, Hradec Králové, Czech Republic

ABSTRACT

This work is concerned with the serious games intended as a supplement to National History lessons at primary schools and it also examines the influence on the instruction of these lessons. According to the project, 3D models of significant historic buildings, mainly from the territory of the Czech Republic are developed and they are integrated to evolving SG.

KEYWORDS

Serious games, 3D technologies, Cultural Heritage, Education

1. INTRODUCTION

The aim of this work is to ascertain whether the usage of 3D technologies in the form of serious games has an influence on the instruction of National History of primary school pupils at 4th and 5th grade. Whether this type of instruction would change the communication between the teacher and his/her pupil, whether and how the rate of activation is influenced and whether the pupil's activation is changed during the instruction. According to the measurement and observing is then possible to consider whether it is appropriate to reflect the latest technological trends (especially 3D technologies) which surround us not only in our common life but also while instructing at primary schools. This project is framed on the mixed design [Vlc11] where the qualitative research is represented by the pedagogical experiment.

Historic buildings from the Czech Republic (for now) were chosen to be used in the development of these serious games. There are mainly represented castles and ruins of castles which are historically important (state-wide or locally). Moreover, religious buildings are also among the selected buildings. Interaction in these serious games is based on that each of the important elements (historic, architectonical etc.) in the building is possible to activate and either obtain detailed pieces of information or answer the questions.

2. THE CREATION OF 3D MODELS OF HISTORIC BUILDINGS AND THE CREATION OF SERIOUS GAMES

For the purposes of serious games, it is appropriate to create a lot of authentic and relevant details (as much as possible) of the historic building in the virtual environment due to the fact that they are an essential and inseparable part of that building as well it is important for understanding of its architecture and history. On the other hand, it is possible not to obey the exact castle's dimensions, altitudes and other figures (these exact numbers are significant during the digitalization for the historic preservation and archival purposes but not for serious games). Neither is possible to maintain the exact dimensions of the historic building nor to acquire the digital space shape of building details in some cases, mainly if it is a reconstruction of a vanished historic building or ruins of a castle where it is hard to know these details.

There are several methods of creating the 3D models of historic buildings. The creation depends mainly on the documentation and it also depends on technical, occasionally, financial base of the historic building or of the 3D model creator.

The usage of a long range 3D scanner to get the exact „digital 3D copy“ of the present day state of the chosen historic building is advised. Another possibility is to obtain relatively exact „digital 3D copy“ of present day state of the historic building is to used the camera hanged on the drone.

The most widely used is the usage of the ground documentation of the historic building to create the 3D model. This type of modelling is done in the "free modeller" 3D software (for our purposes was chosen AutoDesk 3DS MAX). Although, a "free modeller" is not restrictived using a parametric system, which does not matter for the purposes of the serious games. And it allows better creating of atypical shapes (atypical in modern architecture). All modelling works including textures, eventual illumination of the building are done in 3DS MAX.

Figure 1. The example of 3D model of rotundy St. George from software 3DS MAX

The completed and textured 3D model of historic building is exported into the FBX format and then imported into the game engine UNITY3D. All the interaction elements are added in this developmental environment, e. g. an avatar that walks through the historic building and is fully controlled by the user. The avatar can examine exteriors as well as interiors. The avatar will get information about history of that part of the building (eventually history of the region or state) to which he enters. Extra details about the architecture, arts etc. are given to the user after clicking on highlighted elements (for example in the room). To enter other parts of the building is necessary to answer several questions related to the newly acquired knowledge. All scripts necessary for developing of such serious games were written in JavaSript and C#.

3. PEDAGOGICAL EXPERIMENT IN THE INSTRUCTION OF NATIONAL HISTORY AT THE FIRST STAGE OF PRIMARY SCHOOL

The pilot game was included into a several independent National History lessons at primary schools during which the behaviour of pupils was structurally observed. This observation was analysed whose aim was to ascertain the pupils' activity and their activation. A modified Flanders' system of interactive analysis was used to acquire demanded data. According to this analysis we can generally say, that if the index of interaction is equal to 1 the communication between the teacher and his/her pupil was equal during the instruction. If the index is lower than 1 the teacher is more active during the instruction and if the index if higher than 1 then the pupils were more active during the instruction [Fla70].

It was discovered that the index was higher than 1 when the serious games were included in the instruction (pupils were more active) after evaluation of results of the analysis.

4. CONCLUSION

Even if we encouraging results, it was only a pilot analysis and that is why the conclusion cannot be generalised [MC15]. It is necessary to perform another observing and analyses to get the final knowledge whether to include or not these modern technologies into the instruction, e. g.: whether the form of instruction (usage of the familiar environment of computer games) influence on the number of remembered facts by the pupils. The other variables appropriate for observing are time in which the pupils acquire the new topic and whether or not is the time of acquiring influenced by the form of instruction (computer game vs. classical form of instruction), measurement of pupils' activity and the rate of their activation and etc.

REFERENCES

[Vlc11] VLČKOVÁ, K. 2011. *Smíšený výzkum: Jedná se o nové a závažné téma?* In T. Janík, P. Knecht, & S. Šebestová (Eds.), *Smíšený design v pedagogickém výzkumu*: Sborník příspěvků z 19. výroční konference České asociace pedagogického výzkumu (s. 1–6). Brno: Masarykova univerzita. Dostupné z: http://www.ped.muni.cz/capv2011/sbornikprispevku/vlckova.pdf

[Fla70] Flanders, N. A., 1970. *Analyzing Teaching Behavior*. London : Addison-Wesley,1970.

[MC15] Maněnová, M and Chadimová, L., 2015 *'3D Models of Historical Objects in Teaching at the 1 st Level of Primary School'*, Procedia – Social and Behavioral Sciences - 5th ICEEPSY International Conference on Education & Education Psychology (ICEEPSY 2014), Vol. 171, 16 January 2015, pp. 830-836

[Det11] DETERDING, Sebastian, et al., 2011. *From game design elements to gamefulness: defining gamification*. In: Proceedings of the 15th International Academic MindTrek Conference: Envisioning Future Media Environments. ACM, 2011. p. 9-15.

[Doo97] DORMAN, Steave M. http://onlinelibrary.wiley.com/doi/10.1111/j.1746-1561.1997.tb03432.x/abstract

[TYK*09] TÜZÜN, H., YILMAZ-SOYLU, M., KARAKUS, ÍNAL,Y., KIZILKAYA, G., 2009. *The effects of computer games on primary school students' achievement and motivation in geography learning.* Computers & Education 52 (s. 68-77), 2009. Ankara. Dostupné z WWW: http://www.sciencedirect.com/science/article/pii/S0360131508000985

AUTHOR INDEX

International Association for Development of the Information Society (IADIS)
Rua Sao Sebastiao Da Pedreira
No. 100, 30, 1050-209
Lisbon, Portugal

ISBN 978-1-5108-6527-3

CURRAN ASSOCIATES INC.
proceedings.com

9th Conferencia Iberoamericana en Software Engineering (CIbSE 2006)

La Plata, Argentina
24 – 28 April 2006